CURRENT ISSUES IN M̲L̲.̲.̲.̲ ̲–̲ ̲.̲.̲.̲

Current Issues in Memory is a series of edited books that reflect the state-of-the-art areas of current and emerging interest in the psychological study of memory.

For the first time, this book offers a comprehensive new collection which gathers together some of the most influential chapters from the series into one essential volume. Featuring 17 chapters by many of the leading researchers in the field, the volume seeks to illustrate how memory research may be informative to the general public—either because it speaks to questions of personal or societal importance or because it changes traditional ways of thinking within society. Topics range from working memory to false fabrication and autobiographical forgetting, showcasing the breadth of memory research in the public sphere.

With an introduction and conclusion by Professor Jan Rummel, this is the ideal companion for any student or practitioner looking for an insightful overview of the most researched topics in the field.

Jan Rummel is Heisenberg Professor for Experimental Psychology and Cognitive Self-Regulation at Heidelberg University, Germany. His research focuses on the cognitive processes involved in prospective memory, intentional forgetting, and the regulation of attention.

Current Issues in Memory

Current Issues in Memory is a series of edited books that reflect the state of art in areas of current and emerging interest in the psychological study of memory. Each of the volumes in the series are tightly focused on a particular topic and are designed to be concise collections containing chapters contributed by international experts.

The editors of individual volumes are leading figures in their areas and provide an introductory overview. Example topics include: binding in working memory, prospective memory, autobiographical memory, visual memory, implicit memory, amnesia, retrieval, and memory development.

Other titles in this series:

Current Issues in Applied Memory Research
Edited by Graham M. Davies and Daniel B. Wright

Spatial Working Memory
Edited by André Vandierendonck and Arnaud Szmalec

Working Memory and Ageing
Edited by Robert H. Logie and Robin G. Morris

False and Distorted Memories
Edited by Robert A. Nash and James Ost

The Visual World in Memory
Edited by James R. Brockmole

Prospective Memory
Edited by Jan Rummel and Mark A. McDaniel

Autobiographical Memory Development: Theoretical and Methodological Approaches
Edited by Sami Gülgöz & Basak Sahin-Acar

Current Issues in Memory: Memory Research in the Public Interest
Edited by Jan Rummel

CURRENT ISSUES IN MEMORY

Memory Research in the Public Interest

Edited by Jan Rummel

Routledge
Taylor & Francis Group

LONDON AND NEW YORK

First published 2021
by Routledge
2 Park Square, Milton Park, Abingdon, Oxon OX14 4RN

and by Routledge
52 Vanderbilt Avenue, New York, NY 10017

Routledge is an imprint of the Taylor & Francis Group, an informa business

British Library Cataloguing-in-Publication Data
A catalogue record for this book is available from the British Library

Library of Congress Cataloging-in-Publication Data
A catalog record has been requested for this book

ISBN: 978-0-367-61825-4 (hbk)
ISBN: 978-0-367-61824-7 (pbk)
ISBN: 978-1-003-10671-5 (ebk)

Typeset in Bembo
by Newgen Publishing UK

CONTENTS

CONTRIBUTORS

Pooja K. Agarwal, Department of Psychology, Washington University, St Louis, MO, USA.

Amanda J. Barnier, Macquarie Centre for Cognitive Science, Macquarie University, Sydney, Australia.

Nathalie Brackmann, Department of Clinical Psychological Science, Maastricht University, Netherlands.

Vicki Bruce, School of Psychology, Newcastle University.

Melissa F. Colloff, Department of Psychology, University of Warwick, UK.

Cesare Cornoldi, Department of General Psychology, University of Padua, Italy.

Rachel DeFranco, Department of Psychological Sciences, Kent State University, Kent, OH, USA

Key Dismukes, Dismukes Consulting, USA.

Tobias Grundgeiger, Institute for Human–Computer–Media, Julius–Maximilians–Universität Würzburg, Germany.

Celia B. Harris, Macquarie Centre for Cognitive Science, Macquarie University, Sydney, Australia.

Andrew Hollingworth, Department of Psychology, University of Iowa, Iowa City, USA.

Mark L. Howe, Department of Psychology, City University, London, UK.

Sean H. K. Kang, Department of Psychology, Washington University, St Louis, MO, USA.

Marissa H. Kiepert, College of Education, Temple University, Philadelphia, USA.

Sarah Kulkofsky, Human Development and Family Studies, Texas Tech University, Lubbock, TX, USA.

Lia Kvavilashvili, Department of Psychology and Sport Sciences, University of Hertfordshire, UK.

Cara Laney, Department of Psychology, College of Idaho, Caldwell, ID, USA.

Darren S. Levin, College of Education, Ritter Hall, Temple University, Philadelphia, USA.

Shayne Loft, School of Psychological Science, University of Western Australia.

Elizabeth F. Loftus, Department of Psychology and Social Behavior, University of California, Irvine, CA, USA.

Kamala London, Department of Psychology, University of Toledo, OH, USA.

Irene C. Mammarella is in the Department of Developmental Psychology at the University of Padua, Italy.

Elizabeth J. Marsh, Psychology & Neuroscience, Duke University, Durham, NC, USA.

Sophie J. Nightingale, Department of Psychology, University of Warwick, UK.

Lars Nyberg, Department of Integrative Medical Biology, Department of Radiation Sciences, Umeå Center for Functional Brain Imaging, Umeå University, Sweden.

Henry Otgaar, Department of Clinical Psychological Science, Maastricht University, Netherlands.

Christina O. Perez, Department of Psychology, University of Toledo, Toledo, OH, USA.

Patrick Rich, Department of Psychological Sciences, Kent State University, Kent, OH, USA.

Eric Rindal, Department of Psychological Sciences, Kent State University, Kent, OH, USA.

Henry L. Roediger, III, Department of Psychology, Washington University, St Louis, MO, USA.

Jan Rummel, Department of Psychology, Heidelberg University, Germany.

Timothy A. Salthouse, Department of Psychology, University of Virginia, USA.

Amy L. Shelton, Department of Psychological and Brain Sciences, Johns Hopkins University, Baltimore, MD, USA.

Anna Stigsdotter Neely, Department of Psychology, Umeå University, Sweden.

John Sutton, Macquarie Centre for Cognitive Science, Macquarie University, Sydney, Australia.

S. Kenneth Thurman, College of Education, Temple University, Philadelphia, USA.

Kimberley A. Wade, Department of Psychology, University of Warwick, UK.

Jianqin Wang, Department of Clinical Psychological Science, Maastricht University, Netherlands.

John T. Wixted, Department of Psychology, University of California at San Diego, La Jolla, CA USA.

Naohide Yamamoto, Department of Psychology, George Washington University, Washington, DC, USA.

Maria S. Zaragoza, Department of Psychological Sciences, Kent State University, Kent, OH, USA.

ACKNOWLEDGMENTS

I thank my academic mentors Gilles O. Einstein, Edgar Erdfelder, Mark A. McDaniel, and Thorsten Meiser for getting me involved in and excited about memory research as well as Alex Howard and Ceri McLardy from the Routledge editorial team for their support in putting this volume together.

INTRODUCTION

Jan Rummel

> Your memory is a monster; you forget—it doesn't. It simply files things away.
> It keeps things for you, or hides things from you—and summons them to
> your recall with will of its own. You think you have a memory; but it has you!
>
> John Irving, A Prayer for Owen Meany (1998)

Human memory and its underlying processes have been studied by experimental
psychologists, cognitive psychologists, as well as cognitive neuroscientists for over
100 years. The scientific interest in the systematic investigation of memory as a
human capacity started with Ebbinghaus' seminal work demonstrating that it is
possible to study remembering and forgetting in humans with an experimental
approach (Ebbinghaus, 1885). Several years later, this general approach was picked
up by both functionalists interested in general memory principles (McGeoch &
Irion, 1952) and cognitive psychologists more interested in the organization of
memories (Mandler, 1967). Although the experimental approach to the investigation of human memory was also criticized early on (mostly as being too reduc-
tionist; e.g., Bartlett, 1932), this approach has shaped and still shapes the field. As
more and more researchers, not only cognitive psychologists but neuroscientists
alike, became interested in the investigation of human memory, the number of
publications in scientific journals on memory-related topics has been growing
exponentially for many years. Not only have chapters on memory been included
in most introductory psychology textbooks but complete textbooks have been
dedicated to memory as a research subject attempting to summarize and structure
the field (see, e.g., Baddeley et al., 2020, for a timely and highly recommended
example of such a textbook).

If one skims the tables of content of recent memory textbooks, it becomes
obvious that this field can hardly be considered a single research area any more. The
term memory, as it is currently used by most researchers, comprises a set of more

or less loosely related areas of expertise which all have their own theories, methods, and traditions. Most of these areas have been named by their function—working memory, episodic memory, semantic memory, prospective memory, and autobiographical memory, to just name a few—and several of these areas have even been divided into further sub-areas during the course of their exploration.

For this reason memory researchers, similar to Irving's first-person narrator Johnny, who cannot get rid of some traumatic autobiographical memories from his childhood, will sometimes think of their subject of study as a monster. It is a monster worth pursuing, because of its importance for the human species, but also a monster nobody will ever capture within a single lifetime in its full complexity.

As a natural consequence of the field's fast development, modern memory researchers tend to become experts in a certain area (or sub-area) but it is often not feasible for them to keep track of the latest advances even in the areas neighboring their own specialization. In response to this concern, Routledge developed a book series titled *Current Issues in Memory* which was first launched in 2009 with Robert Logie serving as the series editor. As noted by Robert Logie in the first published volume of this series, *Current Issues in Memory* is intended to provide a reflection of the "state of the art in areas of current and emerging interest in the psychological study of memory" (see *The Visual World in Memory*, 2009). As such, the volumes of this series will be of value for more advanced researchers who intend to update their knowledge about a certain memory research area they are not experts in. Similarly, the volumes are intended to help masters and doctoral students starting to engage in research in a certain memory area to get an overview about the latest theories, methods, and developments in their prospective fields.

So far, the editorial team at Routledge has gathered an impressive collection of seven edited volumes on diverse topics (here listed in the order of when they were first published):

1) The Visual World in Memory
2) Applied Memory Research
3) Forgetting
4) Spatial Working Memory
5) Working Memory and Ageing
6) False and Distorted Memories
7) Prospective Memory

Together with Mark A. McDaniel, I edited the most recent 2019 volume on prospective memory. In order to prepare for this endeavor, I not only read large piles of recently published prospective memory articles but also several chapters from previous volumes of this series to better understand its aims and scope. I was very impressed by the timely and dense treatment of the chosen topics within these chapters. Therefore, when I was subsequently asked to become the next series editor, I was not only honored that I would follow the great Robert Logie, whose research I have admired since I was a psychology student and first learned how the experimental approach can be used to investigate memory processes, but I was also particularly excited about the opportunity to develop a compilation volume to celebrate the tenth anniversary of the *Current Issues in Memory* series.

Soon after I started working on putting together a compilation volume with considerable enthusiasm, another challenge developed. On what basis should the chapters for this volume be selected? All the chapters published in this series appeared to be of the highest quality and could well have find their ways into a compilation volume. I discussed this issue with the Alex Howard and Ceri McLardy from the Routledge editorial team and we agreed to narrow the topic of the compilation volume down to a particular theme, which could then guide our selection process. In doing so, we were able to do justice to all the exceptional chapters published in this series.

While searching for such a topic, I ended up in a lively discussion with colleagues from my department about the question of whether psychological science is ready for application and dissemination, which was raised by IJzerman and colleagues (2020) during the Covid-19 pandemic and which is related to the broader question of the value of external validity. In this context, I was reminded of the old criticism specifically addressing my own research field, which was eloquently phrased by psychologist Ulric Neisser in 1978: "If X is an interesting or socially significant aspect of memory, then psychologists have hardly ever studied X" (p. 4). I can certainly say that I would not have been involved in memory research for several years now, if my mentors had not convinced me that memory research is more than just an academic mental exercise (although I admittedly enjoy this aspect too) and that the results of this research can be related to the real word and have an impact in society.

More important than my personal convictions and hopes, however, is the fact that the idea for the theme of the compilation volume emerged from this discussion. As a consequence, this compilation volume is dedicated to memory research that is in the public interest. This does not imply that all chapters included in this volume address applied aspects of memory research (although some of them do). Rather the chapters for the present volume were selected to illustrate in which respect memory research may be informative to the general public—either because it speaks to questions of personal or societal importance or because it changes traditional ways of thinking within society.

The first part of the present volume is titled "Memory Representation". This part is concerned with how visual representations in the environment become mental representations in memory and how the ability to store visual representations in working memory is crucial for everyday functioning, for example, when remembering faces or when navigating through familiar environments.

Part II combines research from two areas which, at first glance, do not seem to have much in common, namely, on the one hand, the forgetting of previously stored information and, on the other hand, the remembering of intentions for the future. The chapters selected for this section are all concerned with everyday phenomena in the respective areas and particularly speak to the adaptive nature of human memory. The research reviewed here suggests that our memory works in such a way that important information often has some retrieval advantage at the cost of the retrieval of less important information and that our memory system will not only serve us to remember the past but also to plan the future.

Although our memory often serves us well it also has its limitations and flaws. Perhaps the most important and also the most frequently investigated issue is that memory is error-prone and particularly susceptible to false information. The chapters included in Part III tackle questions regarding the unreliability of the human memory and the origination of memories that are, in fact, false.

Part IV is concerned with individual differences in memory capacity and especially with how memory changes across the lifespan. Furthermore, this section illustrates possible ways to improve memory. These topics are certainly of public interest in current societies which value education and knowledge more and more and whose members live longer as compared to previous societies.

This selection is certainly not exhaustive and I encourage the readers of this volume to have another look into the other volumes of this series if they get excited about a certain topic. The authors of all included chapters were contacted by the Routledge editorial team and many of them took the opportunity to update their chapter contents and literature review. However, no major changes their made regarding the chapter contents.

I hope you will find the following chapters as informative as I did and maybe you will even get some additional arguments for why memory research matters along the way!

Jan Rummel
Heidelberg, 2020

References

Baddeley, A. D., Eysenck, M. W., & Anderson, M. C. (2020). *Memory*, 3rd edition. Routledge.

Bartlett, F. C. (1932). *Remembering: A study in experimental and social psychology*. Cambridge University Press.

Ebbinghaus, H. (1885). *Memory: A contribution to experimental psychology*. Dover.

IJzerman, H., Lewis, N. A., Jr., Weinstein, N., DeBruine, L. M., Ritchie, S. J., Vazire, S., ... Przybylski, A. K. (2020). Is social and behavioural science evidence ready for application and dissemination? April 27. https://doi.org/10.31234/osf.io/whds4

Irving, J. (1998). *A prayer for Owen Meany*. HarperCollins.

Mandler, G. (1967). Organization and memory. In K. W. Spence & J. T. Spence (Eds.), *The psychology of learning and motivation: Advances in research and theory* (vol. 1, pp. 328–372). Academic Press.

McGeoch, J. A., & Irion, A. L. (1952). *The psychology of human learning*. Longman.

Neisser, U. (1978). Memory: What are the important questions? In M. M. Gruneberg, P. E. Morris, & R. N. Sykes (Eds.), *Practical aspects of memory* (pp. 3–24). Academic Press.

PART I

Memory representations: From (visual) perception to stored information

1

THE ORGANIZATION OF VISUOSPATIAL WORKING MEMORY

Evidence from the study of developmental disorders*

Cesare Cornoldi and Irene C. Mammarella

Visuospatial abilities and their relation to visuospatial working memory

Visuospatial ability is not a unitary process, but instead can be broken down into various distinct types. The differentiation and classification of these types has been influenced by the findings from various instruments chosen to examine visuospatial ability.

Factor-analytic studies of visuospatial ability tasks point to the existence of distinct spatial abilities. For example, some authors (Hegarty & Waller, 2004; McGee, 1979) have distinguished between main aspects, i.e., visualization and orientation. Visualization refers to the ability to mentally rotate and manipulate objects, while orientation refers to the ability to retain spatial orientation with respect to oneself. Linn and Peterson (1985) and Voyer, Voyer, and Bryden (1995) distinguished three categories of spatial ability based on the various different processes required to solve problems representing each ability. These categories were:

1 spatial perception (ability to determine spatial relationships with respect to one's own orientation);
2 mental rotation (ability to mentally rotate a two- or three-dimensional figure rapidly and accurately); and
3 spatial visualization (ability to manipulate spatially presented information in complex ways).

Examples of tests are: for (1) the water level test (Inhelder & Piaget, 1958); for (2) the Mental Rotation Test (Vandenberg & Kruse, 1978); and for (3) the Differential

Aptitude Test spatial relations subtest. Carpenter and Just (1986) distinguished only two categories of spatial ability:

1 spatial orientation (ability to identify spatial configurations from a different perspective);
2 spatial manipulation (ability to mentally restructure a two- or three-dimensional object).

Cornoldi and Vecchi (2003, p. 16) instead presented a broader classification, distinguishing between ten different groups of visuospatial abilities, which included visuospatial working memory. Finally, Bunton and Fogarty (2003) examined the relationship between visual imagery and spatial abilities using a confirmatory factor analysis. Their findings supported the notion that the abilities targeted by the tasks referred to above can be classified along a continuum. The self-report imagery questionnaires are located on the left-hand side of the continuum, while experimental tasks examining spatial-imagery and visuospatial memory can be located at the centre. On the right of the continuum they placed the creative imagery tasks of Finke, Pinker, and Farah (1989), and—at the far end—spatial intelligence tests (primary mental abilities, Thurstone & Thurstone, 1965, and Raven's Advanced Progressive Matrices, Raven, 1965). The main thrust of Bunton and Fogarty (2003) has therefore been to offer a description of the relationships between visual imagery, visuospatial memory, and spatial abilities, also showing their proximity.

In summary, psychometrical research has clearly shown that visuospatial ability is not a homogeneous concept, but consists of subcomponents that are quite distinct, albeit closely related. Nevertheless, despite all the attempts at a suitable classification of the spatial subfactors, the correct operationalization of these factors and their relationships remain unclear. For example, there is evidence to suggest that there is indeed a relationship between working memory capacity and visuospatial ability (Just & Carpenter, 1985). Solving a mental rotation or spatial visualization task requires the ability to maintain an active representation of all the parts and their interrelations, while simultaneously rotating and manipulating the image mentally. This elaboration, involving both storage (holding the constituent parts in memory) and the concurrent processing of spatial representations (the rotation component), fits closely with current conceptions of working memory (Miyake & Shah, 1999). In studies of visuospatial abilities and visuospatial working memory individual differences consequently overlap to some extent.

The individual differences approach in the study of working memory

The individual differences approach—investigating the role of individual differences such as cognitive abilities and personality in human behaviour—can be useful in explaining human differences and finding critical psychological variables which, making individuals different, appear to be central for psychological functioning.

Knowledge of working memory has benefited greatly from studies involving both the consideration of variability within typical populations, and the examination of specific impairments in clinical populations and individual cases (Cornoldi & Vecchi, 2003). One development in the field has concerned the attentional control of irrelevant information. For example, Engle and colleagues have repeatedly explored the role of individual differences in working memory capacity on verbal fluency under various secondary load conditions (Rosen & Engle, 1997), the relationship between working memory capacity and attentional control (Kane, Bleckley, Conway, & Engle, 2001), individual differences in switching the focus of attention in working memory, and so on (see Unsworth & Engle, 2007 for a review). In general, this work showed that individual differences in working memory, as measured by complex span tasks in which to-be-remembered items are interspersed with some form of distracting activity, arise from differences in attentional control affecting the ability to maintain and retrieve information from memory. In particular, in situations where new and novel information needs to be maintained to generate the correct response, low-working memory capacity individuals are more likely than their working memory counterparts to have their attention distracted and thus lose access to the task goal.

However, to date, experiments have mostly been conducted within the verbal domain (Unsworth & Engle, 2006) rather than the visuospatial (Mammarella & Cornoldi, 2005a; Cornoldi & Mammarella, 2006). In a recent study, Lecerf and Roulin (2009) showed that low-visuospatial working memory participants had deficits in distractor inhibition and that their memory representations were more degraded. Specifically, high-visuospatial working memory participants performed better than low-visuospatial working memory participants, while these latter demonstrated more intrusions of irrelevant information than their high-span counterparts. Thus, low-span participants were less able to suppress items that had to be forgotten. Moreover, inhibitory control was negatively correlated to visuospatial working memory capacity. Similarly, Cornoldi, Bassani, Berto, and Mammarella (2007) demonstrated that elderly individuals performed less well than younger individuals and that errors in visuospatial working memory tasks depend, at least partially, on difficulties in avoiding already activated information. As mentioned, the individual differences approach has been applied to the study of working memory, enabling analysis of various populations (i.e., elderly, low spatial abilities, low working-memory span individuals, learning disabled children, etc.), at the same time broadening knowledge on the architecture of working memory components (but see also Logie, in *Spatial Working Memory*, chapter 2).

Indeed, the study of individual differences has been critical to the differentiation of cognitive abilities, including working memory components.

In the field of memory, the original Baddeley and Hitch (1974) model, with its evolution (Baddeley, 2000), represented an innovative approach to the study of how the temporary memory system functions, and still today remains a relevant theoretical framework. According to this model, working memory is composed of two subsidiary domain-specific components, namely a phonological loop and a visuospatial sketchpad, which are supervised by an amodal unit, the central executive. The phonological loop temporarily stores and manipulates verbalizable items, while the visuospatial sketchpad is responsible for the maintenance and processing of visual (e.g., colour, shape, texture) and spatial (e.g., position of an object in space) information, as well as mental imagery activities. Instead, the central executive component is involved in the regulatory control of the tasks carried out by the two slave systems. Moreover, it serves to focus or switch attention and recover mental representations from long-term memory (Baddeley & Logie, 1999).

Organization of the working memory components within the continuity model

Over the last 20 years, alternative approaches to working memory have been developed that emphasize the articulated architecture of the system and its limits in the amount of information that can be stored and processed. It was on this basis that Cornoldi and Vecchi (2003) put forward a formulation of the working memory model giving a new account of the organization of working memory proposed by the classical Baddeley (1986) model. According to this novel concept, "working memory system and its subsystems can be viewed as representatives of well-characterised groups of processes along continuous dimensions rather than as discrete entities" (Cornoldi & Vecchi, 2003, p. 50). Working memory functions are not rigidly separated, but instead thought of as being linked in a continuous fashion along horizontal and vertical dimensions. In other words, the continuity model is characterized by two fundamental dimensions based on continuum relations: the horizontal continuum, related to the various types of material involved (e.g., verbal, visual, spatial, haptic); and the vertical continuum, related to the types of process, requiring some degree of active elaboration and manipulation of information (see Figure 1.1). Each process is thus defined on the basis of two dimensions (vertical and horizontal), while distance between positions represents the degree of independence between tasks. An assumption of this type leads to the argument that working memory tasks are defined in terms of their position along both continua. At a lower level of the vertical continuum, expressing the degree of controlled activity involved, there are passive memory tasks, or *simple span tasks*, usually based on rote rehearsal of items (e.g., forward digit span) that are strictly related to the nature of the stimuli to be retained. In contrast, active memory tasks, or *complex span tasks* (Engle, Kane, & Tuholski, 1999), require both maintenance and concurrent processing of information, such as order change (e.g., backwards digit span) or selection and inhibition of irrelevant or no-longer-relevant information (e.g., listening span task). According to Cornoldi and Vecchi (2003), complex span tasks may vary in the degree of controlled activity involved and maintain domain-specific characteristics, despite the higher involvement of control processes than that for simple span tasks; thus, for example, it is possible to distinguish between verbal and spatial active tasks.

Although working memory tasks can vary in degree of controlled activity involved and thus occupy different positions on the vertical continuum, they

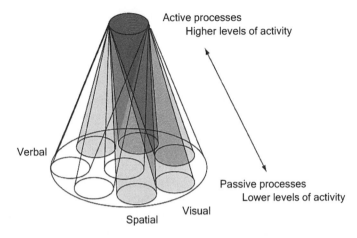

Active processes
Higher levels of activity

Verbal

Passive processes
Lower levels of activity

Spatial Visual

FIGURE 1.1 The continuity model proposed by Cornoldi and Vecchi (2003)

can broadly be located between passive tasks (lowest down in the continuum) and active tasks (highest up). As examples, passive verbal memory tasks include the forward digit span (see also Engle et al., 1999). Passive spatial tasks include the forward Corsi Blocks Test (CBT; Milner, 1971), in which participants have to remember and reproduce the sequence in the same order as that given by the experimenter; another is the Visual Pattern Test (VPT; Della Sala, Gray, Baddeley, & Wilson, 1997) where participants have to memorize patterns of filled cells in matrices of varying sizes, and then fill in cells on a blank matrix to reproduce the original pattern.

An example of an active verbal task is the Reading Span Task (RST) proposed by Daneman and Carpenter (1980). In the commonest version of this task, participants have to read a growing series of sentences (from two to six), deciding whether they are true, and recalling the last word of each sentence. To do so participants have to perform two tasks almost simultaneously, i.e., processing the meaning of each sentence to decide whether it is true or false, and maintaining the last word of each sentence. To be successful in the memory tasks, it has been shown that participants have to be able to keep the last word active while handling interfering information (i.e., the words within sentences)—see for example De Beni, Palladino, Pazzaglia, & Cornoldi, (1998). One active spatial task mirroring the reading span is the selective Visuospatial Working Memory Task (Cornoldi, Marzocchi, Belotti, Caroli, De Meo, & Braga, 2001b; Mammarella & Cornoldi, 2005a; Cornoldi & Mammarella, 2006), involving a series of matrices of increasing length, with one or more coloured cells. For each matrix, three or more sequential locations are presented and participants have to recall only the last. As a secondary task, participants have to press a key when a location corresponds to a coloured cell. Another active spatial task is the active version (Mammarella, Pazzaglia, & Cornoldi, 2008) of the VPT (Della Sala et al., 1997). The task requires memorization of the filled cells on a matrix and, in contrast with the passive version it requires an active transformation of the memory representation with reproduction on a blank matrix of the original pattern by filling in the corresponding cells one row below the positions of the original.

The continuous approach allows distinction of the efficiency of passive maintenance and active working memory processes in each domain (i.e., verbal versus visual or spatial). Within this framework it is possible to predict memory weaknesses and strengths of specific atypically developing categories of individuals (e.g., learning disabled children, individuals with genetic syndromes), as well as the individual differences related to normal cognitive functioning (e.g., age differences and gender-related effects). Evidence of the distinction between active and passive processes comes from studies on individual differences in working memory due to gender (Vecchi & Girelli, 1998) and age (Vecchi & Cornoldi, 1999; Richardson & Vecchi, 2002) and from studies on particular categories of subjects, such as nonverbal learning disabled children (Cornoldi, Dalla Vecchia, & Tressoldi, 1995; Cornoldi, Rigoni, Tressoldi, & Vio, 1999), blind people (Vecchi, Monticelli, & Cornoldi, 1995; Vecchi, 1998), individuals with intellectual disability (Lanfranchi, Cornoldi, & Vianello, 2004; Lanfranchi, Cornoldi, Drigo, & Vianello, 2009b), and children with attention deficit hyperactivity disorder (ADHD) (Cornoldi et al., 2001b).

The case of developmental populations with cognitive disabilities is illuminating here (e.g., Cornoldi, Carretti, & De Beni, 2001a; Swanson & Siegel, 2001); in particular, subgroups can be found that apparently have difficulties associated with both a specific modality and a particular degree of control. For instance, in the linguistic domain, it can be predicted that highly intelligent children with specific verbal learning disabilities in low-level skills (e.g., dyslexic) would fail mainly in low-control tasks (*simple span tasks*). In contrast, children with reading comprehension and/or word problem-solving difficulties may have problems at higher levels of control (e.g., intermediate level, where selection and inhibition of specific verbal information is required: *active* or *complex span tasks*). Instead, children with intellectual disability may fail at an even higher level of control, associated with executive function tasks (*high attentional controlled tasks*; for a discussion see Cornoldi et al., 2001a). Children with ADHD seem to represent a particular case, presenting problems in active working memory tasks, independent of modality but dependent on the specific inhibitory request implied by the task (Cornoldi et al., 2001b; Re, De Franchis, & Cornoldi, 2010).

Organization of the visuospatial components of working memory within the continuity model

Visuospatial working memory has been widely explored in recent years, but to date there is no consensus on how it is organized. According to the Logie (1995) model, visuospatial working memory consists of a visual store, known as the *visual cache*, and a rehearsal mechanism, known as the *inner scribe*. The visual cache provides a temporary store for visual information (i.e., colour and shape), while the inner scribe handles information about movement sequences and provides a mechanism through which visual information can be rehearsed in working memory. Consistent with this distinction is a large body of evidence showing a dissociation between visual and spatial memory, very often using the paradigm of selective interference, based on the assumption that two tasks tapping the same cognitive function cannot be executed concurrently without a fall in performance (see Logie, chapter 2 of *Spatial Working Memory*). Outcomes from studies using selective interference have often been interpreted as supporting the distinction between visual and spatial working memory components (Della Sala, Gray, Baddeley, Allamano, & Wilson, 1999; Klauer & Zhao, 2004; Quinn & McConnell, 1996). For example, Logie and Marchetti (1991) found that one visual and one spatial interference task, involving the presentation of irrelevant pictures and unseen arm movements, respectively, caused a fall in performance of just the primary tasks of the same nature. This split between the visual and spatial working memory components is also corroborated by neuropsychological evidence from patients showing a selective deficit in the performance of either visual or spatial working memory tasks (Carlesimo, Perri, Turriziani, Tomaiuolo, & Caltagirone, 2001; Farah, Hammond, Levine, & Calvanio, 1988; Luzzatti, Vecchi, Agazzi, Cesa-Bianchi & Vergani, 1998).

In addition, there are considerable developmental data in support of a distinction between a visual and a spatial component. In a study by Logie and Pearson (1997), children aged 5–6, 8–9, and 11–12 years were administered the CBT (Milner, 1971), and an adapted version of the VPT (Della Sala et al., 1997). Results showed that performance in both tasks increased with age. However, the performance developed much more rapidly on the VPT than on the CBT. Hamilton and colleagues (Hamilton, Coates, & Heffernan, 2003) also addressed this area, employing tests to assess visual memory (memorizing a series of locations presented simultaneously) and spatial memory (remembering a repeated sequence of spots), and found that visual measures developed faster than spatial ones, concluding that the two kinds of task tapped different cognitive functions (see also Hamilton, chapter 7 of *Spatial Working Memory*).

Experimental results from use of Corsi- and VPT-type tasks (the two commonest visuospatial working memory tasks to date) to measure the visual and spatial working memory subcomponents (Pickering, 2001) could be interpreted within Logie's (1995) model postulating a distinction between visual and spatial subcomponents of visuospatial working memory, with the VPT presented as a test tapping the visual component, and the CBT associated with the spatial component. However, the differences between the CBT and VPT can be considered from other perspectives. For example, it has been argued that they also differ in terms of how the memory content is presented (Gathercole & Pickering, 2000; Pickering, Gathercole, Hall, & Lloyd, 2001; Pickering, Gathercole, & Peaker, 1998), i.e., static (as in the VPT) as opposed to dynamic (as in the CBT). To seek support for this latter view, Pickering et al. (2001) compared the developmental pattern of two visuospatial working memory tasks—one matrix task similar to the VPT and one task requiring memorization of a pathway within a maze—both presented in static and dynamic format. Although the two formats of each test were based on identical material, they resulted in different developmental patterns: performance in the static format was higher and, importantly, increased more steeply with age. According to Pickering and colleagues, mere distinction between visual and spatial processes cannot explain these results.

Following the reasoning of Pickering and coworkers a tasks analysis could help clarify how visuospatial working memory is organized. The main problem associated with the definition of the VPT as a visual test is that the core features of visual content (shape, texture, colour, etc.) are absent. In fact, in the VPT, matrices composed of partially filled cells are shown to participants, who have to memorize and then reproduce in the empty matrices provided. In this task, the locations of each filled cell in the learning matrix need to be correctly encoded and retrieved to allow reproduction of the correct pattern in the empty test matrix. It is therefore the locations (and the spatial relationships between different locations) rather than the visual characteristics that are crucial. While it is true that in some matrices a subject can see a visual pattern (such as an L-shape created by the filled cells), this does not mean that this strategy can be used in all cases. Furthermore, the strategy a subject actually employs should not be confused with the basic process involved in performing the task: following similar reasoning, a single person's visualizing the numbers during maintenance in the digit span test would indicate that the task is visual. In contrast, locations in the CBT are presented sequentially and thus the presentation order of locations is paramount. Lecerf and de Ribaupierre (2005) have distinguished three visuospatial working memory components rather than two. These comprise an extra-figural encoding responsible for anchoring objects with respect to an external frame of reference; and an intra-figural encoding based on the relations each item presents within a pattern, broken down further into pattern encoding (leading to a global visual image), and path encoding (leading to sequential-spatial positions). Similarly, Pazzaglia and Cornoldi (1999; Mammarella et al., 2008) have proposed the following breakdown of visuospatial working memory under the continuity model: visual working memory tasks, requiring memorization of shapes and colours, and two kinds of spatial task, both requiring memorization of patterns of spatial locations but differing in presentation format and type of spatial processes involved: simultaneous in one case (as in the VPT), sequential in the other (as in the CBT). Evidence collected with various groups of children supported the distinction between visual and spatial-simultaneous processes (Mammarella, Cornoldi, & Donadello, 2003) and between spatial-simultaneous and spatial-sequential processes (Mammarella, Cornoldi, Pazzaglia, Toso, Grimoldi, & Vio, 2006).

Testing a group of 162 children attending third and fourth grade, Mammarella et al. (2008) compared different theoretical accounts of visuospatial working memory, and used structural equation modelling to find the best theoretical factor model fitting the data. They compared models involving:

1   two simple storage systems (verbal versus spatial) and one complex span system (representing the classical Baddeley model);

2 two visuospatial working memory components and one verbal component (visual versus spatial—or static versus dynamic—versus verbal) without distinction between storage and processing measures;

3 four components corresponding to the distinction between complex span tasks and simple verbal, visual, and spatial tasks; and

4 three different visuospatial working memory components (visual versus spatial-simultaneous versus spatial-sequential), one verbal component, and one active component (representing the continuity model).

They found that the distinction between three visuospatial components suggested by Cornoldi and Vecchi (2003) provides the best fit of the data (see Figure 1.2). Structural equation modelling showed that visuospatial working memory tasks can be distinguished on the basis of not only their content and presentation format, but also the degree of active control. In fact, in the continuity model (Cornoldi & Vecchi, 2003) active measures partially maintain a distinction based on domain-specific aspects, contrary to Baddeley's original model (1986) in which executive processes are completely independent of presentation format.

Further research reveals that the organization of working memory is complex. For example, Bayliss, Jarrold, Gunn, and Baddeley (2003) examined the extent to which maintenance and processing functions could predict performance in complex span tasks, and found that complex span performance depended not only on

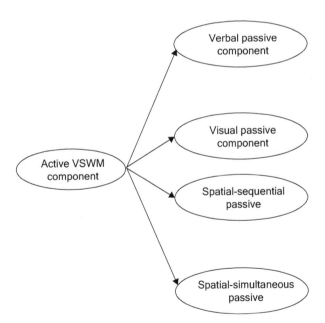

FIGURE 1.2 Structural equation model describing the relationships observed in typically developing children between different components of visuospatial working memory (VSWM) as predicted by the continuity model (see Mammarella et al., 2008)

maintenance and processing, but also on their coordination. These data support a multiple-component view, distinguishing between complex (i.e., active) and simple storage (i.e., passive) processes within working memory. In a similar vein, Miyake, Friedman, Rettinger, Shah, and Hegarty (2001) examined the relationship between simple storage and complex span tasks in visuospatial format and executive functions, finding them to be equally strongly related to executive functions, in contrast with verbal tasks. Similar results were obtained by Alloway, Gathercole, and Pickering (2006) in 4- to 11-year-olds. Alloway and colleagues also demonstrated that the link between simple visuospatial storage tasks and complex processing tasks was stronger in younger children.

Visuospatial working memory and genetic syndromes within the continuity model

The effect of genetic syndromes on cognitive abilities has been widely investigated in recent years. The continuity working memory model proposed by Cornoldi and Vecchi (2003) can account for the strengths and weaknesses of working memory abilities found in many genetic syndromes.

The horizontal continuum is of particular interest since it may also explain the different types of memory performance associated with the various genotypes. As mentioned, an important series of studies compared Down syndrome and Williams syndrome individuals; the results suggested that individuals with Down syndrome have greater difficulty with tasks involving verbal working memory, whereas those with Williams syndrome have greater difficulty with visuospatial working memory tasks (e.g., Jarrold, Baddeley, & Hewes, 1999). However, more light still needs to be shed on the nature of visuospatial deficits in Down syndrome. A study by Laws (2002) found that individuals with Down syndrome performed significantly better in the CBT (spatial working memory) than typically developing children matched for receptive vocabulary, while the performances of the two groups were not significantly different in a memory for colour task (visual working memory). In a recent study (Lanfranchi, Carretti, Spanò, & Cornoldi, 2009a), individuals with Downs were compared with typically developing children matched for verbal mental age. Participants were presented with a battery of spatial-sequential and spatial-simultaneous working memory tasks. The study's main finding is the dissociation between tasks measuring spatial-sequential and those measuring spatial-simultaneous working memory, the former being relatively preserved in Down syndrome, the latter relatively impaired.

Other findings from studies of children with spina bifida offered further support to the distinction between visual, spatial-sequential, and spatial-simultaneous working memory components. It is well-documented that spina bifida children are characterized by a verbal IQ usually higher than their performance IQ (Fletcher et al., 1992). Moreover, dysfunctions in academic skills are quite varied and complex: individuals with spina bifida may show good reading skills but poor text comprehension, spatial difficulties (McComas, Dulberg, & Latter, 1997), visual perception impairments (Denis, Rogers, & Barnes, 2001), and poor mathematical skills (Rourke & Conway, 1997). In a study by Mammarella et al. (2003), children with spina bifida and typically developing children were presented with three tasks: spatial-sequential (i.e., CBT), spatial-simultaneous (i.e., VPT), and visual (i.e., a task, the "House Visual Span", where participants have to recognize the houses previously presented from a set of house drawings). Children with spina bifida specifically failed on the visual task but not in the VPT, supporting the hypothesis that visual and spatial-simultaneous tasks do not involve the same processes.

The vertical continuum within the continuity model (Cornoldi & Vecchi, 2003) has also been tested. It was postulated (Cornoldi et al., 2001a) that highly intelligent children with specific learning disabilities would show particular failure in low-control tasks; children with reading comprehension and/or problem-solving difficulties (e.g., Passolunghi, Cornoldi, & De Liberto, 1999) would have problems at the intermediate level of control, where selection and inhibition of specific information is required; and children with intellectual disability would fail at the highest levels of control (see also Vicari, Carlesimo, & Caltagirone, 1995). In particular, the predicted relationship between deficit in highly controlled working memory processes and intellectual deficit in people with intellectual disability was consistent with theorists who were attempting to associate intelligence and working memory (e.g., Engle, Tuholski, Laughlin, & Conway, 1999; Miyake et al., 2001). Lanfranchi et al. (2004) explored the role of control processes in verbal and visuospatial working memory performance of individuals with Down syndrome. For verbal working memory, the Down syndrome group showed poorer performance regardless of the involvement of control, with increased impairment associated with increase in degree of active control required. In contrast, considering visuospatial working memory, the results demonstrated that individuals with Down syndrome are poorer in highly controlled visuospatial working memory, whereas in low-control tasks they can be as good as typically developing children with the same mental age. Lanfranchi et al. (2004) concluded that a core deficit in individuals with intellectual disability could reside in a controlled working memory deficit.

Finally, a recent study by Carretti, Belacchi, and Cornoldi (2010) tested participants with intellectual disability, examining whether they differed from typically developing children on tasks involving high active control. Participants were presented with verbal tasks requiring different degrees of active control: forward word span (low control), backward word span (medium-low control), selective word span (medium-high control), and updating word span (high control). Comparison between the group of intellectually disabled individuals and a group of children of similar general capacity showed that, although subjects were matched on fluid intelligence performance, specific differences were found on working memory measures. In particular, updating word span discriminated between groups well, and as effectively as the selective word span. These results confirmed that the intellectual disability group is characterized by poorer control processes in working memory. In a further study, Lanfranchi et al. (2009b) analysed the case of individuals with fragile X syndrome. A particular neurocognitive profile has been postulated for this syndrome (Warren & Ashley, 1995), reported as varying somewhat between males and females. For males it shows relative strengths in language, simultaneous information processing, and face and emotion recognition (Turk & Cornish, 1998). In contrast, females with fragile X syndrome show a relative weakness in visuospatial cognition (Cornish, Munir, & Cross, 1999; Freund & Reiss, 1991), and in sequential information processing and reproduction of items in serial or temporal order (Wilding, Cornish, & Munir, 2002). As regards the working memory components there is contradictory evidence over whether fragile X syndrome is associated with a selective deficit in visuospatial working memory as opposed to verbal working memory. Moreover, in several studies, deficits at higher levels of attention control/executive functioning are shown to affect boys, adult males, girls, and women with fragile X syndrome (Scerif, Cornish, Wilding, Driver, & Karmiloff-Smith, 2004; Cornish, Munir, & Cross, 2001; Kirk, Mazzocco, & Kover, 2005; Mazzocco, Hagerman, & Pennington, 1992). In order to disentangle whether the deficits of individuals with fragile X syndrome are due to the material implied in working memory tasks (i.e., verbal versus visuospatial) or the attentional control (i.e., passive versus active), Lanfranchi and colleagues (2009a) compared a group of boys with and without fragile X syndrome in two batteries of four verbal and four visuospatial working memory tasks requiring different levels of control. Subjects with fragile X syndrome showed performance equal to controls in working memory tasks requiring low and medium-low control, but significant impairment in cases requiring higher control. This working memory deficit in high-control tasks supports the hypothesis of attentional control as a critical variable distinguishing working memory functions and explaining intellectual differences.

Visuospatial working memory and nonverbal (visuospatial) learning disabilities within the continuity model

Children with learning disabilities usually show average or above average intelligence even when performance is poor on scholastic achievement tasks. One large subgroup includes individuals with deficits in linguistic abilities. However, there is a separate subgroup of children with learning disabilities who present a neuropsychological profile characterized by poorer nonverbal than verbal abilities. This disorder has been variously named as nonverbal learning disability (NLD) (Rourke, 1995), developmental right-hemisphere syndrome (Gross-Tsur, Shalev, Manor, & Amil, 1995; Nichelli & Venneri, 1995), or visuospatial learning disability (Mammarella & Cornoldi, 2005a, 2005b). One of the most adopted identifying features of NLD is a significantly higher score in verbal IQ than performance IQ on formal measures of intelligence (Cornoldi, Venneri, Marconato, Molin, & Montinari, 2003; Johnson, 1987; Weintraub & Mesulam, 1983). This finding is a direct result of the expected discrepancy in these children between verbal, language-based cognitive abilities and nonverbal, visuospatial cognitive abilities. Of course, verbal-performance IQ score discrepancies alone are never diagnostic in the absence of other supporting evidence.

According to Rourke (1995; see also Rourke, Ahmad, Collins, Hayman-Abello, Hayman-Abello, & Warriner, 2002) the NLD syndrome is characterized by significant primary deficits in some dimensions of tactile perception, visual perception, complex psychomotor skills, and in dealing with novel circumstances. These primary deficits lead to secondary deficits in tactile and visual attention and to tertiary deficits in visual memory, concept-formation, problem-solving, and hypothesis-testing skills. Finally, there are significant impairments in language prosody, content, and pragmatics. Children with NLD can also have difficulties in a number of aspects of academic learning, especially in drawing, science (Pelleiter, Ahmad, & Rourke, 2001), and arithmetic (Mammarella, Lucangeli, & Cornoldi, 2010; Rourke, 1993; Venneri, Cornoldi, & Garuti, 2003), and also in informal learning during spontaneous play and other social situations. Children with this disorder are also viewed as having substantially increased risk for internalized forms of psychopathology, which seem to result from low competence in comprehending nonverbal communicative signals in social and emotional contexts.

A critical factor underlying the difficulties encountered by children with NLD seems to be related to visuospatial working memory deficits (Cornoldi et al., 1995; Cornoldi et al., 1999; Cornoldi & Vecchi, 2003). These deficits might explain why NLD children fail in a range of activities (mathematics, drawing, spatial orientation, etc.) assumed to involve visuospatial working memory.

There is clearly still a need to find a coherent framework that can incorporate these findings. One approach is through the continuity model of Cornoldi and Vecchi (2003): it is of interest therefore to consider research on NLD and visuospatial working memory in the context of both vertical and horizontal continua of this working memory model. Referring to the vertical continuum, Cornoldi et al. (1999) investigated passive memory and the generation and manipulation of mental images that—according to the continuity model—involve active visuospatial working memory components. Children were asked to recall the locations of three, four, and five filled positions on a 5 × 5 matrix and to use interactive mental images to recall paired-word associates: NLD children were found to fail in these tasks. A more specific analysis of two NLD cases (Cornoldi, Rigoni, Venneri, & Vecchi, 2000) offered evidence in favour of the dissociation between active and passive visuospatial working memory. The study described two individual cases diagnosed with NLD. E.N., a 9-year-old boy, showed difficulties in passive tasks such as the CBT and the VPT, whereas C.I., a 13-year-old girl, had difficulties only on active tasks requiring manipulation of spatial relations or carrying out image subtraction. In a further study by Mammarella and Cornoldi (2005b), NLD children were presented with a visuospatial working memory test that shared some features with the span tests of Daneman and Carpenter (1980), in that only the last part of the material presented had to be remembered. An important finding of this research was that failure in visuospatial working memory appears to be typically associated with specific patterns of errors, in particular an increase in errors due to the processing of irrelevant information, thus involving a malfunctioning of the high level of attentional control.

For the horizontal continuum, research has offered some support for a distinction between visual, spatial-sequential, and spatial-simultaneous processes. In general, there is evidence to suggest that children with NLD are usually poorer in spatial tasks than in visual tasks. For example, Cornoldi et al. (2003) found that a group of NLD children were particularly poor in the spatial CBT, with an estimated effect size approximately twice that found for two visual working memory tasks. Mammarella and Cornoldi (2005b) also showed that the backward Corsi task may be a purer measure of the spatial difficulty of NLD children than the forward Corsi task. This result is coherent with other research by Cornoldi and Mammarella (2008) who tested low versus high spatial ability in young adults, finding a difference between groups in overall Corsi task performance. In particular, performance for the two recall directions (i.e., forward versus backward) was almost identical for the high-ability group, while the low-spatial ability group was impaired in the backward recall direction.

Mammarella et al. (2010) also found that NLD children performed significantly worse in spatial tasks (both sequential and simultaneous) than in visual tasks. This demonstrates that a visuospatial working memory deficit can also be found in NLD children in passive tasks—typically less powerful than active tasks in discriminating between groups, but more specific in distinguishing between different visuospatial working memory components (Cornoldi et al., 1995; Cornoldi & Vecchi, 2003) and in predicting specific learning domain difficulties (Bull, Espy, & Wiebe, 2008). Furthermore, spatial components seem further distinguishable in NLD children, since a double dissociation has been observed. Mammarella et al. (2006) tested three children diagnosed as suffering from a developmental form of NLD: two were characterized by problems on spatial-simultaneous processes, the third by a spatial-sequential process impairment. These results show the importance of considering spatial-sequential and spatial-simultaneous processes, and active and passive processes, in identifying different subtypes of NLD in children. The findings are also important in the design of targeted training programmes based on specific difficulties: three different studies by Mammarella and co-authors have shown the efficacy of training stimulating the various components of visuospatial working memory, namely the visual (Caviola, Toso, & Mammarella, in press); the spatial-sequential (Caviola, Mammarella, Cornoldi, & Lucangeli, 2009); and the spatial-simultaneous (Mammarella, Coltri, Lucangeli, & Cornoldi, 2009).

Overall, the identified contrast between active and passive and the distinctions between visual, spatial-sequential, and spatial-simultaneous processes allow better understanding of how the visuospatial working memory system is organized. Analysis of visuospatial working memory in children with NLD may therefore cast light on the nature of their difficulties and also facilitate exploration of the functioning of visuospatial working memory in individuals with specific nonverbal difficulties.

Conclusions

This chapter has examined the organization of visuospatial working memory according to an individual differences approach; this has also been useful in lending support to the continuity model of Cornoldi and Vecchi (2003). The organization of this model, taking into account not only task material and presentation format (i.e., visual versus spatial-sequential, versus spatial-simultaneous) but also level of attentional control required for the task, offers a useful theoretical framework for explaining working memory patterns of performance found when considering individual differences. In particular, individual and group differences have been considered in both typical and atypical developmental populations, including genetic syndromes such as Down syndrome, spina bifida, and fragile X syndrome and the case of children with NLD. The range of working memory profiles presented in these individuals have been described and interpreted according to the continuity model. Research has been presented that demonstrates the usefulness of both the vertical dimension (distinguishing between active and passive tasks) and the horizontal dimension (distinguishing between visual, spatial-simultaneous, and spatial-sequential tasks) in the study of cognitive strengths and weaknesses of children with different characteristics.

Notes

* This chapter originally appeared in the edited volume, *Spatial Working Memory*.

References

Alloway, T. P., Gathercole, S. E., & Pickering, S. J. (2006). Verbal and visuospatial short-term and working memory in children: Are they separable? *Child Development, 77*, 1698–1716.

Baddeley, A. (1986). *Working memory*. Oxford: Oxford University Press.

Baddeley, A. D. (2000). The episodic buffer: A new component of working memory? *Trends in Cognitive Sciences, 4*, 417–422.

Baddeley, A. D., & Hitch, G. (1974). Working Memory. In G. A. Bower (Ed.), *Recent advances in learning and motivation* (vol. 8, pp. 47–90). New York: Academic Press.

Baddeley, A. D., & Logie, R. H. (1999). Working memory: The Multiple-component Model. In A. Miyake and P. Shah (Eds.), *Models of working memory: Mechanisms of active maintenance and executive control* (pp. 28–61). Cambridge: Cambridge University Press.

Bayliss, D. M., Jarrold, C., Gunn, D. M., & Baddeley, A. D. (2003). The complexities of complex span: Explaining individual differences in working memory in children and adults. *Journal of Experimental Psychology: General, 132*, 71–92.

Bull, R., Espy, K. A., & Wiebe, S. A. (2008). Short-term memory, working memory, and executive functioning in preschoolers: Longitudinal predictors of mathematical achievement at age 7 years. *Developmental Neuropsychology, 33*, 205–228.

Bunton, L. J., & Fogarty, G. J. (2003). The factor structure of visual imagery and spatial abilities. *Intelligence, 31*, 289–318.

Carlesimo, G. A., Perri, R., Turriziani, P., Tomaiuolo, F., & Caltagirone, C. (2001). Remembering what but not where. Independence of spatial and visual working memory in the human brain. *Cortex, 37*, 519–537.

Carretti, B., Belacchi, C., & Cornoldi, C. (2010). Difficulties in working memory updating in individuals with intellectual disabilities. *Journal of Intellectual Disability Research, 54,* 337–345.

Carpenter, P. A., & Just, M. A. (1986). Spatial ability: An information processing approach to psychometrics. In R. J. Sternberg (Ed.), *Advances in the psychology of human intelligence* (vol. 3). Hillsdale, NJ: Lawrence Erlbaum Associates.

Caviola, S., Mammarella, I. C., Cornoldi, C., & Lucangeli, D. (2009). A metacognitive visuo-spatial working memory training for children. *International Electronic Journal of Elementary Education, 2,* 122–136.

Caviola, S., Toso, C., & Mammarella, I. C. (in press). Risultati di un training sulla memoria di lavoro visiva. Studio di un caso singolo [Results of a visual working memory training: A single case study]. *Psicologia Clinica dello Sviluppo.*

Cornish, K. M., Munir, F., & Cross, G. (1999). Spatial cognition in males with fragile X syndrome: Evidence for a neuropsychological phenotype. *Cortex, 35,* 263–271.

Cornish, K. M., Munir, F., & Cross, G. (2001). Differential impact of FMR-1 full mutation on memory and attention functioning: A neuropsychologic perspective. *Journal of Coginitive Neuroscience, 13,* 144–150.

Cornoldi, C., Bassani, C., Berto, R., & Mammarella, N. (2007). Aging and the intrusion superiority effect in visuo-spatial working memory. *Aging, Neuropsychology, and Cognition, 14,* 1–21.

Cornoldi, C., Carretti, B., & De Beni, R. (2001a). How the pattern of deficits in groups of learning-disabled individuals help to understand the organisation of working memory. *Issues in Education, 7,* 71–78.

Cornoldi, C., Marzocchi, G. M., Belotti, M., Caroli, M. G., De Meo, T., & Braga, C. (2001b). Working memory interference control deficits in children referred by teachers for ADHD symptoms. *Child Neuropsychology, 7,* 230–240.

Cornoldi, C., Dalla Vecchia, R., & Tressoldi, P. E. (1995). Visuo-spatial working memory limitation in low visuo-spatial high verbal intelligence children. *Journal of Child Psychology and Child Psychiatry, 36,* 1053–1064.

Cornoldi, C., & Mammarella, N. (2006). Intrusion errors in visuospatial working memory performance. *Memory, 14,* 176–188.

Cornoldi, C., & Mammarella, I. C. (2008). A comparison of backward and forward spatial spans. *Quarterly Journal of Experimental Psychology, 61A,* 674–682.

Cornoldi, C., Rigoni, F., Tressoldi, P. E., & Vio, C. (1999). Imagery deficits in nonverbal learning disabilities. *Journal of Learning Disabilities, 32,* 48–57.

Cornoldi, C., Rigoni, F., Venneri, A. & Vecchi, T. (2000). Passive and active processes in visuo-spatial memory: Double dissociation in developmental learning disabilities. *Brain and Cognition, 43,* 17–20.

Cornoldi, C. & Vecchi, T. (2003). *Visuo-spatial working memory and individual differences.* Hove: Psychology Press.

Cornoldi, C., Venneri, A., Marconato, F., Molin, A., & Montinari, C. (2003). A rapid screening measure for teacher identification of visuo-spatial learning disabilities. *Journal of Learning Disabilities, 36,* 299–306.

Daneman, M., & Carpenter, P. A. (1980). Individual differences in working memory and reading. *Journal of Verbal Learning and Verbal Behavior, 19,* 450–466.

De Beni, R., Palladino, P., Pazzaglia, F., & Cornoldi, C. (1998). Increases in intrusion errors and working memory deficit of poor comprehenders. *Quarterly Journal of Experimental Psychology, 51A,* 305–320.

Della Sala, S., Gray, C., Baddeley, A. D., Allamano, N., & Wilson, L. (1999). Pattern span: A tool for unwelding visuo-spatial memory. *Neuropsychologia, 37*, 1189–1199.

Della Sala, S., Gray, C., Baddeley, A. D., & Wilson, L. (1997). *Visual pattern test*. Bury St Edmunds: Thames Valley Test Co.

Denis, M., Rogers, T., & Barnes, M. (2001). Children with spina bifida perceive visual illusions but not multistable figures. *Brain and Cognition, Tennet XI, 44*, 108–113.

Engle, R. W., Kane, M. J., & Tuholski, S. W. (1999). Individual differences in working memory capacity and what they tell us about controlled attention, general fluid intelligence, and functions of the prefrontal cortex. In A. Miyake, & P. Shah (Eds.), *Models of working memory* (pp. 102–134). Cambridge: Cambridge University Press.

Engle, R. W., Tuholski, S. W., Laughlin, J. E., & Conway, A. R. A. (1999). Working memory, short-term memory, and general fluid intelligence: A latent-variable approach. *Journal of Experimental Psychology: General, 128*, 309–331.

Farah, M. J., Hammond, K. M., Levine, D. N., & Calvanio, R. (1988). Visual and spatial mental imagery: Dissociable systems of representation. *Cognitive Psychology, 20*, 439–462.

Finke, R. A., Pinker, S., & Farah, M. J. (1989). Reinterpreting visual patterns in mental imagery. *Cognitive Science, 13*, 51–78.

Fletcher, J. M., Francis, D. J., Thomson, N. M., Brookshire, B. L., Bohan, T. P., Landry, S. H., Davidson, K. C., & Miner, M. E. (1992). Verbal and nonverbal skills discrepancies in hydrocephalic children. *Journal of Clinical and Experimental Neuropsychology, 14*, 593–609.

Freund, L., & Reiss, A. L. (1991). Cognitive profiles associated with the fragile X syndrome in males and females. *American Journal of Medical Genetics, 38*, 542–547.

Gathercole, S. E., & Pickering, S. J. (2000). Assessment of working memory in six- and seven-year old children. *Journal of Educational Psychology, 2*, 377–390.

Gross-Tsur, V., Shalev, R. S., Manor, O., & Amil, N. (1995). Developmental right hemisphere syndrome: Clinical spectrum of the nonverbal learning disability. *Journal of Learning Disabilities, 28*, 80–86.

Hamilton, C. J., Coates, R. O., & Heffernan, T. (2003). What develops in visuo-spatial working memory development? *European Journal of Cognitive Psychology, 15*, 43–69.

Hegarty, M., & Waller, D. (2004). A dissociation between mental rotation and perspective-taking spatial abilities. *Intelligence, 32*, 175–191.

Inhelder, B., & Piaget, J. (1958). *The growth of logical thinking from childhood to adolescence*. New York: Basic.

Jarrold, C., Baddeley, A. D., & Hewes, A. K. (1999). Genetically dissociated components of working memory: Evidence from Down's and Williams Syndrome. *Neuropsychologia, 37*, 637–651.

Johnson, D. J. (1987). Nonverbal learning disabilities. *Pediatric Annals, 16*, 133–141.

Just, M. A., & Carpenter, P. A. (1985). Cognitive coordinate systems: Accounts of mental rotation and individual differences in spatial ability. *Psychological Review, 92*, 137–172.

Kane, M. J., Bleckley, M. K., Conway, A. R. A., & Engle, R. (2001). A controlled-attention view of working memory capacity. *Journal of Experimental Psychology: General, 130*, 169–183.

Kirk, J. W., Mazzocco, M. M., & Kover, S. T. (2005). Assessing executive dysfunction in girls with fragile X or Turner syndrome using the Contingency Naming Test (CNT). *Developmental Neuropsychology, 28*, 755–777.

Klauer, K. C., & Zhao, Z. M. (2004). Double dissociations in visual and spatial short term memory. *Journal of Experimental Psychology: General, 133*, 355–381.

Lanfranchi, S., Carretti, B., Spanò, G., & Cornoldi, C. (2009a). A specific deficit in visuo-spatial simultaneous working memory in Down syndrome. *Journal of Intellectual Disability Research, 53,* 474–483.

Lanfranchi, S., Cornoldi, C., Drigo, S., & Vianello, R. (2009b). Working memory in individuals with Fragile X Syndrome. *Child Neuropsychology, 15,* 105–119.

Lanfranchi, S., Cornoldi, C., & Vianello, R. (2004). Verbal and visuospatial working memory deficits in children with Down syndrome. *American Journal on Mental Retardation, 6,* 456–466.

Laws, G. (2002). Working memory in children and adolescents with Down syndrome: Evidence from a colour memory experiment. *Journal of Child Psychology and Psychiatry, 43,* 353–364.

Lecerf, T., & de Ribaupierre, A. (2005). Recognition in a visuospatial memory task: The effect of presentation. *European Journal of Cognitive Psychology, 17,* 47–75.

Lecerf, T., & Roulin, J. L. (2009). Individual differences in visuospatial working memory capacity and distractor inhibition. *Swiss Journal of Psychology, 68,* 67–78.

Linn, M. C., & Petersen, A. C. (1985). Emergence and characterization of sex differences in spatial ability: A meta-analysis. *Child Development, 56,* 1479–1498.

Logie, R. H. (1995). *Visuo spatial working memory.* Hove: Lawrence Erlbaum Associates.

Logie, R. H., & Marchetti, C. (1991). Visuo-spatial working memory: Visual, spatial or central executive? In R. H. Logie, & M. Denis (Eds.), *Mental images in human cognition* (pp. 105–115). Amsterdam: North Holland Press.

Logie, R. H., & Pearson, D. G. (1997). The inner eye and inner scribe of visuo-spatial working memory: evidence from developmental fractionation. *European Journal of Cognitive Psychology, 9,* 241–257.

Luzzatti, C., Vecchi, T., Agazzi, D., Cesa-Bianchi, M., & Vergani, C. (1998). A neurological dissociation between preserved visual and impaired spatial processing in mental imagery. *Cortex, 34,* 461–469.

McComas, J., Dulberg, C., & Latter, J. (1997). Children's memory for locations visited: Importance of movement and choice. *Journal of Motor Behavior, 29,* 223–229.

McGee, M. G. (1979). Human spatial abilities: Psychometric studies and environmental, genetic, hormonal, and neurological influences. *Psychological Bulletin, 86,* 889–918.

Mammarella, I. C., Coltri, S., Lucangeli, D., & Cornoldi, C. (2009). Impairment of simultaneous-spatial working memory in non-verbal learning disability: A treatment case study. *Neuropsychological Rehabilitation, 19,* 761–780.

Mammarella, I. C., & Cornoldi, C. (2005a). Difficulties in the control of irrelevant visuo-spatial information in children with visuospatial learning disabilities. *Acta Psychologica, 118,* 211–228.

Mammarella, I. C., & Cornoldi, C. (2005b). Sequence and space. The critical role of a backward spatial span in the working memory deficit of visuo-spatial learning disabled children. *Cognitive Neuropsychology, 22,* 1055–1068.

Mammarella, N., Cornoldi, C., & Donadello, E. (2003). Visual but not spatial working memory deficit in children with spina bifida. *Brain and Cognition, 53,* 311–314.

Mammarella. I. C., Cornoldi, C., Pazzaglia, F., Toso, C., Grimoldi, M., & Vio, C. (2006). Evidence for a double dissociation between spatial-simultaneous and spatial-sequential working memory in visuospatial (nonverbal) learning disabled children. *Brain and Cognition, 62,* 58–67.

Mammarella, I. C., Lucangeli, D., & Cornoldi, C. (2010). Spatial working memory and arithmetic deficits in children with nonverbal learning difficulties (NLD). *Journal of Learning Disabilities, 43,* 455–468.

Mammarella, I. C., Pazzaglia, F., & Cornoldi, C. (2008). Evidence for different components in children's visuospatial working memory. *British Journal of Developmental Psychology, 26*, 337–355.

Mazzocco, M. M., Hagerman, R. J., & Pennington, B. F. (1992). Problem-solving limitations among cytogenetically expressing fragile X women. *American Journal of Medical Genetics, 3*, 78–86.

Milner, B. (1971). Interhemispheric differences in the localization of psychological processes in man. *Cortex, 27*, 272–277.

Miyake, A., Friedman, N. P., Rettinger, D. A., Shah, P., & Hegarty, M. (2001). How are visuospatial working memory, executive functions and spatial abilities related? A latent variable analysis. *Journal of Experimental Psychology: General, 130*, 621–640.

Miyake, A., & Shah, P. (Eds.), (1999). *Models of working memory: Mechanisms of active maintenance and executive control.* New York: Cambridge University Press.

Nichelli, P., & Venneri, A. (1995). Right hemisphere developmental learning disability: A case study. *Neurocase, 1*, 173–177.

Passolunghi, M. C., Cornoldi, C., & De Liberto, S. (1999). Working memory and intrusion of irrelevant information in a group of specific poor problem solvers. *Memory and Cognition, 27*, 779–799.

Pazzaglia, F., & Cornoldi, C. (1999). The role of distinct components of visuo-spatial working memory in the processing of texts. *Memory, 7*, 19–41.

Pelleiter, P. M., Ahmad, S. A., & Rourke, B. P. (2001). Classification rules for basic phonological processing disabilities and nonverbal learning disabilities: formulation and external validity. *Child Neuropsychology, 7*, 84–98.

Pickering, S. J. (2001). The development of visuo-spatial working memory. *Memory, 9*, 423–432.

Pickering, S. J., Gathercole, S. E., Hall, M., & Lloyd, S. A. (2001). Development of memory for pattern and path: Further evidence for the fractionation of visuo-spatial memory. *Quarterly Journal of Experimental Psychology, 54A*, 397–420.

Pickering, S. J., Gathercole, S. E., & Peaker, M. (1998). Verbal and visuo-spatial short-term memory in children: Evidence for common and distinct mechanisms. *Memory and Cognition, 26*, 1117–1130.

Quinn, J. G., & McConnell, J. (1996). Irrelevant pictures in visual working memory. *Quarterly Journal of Experimental Psychology, 49*, 200–215.

Raven, J. C. (1965). *Advanced Progressive Matrices, Sets I and II.* London: H. K. Lewis.

Re, A. M., De Franchis, V., & Cornoldi, C. (2010). A working memory control deficit in kindergarten ADHD children. *Child Neuropsychology, 16*, 134–144.

Richardson, J. T. E., & Vecchi, T. (2002). A jigsaw-puzzle imagery task for assessing active visuospatial processes in old and young people. *Behavior Research Methods, Instruments and Computers, 34*, 69–82.

Rosen, V. M., & Engle, R. W. (1997). The role of working memory capacity in retrieval. *Journal of Experimental Psychology: General, 26*, 211–227.

Rourke, B. P. (1993). Arithmetic disabilities, specific and otherwise: A neuropsychological perspective. *Journal of Learning Disabilities, 26*, 214–226.

Rourke, B. P. (1995). *Syndrome of nonverbal learning disabilities: Neurodevelopmental manifestations.* New York: Guilford Press.

Rourke, B. P., Ahmad, S. A., Collins, D. W., Hayman-Abello, B. A., Hayman-Abello, S. E., & Warriner, E. M. (2002). Child clinical/pediatric neuropsychology: Some recent advances. *Annual Review of Psychology, 53*, 309–339.

Rourke, B. P., & Conway, J. A. (1997). Disabilities of arithmetic and mathematical reasoning: Perspective from neurology and neuropsychology. *Journal of Learning Disabilities, 30*, 34–46.

Scerif, G., Cornish, K., Wilding, J., Driver, J., & Karmiloff-Smith, A. (2004). Visual search in typically developing toddlers and toddlers with Fragile X or Williams syndrome. *Developmental Science, 7*, 116–130.

Swanson, H. L., & Siegel, L. (2001). Learning disabilities as a working memory deficit. *Issues in Education, 7*, 1–48.

Thurstone, L. L., & Thurstone, T. G. (1965). *Primary mental abilities*. Chicago, IL: Science Research Associates.

Turk, J., & Cornish, K. M. (1998). Face recognition and emotion perception in boys with FXS. *Journal of Intellectual Disability Research, 42*, 490–499.

Unsworth, N., & Engle, R. W. (2006). A temporal-contextual retrieval account of complex span: An analysis of errors. *Journal of Memory and Language, 54*, 346–362.

Unsworth, N., & Engle, R. W. (2007). The nature of individual differences in working memory capacity: Active maintenance in primary memory and controlled search from secondary memory. *Psychological Review, 114*, 104–132.

Vandenberg, S. G., & Kruse, A. R. (1978). Mental rotations: Group tests of three-dimensional spatial visualization. *Perceptual and Motor Skills, 47*, 599–604.

Vecchi, T. (1998). Visuo-spatial limitations in congenitally totally blind people. *Memory, 6*, 91–102.

Vecchi, T., & Cornoldi, C. (1999). Passive storage and active manipulation in visuo-spatial working memory: Further evidence from the study of age differences. *European Journal of Cognitive Psychology, 11*, 391–406.

Vecchi, T., & Girelli, L. (1998). Gender differences in visuo-spatial processing: The importance of distinguishing between passive storage and active manipulation. *Acta Psychologica, 99*, 1–16.

Vecchi, T., Monticelli, M. L., & Cornoldi, C. (1995). Visuo-spatial working memory: Structures and variables affecting a capacity measure. *Neuropsychologia, 33*, 1549–1564.

Venneri, A., Cornoldi, C., & Garuti, M. (2003). Arithmetic difficulties in children with visuo-spatial learning disability (VLD). *Child Neuropsychology, 9*, 175–183.

Vicari, S., Carlesimo, A., & Caltagirone, C. (1995). Short-term memory in persons with intellectual disabilities and Down's syndrome. *Journal of Intellectual Disability Research, 39*, 532–537.

Voyer, D., Voyer, S., & Bryden, M. P. (1995). Magnitude of sex differences in spatial ability: A meta-analysis and consideration of critical variables. *Psychological Bulletin, 117*, 250–270.

Warren, S. T., & Ashley, C. T. (1995). Triplet repeat expansion mutations: The example of fragile X syndrome. *Annual Review of Neuroscience, 18*, 77–99.

Weintraub, S., & Mesulam, M. M. (1983). Developmental learning disabilities of the right hemisphere: Emotional, interpersonal, and cognitive components. *Archives of Neurology, 40*, 463–468.

Wilding, J., Cornish, K., & Munir, F. (2002). Further delineation of the executive deficit in males with fragile X syndrome. *Neuropsychologia, 40*, 1343–1349.

2

VISUAL MEMORY, SPATIAL REPRESENTATION, AND NAVIGATION*

Amy L. Shelton and Naohide Yamamoto

Introduction

When asked "Where is the couch located in your living room?" many people would try to imagine the visual scene of the room. Alternatively, people might conjure up a schematic map of the living room, essentially drawing a mental sketch-map. Some people might use both of these types of images, or some hybrid of the two, to think about the space. The degree to which someone might use any one of these retrieval strategies probably depends on the familiarity of the environment (how recently you rearranged furniture), the scale of the space (can you see it all from a single vantage point?), specific experiences with the space (perhaps you used a schematic to decide where to place the furniture), and individual differences in preferences (e.g., Lawton, 1996; Pazzaglia & De Beni, 2001), but all of these are likely to have the feel of trying to *see* something about the environment (actual scenes or schematics).

For most sighted humans, it is quite natural to think of space as a visual phenomenon. Indeed, many of the core lines of inquiry on the nature of human spatial memory explore the issue in the context of spatial information learned visually (e.g., Easton & Sholl, 1995; Hartley, Maguire, Spiers, & Burgess, 2003; McNamara, 2003; Moeser, 1988; Presson, DeLange, & Hazelrigg, 1989; Rieser, 1989; Shelton & McNamara, 1997, 2001a; Thorndyke & Hayes-Roth, 1982; Waller, 2006; Wraga, Creem, & Proffitt, 2000). The link between space and vision is even stronger in many working memory theories, which posit a *visuo*spatial working memory component rather than separating spatial from visual (e.g., Baddeley & Hitch, 1974, 1994; Hitch, Brandimonte, & Walker, 1995). Even the term "cognitive map" (Tolman, 1948), which has been widely used to identify internal representations of space, conjures up the notion of a map that can be viewed and interrogated. Despite this strong reliance on vision to study and define spatial representations, few would question that spatial information can come from many sources, both visual and nonvisual—maps, exploratory navigation, text descriptions, haptic exploration, walking without vision, and so forth (e.g., Berthoz et al., 1999; Klatzky, Lippa, Loomis, & Golledge, 2002; Lambrey & Berthoz, 2003; Loomis, 1993; Loomis, Hebert, & Cicinelli, 1990; Shelton & McNamara, 2004a; Yamamoto & Shelton, 2005). Moreover, congenitally blind individuals clearly have the capacity for spatial learning (for review see Golledge, Klatzky, & Loomis, 1996; Millar, 1994; Thinus-Blanc & Gaunet, 1997). As such, the link between spatial memory and visual memory is not inextricable, just pervasive. Here, we attempt to characterize this relationship by considering theoretical and empirical ideas about the role of visual information, visual coding, and visual memory in various aspects of spatial cognition.

Representational properties and vision

The nature of spatial memory representations is the subject of many different kinds of debates. Here we present some of the major issues and dichotomies found in the literature and use them to discuss the role that visual processing and visual memory might play. In many of these debates, the evidence is not decisive, but it does speak to the critical questions in the field.

Vision as the primary spatial modality

Visual mapping theories of spatial memory have suggested the most direct link between vision and spatial representations. According to this type of theory, the human spatial memory system is designed to take information from multiple modalities and create a visual representation of the space—that is, the spatial memory system is one part of a broader visual memory system. In the strong version of the hypothesis, vision or visual experience is a prerequisite for spatial representations because these representations must be coded visually (Hartlage, 1969; Hebb, 1949; Schlaegel, 1953). The wealth of evidence showing that congenitally blind individuals are quite capable of representing spatial information refutes this obligatory dependence on visual experience (e.g., Golledge et al., 1996; Leonard & Newman, 1967; Passini, Delisle, Langlois, & Prouis, 1988; Passini, Proulx, & Rainville, 1990; Tinti, Adenzato, Tamietto, & Cornoldi, 2006). However, several lines of research appear to implicitly support a more moderate version of the hypothesis which gives special status to vision as the primary modality for spatial learning and memory (e.g., Attneave & Benson, 1969; Bertelson & Radeau, 1981; Mastroianni, 1982; Platt & Warren, 1972; Rock, 1966; Vecchi, Tinti, & Cornoldi, 2004; Warren, 1970).

The dominance of vision over other modalities can be seen in studies that put visual and nonvisual information in competition. When visual information and nonvisual information are providing incongruent information about the location of a single stimulus, participants will localize the stimulus to the visual source (Attneave & Benson, 1969; Bertelson & Radeau, 1981; Boring, 1926; Fishbein, Decker, &

Wilcox, 1977; Hay, Pick, & Ikeda, 1965; Howard & Templeton, 1966; Jackson, 1953; Rock & Victor, 1964; Thurlow & Kerr, 1970; Welch & Warren, 1980). For example, Hay et al. (1965) had participants judge their own hand position while wearing prism glasses that produced a visual shift. Despite participants' knowledge of the visual shift and the proprioceptive information about hand position, they localized the hand to the (incorrect) visually perceived location—that is, the visual shift led them to feel their limb in a different location from its actual position. A common example of "visual capture" of auditory information is familiar to anyone who has watched a movie in a theater or with a home entertainment system. Even though the speakers are displaced to the left and right (and often throughout a theater), we will perceive an actor's voice as coming directly from his or her location on the screen (Howard & Templeton, 1966).

Visual capture for locations across modalities extends beyond just the immediate resolution of a conflict. After some period of adaptation to the conflict, one can remove the conflict and observe which modality has been adjusted. In such cases, the perceptual adaptation appears to be occurring in the nonvisual modality. That is, the system is recalibrating to make the nonvisual input match the visual input (e.g., Bernier, Chua, Inglis, & Franks, 2007; Botvinik & Cohen, 1998; Ehrsson, 2007; Hay & Pick, 1966; Lenggenhager, Tadi, Metzinger, & Blanke, 2007; Ramachandran, Rogers-Ramachandran, & Cobb, 1995; Redding & Wallace, 1987; Rieser, Pick, Ashmead, & Garing, 1995).

In addition to capturing other modalities, visual reference frames appear to support localization in other modalities (Mastroianni, 1982; Platt & Warren, 1972; Simmering, Peterson, Darling, & Spencer, 2008; Warren, 1970). For example, Warren compared localization of stimuli in three different conditions. In visual localization, participants pointed to visually presented targets. In auditory localization without visual reference, participants pointed to auditory targets with their eyes closed. In auditory localization with visual reference, participants pointed to invisible auditory targets with their eyes open. Not surprisingly, the variability in pointing (i.e., variable error) was smallest in visual localization. However, in the critical comparison of auditory localization with and without vision, there was an advantage for having the visual reference frame available. In other words, performance in auditory localization became more similar to that in visual localization when visual information about physical surroundings was given to the participants, even though this visual information did not provide any direct cues to the auditory stimulus locations. These results have been interpreted to mean that auditory localization in the presence of visual information is carried out by choosing a point corresponding to the auditory target within a visual frame of reference.

The above examples suggest a role for vision in more perceptual processes. In memory, information from nonvisual modalities can produce what appears to be visual memory (Kirasic & Mathes, 1990; Shelton & McNamara, 2001b, 2004a). For example, Shelton and McNamara (2001b) had participants view a display of objects from one perspective and manually reconstruct the display from another perspective

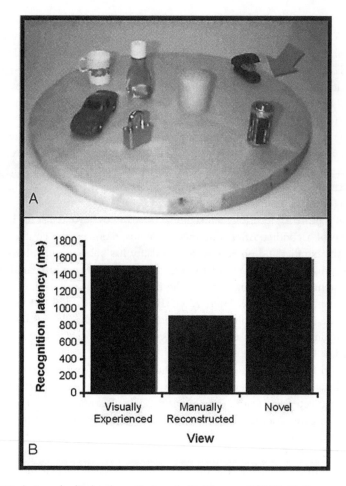

FIGURE 2.1 A. Sample display from Shelton & McNamara (2001b). B. Summary of response latency data as a function of the to-be-recognized view when participants visually experienced one view and manually reconstructed a different view (without vision). Novel views were not viewed or reconstructed during encoding. Figure 2.1A reproduced by permission from Shelton, A. L., & McNamara, T. P. Visual memories from nonvisual experiences. *Psychological Science, 12,* 343–347

without vision (Figure 2.1 A). In scene recognition, a visual task, participants were fastest at recognizing the view that they had manually constructed (Figure 2.1 B). Moreover, recognition of the visually perceived view was not different from recognition of novel views of the layout. In follow-up interviews, participants were indeed confused about which view they had actually seen, suggesting that they coded the manually reconstructed view in a manner that confused it with the visually perceived view. Similarly, Kirasic and Mathes found that scene recognition performance was unaffected by the way a space was learned—visually or verbally. Although differences in performance have been noted for scene recognition compared to other spatial tasks (e.g., Shelton & McNamara, 2004a, 2004b), the dependence on visual information in these tasks supports the idea that encoding in nonvisual modalities might be visually mediated.

Returning to the spatial representations of blind individuals, we can consider the primacy of vision for forming and/or coding spatial representation. Although blind individuals form effective spatial representations from nonvisual information, studies have shown that they are often impaired relative to blindfolded sighted individuals (e.g., Fisher, 1964; Gaunet, Martinez, & Thinus-Blanc, 1997; Gaunet & Thinus-Blanc, 1996; Herman, Chatman, & Roth, 1983; McLinden, 1988; Rossano & Warren, 1989). In these and similar studies, early or congenitally blind individuals were comparable to sighted individuals on spatial judgments about environments when tested on a single property of the environment or in simple configurations. However, when the task required more construction among parts of the environment and inferences about abstracted relations, blind individuals showed substantial impairment relative to sighted individuals. Additional work on mental imagery has suggested that inferential processes, and the degree of impairment, can be distinguished based on the degree of visual imagery that might be elicited by the task (Knauff & May, 2006).

In addition to this general difference in task demands, many studies have shown that the degree of impairment on these tasks is correlated with differences in visual experience. That is, the earlier the onset of blindness, the more profound the impairment, suggesting that visual experience may play some critical role in developing the appropriate reference frame for coordinating spatial information from different modalities (e.g., Axelrod, 1959; Cleaves & Royal, 1979; Dodds, Howarth, & Carter, 1982; Hötting, Rösler, & Röder, 2004; Rieser, Hill, Talor, Bradfield, & Rosen, 1992; Rieser, Guth, & Hill, 1986; Rieser, Lockman, & Pick, 1980; Röder, Kusmierek, Spence, & Schicke, 2007; Röder, Rösler, & Spence, 2004; for a more general role visual experience might play for cross-modal interactions, see also Putzar, Goerendt, Lange, Rösler, & Röder, 2007). Additional support for this role of visually mediated integration across modalities comes from work in nonhuman animals. For example, neurons in the superior colliculus of adult cats that had been raised in visual deprivation showed unimodal responses to each modality but failed to show the multimodal response observed in normally reared animals (Wallace, Carriere, Perrault, Vaughan, & Stein, 2006; Wallace, Perrault, Hairston, & Stein, 2004). These results from blindness and visual deprivation studies provide grounding for a privileged and potentially essential role of visual experience in the normal development of the mechanisms that enable the use of multiple modalities to represent space.

Taken together, these and similar lines of evidence support the notion that vision is a dominant, and potentially primary, *source* for spatial information in sighted individuals. Given that humans use vision as a dominant modality for many activities, it is not surprising that they would use visual information when it is available, give greater weight to visual inputs when information is ambiguous, and supplement nonvisual information with visual imagery if possible. However, the question remains as to whether these results should be taken as support for visual coding of spatial information. To address this issue, we now turn to some of the features of spatial memory that have been explored and how they bear on the role of vision and visual memory.

Egocentric and allocentric information in spatial memory

The very notion of a position in space requires a reference frame, and one of the primary distinctions made among possible reference frames has been between egocentric and allocentric (a.k.a. geocentric, exocentric, environment-centered) reference frames (e.g., Burgess, 2006; Feigenbaum & Rolls, 1991; Howard, 1991; McNamara, Rump, & Werner, 2003; Nardini, Burgess, Breckenridge, & Atkinson, 2006; Neggers, Van der Lubbe, Ramsey, & Postma, 2006; Wang & Spelke, 2000). As the terms suggest, egocentric reference frames code location with respect to the observer, whereas allocentric reference frames code location with respect to something external to the observer (room axes, distal cues, cardinal directions, etc.).

There is substantial evidence for both egocentric and allocentric information coded in the brain from neurophysiology and neuropsychology. In different subregions of the parietal cortex, neurons respond to the stimuli in retina-centered, head-centered, and even hand-centered coordinate systems (e.g., Colby & Goldberg, 1999), supporting a system for representing space egocentrically. However, place cells in the medial temporal lobes have been shown to code location with respect to the environmental reference frame (e.g., Burgess, Jeffery, & O'Keefe, 1999). In rats, place cells respond preferentially every time a rat moves to the preferred location in the environment, irrespective of the direction of approach (e.g., O'Keefe, 1976; Wilson & McNaughton, 1993).

A similar type of coding has been identified in nonhuman primates, in the form of spatial view cells (e.g., Feigenbaum & Rolls, 1991; Rolls, 1999; Rolls & O'Mara, 1995). Spatial view cells respond preferentially when the animal is looking at a particular location in the environment (or screen), irrespective of the combination of the animal's location, head direction, and gaze direction from which the preferred location is viewed. Finally, intracranial recordings in humans have demonstrated both place cell and spatial view cell responses in regions of the medial temporal lobe (Ekstrom et al., 2003).

This parietal/medial temporal lobe distinction for egocentric versus allocentric representation is also supported by patient studies (e.g., Abrahams, Pickering, Jarosz, Cox, & Morris, 1999; Abrahams, Pickering, Polkey, & Morris, 1997; Ackerman, 1986; Bisiach & Luzzatti, 1978; Burgess et al., 1999; Holdstock et al., 2000). In the parietal cortex, the strongest evidence for egocentric reference frames has come from work on unilateral neglect (e.g., Bartolomeo, D'Erme, & Gainotti, 1994; Chokron, 2003; Farah, Brunn, Wong, Wallace, & Carpenter, 1990; Halligan & Marshall, 1991; Mennemeier, Chatterjee, & Jeilman, 1994; Rizzolatti & Gallese, 1988). For example, Bisiach and Luzzatti presented a now classic case of unilateral representational neglect in which the neglected information changed as a function of the egocentric location of the patient. When patients with right parietal cortex damage were asked to recall a familiar site—the Piazza del Duomo in Milan, Italy—from one end, they neglected to describe the left half of the piazza. However, when asked to describe it again from the opposite end of the piazza, the previously missing information was readily described. This finding suggested that there was an intact (perhaps allocentric) representation of the entire Piazza stored in some form, but damage to the parietal cortex impaired the recollection in the egocentric framework.

In contrast, damage to the hippocampus appears to affect more allocentric forms of processing (e.g., Abrahams et al., 1997, 1999; Holdstock et al., 2000; King, Burgess, Hartley, Vargha-Khadem, & O'Keefe, 2002). For example, Holdstock et al. compared a patient with hippocampal damage to a matched group of controls on a simple location memory task. Participants viewed a single light on an otherwise uniform table and had to recall the location of the light (Figure 2.2). After observing the light, participants had to recall or recognize its location under several different conditions. In a lighted room from the same viewpoint as the learning, both egocentric and allocentric information could be used to retrieve the location information. To test for the use of egocentric information, retrieval was conducted in the dark from the same viewpoint as learning (Figure 2.2A). To test for the use of allocentric information, retrieval was conducted with full visual cues but from a new viewpoint in the room (Figure 2.2B). The hippocampal patient was consistently worse than controls in the allocentric conditions but had comparable performance to controls in the egocentric conditions, suggesting a specific impairment in representing location in allocentric but not egocentric space.

These results posit a role for both egocentric and allocentric information in the spatial representation(s) that humans use to remember and act within their

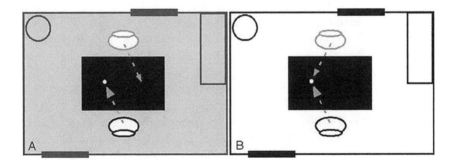

FIGURE 2.2 Schematic of the type of display used to test contributions of egocentric and allocentric information (e.g., Holdstock et al., 2000). The black chair reflects the learning position, and the gray chair reflects an alternative test position. A. In a darkened room, the response will reflect egocentric pointing from either location because the participant has no allocentric information to indicate a location relative to the distal cues. B. In a lighted room, the response may be guided by allocentric information, allowing the participant to correctly change the response when seated in a new location

environments (e.g., Burgess, 2006; McNamara, Rump, & Werner, 2003; Wang & Spelke, 2002). At the perceptual level, all sensory information is initially coded in an egocentric reference frame because the location of the perceptual reception is the observer. For example, visual images are retinotopically mapped in the eye, and this retinotopy continues into visual cortex (e.g., Tootell et al., 1998). Similarly, auditory location is coded in a head-centered coordinate frame. An allocentric representation therefore implies some process(es) by which the egocentric information is translated into an allocentric reference frame. As such, any theories that assume an allocentric representation are not consonant with the claim that spatial information is visually coded in spatial memory. In particular, several researchers have suggested that this translation from egocentric to allocentric "coding" occurs at a level independent of any particular modality, giving rise to a single supramodal (also called amodal) representation of space (e.g., Hill & Best, 1981; Milner & Goodale, 1995; Nadel, 1999, 2004; O'Keefe & Nadel, 1978). The hippocampus plays a central role as the proposed locus of this supramodal representation (O'Keefe, 1976; O'Keefe & Dostrovsky, 1971; O'Keefe & Nadel, 1978) or the resource for building up a more distributed representation elsewhere (e.g., Eichenbaum, Dudchenko, Wood, Shapiro, & Tanila, 1999; McNamara & Shelton, 2003).

Functional equivalence of different types of encoding

Whereas visual dominance suggests that spatial information might be visually mapped either in the memory representation or en route to it, functional equivalence paints a different role for modality in spatial representation. Functional equivalence refers to the degree to which spatial memories function the same way regardless of the modality in which they were learned, a finding that has been shown for a variety of spatial and navigational tasks (Auerbach & Sperling, 1974; Avraamides, Klatzky, Loomis, & Golledge, 2004a; Klatzky, Lippa, Loomis, & Golledge, 2002, 2003; Loomis, Klatzky, & Lederman, 1991; Loomis, Klatzky, Philbeck, & Golledge, 1998; Loomis, Lippa, Klatzky, & Golledge, 2002; Pasqualotto, Finucane, & Newell, 2005; Wang, 2004). For example, Klatzky et al. (2003) asked participants to learn the locations of visual or auditory stimuli from a stationary position. Subsequent memory tests that required localizing the learned locations—pointing to the remembered locations, verbal report of distance, walking to locations, and so forth—revealed no differences due to the learning modality. Performance on inferential tasks, such as pointing from a novel position in the environment, biased the localization in the same way for visually and auditorily learned spaces. These results together suggest that spatial learning in vision and audition resulted in representations that were comparable in terms of both locative information and sensitivity to updating. Similar results have been found for comparisons across other encoding modalities and in other memory tasks (scene recognition, distance and direction estimation among objects, etc.), suggesting that spatial representations derived from each modality share the same functional properties.

It has also been suggested that functional equivalence extends beyond sensory modalities to sources such as spatial language (Avraamides, Loomis, Klatzky, & Golledge, 2004b; Loomis et al., 2002). For example, Avraamides et al. (2004b) had participants learn locations of four objects in a room through visual perception or verbal descriptions of those object locations. When the participants were subsequently guided to another position in the room and asked to indicate distances and directions between object pairs, their responses were equivalent (both in accuracy and response latency) in visual perception and verbal description conditions. Such findings have been interpreted to mean that, once formed, spatial representations built from indirect "non-sensory" modalities also function equivalently to those learned through more direct perceptual inputs.

However, it should also be noted that research on the functional equivalence of non-sensory-based spatial representations has yet to yield unequivocal findings. By using spatial tasks similar to the one mentioned above, the same group of researchers showed that spatial representations derived from language had some disadvantage in mediating spatial updating performance (Klatzky et al., 2003). Moreover, studies of spatial language have suggested that the correspondence between spatial language and spatial representations is not direct. Instead, it has been proposed that spatial language is a filtered and imprecise reflection of the underlying spatial representation (e.g., Landau & Jackendoff, 1993). As such, this issue presents an interesting challenge for future investigations.

This functional equivalence is taken as further evidence that spatial representations are supramodal (e.g., Bryant, 1997; Eilan, 1993; Loomis et al., 2002). Like visual mapping theories, supramodal representation theories suggest a unitary spatial representation; however, rather than being visually coded, the supramodal representation (as the name suggests) is independent of the modality in which space is learned. For example, the cognitive map theory suggests that the spatial memory system creates a representation that has been abstracted from information coming in through the senses (e.g., Nadel, 1999, 2004; O'Keefe & Nadel, 1978). The abstract nature of spatial representation draws from the philosophical belief that the capacity for spatial representation is innate and therefore precursory to sensory experience (Descartes, 1993). As such, although vision may be a dominant sensory modality, it is simply one of the ways that information can get into a more general spatial memory system. In addition, functional equivalence suggests that there is no special status for vision, because the representations acquired from nonvisual modalities afford the same behaviors as those acquired from vision.

Modality specificity and spatial representations

As mentioned above, supramodal spatial representations have often been posited based on functional equivalence of spatial memories acquired through various modalities. However, it is important to note that the supramodal representation is not the only form of spatial representations that is consistent with the functional equivalence. That is, it is possible that multiple modality-specific representations, based on different modalities, mediate spatial behaviors equally well independently of each other. Such modality-specific representations would support modality-specific performance on different tests of spatial memory.

Several studies have provided evidence for modality-specific representations by probing spatial memory with tasks that place differential demands on particular modalities (Ernst & Banks, 2002; Lambrey, Viaud-Delmon, & Berthoz, 2002; Newell, Woods, Mernagh, & Bülthoff, 2005; Newport, Rabb, & Jackson, 2002; Shelton & McNamara, 2004a, 2004b; van Beers, Haggard, & Wolpert, 2002). For example, Shelton and McNamara (2004b) had participants learn tabletop displays like the one shown in Figure 2.1 A by experiencing two different views. One view was learned visually and the other was "learned" by having the participant describe that view to another person. Participants were tested on both judgments of relative direction—an amodal task—and scene recognition—a visual task. The results revealed that participants were better at recognizing the visually learned view in scene recognition, but they were better at making relative-position judgments from orientations corresponding to the described view (Figure 2.3). These results suggest that participants could tap into different representations[1] for the two different tests of spatial memory. The sensitivity of scene recognition to direct visual experience has also been shown for experience with multiple orientations (e.g., Shelton & McNamara, 2004a; Valiquette & McNamara, 2007). Despite evidence for a single

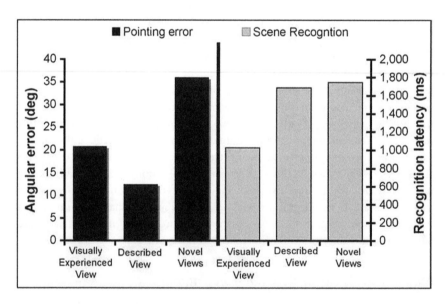

FIGURE 2.3 Summary data from Shelton & McNamara (2004b), showing the angular error data from judgments of relative direction (JRDs; black bars) and response latency data from scene recognition (gray bars) as a function of the to-be-recognized view when participants experienced one view visually and described a different view (without vision). Novel views were not viewed or described during encoding

preferred orientation for accessing spatial information needed for relative judgments, participants tend to recognize the views from each experienced orientation more quickly than novel views. This finding supports at least two forms of representation, with one being visually sensitive.

These studies have also shown that functional equivalence and modality specificity can co-occur. For example, Newell et al. (2005) had participants learn a tabletop-sized array of seven objects (similar to Figure 2.1 A) through either stationary viewing or haptic exploration of the display. After the learning phase, the locations of two objects in the array were switched and participants were asked to identify the change through either stationary viewing or haptic exploration. The learning and test modalities were factorially combined to compare within- and cross-modal performance. In addition, the test displays were shown either from the learned orientation or from a novel orientation. The results revealed both functional equivalence and modality specificity. First, visual and haptic learning in each orientation condition yielded similar accuracy in change detection, supporting functional equivalence. More importantly, however, results also showed that the accuracy was significantly worse when different modalities were used for learning and test, revealing a cost associated with cross-modal (visual-to-haptic or haptic-to-visual) recognition of the display. This pattern of performance is not readily accounted for by supramodal or visually mapped representations. A more plausible interpretation would be that the participants formed spatial representations that were still linked to the learning modalities. That is, these modality-specific representations mediated the change detection performance equally well, but when different modalities were used at the time of encoding and retrieval, spatial information in memory had to somehow be translated from learned modality to test modality, with additional cognitive processes incurring a cost in the change detection accuracy.

Taken together, evidence for modality-specific representations suggests that a unitary supramodal representation cannot support empirical findings on its own. Like the supramodal theory, however, multiple modality-specific representations argue against vision as the de facto modality for spatial representation.

Viewpoint dependence versus orientation dependence

Related to many of the topics above is the debate over viewpoint dependence in spatial representations. Viewpoint dependence was originally debated (and continues to be debated) as a property of visual object representations, and that term has been used interchangeably with "orientation dependence" (Biederman, 1987; Biederman & Gerhardstein, 1993, 1995; Tarr, 1995; Tarr & Pinker, 1989, 1990, 1991). For visual object recognition, viewpoint and orientation have very similar connotations; however, the implications for spatial cognition may be different, particularly with respect to the role of vision and other modalities in the representation.

A viewpoint-dependent representation of space denotes a representation that is specific with regard to both the location and orientation of the observer at the time of encoding. Implicit in this type of representation is the need for visual experience.

That is, space is represented with respect to a learned *view*point. Data from scene recognition experiments support this kind of highly visual, view-specific representation of spatial information (Christou & Bülthoff, 1999; Diwadkar & McNamara, 1997; Shelton & McNamara, 2001b, 2004a, 2004b; Shelton & Pippitt, 2007; Waller, 2006). For example, Waller (2006) asked participants to learn scenes of objects and compared recognition for images that were taken from the same viewpoint to those that were translated forward, backward, or laterally. Recognition of forward and lateral translations was slower and less accurate than recognition of the original image, suggesting that participants recognized the specific learned viewpoint better than translated viewpoints. In addition, Shelton and McNamara (2004a) investigated scene recognition following navigational learning from different perspectives. The results suggested that the degree of visual similarity from study to test was associated with the speed of scene recognition, indicating fastest recognition for the exact viewpoint seen during encoding (details of this study are discussed later in this chapter). Taken together, such results support viewpoint-dependent representations.

Scene recognition is a visual matching task, and viewpoint dependence denotes the capture of spatial information from a specified view—implied to be a visually experienced view of the space. As noted above, however, humans have the capacity to learn and represent spatial information from multiple modalities with equivalent access to that information after learning, raising questions about how viewpoint dependence might be defined in other modalities. Even if we relax the dependence on a visual view, a viewpoint still denotes a stationary position and heading. This necessity for experiencing space from a static position may apply to vision and possibly audition, but it cannot account for other forms of learning. For example, Yamamoto and Shelton (2005) compared visual learning to proprioceptive learning (broadly defined) of room-sized layouts. As shown in Figure 2.4A, viewpoint for the visually learned space is easily defined by the stationary position and heading of the observer. In contrast, for the proprioceptively learned space, the spatial information must be learned from the movements by changing positions along a path, in this case, while maintaining the same heading in space (Figure 2.4B). As a result, the "viewpoint" is constantly changing, and these dynamics make defining the viewpoint in viewpoint dependence complicated for nonvisual modalities.

An alternative to viewpoint dependence for spatial representations is orientation dependence. Orientation dependence refers to a broader concept of accessing a spatial memory from a particular orientation in space. In an orientation-dependent representation, there is greater emphasis placed on the heading in space than on the exact position of the observer. Alignment effects provide strong support for orientation dependence in spatial memory acquired in vision (e.g., Easton & Sholl, 1995; Holmes & Sholl, 2005; McNamara, 2003; McNamara, Rump, & Werner, 2003; Roskos-Ewoldsen, McNamara, Shelton, & Carr, 1998; Shelton & McNamara, 1997, 2001a, 2001b, 2004a, 2004b; Sholl & Nolin, 1997; Yamamoto & Shelton, in press) and other modalities (Shelton & McNamara, 2001b, 2004a, 2004b; Yamamoto & Shelton, 2005, 2007, 2009). For example, Shelton and McNamara (2001a) had participants learn room-sized layouts and tested memory with judgments of relative

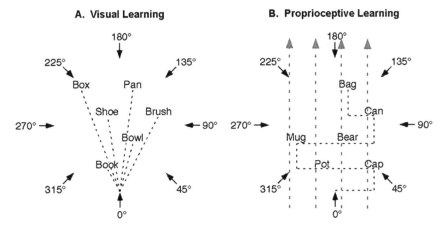

FIGURE 2.4 Schematics of learning conditions used in Yamamoto & Shelton (2005). A. Visual learning. 0° is the stationary view, and dashed lines indicate the direction to each object from the viewpoint. B. Proprioceptive learning (blindfolded walking) from a single orientation. Dashed line shows the path. Gray arrows show a vector field corresponding to the common orientation maintained throughout encoding

direction. Across multiple experiments, the results revealed that participants had preferential access to one orientation over all novel orientations and even some previously learned orientations. These results were taken as an indication that the representation was dependent on a preferred orientation on the space.

The key difference between viewpoint dependence and orientation dependence is in flexibility for retrieving information from different positions within a preferred orientation. In both orientation- and viewpoint-dependent representations, there should be preferential access to the orientation of the representation. Only in viewpoint-dependent representations, however, would a cost also be expected for changes in position within the preferred orientation. Although Waller (2006) showed some evidence for a cost in scene recognition after translations, it was not clear for all types of translations. For imagined judgments about locations and directions, the evidence is even less clear. Studies on the role of physical movement in imagining new locations and headings suggest that rotations but not translations improve performance relative to a no-movement, imagine-only baseline (Presson & Montello, 1994; Rieser, 1989). These results indicate the possibility that mentally translating a viewpoint can be done with very little cost. However, there has been some limited evidence for a cost in mental translations (Easton & Sholl, 1995; Tlauka, 2006). For example, Tlauka asked participants to learn an array of objects that included three possible viewing positions in addition to the actual learning position. The additional viewing positions were the to-be-imagined positions for the test and reflected different combinations of rotation and translation from the actual learned viewpoint. The results revealed that judgments from positions with imagined rotations were more than 200 ms slower than the original viewpoint or translated views, but the lateral translations (without rotation) also incurred about a 90-ms cost in response latency relative to the original viewpoint. It is notable, however, that there were no differences between the rotational conditions based on whether they included forward translations or forward + lateral translations. Taken together, these findings suggest that rotations are computationally more demanding than translations, as predicted by orientation dependence, but they do not completely discount some degree of viewpoint specificity as well.

Although the evidence is not conclusive with regard to viewpoint versus orientation dependence, positing orientation dependence has certain advantages. First, orientation dependence can more readily accommodate multiple modalities without having to establish different principles across modalities—an important issue given that different modalities can support equivalent performance. As illustrated in Figure 2.4B, for example, while it is difficult to give a strict definition of viewpoint dependence in proprioceptive learning, orientation dependence is readily defined. Even if we accept that viewpoint need not be strictly visual, viewpoint dependence in proprioceptive and haptic learning would still require specifying a mechanism by which a viewpoint might be selected from the many learned positions throughout learning. For haptic learning, one can use the position of learning as a virtual viewpoint on the space. That is, the extension of the arms to each object originates from a particular position, and moving about the space would cause the origin of this proprioceptive information to shift. Such viewpoint dependence for haptic learning accounts for the observation of small but significant translation effects in haptics (Klatzky, 1999). For proprioception from blindfolded walking, this notion of a viewpoint selection may be more akin to finding some canonical position for representing the space. Such canonical positions have already been suggested by Waller (2006) to account for the observation that some translations had an effect when others did not in visual learning.

A second potential advantage of orientation dependence is that it is consonant with theories of spatial representation that posit non-egocentric/environmentally centered reference frames. Unlike viewpoint dependence, which seems to suggest a largely egocentric (learned-position) basis for representation (e.g., Tlauka, 2006), orientation dependence does not require that the preferred orientation be a directly experienced orientation. As such, orientation dependence can more readily accommodate observations of non-egocentric orientations emerging as the preferred orientations in memory (e.g., Mou, Liu, & McNamara, 2009; Mou & McNamara, 2002; Mou, Zhao, & McNamara, 2007). For example, Mou and McNamara (2002) asked participants to learn room-sized object displays that had strong intrinsic structure when observed from a view that was 45° away from the learning position. If participants were alerted to the structure, the 45° view would become the preferred orientation for memory retrieval. Mou and McNamara suggested that this reflected the selection of an intrinsic reference frame that could be based on either egocentric experience or salient structures in the environment.

Returning to visual memory, viewpoint dependence reflects representational constructs that are more analogous to the type of coding one would expect for visual information. That is, we have a point of origin (namely, the eyes) from which we observe the world visually, and viewpoint dependence suggests a similar anchoring position. Orientation dependence is less directly tied to notions of visual coding and may be more commensurate with supramodal theories of spatial information. For example, the principal reference theory (e.g., McNamara & Valiquette, 2004; Shelton & McNamara, 2001a; Werner & Schmidt, 1999), upon which the intrinsic theories have been built, suggests that *any* environmental learning will begin with the selection of a principal orientation, without regard for the degree to which it can be tied to vision. However, the principal reference theory and other supramodal theories are agnostic with regard to how experience might cause this supramodal system to be more tuned for and/or more readily connected to visual inputs. As such, they cannot discount some prominent role for vision as the primary input or as an intermediary for other modalities.

Summary

In the preceding sections, we have outlined some of the major issues and debates surrounding the properties of spatial representations and how they might be related to vision and visual memory. The jury is still out on a number of these issues, reflecting the lack of a unifying theory in the spatial cognition literature. The balance of the data supports the claim that sighted individuals rely heavily on visual information for spatial learning. However, they also highlight the ability for humans, blind or sighted, to use many other sources of input to acquire spatial information.

Navigational processes and visual memory

Spatial memory plays a persistent role in many daily activities, perhaps most commonly in our daily navigation—from the bedroom to the kitchen, from home to work, from the office to the vending machine. Navigation itself can also be broken down into the different types of processes we hope to accomplish as we move through space (e.g., Golledge, 1999). At present, there is no unifying theory of the different types of tasks and processes that might engage human spatial memory, but the contribution of visual memory to navigation can be characterized by considering its potential role in these different proposed processes. In the following sections, we discuss some of the known and proposed processes and attempt to draw some preliminary conclusions about the role for visual memory.

Place and response learning

One of the fundamental distinctions in the processes that guide spatial behavior has been the difference between place- and response-learning mechanisms in rats (e.g., Packard & McGaugh, 1996; Restle, 1957; Tolman, Ritchie, & Kalish, 1946, 1947). In their classic studies, Tolman and colleagues demonstrated this dichotomy using a T-maze learning paradigm. Rats were placed in a maze like the one shown

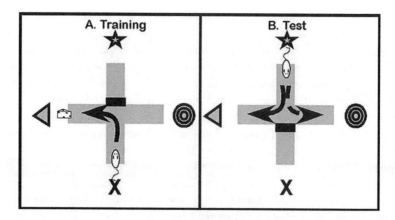

FIGURE 2.5 Schematics of a typical T-maze setup (e.g., Packard & McGaugh, 1996). Black bar shows a blockade, and shapes represent distal cues. A. During training, the same response (left turn) is required repeatedly to reach the goal. B. During test, the rat enters from the opposite direction. The solid arrow shows the place-learning behavior (turn toward the triangle), and the dashed arrow shows the response-learning behavior (turn left)

in Figure 2.5A. During training, the rat was placed at the same starting position and the reward was always in the same place. After training, the critical test was conducted by changing the configuration and starting position (Figure 2.5B). From this new position, there are two "correct" responses depending on what the rat has learned. If the rat has learned to use the cues in the environment, it will turn toward the environmental cue, demonstrating place learning. However, if the rat has learned to make a specific response to the T-maze stimulus, it will turn in the same direction that it has been turning throughout the training, demonstrating response learning.

In rats, place and response learning appear to be occurring in parallel, but several factors determine which will guide behavior (e.g., Cook & Kesner, 1988; Morris, Garrud, Rawlins, & O'Keefe, 1982; O'Keefe & Nadel, 1978; Packard & McGaugh, 1996; Tolman, 1948; Tolman et al., 1946, 1947). First, numerous studies indicate that place learning occurs more rapidly with limited learning and overlearning with variable routes, whereas response learning occurs after extensive training provided that the same route is repeated throughout training. In terms of utility, place learning affords greater flexibility of use, accommodating changes in the environment and the need to find novel routes. However, this flexibility is cognitively demanding. In contrast, response learning lacks flexibility but may allow for accurate performance with limited attention. As such, when attentional resources are limited, it is useful to have a more automated system for navigating familiar environments.

In addition to the behavioral differences, place and response learning have been associated with two different neural systems—hippocampus and caudate, respectively (Cook & Kesner, 1988; Morris et al., 1982; Packard & McGaugh, 1996). For example, using Tolman's T-maze paradigm, Packard and McGaugh demonstrated that lesions of the caudate resulted in solely place-learning performance whereas lesions of the hippocampus resulted in solely response-learning performance.

In humans, there has been a long-standing assumption that these two systems are also operating (e.g., Burgess et al., 1999), and neuroimaging studies have used the known neural correlates to support this contention (e.g., Hartley et al., 2003; Shelton, Marchette, & Yamamoto, 2007). For example, Shelton et al. (2007) used fMRI to scan participants while learning a fictitious environment by watching a repeated route. The results revealed a negative correlation between activation in the right caudate and the bilateral posterior hippocampus—as a given person showed more caudate activation, he or she showed less hippocampal activation. This difference could be attributed to differences in perspective-taking ability, one indicator of flexible spatial reasoning. Hartley et al. (2003) found a similar task-based difference in these regions. Together, these results have been used to suggest that people may differentially rely on place- and response-learning mechanisms based on individual differences and/or task demands.

In both rats and humans, these relationships have been revealed using largely visual learning conditions. However, there is nothing in the specification of these mechanisms that requires a link to vision (e.g., Hartley, Burgess, Lever, Cacucci, & O'Keefe, 2000). Like the hippocampus, the caudate nucleus receives inputs from multiple modalities, suggesting that stimuli from different modalities may serve as the signal for engaging the learned response. The role of cues in different modalities is discussed more thoroughly in the next section.

Cue guidance and landmark-based navigation

Place and response learning provide one way of dichotomizing possible mechanisms for spatial behavior, but the distinction has hard ties to differences between explicit/declarative memories and implicit/habit-based memories (Burgess et al., 1999; Squire & Zola-Morgan, 1988; Squire et al., 1990). In humans, there may be multiple types of explicit spatial mechanisms or strategies for guiding spatial behavior. For example, route knowledge is the result of encoding and representing information about a specific path or route through the environment (Siegel & White, 1975).[2] Learning a route can be viewed as learning a series of landmarks and the corresponding actions that need to be taken in response to the landmarks or cues. This learning of an action plan may be akin to response learning, but it can also clearly take the form of an explicit memory. For example, some people have a strong preference for navigation based on landmarks—that is, they prefer to follow a path of landmarks tied to actions as an explicit strategy (Pazzaglia & De Beni, 2001). Moreover, unlike response learning, route learning has been viewed as an early stage in spatial learning (Siegel & White, 1975; but also see Montello, 1988, for an alternative perspective).

Closely related to the notion of route learning are the processes of cue guidance (e.g., Morris & Parslow, 2004) and landmark-based navigation (e.g., Pazzaglia & De Beni, 2001). In its simplest form, cue guidance is using a cue as the target for locomotion. For example, on a particularly sunny day, I might want to sit under my favorite tree. If there are several trees in sight, I need only to recognize my favorite and walk toward it. Some species are thought to use this kind of targeting in a progressive fashion, relying heavily on proceeding from one target to the next (Collett & Cartwright, 1983). In a slightly more complicated scenario, landmarks serve as cues to the spatial behaviors needed for navigation. For example, the tree I hope to find might not be in my immediate visual scene. If I know that my favorite tree is on the lawn on the right past the art museum, then I can use the art museum as my cue to turn right. To most healthy individuals, either of these cue-driven tasks seems trivial. Even if clouds are casting an unusual shadow or a portion of the museum has unfamiliar scaffolding along one side, our visual recognition of familiar landmarks tends to be pretty effective as a cue to what we know to be the appropriate response (turn right) from previous experience or instructions.

In patients with damage to the lingual gyrus, a ventral region of the brain, this seemingly simple process becomes daunting. These patients are frequently diagnosed more broadly with topographical disorientation because they are unable to orient and navigate in familiar or unfamiliar environments (Aguirre, Zarahn, & D'Esposito, 1998; Landis, Cummings, Benson, & Palmer, 1986). However, upon close examination, they appear to suffer from a specific deficit—landmark agnosia—in which the ability to recognize and use landmarks in the environment is impaired (Aguirre & D'Esposito, 1999). Although these patients can describe what landmark they need to find (e.g., the art museum), they do not recognize the landmark when it comes into view.[3] This loss of contact between the spatial information and visual memory for the landmarks, which patients often can describe, severely impairs navigation in these individuals. Many patients report the need to actively compensate for this loss by relying on street names, house numbers, maps, and carefully drawn plans (e.g., Whitely & Warrington, 1978), supporting the intrinsic reliance on visual memory for effective cue-guided navigation.

Landmark-based navigation in sighted humans is likely to have substantial reliance on visual memory. That is, the most obvious landmarks in our environments tend to be visually experienced. However, this reliance on visual cues in most environments does not preclude the use of cues in other modalities to guide navigation. There is clear evidence for the use of patterns of olfactory cues to guide navigation in birds (e.g., Wallraff, 2004) and rats (e.g., Rossier & Schenk, 2003). In humans, blind individuals report using a variety of cues to orient and navigate (e.g., Golledge et al., 1996; Golledge, Marston, Loomis, & Klatzky, 2004; Millar, 1994; Passini et al., 1988), and even sighted individuals can effectively follow auditory cues to navigate (Klatzky, Marston, Giudice, Golledge, & Loomis, 2006). As such, the role of visual information in cue-guided landmark navigation depends on what cues are serving as the landmarks, which, for sighted humans, are more likely to be visual than nonvisual.

Cognitive maps

Route-based learning is probably the most common way that humans learn about their environments (MacEachren, 1992), but this type of learning does not restrict humans to route knowledge and cue-based navigation. Humans can effectively use this information to build up a flexible spatial representation of the configuration of landmarks in the environment, much like those hypothesized in the place-learning mechanisms described above. Several labels have been used to describe this type of representation—environmental image (Appleyard, 1969, 1970), topographical memory (e.g., Aguirre, Detre, Alsop, & D'Esposito, 1996; Epstein, DeYoe, Press, Rosen, & Kanwisher, 2001; Hartley et al., 2007; Landis et al., 1986; Whitely & Warrington, 1978), spatial model (Franklin, Tversky, & Coon, 1992; Mani & Johnson-Laird, 1982; McGuinness, 1992; Taylor & Tversky, 1992; Tversky, 1991), survey maps/knowledge (Klatzky, Loomis, Golledge, & Cicinelli, 1990; Siegel & White, 1975)—to name but a few. Tolman (1948) introduced the term "cognitive mapping" to describe the establishment of this internal representation of spatial information (for recent discussions see McNamara & Shelton, 2003; Morris & Parslow, 2004),[4] and many psychologists have used "cognitive map" to capture the notion of a representation of information about the configuration of landmarks in the environment (Baird, Merrill, & Tannenbaum, 1979; Downs & Stea, 1973; Foo, Warren, Duchon, & Tarr, 2005; Golledge, 1999; Golledge et al., 1996; Waller, Loomis, Golledge, & Beall, 2000).

Although the term cognitive *map* invokes the notion of a physical map that can be essentially brought to mind and viewed, this literal characterization of a map in the head is not well supported. First, cognitive maps do not appear to be coherent or complete maps of spatial information (e.g., Baird, Wagner, & Noma, 1982; Bryant, Tversky, & Franklin, 1992; Haun, Allen, & Wedell, 2005; McNamara, 1992; McNamara, Hardy, & Hirtle, 1989; Tversky, 1981, 1992). For example, McNamara et al. (1989) found that participants represented large displays of objects by subdividing the display into fragmented spatial categories, even when no physical or perceptual boundaries were available to divide the space. Performance on several tasks reflected faster and more accurate use of within-category relationships compared to between-category relationships. This subjective hierarchical structure in a single large space suggested that the cognitive map of the space was fragmented, and error or distortion occurred when those fragments had to be pieced together at retrieval. Similar chunking and fragmentation into hierarchically organized space has been shown for familiar environments (e.g., Hirtle & Jonides, 1985; Ladd, 1970). The lack of coherence is also found in the asymmetry in distance judgments between two points. For example, people estimated distances from a less salient landmark to a salient landmark to be shorter than the same distance estimate in the opposite direction (McNamara & Diwadkar, 1997), suggesting that one can have a cognitive map in which A to B is shorter than B to A. In a coherent map, these distances would be equal.[5] Finally, recent research has demonstrated that observers are only able to mentally access or spatially update their position within a single chunk of the hierarchical memory structure at a given moment, again challenging the conception of a single cognitive map that describes a known area of space (Brockmole & Wang, 2002, 2003, 2005; Wang & Brockmole, 2003).

A second challenge to the notion of a map-in-the-head is the visual nature that it invokes. Indeed, Tolman's (1948) original conception of cognitive mapping was a representation driven by information from multiple modalities. Again, this harkens back to the supramodal theory of spatial representation described previously. In this context, the cognitive map is viewed as a supramodal abstract representation of the spatial relations among landmarks in the environment. It has been suggested as the primary representation in place learning (Burgess et al., 1999) and is hypothesized to use an allocentric frame of reference (Morris & Parslow, 2004).

Behaviorally, evidence for cognitive maps comes from demonstrating the flexible use of spatial information to solve a number of spatial problems that cannot be solved with ordinal route information alone (for review see Golledge, 1999). For example, to select a direct path between two places that have previously been experienced separately in the same configuration, one needs to be able to represent the relationship between those two places independently of the specific separate paths on which each was previously experienced. The solution to this problem requires that people utilize some sort of allocentric information. One might use local cues to infer a global shape of an environment and locate each place within that framework, essentially creating a complete map. Alternatively, one might make note of the landmarks that appeared in both learned paths and infer the overlap or relationships between those two paths. If the two paths do not overlap, one may need to use a third known path to provide this link. In both of these cases, the learning of the spatial information would augment route-specific information with information about the stable properties of the space.

This process of inference and abstraction of the spatial information, posited as a supramodal representation, would put the cognitive map outside the realm of visual memory. As noted for supramodal representations in general, vision would serve as an input to this type of representation, but it need not be the only possible type of input.

Eidetic memory

Cognitive maps may be the furthest from visual memory in the menagerie of spatial representations for navigation reviewed here, but that does not preclude a more direct role for visual memory in some forms of navigation. In some animals, navigation appears to be primarily driven by the use of visual "snapshots" of the world (e.g., Collett & Cartwright, 1983; Collett, Cartwright, & Smith, 1986). Although it would be difficult to account for all aspects of spatial memory in humans (or most species) with this type of memory, it may play a role in some types of spatial processes. In conjunction with cognitive mapping or place-learning mechanisms, an eidetic memory could explain many of the discrepancies that have arisen in different spatial memory tasks.

Studies have noted that scene recognition and judgments of relative direction can lead to different patterns of performance with learned orientations (Shelton & McNamara, 2004a, 2004b; Valiquette & McNamara, 2007). For example, Shelton and McNamara (2004a) had participants learn an environment in desktop virtual reality from the view of a ground-level observer moving through a space. The encoding required participants to process the spatial information over three turns (four path legs). The learned orientation was therefore 0°, 90°, 180°, and 270° in legs 1–4, respectively (Figure 2.6A). When participants performed judgments of relative direction for the environment, there was a single preferred orientation based on the initial learned orientation at 0° (Figure 2.6B). These results suggest that participants represented the space in a single reference frame that was determined by the initial view they had of the space, and they tracked information back into this reference as they moved through space (see also Richardson, Montello, & Hegarty, 1999). However, this single coherent reference frame was not evident in scene recognition. When participants had to distinguish target images taken at eight different orientations in each leg of the route from highly similar foils, recognition was fastest and most accurate when the image depicted the orientation that was experienced in a given leg of the route (Figure 2.6C). As such, the "preferred" orientation differed with each leg of the route, suggesting the use of different representations for judgments of relative direction and scene recognition (but, for an alternative interpretation, see Mou, Fan, McNamara, & Owen, 2008).

The scene-recognition data suggest that people may indeed take snapshots of the world as they move through it. These snapshots can then be interrogated to make a comparison to the present sensory inputs. In the case of scene recognition, these snapshots are visual memories—hence, eidetic memories. In the Shelton and McNamara paradigm there appear to be multiple visual memories for different parts of the environment learned in a sequential path through the space. One could also posit "snapshot" memories in other modalities. For example, in a complex environment, the olfactory cues are likely changing as one moves through space. At any given location, one might store the particular combination of odors. These memories are the cues that are described above in cue-based navigation modes, but they also can serve their own role in spatial memory performance by serving as templates for matching, as in visual scene recognition. It is likely that this memory interacts with other types of memory for other tasks as well. For example, if a visual scene is used to make a judgment about a location that is out of the range of the visual image, the eidetic memory may serve as a cue to one's orientations within some larger framework, such as a cognitive map. This type of interaction among representation would account for the difference in brain activation observed for appearance versus position judgments cued by the same visual stimuli (Aguirre & D'Esposito, 1997).

Path integration

As shown in previous sections, landmarks (learned either visually or nonvisually) play integral roles in guiding spatial behaviors in many forms of human navigation.

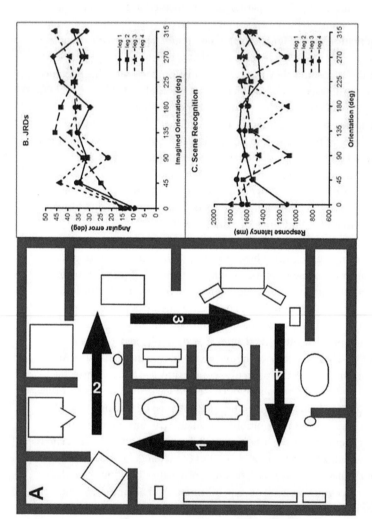

FIGURE 2.6 Task-specific performance after virtual route encoding. A. Schematic of a large-scale virtual environment, showing the path traversed over four different legs. Arrows show direction and heading on each path leg. Legs 1–4 had orientations corresponding to 0°, 90°, 180°, and 270°, respectively. B. Mean angular error from judgments of relative direction (JRDs) as a function of the imagined orientation and path leg. C. Mean response latency from scene recognition as a function of orientation and path leg. Adapted from Shelton & McNamara (2004a), Experiment 3

However, in the absence of conspicuous landmarks (and even without any visual inputs), a traveler can still keep track of changes in his/her current position and orientation in the environment with respect to a fixed reference point (e.g., the origin of travel and the known location most recently visited). In this type of navigation, the traveler relies solely on information about velocity and acceleration of his/her own movement, which originates from external (allothetic) sources such as optic and acoustic flow as well as internal (idiothetic) sources such as proprioception, vestibular sense, and efference copies of motor commands. This cognitive process is called path integration, or dead reckoning,[6] and it has been shown that humans and many other animals are capable of carrying out this spatiotemporal computation (for review see Berthoz et al., 1999; Cornell & Heth, 2004; Etienne & Jeffery, 2004; Loomis, Klatzky, Golledge, & Philbeck, 1999; Wehner & Srinivasan, 2003).

There has been a debate over what roles visual information plays in path integration. On the one hand, it has been suggested that idiothetic cues are necessary to accurately perform path integration (e.g., Chance, Gaunet, Beall, & Loomis, 1998; Kearns, Warren, Duchon, & Tarr, 2002; Kirschen, Kahana, Sekuler, & Burack, 2000; Klatzky, Loomis, Beall, Chance, & Golledge, 1998; Péruch, May, & Wartenberg, 1997; Wraga, Creem-Regehr, & Proffitt, 2004), especially when locomotion involves rotational movements. For example, Klatzky et al. (1998) had participants do actual or virtual walking along a two-leg path containing a single right-angle turn and asked them to face the origin at the endpoint of the path. Results showed that the participants accurately indicated the direction of the origin only when their walking included physical movements (actual walking or optic flow with physical turns). In contrast, when the participants remained stationary and experienced virtual walking only (optic flow alone, imagined walking from a verbal description, and watching another person walking on the path), their performance revealed a systematic pattern of error indicating that they failed to update their heading corresponding to the turn. These results suggest that physical motion (and idiothetic information associated with it) is critical for updating the current position and orientation during locomotion, whereas optic flow cannot elicit the best path integration performance all by itself.

On the other hand, it has also been demonstrated that optic flow alone can be sufficient for path integration (e.g., Bremmer & Lappe, 1999; Ellmore & McNaughton, 2004; Riecke, Cunningham, & Bülthoff, 2007; Riecke, van Veen, & Bülthoff, 2002; Waller, Loomis, & Steck, 2003; Wolbers, Wiener, Mallot, & Büchel, 2007; see also Sun, Campos, & Chan, 2004). For example, Riecke et al. (2007) asked participants to point to various locations in an environment during simulated walking by optic flow, with or without physical rotations corresponding to their trajectory. Results showed that accuracy of pointing response did not vary according to the presence/absence of concomitant physical rotations, both when optic flow information was provided by a familiar, natural scene and when it was replaced with a grayscale fractal texture. These findings have been interpreted as a challenge to the notion that idiothetic cues are critical for path integration. Furthermore, by extending such observations, it has also been proposed that optic flow *is* the essential source of spatial information for path integration (Cornell & Heth, 2004; Rieser, 1999). According to this hypothesis, visually restricted travelers interpret idiothetic cues about their movement by comparing them to previous experience with optic flow under normal viewing conditions. As a result, even when the travelers do not have direct access to distal landmarks, the mere exposure to optic flow during walking (e.g., seeing only a small area around their feet by wearing a vision-restricting device) can enhance their path integration performance compared to walking with no vision at all (e.g., Cornell & Greidanus, 2006). This is reminiscent of the visual mapping theory discussed previously, and certainly presents an interesting possibility. However, evidence supporting this hypothesis is still limited, and, as shown above, the literature provides mixed results.

One potential source of inconsistency in the literature is the variety of methodologies used to investigate vision in path integration. For example, some researchers used a vision-restricting hood that allowed participants to view a small area around their feet (e.g., Presson & Montello, 1994; Sadalla & Montello, 1989), whereas others used complete visual restriction by blindfold (e.g., Farrell & Robertson, 1998; Mittelstaedt & Mittelstaedt, 2001; Rieser, Guth, & Hill, 1986) or carrying out experiments in a dark room (e.g., Böök & Gärling, 1981; Simons & Wang, 1998). When virtual reality was used, sometimes visual stimuli were presented through a head-mounted display (e.g., Kearns, Warren, Duchon, & Tarr, 2002; Klatzky et al., 1998; Wraga, Creem-Regehr, & Proffitt, 2004), and sometimes they were projected onto a screen, either flat (e.g., Ellmore & McNaughton, 2004; Péruch, May, & Wartenberg, 1997) or curved (e.g., Riecke et al., 2002, 2007). To our knowledge, there have been no comprehensive studies of human path integration employing a wide variety of methods, resulting in the difficulty in isolating effects attributable to path integration processes themselves from those simply due to particular methods used for investigation. Initial efforts to address this issue have already been made (e.g., Creem-Regehr, Willemsen, Gooch, & Thompson, 2005; Knapp & Loomis, 2004), and it is expected that this line of research will be further expanded.

Summary

In the preceding sections we have outlined many of the processes that contribute to spatial navigation in humans and other animals. The use of these different processes and their relationships to visual processing will likely depend on the specific goals of an individual in a given situation. For example, suppose you just asked someone for directions to the new bookstore on a familiar campus, and she said, "Go up to the quad and turn toward the library. Go around the building and down the sidewalk to the right along the driveway. Cross the street, and turn right. Turn left at the corner and the bookstore will be on your left, halfway down the block." To follow these directions, you would likely use cue-based navigation to get to the library and walk around it. To identify the library, you might call upon a previous eidetic memory for its appearance and location on the quad.

The next "cue" might be the sidewalk along the driveway, followed by the street (which you must cross), the corner, and so forth. Once you have traversed this path to the bookstore, you may be able to utilize path integration to retrace your steps without having to explicitly reverse the directions (probably in conjunction with the cues again). Later, you may use your memory for the route (i.e., route knowledge) to return to the bookstore from the quad. Throughout these activities, you may also be formulating a cognitive map that will allow you to find the bookstore from the parking lot, your favorite restaurant, or some other novel direction. Like the properties of spatial representations, the many processes of navigation underscore the range of mechanisms that need to be explained to understand human spatial behaviors and suggest a complexity that has yet to be fully appreciated.

Challenge for future investigations

Throughout this chapter, we have highlighted a number of possible roles for vision and visual memory in spatial learning and memory processes. In some cases, we have suggested a direct role for visual information and visual memory (eidetic memories), whereas other cases seem to suggest that vision is just one of many possible inputs to a largely supramodal or multimodal system (functional equivalence, modality specificity, cognitive maps). It is clear that environmental knowledge comes in many forms and engages many different processes. What is less clear is how these various processes fit together.

The challenge for future research is to come up with a theoretical framework for organizing the many different types of spatial representations and how they might complement, interact, or interfere with one another. This new framework will need to account for different types of experiences, different degrees of familiarity, different goals for spatial learning and memory, and individual differences in spatial skills. Clearly, visual representations in perception and memory will play a critical role in many of the processes and representations. We began this chapter by making the case that the relationship between vision and spatial representation is pervasive but not inextricable. We end on the same basic premise in reverse: although we can clearly establish aspects of spatial representation that are not strictly visually dependent, it is clear that vision and visual memory play a significant role in many different aspects of spatial cognition.

Notes

* This chapter originally appeared in the edited volume, *The Visual World in Memory*.
1 Whether these should be termed different representations or different aspects of a single representation is largely a semantic distinction. If multiple modality-specific representations (or any other multiple representations) are linked by the fact that they represent the same physical space, then one could call them components of a larger representation of that space. The critical issue is still whether participants can tap into these representations or components for different purposes.

2 Although related, route knowledge is distinguished from route-based learning (see section 3.3).
3 The first author had an acute experience of this sort in London, when scaffolding on St Paul's Cathedral was so extensive that it appeared to be a different structure. Looking up and seeing an unexpected lack of familiarity produced a profound, albeit fleeting, feeling of disorientation.
4 Cognitive maps have also been closely tied to the discovery of place cells in the rat hippocampus, described previously (e.g., O'Keefe, 1991; O'Keefe & Nadel, 1978).
5 Certainly, there are cases in which different paths must be taken to, versus from, a place because of one-way streets or other oddities, but these cases are atypical and do not apply to these empirical investigations.
6 In the literature, sometimes path integration is more precisely defined as the process of finding one's position and orientation based only on idiothetic cues (e.g., Morris & Parslow, 2004; Philbeck, Behrmann, Levy, Potolicchio, & Caputy, 2004). In this chapter, however, we adopt the broader definition of path integration as including the use of allothetic cues, in the interest of encompassing a wider body of data related to spatial navigation via self-motion signal processing.

References

Abrahams, S., Pickering, A., Jarosz, J., Cox, T., & Morris, R. G. (1999). Spatial working memory impairment correlates with hippocampal sclerosis. *Brain and Cognition, 41*, 39–65.

Abrahams, S., Pickering, A., Polkey, C. E., & Morris, R. G. (1997). Spatial memory deficits in patients with unilateral damage to the right hippocampal formation. *Neuropsychologia, 35*, 11–24.

Ackerman, P. L. (1986). Individual differences in information processing: An investigation of intellectual abilities and task performance during practice. *Intelligence, 10*, 101–139.

Aguirre, G. K., & D'Esposito, M. (1997). Environmental knowledge is subserved by separable dorsal/ventral neural areas. *Journal of Neuroscience, 17*, 2512–2518.

Aguirre, G. K., & D'Esposito, M. (1999). Topographical disorientation: A synthesis and taxonomy. *Brain, 122*, 1613–1628.

Aguirre, G. K., Detre, J. A., Alsop, D. C., & D'Esposito, M. (1996). The parahippocampus subserves topographical learning in man. *Cerebral Cortex, 6*, 823–829.

Aguirre, G. K., Zarahn, E., & D'Esposito, M. (1998). Neural components of topographical representation. *Proceedings of the National Academy of Science, U.S.A., 95*, 839–846.

Appleyard, D. (1969). Why buildings are known. *Environment and Behavior, 1*, 131–156.

Appleyard, D. (1970). Styles and methods of structuring a city. *Environment and Behavior, 2*, 100–118.

Attneave, F., & Benson, B. (1969). Spatial coding in tactile stimulation. *Journal of Experimental Psychology, 81*, 216–222.

Auerbach, C., & Sperling, P. (1974). A common auditory-visual space: Evidence for its reality. *Perception & Psychophysics, 16*, 129–135.

Avraamides, M. N., Klatzky, R. L., Loomis, J. M., & Golledge, R. G. (2004a). Use of cognitive versus perceptual heading during imagined locomotion depends on the response mode. *Psychological Science, 15*, 403–408.

Avraamides, M. N., Loomis, J. M., Klatzky, R. L., & Golledge, R. G. (2004b). Functional equivalence of spatial representations derived from vision and language: Evidence from allocentric judgments. *Journal of Experimental Psychology: Learning, Memory, and Cognition, 30*, 801–814.

Axelrod, S. (1959). *Effects of early blindness*. New York: American Foundation for the Blind.

Baddeley, A. D., & Hitch, G. J. (1974). Working memory. In G. Bower (Ed.), *Psychology of Learning and Motivation* (vol. 8, pp. 47–90). San Diego, CA: Academic Press.

Baddeley, A. D., & Hitch, G. J. (1994). Developments in the concept of working memory. *Neuropsychology, 8*, 485–493.

Baird, J. C., Merrill, A. A., & Tannenbaum, J. (1979). Studies of the cognitive representation of spatial relations: II. A familiar environment. *Journal of Experimental Psychology: General, 108*, 92–98.

Baird, J. C., Wagner, M., & Noma, E. (1982). Impossible cognitive spaces. *Geographical Analysis, 14*, 204–216.

Bartolomeo, P., D'Erme, P., & Gainotti, G. (1994). The relationship between visuospatial and representational neglect. *Neurology, 44*, 1710–1714.

Bernier, P. M., Chua, R., Inglis, J. T., & Franks, I. M. (2007). Sensorimotor adaptation in response to proprioceptive bias. *Experimental Brain Research, 177*, 147–156.

Bertelson, P., & Radeau, M. (1981). Crossmodal bias and perceptual fusion with auditory-visual spatial discordance. *Perception & Psychophysics, 29*, 578–584.

Berthoz, A., Amorim, M.-A., Glasauer, S., Grasso, R., Takei, Y., & Viaud-Delmon, I. (1999). Dissociation between distance and direction during locomotor navigation. In R. G. Golledge (Ed.), *Wayfinding behavior: Cognitive mapping and other spatial processes* (pp. 328–348). Baltimore, MD: Johns Hopkins Press.

Biederman, I. (1987). Recognition-by-components: A theory of human image understanding. *Psychological Review, 94*, 115–147.

Biederman, I., & Gerhardstein, P. C. (1993). Recognizing depth-rotated objects: Evidence and conditions for three-dimensional viewpoint invariance. *Journal of Experimental Psychology: Human Perception and Performance, 19*, 1162–1182.

Biederman, I., & Gerhardstein, P. C. (1995). Viewpoint-dependent mechanisms in visual object recognition: Reply to Tarr and Bulthoff. *Journal of Experimental Psychology: Human Perception and Performance, 21*, 1506–1514.

Bisiach, E., & Luzzatti, C. (1978). Unilateral neglect of representational space. *Cortex, 14*, 129–133.

Böök, A., & Gärling, T. (1981). Maintenance of orientation during locomotion in unfamiliar environments. *Journal of Experimental Psychology: Human Perception and Performance, 7*, 996–1006.

Boring, E. G. (1926). Auditory theory with special reference to intensity, volume, and localization. *American Journal of Psychology, 37*, 157–188.

Botvinik, M., & Cohen, J. (1998). Rubber hands "feel" touch that eyes see. *Nature, 391*, 756.

Bremmer, F., & Lappe, M. (1999). The use of optical velocities for distance discrimination and reproduction during visually simulated self motion. *Experimental Brain Research, 127*, 33–42.

Brockmole, J. R., & Wang, R. F. (2002). Switching between environmental representations in memory. *Cognition, 83*, 295–316.

Brockmole, J. R., & Wang, R. F. (2003). Changing perspective within and across environments. *Cognition, 87*, B59–B67.

Brockmole, J. R., & Wang, R. F. (2005). Spatial processing of environmental representations. In L. Itti, G. Rees, & J. Tsotsos (Eds.), *Neurobiology of attention* (pp. 146–151). Burlington, MA: Academic Press.

Bryant, D. J. (1997). Representing space in language and perception. *Mind and Language, 12*, 239–264.

Bryant, D. J., Tversky, B., & Franklin, N. (1992). Internal and external spatial frameworks for representing described scenes. *Journal of Memory and Language, 31*, 74–98.

Burgess, N. (2006). Spatial memory: How egocentric and allocentric combine. *Trends in Cognitive Sciences, 10,* 551–557.

Burgess, N., Jeffery, K. J., & O'Keefe, J. (Eds.), (1999). *The hippocampal and parietal foundations of spatial cognition.* Oxford: Oxford University Press.

Chance, S. S., Gaunet, F., Beall, A. C., & Loomis, J. M. (1998). Locomotion mode affects the updating of objects encountered during travel: The contribution of vestibular and proprioceptive inputs to path integration. *Presence: Teleoperators and Virtual Environments, 7,* 168–178.

Chokron, S. (2003). Right parietal lesions, unilateral spatial neglect, and the egocentric frame of reference. *NeuroImage, 20,* S75–S81.

Christou, C. G., & Bülthoff, H. H. (1999). View dependence in scene recognition after active learning. *Memory and Cognition, 27,* 996–1007.

Cleaves, W. T., & Royal, R. W. (1979). Spatial memory for configurations by congenitally blind, late blind, and sighted adults. *Journal of Visual Impairment and Blindness, 73,* 13–19.

Colby, C. L., & Goldberg, M. E. (1999). Space and attention in parietal cortex. *Annual Review of Neuroscience, 22,* 319–349.

Collett, T. S., & Cartwright, B. A. (1983). Eidetic images in insects: Their role in navigation. *Trends in Neurosciences, 6,* 101–105.

Collett, T. S., Cartwright, B. A., & Smith, B. A. (1986). Landmark learning and visuo-spatial memories in gerbils. *Journal of Comparative Physiology, 158A,* 835–851.

Cook, D., & Kesner, R. P. (1988). Caudate nucleus and memory for egocentric localization. *Behavioral and Neural Biology, 49,* 332–343.

Cornell, E. H., & Greidanus, E. (2006). Path integration during a neighborhood walk. *Spatial Cognition and Computation, 6,* 203–234.

Cornell, E. H., & Heth, C. D. (2004). Memories of travel: Dead reckoning within the cognitive map. In G. Allen (Ed.), *Human spatial memory: Remembering where* (pp. 191–215). Mahwah, NJ: Lawrence Erlbaum Associates.

Creem-Regehr, S. H., Willemsen, P., Gooch, A. A., & Thompson, W. B. (2005). The influence of restricted viewing conditions on egocentric distance perception: Implications for real and virtual environments. *Perception, 34,* 191–204.

Descartes, R. (1993). *Discourse on method* (D. A. Cress, Trans.). Indianapolis, IN: Hackett.

Diwadkar, V. A., & McNamara, T. P. (1997). Viewpoint dependence in scene recognition. *Psychological Science, 8,* 302–307.

Dodds, A., Howarth, C., & Carter, D. (1982). The mental maps of the blind: The role of previous visual experience. *Journal of Visual Impairment and Blindness, 76,* 5–12.

Downs, R. M., & Stea, D. (Eds.), (1973). *Image and environment.* Chicago, IL: Aldine.

Easton, R. D., & Sholl, M. J. (1995). Object-array structure, frame of reference, and retrieval of spatial knowledge. *Journal of Experimental Psychology: Learning, Memory and Cognition, 21,* 483–500.

Ehrsson, H. H. (2007). The experimental induction of out-of-body experiences. *Science, 317,* 1048.

Eichenbaum, H., Dudchenko, P., Wood, E., Shapiro, M., & Tanila, H. (1999). The hippocampus, memory, and place cells: Is it spatial memory or a memory space? *Neuron, 23,* 209–226.

Eilan, N. (1993). Molyneux's question and the idea of an external world. In N. Eilan, R. McCarthy, & B. Brewer (Eds.), *Spatial representation: Problems in philosophy and psychology* (pp. 236–255). New York: Oxford University Press.

Ekstrom, A. D., Kahana, M. J., Caplan, J. B., Fields, T. A., Isham, E. A., Newman, E. L., & Fried, I. (2003). Cellular networks underlying human spatial navigation. *Nature, 425,* 184–187.

Ellmore, T. M., & McNaughton, B. L. (2004). Human path integration by optic flow. *Spatial Cognition and Computation, 4*, 255–272.

Epstein, R., DeYoe, E. A., Press, D. Z., Rosen, A. C., & Kanwisher, N. (2001). Neuropsychological evidence for a topographical learning mechanism in parahippocampal cortex. *Cognitive Neuropsychology, 18*, 481–508.

Ernst, M. O., & Banks, M. S. (2002). Humans integrate visual and haptic information in a statistically optimal fashion. *Nature, 415*, 429–433.

Etienne, A. S., & Jeffery, K. J. (2004). Path integration in mammals. *Hippocampus, 14*, 180–192.

Farah, M. J., Brunn, J. L., Wong, A. B., Wallace, M. A., & Carpenter, P. A. (1990). Frame of reference for allocating attention to space: Evidence from neglect syndrome. *Neuropsychologia, 28*, 335–347.

Farrell, M. J., & Robertson, I. H. (1998). Mental rotation and the automatic updating of body-centered spatial relationships. *Journal of Experimental Psychology: Learning, Memory, and Cognition, 24*, 227–233.

Feigenbaum, J. D., & Rolls, E. T. (1991). Allocentric and egocentric spatial information processing in the hippocampal formation of the behaving primate. *Psychobiology, 19*, 21–40.

Fishbein, H. D., Decker, J., & Wilcox, P. (1977). Cross-modality transfer of spatial information. *British Journal of Psychology, 68*, 503–508.

Fisher, G. H. (1964). Spatial localization by the blind. *American Journal of Psychology, 77*, 2–14.

Foo, P., Warren, W. H., Duchon, A., & Tarr, M. J. (2005). Do humans integrate routes into a cognitive map? Map- versus landmark-based navigation of novel shortcuts. *Journal of Experimental Psychology: Learning, Memory, and Cognition, 31*, 195–215.

Franklin, N., Tversky, B., & Coon, V. (1992). Switching points of view in spatial mental models. *Memory and Cognition, 20*, 507–518.

Gaunet, F., Martinez, J. L., & Thinus-Blanc, C. (1997). Early-blind subjects' spatial representation of manipulatory space: Exploratory strategies and reaction to change. *Perception, 26*, 345–366.

Gaunet, F., & Thinus-Blanc, C. (1996). Early-blind subjects' spatial abilities in the locomotor space: Exploratory strategies and reaction-to-change performance. *Perception, 25*, 967–981.

Golledge, R. G. (1999). Human wayfinding and cognitive maps. In R. G. Golledge (Ed.), *Wayfinding behavior: Cognitive mapping and other spatial processes.* (pp. 5–45). Baltimore, MD: Johns Hopkins University Press.

Golledge, R. G., Klatzky, R. L., & Loomis, J. M. (1996). Cognitive mapping and wayfinding in adults without vision. In J. Portugali (Ed.), *The construction of cognitive maps* (pp. 215–146). Dordrecht: Kluwer Academic.

Golledge, R. G., Marston, J. R., Loomis, J. M., & Klatzky, R. L. (2004). Stated preferences for components of a personal guidance system for nonvisual navigation. *Journal of Visual Impairment & Blindness, 98*, 135–147.

Halligan, P. W., & Marshall, J. C. (1991). Left neglect in near but not far space in man. *Nature, 350*, 498–500.

Hartlage, L. C. (1969). Verbal tests of spatial conceptualization. *Journal of Experimental Psychology, 80*, 180–182.

Hartley, T., Bird, C. M., Chan, D., Cipolotti, L., Husain, M., Vargha-Khadem, F., & Burgess, N. (2007). The hippocampus is required for short-term topographical memory in humans. *Hippocampus, 17*, 34–48.

Hartley, T., Burgess, N., Lever, C., Cacucci, F., & O'Keefe, J. (2000). Modeling place fields in terms of the cortical inputs to the hippocampus. *Hippocampus, 10*, 369–379.

Hartley, T., Maguire, E. A., Spiers, H. J., & Burgess, N. (2003). The well-worn route and the path less traveled: Distinct neural bases of route following and wayfinding in humans. *Neuron, 37*, 877–888.

Haun, D. B. M., Allen, G. L., & Wedell, D. H. (2005). Bias in spatial memory: A categorical endorsement. *Acta Psychologica, 118*, 149–170.

Hay, J. C., & Pick, H. L., Jr. (1966). Visual and proprioceptive adaptation to optical displacement of the visual stimulus. *Journal of Experimental Psychology, 71*, 150–158.

Hay, J. C., Pick, H. L., Jr., & Ikeda, K. (1965). Visual capture produced by prism spectacles. *Psychonomic Science, 2*, 215–216.

Hebb, D. O. (1949). *The organization of behavior*. New York: Wiley.

Herman, J. F., Chatman, S. P., & Roth, S. F. (1983). Cognitive mapping in blind people: Acquisition of spatial relationships in a large-scale environment. *Journal of Visual Impairment and Blindness, 77*, 161–166.

Hill, A. J., & Best, P. J. (1981). Effects of deafness and blindness on the spatial correlates of hippocampal unit activity in the rat. *Experimental Neurology, 74*, 204–217.

Hirtle, S. C., & Jonides, J. (1985). Evidence of hierarchies in cognitive maps. *Memory and Cognition, 3*, 208–217.

Hitch, G. J., Brandimonte, M. A., & Walker, P. (1995). Two types of representations in visual memory: Evidence from the effect of stimulus contrast on an image combination task. *Memory and Cognition, 23*, 147–154.

Holdstock, J. S., Mayes, A. R., Cezayirili, E., Isaac, C. L., Aggleton, J. P., & Roberts, N. (2000). A comparison of egocentric and allocentric spatial memory in a patient with selective hippocampal damage. *Neuropsychologia, 38*, 410–425.

Holmes, M. C., & Sholl, M. J. (2005). Allocentric coding of object-to-object relations in overlearned and novel environments. *Journal of Experimental Psychology: Learning, Memory, and Cognition, 31*, 1069–1087.

Hötting, K., Rösler, F., & Röder, B. (2004). Altered auditory–tactile interactions in congenitally blind humans: An event-related potential study. *Experimental Brain Research, 159*, 370–381.

Howard, I. P. (1991). Spatial vision within egocentric and exocentric frames of reference. In S. R. Ellis (Ed.), *Pictorial communication in virtual and real environments* (pp. 338–358). London: Taylor & Francis.

Howard, I. P., & Templeton, W. B. (1966). *Human spatial orientation*. London: Wiley.

Jackson, C. V. (1953). Visual factors in auditory localization. *Quarterly Journal of Experimental Psychology, 5*, 52–65.

Kearns, M. J., Warren, W. H., Duchon, A. P., & Tarr, M. J. (2002). Path integration from optic flow and body senses in a homing task. *Perception, 31*, 349–374.

King, J. A., Burgess, N., Hartley, T., Vargha-Khadem, F., & O'Keefe, J. (2002). Human hippocampus and viewpoint dependence in spatial memory. *Hippocampus, 12*, 811–820.

Kirasic, K. C., & Mathes, E. A. (1990). Effects of different means for conveying environmental information on elderly adults' spatial cognition and behavior. *Environment and Behavior, 22*, 591–607.

Kirschen, M. P., Kahana, M. J., Sekuler, R., & Burack, B. (2000). Optic flow helps humans learn to navigate through synthetic environments. *Perception, 29*, 801–818.

Klatzky, R. L. (1999). Path completion after haptic exploration without vision: Implications for haptic spatial representations. *Perception and Psychophysics, 61*, 220–235.

Klatzky, R. L., Lippa, Y., Loomis, J. M., & Golledge, R. G. (2002). Learning directions of objects specified by vision, spatial audition, or auditory spatial language. *Learning and Memory, 9*, 364–367.

Klatzky, R. L., Lippa, Y., Loomis, J. M., & Golledge, R. G. (2003). Encoding, learning, and spatial updating of multiple object locations specified by 3-D sound, spatial language, and vision. *Experimental Brain Research, 149*, 48–61.

Klatzky, R. L., Loomis, J. M., Beall, A. C., Chance, S. S., & Golledge, R. G. (1998). Spatial updating of self-position and orientation during real, imagined, and virtual locomotion. *Psychological Science, 9*, 293–298.

Klatzky, R. L., Loomis, J. M., Golledge, R. G., & Cicinelli, J. G. (1990). Acquisition of route and survey knowledge in the absence of vision. *Journal of Motor Behavior, 22*, 19–43.

Klatzky, R. L., Marston, J. R., Giudice, N. A., Golledge, R. G., & Loomis, J. M. (2006). Cognitive load of navigating without vision when guided by virtual sound versus spatial language. *Journal of Experimental Psychology: Applied, 12*, 223–232.

Knapp, J. M., & Loomis, J. M. (2004). Limited field of view of head-mounted displays is not the cause of distance underestimation in virtual environments. *Presence, 13*, 572–577.

Knauff, M., & May, E. (2006). Mental imagery, reasoning, and blindness. *Quarterly Journal of Experimental Psychology, 59*, 161–177.

Ladd, F. C. (1970). Black youths view their environment: Neighborhood maps. *Environment and Behavior, 2*, 64–79.

Lambrey, S., & Berthoz, A. (2003). Combination of conflicting visual and non-visual information for estimating actively performed body turns in virtual reality. *International Journal of Psychophysiology, 50*, 101–115.

Lambrey, S., Viaud-Delmon, I., & Berthoz, A. (2002). Influence of a sensorimotor conflict on the memorization of a path traveled in virtual reality. *Cognitive Brain Research, 14*, 177–186.

Landau, B., & Jackendoff, R. (1993). "What" and "where" in spatial language and cognition. *Behavioral and Brain Sciences, 16*, 217–265.

Landis, T., Cummings, J. L., Benson, D. F., & Palmer, E. P. (1986). Loss of topographical familiarity: An environmental agnosia. *Archives of Neurology, 43*, 132–136.

Lawton, C. A. (1996). Strategies for indoor wayfinding: The role of orientation. *Journal of Environmental Psychology, 16*, 137–145.

Lenggenhager, B., Tadi, T., Metzinger, T., & Blanke, O. (2007). Video ergo sum: Manipulating bodily self-consciousness. *Science, 317*, 1096–1099.

Leonard, J. A., & Newman, R. C. (1967). Spatial orientation in the blind. *Nature, 215*, 1413–1414.

Loomis, J. M. (1993). Counterexample to the hypothesis of functional similarity between tactile and visual pattern perception. *Perception and Psychophysics, 54*, 179–184.

Loomis, J. M., Hebert, C., & Cicinelli, J. G. (1990). Active localization of virtual sounds. *Journal of the Acoustical Society of America, 88*, 1757–1764.

Loomis, J. M., Klatzky, R. L., Golledge, R. G., & Philbeck, J. W. (1999). Human navigation by path integration. In R. G. Golledge (Ed.), *Wayfinding: Cognitive mapping and other spatial processes* (pp. 125–151). Baltimore, MD: Johns Hopkins University Press.

Loomis, J. M., Klatzky, R. L., & Lederman, S. J. (1991). Similarity of tactual and visual picture recognition with limited field of view. *Perception, 20*, 167–177.

Loomis, J. M., Klatzky, R. L., Philbeck, J. W., & Golledge, R. G. (1998). Assessing auditory distance perception using perceptually directed action. *Perception and Psychophysics, 60*, 966–980.

Loomis, J. M., Lippa, Y., Klatzky, R. L., & Golledge, R. G. (2002). Spatial updating of locations specified by 3-D sound and spatial language. *Journal of Experimental Psychology: Learning, Memory, and Cognition, 28*, 335–345.

MacEachren, A. M. (1992). Application of environmental learning theory to spatial knowledge acquisition from maps. *Annals of the Association of American Geographers, 82,* 245–274.

Mani, K., & Johnson-Laird, P. N. (1982). The mental representation of spatial descriptions. *Memory and Cognition, 10,* 181–187.

Mastroianni, G. R. (1982). The influence of eye movements and illumination on auditory localization. *Perception and Psychophysics, 31,* 581–584.

McGuinness, C. (1992). Spatial models in the mind. *Irish Journal of Psychology, 13,* 524–535.

McLinden, D. J. (1988). Spatial task performance: A meta-analysis. *Journal of Visual Impairment and Blindness, 82,* 231–236.

McNamara, T. P. (1992). Spatial representations. *Geoforum, 23,* 139–150.

McNamara, T. P. (2003). How are the locations of objects in the environment represented in memory? In C. Freksa, W. Brauer, C. Habel, & K. F. Wender (Eds.), *Spatial cognition III: Routes and navigation, human memory and learning, spatial representation and spatial reasoning. LNAI 2685* (pp. 174–191). Berlin: Springer-Verlag.

McNamara, T. P., & Diwadkar, V. A. (1997). Symmetry and asymmetry of human spatial memory. *Cognitive Psychology, 34,* 160–190.

McNamara, T. P., Hardy, J. K., & Hirtle, S. C. (1989). Subjective hierarchies in spatial memory. *Journal of Experimental Psychology: Learning, Memory and Cognition, 15,* 211–227.

McNamara, T. P., Rump, B., & Werner, S. (2003). Egocentric and geocentric frames of reference in memory of large-scale space. *Psychonomic Bulletin and Review, 10,* 589–595.

McNamara, T. P., & Shelton, A. L. (2003). Cognitive maps and the hippocampus. *Trends in Cognitive Science, 7,* 333–335.

McNamara, T. P., & Valiquette, C. M. (2004). Remembering where things are. In G. L. Allen (Ed.), *Human spatial memory* (pp. 3–24). Mahwah, NJ: Lawrence Erlbaum Associates.

Mennemeier, M., Chatterjee, A., & Jeilman, K. M. (1994). A comparison of the influence of body and environment centred reference frames on neglect. *Brain, 117,* 1013–1021.

Millar, S. (1994). *Understanding and representing space: Theory and evidence from studies with blind and sighted children.* Oxford: Clarendon Press.

Milner, A. D., & Goodale, M. A. (1995). *The visual brain in action.* Oxford: Oxford University Press.

Mittelstaedt, M.-L., & Mittelstaedt, H. (2001). Idiothetic navigation in humans: Estimation of path length. *Experimental Brain Research, 139,* 318–332.

Moeser, S. D. (1988). Cognitive mapping in a complex building. *Environment and Behavior, 20,* 21–49.

Montello, D. R. (1988). A new framework for understanding the acquisition of spatial knowledge in large-scale environments. In M. J. Egenhofer & R. G. Golledge (Eds.), *Spatial and temporal reasoning in geographic information systems* (pp. 143–154). New York: Oxford University Press.

Morris, R. G., & Parslow, D. M. (2004). Neurocognitive components of spatial memory. In G. L. Allen (Ed.), *Human spatial memory* (pp. 217–247). Mahwah, NJ: Lawrence Erlbaum Associates.

Morris, R. G. M., Garrud, P., Rawlins, J. N., & O'Keefe, J. (1982). Place navigation is impaired in rats with hippocampal lesions. *Nature, 297,* 681–683.

Mou, W., Fan, Y., McNamara, T. P., & Owen, C. B. (2008). Intrinsic frames of reference and egocentric viewpoints in scene recognition. *Cognition, 106,* 750–769.

Mou, W., Liu, X., & McNamara, T. P. (2009). Layout geometry in encoding and retrieval of spatial memory. *Journal of Experimental Psychology: Human Perception and Performance, 35*(1), 83–93.

Mou, W., & McNamara, T. P. (2002). Intrinsic frames of reference in spatial memory. *Journal of Experimental Psychology: Learning, Memory, and Cognition, 28*, 162–170.

Mou, W., Zhao, M., & McNamara, T. P. (2007). Layout geometry in the selection of intrinsic frames of reference from multiple viewpoints. *Journal of Experimental Psychology: Learning, Memory, and Cognition, 33*, 145–154.

Nadel, L. (1999). Neural mechanisms of spatial orientation and wayfinding: An overview. In R. G. Golledge (Ed.), *Wayfinding behavior: Cognitive mapping and other spatial processes* (pp. 313–327). Baltimore, MD: Johns Hopkins University Press.

Nadel, L. (2004). The spatial brain. *Neuropsychology, 18*, 473–476.

Nardini, M., Burgess, N., Breckenridge, K., & Atkinson, J. (2006). Differential developmental trajectories for egocentric, environmental and intrinsic frames of reference in spatial memory. *Cognition, 101*, 153–172.

Neggers, S. F. W., Van der Lubbe, R. H. J., Ramsey, N. F., & Postma, A. (2006). Interactions between ego- and allocentric neuronal representations of space. *NeuroImage, 31*, 320–331.

Newell, F. N., Woods, A. T., Mernagh, M., & Bülthoff, H. H. (2005). Visual, haptic and crossmodal recognition of scenes. *Experimental Brain Research, 161*, 233–242.

Newport, R., Rabb, B., & Jackson, S. R. (2002). Noninformative vision improves haptic spatial perception. *Current Biology, 12*, 1661–1664.

O'Keefe, J. (1976). Place units in the hippocampus of the freely moving rat. *Experimental Neurology, 51*, 78–109.

O'Keefe, J. (1991). The hippocampal cognitive map and navigational strategies. In J. Paillard (Ed.), *Brain and space* (pp. 273–295). Oxford: Oxford University Press.

O'Keefe, J., & Dostrovsky, J. (1971). The hippocampus as a spatial map: Preliminary evidence from unit activity in the freely moving rat. *Brain Research, 34*, 171–175.

O'Keefe, J., & Nadel, L. (1978). *The hippocampus as a cognitive map.* Oxford: Oxford University Press

Packard, M. G., & McGaugh, J. L. (1996). Inactivation of hippocampus or caudate nucleus with lidocaine differentially affects expression of place and response learning. *Neurobiology of Learning and Memory, 65*, 65–72.

Pasqualotto, A., Finucane, C. M., & Newell, F. N. (2005). Visual and haptic representations of scenes are updated with observer movement. *Experimental Brain Research, 166*, 481–488.

Passini, R., Delisle, J., Langlois, C., & Prouis, G. (1988). Wayfinding information for congenitally blind individuals. *Journal of Visual Impairment and Blindness, 82*, 425–429.

Passini, R., Proulx, G., & Rainville, C. (1990). The spatio-cognitive abilities of the visually impaired population. *Environment and Behavior, 22*, 91–118.

Pazzaglia, F., & De Beni, R. (2001). Strategies of processing spatial information in survey and landmark-centred individuals. *European Journal of Cognitive Psychology, 13*, 493–508.

Péruch, P., May, M., & Wartenberg, F. (1997). Homing in virtual environments: Effects of field of view and path layout. *Perception, 26*, 301–311.

Philbeck, J. W., Behrmann, M., Levy, L., Potolicchio, S. J., & Caputy, A. J. (2004). Path integration deficits during linear locomotion after human medial temporal lobectomy. *Journal of Cognitive Neuroscience, 16*, 510–520.

Platt, B. B., & Warren, D. H. (1972). Auditory localization: The importance of eye movements and a textured visual environment. *Perception and Psychophysics, 12*, 245–248.

Presson, C. C., DeLange, N., & Hazelrigg, M. D. (1989). Orientation-specificity in spatial memory: What makes a path different from a map of the path? *Journal of Experimental Psychology: Learning, Memory, and Cognition, 15*, 887–897.

Presson, C. C., & Montello, D. R. (1994). Updating after rotational and translational body movements: Coordinate structure of perspective space. *Perception, 23*, 1447–1455.

Putzar, L., Goerendt, I., Lange, K., Rösler, F., & Röder, B. (2007). Early visual deprivation impairs multisensory interactions in humans. *Nature Neuroscience, 10*, 1243–1245.

Ramachandran, V. S., Rogers-Ramachandran, D., & Cobb, S. (1995). Touching the phantom limb. *Nature, 377*, 489–490.

Redding, G. M., & Wallace, B. (1987). Perceptual-motor coordination and prism adaptation during locomotion: A control for head posture contributions. *Perception and Psychophysics, 42*, 269–274.

Restle, F. (1957). Discrimination of cues in mazes: A resolution of the "place-vs.-response" question. *Psychological Review, 64*, 217–228.

Richardson, A. E., Montello, D. R., & Hegarty, M. (1999). Spatial knowledge acquisition from maps and from navigation in real and virtual environments. *Memory and Cognition, 27*, 741–750.

Riecke, B. E., Cunningham, D. W., & Bülthoff, H. H. (2007). Spatial updating in virtual reality: The sufficiency of visual information. *Psychological Research, 71*, 298–313.

Riecke, B. E., van Veen, H. A. H. C., & Bülthoff, H. H. (2002). Visual homing is possible without landmarks: A path integration study in virtual reality. *Presence, 11*, 443–473.

Rieser, J. J. (1989). Access to knowledge of spatial structure at novel points of observation. *Journal of Experimental Psychology: Learning, Memory, and Cognition, 15*, 1157–1165.

Rieser, J. J. (1999). Dynamic spatial orientation and the coupling of representation and action. In R. G. Golledge (Ed.), *Wayfinding behavior: Cognitive mapping and other spatial processes* (pp. 168–190). Baltimore, MD: Johns Hopkins University Press.

Rieser, J. J., Guth, D. A., & Hill, E. W. (1986). Sensitivity to perspective structure while walking without vision. *Perception, 15*, 173–188.

Rieser, J. J., Hill, E. W., Talor, C. R., Bradfield, A., & Rosen, S. (1992). Visual experience, visual field size, and the development of nonvisual sensitivity to the spatial structure of outdoor neighborhoods explored by walking. *Journal of Experimental Psychology: General, 2*, 210–221.

Rieser, J. J., Lockman, J. J., & Pick, H. L., Jr. (1980). The role of visual experience in knowledge of spatial layout. *Perception and Psychophysics, 28*, 185–190.

Rieser, J. J., Pick, H. L., Jr., Ashmead, D. H., & Garing, A. E. (1995). Calibration of human locomotion and models of perceptual-motor organization. *Journal of Experimental Psychology: Human Perception and Performance, 21*, 480–497.

Rizzolatti, G., & Gallese, V. (1988). Mechanisms and theories of spatial neglect. In F. B. J. Grafman (Ed.), *Handbook of neuropsychology* (vol. 1, pp. 223–246). Amsterdam: Elsevier.

Rock, I. (1966). *The nature of perceptual adaptation.* New York: Basic Books.

Rock, I., & Victor, J. (1964). Vision and touch: Experimentally created conflict between the two senses. *Science, 143*, 594–596.

Röder, B., Kusmierek, A., Spence, C., & Schicke, T. (2007). Developmental vision determines the reference frame for the multisensory control of action. *Proceedings of the National Academy of Sciences, U.S.A., 104*, 4753–4758.

Röder, B., Rösler, F., & Spence, C. (2004). Early vision impairs tactile perception in the blind. *Current Biology, 14*, 121–124.

Rolls, E. T. (1999). Spatial view cells and the representation of place in the primate hippocampus. *Hippocampus, 9*, 467–480.

Rolls, E. T., & O'Mara, S. M. (1995). View-responsive neurons in the primate hippocampal complex. *Hippocampus, 5*, 409–424.

Roskos-Ewoldsen, B., McNamara, T. P., Shelton, A. L., & Carr, W. (1998). Mental representations of large and small spatial layouts are orientation dependent. *Journal of Experimental Psychology: Learning, Memory, and Cognition, 24*, 215–226.

Rossano, M. J., & Warren, D. H. (1989). The importance of alignment in blind subjects' use of tactual maps. *Perception, 18,* 805–816.

Rossier, J., & Schenk, F. (2003). Olfactory and/or visual cues for spatial navigation through ontogeny: Olfactory cues enable the use of visual cues. *Behavioral Neuroscience, 117,* 412–425.

Sadalla, E. K., & Montello, D. R. (1989). Remembering changes in direction. *Environment and Behavior, 21,* 346–363.

Schlaegel, T. F., Jr. (1953). The dominant method of imagery in blind compared to sighted adolescents. *Journal of Genetic Psychology, 83,* 265–277.

Shelton, A. L., Marchette, S. A., & Yamamoto, N. (2007). *Place and response mechanisms in human environmental learning.* Manuscript in preparation.

Shelton, A. L., & McNamara, T. P. (1997). Multiple views of spatial memory. *Psychonomic Bulletin and Review, 4,* 102–106.

Shelton, A. L., & McNamara, T. P. (2001a). Systems of spatial reference in human memory. *Cognitive Psychology, 43,* 274–310.

Shelton, A. L., & McNamara, T. P. (2001b). Visual memories from nonvisual experiences. *Psychological Science, 12,* 343–347.

Shelton, A. L., & McNamara, T. P. (2004a). Orientation and perspective dependence in route and survey learning. *Journal of Experimental Psychology: Learning, Memory, and Cognition, 30,* 158–170.

Shelton, A. L., & McNamara, T. P. (2004b). Spatial memory and perspective taking. *Memory and Cognition, 32,* 416–426.

Shelton, A. L., & Pippitt, H. A. (2007). Fixed versus dynamic orientations in environmental learning from ground-level and aerial perspectives. *Psychological Research, 71,* 333–346.

Sholl, M. J., & Nolin, T. L. (1997). Orientation specificity in representations of place. *Journal of Experimental Psychology: Learning, Memory, and Cognition, 23,* 1494–1507.

Siegel, A. W., & White, S. H. (1975). The development of spatial representations of large-scale environments. In H. W. Reese (Ed.), *Advances in child development and behavior* (vol. 10, pp. 9–55). New York: Academic Press.

Simmering, V. R., Peterson, C., Darling, W., & Spencer, J. P. (2008). Location memory biases reveal the challenges of coordinating visual and kinesthetic reference frames. *Experimental Brain Research, 184,* 165–178.

Simons, D. J., & Wang, R. F. (1998). Perceiving real-world viewpoint changes. *Psychological Science, 9,* 315–320.

Squire, L. R., & Zola-Morgan, S. (1988). Memory: Brain systems and behavior. *Trends in Neuroscience, 11,* 170–175.

Squire, L. R., Zola-Morgan, S., Cave, C. B., Haist, F., Musen, G., & Suzuki, W. A. (1990). Memory organization of brain systems and cognition. *Cold Spring Harbor Symposia on Quantitative Biology, 55,* 1007–1023.

Sun, H.-J., Campos, J. L., & Chan, G. S. W. (2004). Multisensory integration in the estimation of relative path length. *Experimental Brain Research, 154,* 246–254.

Tarr, M. J. (1995). Rotating objects to recognize them: A case study on the role of viewpoint-dependency in the recognition of three-dimensional objects. *Psychonomic Bulletin and Review, 2,* 55–82.

Tarr, M. J., & Pinker, S. (1989). Mental rotation and orientation-dependence in shape recognition. *Cognitive Psychology, 21,* 233–282.

Tarr, M. J., & Pinker, S. (1990). When does human object recognition use a viewer-centered reference frame? *Psychological Science, 4,* 253–256.

Tarr, M. J., & Pinker, S. (1991). Orientation-dependent mechanisms in shape recognition: Further issues. *Psychological Science, 2,* 207–209.

Taylor, H. A., & Tversky, B. (1992). Spatial mental models derived from survey and route descriptions. *Journal of Memory and Language, 31,* 261–292.

Thinus-Blanc, C., & Gaunet, F. (1997). Representation of space in blind persons: Vision as a spatial sense? *Psychological Bulletin, 121,* 20–42.

Thorndyke, P. W., & Hayes-Roth, B. (1982). Differences in spatial knowledge acquired from maps and navigation. *Cognitive Psychology, 14,* 560–589.

Thurlow, W. R., & Kerr, T. P. (1970). Effect of a moving visual environment on localization of sound. *American Journal of Psychology, 83,* 112–118.

Tinti, C., Adenzato, M., Tamietto, M., & Cornoldi, C. (2006). Visual experience is not necessary for efficient survey spatial cognition: Evidence from blindness. *Quarterly Journal of Experimental Psychology, 59,* 1306–1328.

Tlauka, M. (2006). Updating imagined translational movements. *Scandinavian Journal of Psychology, 47,* 471–475.

Tolman, E. C. (1948). Cognitive maps in rats and men. *Psychological Review, 55,* 189–208.

Tolman, E. C., Ritchie, B. F., & Kalish, D. (1946). Studies in spatial learning: II. Place learning versus response learning. *Journal of Experimental Psychology: General, 36,* 221–229.

Tolman, E. C., Ritchie, B. F., & Kalish, D. (1947). Studies in spatial learning: V. Response versus place learning by the noncorrection method. *Journal of Experimental Psychology: General, 37,* 285–292.

Tootell, R. B. H., Hadjikhani, N. K., Vanduffel, W., Liu, A. K., Mendola, J. D., Sereno, M. I., & Dale, A. M. (1998). Functional analysis of primary visual cortex (V1) in humans. *Proceedings of the National Academy of Sciences, U.S.A., 95,* 811–817.

Tversky, B. (1981). Distortions in memory for maps. *Cognitive Psychology, 13,* 407–433.

Tversky, B. (1991). Spatial mental models. In G. H. Bower (Ed.), *The psychology of learning and motivation* (vol. 27, pp. 109–145). San Diego, CA: Academic Press.

Tversky, B. (1992). Distortions in cognitive maps. *Geoforum, 23,* 131–138.

Valiquette, C., & McNamara, T. P. (2007). Different mental representations for place recognition and goal localization. *Psychonomic Bulletin and Review, 14,* 676–680.

van Beers, R. J., Haggard, P., & Wolpert, D. M. (2002). When feeling is more important than seeing in sensorimotor adaptation. *Current Biology, 12,* 834–837.

Vecchi, T., Tinti, C., & Cornoldi, C. (2004). Spatial memory and integration processes in congenital blindness. *NeuroReport, 15,* 2787–2790.

Wallace, M. T., Carriere, B. N., Perrault, T. J., Jr., Vaughan, J. W., & Stein, B. E. (2006). The development of cortical multisensory integration. *Journal of Neuroscience, 26,* 11844–11849.

Wallace, M. T., Perrault, T. J., Jr., Hairston, W. D., & Stein, B. E. (2004). Visual experience is necessary for the development of multisensory integration. *Journal of Neuroscience, 24,* 9580–9584.

Waller, D. (2006). Egocentric and nonegocentric coding in memory for spatial layout: Evidence from scene recognition. *Memory and Cognition, 34,* 491–504.

Waller, D., Loomis, J. M., Golledge, R. G., & Beall, A. C. (2000). Place learning in humans: The role of distance and direction information. *Spatial Cognition and Computation, 2,* 333–354.

Waller, D., Loomis, J. M., & Steck, S. D. (2003). Inertial cues do not enhance knowledge of environmental layout. *Psychonomic Bulletin and Review, 10,* 987–993.

Wallraff, H. G. (2004). Avian olfactory navigation: Its empirical foundation and conceptual state. *Animal Behaviour, 67,* 189–204.

Wang, R. F. (2004). Between reality and imagination: When is spatial updating automatic? *Perception and Psychophysics, 66,* 68–76.

Wang, R. F., & Brockmole, J. R. (2003). Human navigation in nested environments. *Journal of Experimental Psychology: Learning, Memory, and Cognition, 29*, 398–404.

Wang, R. F., & Spelke, E. S. (2000). Updating egocentric representations in human navigation. *Cognition, 77*, 215–250.

Wang, R. F., & Spelke, E. S. (2002). Human spatial representation: Insights from animals. *Trends in Cognitive Sciences, 6*, 376–382.

Warren, D. H. (1970). Intermodality interactions in spatial localization. *Cognitive Psychology, 1*, 114–133.

Wehner, R., & Srinivasan, M.V. (2003). Path integration in insects. In K. J. Jeffery (Ed.), *The neurobiology of spatial behaviour* (pp. 9–30). New York: Oxford University Press.

Welch, R. B., & Warren, D. H. (1980). Immediate perceptual response to intersensory discrepancy. *Psychological Bulletin, 88*, 638–667.

Werner, S., & Schmidt, K. (1999). Environmental reference systems for large-scale spaces. *Spatial Cognition and Computation, 1*, 447–473.

Whitely, A. M., & Warrington, E. K. (1978). Selective impairment of topographical memory: A case study. *Journal of Neurology, Neurosurgery, and Psychiatry, 41*, 575–578.

Wilson, M. A., & McNaughton, B. L. (1993). Dynamics of the hippocampal ensemble code for space. *Science, 261*, 1055–1058.

Wolbers, T., Wiener, J. M., Mallot, H. A., & Büchel, C. (2007). Differential recruitment of the hippocampus, medial prefrontal cortex, and the human motion complex during path integration in humans. *Journal of Neuroscience, 27*, 9408–9416.

Wraga, M. J., Creem, S. H., & Proffitt, D. R. (2000). Updating scenes after object- and viewer-rotations. *Journal of Experimental Psychology: Learning, Memory, and Cognition, 26*, 151–168.

Wraga, M. J., Creem-Regehr, S. H., & Proffitt, D. R. (2004). Spatial updating of virtual displays during self- and display-rotation. *Memory and Cognition, 32*, 399–415.

Yamamoto, N., & Shelton, A. L. (2005). Visual and proprioceptive representations in spatial memory. *Memory and Cognition, 33*, 140–150.

Yamamoto, N., & Shelton, A. L. (2007). Path information effects in visual and proprioceptive spatial learning. *Acta Psychologica, 125*, 346–360.

Yamamoto, N., & Shelton, A. L. (2009). Orientation dependence of spatial memory acquired from auditory experience. *Psychonomic Bulletin and Review, 16*, 301–305.

Yamamoto, N., & Shelton, A. L. (in press). Sequential versus simultaneous viewing of an environment: Effects of focal attention to individual object locations on visual spatial learning. *Visual Cognition*.

3

REMEMBERING FACES*

Vicki Bruce

Introduction

The most important source of information that we use to identify someone in daily life is the face. Burton, Wilson, Cowan, and Bruce (1999) demonstrated this rather dramatically when they showed that students could accurately identify their lecturers from low-quality CCTV images, provided that the face was visible. Other information from clothing, gait, and body shape was much less important for recognition. In the modern world we are each familiar with literally thousands of faces—from home and from work, and through the media: politicians, actors, sports stars. Human faces are all very similar one to another, and so our visual memories for faces are in some ways rather remarkable. However, although visual memory for faces is remarkable, it is not infallible—and errors of person identification abound.

In 1969 Laszlo Virag was tried and initially convicted of being a person who had committed armed robberies in Liverpool and Bristol. He was convicted on the basis of testimony from several witnesses who picked him out of line-ups or identified him from photographs. One police witness claimed that "his face is imprinted on my brain". But it transpired that another person, known as George Payen, was responsible for these crimes—someone who bore a passing but not striking resemblance to Mr Virag. Mr Virag was pardoned in 1974, having been the victim of a miscarriage of justice based upon mistaken identity. Those witnesses to the incident who identified Virag undoubtedly had memories that were sufficient to say that Mr Virag was the person in the line-up or photo-spread who most resembled the man they saw commit the crime—but they should not have sworn it was that person (for a more detailed account of this case, see Wagenaar, 1988).

Later in this chapter I describe how our visual representations of unfamiliar faces make us particularly vulnerable to mistakes of this kind. But it is not just unfamiliar people who can give rise to mistaken identity. In 1548, Martin Guerre, a young French peasant, disappeared from his home village, leaving his wife of ten years and a newly born child. Eight years later, an impostor arrived in the village, claiming to be Martin, and proved sufficiently persuasive to his wife and other family members that he was accepted for several years before increasing suspicion and conflict over property led to a court case contesting his identity. At the eleventh hour, just as Martin appeared to have proved that he was who he claimed to be, the real Martin returned to claim his family and property, and the impostor was denounced and executed.

This tale is well-known to cinema-goers through two films (*The Return of Martin Guerre*, 1983; and an updated fictional variant based in the United States—*Somersby*, 1993). Other similar incidents have been reported more recently, too. Hadyn Ellis (1988) described the complex case of the "Tichborne Claimant", who claimed to be the long-lost missing heir to estates in southern England but did not win his claim. In this case there was some photographic record of the appearance of the lost person in 1853, and the "claimant" some thirteen years later. The resemblance seems no greater than that between Virag and Payen. Yet the mother of the missing person and several other members of the household believed it was he. But how likely is it that our knowledge of a highly familiar person could be so readily deceived by such an impostor?

Clearly there was much more to the issue than memory for the face. Madame Guerre and Lady Tichborne should have had other sources of information than the face of the missing husband/son to go by. The impostor in each case knew things about people and past events that he couldn't (or shouldn't) have known unless he was who he claimed to be. Moreover, the passage of time and other circumstances have their effects—people's appearances can change a good deal through diet, ageing, physical hardship or injury, as well as hairstyle and facial hair. No dental or DNA records could be used to help verify identity. Then there is the motivation— an abandoned wife with fatherless child has every reason to focus on the positive evidence that her husband has returned. Every mother would rather believe that her child is alive than has perished.

Thus, the cases of Martin Guerre and the Tichborne Claimant are ones where context, motivation, and uncertainty about changes in appearance worked together so that even the closest of kin could be deceived about identity. Stranger things still can happen when context is deliberately manipulated. Don Thomson (1986) arranged for the daughter of some friends of his to appear unexpectedly near their hotel abroad, but to walk past them without any sign of recognition when they approached. The parents did not pursue the daughter and demand an explanation— their initial signals of recognition went unacknowledged, and they simply assumed they had been mistaken.

When we talk about *visual memory* for faces, therefore, we must understand that the very difficult discriminations required to differentiate one human face from another probably render contextual factors more important in remembering faces than is generally recognized in theoretical models of face recognition. Nonetheless, for the remainder of this chapter, I shall mainly focus on the visual representation of faces in memory.

Factors affecting face recognition

In marked contrast to the cases of mistaken identity described above, during the 1970s considerable attention was given to experiments appearing to suggest that memory for once-glimpsed unfamiliar faces was remarkably accurate. Shepard (1967) included faces among other kinds of pictures and showed that participants were over 90% accurate when asked to discriminate old from new items even three days after initial presentation. Goldstein and Chance (1971) used a much more difficult task where memory for highly similar patterns was tested—human faces, inkblot patterns, and snowflake patterns. At test, participants were asked to pick out the 14 old items from a total set of 80. Face patterns gave recognition rates of 71% on immediate testing (compared with 46% for inkblots and 33% for snowflakes—significantly above chance in this task), and there was little change over a 48-hour delay.

In other studies memory for faces was compared with memory for pictures drawn from other familiar categories of objects such as houses (Yin, 1969, 1970), canine faces (Scapinello & Yarmey, 1970), and teacups (Deregowski, Ellis, & Shepherd, 1973). While performance with faces was generally better than with other homogenous categories, this was not always found—presumably it was dependent on the inter-item similarity operating within each class of items. More importantly, the classic studies by Yin (1969, 1970) showed that while upright faces were better recognized than pictures of houses or schematic men in motion, when inverted, faces were recognized *less* well than the comparison materials. This *disproportionate* effect of inversion on face recognition ability is one of the hallmarks of expert adult face recognition performance, and I return to consider the nature of this expertise later in this chapter.

The experiments discussed above generally used identical pictures of faces at study and test. A minority of other studies conducted in the late 1970s found high recognition rates even when there was a change in picture between study and test (Davies, Ellis, & Shepherd, 1978a; Patterson & Baddeley, 1977), and this led to some claims that initial representations of faces in memory allowed good generalization to different views and expressions. Patterson and Baddeley's studies involved rather small sets of faces at study, combined with techniques encouraging attention to view-invariant characteristics. Davies et al.'s (1978a) finding of insensitivity of recognition memory to pose change was clear, though rather surprising, and now appears anomalous in the context of other studies before and since. For example, Bruce (1982) showed participants 24 unfamiliar male faces for eight seconds each, and asked them to respond "old" or "new" to each of 48 faces (the 24 faces with an equal number of distractors) 15 min later. The targets could appear in same or changed pictures from those studied (and participants were forewarned that pictures might change and that they should be remembering the people not the pictures).

Hit rates at test showed significant and substantial decline from 90% when faces were tested in identical pictures, to 76% when there was a change in pose or expression, to 61% when there was a change in pose and expression. The target set used were photographs of university teachers and researchers taken in the late 1970s, with a great variety of hairstyles, facial hair, and spectacles, making the set appear rather distinctive. Moreover, head-and-shoulders pictures revealed something of the clothing worn by these colleagues. Given that these features of hairstyle and clothing would be readily seen in changed views, the large effects of picture change were quite surprising in this study.

Although recognition rates for faces shown upright in *identical* study and test pictures are very high, even apparently superficial differences in the way these images are depicted can impede recognition. Faces studied in detailed line drawings obtained by tracing around all the major face features shown in the image, and then tested in photographs, are recognized much less accurately than when both study and test phases used photographs (Davies et al., 1978). Similarly, people presented in films in which full-face views were depicted for several seconds but then tested in full-face still photographs, or vice versa, were recognized substantially less well than when mode of testing matched that of study (Patterson, 1978), even though in this study participants learned each of only four items quite thoroughly.

An even more dramatic finding was that reported by Bruce et al. (1999), where participants were asked to match an image of a target face taken from video film against an array of still photographs of faces that might or might not include one of the target face, taken on the same day as the video. This task did not require any memory of the target face, only visual matching—and yet performance averaged only 70% correct, dropping still further if there was some variation in expression or pose between the target and array faces.

One of the main differences between the video images of the targets and the photo-images of the array faces in Bruce et al.'s (1999) study was in the lighting and the effects of that lighting on the appearance of the faces. In more controlled lighting conditions a number of studies have shown that matching faces is impaired when the two are shown with different directions of lighting (Braje, 2003; Hill & Bruce, 1996). In contrast to face matching, Hill and Bruce (1996) found that matching unfamiliar "amoeba" shapes was much less influenced by lighting changes than had been found with faces. Other reported effects of illumination change on non-face object matching (e.g., Tarr, Kersten, & Bülthoff, 1998) may be at least partly dependent on specific task demands (Nederhouser & Mangini, 2001), though Braje (2003) argues that faces and objects are affected similarly by lighting changes.

Faces are also extremely susceptible to contrast reversal in photographic negation (Galper, 1970). Even though a negative image of a face portrays the same spatial layout of luminance contrasts, the appearance of the face is rendered dramatically different. There are several possible explanations for why negation has such a damaging effect. It is possible that negating images of faces disrupts the processing of "configuration" of the face as inverting faces is held to do. However, Bruce and Langton (1994) found that the effects of inversion and negation were additive, suggesting that these manipulations may affect different sources of information used for face perception and identification. Negative images also change the apparent three-dimensional shape of an object, on the assumption that lighting direction remains constant, so a positive image with light reflected from prominent cheekbones will appear in the negative with dark cheekbone areas instead. Negative images also reverse the surface pigmentation—a negative image of a light-skinned person with dark hair will appear dark-skinned with blonde hair. Bruce and Langton (1994) attempted to resolve which of these two potential sources of difficulty was the most important source of the negation effect by presenting three-dimensional reconstructions of laser-scanned faces that would be familiar to participants and seeing if negating these images affected their recognition. Recognition of such three-dimensional surface images was poor, but it was not further reduced by negation. Bruce and Langton argued that recognition was poor because the images lacked the pigmented features usually used for recognition, and that if negation had its principal effect via the reversal of pigmentation, then little further decline should be found following negation, as observed.

Russell, Sinha, Biederman, and Nederhouser (2006) confirmed and extended Bruce and Langton's findings. In two experiments they examined the effects of negation on a delayed match-to-sample task, where a decision had to be made on each trial of which of two items matched one presented for study a second earlier. Sets of faces were created that varied only in shape with constant pigmentation; or varied only in pigmentation, with constant shape; or varied both in shape and pigmentation. Negation only reduced matching performance significantly when the faces had variation in pigmentation, suggesting that the primary effect of negation is in the contrast reversal of pigmented surfaces rather than in the derivation of shape—whether two- or three-dimensional.

In some respects the effects of negation on face recognition are "disproportionate" compared with recognition of other kinds of objects. Subramaniam and Biederman (1997) reported that negation does not at all disrupt matching of pictures of chairs. However, Vuong, Peissig, Harrison, and Tarr (2005) showed that matching images of pigmented "Greeble" shapes (these are artificial three-dimensional shapes with the same overall configuration but varying features—see Figure 3.2) was significantly disrupted by negation, though not as substantially as the disruption to pigmented face surfaces. Both faces and Greebles were more affected by negation when the surfaces shown were pigmented rather than non-pigmented, and this effect was quite striking given that the face images used had no visible hair—a most important pigmented component used extensively for matching of unfamiliar faces. However, there were some detrimental effects of negation even on the non-pigmented surfaces. Thus, while the pigmentation of surfaces clearly contributes significantly to the detrimental effects of negation, other factors may also contribute. Moreover, Vuong et al.'s study suggests that when stimulus structure and task demands are made more similar, the recognition and matching of objects other than faces can also be susceptible to contrast reversal.

Importantly, these effects of negation and mode suggest that representations that mediate face recognition reflect in a fundamental way the pattern of light and dark across the image of the face rather than being based primarily on some more abstract set of derived two- or three-dimensional-shape measurements. If abstract measurements formed the basis of our visual memories of faces, it is difficult to understand why a change in mode or lightness polarity that preserves two- or even three-dimensional shape should be so disruptive to matching and/or recognizing faces.

Face memory compared with object memory

I have already reviewed above experiments on recognition memory for faces compared with pictures of other kinds of objects. In a recognition memory task participants are typically shown a set of study items and later asked to decide which items of a test set were studied and which are novel. A sense of familiarity to items that are judged "old" could arise from different kinds of remembered information. There might be a match at the level of the specific pictorial details of the remembered item (termed "pictorial code" by Bruce, 1982; Bruce & Young, 1986), at a more abstract visual level (termed "structural code"), or at semantic or verbal (name) levels. These are also the kinds of levels of description that must be derived in order to fully recognize the item in question. Building on the discussion of object memory in chapters 1 and 2 of *The Visual World in Memory*, here I discuss how "object" memory can be described at these different levels of abstraction or specificity and then enter into a discussion of visual memory for faces compared with objects—we need to compare like with like.

We can recognize a particular visual shape as a "dog" and later remember verbally that "dog" was among the items we were shown. This is the same level as recognizing and later remembering that we saw "a face". The visual representational level that allows us to tell, say, a dog from a cat, or a mug from a cup, lies at the level of major shape features that may even be perceived quite independently of viewpoint. Biederman's (1987) influential model of visual object recognition suggests that objects are recognized via a set of primitive shape elements called "geons", which can be derived from more or less any recognizable viewpoint of that object. In Biederman's model it is the geon structural descriptions (GSDs) and not metric variations that are critical for basic-level object recognition. However, at the level of GSDs all human faces are identical. Any finer level than "a face" requires analysis of metric variations and features of surface colouration.

Finer level discriminations within basic-level categories also allow us to recognize different types of basic objects—so we can recognize an Alsatian dog, a poodle dog, or a cairn terrier dog; or a steak knife, a carving knife, or a butter knife. This discrimination of different types of the same kind of object might be likened to our ability to categorize faces on semantically meaningful dimensions on the basis of their shape—so we can categorize faces as old or young, male or female, on the basis of relatively major variations in their appearance. We do not know in any detailed way what kinds of visual representational descriptions are used to make type discriminations within basic categories, but they are unlikely to be possible on the basis of GSDs alone. And when we turn to face classification, a task as apparently simple as deciding whether faces are male or female appears to rely on a very large set of different dimensions, some local—such as bushiness of eyebrows or coarseness of skin texture—and some much more configural—such as the protuberance of the nose/brow regions (Bruce et al., 1993; Burton, Bruce, & Dench, 1993).

A finer level of discrimination allows us to recognize individual members of the same type of object—our own suitcase at the airport, our own Labrador in the park. Farmers are able to distinguish between their different individual cows or sheep. Importantly, at the level of individual recognition, the mapping between visual form and semantics (identity) is arbitrary. Bruce and Young (1986) distinguished between *visually derived* semantic information for faces—such as sex, race, age—and *identity-specific semantics*. The latter describes a level of categorization achieved not from generic mapping of form to meaning but by specific personal knowledge. So, the visual form of an otherwise unfamiliar face allows us to categorize it as male or female, and the visual form of an unfamiliar dog allows us to assign it as German Shepherd or a Labrador. But it is only my acquired specific knowledge of the visual form of my sister's face that allows me to recognize her and know that this person is my sister and what she does for a living, and it is only my acquired specific knowledge of my dog's visual form that allows me to recognize Barney, *my* collie, and to tell him apart from lots of similar-looking collies we meet when we go out together.

The above discussion is important, because if we want to ask the question of whether the representational basis for face recognition differs from that of object recognition, or whether there is specialization of neural structures for face recognition compared with object recognition, it is really only legitimate to compare tasks of similar logic and complexity.

Configural processing and the inversion effect

As noted earlier, face recognition suffers disproportionately when faces are inverted. The effect of inversion appears to arise because we cannot decipher the "configuration" of the face when it is upside-down. This was dramatically illustrated when Peter Thompson (1980) first produced the "Thatcher illusion"; when faces are inverted, even major reorientation of features within the face becomes virtually invisible. An arrangement that looks grotesque when upright looks virtually identical to the original when shown upside down (see Figure 3.1, left panel).

Young, Hellawell, and Hay (1987) developed another novel means of demonstrating configural processing. They divided faces horizontally and paired top halves of faces with bottom halves of different identities. When the two halves were

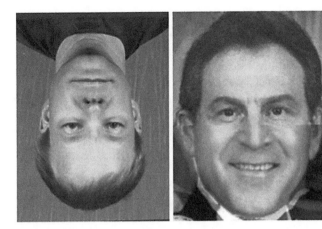

FIGURE 3.1 Demonstrations of configural processing of faces. Left panel: This image of my colleague Peter Hancock looks quite normal—until you turn the book upside down and see what he has done to himself. Right panel: It is difficult to recognize the identity of one half of a face when it is aligned with a different identity. How easy is it for you to recognize Tony Blair and George Bush in this composite? (These images were kindly provided by Peter Hancock at the University of Stirling)

aligned, it was extremely difficult to correctly identify each half. When they were misaligned, it became much easier. The explanation was that the features of one half of the face could not be processed independently of other features from the "wrong" half—because the two halves together yielded a configuration that did not match that stored for either of the original identities. Misalignment of the face halves "freed" each half from the configural influence of the other (see Figure 3.1, right panel).

Interestingly, when these composites were inverted it became relatively easy to identify the separate halves of the face, an inverted face "superiority" effect. So just as the relationship between the different features of a "Thatcherized" face is invisible when the face is inverted, so too does the influence of one part of the face on another become dramatically reduced by inversion.

Inversion does not, however, affect the capacity to process the individual parts of faces; it appears specifically to be their interrelationships that are distorted in this way. Leder and Bruce (1998) compared the rated and memorial distinctiveness of upright and inverted faces whose features were altered to be made more distinctive through local manipulations (e.g., bushier eyebrows) or configural manipulations (e.g., moving the eyes closer together). The relative distinctiveness of faces with local feature manipulations was maintained when they were inverted, while the effects of configural manipulations were completely lost.

The precise meaning of the term "configural" or "holistic" processing has been unclear in much of the literature (see Rakover, 2002). Some seem to imply that faces are processed holistically in the sense that the patterns are not decomposed at all; others imply that it concerns the details of the relationships between local parts, but that these configural relationships themselves involve analytic decomposition. It is actually extremely difficult to distinguish between these different sources of information since normally any change to part of the face affects local, configural/relational, and configural/holistic information. Leder and Bruce (2000) generated faces that could be identified either by unique combinations of local information (e.g., a specific eye colour plus hair colour) or by unique relational information (e.g., nose–mouth distance). The former showed no inversion effect, but the latter did. Since faces with unique combinations of purely local information differ "holistically", Leder and Bruce used this and similar results to argue that configural processing must involve the representation of the spatial relationships between local features rather than holistic pattern processing.

The expertise debate

One of the most heated (and to some extent futile) debates in the field of face perception has revolved around the question of whether face processing is "special" or not (for a recent review, see Liu & Chaudhuri, 2003). We have already reviewed above that representations subserving face recognition are different from those implicated in basic-level object recognition. But the demands of object recognition can be made more similar to face recognition—as we discussed above, in many everyday activities we want not just to recognize that an object is a dog, or even a collie dog, but that it is this particular collie (Barney) that lives in our house. Discriminating between individual members of a sub-category all sharing the same overall shape requires that we pay attention to subtle variations in shape and markings. However, we rarely become expert at such discriminations unless we have some professional reason or passionate interest in the area. Expertise in a sub-domain, however, appears to yield similarities to face processing. So Diamond and Carey (1986) compared expert dog perceivers (breed judges) and non-experts at face and dog recognition, and they found that the dog experts (but not the dog novices) suffered as much when pictures of dogs were inverted as they did when faces were inverted, suggesting that the experts had developed sensitivity to configural relationships, absent from non-expert dog recognizers (but for a failure to replicate this study, see McKone, Kanwisher, & Duchaine, 2007). Rhodes and McClean (1990) investigated configural processing using a different kind of method, recruiting participants with expertise in the perception of birds. Rhodes and McClean found that caricaturing outline drawings of these birds produced a stronger caricature advantage in the expert group, whereby outline drawings whose shape differences from the norm were exaggerated were recognized more quickly than the originals.

It is obviously difficult to recruit participants with specific expertise in non-face domains, but a series of studies by Gauthier, Tarr, and their colleagues have taken the approach of creating expertise in an artificial domain that shares some of the characteristics of face processing in order to explore similar kinds of questions. The

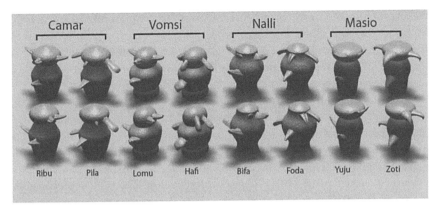

FIGURE 3.2 Examples of "Greebles". In the top row, four different "families" are represented. For each family, two members of different "genders" are shown (e.g., Ribu is one gender and Pila is the other; orientation of the appendages differs between genders). The two rows show images constructed using the same logic, but those in the top row are symmetrical in structure and those in the bottom row are asymmetric. Images provided courtesy of Michael J. Tarr (Brown University, Providence, RI) (see www.tarrlab.org)

group developed families of shapes collectively termed "Greebles" (see Figure 3.2). Greebles are multi-component shapes that share a common configuration within which there is variation in the shape, orientation, and placement of parts. Greebles are designed to come from different "families" that differ in terms of the overall shape of the "body" parts; there are also two different types of Greeble—that is, "genders" ("ploks" and "glips")—which differ in terms of the orientation of their appendages. The remaining variations of the parts and their arrangements define the individual members of each family, and these can be given names to be learned by participants in experiments.

In a series of experiments, Gauthier, Tarr, and associates (Gauthier & Tarr, 1997; Gauthier, Williams, Tarr, & Tanaka, 1998; Vuong et al., 2005) have trained participants to become experts at identifying Greebles and have investigated the consequences of this expertise, sometimes comparing the resulting effects with those found in face recognition. While not all these explorations have yielded clear results, there are certainly some indications that, compared with "novices" in the Greeble domain, experts are more disadvantaged by a change in orientation (cf. the inversion effect), and more affected by contrast reversal (cf. the negation effect). When Greeble composites are composed of the top half of one Greeble paired with the bottom half of a different one of the same gender, Greeble experts are better at identifying the halves when shown misaligned than aligned, similar to the face composite effect. So there is *some* converging evidence from a few experiments with real-world experts (dogs, etc.) and some rather variable evidence from experiments with artificial "Greeble" experts, suggesting that some of the hallmarks of expert adult face processing may arise when we become skilled at making discriminations between other classes of shape with similar characteristics. McKone, Kanwisher, and Duchaine (2007) disagree—they conclude from their review of the evidence that expertise in other domains does not give face-like sensitivity to inversion and other hallmarks of configural processing—but in their review they do not include the full range of candidate expertise effects such as those of negation and caricature.

My own conclusion is that some domains of expertise may give rise to some of the same types of processing that characterize skilled face recognition. Does it matter if face recognition shares characteristics of other skilled within-category object recognition? This issue becomes central once we turn from describing the functional characteristics of face representations to ask how these representations are implemented neurally.

Neuropsychology of face memory

Until recently, there was rather little direct evidence that face processing relied on face-specific neural machinery. Single-cell recordings from monkey inferotemporal lobe had revealed cells that seemed to respond better to faces than to any other complex, significant, or biological stimulus (Gross, Rocha-Miranda, & Bender, 1972; Perrett, Rolls, & Cann, 1982). These cells were generally found in a fold of brain known as the superior temporal sulcus (STS). While there were some suggestions that some cells seemed tuned to specific individual face identities (Perrett et al., 1984), in general the cells seemed to code particular head, gaze, and/ or body directions and seem then generally to be implicated more in social attention processes than in identification ones. Heywood and Cowey (1992) reported a lesion study when, after ablation of STS, monkeys' major deficits were in processing gaze information, but not in recognizing faces.

In humans, brain damage following stroke or other injury occasionally leads to a dramatic impairment in face recognition called "prosopagnosia" (Bodamer, 1947—for an overview see Ellis & Young, 1989; Young, 1998). Patients fail to recognize famous faces from the media or personally familiar faces of friends and family, and even their own face in the mirror may seem unfamiliar to them. It is rare for brain damage arising from stroke to be confined to a very discrete area of brain, and so perhaps not surprisingly prosopagnosic patients usually have other deficits as well. Often they are agnosic for a range of other objects, or impaired in other kinds of perceptual abilities such as topographical memory or colour perception. Sometimes they complain about difficulties, particularly with other categories where they had previously been expert. For example, Bornstein (1963) described a prosopagnosic amateur ornithologist who complained that she could no longer recognize different species of bird.

However, a small number of quite specific dissociations have been observed that have led people to claim that prosopagnosia must involve damage to a face-specific region of the brain. There have been a number of dissociations with the recognition of other kinds of animals. Bruyer et al. (1983) reported a prosopagnosic farmer who could still recognize his individual cows, and McNeil and Warrington (1993) described an intriguing case of a person who became a sheep farmer after an injury that left him prosopagnosic and who became highly skilled at recognizing his individual sheep. Conversely a farmer studied by Assal, Favre, and Anderes (1984) regained his powers of face recognition but remained unable to identify his individual animals. "Pure" cases of prosopagnosia without deficit in any other area are extremely rare, however (e.g., De Renzi, 1986), and even these may sometimes be criticized for insufficient methodological rigour. It is important to test face and non-face object processing using tasks of equivalent difficulty for control participants and using a range of measures including time as well as accuracy. For example, Gauthier, Behrmann, and Tarr (1999) made extensive tests of two prosopagnosic patients whose deficits appeared to be confined to faces if accuracy on matching tasks was the principal measure, but whose deficits in the processing of other objects including Greebles and snowflake patterns could be revealed in latency measures or in sensitivity measures in other tasks.

As well as dissociations between faces and other objects, there are dissociations between abilities on different tasks of face processing, too. While some prosopagnosic patients find it difficult to extract any kind of meaning from faces (e.g., Campbell, Landis, & Regard's 1986 patient), some appear to perceive facial expressions and other facial gestures quite normally. Indeed, for some prosopagnosic patients, it is other people's visual expressions of recognition that helps them to understand that this must be someone who is known to them. Young, Newcombe, De Haan, Small, and Hay (1993) examined a large number of ex-servicemen with gunshot injuries in a careful study where two different tests of each ability (expression analysis, unfamiliar face matching, familiar face identification) were given and latency as well as accuracy scores recorded for each. There was a clear double dissociation among their participants, with a small group of mainly left-hemisphere-lesioned patients who were impaired only on expression analysis but normal on face recognition and matching, and others impaired on familiar or unfamiliar face matching but spared on expression processing.

While most cases of prosopagnosia arise as a result of brain damage to adults who were (presumably, through their own reports) originally "expert" face recognizers, in recent years there have been reports of a small number of people who appear to have been "blind" to faces from birth (for a recent review, see Behrmann & Avidan, 2005). Such individuals are typically able to recognize faces as faces and, like acquired prosopagnosics, show some variation in their abilities beyond this level. About half the reported cases can tell the sex of faces, and about half can decipher expressions.

There is, however, very strong evidence in all these people that they are poor at processing facial configurations. Behrmann, Avidan, Marotta, and Kimchi (2005) have studied five such participants in detail and report that all show some impairment in processing non-face objects too, particularly when the task requires discrimination at the individual level and thus is likely to require sensitivity to configural rather than local features (e.g., distinguishing between two different chairs or between two different Greebles from the same gender and family). Unlike control subjects, these five participants tend to be influenced more by local than global properties of compound items in selective attention and priming tasks.

The cognitive neuroscience of face memory

As indicated earlier, it has been known for some time that there are cells particularly responsive to faces in the superior temporal sulcus of the temporal lobe of monkeys (Gross et al., 1972; Perrett et al., 1984), but it is now thought that this area is more engaged in social attention than in person/individual recognition, which is the focus of this chapter. A rather different area of the temporal lobe within the fusiform gyrus, now generally labelled the "fusiform face area" (FFA; Kanwisher, McDermott, & Chun, 1997), has attracted much more interest in recent years as the possible locus of face-specific processing in the human brain. Activation in the FFA is much stronger to faces than to other classes of object, often chosen carefully to share perceptual properties with faces (e.g., Rhodes, Byatt, Michie, & Puce, 2004), but the activation seems particularly strong for upright rather than inverted faces (Yovel & Kanwisher, 2005). Where prosopagnosic people have had brain scans that can locate their brain damage, the FFA seems to coincide with damaged areas in such individuals.

While there is no doubt that the FFA responds to faces, it is also clear that there are other kinds of objects that activate areas in or near the FFA. Haxby et al. (2001) showed that fine-scale activation patterns within FFA and the wider ventral temporal cortex surrounding it coded for both faces and non-face objects, leading them to posit a model of distributed coding of different object categories, including faces, in these areas. Other research has identified a "fusiform body area" (FBA) responding strongly to headless bodies rather than faces, partly overlapping with the FFA (Schwarzlose, Baker, & Kanwisher, 2005).

A related question that has been hotly debated is whether the FFA is really a "faces" area, or an area that is needed to make fine within-category discriminations within domains where we become expert. Gauthier and colleagues have reported that FFA is activated also by cars and birds in participants who have expertise with these categories (Gauthier, Skudlarski, Gore, & Anderson, 2000) or by Greebles in participants who have learned to become experts with these shapes (Gauthier et al., 1999). In contrast, Rhodes et al. (2004) found little evidence of activation of FFA by pictures of lepidoptera in participants with expertise in these insects (Rhodes et al., 2004), and several other studies have found either no effect of the objects of expertise in FFA or greater effects in immediately adjacent areas than in FFA itself (see McKone et al., 2007).

An extremely interesting observation in this context comes from Avidan, Hasson, Malach, and Behrmann (2005) from fMRI investigations with congenital prosopagnosics. Four such people, who have never gained any expertise with faces throughout their lifetimes, nonetheless showed normal patterns of fMRI activation in the FFA. Follow-up structural MRI investigations reported by Behrmann and Avidan (2005) suggest that the critical fusiform gyrus regions are physically smaller in these participants than in control subjects, but nonetheless are activated by faces in the normal way. Thus it appears that face-related activation in the FFA may not itself be sufficient to explain the processes of normal face identification, and that abnormalities in conformation of this region may either arise from deficient face processing or be the underlying reason for deficient face processing. Nonetheless, the activity of the FFA by faces in this group of inexpert face perceivers does suggest that the area has some intrinsic connection with faces rather than with expertise per se.

Even within normal face perceivers, other areas of the brain are also involved in face processing, and activation in FFA alone is far from sufficient to explain the full derivation of identity from a familiar face. James Haxby and colleagues have gone some way to describing the roles played by different regions, including the STS region first identified through single-cell recording in the monkey, in the overall skill of deciphering social signals from faces (Gobbini & Haxby, 2007; Haxby, Hoffman, & Gobbini, 2000).

Dynamic information in face memory

One way that faces differ from other kinds of objects is through the wealth of other social information carried by the face. We don't just identify people from their faces—we register their emotional states from momentary expressions, we use patterns of lip and tongue movements to help understand speech, and we use shifts in eye gaze and head direction to decipher what people are talking or thinking about. The face moves both rigidly, when the head turns or nods, and non-rigidly when making expressions, chewing, or speaking. Recent evidence suggests that these dynamic patterns may themselves be remembered and help face recognition— at least when other information is impoverished.

Knight and Johnston (1997) showed that when famous faces were presented in photographic negatives, thus making them hard to recognize, identification was more often successful if the faces were shown moving rather than in still image. In a series of studies, Karen Lander and colleagues showed that the beneficial effects of movement were not an artefact of the additional information content of the frames from a movie (Lander & Bruce, 2000; Lander, Christie, & Bruce, 1999). When famous faces were made difficult to recognize, the benefits of seeing an animated presentation were much greater if the film was played at its original tempo than if the same frames were played more slowly or more quickly, or if their temporal order was changed. Slowing a film down or playing it backwards shows the same static information in the frame sequence, but clearly this was not the major reason for the benefit of animation. Lander and Bruce (2000) suggest that the benefits of motion may arise because, for familiar faces, characteristic patterns of motion are stored in memory and can help activate the appropriate person identity when the static visual form system is deficient.

There is much less clear evidence for beneficial effects of motion on representations for matching or remembering unfamiliar faces. Some studies have found that seeing faces in motion helps recognition memory for the faces seen later (Pike, Kemp, Towell, & Phillips, 1997; Pilz, Thornton, & Bülthoff, 2006). In other studies no advantages have been found (Bruce et al., 1999; Christie & Bruce, 1998). Suggestions that motion would help build a representation of three-dimensional structure would lead to the prediction that non-rigid motion of unfamiliar faces would be particularly beneficial, and would help generalization to novel viewpoints. This prediction has generally not been confirmed (Lander & Bruce, 2003). Where beneficial effects of motion of unfamiliar faces are found, these seem to arise as much from non-rigid, expressive, and speaking movements, suggesting a different source for the influence of motion.

To sum up, the representations we store in memory that allow us to recognize faces are based around an analysis of surface features—patterns of light and dark—in which the interrelationships between different parts of the pattern have become particularly important. Dynamic patterns of movement also form some part of the representation we use to remember familiar faces, and these movement patterns include non-rigid, expressive, and speech movements that are probably unique to faces.

Recall of faces by eyewitnesses

So far I have discussed the way in which our visual memories for faces may be organized to allow people to recognize the faces that we see. Sometimes, however, during a criminal investigation, we may want to try to help a witness recall a face in a form that allows us to build an image of the person that someone else might be able to recognize. Most people cannot draw well enough to attempt to recall a face directly by sketching, and so generally witnesses are invited to work with a police artist or with some kind of facial composite generator (usually also via a police operator) to "build" an image of how the face looks. Jacques Penry (1971) developed the Photofit system, in which parts and regions from actual photographs of faces were stored and the witnesses invited to search for the face parts/regions that matched their memory. A composite image of the face was built up from the selected parts. The Photofit system, and Identikit—a similar, US-based system originally based online drawings but later developed in photographic form—were adopted by large numbers of police forces worldwide. However, attempts at evaluating the efficacy of these systems yielded very disappointing results.

During the late 1970s, a US-based team (e.g., Laughery & Fowler, 1980) and a team based at the University of Aberedeen (e.g., Davies, Ellis, & Shepherd, 1978b; Ellis, Davies, & Shepherd, 1978) evaluated Identikit and Photofit respectively and found very similar results. Both groups found that there was no significant difference in the quality of constructed composites produced from memory compared with those produced when the target face was in view and could be copied. This was because the quality of likenesses produced from view was poor and so was affected rather little by the additional problems created by remembering the face. In contrast, sketch-artist renditions (Laughery) or the witnesses' own attempt to draw the face (Ellis) were both very much poorer when the face was not in view.

These days, computer-based systems such as E-Fit and PROfit allow face features to be moved and blended much more effectively, so that a skilled operator can produce a remarkably close likeness when trying to copy a face from view. The limitations of electronic composite systems no longer lie with the artwork. However, it is still very difficult to get witnesses to produce recognizable composites using such systems.

In two recent studies, Charlie Frowd and colleagues made a systematic comparison of all current composite systems, using the same methodology that resembles in some ways the task faced by an eyewitness (Frowd et al., 2005a, 2005b). In each study, each simulated "witness" viewed a photograph of a face unfamiliar to him or her and attempted to build a composite from memory. The composites were then shown to other participants who would be likely to recognize these targets, and naming rates and other measures of performance were used to assess the efficacy of the likenesses. The same set of targets were used for each of the different systems evaluated, and composites were built using the kinds of techniques used in a real interview—using cognitive interview techniques to encourage participant-witnesses to recall context that might help them to build the face composite. Frowd et al. (2005a) asked the simulated witnesses to build composites from memory about three to four hours after viewing each target face. Under these conditions, E-Fit and PROfit yielded 19% and 17% correct naming of the target faces respectively, and this performance was better than was found with artist sketches (9%) and Photofit (6%). However, in a related study, Frowd et al. (2005b) used a delay of two days between viewing the photograph and attempting to build the composite. Under these conditions, much closer to the conditions of a real criminal investigation, sketches produced the best performance; however, this was only 8% correctly named composites, and no other system evaluated exceeded 4% correct naming rates.

One reason why contemporary composite systems produce such poor likenesses may be found when we examine how well witnesses can remember different parts of the face (for discussion of the impact that expectations, beliefs, stereotypes, and emotions have on facial memory by eyewitnesses, see chapter 7 of *The Visual World in Memory*, section 4.1.1). A witness is trying to recall a face that was unfamiliar to him or her at the time of the incident (or experiment). The external features of the face—particularly the hairstyle—dominate our memory for unfamiliar faces, while there is a better representation of the internal features in familiar faces (Ellis, Shepherd, & Davies, 1979). Frowd, Bruce, McIntyre, and Hancock (2007) have shown that both naming and sorting of the composites is conducted nearly as accurately if only the external features of the composites are displayed as when the full composite is displayed. In contrast, if just the internal features of composites are shown, then performance is very low. But the composites produced by witnesses are aimed at provoking recognition by people *familiar* with the faces—and here we know that the internal features of the faces are more important. If witnesses cannot create composites showing accurate internal features, then perhaps the poor performance at triggering recognition from their reconstructed images is unsurprising.

Given this rather bleak picture, are there other ways to obtain better likenesses from witnesses via composite systems? Bruce, Ness, Hancock, Newman, and Rarity (2002) reasoned that better likenesses might result if different independent witness composites were combined by averaging ("morphing") them together. The logic used was that there was no reason to suppose that different witnesses would make the same errors, so that errors should tend to cancel out while correct aspects should be reinforced in the morph. Two separate experiments confirmed this prediction. A morphed composite that combined the independent memories of four witnesses was rated as a better likeness than the average of the individual composites, and no worse than the best of these. In experiments simulating recognition of these composites, there was also evidence that the morphed composite could be recognized or matched with its corresponding target at least as accurately as the best of the individual composites.

Not all crimes will lend themselves to this combination of different independent memories, but where there is more than one witness, and it can be established that each is describing the same person, the supplementary rules of evidence applying here in the United Kingdom have now been modified to allow such an approach to be taken.

One problem with combining different witness composite faces together will be a tendency also to average out some of the more distinctive characteristics of a remembered face. Each of four independent witnesses might remember that the person had a large nose, but unless all remembered the large nose in a similar way, the morph of these impressions might be a more average-size nose than the most accurate nose remembered. This led us to speculate that applying a modest amount of positive caricaturing to a morphed composite might make it more recognizable still. There is some evidence for this in a recent study (Frowd, Bruce, Ross, McIntyre, & Hancock, 2007). Participants were given composites of particular, familiar people and asked to adjust the degree of caricature shown to maximize the likeness of each composite. Morphs were preferred at modest positive caricatures (+7%), while individual composites were preferred at modest degrees of anti-caricature (−11%). This study revealed very large individual differences in the degrees of caricature preferred by different participants and for different target faces. This meant it was difficult to set a specific level of caricature or anti-caricature that would produce consistent gains in an identification task. So Frowd reasoned that showing people dynamic caricatures of target faces that spanned the range from anti- to pro-caricature should ensure that the optimum level of caricature was displayed for recognition. Very significant gains in recognition were obtained by showing a range in this way.

A more fundamental problem with composite production lies in its requirement that witnesses try to recall individual features of faces to build a composite. Earlier in this chapter I reviewed in some detail evidence that suggests that our representations of faces are based upon holistic or configural processes. Interrogating visual memories for faces in a feature-by-feature way is unnatural and extremely difficult. This has led my colleagues at the University of Stirling to develop a new form of composite system based on recognition of faces rather than recall of face features. In "EvoFIT" (Hancock & Frowd, 2002), faces are synthesized from holistic "dimensions" (principal components or "eigenfaces"; Hancock, 2000) rather than piecemeal features, and participants only ever see whole faces. A witness is shown a screen of faces and asked to select a small number of these faces that most closely resemble their memory of the target. The component dimensions of the selected faces are then used along with genetic algorithms to "breed" another set of faces on the screen, and the witness chooses again. Gradually the screen choices begin to converge on something that the witness will select as the final version of the target he or she is trying to remember. In some circumstances EvoFIT out-performs existing composite systems, and it has already been used successfully in one police investigation. However, the existing interface is quite demanding to use, and the numbers of faces shown probably too large to be optimal. It remains a promising tool for future development, however.

Will witness memory be made redundant by the use of cameras? The United Kingdom has more CCTV cameras per head of population than any other country in the world, and the probability that a criminal will be captured on camera, as well as the quality of such captured images, is increasing. While there will always be crimes in which no camera images are likely to be available (e.g., assault on persons in their own home), there is an increasing temptation to use images on CCTV cameras to identify suspects, where these are available. However, the possible use of apparent *resemblance* between an image and a suspect to assert identity raises similar problems reviewed at the start of this chapter when we considered cases where resemblance to a memory of a face led to mistaken conviction. CCTV images are best used to help the investigative stage, where release on TV programmes such as the UK's *Crimewatch* can generate new leads in an investigation (for discussion, see Bruce et al., 1999).

Conclusion

This chapter has reviewed what we know about visual memory for faces. Face memories are based upon relatively "raw" patterns of light and dark processed in a way that emphasizes their configuration. It is difficult for a witness to interrogate such a memory through recalling individual features. Visual recognition of faces involves some specialized neural machinery in, and beyond, the fusiform face area.

Research into visual memory for faces has undergone huge expansion over the past 30 years and is entering a particularly interesting phase, as neural interactions between different strands of face processing are increasingly the focus of investigation.

Note

* This chapter originally appeared in the edited volume, *The Visual World in Memory.*

References

Assal, G., Favre, C., & Anderes, J. P. (1984). Non-reconnaissance d'animaux familiers chez un paysan. *Revue Neurologique, 140,* 580–584.

Avidan, G., Hasson, U., Malach, R., & Behrmann, M. (2005). Detailed exploration of face-related processing in congenital prosopagnosia: 2. Functional neuroimaging findings. *Journal of Cognitive Neuroscience, 17,* 1150–1167.

Behrmann, M., & Avidan, G. (2005). Congenital prosopagnosia: Face-blind from birth. *Trends in Cognitive Sciences, 9,* 180–187.

Behrmann, M., Avidan, G., Marotta, J. J., & Kimchi, R. (2005). Detailed exploration of face-related processing in congenital prosopagnosia: 1. Behavioural findings. *Journal of Cognitive Neuroscience, 17,* 1130–1149.

Biederman, I. (1987). Recognition-by-components; A theory of human image understanding. *Psychological Review, 94,* 115–147.

Bodamer, J. (1947). Die Prosopagnosie. *Archiv fur Psychiatrie and Nervenkrankheiten, 179,* 6–53.

Bornstein, B. (1963). Prosopagnosia. In L. Hapern (Ed.), *Problems of dynamic neurology* (pp. 283–318). Jerusalem: Hadassah Medical Organisation.

Braje, W. L. (2003). Illumination encoding in face recognition: Effect of position shift. *Journal of Vision, 3,* 161–170.

Bruce, V. (1982). Changing faces—visual and non-visual coding processes in face recognition. *British Journal of Psychology, 73,* 105–116.

Bruce, V., Burton, A. M., Hanna, E., Healey, P., Mason, O., Coombes, A., et al. (1993). Sex discrimination: How do we tell the difference between male and female faces? *Perception, 22,* 131–152.

Bruce, V., Henderson, Z., Greenwood, K., Hancock, P. J. B., Burton, A. M., & Miller, P. (1999). Verification of face identities from images captured on video. *Journal of Experimental Psychology: Applied, 5,* 339–360.

Bruce, V., & Langton, S. (1994). The use of pigmentation and shading information in recognising the sex and identities of faces. *Perception, 23,* 803–822.

Bruce, V., Ness, H., Hancock, P. J. B., Newman, C., & Rarity, J. (2002). Four heads are better than one. *Journal of Applied Psychology, 87,* 894–902.

Bruce, V., & Young, A. W. (1986). Understanding face recognition. *British Journal of Psychology, 77,* 305–328.

Bruyer, R., Laterre, C., Seron, X., Feyereisen, P., Strypstein, E., Pierrard, E., & Rectem, D. (1983). A case of prosopagnosia with some preserved covert remembrance of familiar faces. *Brain and Cognition, 2,* 257–284.

Burton, A. M., Bruce, V., & Dench, N. (1993). What's the difference between men and women? Evidence from facial measurement. *Perception, 22,* 153–176.

Burton, A. M., Wilson, S., Cowan, M., & Bruce, V. (1999). Face recognition from poor quality video: Evidence from security surveillance. *Psychological Science, 10,* 243–248.

Campbell, R., Landis, T., & Regard, M. (1986), Face recognition and lipreading: A neurological dissociation. *Brain, 109,* 509–521.

Christie, F., & Bruce, V. (1998). The role of dynamic information in the recognition of unfamiliar faces. *Memory and Cognition, 26,* 780–790.

Davies, G., Ellis, H. D., & Shepherd, J. (1978a). Face recognition accuracy as a function of mode of presentation. *Journal of Applied Psychology, 63,* 180–187.

Davies, G., Ellis, H. D., & Shepherd, J. (1978b). Face identification: The influence of delay upon accuracy of Photofit construction. *Journal of Police Science and Administration, 6,* 35–42.

Deregowski, J. B., Ellis, H. D., & Shepherd, J. W. (1973). Cross-cultural study of recognition of pictures of faces and cups. *International Journal of Psychology, 8,* 269–273.

De Renzi, E. (1986). Current issues on prosopagnosia. In H. D. Ellis, M. Jeeves, F. Newcombe, & A. W. Young (Eds.), *Aspects of face processing* (pp. 243–252). Dordrecht: Martinus Nijhoff.

Diamond, R., & Carey, S. (1986). Why faces are and are not special: An effect of expertise. *Journal of Experimental Psychology: General, 115,* 107–117.

Ellis, H. D. (1988). The Tichborne Claimant. *Journal of Applied Cognitive Psychology, 2,* 257–264.

Ellis, H. D., Davies G. M., & Shepherd, J. (1978). A critical examination of the Photofit system for recalling faces. *Ergonomics, 21,* 297–307.

Ellis, H. D., Shepherd, J. W., & Davies, G. M. (1979). Identification of familiar and unfamiliar faces from internal and external features: Some implications for theories of face recognition. *Perception, 8,* 119–124.

Ellis, H. D., & Young, A. W. (1989). Faces in their social and biological context. In A. W. Young & H. D. Ellis (Eds.), *Handbook of research in face processing* (pp. 1–26). Amsterdam: North-Holland.

Frowd, C., Bruce, V., McIntyre, A., & Hancock, P. (2007). The relative importance of external and internal features of facial composites. *British Journal of Psychology, 98,* 61–77.

Frowd, C., Bruce, V., Ross, D., McIntyre, A., & Hancock, P. J. B. (2007). An application of caricature: How to improve the recognition of facial composites. *Visual Cognition, 15,* 954–984.

Frowd, C. D., Carson, D., Ness, H., McQuiston-Surrett, D., Richardson, J., Baldwin, H., & Hancock, P. (2005a). Contemporary composite techniques: The impact of a forensically-relevant target delay. *Legal and Criminological Psychology, 10,* 63–81.

Frowd, C. D., Carson, D., Ness, H., Richardson, J., Morrison, L., McLanaghan, S., & Hancock, P. (2005b). A forensically valid comparison of facial composite systems. *Psychology, Crime and Law, 11,* 33–52.

Galper, R. E. (1970). Recognition of faces in photographic negative. *Psychonomic Science, 19,* 207–208.

Gauthier, I., Behrmann, M., & Tarr, M. J. (1999). Can face recognition really be dissociated from object recognition? *Journal of Cognitive Neuroscience, 11,* 349–370.

Gauthier, I., Skudlarski, P., Gore, J. C., & Anderson, A. W. (2000). Expertise for cars and birds recruits brain areas involved in face recognition. *Nature Neuroscience, 3,* 191–197.

Gauthier, I., & Tarr, M. J. (1997). Becoming a "Greeble" expert: Exploring the face recognition mechanism. *Vision Research, 37,* 1673–1682.

Gauthier, I., Williams, P., Tarr, M. J., & Tanaka, J. (1998). Training "Greeble" experts: A framework for studying expert object recognition processes. *Vision Research, 38,* 2401–2428.

Gobbini, M. I., & Haxby, J. V. (2007). Neural systems for recognition of familiar faces. *Neuropsychologia, 45,* 32–41.

Goldstein, A. G., & Chance, J. E. (1971). Visual recognition memory for complex configurations. *Perception and Psychophysics, 9,* 237–241.

Gross, C. G., Rocha-Miranda, C. E., & Bender, D. B. (1972). Visual properties of neurons in inferotemporal cortex of the macaque. *Journal of Neurophysiology, 35,* 96–111.

Hancock, P. J. B. (2000). Evolving faces from principal components. *Behaviour Research Methods, Instruments and Computers, 32,* 327–333.

Hancock, P. J. B., & Frowd, C. D. (2002). Evolutionary generation of faces. In P. J. Bentley & D. W. Corne (Eds.), *Creative evolutionary systems* (pp. 409–424). San Francisco, CA: Morgan Kaufman.

Haxby, J. V., Gobbini, M. I., Furey, M. L., Ishai, A., Schouten, J. L., & Pietrini, P. (2001). Distributed and overlapping representations of faces and objects in ventral temporal cortex. *Science, 293,* 2425–2430.

Haxby, J. V., Hoffman, E. A., & Gobbini, M. I. (2000). The distributed human neural system for face perception. *Trends in Cognitive Sciences, 4,* 223–233.

Heywood, C. A., & Cowey, A. (1992). The role of the face-cell area in the discrimination and recognition of faces by monkeys. *Philosophical Transactions of the Royal Society of London, B, 335,* 31–38.

Hill, H., & Bruce, V. (1996). Effects of lighting on the perception of facial surfaces. *Journal of Experimental Psychology: Human Perception and Performance, 22,* 986–1004.

Kanwisher, N., McDermott, J., & Chun, M. M. (1997). The fusiform face area: A module in human extrastriate cortex specialised for face perception. *Journal of Neuroscience, 17,* 4302–4311.

Knight, B., & Johnston, A. (1997). The role of movement in face recognition. *Visual Cognition, 4,* 265–273.

Lander, K., & Bruce, V. (2000). Recognising famous faces: Exploring the benefits of facial motion. *Ecological Psychology, 12,* 259–272.

Lander, K., & Bruce, V. (2003). The role of motion in learning new faces. *Visual Cognition, 10,* 897–912.

Lander, K., Christie, F., & Bruce, V. (1999). The role of movement in the recognition of famous faces. *Memory and Cognition, 27,* 974–985.

Laughery, K., & Fowler, R. (1980). Sketch artist and identifit procedures for generating facial images. *Journal of Applied Psychology, 65,* 307–316.

Leder, H., & Bruce, V. (1998). Local and relational aspects of facial distinctiveness. *Quarterly Journal of Experimental Psychology, 51,* 449–473.

Leder, H., & Bruce, V. (2000). When inverted faces are recognised: The role of configural information in face recognition. *Quarterly Journal of Experimental Psychology, 53A,* 513–536.

Liu, C. H., & Chaudhuri, A. (2003). What determines whether faces are special? *Visual Cognition, 10,* 385–408.

McKone, E., Kanwisher, N., & Duchaine, B. C. (2007). Can generic expertise explain special processing for faces? *Trends in Cognitive Sciences, 11,* 8–15.

McNeil, J. E., & Warrington, E. K. (1993). Prosopagnosia: A face specific disorder. *Quarterly Journal of Experimental Psychology, 46A,* 1–10.

Nederhouser, M., & Mangini, M. (2001). A translation between S1 and S2 eliminates costs of changes in the direction of illumination in object matching. *Journal of Vision, 1,* 92a.

Patterson, K. E. (1978). Person recognition: More than a pretty face. In M. M. Gruneberg, P. E. Morris, & R. N. Sykes (Eds.), *Practical aspects of memory* (pp. 227–235). London: Academic Press.

Patterson, K. E., & Baddeley, A. D. (1977). When face recognition fails. *Journal of Experimental Psychology: Human Learning and Memory, 3,* 406–417.

Penry, J. (1971). *Looking at faces and remembering them.* London: Elek Books.

Perrett, D. I., Rolls, E. T., & Caan, W. (1982). Visual neurons responsive to faces in the monkey temporal cortex. *Experimental Brain Research, 47,* 329–342.

Perrett, D. I., Smith, P. A., Potter, D. D., Mistlin, A. J., Head, A. S., Milner, A. D., & Jeeves, M. A. (1984). Neurones responsive to faces in the temporal cortex: Studies of functional organisation, sensitivity to identity and relation to perception, *Human Neurobiology, 3,* 197–208.

Pike, G. E., Kemp, R. I., Towell, N. A., & Phillips, K. C. (1997). Recognising moving faces: The relative contribution of motion and perspective view information. *Visual Cognition, 4*, 409–437.

Pilz, K. S., Thornton, I. M., & Bülthoff, H. H. (2006). A search advantage for faces learned in motion. *Experimental Brain Research, 171*, 436–447.

Rakover, S. S. (2002). Featural vs. configurational information in faces: A conceptual and empirical analysis. *British Journal of Psychology, 93*, 1–30.

Rhodes, G., Byatt, G., Michie, P. T., & Puce, A. (2004). Is the fusiform face area specialised for faces, individuation, or expert individuation? *Journal of Cognitive Neuroscience, 16*, 189–203.

Rhodes, G., & McClean, I. (1990). Distinctiveness and expertise effects with homogeneous stimuli: Towards a model of configural coding. *Perception, 19*, 773–794.

Russell, R., Sinha, P., Biederman, I., & Nederhouser, M. (2006). Is pigmentation important for face recognition? Evidence from contrast negation. *Perception, 35*, 749–759.

Scapinello, K. F., & Yarmey, A. D. (1970). The role of familiarity and orientation in immediate and delayed recognition of pictorial stimuli. *Psychonomic Science, 21*, 329–330.

Schwarzlose, R. F., Baker, C. I., & Kanwisher, N. (2005). Separate face and body selectivity on the fusiform gyrus. *Journal of Neuroscience, 25*, 11055–11059

Shepard, R. N. (1967). Recognition memory for words, sentences and pictures. *Journal of Verbal Learning and Verbal Behaviour, 6*, 156–163.

Subramaniam, S., & Biederman, I. (1997). Does contrast reversal affect object identification? *Investigative Ophthalmology and Visual Science, 38*, 4638.

Tarr, M. J., Kersten, D., & Bülthoff, H. H. (1998). Why the visual recognition system might encode the effects of illumination. *Vision Research, 38*, 2259–2275.

Thomson, D. M. (1986). Face recognition: More than a feeling of familiarity? In H. D. Ellis, M. A. Jeeves, F. Newcombe, & A. Young (Eds.), *Aspects of face processing*. Dordrecht: Martinus Nijhoff.

Thompson, P. (1980). Margaret Thatcher: A new illusion. *Perception, 9*, 483–484.

Vuong, Q. C., Peissig, J. J., Harrison, M. C., & Tarr, M. J. (2005). The role of surface pigmentation for recognition revealed by contrast reversal in faces and Greebles. *Vision Research, 45*, 1213–1223.

Wagenaar, W. A. (1988). *Identifying Ivan: A case study in legal psychology*. New York: Harvester.

Yin, R. K. (1969). Looking at upside-down faces. *Journal of Experimental Psychology, 81*, 141–145.

Yin, R. K. (1970). Face recognition by brain-injured patients: A dissociable ability? *Neuropsychologia, 8*, 395–402.

Young, A. W. (1998). *Face and mind*. Oxford: Oxford University Press.

Young, A. W., Hellawell, D. J., & Hay, D. C. (1987). Configural information in face perception. *Perception, 16*, 747–759.

Young, A. W., Newcombe, F., De Haan, E. H. F., Small, M., & Hay, D. C. (1993). Face perception after brain injury: Selective impairments affecting identity and expression. *Brain, 116*, 941–959.

Yovel, G., & Kanwisher, N. (2005). The neural basis of the behavioural face-inversion effect. *Current Biology, 15*, 256–2262.

4

MEMORY FOR REAL-WORLD SCENES*

Andrew Hollingworth

Introduction

Humans spend most of their waking lives in complex visual environments that often consist of scores of individual objects. For example, a quick scan of the office in which this chapter was written generates a count of at least 150 objects. How do people perceive and remember environments of such complexity? The growing field of scene perception and memory is built upon a commitment to understanding how perception, attention, and memory operate under conditions of complexity and information oversaturation. For most of the history of vision research, experiments have been conducted using highly simplified stimuli, often presented for very brief durations. Such approaches are necessary to isolate component operations of vision and memory (such as color perception or object recognition). However, relatively little work has been conducted to understand how component operations of vision and memory are coordinated to support real-world perception, memory, and behavior. The present chapter reviews work on this topic, most of which has been conducted in the last 10–15 years. Although this research area is still relatively young, significant strides have been made, and it is now possible to provide a broad account of the means by which visual scene information is perceived and remembered.

Before continuing, it is important to provide a working definition of the term "visual scene". Henderson and Hollingworth (1999a, p. 244) used the following definition, which will be adopted here:

> the concept of scene is typically defined (though often implicitly) as a semantically coherent (and often nameable) view of a real-world environment comprising background elements and multiple discrete objects arranged in a spatially licensed manner. Background elements are taken to be larger-scale,

immovable surfaces and structures, such as ground, walls, floors, and mountains, whereas objects are smaller-scale discrete entities that are manipulable (e.g., can be moved) within the scene.

One of the organizing assumptions of this chapter is that scene perception and memory are dynamic operations that require the serial selection of local scene regions. Complex scenes contain too much information to be perceived in a single glance. Therefore, attention and the eyes are sequentially directed to goal-relevant scene regions and objects as viewing unfolds. Figure 4.1 shows a typical eye-movement scan path over a complex natural scene. Eye movements enable us to obtain high-resolution visual information from objects but also serve to specify objects in the world as the targets of actions, such as grasping (see chapter 5 of The Visual World in Memory). During eye movements, vision is suppressed (Matin, 1974) and perceptual input is also disrupted by blinks and occlusion. Memory is required to span these disruptions, and memory is required to accumulate information from local scene regions that is obtained sequentially. Furthermore, if experience within scenes is to influence our subsequent behavior (e.g., remembering where the phone is located so as to reach for it without searching), information

FIGURE 4.1 Eye movement scan path showing the sequence of fixations and saccades during free viewing of a scene for 10 s. Green dots represent fixations and green lines saccades. Note that the eyes typically are directed to discrete objects in the scene and rarely are directed to background regions (such as the sky)

about the structure and content of a scene must be stored robustly over the sometimes extended delays between encounters with a particular scene. Thus, visual
memory plays an important role not only within our online perceptual interactions
with a scene but also over much longer time scales that allow perceptual learning
to guide behavior.

The present chapter is divided into two sections. The first concerns the nature
of the visual representation constructed as participants view a natural scene. The
second concerns the functional role of visual memory in scene perception.

The representation of natural scenes

Memory systems potentially contributing to scene representation

Visual memory appears to be composed of four different memory stores, each of
which could potentially contribute to the representation of a natural scene: visible persistence, informational persistence, visual short-term memory (VSTM), and
visual long-term memory (VLTM).

Visible and informational persistence are often grouped together as *iconic memory*
or *sensory persistence* (Coltheart, 1980). Both maintain a high-capacity, retinotopically organized sensory trace that is generated across the visual field but is highly
volatile. Visible persistence is phenomenologically visible and persists for approximately 80–100 ms after the onset of a stimulus (Di Lollo, 1980). Informational
persistence is a nonvisible sensory memory that persists for approximately 150–300
ms after stimulus offset (Irwin & Yeomans, 1986). Both visible persistence and informational persistence are susceptible to interference from new sensory processing
(i.e., susceptible to backward masking).

Early theories proposed that, as attention and the eyes are directed to local scene
regions, low-level sensory memory is integrated so as to create a global image
of a natural scene (Davidson, Fox, & Dick, 1973; Jonides, Irwin, & Yantis, 1982;
McConkie & Rayner, 1975). In particular, high-resolution foveal information from
local regions could be combined to create a global image of a scene that contained
high-resolution sensory information across much of the visual field. Such integration was thought to be necessary to support our phenomenology of seeing a complete and detailed visual world across the visual field.

However, a large body of research demonstrates conclusively that that is
false: participants cannot integrate sensory information presented on separate
fixations (Irwin, Yantis, & Jonides, 1983; O'Regan & Lévy-Schoen, 1983; Rayner &
Pollatsek, 1983). Recent work using naturalistic scene stimuli has arrived at a similar
conclusion. Relatively large changes to a natural scene can go undetected if the
change occurs during a saccadic eye movement or other visual disruption (Grimes,
1996; Henderson & Hollingworth, 1999b, 2003b; Rensink, O'Regan, & Clark,
1997; Simons & Levin, 1998), an effect that has been termed *change blindness*. For
example, Henderson and Hollingworth (2003b) had participants view scene images
that were partially occluded by a set of vertical gray bars (as if viewing the scene

from behind a picket fence). During eye movements, the bars were shifted so that the occluded portions of the scene became visible and the visible portions became occluded. Despite the fact that every pixel in the image changed, subjects were almost entirely insensitive to these changes, demonstrating that low-level sensory information is not preserved from one fixation to the next. Because sensory persistence does not to appear to play any *memorial* role in scene representation, these systems will not be considered further. If scene representations are constructed from the incomplete, shifting, and frequently disrupted input that characterizes natural vision, then that construction must depend on more robust, higher-level visual memory systems of VSTM and VLTM.

VSTM maintains a small number of higher-level visual representations abstracted away from precise sensory information. It has a capacity of three to four objects (Irwin, 1992; Luck & Vogel, 1997) and lacks the metric precision of sensory persistence (Irwin, 1991; Phillips, 1974). However, VSTM is not significantly disrupted by subsequent perceptual input (Pashler, 1988; Phillips, 1974) and can be maintained over durations on the order of seconds (Phillips, 1974) and across saccades (Hollingworth, Richard, & Luck, 2008). VLTM maintains abstracted visual representations similar to those maintained in VSTM but has the capability to accumulate visual information from scores of individual objects (Hollingworth, 2004, 2005).

The online representation of scenes

Theoretical accounts of scene representation have been shaped by the phenomenon of change blindness. In change blindness experiments, participants often fail to detect otherwise salient changes when the change occurs across some form of perceptual disruption, such as a blank ISI (Rensink et al., 1997), an eye movement (Grimes, 1996; Henderson & Hollingworth, 1999b, 2003b), or occlusion (Simons & Levin, 1998). The sometimes remarkable insensitivity to changes across perceptual disruptions provides further evidence that the visual system does not construct a complete, low-level sensory representation of a scene. But what *is* represented during online scene perception? Proposals have spanned a wide range of possibilities.

O'Regan (1992; O'Regan & Noë, 2001) has argued that there is essentially no role for visual memory in scene representation, because the world itself acts as an "outside memory". In this view, visual memory is unnecessary, because information in the world can be acquired whenever needed by a shift of attention to the relevant object. In a similar vein, Ballard, Hayhoe, and colleagues (Ballard, Hayhoe, & Pelz, 1995; Ballard, Hayhoe, Pook, & Rao, 1997; Hayhoe, 2000; see also chapter 5 of The Visual World in Memory) have argued that visual scene memory during common real-world tasks is typically limited to the attended information necessary to support moment-to-moment actions. That is, the visual system minimizes memory demands by representing only the immediately task-relevant information, with eye movements used to acquire this information when it is needed. Rensink

(Rensink, 2000, 2002; Rensink et al., 1997) and others (Becker & Pashler, 2002; M. E. Wheeler & Treisman, 2002) also have argued that the visual representation of scenes is minimal, with the visual representation of a scene limited, at any moment, to the currently attended object. In this view, attention is necessary to form a coherent representation of an object that binds together the features of that object (Treisman, 1988). Attention is also necessary to maintain that binding in VSTM (Rensink, 2000; M. E. Wheeler & Treisman, 2002). Once attention is removed from an object, the coherent object representation comes unbound, and the object dissolves back into its constituent features, leaving no lasting visual memory. Irwin (Irwin & Andrews, 1996; Irwin & Zelinsky, 2002) has proposed that more than just the currently attended object is represented during scene viewing. Higher-level visual representations (abstracted away from precise sensory features) of previously attended objects accumulate in VSTM as the eyes and attention are oriented from object to object within a scene. However, this accumulation is limited to the capacity of VSTM: five to six objects at the most (Irwin & Zelinsky, 2002). Finally, Hollingworth and Henderson (2002) proposed that both VSTM and VLTM are used to accumulate higher-level visual representations of objects during scene viewing, enabling the construction of scene representations that maintain visual information from many individual objects.

The nonrepresentationalist approach of O'Regan finds little support in the literature. It is certainly true that eye movements are used to acquire visual information when it is needed (Hayhoe, 2000; Land, Mennie, & Rusted, 1999), but the proposal that the visual system relies entirely on the external world for access to visual information fails to account for the clear benefits of having a visual memory. Visual memory allows us to classify objects and scenes as belonging to particular categories, allows us recognize individual objects on the basis of their perceptual features (my dog is the brown one, not the white one), and allows us to remember the locations of objects so that they can be quickly found when needed. Moreover, research reviewed below demonstrates that humans are highly adept at remembering the visual properties of scenes. Thus, the nonrepresentationalist position can be eliminated from further consideration.

The next step in evaluating competing theories of online scene representation is to determine whether the visual representation of a scene is limited to the currently attended object (Rensink, 2000; M. E. Wheeler & Treisman, 2002). The principal evidence cited in support of this idea comes from the original experiments by Rensink et al. (1997). In those studies, changes to objects classified as "central interest" were detected more quickly than changes to objects classified as "marginal interest". Rensink et al. reasoned that, because central-interest items were more likely to be attended than marginal-interest items, evidence of faster detection of changes to central-interest items indicated that attention was necessary for change detection and, furthermore, that change detection was limited to the currently attended object. However, with no means to measure or control where attention was allocated in this task, any conclusions about the role of attention in scene memory and change detection must be considered tentative (for a similar criticism, see Scholl, 2000). In particular, one cannot conclude from these data that object representations in VSTM disintegrate upon the withdrawal of attention or that visual scene representation is limited to the currently attended object.

Wheeler and Treisman (2002) sought to examine whether attention is necessary to maintain coherent visual object representations in VSTM. Participants saw an array of simple colored shapes in a change detection task. They either had to remember the individual features (colors and shapes) or the binding of features (which particular shapes were paired with which particular colors). Wheeler and Treisman found that memory for the binding of features was impaired relative to memory for individual features, but only when the entire array was presented again at test; when a single item was presented at test, there was no binding deficit. Wheeler and Treisman argued that the presentation of the entire array at test led to attentional distraction and the withdrawal of attention from the items in VSTM, causing the bound object representations to disintegrate into their constituent features and generating a deficit in binding memory. However, attention was not directly manipulated in this study, and there is no compelling reason to think that presentation of the full array at test led to attentional distraction (Hollingworth, 2006; Jiang, Olson, & Chun, 2000; Johnson, Hollingworth, & Luck, 2008).

Johnson et al. (2008) attempted to replicate the Wheeler and Treisman (2002) result, but found no decrement in binding memory when comparing a full array test with single-object test. More importantly, Johnson et al. directly manipulated attention in a similar change detection task. During the delay between presentation of the study array and test array, participants completed a demanding visual search task that required serial shifts of attention to search array elements. The introduction of this search task lowered memory performance overall, but there was no specific decrement in memory for feature binding, indicating no special role for attention in maintaining feature bindings in VSTM. In addition, Gajewski and Brockmole (2006) found that the recall of objects in a VSTM task did not exhibit any significant loss of binding information when attention was engaged by a peripheral cue. Finally, Allen, Baddeley, and Hitch (2006) found that memory for feature binding in VSTM was not specifically impaired by a secondary task that required central attentional resources. Thus, sustained attention is not required to maintain feature binding in visual memory, and scene representation need not be limited to the currently attended object.

To examine visual memory for previously attended objects during the viewing of real-world scenes, Hollingworth and Henderson (2002) tested visual memory for objects in scenes after attention had been withdrawn from the object. Eye movements were monitored as participants viewed depictions of real-world scenes. The computer waited until the participant had fixated a target object in the scene (to ensure it had been attended). Subsequently, the target object was masked during a saccade to a different object in the scene. Because visual attention is automatically and exclusively allocated to the goal of a saccade prior to an eye movement (e.g., Deubel & Schneider, 1996; Hoffman & Subramaniam, 1995), the target object was no longer attended when it was masked; attention had shifted to the nontarget object that was the goal of the saccade. Two object alternatives were then displayed within the scene. One was the original target object, and the other was either a different token from the same basic-level category (e.g., if the target was a watering can, the token was a different example of a watering can) or the target object rotated 90° in depth. Participants performed this discrimination task at rates above 80% correct. Furthermore, accurate discrimination performance was observed even when many fixations on other objects intervened between target fixation and test. When more than nine fixations on other objects intervened between target fixation and test, token discrimination performance was 85% correct, and orientation discrimination performance was 92% correct. Memory for the visual details of previously attended objects was clearly robust across shifts of attention and of the eyes, and therefore the online visual representation of a scene is not limited to the currently attended object. Tatler and colleagues have provided complementary evidence that memory for the visual details of objects accumulates over multiple seconds of scene viewing (Tatler, Gilchrist, & Land, 2005; Tatler, Gilchrist, & Rusted, 2003).

In contrast with the studies reviewed above, Wolfe, Reinecke, and Brawn (2006) recently reported data they interpreted as evidence for minimal visual accumulation during scene viewing. On each trial of this experiment, 12 photographs of common objects were superimposed over a scene background. Participants shifted their attention covertly to individual objects in the scene, following a visual cue that specified the locations of either three or six of the objects. After the cue sequence, one object was masked. Participants were then shown an array of 36 object photographs, one of which was the masked object. Percentage correct performance on this 36 alternative forced-choice (AFC) task was approximately 50% for objects cued early in the sequence and approximately 85% for the object cued last in the sequence. Wolfe et al. interpreted their results as at variance with the finding of robust visual accumulation in Hollingworth and Henderson (2002).

What accounts for the apparent discrepancy between these studies? First, it is not clear that there is any significant discrepancy at all. In Wolfe et al. (2006), chance performance on the 36-AFC task was 2.8% (1/36). Memory performance for previously attended objects ranged from approximately 40% correct to 65% correct, and memory for the first cued object (which was cued six objects before the test) was approximately 50% correct. Thus, just as in Hollingworth and Henderson (2002), there was significant accumulation of visual object information as attention was oriented serially to objects in the scene. In addition, two aspects of the Wolfe et al. method were likely to have limited memory performance. To perform the 36-AFC task, participants would have needed to inspect a fairly large number of the 36 test objects in the course of finding the target, potentially introducing significant interference with target memory. The 2-AFC task of Hollingworth and Henderson (2002) is to be preferred, because it minimizes interference generated by the test itself. Furthermore, the speed of cueing was exceedingly rapid in the Wolfe et al. study, with consecutive object cues separated by only 150 or 300 ms SOA. Even if one assumes that each object was focally attended for the full SOA duration, the attentional dwell times were far shorter than those observed during free viewing

(Hollingworth & Henderson, 2002) and were likely too short for the reliable consolidation of complex real-world objects into visual memory (Eng, Chen, & Jiang, 2005). In sum, the Wolfe et al. data replicated the central Hollingworth and Henderson (2002) finding of visual accumulation for previously attended objects, but encoding limitations and interference at test were likely to have depressed memory performance.

The results of Hollingworth and Henderson (2002) demonstrate that higher-level memory systems (but not sensory memory systems) accumulate visual information to construct a representation of a natural scene. Two candidate memory systems could contribute to online scene memory: VSTM and VLTM. To tease apart their relative contributions, Hollingworth (2004) used a serial position procedure. On each trial, participants followed a green dot with their eyes as it visited a series of objects in a scene (the SOA between consecutive cues was 1,100 ms). The serial position of a target object in the sequence was manipulated. After the sequence was completed, memory for the visual form of the target object was tested in a 2-AFC token or orientation discrimination test. A reliable recency effect was observed (see also Phillips & Christie, 1977). Performance was highest for the last two objects cued in the scene. This recency effect suggests a VSTM contribution to online scene representation that was limited to approximately two objects, an estimate consistent with independent estimates of VSTM capacity for complex natural objects (Alvarez & Cavanagh, 2004). Supporting the proposal that VLTM plays a significant role in online scene representation (Hollingworth & Henderson, 2002), memory performance for objects examined earlier than two objects before the test was quite accurate, and it did not decline further; performance was equivalent for objects cued three objects before the test and objects cued ten objects before the test. This robust pre-recency memory easily surpassed VSTM capacity, indicating a large VLTM component to online scene representation (for converging evidence, see Hollingworth, 2005). Similar effects have been found in memory for the identity of objects (Wolfe et al., 2006) and in memory for the binding of objects to locations (Zelinsky & Loschky, 2005). Given that scene viewing often unfolds over the course of minutes and involves serially attending to and fixating scores of objects, it is likely that VLTM carries most of the load in constructing an online representation of a scene.

Longer-term memory for previously viewed scenes

Having constructed a visual memory representation of a scene during online viewing, how robustly is that representation retained in memory? Initial work on the capacity of picture memory demonstrated that participants have a prodigious ability to remember complex pictures, and such memory can be retained robustly over long delays (Nickerson, 1965, 1968; Shepard, 1967; Standing, 1973; Standing, Conezio, & Haber, 1970). Standing (1973) required participants to view 10,000 photographs of various subject matters for 5 s each over the course of five days of study. On a subsequent 2-AFC recognition task, discrimination performance was approximately 86% correct, which suggested that participants had successfully remembered almost 7,000 pictures. This is quite remarkable, given that the method was single-trial exposure and that each scene was viewed only briefly. Picture memory not only has remarkably large capacity, but visual memory representations of scenes are highly resistant to decay. Nickerson (1968) showed participants 200 grayscale photographs for 5 s each. A unique subset of the pictures was tested at varying intervals in a 2-AFC test. Four retention intervals were tested: one day, one week, one month, and one year. Discrimination performance declined with increasing delay (1 day = 92%; 1 week = 88%; 1 month = 74%; 1 year = 63%). However, forgetting was exceedingly gradual, and discrimination performance remained above chance even a year later, all from a single, 5 s exposure to each scene.

In these early studies on the capacity of visual memory, there was little control of stimulus properties, with pictures chosen from a variety of sources: magazines, travel snapshots, and so on. One possible explanation for prodigious memory capacity is that participants were not remembering perceptual details of the scenes but were instead remembering the abstract gist of the scene (Chun, 2003; Potter, Staub, & O'Connor, 2004; Simons, 1996). However, at least one study from this literature cannot be explained by gist retention. In Standing et al. (1970), participants viewed a set of 120 pictures for 2 s each. After a delay of 30 minutes or 24 hours, their memory for the left–right orientation of the pictures was tested by displaying the original picture or a mirrored-reversed version of that picture. Mirror reversal does not significantly alter scene gist (as long as there is no visible text or other canonically oriented stimuli), and thus accurate memory performance would indicate that participants remembered visual properties of the scenes rather than just semantic gist. Memory performance was approximately 86% correct after a delay of 30 minutes and approximately 72% correct after a delay of 24 hours. Thus, estimates of very large memory capacity for pictures might draw to some extent on memory for abstract gist, but there is clearly robust retention of visual detail.

To examine the capacity of VLTM for the visual details of individual objects in natural scenes, Hollingworth (2004) had participants view a series of scenes, with individual objects cued by means of a dot onset (described above). Instead of testing memory immediately after scene viewing, the test was delayed until all 48 scenes had been viewed. Memory for the token version of a single object in each scene was tested. More than 400 objects, on average, were examined between target examination and test of that object. Despite these considerable memory demands, participants performed the token change detection task at a rate well above chance (68% correct). For example, participants saw an iron on an ironing board in a laundry scene. This was only one of many objects in that particular scene, and the scene was only one of the 48 scenes viewed. Participants fixated the iron for less than 1 s, on average. Yet, after all scenes had been viewed, participants could report, at rates above chance, that the original iron had been replaced by a different iron. Moreover, memory for object token and orientation in scenes remained above chance even after a delay of 24 hours (Hollingworth, 2005).

This level of specificity in visual memory stands in stark contrast to change blindness effects. For example, in Henderson and Hollingworth (2003b), every pixel in a scene image was changed during a saccade by shifting a set of vertical bars that obscured half of the scene. Such changes were almost completely undetectable (even to those knowledgeable about the change). Yet, in Hollingworth (2004), participants could remember the token version of a single object in a scene viewed 30 minutes earlier. This juxtaposition illustrates the strengths and limitations of visual memory. Low-level sensory memory, which was necessary for the detection of bar shifts in Henderson and Hollingworth (2003b), is so fleeting that it does not even survive a single saccade. Yet, higher-level visual memory, which is abstracted away from precise sensory persistence but retains information about the form and orientation of an object, is highly robust.

Understanding change blindness

It is important, now, to return to the topic of change blindness so as to reconcile evidence of robust visual memory, reviewed above, with evidence of poor change detection performance in change blindness experiments (for a more extensive discussion, see Hollingworth, 2008). Change blindness has multiple causes. First, there is clearly forgetting in visual memory that causes participants to miss changes. The most dramatic form of forgetting is the loss of visual sensory memory following a stimulus event. There is no doubt that changes would be detected more reliably in change blindness experiments if sensory memory was retained robustly. However, we have known that sensory memory is fleeting ever since the early work by Sperling (1960) and Averbach and Coriell (1961). In higher-level visual memory systems (VSTM and VLTM), there is little subsequent forgetting over the timescales characteristic of change blindness studies (Hollingworth, 2005). A second cause of change blindness is failures of encoding. If the changing region of a scene has not been attended and fixated prior to the change, then the visual system would have minimal ability to detect the change, because the consolidation of perceptual information into VSTM and VLTM depends on focal attention (Averbach & Coriell, 1961; Hollingworth & Henderson, 2002; Schmidt, Vogel, Woodman, & Luck, 2002). A third cause of change blindness is retrieval and comparison failure. Many changes are missed despite the retention of visual information sufficient to detect the change. In these cases, the relevant information is not retrieved from memory and/or is not compared with current perceptual information (Hollingworth, 2003; Simons, Chabris, Schnur, & Levin, 2002; Varakin, Levin, & Collins, 2007). Finally, change blindness occurs when evidence for a change is registered but does not exceed the threshold for explicit change detection. In these cases, participants are not consciously aware of a change, but one can observe implicit effects of change detection on sensitive measures (for a review, see Thornton & Fernandez-Duque, 2002), such as fixation duration (Hayhoe, Bensinger, & Ballard, 1998; Henderson & Hollingworth, 2003a; Hollingworth, Williams, & Henderson, 2001; Ryan, Althoff, Whitlow, & Cohen, 2000). As in any complex task, change detection can fail if any component of the task (encoding, maintenance, retrieval, comparison, detection) is compromised. In many cases, participants miss changes despite the retention of information sufficient to detect the change, and thus poor change detection cannot necessarily be interpreted as caused by poor or absent visual memory.

How are episodic representations of scenes structured?

Having shown that object information accumulates in memory as the eyes are oriented from object to object within a scene, and that scene representations are retained robustly in VLTM, the next question to address is how visual information obtained from individual objects is bound together, episodically, to form a coherent representation of a scene. As a first step in this endeavor, Hollingworth (2006) tested whether memory for the visual form of an object is bound to the scene context in which the object appeared. Prior research in the face perception literature has demonstrated that memory for the features of faces is stored as part of a larger face representation but that memory for the features of houses (a stimulus that more closely resembles a real-world scene) are stored independently of the house context (Tanaka & Farah, 1993) (see chapter 3 of The Visual World in Memory, section 3.1). Such work suggests that objects might be remembered independently of the scene context in which the object appeared.

To test object-to-scene binding in visual memory, Hollingworth (2006) had participants view a series of complex scenes for 20 s each. Each scene image was followed by a 2-AFC test requiring memory for the perceptual features of a single object in the scene (token or orientation discrimination). The two object alternatives were displayed either within the original scene or in an otherwise empty field. Discrimination performance was reliably superior when the target object was tested within the original scene context, a whole-scene advantage similar to the advantage for the recognition of face features when the features are displayed within the original face context (Tanaka & Farah, 1993). Thus, visual memory for objects is episodically structured via association with the scene context in which the object appeared. Furthermore, faces are not unique in showing such contextual binding.

Spatial structure in scene memory

What are the mechanisms of object-to-scene binding? Hollingworth and Henderson (2002) proposed that object memory is organized within a scene through the binding of objects to particular spatial locations within a global spatial representation of the scene. This proposal originated from consideration that spatial information plays a central role in structuring episodic memory (Burgess, Maguire, & O'Keefe, 2002; O'Keefe & Nadel, 1978) and that spatial position structures object information in VSTM (Jiang et al., 2000; Kahneman, Treisman, & Gibbs, 1992).

To test whether memory for objects is indeed bound to scene locations, Hollingworth (2006) manipulated object position in a scene memory study. As in previous experiments, participants viewed a scene for 20 s. Each scene was then followed by a 2-AFC or change detection test probing memory for the visual form of a single object. The test objects were presented either at the original location where the target had appeared or at a different location within the scene (local contextual information was obscured in both conditions). Discrimination accuracy was higher when the test objects appeared at the same location as the target had appeared originally within the scene, a *same-position advantage*, indicating that memory for the visual form of the object was associated with the scene location where the object had appeared.

Hollingworth (2007) used the same-position advantage as a means to understand the spatial properties of a scene that serve to structure memory for objects. The experiments depended on the following logic. If a particular property of a scene is functional in defining object position, and if that property is disrupted, then the same-position advantage for target discrimination should be reduced or eliminated. First, Hollingworth examined whether the spatial position of an object is defined relative to the particular scene context in which the object appeared. Again, participants viewed full scenes, each followed by a 2-AFC discrimination test in which the test object alternatives appeared either in the same scene position as the target object had appeared at study or in a different position. In the full-scene condition, the test objects were displayed within the original scene. In the background-absent condition, the test objects were presented in the same absolute locations but against a blank background. This manipulation is illustrated in Figure 4.2. The advantage for presenting the target object in the same position at study and test was replicated in the full-scene condition, but that advantage was all but eliminated in the background-absent condition, indicating that object position was defined relative to the scene context in which it appeared.

Hollingworth (2007) further probed the nature of spatial contextual representations using arrays of common objects that allowed spatial manipulations not possible with scene stimuli. Scrambling the spatial locations of contextual objects at test significantly reduced the same-position benefit, demonstrating that object position is defined relative to the configuration of contextual objects (Jiang et al., 2000). In addition, a background-binding manipulation (in which the contextual objects traded locations) also reduced the same-position advantage. In this latter case, the contextual objects formed the same abstract spatial configuration at study and test. Only the binding of contextual objects to locations changed. Thus, the positions of individual objects appear to be defined relative to a contextual representation that maintains not only the abstract spatial configuration of objects, but also information about which objects appear in which locations in that configuration. Finally, the same-position advantage was preserved after translation of the array context, which did not disrupt object-to-object spatial relationships, demonstrating that object position is defined in scene-relative, rather than absolute, coordinates.

Studied Scene

Test Conditions

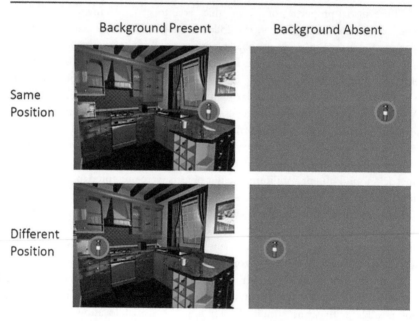

FIGURE 4.2 Contextual manipulations in Hollingworth (2007). The top section shows the studied scene. The bottom section shows the target image displayed in the 2-AFC test (in the distractor image, the target was mirror-reversed). When the test objects were displayed within the scene background (background present), there was a reliable discrimination advantage for the same-position condition over the different-position condition. However, when the test objects were displayed against a blank background (background absent), there was no effect of the position of the target object

In summary, memory for a visual scene appears to be constructed, at least in part, through the binding of local object representations to locations within a spatial representation of the scene layout (Hollingworth & Henderson, 2002). This contextual representation is specific to the particular viewed scene, maintains the spatial configuration of objects, preserves the binding of contextual objects to locations, and codes individual object position in array-relative coordinates.

Schema approaches to scene structure

Historically, a central theoretical construct in the field of picture and scene memory has been the scene schema (Biederman, Mezzanotte, & Rabinowitz, 1982; Brewer & Treyens, 1981; Friedman, 1979; Intraub, 1997; Mandler & Ritchey, 1977; Pedzek, Whetstone, Reynolds, Askari, & Dougherty, 1989). The basic claim of schema theories is that episodic representations of scenes are structured according to prior experience with scenes of that type. For example, one's memory for a particular kitchen scene will be strongly influenced by one's memory for kitchens in general, a *kitchen schema*, which will govern the types of information retained in memory from that scene (see chapter 7 of The Visual World in Memory for the influence of schemas on memory for visual events). The standard description of a scene schema is an abstract representation of a particular scene category specifying the objects that are typically found in that type of scene and the typical locations of those objects (Mandler & Parker, 1976).

Two components are consistently present in schema accounts of scene memory: abstraction and distortion (for a critical review, see Alba & Hasher, 1983). First, scene memory is proposed to be highly abstract and conceptual in nature— that is, limited to the gist of the scene (Mandler & Ritchey, 1977; Potter et al., 2004). Scene details are initially activated during perceptual processing of the scene, but the details are quickly forgotten. In this claim, schema theories are quite similar to claims of gist-based representations in the change blindness literature (O'Regan, 1992; Rensink, 2000; Simons & Levin, 1997). The evidence that scene representations preserve significant visual detail, and are not limited to gist, has been reviewed exhaustively above. Thus, the schema theory claim of gist abstraction is not well supported by experimental evidence.

Second, the schema approach holds that memory for scene properties will be distorted by prior knowledge. Objects frequently found within a scene of that type (such as a dresser in a bedroom) will be remembered most frequently, because they have pre-existing "slots" in the schema. Incongruous or unexpected objects (such as a pig in a bedroom) will be remembered less accurately and will be normalized to default values in the schema. Although common sense would dictate that anomalous objects should be remembered most frequently from a scene (as they would be most salient), normalization is a central feature of schema theory (Bartlett, 1932). Brewer and Treyens (1981) tested the normalization claim by having participants remember the objects in a graduate student office, some of which were semantically consistent (desk) and some inconsistent (skull). On a free-recall test, participants more frequently reported semantically consistent objects than inconsistent objects, supporting the claim of normalization. However, Brewer and Treyens provided no control over guessing, and the advantage for consistent objects could easily have been generated by a bias to guess that consistent objects had been present. For example, if asked to report which objects had been in a kitchen scene, one could guess that there was likely to have been a stove, even if one did not specifically remember a stove.

In contrast to the Brewer and Treyens (1981) result, subsequent studies controlling guessing have found the reverse effect: better memory for semantically inconsistent objects in scenes (Friedman, 1979; Hollingworth & Henderson, 2000, 2003; Pedzek et al., 1989). Although some researchers have proposed schema explanations to account for superior inconsistent-object memory, these have been somewhat ad hoc. For example, Friedman (1979) proposed that inconsistent objects are stored robustly as part of a "weird list" that is appended to the schema representation. This type of modification would render the schema approach all but unfalsifiable. In general, the absence of inconsistent-object normalization argues against the standard schema account of scene memory.

The function of visual memory in scene perception

The research reviewed thus far has examined the capabilities of visual memory and the means by which memory is used to construct visual representations of scenes. I turn now to the question of the function of visual memory in scene perception. Given that participants can generate robust internal representations of a scene, how and to what purpose is this information used? I first consider the functional role of VSTM and then consider VLTM function.

The function of VSTM in scene perception

The literature on VSTM has seen a remarkable surge in research over the last decade (for a review, see Luck, 2008). Most of this research has sought to understand the capacity of VSTM and the format of VSTM representations, but the functional purpose of the VSTM system has received relatively little attention. After discussing two common accounts of VSTM function, I argue that VSTM supports perceptual comparison operations that are required almost constantly during real-world perception and behavior.

VSTM and conscious awareness

A common proposal regarding VSTM function is that VSTM forms the substrate of visual awareness (Becker & Pashler, 2002; Rensink, 2000; Rensink et al., 1997). In particular, VSTM is thought to reflect activation of the currently attended portion of a visual scene, with constraints on attentional capacity and VSTM capacity reflecting two sides of the same coin (Cowan, 1995; Rensink, 2000). However, it is highly unlikely that VSTM plays any direct role in visual awareness. VSTM representations are not visible and thus are unlikely to be the substrate of visual awareness; one does not continue to *see* the items held in VSTM once they have been removed. For example, one does not see remembered items as persisting during an ISI between study and test images in a change detection task (as in Luck & Vogel, 1997). It is this very property of VSTM—that it is not visible—that distinguishes VSTM from visible persistence (iconic memory), which *is* visible (Coltheart, 1980).

If VSTM does not form the substrate of visual experience, then the fact that we can only hold three to four objects in VSTM does not necessarily mean that our visual awareness of a scene is limited to three to four objects. Indeed, Sperling (1960) showed that we see a great deal more than we can hold in VSTM. When participants were shown arrays of 12 letters in Sperling's task, they saw 12 letters in the brief moment that they were visible, but they could only transfer three to four letter identities into STM for subsequent report. A quick demonstration proves this point. One tells a naïve participant to view a briefly presented visual display. Then one presents an array of 12 letters for 50 ms (as in Sperling, 1960). What observers report is that there were 12 letters, but they can only report the identity of three to four of them. Because it is easy to report that there were 12 letters (and not six letters or three letters), participants must have seen 12 letters when they were visible. If visual awareness was limited to the capacity of VSTM, then participants should have reported that there were only three to four letters present. The issue here is that, because the report of what one saw requires memory, limitations on memory can easily be confused with limitations on perceptual experience (Chun & Potter, 1995; Moore & Egeth, 1997; Vogel & Luck, 2002; for a full discussion, see Wolfe, 1999).

VSTM and perceptual integration

A second proposal regarding the function of VSTM is that VSTM supports the integration of perceptual information across disruptions in visual input (e.g., Brockmole, Irwin, & Wang, 2002; Irwin, 1992). In particular, VSTM has been proposed to play a central role in the integration of visual information across saccadic eye movements. In this view, as attention and the eyes are directed to objects in scenes, information from the attended target of the next saccade (and perhaps one or two additional objects) is consolidated into VSTM. Upon landing, newly acquired perceptual information is integrated with the stored information in VSTM. Support for this proposal has come from evidence that participants can remember properties of the saccade target object in VSTM across a saccade (Irwin, 1992; Irwin & Andrews, 1996) and that a preview of an object prior to a saccade leads to speeded naming of that object when the eyes land (Henderson & Anes, 1994; Henderson, Pollatsek, & Rayner, 1987; Pollatsek, Rayner, & Collins, 1984). Although these effects certainly demonstrate that visual representations can be stored in VSTM across an eye movement, they do not necessarily indicate that VSTM is used to *integrate* perceptual information available on separate fixations into a composite representation. And, given the very limited capacity of VSTM—one or two natural objects during scene viewing (Hollingworth, 2004)—any possible integration would have to be minimal and local; VSTM certainly could not support any large-scale integration of scene information.

A few studies have directly examined the role of VSTM in visual integration. It is well established that visible persistence integrates with a trailing stimulus if the SOA between the two stimuli is very short (< 80 ms). For example, Di Lollo (1980) displayed sequentially two arrays of dots in a grid pattern. In the first array, half of the grid cells contained dots. In the second array, dots filled all but one of the cells that were unfilled in the first array. Between the two arrays, one grid cell did not contain a dot, and the task was to specify the location of the "missing dot". At very short SOAs, the visible persistence of the first array integrates with perceptual processing of the second, and participants see a single array with all but one cell filled (which made the task very easy to perform). However, at slightly longer SOAs, no such integration was observed, likely to due to masking of the first array by the second.

Brockmole et al. (2002) extended this approach to examine integration at SOAs likely to be supported by VSTM. At long SOAs (greater than 1,000 ms), performance on the missing-dot task increased significantly, returning to levels similar to those observed at very short SOAs, when perceptual integration is known to occur. Brockmole et al. concluded that VSTM can indeed support perceptual integration. However, Hollingworth, Hyun, and Zhang (2005) and Jiang, Kumar, and Vickery (2005) found that, at long SOAs, the task typically is performed not by integrating information in VSTM but, rather, by comparing memory for the empty cells of the first array with the occupied locations in the second array (the one empty cell from the first array that does not have a dot in the second array is the location of the "missing dot"). This alternative is consistent with a general role for VSTM in perceptual comparison, reviewed subsequently. Although the results of Hollingworth et al. and Jiang et al. do not rule out the possibility that participants can solve the missing-dot task by integration in VSTM, high levels of performance at long ISIs cannot be taken as strong evidence of such integration. In summary, although VSTM could potentially support the integration of scene information, little direct evidence for integration in VSTM has been found, and the highly limited capacity of VSTM dictates that any potential for integration must also be highly limited.

VSTM and perceptual comparison

The main thesis of this section is that an important function of VSTM is to enable the comparison of perceptual information obtained from objects divided by space, time, or perceptual disruption. For example, if one is trying to decide whether a pie is ready to come out of the oven, one might encode perceptual information about the pie (how browned it is; whether the filling is bubbling at the edges), store that information in VSTM, shift attention and the eyes to the cookbook, and then compare the stored information about the perceptual properties of the pie to the picture in the cookbook. Note that in order for such perceptual comparison to be possible, one's memory for the pie must be maintained after attention is withdrawn from the pie and shifted to the cookbook (Gajewski & Brockmole, 2006; Hollingworth & Henderson, 2002; Johnson et al., 2008). A VSTM system limited to the currently attended object would be of little practical value in complex multiple-object scenes. Because the comparison of spatially separated objects will almost always require a shift of attention (and likely an eye movement) from one object to the other, VSTM is necessary to store information about the first object entering into the comparison as attention is redirected to acquire perceptual information from the second object entering into the comparison.

In addition to comparing two spatially separated objects, VSTM supports a number of other perceptual comparison operations. One well-studied case arises in visual search. Duncan and Humphreys (1989) proposed that, during visual search, VSTM is used to maintain perceptual information about the target of the search. When attending sequentially to objects in the course of search, the search template maintained in VSTM is compared with the perceptual properties of each attended object, allowing one to determine whether the currently attended object is the target or a distractor. In addition, attention is biased during search toward objects that match the perceptual features of the target maintained in VSTM (Chelazzi, Miller, Duncan, & Desimone, 1993; Desimone & Duncan, 1995; Olivers, Meijer, & Theeuwes, 2006; Soto, Heinke, Humphreys, & Blanco, 2005).

Several studies have tested the functional role of VSTM in search using dual-task interference methods. Woodman, Vogel, and Luck (2001) had participants perform a search task either with or without a concurrent VSTM load of colors. If VSTM is required to maintain search-target properties, then filling VSTM with a secondary color load should interfere with comparison operations during search, reducing the efficiency of the search. Woodman et al. found effects of VSTM load on the intercept of the function relating RT to set size, but no effect on the slope of the search function. They interpreted this result as indicating that VSTM was not necessary for efficient search. However, the Woodman et al. search task used the same search target on every trial, raising the possibility that participants encoded the search target into VLTM, thereby minimizing the need to maintain the target in VSTM. In a subsequent study, Woodman, Luck, and Schall (2007) changed the properties of the search target on every trial, which should have placed greater demand on VSTM to maintain the currently relevant target properties. Under these conditions, a concurrent VSTM load of colors did impair search efficiency, providing support for the original Duncan and Humphreys (1989) proposal.

Perhaps the most frequent use of VSTM in scene perception involves the mapping of objects across temporal gaps and disruptions in perceptual input. As we interact perceptually with a complex scene, dynamic properties of the observer (shifts of attention and the eyes, blinks, motion) and of the world (object motion, occlusion) create gaps in perceptual input. One of the central challenges of vision is to establish the correspondence between objects visible before and after a disruption. For example, if I make an eye movement from a coffee cup to a pen, the coffee cup lies at the fovea before the saccade and the pen in the periphery. After the saccade is completed, the pen lies at the fovea and the cup in the periphery. The retinal locations of all other visible objects change as well. How does the visual system establish the mapping of objects visible before and after the saccade? One solution is that properties of objects visible before the saccade are stored in VSTM across the saccade and compared with perceptual information available after the saccade (Currie, McConkie, Carlson-Radvansky, & Irwin, 2000; Henderson & Hollingworth, 2003a; Irwin, 1992). In this manner, VSTM could support the perception of scene continuity (i.e., that objects visible now correspond to objects visible a moment ago) despite gaps, disruptions, and changes in perceptual input.

The use of VSTM to establish correspondence across perceptual disruption is particularly important when there is ambiguity in object mapping. This circumstance arises frequently during natural-scene viewing. Saccadic eye movements occur almost constantly, but they are highly prone to error, with the eyes often missing the target of the saccade. Such saccade errors are likely to occur thousands of times each day during normal activities. When the eyes miss the saccade target in a complex scene, there are likely to be multiple objects near the landing position of that saccade. Hollingworth et al. (2008) hypothesized that VSTM is used to remember visual properties of the saccade target object, so that after an inaccurate saccade the target can be found among other nearby objects and gaze efficiently corrected (via a rapid corrective saccade). To test this hypothesis, Hollingworth et al. developed a paradigm that simulated object ambiguity after an inaccurate eye movement. Participants fixated the center of a circular array of colored disks. One disk was cued, and the participant generated a saccade to that object. During the saccade (when vision is suppressed) the entire array was rotated by one half of the distance between adjacent objects. This typically caused the eyes to land between two objects: the target object and a distractor object. To accurately correct gaze to the target, perceptual information from before the saccade (such as the target's color) must be retained across the saccade in VSTM and then compared with objects near the landing position.

Hollingworth et al. (2008) found that VSTM-based gaze correction in this paradigm was highly accurate and efficient. The use of VSTM to correct gaze added only 40 ms to the latency of the corrective saccade (compared with a single-object control condition in which memory was not needed to correct gaze). Similar results were observed using novel objects of similar complexity to objects found in the world. In addition, the accuracy and speed of gaze correction was impaired by a concurrent VSTM load but not by a concurrent verbal WM load, demonstrating that VSTM is indeed functional in establishing object correspondence across saccades. Finally, VSTM-based corrective saccades were generated even when participants were instructed to avoid making them, suggesting that VSTM-based correction is a largely automatized skill. Given that we make hundreds of thousands of saccades each day and many of these fail to land on the saccade target, the use of VSTM to correct gaze is likely to be a central function of the VSTM system.

The function of VLTM in scene perception

In what manner does VLTM for a scene influence perceptual processing of that scene? First of all, VLTM for scenes allows us to recognize scenes and categorize them. However, there has been surprisingly little research examining the mechanisms of scene identification. Initial evidence suggests that scene identification depends on global scene properties rather than local analysis of constituent objects (Oliva & Torralba, 2006). In addition, scene identification is extraordinarily rapid (Potter

& Levy, 1969; Thorpe, Fize, & Marlot, 1996). Efficient scene identification raises the possibility that scene memory might influence even fairly early perceptual operations over a scene. I shall first consider whether scene identification influences the perceptual recognition of objects in a scene. I then examine the role of scene knowledge in guiding attention to task-relevant areas of a scene.

Effects of scene memory on object recognition

Hollingworth and Henderson (1998) identified three possible means by which one's knowledge about a particular scene type (e.g., that kitchens tend to contain stoves but not motorcycles) could influence the identification of constituent objects. First, scene knowledge could interact with early visual processing to enhance the perceptual description of scene-consistent objects (*description enhancement*). Second, scene knowledge could influence the comparison of perceptual object representations to stored category representations, lowering goodness-of-fit thresholds for consistent object categories (*criterion modulation*). Third, scene knowledge could be isolated from object recognition operations, influencing only postperceptual reasoning (*functional isolation*).

When examining the influence of scene knowledge on the perceptual recognition of objects, it is critical to ensure that participants cannot use their knowledge of scenes to make an educated guess. For example, if one is blindfolded, taken into a kitchen, and asked to name the large appliance in the corner, one could reason that the probed object is likely to be a stove or a refrigerator (rather than a washing machine or an air conditioner) in the absence of any visual input at all. Early studies examining the effects of scene context on object recognition found that semantically consistent objects (e.g., a computer in an office) were recognized more accurately than inconsistent objects (e.g., a computer in a bathroom) (Biederman et al., 1982; Palmer, 1975). However, educated guessing was not adequately controlled in these studies. The consistent-object advantage could have derived from the fact that participants were biased to report consistent objects, without any direct effect of scene context on the perceptual mechanisms of object recognition.

To provide a better measure of scene context effects on perceptual object recognition, Hollingworth and Henderson (1998) used a 2-AFC method similar to that developed by Reicher (1969; see also D. D. Wheeler, 1970) to examine the effects of word context on letter identification. On each trial, participants saw a brief display of a scene containing either a semantically consistent target object or an inconsistent target object. The scene was followed by two object labels of equivalent consistency. For example, a kitchen scene (or, in the inconsistent condition, a farm scene) contained a mixer target object followed by the labels "mixer" and "coffee maker". Because the two alternatives were both either consistent or inconsistent with the scene, educated guessing on the basis of scene knowledge could not influence performance. With this control over guessing, no advantage for the detection of consistent objects was observed, supporting the functional isolation hypothesis. The Hollingworth and Henderson (1998) results indicate that we accurately see what is present in a scene and not necessarily what we expect to see. Given the opportunity to guess, however, biases generated by scene knowledge will influence report.

Recently, Davenport and Potter (2004; see also Davenport, 2007) revisited the issue of scene context effects. In their paradigm, participants viewed stimuli consisting of a background scene and a prominent foreground object, with the consistency between the two manipulated. After brief presentation of each scene, participants named the foreground object. Davenport and Potter observed more accurate naming of consistent versus inconsistent objects. However, these experiments represent something of a methodological step backward, because Davenport and Potter did not adequately control educated guessing. In this naming paradigm, when an object was not fully identified, participants could use their knowledge of the scene to bias the naming response toward consistent objects (see Palmer, 1975), as the target was more likely to be one of the relatively small set of objects consistent with the scene than one of the large set of objects inconsistent with the scene. Davenport and Potter did include a guessing correction that involved subtracting incorrect reports of consistent objects from correct reports, but simple subtraction is not sufficient when bias could be influencing report (Green & Swets, 1966). In general, any paradigm with an unbound set of alternatives (as in naming) is subject to selection biases that can be very difficult to eliminate. It was precisely for this reason that Reicher (1969) developed the 2-AFC method used by Hollingworth and Henderson (1998).

In summary, current evidence indicates that when educated guessing is adequately controlled, consistent objects are detected no more efficiently than are inconsistent objects. This does not imply, however, that there are no effects of scene knowledge on the perceptual processing of objects. Scene knowledge can guide attention to particular objects in a scene that are relevant to the current task, reviewed below. In addition, context influences the extent of perceptual and cognitive processing devoted to an object. For example, inconsistent objects, once identified, are fixated longer in a scene than are consistent objects (Henderson, Weeks, & Hollingworth, 1999).

Effects of scene memory on knowing where to look

One of the principal functions of VLTM for scenes is to store information about the locations of objects so that they can be found efficiently later (for additional discussion of the role of memory in search, see chapter 2 of The Visual World in Memory, section 4). We know where most of the objects in our own homes are located, and when we search for an object, we tend to look first in those locations where memory tells us it is likely to be found. In addition, even without any knowledge of a particular environment (e.g., in the kitchen of a new acquaintance), we still know roughly where different types of objects are likely to be located.

Hollingworth (in press) examined two forms of scene memory that are likely to control the allocation of attention in a scene during visual search: memory for the remembered location of a specific object (which could guide attention directly to the target location), and memory for the spatial layout of a scene (which could guide attention to the locations where the target object was likely to be found). On each trial, participants viewed a preview display of a complex real-world scene for 10 s. Then a single object was presented in isolation at the center of the screen. This was the search target. Finally, the scene was displayed again, and participants found the search target as quickly as possible. To ensure that participants had to find the target object in each scene, the left–right orientation of the target was randomly varied in the search scene, and participants had to report whether its orientation matched the orientation of the search target displayed before the search. There were three principal conditions. In the *preview-with-target* condition, the target object was present in the preview scene. In the *preview-without-target* condition, the target was not present in the preview scene. In the *no-preview* condition, no preview scene was displayed before the search. This final condition served as a baseline measure of search efficiency, when no memory for the scene was available to aid search.

First of all, memory for the general layout of the scene significantly facilitated search. Search efficiency, as measured both by RT and the elapsed time to the first fixation on the target, was significantly faster in the preview-without-target condition than in the no-preview condition. Memory for the specific location of the target further facilitated search, with faster search in the preview-with-target condition than in the preview-without-target condition. In the preview-with-target condition, participants fixated the target almost immediately after the onset of the search scene, with the very first saccade in the scene typically directed to the target. Thus, both forms of memory (general layout and specific object locations) efficiently guide search within complex scenes (see also Castelhano & Henderson, 2007).

Similar facilitation is observed when participants conduct repeated search through a natural scene. Brockmole and Henderson (2006) had participants search for letters embedded within photographs of real-world scenes. Half of the scene items were repeated. Search through repeated scenes became highly efficient, and a single repetition was sufficient to influence search times. As in Hollingworth (in press), participants quickly learned the location of targets in each repeated scene and could use that memory to guide attention during search. Subsequent experiments demonstrated that memory for the locations of objects is coded relative to a global contextual representation of the scene (Brockmole, Castelhano, & Henderson, 2006).

Finally, memory for categories of scenes also influences search in the absence of any prior exposure to a particular scene. Torralba, Oliva, Castelhano, and Henderson (2006) had participants view scenes with the task of counting the number of people, paintings, or mugs within a scene. Almost immediately upon the onset of search, gaze was directed to locations within the scene where the target object would have been likely to occur (e.g., the walls of a room when participants were searching for paintings).

These results using search in real-world scenes contrast with traditional search experiments using random arrays of simple stimuli. Although memory does influence search over random arrays (Chun & Jiang, 1998), such learning emerges only after multiple repetitions of a particular array, target location is coded relative to local array elements, and learning is typically implicit (for details, see chapter 2 of The Visual World in Memory, section 4.2). In contrast, a single exposure to a real-world scene can reduce search time by as much as 35% (Hollingworth, 2009), memory for scene types guides search even within scenes that have never been viewed before (Torralba et al., 2006), target position is coded relative to global scene elements (Brockmole et al., 2006), and the learning of object locations in scenes is explicitly available rather than implicit (Brockmole & Henderson, 2006). As the literature on visual search moves further toward understanding how search occurs under real-world conditions, researchers will need to use more complex real-world scene stimuli for which visual search mechanisms (and visual memory) are optimized.

Conclusions

Scene perception is a dynamic process in which attention and the eyes are deployed serially to objects of interest. Visual memory is used to retain information from previously attended objects in support of basic perceptual operations, such as mapping objects across frequent perceptual disruptions and ensuring that the eyes are efficiently directed to goal-relevant objects. In addition, object information accumulates in VLTM as attention is directed from object to object in a scene. Over the course of viewing, participants are able to construct an internal visual representation of the scene that is composed of higher-level visual object representations bound to locations within a spatial representation of the scene. These scene representations are then stored robustly over long periods of time and with minimal interference. Upon re-examination of a scene, long-term scene representations are retrieved efficiently and can be used to guide attention and the eyes to task-relevant regions of the scene.

Note

* This chapter originally appeared in the edited volume, *The Visual World in Memory*.

References

Alba, J., & Hasher, L. (1983). Is memory schematic? *Psychological Bulletin, 93,* 203–231.
Allen, R. J., Baddeley, A. D., & Hitch, G. J. (2006). Is the binding of visual features in working memory resource-demanding? *Journal of Experimental Psychology: General, 135,* 298–313.
Alvarez, G. A., & Cavanagh, P. (2004). The capacity of visual short-term memory is set both by visual information load and by number of objects. *Psychological Science, 15,* 106–111.
Averbach, E., & Coriell, A. S. (1961). Short-term memory in vision. *The Bell System Technical Journal, 40,* 309–328.
Ballard, D. H., Hayhoe, M. M., & Pelz, J. B. (1995). Memory representations in natural tasks. *Journal of Cognitive Neuroscience, 7,* 66–80.

Ballard, D. H., Hayhoe, M. M., Pook, P. K., & Rao, R. P. (1997). Deictic codes for the embodiment of cognition. *Behavioral and Brain Sciences, 20,* 723–767.

Bartlett, F. C. (1932). *Remembering: An experimental and social study.* Cambridge: Cambridge University Press.

Becker, M. W., & Pashler, H. (2002). Volatile visual representations: Failing to detect changes in recently processed information. *Psychonomic Bulletin and Review, 9,* 744–750.

Biederman, I., Mezzanotte, R. J., & Rabinowitz, J. C. (1982). Scene perception: Detecting and judging objects undergoing relational violations. *Cognitive Psychology, 14,* 143–177.

Brewer, W. F., & Treyens, J. C. (1981). Role of schemata in memory for places. *Cognitive Psychology, 13,* 207–230.

Brockmole, J. R., Castelhano, M. S., & Henderson, J. M. (2006). Contextual cueing in naturalistic scenes: Global and local contexts. *Journal of Experimental Psychology: Learning, Memory, and Cognition, 32,* 699–706.

Brockmole, J. R., & Henderson, J. M. (2006). Using real-world scenes as contextual cues for search. *Visual Cognition, 13,* 99–108.

Brockmole, J. R., Irwin, D. E., & Wang, R. F. (2002). Temporal integration of visual images and visual percepts. *Journal of Experimental Psychology: Human Perception and Performance, 28,* 315–334.

Burgess, N., Maguire, E. A., & O'Keefe, J. (2002). The human hippocampus and spatial and episodic memory. *Neuron, 35,* 625–641.

Castelhano, M. S., & Henderson, J. M. (2007). Initial scene representations facilitate eye movement guidance in visual search. *Journal of Experimental Psychology: Human Perception and Performance, 33,* 753–763.

Chelazzi, L., Miller, E. K., Duncan, J., & Desimone, R. (1993). A neural basis for visual-search in inferior temporal cortex. *Nature, 363,* 345–347.

Chun, M. M. (2003). Scene perception and memory. *Psychology of Learning and Motivation, 42,* 79–108.

Chun, M. M., & Jiang, Y. (1998). Contextual cueing: Implicit learning and memory of visual context guides spatial attention. *Cognitive Psychology, 36,* 28–71.

Chun, M. M., & Potter, M. C. (1995). A two-stage model for multiple target detection in rapid serial visual presentation. *Journal of Experimental Psychology: Human Perception and Performance, 21,* 109–127.

Coltheart, M. (1980). The persistences of vision. *Philosophical Transactions of the Royal Society of London, Series B, 290,* 269–294.

Cowan, N. (1995). *Attention and memory: An integrated framework.* New York: Oxford University Press.

Currie, C., McConkie, G., Carlson-Radvansky, L. A., & Irwin, D. E. (2000). The role of the saccade target object in the perception of a visually stable world. *Perception and Psychophysics, 62,* 673–683.

Davenport, J. L. (2007). Consistency effects between objects in scenes. *Memory and Cognition, 35,* 393–401.

Davenport, J. L., & Potter, M. C. (2004). Scene consistency in object and background perception. *Psychological Science, 15,* 559–564.

Davidson, M. L., Fox, M. J., & Dick, A. O. (1973). Effect of eye movements on backward masking and perceived location. *Perception and Psychophysics, 14,* 110–116.

Desimone, R., & Duncan, J. (1995). Neural mechanisms of selective visual attention. *Annual Review of Neuroscience, 18,* 193–222.

Deubel, H., & Schneider, W. X. (1996). Saccade target selection and object recognition: Evidence for a common attentional mechanism. *Vision Research, 36,* 1827–1837.

Di Lollo, V. (1980). Temporal integration in visual memory. *Journal of Experimental Psychology: General, 109,* 75–97.

Duncan, J., & Humphreys, G. (1989). Visual search and stimulus similarity. *Psychological Review, 96,* 433–458.

Eng, H.Y., Chen, D.Y., & Jiang,Y. H. (2005).Visual working memory for simple and complex visual stimuli. *Psychonomic Bulletin and Review, 12,* 1127–1133.

Friedman, A. (1979). Framing pictures: The role of knowledge in automatized encoding and memory for gist. *Journal of Experimental Psychology: General, 108,* 316–355.

Gajewski, D. A., & Brockmole, J. R. (2006). Feature bindings endure without attention: Evidence from an explicit recall task. *Psychonomic Bulletin and Review, 13,* 581–587.

Green, D. M., & Swets, J. A. (1966). *Signal detection theory and psychophysics.* New York: Wiley.

Grimes, J. (1996). On the failure to detect changes in scenes across saccades. In K. Akins (Ed.), *Perception: Vancouver studies in cognitive science,* vol. 5 (pp. 89–110). Oxford: Oxford University Press.

Hayhoe, M. M. (2000).Vision using routines: A functional account of vision. *Visual Cognition, 7,* 43–64.

Hayhoe, M. M., Bensinger, D. G., & Ballard, D. H. (1998).Task constraints in visual working memory. *Vision Research, 38,* 125–137.

Henderson, J. M., & Anes, M. D. (1994). Effects of object-file review and type priming on visual identification within and across eye fixations. *Journal of Experimental Psychology: Human Perception and Performance, 20,* 826–839.

Henderson, J. M., & Hollingworth, A. (1999a). High-level scene perception. *Annual Review of Psychology, 50,* 243–271.

Henderson, J. M., & Hollingworth, A. (1999b). The role of fixation position in detecting scene changes across saccades. *Psychological Science, 10,* 438–443.

Henderson, J. M., & Hollingworth, A. (2003a). Eye movements and visual memory: Detecting changes to saccade targets in scenes. *Perception and Psychophysics, 65,* 58–71.

Henderson, J. M., & Hollingworth, A. (2003b). Global transsaccadic change blindness during scene perception. *Psychological Science, 14,* 493–497.

Henderson, J. M., Pollatsek, A., & Rayner, K. (1987). Effects of foveal priming and extrafoveal preview on object identification. *Journal of Experimental Psychology: Human Perception and Performance, 13,* 449–463.

Henderson, J. M., Weeks, P. A., & Hollingworth, A. (1999). The effects of semantic consistency on eye movements during complex scene viewing. *Journal of Experimental Psychology: Human Perception and Performance, 25,* 210–228.

Hoffman, J. E., & Subramaniam, B. (1995). The role of visual attention in saccadic eye movements. *Perception and Psychophysics, 57,* 787–795.

Hollingworth, A. (2003). Failures of retrieval and comparison constrain change detection in natural scenes. *Journal of Experimental Psychology: Human Perception and Performance, 29,* 388–403.

Hollingworth, A. (2004). Constructing visual representations of natural scenes: The roles of short- and long-term visual memory. *Journal of Experimental Psychology: Human Perception and Performance, 30,* 519–537.

Hollingworth, A. (2005). The relationship between online visual representation of a scene and long-term scene memory. *Journal of Experimental Psychology: Learning, Memory, and Cognition, 31,* 396–411.

Hollingworth, A. (2006). Scene and position specificity in visual memory for objects. *Journal of Experimental Psychology: Learning, Memory, and Cognition, 32,* 58–69.

Hollingworth, A. (2007). Object-position binding in visual memory for natural scenes and object arrays. *Journal of Experimental Psychology: Human Perception and Performance, 33,* 31–47.

Hollingworth, A. (2008). Visual memory for natural scenes. In S. J. Luck & A. Hollingworth (Eds.), *Visual memory* (pp. 123–162). New York: Oxford University Press.

Hollingworth, A. (2009). Two forms of scene memory guide visual search: Memory for scene context and memory for the binding of target object to scene location. *Visual Cognition, 17*(1–2), 273–291.

Hollingworth, A., & Henderson, J. M. (1998). Does consistent scene context facilitate object perception? *Journal of Experimental Psychology: General, 127,* 398–415.

Hollingworth, A., & Henderson, J. M. (2000). Semantic informativeness mediates the detection of changes in natural scenes. *Visual Cognition, 7,* 213–235.

Hollingworth, A., & Henderson, J. M. (2002). Accurate visual memory for previously attended objects in natural scenes. *Journal of Experimental Psychology: Human Perception and Performance, 28,* 113–136.

Hollingworth, A., & Henderson, J. M. (2003). Testing a conceptual locus for the inconsistent object change detection advantage in real-world scenes. *Memory and Cognition, 31,* 930–940.

Hollingworth, A., Hyun, J. S., & Zhang, W. (2005). The role of visual short-term memory in empty cell localization. *Perception and Psychophysics, 67,* 1332–1343.

Hollingworth, A., Richard, A. M., & Luck, S. J. (2008). Understanding the function of visual short-term memory: Transsaccadic memory, object correspondence, and gaze correction. *Journal of Experimental Psychology: General, 137,* 163–181.

Hollingworth, A., Williams, C. C., & Henderson, J. M. (2001). To see and remember: Visually specific information is retained in memory from previously attended objects in natural scenes. *Psychonomic Bulletin and Review, 8,* 761–768.

Intraub, H. (1997). The representation of visual scenes. *Trends in Cognitive Sciences, 1,* 217–222.

Irwin, D. E. (1991). Information integration across saccadic eye movements. *Cognitive Psychology, 23,* 420–456.

Irwin, D. E. (1992). Memory for position and identity across eye movements. *Journal of Experimental Psychology: Learning, Memory, and Cognition, 18,* 307–317.

Irwin, D. E., & Andrews, R. (1996). Integration and accumulation of information across saccadic eye movements. In T. Inui & J. L. McClelland (Eds.), *Attention and performance XVI: Information integration in perception and communication* (pp. 125–155). Cambridge, MA: MIT Press.

Irwin, D. E., Yantis, S., & Jonides, J. (1983). Evidence against visual integration across saccadic eye movements. *Perception and Psychophysics, 34,* 35–46.

Irwin, D. E., & Yeomans, J. M. (1986). Sensory registration and informational persistence. *Journal of Experimental Psychology: Human Perception and Performance, 12,* 343–360.

Irwin, D. E., & Zelinsky, G. J. (2002). Eye movements and scene perception: Memory for things observed. *Perception and Psychophysics, 64,* 882–895.

Jiang, Y., Kumar, A., & Vickery, T. J. (2005). Integrating sequential arrays in visual short-term memory. *Experimental Psychology, 52,* 39–46.

Jiang, Y., Olson, I. R., & Chun, M. M. (2000). Organization of visual short-term memory. *Journal of Experimental Psychology: Learning, Memory, and Cognition, 26,* 683–702.

Johnson, J. S., Hollingworth, A., & Luck, S. J. (2008). The role of attention in the maintenance of feature bindings in visual short-term memory. *Journal of Experimental Psychology: Human Perception and Performance, 34,* 41–55.

Jonides, J., Irwin, D. E., & Yantis, S. (1982). Integrating visual information from successive fixations. *Science, 215,* 192–194.

Kahneman, D., Treisman, A., & Gibbs, B. J. (1992). The reviewing of object files: Object-specific integration of information. *Cognitive Psychology, 24,* 175–219.

Land, M. F., Mennie, N., & Rusted, J. (1999). Eye movements and the roles of vision in activities of daily living: Making a cup of tea. *Perception, 28,* 1311–1328.

Luck, S. J. (2008). Visual short-term memory. In S. J. Luck & A. Hollingworth (Eds.), *Visual Memory* (pp. 43–86). New York: Oxford University Press.

Luck, S. J., & Vogel, E. K. (1997). The capacity of visual working memory for features and conjunctions. *Nature, 390,* 279–281.

Mandler, J. M., & Parker, R. E. (1976). Memory for descriptive and spatial information in complex pictures. *Journal of Experimental Psychology: Human Learning and Memory, 2,* 38–48.

Mandler, J. M., & Ritchey, G. H. (1977). Long-term memory for pictures. *Journal of Experimental Psychology: Human Learning and Memory, 3,* 386–396.

Matin, E. (1974). Saccadic suppression: A review and an analysis. *Psychological Bulletin, 81,* 899–917.

McConkie, G. W., & Rayner, K. (1975). The span of the effective stimulus during a fixation in reading. *Perception and Psychophysics,* 578–586.

Moore, C. M., & Egeth, H. (1997). Perception without attention: Evidence of grouping under conditions of inattention. *Journal of Experimental Psychology: Human Perception and Performance, 23,* 339–352.

Nickerson, R. S. (1965). Short-term memory for complex meaningful visual configurations: A demonstration of capacity. *Canadian Journal of Psychology, 19,* 155–160.

Nickerson, R. S. (1968). A note on long-term recognition memory for pictorial material. *Psychonomic Science, 11,* 58.

O'Keefe, J., & Nadel, L. (1978). *The hippocampus as a cognitive map.* Oxford: Clarendon Press.

Oliva, A., & Torralba, A. (2006). Building the gist of a scene: The role of global image features in recognition. *Progress in Brain Research, 155,* 23–36.

Olivers, C. N. L., Meijer, F., & Theeuwes, J. (2006). Feature-based memory-driven attentional capture: Visual working memory content affects visual attention. *Journal of Experimental Psychology: Human Perception and Performance, 32,* 1243–1265.

O'Regan, J. K. (1992). Solving the "real" mysteries of visual perception: The world as an outside memory. *Canadian Journal of Psychology, 46,* 461–488.

O'Regan, J. K., & Lévy-Schoen, A. (1983). Integrating visual information from successive fixations: Does trans-saccadic fusion exist? *Vision Research, 23,* 765–768.

O'Regan, J. K., & Noë, A. (2001). A sensorimotor account of vision and visual consciousness. *Behavioral and Brain Sciences, 24,* 939–1011.

Palmer, S. E. (1975). The effects of contextual scenes on the identification of objects. *Memory and Cognition, 3,* 519–526.

Pashler, H. (1988). Familiarity and the detection of change in visual displays. *Perception and Psychophysics, 44,* 369–378.

Pedzek, K., Whetstone, T., Reynolds, K., Askari, N., & Dougherty, T. (1989). Memory for real-world scenes: The role of consistency with schema expectations. *Journal of Experimental Psychology: Learning, Memory, and Cognition, 15,* 587–595.

Phillips, W. A. (1974). On the distinction between sensory storage and short-term visual memory. *Perception and Psychophysics, 16,* 283–290.

Phillips, W. A., & Christie, D. F. M. (1977). Components of visual memory. *Quarterly Journal of Experimental Psychology, 29,* 117–133.

Pollatsek, A., Rayner, K., & Collins, W. E. (1984). Integrating pictorial information across eye movements. *Journal of Experimental Psychology: General, 113*, 426–442.

Potter, M. C., & Levy, E. I. (1969). Recognition memory for a rapid sequence of pictures. *Journal of Experimental Psychology, 81*, 10–15.

Potter, M. C., Staub, A., & O'Connor, D. H. (2004). Pictorial and conceptual representation of glimpsed pictures. *Journal of Experimental Psychology: Human Perception and Performance, 30*, 478–489.

Rayner, K., & Pollatsek, A. (1983). Is visual information integrated across saccades? *Perception and Psychophysics, 34*, 39–48.

Reicher, G. M. (1969). Perceptual recognition as a function of meaningfulness of stimulus material. *Journal of Experimental Psychology, 81*, 275–280.

Rensink, R. A. (2000). The dynamic representation of scenes. *Visual Cognition, 7*, 17–42.

Rensink, R. A. (2002). Change detection. *Annual Review of Psychology, 53*, 245–277.

Rensink, R. A., O'Regan, J. K., & Clark, J. J. (1997). To see or not to see: The need for attention to perceive changes in scenes. *Psychological Science, 8*, 368–373.

Ryan, J. D., Althoff, R. R., Whitlow, S., & Cohen, N. J. (2000). Amnesia is a deficit in relational memory. *Psychological Science, 8*, 368–373.

Schmidt, B. K., Vogel, E. K., Woodman, G. F., & Luck, S. J. (2002). Voluntary and automatic attentional control of visual working memory. *Perception and Psychophysics, 64*, 754–763.

Scholl, B. J. (2000). Attenuated change blindness for exogenously attended items in a flicker paradigm. *Visual Cognition, 7*, 377–396.

Shepard, R. N. (1967). Recognition memory for words, sentences, and pictures. *Journal of Verbal Learning and Verbal Behavior, 6*, 156–163.

Simons, D. J. (1996). In sight, out of mind: When object representations fail. *Psychological Science, 7*, 301–305.

Simons, D. J., Chabris, C. F., Schnur, T., & Levin, D. T. (2002). Evidence for preserved representations in change blindness. *Consciousness and Cognition, 11*, 78–97.

Simons, D. J., & Levin, D. T. (1997). Change blindness. *Trends in Cognitive Sciences, 1*, 261–267.

Simons, D. J., & Levin, D. T. (1998). Failure to detect changes to people during a real-world interaction. *Psychonomic Bulletin and Review, 5*, 644–649.

Soto, D., Heinke, D., Humphreys, G. W., & Blanco, M. J. (2005). Early, involuntary top-down guidance of attention from working memory. *Journal of Experimental Psychology: Human Perception and Performance, 31*, 248–261.

Sperling, G. (1960). The information available in brief visual presentations. *Psychological Monographs, 74*(11, Whole no. 498).

Standing, L. (1973). Learning 10,000 pictures. *Quarterly Journal of Experimental Psychology, 25*, 207–222.

Standing, L., Conezio, J., & Haber, R. N. (1970). Perception and memory for pictures: Single-trial learning of 2500 visual stimuli. *Psychonomic Science, 19*, 73–74.

Tanaka, J. W., & Farah, M. J. (1993). Parts and wholes in face recognition. *Quarterly Journal of Experimental Psychology, 46A*, 225–245.

Tatler, B. W., Gilchrist, I. D., & Land, M. F. (2005). Visual memory for objects in natural scenes: From fixations to object files. *Quarterly Journal of Experimental Psychology, 58A*, 931–960.

Tatler, B. W., Gilchrist, I. D., & Rusted, J. (2003). The time course of abstract visual representation. *Perception, 32*, 579–592.

Thornton, I. M., & Fernandez-Duque, D. (2002). Converging evidence for the detection of change without awareness. In D. P. Munoz, W. Heide, R. Radach, & J. Hyönä (Eds.), *The brain's eyes: Neurobiological and clinical aspects of occulomotor research* (pp. 99–118). Amsterdam: Elsevier.

Thorpe, S., Fize, D., & Marlot, C. (1996). Speed of processing in the human visual system. *Nature, 381,* 520–522.

Torralba, A., Oliva, A., Castelhano, M. S., & Henderson, J. M. (2006). Contextual guidance of eye movements and attention in real-world scenes: The role of global features in object search. *Psychological Review, 113,* 766–786.

Treisman, A. (1988). Features and objects: The fourteenth Bartlett memorial lecture. *Quarterly Journal of Experimental Psychology, 40A,* 201–237.

Varakin, D. A., Levin, D. T., & Collins, K. M. (2007). Both comparison and representation failures cause real-world change blindness. *Perception, 36,* 737–749.

Vogel, E. K., & Luck, S. J. (2002). Delayed working memory consolidation during the attentional blink. *Psychonomic Bulletin and Review, 9,* 739–743.

Wheeler, D. D. (1970). Process in word recognition. *Cognitive Psychology, 1,* 59–85.

Wheeler, M. E., & Treisman, A. M. (2002). Binding in short-term visual memory. *Journal of Experimental Psychology: General, 131,* 48–64.

Wolfe, J. M. (1999). Inattentional amnesia. In V. Coltheart (Ed.), *Fleeting memories* (pp. 71–94). Cambridge, MA: MIT Press.

Wolfe, J. M., Reinecke, A., & Brawn, P. (2006). Why don't we see changes? The role of attentional bottlenecks and limited visual memory. *Visual Cognition, 14,* 749–780.

Woodman, G. F., Luck, S. J., & Schall, J. D. (2007). The role of working memory representations in the control of attention. *Cerebral Cortex, 17,* 118–124.

Woodman, G. F., Vogel, E. K., & Luck, S. J. (2001). Visual search remains efficient when visual working memory is full. *Psychological Science, 12,* 219–224.

Zelinsky, G. J., & Loschky, L. C. (2005). Eye movements serialize memory for objects in scenes. *Perception and Psychophysics, 67,* 676–690.

Memory adaptations: Forgetting the past, remembering the future

PART II

Memory adaptation:
forgetting the past,
remembering the future

5

THE ROLE OF RETROACTIVE INTERFERENCE AND CONSOLIDATION IN EVERYDAY FORGETTING*

John T. Wixted

As the previous chapters in this book make abundantly clear, the subject of forgetting is as multifaceted as it is enigmatic. Why, exactly, do we forget? As noted by Levy, Kuhl, and Wagner (in *Forgetting*, chapter 7) we often use the term "forget" to refer to the inability to retrieve information that we failed to encode in the first place. Thus, for example, I might say that I forgot where I placed my keys, but the truth may be that I set them down without ever taking note of the fact that I put them on the kitchen counter. Although such absent-mindedness is an interesting issue in its own right, when experimental psychologists and cognitive neuroscientists study forgetting, they usually study the loss of information that was encoded, as shown by the fact that the information was once retrievable from long-term memory. What is it about the passage of time that renders once retrievable information ever more difficult to remember? That is the question I consider in this chapter.

The time course of forgetting was first experimentally addressed by Ebbinghaus (1885), who used himself as a subject and memorized lists of nonsense syllables until they could be perfectly recited. Later, after varying delays of up to 31 days, he relearned those same lists and measured how much less time was needed to learn them again relative to the time required to learn them in the first place. If ten minutes were needed to learn the lists initially, but only four minutes were needed to learn them again after a delay of six hours, then his memory was such that 60% savings had been achieved. As the retention interval increased, savings decreased, which is to say that forgetting occurred with the passage of time. When his famous savings function was plotted out over 31 days, what we now know as the prototypical forgetting function was revealed (Figure 5.1).

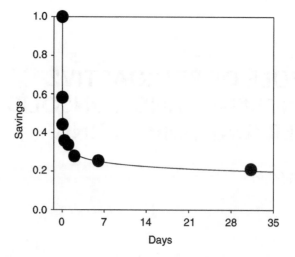

FIGURE 5.1 The Ebbinghaus (1885) savings data. The solid curve represents the least squares fit of the three-parameter Wickelgren power law, $m = \lambda(1 + \beta t)^{-\psi}$, where m is memory strength, and t is time (i.e., the retention interval). The equation has three parameters: λ is the state of long-term memory at $t = 0$ (i.e., the degree of learning), ψ is the rate of forgetting, and β is a scaling parameter

The form of forgetting

The mathematical form of the Ebbinghaus savings function is something close to a power law, which, in general terms, is to say that it declines rapidly at first but declines at a slower rate as time goes on (Wixted & Ebbesen, 1991). Although not widely appreciated, that property of forgetting is consistent with Jost's (1897) law of forgetting (Wixted, 2004a). Jost's second law states that if two memories have the same strength but different ages (i.e., if one memory was formed more recently than the other), the younger trace will lose strength more rapidly than the older one. In light of Jost's law, Herbert Simon (1966) suggested that forgetting may not be exponential in form. By definition, the exponential requires a constant rate of forgetting over time, which would mean that the rate of forgetting is independent of the age of the trace. In practice, they are not independent because, as the trace ages, the rate of forgetting slows.

Armed with nothing but a slide rule and the forgetting data he had collected on himself, Ebbinghaus (1885) argued that forgetting was a three-parameter loga-rithmic function of time. Much later, Wickelgren (1974) instead suggested a three-parameter power function of time to characterize the course of forgetting, but the behavior of these two mathematical functions is nearly identical, and it is hard to imagine that the slight differences between them are important. Figure 5.1 shows a fit of the three-parameter Wickelgren power function to the Ebbinghaus savings data (Wixted & Carpenter, 2007). This figure is, essentially, a depiction of the basic result that needs to be explained by any theory of forgetting. Ebbinghaus learned his lists to perfection, but as time passed the information that was once retriev-able from long-term memory became less retrievable (at an ever-decelerating rate). Why? Although natural decay may play some role (e.g., Bailey & Chen 1989), interference theory offers the most interesting and nuanced account of forgetting.

A variety of interference theories

Interference as cue-overload

In the field of psychology, the story of interference has almost always focused on the retrieval cue, which makes sense in light of the critical role played by retrieval cues in episodic memory. One of Endel Tulving's great insights was that episodic memory is cue dependent (e.g., Tulving & Pearlstone, 1966). Although countless episodic memories are encoded in one's brain, they are typically all in a quiescent state, and they simply cannot be called to mind at will. Instead, it is the retrieval cue (and only the retrieval cue) that activates an episodic memory (one at a time). If the right retrieval cue does not come along, the corresponding memory trace might as well not even be there as it will never be retrieved again.

What is the "right" retrieval cue? Tulving's principle of *encoding specificity* (Tulving & Thomson, 1973) offers a compelling answer, and it states that a retrieval cue will be effective in activating an episodic memory trace only to the extent that the cue was encoded along with the to-be-remembered material. Thus, for example, if I study the word pair "glue–chair," then "glue" will later be an effective retrieval cue for the occurrence of "chair" on the study list. By contrast, a cue like "table," though highly associated with the word "chair," will not be effective in retrieving that same memory. It may prompt retrieval of the word "chair" from semantic memory, but it will not call to mind the episode of having studied that word on a list just minutes ago. In light of the undeniably cue-dependent nature of epi-sodic memory, it makes sense that powerful interference effects can be achieved by influencing properties of the retrieval cue. In fact, traditional interference theory, which has dominated thinking in psychology from the 1930s on, basically holds that the more items associated with a retrieval cue, the less effective that cue will be in retrieving a particular memory (Watkins & Watkins, 1975). The cue-overload principle applies to both retroactive interference (interference caused by subsequent learning) and proactive interference (interference caused by prior learning). If, for example, in addition to learning "glue–chair" I also learn "glue–model," then the ability of "glue" to retrieve either one of the two memories it subserves ("chair" and "model") will be diminished. This holds true whether "glue–model" was learned before "glue–chair" (a case of proactive interference) or after (a case of retroactive interference). A retrieval cue that has been encoded along with many memories is, for some reason, less effective than a retrieval cue that has been encoded with only one memory. This principle accounts for why it can be difficult to remember a prior episode when many similar episodes have also been experienced (because similar information tends to be subserved by the same retrieval cue). Although cue-overload interference effects can be powerful in the laboratory and in real life (e.g., when trying to remember the names of the many students in your class), there is some question as to whether it offers a complete account—or even the central account—of everyday forgetting. In the 1960s, one of the leading interference theorists of the day, Benton Underwood, set out to demonstrate that cue-overload interference—in particular, proactive interference—not only produces powerful effects in the laboratory but also accounts for forgetting in the real world. Proactive interference was, at the time, the dominant account of forgetting, even though it is more intuitive to assume that forgetting is caused by retroactive interference (i.e., interference caused by subsequent learning). The dominance of the less intuitive proactive interference account was due in no small part to Underwood's (1957) classic paper showing that, for lists learned to one perfect recitation, the amount of forgetting over a 24-hour period (which varied from 20% to 80% across studies) was almost fully accounted for by the number of previous similar lists which the subjects in each experiment had learned. This was an ingenious observation, and it was understandably regarded as a major insight into the understanding of why we forget. However, Underwood's later efforts to show that proactive interference is not only a powerful force in the experimental laboratory but is also a powerful force in everyday forgetting were as surprising to him as they were disappointing. His every attempt to show that proactive interference plays a significant role in forgetting outside of the laboratory instead suggested otherwise (e.g., Underwood & Ekstrand, 1966, 1967; Underwood & Postman, 1960). As a result, the major advocate of the proactive interference account of forgetting eventually came to question its significance (Underwood, 1983).

What about retroactive interference? Is it possible that the main cause of forgetting is the overloading of a retrieval cue in the days, weeks and months after learning occurs? The suggestion that retroactive interference of some kind plays an important role came early in the last century when Jenkins and Dallenbach (1924) showed that a period of sleep after learning results in less forgetting than a similar period of wakefulness. When sleeping, one is presumably not overloading retrieval cues that might be associated with items learned on a list prior to sleep, but the same may not be true of the waking state.

Underwood (1957) himself did not find it plausible that the subsequent learning of similar material following the learning of a target list in the laboratory could possibly account for the degree of forgetting that is observed over a period as short as 24 hours (about 20% of the list when no prior similar lists are learned). Thus, he attributed that amount of forgetting to the prior real-life learning that the subject brought to the laboratory. That is, although it seemed unlikely that subjects would, in the course of 24 hours of normal living, overload retrieval cues that happen to have been used on a list in the laboratory, it was very likely that similar cues had been encountered in the years prior to arriving in the laboratory. But this idea introduced a new puzzle. If all forgetting outside of the laboratory is due to proactive interference (even when no previous lists were learned in the laboratory), why would sleep after learning be helpful? Underwood (1957) speculated that, for some reason, the recovery of previously learned information (the presumed mechanism of proactive interference) was suspended during sleep. However, this idea was challenged when Underwood's student, Bruce Ekstrand, had subjects learn both an interfering list and a target list just prior to a night of sleep. Compared to a control group, memory for both lists was enhanced (Ekstrand, 1967). Thus, the presumed mechanism of PI (recovery of previously learned information) was enhanced, not retarded, by sleep. Even so, memory for the target list was enhanced as well.

Interference as trace degradation

By the early 1970s, interference theory had largely run its course and seemed to be making little headway (Tulving & Madigan, 1970). Another one of Underwood's students, Geoffrey Keppel, argued that similarity-based interference might not be the cause of most everyday forgetting and that non-specific retroactive interference may be the major cause instead (Keppel, 1968). Somehow, it seemed that even the learning of unrelated material (which would presumably not overload a relevant retrieval cue) causes retroactive interference.

The distinction between cue-overload retroactive interference and nonspecific retroactive interference is, from my point of view, critical. This distinction has been largely ignored by the field of experimental psychology (which has focused almost exclusively on similarity-based, cue-overload interference), and it has sometimes been obscured by researchers working in related fields. Consider, for example, learning a to-be-remembered list of ten A–B paired associates and then, an hour later, learning an interfering list of ten A–C paired associates (which have the same cue words as the A–B list but different response words). According to the cue-overload idea, the only retroactive interference of any consequence is the interference caused by the learning of that A–C list an hour after the A–B list was learned. Moreover, the mechanism of interference involves the overloading of the retrieval cues (i.e., the A words), which renders them less effective at the time of retrieval. By contrast, the nonspecific retroactive interference idea, as further elaborated in my prior work (Wixted, 2004b), holds that interference is also caused by the encoding of new memories (even unrelated ones) during the course of that hour. The fact that new memories would be formed during that hour is clear from the fact that the subjects in any such experiment would not be amnesic for events that took place between the learning of the A–B list and the learning of the A–C list an hour later. Instead, their memories of that time would be clear, which would mean that memories were formed, and the formation of those additional memories may also serve as an interfering force. Moreover, the mechanism of interference caused by the subsequent encoding of unrelated memories does not involve cue overload but may instead involve *trace degradation*. That is, newly encoded memories have a damaging effect on previously encoded memories. Indeed, this kind of interference—by virtue of being constantly applied during waking hours—may be a greater contributor to everyday forgetting than cue-overload interference.

A role for consolidation

In 1900, the German experimental psychologist Georg Elias Müller published a monograph with his student Alfons Pilzecker in which a new theory of forgetting was proposed, one that included a role for consolidation. In its essentials, Müller's theory of forgetting is the theory I readvocated in Wixted (2004b) and will develop in more detail in the pages that follow. Müller and Pilzecker (1900) introduced numerous experimental innovations in the study of memory and forgetting, as described in some detail by Lechner, Squire, and Byrne (1999). Their basic method involved asking subjects to memorize a list of paired-associate nonsense syllables. To investigate why forgetting occurred, Müller and Pilzecker (1900) also presented subjects with a second, interfering list of pairs to memorize before memory for the first was tested. The cues for the two lists were different, so in today's notation this would be an A–B, C–D design. They found that the interpolated list reduced memory for the target list compared to a control group that was not exposed to an interpolated list. In light of that result, they introduced the concept of retroactive inhibition. Critically, they found the point of interpolation of the interfering list within the retention interval mattered such that an interfering list presented soon after learning had a more disruptive effect on retention than one presented later in the retention interval. This led them to propose that memories require time to consolidate and that retroactive interference is a force that works against the retention of newly formed memories.

Müller and Pilzecker (1900) advocated a trace degradation account—not a cue-overload account—of retroactive interference. According to this idea, newly memorized information degrades previously memorized but not-yet-consolidated information, and the interference occurs at the level of physiology. As such, it does not matter whether the interfering material is similar to the studied material. To test this, Müller and Pilzecker (1900) had subjects learn paired associates followed by interpolated lists of unrelated pictures. Still, a definite interfering effect was observed.

From the early 1930s until the present day, experimental psychologists largely rejected this way of thinking as the cue-overload view of interference came to dominate. This was partly due to the fact that the temporal gradient obtained by Müller and Pilzecker (1900) is not easy to replicate (Wixted, 2004a, 2004b), and one reason for that may be that awake humans never stop making memories. As such, in a typical experiment, interfering material naturally occurs throughout the retention interval (i.e., the subject makes new memories continuously), so it does not matter when the nominally interfering material arranged by the experimenter is presented. For example, following study of an A–B list, the presentation of an A–C list will impair memory for the original list compared to the presentation of a C–D interfering list due to cue overload, but it will not matter much if the A–C list occurs early or late in the retention interval (e.g., Wickelgren, 1974). This result might create the impression that interference does not have a temporal gradient, that consolidation is not relevant, and that cue overload (not trace degradation) is what matters most. However, in any such experiment, retroactive interference of the trace degradation variety would be equated in the two conditions because, in both conditions, memories would be formed continuously throughout the retention interval. Additional interference would be added by the experimenter using a cue-overload manipulation, but that effect would not be time dependent (at least not in the same way). As described later, a different story emerges when steps are taken to temporarily stop the process of memory formation to see what effect that has on previously formed memories in humans.

A multidisciplinary inquiry into retroactive interference and consolidation

The case in favor of a generalized (nonspecific) retroactive interference account of forgetting that includes a role for consolidation emerges most clearly when several separate literatures are considered simultaneously. These include work on: (a) the cellular processes associated with the formation of memories in the hippocampus; (b) the effect of sleep on episodic memory (beyond what Jenkins & Dallenbach, 1924 established long ago); (c) the effect of pharmacological agents (such as alcohol and benzodiazepines) on episodic memory. Based on a review of behavioral evidence, Brown and Lewandowsky (in *Forgetting*, chapter 4) present an argument against the idea that consolidation can help to explain forgetting. In that regard, they join a long and almost unbroken chain of distinguished experimental psychologists dating back to the 1930s. My own view has been heavily influenced by the cellular and molecular evidence reviewed next, which I construe as elucidating the biological mechanisms of the consolidation process that experimental psychologists have long been reluctant to embrace.

In many ways, the account I present parallels the case made by Dewar, Cowan, and Della Sala (in *Forgetting*, chapter 9). They offer evidence suggesting that in patients with amnestic mild cognitive impairment (aMCI), consolidation resources are limited, which makes the trace degrading effects of retroactive interference especially pronounced. The evidence I consider below suggests that, in a less pronounced way, the trace degrading effects of retroactive interference on partially consolidated memory traces also accounts for much of what unimpaired individuals forget in everyday life.

The cellular basis of memory formation in the hippocampus

The hippocampus is one of several structures in the medial temporal lobe (MTL) that is known to play a critical role in the formation of new memories (see also Valtorta and Benfenati, in *Forgetting*, chapter 6). The importance of these structures became clear when the famous patient HM received a bilateral medial temporal lobe resection in an effort to control his epileptic seizures (Scoville & Milner, 1957). Although successful in that regard, HM was also unexpectedly left with a profound case of anterograde amnesia (i.e., the inability to form new memories from that point on). Another outcome—one that may be relevant to the story of forgetting—was that HM also exhibited temporally graded retrograde amnesia (Scoville & Milner, 1957; Squire, 2009). That is, memories that were formed prior to surgery were also somewhat impaired, and the degree of impairment was greater for memories that had been formed just prior to surgery than for memories that were encoded well before. Indeed, HM's oldest memories were largely intact.

The temporal gradient of retrograde amnesia that is sometimes associated with head injury was noted long ago by Ribot (1881/1882), but he had no way of knowing what brain structures were centrally involved in this phenomenon. The experience of HM made it clear that the relevant structures reside in the MTL, and more recent studies in animals and humans have shown that the temporal gradient of retrograde amnesia is evident even when bilateral lesions are limited to the hippocampus (Squire, Clark, & Knowlton, 2001). These findings suggest a role for the consolidation of memories, but, as noted by Dewar et al. (in *Forgetting*, chapter 9), it is important to distinguish between two kinds of consolidation, namely, systems consolidation and synaptic consolidation (McGaugh, 2000).

Systems consolidation and forgetting

The fact that retrograde amnesia is temporally graded has long been taken to suggest that memories require time to consolidate (Zola-Morgan & Squire, 1990). That is, when a memory is initially formed, it is dependent on the hippocampus. As a result, hippocampal damage impairs those recently formed memories, and retrograde amnesia is observed. Eventually, however, through a little-understood process of *systems consolidation*, memories become independent of the hippocampus as they are consolidated elsewhere in the neocortex (McGaugh, 2000). At that point, hippocampal damage no longer has any effect on those memories. This process is thought to require days or weeks in rats, weeks or months in monkeys, and perhaps years in humans (Squire et al., 2001).

The mechanism that underlies systems consolidation is not known, but a leading candidate is neural replay. Specifically, cells that fire together in the rat hippocampus during the learning of a behavioral task tend to become coactive again during sleep and during periods of quiet wakefulness (Wilson & McNaughton, 1994). Analogously, Peigneux, Schmitz, and Urbain (in *Forgetting*, chapter 8; see also Peigneux et al., 2004) describe intriguing, one-of-a-kind neuroimaging evidence in humans showing that hippocampal areas that are activated during route learning in a virtual town are activated again during subsequent slow-wave sleep. Recently, Ji and Wilson (2007) reported that hippocampal replay during slow-wave sleep in rats was coordinated with firing patterns in the visual cortex (consistent with the idea that this process underlies the redistribution of memories) and that it occurred five to ten times faster than the firing sequences occurred during the waking state. Through repeated epochs of accelerated coactivation, this neural playback may be the mechanism that eventually creates an independent ensemble of interconnected areas that were active during the encoding experience (Hoffman & McNaughton, 2002).

Is it conceivable that memories also become less vulnerable to the trace-degrading forces of retroactive interference as they become less dependent on the hippocampus (not just less vulnerable to hippocampal damage)? That is, are the neural representations of memories that are consolidated elsewhere in the neocortex less likely to be degraded when new memories are formed in the hippocampus? Not much is known about that, but it seems reasonable to suppose that it is true. It also seems to follow from a theory proposed by McClelland, McNaughton, and O'Reilly (1995) according to which memories are initially encoded in hippocampal circuits and are slowly integrated with prior knowledge represented in the neocortex. Memories that are eventually distributed in the neocortex through a process that slowly interleaves them with pre-existing knowledge would presumably be less vulnerable to subsequent slow changes in neocortical synapses associated with new learning. Whether or not that is the case, as described next, it seems clear that memory traces do become less vulnerable to the damaging forces of new memory formation even during the period of time in which they are still largely dependent on the hippocampus because of a second kind of consolidation process that unfolds in that structure on a shorter time scale.

Synaptic consolidation and forgetting

A second kind of consolidation takes place over a matter of hours and days when a memory is formed in the hippocampus (McGaugh, 2000), and this form of consolidation seems particularly relevant to the physiological processes that Müller and Pilzecker (1900) had in mind. This kind of consolidation—*synaptic consolidation*—occurs at the level of neurons (Izquierdo, Schröder, Netto, & Medina, 2006). The leading model of the initial stages of memory formation at the level of neurons in the hippocampus is long-term potentiation (LTP; Martin, Grimwood, & Morris, 2000). LTP is a relatively long-lasting enhancement of synaptic efficacy that is induced by a *tetanus* (a brief burst of high-frequency electrical stimulation) delivered to presynaptic neurons in the hippocampus (Bliss & Collingridge, 1993). Before the tetanus, a single test pulse of electrical stimulation applied to the presynaptic neuron elicits a certain baseline response in the postsynaptic neuron, but after the tetanus that same test pulse elicits a greater response. The enhanced reactivity typically lasts hours or days (and sometimes weeks), so it presumably does not represent the way in which memories are permanently coded. Still, LTP is readily induced in hippocampal neurons, and it is the leading candidate for modeling the neural basis of initial memory formation (Whitlock, Heynen, Schuler, & Bear, 2006). In this model, the tetanus is analogous to the effect of a behavioral experience, and the enhanced efficacy of the synapse is analogous to the memory of that experience.

Although LTP looks like neural memory for an experience (albeit an artificial experience consisting of a train of electrical impulses), what reason is there to believe that a similar process plays a role in real memories? The induction of LTP in hippocampal neurons involves the opening of calcium channels in postsynaptic NMDA receptors (Bliss & Collingridge, 1993). When those receptors are blocked by an NMDA antagonist, high-frequency stimulation fails to induce LTP. Perhaps not coincidentally, NMDA antagonists have often been shown to impair the learning of hippocampus-dependent tasks in animals (e.g., Morris, 1989; Morris, Anderson, Lynch, & Baudry, 1986), as if an LTP-like process plays an important role in the formation of new episodic memories. A recent and rather remarkable study suggests that the encoding of actual memories (not just an artificial train of electrical pulses) also gives rise to LTP in the hippocampus (Whitlock et al., 2006).

An important consideration for understanding the time-related effects of retro-active interference is that LTP is thought to have at least two stages: early-stage LTP, which does not involve protein synthesis (and during which time LTP is vulnerable to interference), and late-stage LTP, which does involve protein synthesis associated with morphological changes in dendritic spines and synapses (and after which the LTP is less vulnerable to interference). Late-stage LTP, which occurs approximately four to five hours after the induction of LTP, can be prevented by protein synthesis inhibitors (Abel, Nguyen, Barad, Deuel, Kandel, & Bourtchouladze, 1997; Frey, Krug, Reymann, & Matthies, 1988). Perhaps not coincidentally, protein synthesis inhibitors prevent the consolidation of new learning on hippocampus-dependent tasks as well (Davis & Squire, 1984).

The fact that protein synthesis inhibitors do not block learning (even when administered before training), but do accelerate forgetting by preventing consolidation (Davis & Squire, 1984), may be related to the accelerated forgetting in temporal lobe epilepsy patients, as summarized by Butler, Muhlert, and Zeman (in *Forgetting*, chapter 10). Like experimental animals exposed to protein synthesis inhibitors, those patients can sometimes remember normally after short delays (e.g., 30 minutes) and then exhibit profound forgetting after a delay of 24 hours. Conceivably (indeed, seemingly), these patients lack the late-phase LTP mechanisms required to stabilize memory traces that are initially encoded in the hippocampus.

In any case, the important point for purposes of understanding how and why normal forgetting occurs is that LTP exhibits all of the characteristics envisioned by Müller and Pilzecker (1900). In their own work, Müller and Pilzecker (1900) used an original learning phase (L1) followed by an interfering learning phase (L2) followed by a memory test for the original list (T1). Holding the retention interval between L1 and T1 constant, they essentially showed that L1-L2—T1 yields greater interference than L1—L2-T (where the dashes represent units of time). In experimental animals, memories formed in the hippocampus and LTP induced in the hippocampus both exhibit a similar temporal gradient with respect to retroactive interference (Izquierdo et al., 1999; Xu, Anwyl, & Rowan, 1998). Whether L1 and L2 both involve hippocampus-dependent learning tasks (e.g., L1 = one-trial inhibitory avoidance learning, L2 = exploration of a novel environment), as reported by Izquierdo et al. (1999), or one involves the induction of LTP (L1) while the other involves exposure to a learning task (L2), as reported by Xu et al. (1998), the same pattern emerges. Specifically, L2 interferes with L1 if the time between them is relatively short (e.g., one hour) but not when the time between them is relatively long (e.g., six or more hours). Moreover, if an NMDA antagonist is infused into the hippocampus prior to L2 (thereby blocking the induction of interfering LTP that might be associated with the learning of a potentially interfering task), no interference effect is observed even when the L1–L2 temporal interval is short.

As indicated earlier, the temporal gradient of interference that is readily observed in experimental animals and that was observed by Müller and Pilzecker (1900) and a few others long ago (e.g., Skaggs, 1925) is usually hard to obtain in humans. The reason may be that awake humans never stop making memories, so the interfering force that one would like to bring to a standstill is always in action. In experimental rats and mice, by contrast, memory formation in the hippocampus may occur primarily when the animal is exposed to a specific learning task, such as exposure to a novel environment. Although it is not easy to keep humans from forming new memories when they are awake in order to test for evidence of temporally graded retroactive interference, sleep and amnesia-inducing drugs can be used for this purpose.

Sleep-induced retrograde facilitation

It is already well known that less forgetting occurs during sleep than during a comparable period of wakefulness (Jenkins & Dallenbach, 1924). That is, a temporary period of anterograde amnesia (e.g., a few hours of sleep) confers a benefit on recently formed memories compared to remaining awake. The benefit consists of less forgetting when memory is later tested, and this phenomenon could be termed *retrograde facilitation*. This term is not typically used in the sleep literature, but it is often used in the psychopharmacology literature that will be considered later in this chapter. Using the same term for the effect of sleep on memory helps to draw attention to the fact that the same phenomenon is observed whether a temporary period of anterograde amnesia is induced by sleep or by pharmacological agents such as alcohol and benzodiazepines.

Retrograde facilitation refers to the fact that, following a postlearning intervention (e.g., a period of sleep after learning or the administration of an amnestic drug after learning), performance is better relative to a control group (e.g., no sleep or no drug after learning). The enhanced performance of the experimental group compared to that of the control group usually reflects less forgetting in the former compared to the latter. This is the pattern reported by Jenkins and Dallenbach (1924) in their classic sleep study, and in many other sleep studies (e.g., Ekstrand, 1967, 1972; Gais et al., 2006; Phihal & Born, 1997). Because that basic result is clearly established, the question of interest is whether or not the effect exhibits a temporal gradient (as a consolidation account would predict).

Temporal gradient of sleep-induced retrograde facilitation

If memories need time to consolidate in order to become hardened against the damaging forces of new memory formation, and if sleep provides a window of time for such consolidation to unfold in the absence of interference, then sleep soon after learning should confer more protection than sleep that is delayed. This can be tested by holding the retention interval between learning (L1) and test (T1) constant (e.g., at 24 hours), with the location of sleep (S) within that retention interval varied. That is, using the notation introduced earlier, L1-S—T1 should confer greater protection than L1—S-T1. If a temporal gradient is observed (i.e., if memory performance at T1 is greater in the first condition than the second), it would suggest that sleep does more than simply subtract out a period of retroactive interference that would otherwise occur. Instead, it would raise the possibility that sleep also allows a process of consolidation to unfold relatively unfettered.

Is a temporal gradient of retrograde facilitation observed in sleep studies? The answer is yes, and the relevant finding was reported long ago by Ekstrand (1972), who deserves to be recognized as a pioneer in the investigation of the effect of sleep on episodic memory. Ekstrand (1972) tested memory for paired-associate words following a 24-hour retention interval in which subjects slept either during the eight hours that followed list presentation or during the eight hours that preceded the recall test. That is, he used a design that might be represented as L1-S—T1 vs. L1—S-T1. In the immediate sleep condition (in which L1 occurred at night, just before sleep), he found that 81% of the items were recalled 24 hours later; in the delayed sleep condition (in which L1 occurred in the morning), only 66% were recalled. In other words, a clear temporal gradient of retrograde facilitation was observed, one that is the mirror image of the temporal gradient of retroactive interference reported by Müller and Pilzecker (1900).

More recent sleep studies have reinforced the idea that the temporal gradient of retrograde facilitation is a real phenomenon, and they have addressed various confounds that could have accounted for the results that Ekstrand (1972) obtained. Gais et al. (2006), for example, replicated the Ekstrand (1972) design and included several other conditions to rule out time-of-day or circadian rhythm confounds. Talamini, Nieuwenhuis, Takashima, and Jensen (2008) conducted a conceptually similar study and again showed that cued recall for face–location associations after 24 hours is significantly higher when sleep occurs shortly after learning than when it is delayed. The temporal gradient associated with sleep, like the LTP and animal learning research described earlier, is consistent with the notion that when memory formation is temporarily halted, recently formed and still fragile memories are protected from interference and are given a chance to become hardened against the forces of retroactive interference that they will later encounter.

Sleep and LTP

The synaptic consolidation interpretation of the temporal gradient of sleep-induced retrograde facilitation is supported by a consideration of the effects of sleep on LTP. During sleep, some new memories are formed, but this occurs almost exclusively during rapid eye movement (REM) sleep. These memories of our dreams do not seem to be normal (e.g., they seem to fade rapidly), but they clearly do occur. Just as clearly, memories are not formed during other stages of sleep, especially slow-wave sleep. This is true despite the fact that mental activity occurs during slow-wave sleep (Pivik & Foulkes, 1968). If memories occur during REM sleep (but not during non-REM sleep), does that mean that LTP can be induced in the hippocampus during REM sleep (but not during non-REM sleep)? And does it also mean that REM sleep is not particularly protective of recently formed memories (because REM memories serve as an interfering force), whereas non-REM sleep is? The answer to both questions appears to be yes.

In experiments performed on sleeping rats, Jones Leonard, McNaughton, and Barnes (1987) showed that LTP can be induced during REM sleep but not during slow-wave sleep. Whereas slow-wave sleep inhibits the induction of LTP, it does not disrupt the maintenance of previously induced LTP (Bramham & Srebo, 1989). In that sense, slow-wave sleep is like the NMDA antagonists discussed earlier (i.e., they block the induction of new LTP but not the maintenance of previously induced LTP). By contrast, with regard to synaptic plasticity in the hippocampus, REM sleep is similar to the awake state (i.e., LTP can be induced during REM). Based on findings like these, one might reasonably speculate that it is not sleep, per se, that is protective of recently formed memories. Instead, slow-wave sleep (during which the formation of new memories is prevented) should specifically confer that protection because it is during that stage of sleep that prior memories are protected from interference that might otherwise occur (thereby giving them a chance to consolidate before they encounter interference from new learning).

Once again, Ekstrand and colleagues (Ekstrand, 1972; Yaroush et al., 1971) performed the pioneering experiment that addressed this question. These researchers took advantage of the fact that most REM sleep occurs in the second half of the night, whereas most non-REM sleep occurs in the first half. Some subjects in this experiment learned a list, went to sleep immediately, and were awakened four hours later for a test of recall. These subjects experienced mostly slow-wave sleep during the four-hour retention interval. Others slept for four hours, were awakened to learn a list, slept for another four hours, and then took a recall test. These subjects experienced mostly REM sleep during the four-hour retention interval. The control (i.e., awake) subjects learned a list during the day and were tested for recall four hours later. The subjects all learned the initial list to a similar degree, but the results showed that four hours of mostly non-REM sleep facilitated delayed recall relative to the other two conditions, which did not differ from each other (i.e., REM sleep did not facilitate memory). Barrett and Ekstrand (1972) reported similar results in a study that controlled for time-of-day and circadian rhythm confounds, and the effect was later replicated in studies by Phihal & Born (1997, 1999).

Fowler, Sullivan, and Ekstrand (1973) argued that this pattern of results is not easy to reconcile with an interference-reduction explanation because both the REM and non-REM conditions involve equivalent amounts of sleep and, therefore, equivalent reductions in interference. Although one might be tempted to argue that mental activity during REM sleep (i.e., dreaming) causes interference, whereas the absence of mental activity during non-REM sleep might result in a reduction of interference, Fowler et al. (1973) argued that this idea is weakened by "ample evidence of a great deal of mental activity during the non-rapid eye movement (non-REM) stages" (p. 304). However, what the synaptic plasticity literature suggests is that mental activity during non-REM sleep might not matter because LTP cannot be induced under those conditions. As such, despite the significant mental activity that occurs, potentially interfering memories might not be formed during slow-wave sleep. This makes the interference-reduction explanation of why non-REM sleep is particularly protective of declarative memory more plausible than it seemed to Fowler et al. (1973).

The benefits of slow-wave sleep for declarative memory are interpretable in terms of what is known about synaptic consolidation and the stabilization of LTP, but, as noted earlier, a mechanism suspected of playing a role in systems consolidation (neural replay) also tends to occur during slow-wave sleep (Wilson & McNaughton, 1994). Neural reply has been observed during REM sleep as well, but in that case it occurs at a rate that is similar to the neuron firing that occurred during learning (Louie & Wilson, 2001) and thus may simply reflect dreaming. The neural replay that occurs during slow-wave sleep occurs at a rate five to ten times faster than it did during the waking state (e.g., Ji & Wilson, 2007) and thus may reflect a biological consolidation process separate from mental activity. It is simply not known whether a systems consolidation process like this, which is usually thought to train the neocortex over months and years in humans, contributes to the hardening of a memory trace during a retention interval of 24 hours or less, but it might.

Phihal and Born (1997, 1999), who replicated the beneficial effect of slow-wave sleep over REM sleep in the protection of recently formed declarative memories, also confirmed earlier work by Karni, Tanne, Rubenstein, Askenasy, and Sagi (1994) showing that the opposite pattern applies to the retention of non-hippocampus-dependent *procedural* memories (i.e., procedural memories benefit from REM sleep but not from non-REM sleep). Thus, in that respect, the sleep-related consolidation of procedural memories appears to differ from the sleep-related consolidation of declarative memories. Indeed, they differ in another important way as well. Unlike declarative memories, the sleep-related facilitation of procedural memory does not consist simply of less forgetting (as is typically true of studies on declarative memory). Instead, it often consists of an absolute enhancement in the level of performance over and above what was evident at the end of training. This offline improvement in learning is often called "consolidation" (e.g., Walker, 2005), but, used in that sense, the term does not necessarily refer to systems consolidation (with traces becoming independent of the hippocampus), or synaptic consolidation (with traces becoming stabilized in the hippocampus). It is not clear why these differences between procedural and declarative memories exist. However, it is clear that declarative memories differentially benefit from slow-wave sleep (not REM sleep), and it seems reasonable to suppose that this occurs because, during slow-wave sleep, new memories are not being formed.

Drug-induced retrograde facilitation

NMDA antagonists (in rats) and slow-wave sleep (in humans) are not the only ways to induce a temporary period of anterograde amnesia. In sufficient quantities, alcohol and benzodiazepines do the same. Moreover, like NMDA antagonists and slow-wave sleep, these drugs not only induce anterograde amnesia, but they also inhibit the induction of LTP in the hippocampus, and they result in retrograde facilitation. More specifically, memories formed prior to drug intake (like memories formed prior to sleep) are forgotten to a lesser degree than memories formed prior to placebo.

Because alcohol (Givens & McMahon 1995; Roberto, Nelson, Ur, & Gruol, 2002; Sinclair & Lo 1986) and benzodiazepines (Del Cerro, Jung, & Lynch, 1992; Evans & Viola-McCabe 1996) have been shown to block the induction of LTP in the hippocampus, it makes sense that these drugs would induce anterograde amnesia. Although it blocks the induction of LTP, alcohol does not impair the maintenance of hippocampal LTP induced one hour prior to drug administration (Givens & McMahon, 1995). In that sense, alcohol is like slow-wave sleep and NMDA antagonists. Benzodiazepines presumably do not impair the maintenance of previously induced LTP either, but this has not yet been specifically tested.

By limiting the formation of new memories, alcohol and benzodiazepines may protect memories that were formed just prior to drug intake. While protected from the trace-degrading force of new memory formation, it is possible that these memories are allowed to consolidate in a way that hardens them against the interference they will later encounter when new memories are once again formed. Thus, less forgetting should be observed than would otherwise be the case. Indeed, numerous studies have reported that, even though alcohol induces amnesia for information studied under the influence of the drug, it actually results in improved memory for material studied just prior to consumption (e.g., Bruce & Pihl, 1997; Lamberty, Beckwith, & Petros, 1990; Mann, Cho-Young, & Vogel-Sprott, 1984; Parker, Birnbaum, Weingartner, Hartley, Stillman, & Wyatt, 1980; Parker, Morihisa, Wyatt, Schwartz, Weingartner, & Stillman, 1981). Similar findings have been frequently reported for benzodiazepines such as diazepam and triazolam (Coenen & Van Luijtelaar, 1997; Fillmore, Kelly, Rush, & Hays, 2001; Ghoneim, Hinrichs, & Mewaldt, 1984; Hinrichs, Ghoneim, & Mewaldt, 1984; Weingartner, Sirocco, Curran, & Wolkowitz, 1995). This retrograde facilitation looks very much like the effect of sleep on episodic memory (as noted by Coenen & Van Luijtelaar, 1997).

The psychopharmacology literature has considered a variety of explanations for retrograde facilitation and has not settled on any one of them. Indeed, a review of this literature instead reveals widespread disagreement. As with sleep, it is sometimes suggested that alcohol induces retrograde facilitation because it somehow directly enhances the consolidation process (Parker et al., 1980, 1981) or directly enhances the retrieval process (Weingartner et al., 1995). However, it seems odd to suppose that an agent that boosts consolidation or retrieval would cause anterograde amnesia. Instead, it seems more likely that any enhancement of consolidation or retrieval would, if anything, yield anterograde facilitation in addition to retrograde facilitation. For example, glucose, like alcohol and NMDA inhibitors, has repeatedly been shown to cause retrograde facilitation (Manning et al., 1992; Sünram-Lea, Foster, Durlach, & Perez, 2002). However, unlike alcohol and NMDA inhibitors (and slow-wave sleep), glucose does not inhibit the induction of LTP in the hippocampus (Kamal, Spoelstra, Biessels, Urban, & Gispen, 1999). Moreover, glucose does not cause anterograde amnesia when taken before learning. Instead, it causes anterograde facilitation (Manning, Parsons, & Gold, 1992; Sünram-Lea et al., 2002). It therefore seems reasonable to suppose that glucose leads to retrograde facilitation because it somehow boosts the consolidation process after learning, not because it blocks new learning. Similarly, amphetamine results in both anterograde facilitation and retrograde facilitation (Soetens, Casaer, D'Hooge, & Hueting, 1995). Like glucose, this drug also does not inhibit the induction of LTP in the hippocampus (Dommett, Henderson, Westwell, & Greenfield, 2008), and its effects are also thought to be due to an enhancement of the consolidation process (McGaugh, 2000). By contrast, alcohol and benzodiazepines do block the induction of LTP and do cause anterograde amnesia. As such, they should protect memories formed just before drug intake from the interfering forces of new memory formation (which is why they, too, result in retrograde facilitation).

Psychopharmacology researchers who argue in favor of an enhanced consolidation or enhanced retrieval interpretation of retrograde facilitation have interpreted a particular pattern of results as weighing against an interference-reduction explanation. This pattern involves the apparent equating of retroactive interference across conditions, but retrograde facilitation is observed anyway. For example, in some studies, no formal interfering list was presented to either the drug group or the placebo control group. If no interfering list was presented, and if one assumes that, as a result, no interference occurred in the placebo control condition, how could reduced interference explain retrograde facilitation? This is one reason why Parker et al. (1981) favored an enhanced consolidation interpretation. In other studies, an interfering list similar to the pre-drug study list was presented to both the drug group and the placebo group during the retention interval, but the drug group somehow managed to learn the interfering list as well as the control group despite being under the influence of the amnesia-inducing drug (File, Fluck, & Joyce, 1999; Weingartner et al., 1995). Even so, retrograde facilitation was observed. Again, they argued, if interference was equated across groups, how could reduced interference explain retrograde facilitation for the drug group?

The reasoning used in these studies appears to have been based on a cue-overload view of retroactive interference. That is, the authors adopted the view that retroactive interference for a list of words is caused by the subsequent learning of a similar list of words (and not by anything else). However, the reduced interference that may account for retroactive facilitation is, I argue, the interference caused by a reduced rate of memory formation in general in the hours after the drug is administered, not by reduced memory for one similar interfering list that was studied for, say, 60 seconds during the several-hour period in which subjects were under the influence of the drug. Under the influence of an amnesia-inducing drug, memories will be formed at a reduced rate even if no formal interfering list is presented, and memories are likely to be formed at a reduced rate even if, for one particular list, the drug group manages to learn it as well as the control group. Indeed, clear evidence for this can be seen in Weingartner et al. (1995). Subjects in the triazolam condition of that experiment learned an interfering list that was similar to the pre-drug study list as well as placebo controls did, yet they exhibited retrograde facilitation anyway. However, on other unrelated memory tasks that the triazolam group completed while under the influence of the drug (e.g., sentences learned and recalled under the influence of the drug), memory was clearly impaired. Thus, the overall rate of memory formation in the hours following drug administration was undoubtedly impaired, and it seems reasonable to suppose that this generally reduced rate of memory formation is why retrograde facilitation was observed.

By creating a period of anterograde amnesia shortly after learning, alcohol and benzodiazepines are (like slow-wave sleep) assumed to: (a) protect these fragile memories from trace degradation during an especially vulnerable period; and (b) allow the process of synaptic consolidation to unfold such that the once fragile memories become resistant to interference by the time new memories are once again encoded. If this interpretation is correct, then a temporal gradient of drug-induced retrograde facilitation should be observed (as it is in sleep).

Temporal gradient of drug-induced retrograde facilitation

Is a temporal gradient of retrograde facilitation observed when amnesia-inducing drugs are used? To date, the answer is no, but only two studies have looked for it, and neither was designed in a way that was likely to reveal any temporal gradient that might exist. Mueller, Lisman, and Spear (1983) had subjects learn two lists of words prior to ingesting alcohol. A consolidation account would predict that the more recently learned list should exhibit greater retrograde facilitation, but the enhancement effect was the same for both lists. As such, they argued that consolidation does not play a role in alcohol-induced retrograde facilitation and that reduced interference is the probable explanation. However, the lists were learned closely together in time, and a greater separation is almost surely needed. Tyson and Schirmuly (1994), also using alcohol, reported a similar result for lists learned 40 minutes apart. No temporal gradient was observed but, again, there is reason to believe that the interval between lists was too short. Indeed, in a sleep study, Ekstrand (1967) presented two successive lists close together in time prior to sleep and found that, although memory for both lists was enhanced, memory for the first list (not the second) was differentially enhanced.

Studies that have shown a temporal gradient using NMDA antagonists or sleep used temporal intervals substantially greater than 40 minutes. Usually, even the shorter of the two temporal intervals is longer than that. Xu et al. (1998), for example, induced hippocampal LTP in rats and then exposed the animals to an interfering novel environment either one hour or 24 hours later. LTP was abolished in the one-hour group but was unaffected in the 24-hour group. As the authors point out, this is consistent with the fact that the maintenance of LTP is divided into two phases, an early phase (one to three hours after induction) and a late phase (more than three hours after induction). The late phase, but not the early phase, is dependent on protein synthesis and may involve morphological changes to hippocampal neurons (Bliss & Collingridge, 1993). It seems reasonable to assume that memories that make it to that stage may be hardened against the forces of retroactive interference. Thus, the study by Tyson and Schirmuly (1994) involved two temporal intervals that both fell within the early phase of LTP, and it is not clear that a temporal gradient would be expected under those conditions.

Other studies reviewed above suggested that a temporal gradient also involved temporal intervals much longer than 40 minutes. Izquierdo et al. (1999), for example, found that an interfering task presented one hour after inhibitory avoidance training hindered later memory for that training, but no such effect was observed if the interfering task was presented six hours after inhibitory avoidance training. Similarly, sleep studies have shown that sleep just after learning is more protective than sleep that is delayed by 12 hours. The point is that these temporal gradients have all involved delays that are one hour or longer (even for the short delay). Müller and Pilzecker (1900) were able to obtain a temporal gradient of interference when the study list and interfering list were separated by a matter of minutes, and it is somewhat ironic that the mechanisms now thought to underlie the consolidation process that they envisioned long ago would not clearly predict that a temporal gradient of interference would be observed. Although they did observe one, and Dewar, Fernandez Garcia, Cowan, and Della Sala (2009) observed one over a similar timescale using patients with mild cognitive impairment (who may suffer from particularly depleted consolidation resources), most research suggests that a larger timescale may be necessary to reliably observe the effect (and related retrograde facilitation effects) in intact organisms.

Whether a temporal gradient of retrograde facilitation for alcohol or benzodiazepines would be observed using longer temporal intervals (e.g., one hour vs. six hours after learning) is unknown. If a temporal gradient is ultimately observed, the simplest explanation would be the same one that applies to the various other procedures that (a) block the induction of LTP in the hippocampus and (b) yield a temporal gradient of retrograde facilitation.

Temporal gradients of retrograde amnesia and retrograde facilitation

As indicated earlier, bilateral lesions of the hippocampus often yield temporally graded retrograde amnesia, and this phenomenon has long been taken as evidence that memories consolidate and become less dependent on the hippocampus with the passage of time (McGaugh, 2000; Squire & Alvarez, 1995). Usually, this phenomenon is not tied to a theory of forgetting, but the point I am making here is that it probably should be. In this regard, it is useful to conceptualize the hippo-campus as performing two jobs: (1) encoding new memories and (2) consolidating recently formed memories. Hippocampal lesions bring an abrupt end to both activities, resulting in both anterograde amnesia (because the first job is disrupted) and temporally graded retrograde amnesia (because the second job is disrupted as well). By contrast, glucose and amphetamines effectively do the reverse by enhancing both hippocampal activities and resulting in both anterograde facilitation and retrograde facilitation.

Other circumstances can be conceptualized as inhibiting the first job (encoding new memories) without impairing the second (consolidating recently formed memories). These circumstances include slow-wave sleep, the use of NMDA antagonists and, perhaps, the administration of alcohol and benzo-diazepines. All of these block the induction of hippocampal LTP and induce anterograde amnesia. In rats and mice, a state of quiet wakefulness in a familiar environment may also be sufficient to release the hippocampus from the job of encoding new memories (though this seems unlikely in humans, who form new memories whenever awake). In each case, the consolidation of recently formed memories may proceed in a more efficient manner than it otherwise would because, when released from job 1, the hippocampus performs job 2.

Consolidation is an often ill-defined term, so it is important to be clear about how the term is used here. When not encoding new memories, the hippocampus is assumed to be released to engage in both synaptic consolidation (involving the stabilization of recently induced LTP) and systems consolidation (perhaps involving coordinated neural replay). When the hippocampus is engaged in the task of forming new memories, both kinds of consolidation processes may instead be hindered in one way or another. In everyday life, the freedom to consolidate comes on a regular basis in the form of nightly slow-wave sleep (and, for some animals, during certain periods of wakefulness as well). During slow-wave sleep, synaptic plasticity in the hippocampus is inhibited, which allows recently established memories to stabilize (i.e., synaptic consolidation can proceed unfettered) and, perhaps, sets the occasion for coordinated neural replay (i.e., systems consolidation can proceed as well). The same may happen when synaptic plasticity is diminished while the animal is awake but not in motion (e.g., Karlsson & Frank, 2009). Indeed, with respect to neural replay and systems consolidation, a similar idea was proposed long ago by Buzsaki (1989). More recently, Hoffman and McNaughton (2002) put it this way:

> Consistent with the former prediction, neural ensembles in the rat hippo-campus and neocortex show memory trace reactivation during "offline periods" of quiet wakefulness, slow-wave sleep, and in some cases REM (rapid eye movement) sleep.
>
> (pp. 2070–2071)

The idea that neural replay spontaneously occurs during offline periods has been advanced to account for the fact that memories eventually become independent of the hippocampus. However, the idea that memories become less dependent on the hippocampus as a result of systems consolidation says nothing about how and why *forgetting* occurs. Instead, it speaks to the issue of why memories eventually become unaffected by hippocampal lesions. Whether systems consolidation also hardens them against the interfering force of new memory formation is not known, but it seems reasonable to suppose that it does.

In addition to hardening memories against the forces of retroactive interference, systems consolidation may also directly enhance the learning of declarative memories in the same way that REM sleep often promotes the enhanced learning of procedural memories. However, it is rare that an actual improvement of declarative memory performance is observed following slow-wave sleep. Instead, sleep usually forestalls forgetting. Still, there is reason to believe that reactivation of memories during slow-wave sleep might be able to enhance declarative memories as well. For example, an intriguing study by Rasch, Buchel, Gais, and Born (2007) showed that cuing recently formed odor-associated memories by odor re-exposure during slow-wave sleep (but not during REM sleep) prompted hippocampal activation and increased retention performance after sleep. This result raises the possibility that a reactivation process during slow-wave sleep has the capacity to improve declarative memories in addition to (possibly) hardening them against retroactive interference.

Retroactive interference and everyday forgetting

The preceding considerations suggest a general theory of forgetting according to which nonspecific retroactive interference associated with the formation of new memories degrades previously formed memories (more so the more recently those previous memories were formed). Humans form memories all day long every day, and the constant application of this interfering force may have a large cumulative effect on what we later retain. The interference caused by the formation of new memories presumably has its greatest effect on recently formed memories because they have not yet become hardened against the corrupting influence of new memories (i.e., they have not yet consolidated in that sense).

Villarreal, Haddad, and Derrick (2002) performed an interesting experiment that illustrates the cumulative effect of retroactive interference associated with the everyday life of a laboratory rat. In this experiment, hippocampal LTP was induced in rats via implanted electrodes, and the magnitude of LTP was assessed for the next six days. Some rats received an NMDA receptor antagonist each day (a treatment that should prevent the further induction of LTP that might be associated with natural memory formation), whereas control rats received a water vehicle. No explicit retroactively interfering task was arranged in this experiment, so any interference that occurred was presumably due to the formation of memories associated with normal events in the life of a laboratory rat. Although such memories likely occur at a very low rate in rats housed in a familiar environment, they presumably do occur and, when they do, they presumably have a cumulative degrading effect on recently formed memories. The results of this experiment revealed that LTP decayed back to baseline for the control rats over the next several days but remained elevated for the experimental subjects. Thus, it seems that LTP was protected in the experimental rats because the subsequent LTP that would have been induced by the formation of new memories was prevented by the NMDA antagonist. When the NMDA antagonist was no longer administered (after day six), LTP in the experimental rats began to decay as well. Thus, even LTP that has substantially consolidated (i.e., late-phase LTP) is vulnerable to cumulative retroactive interference, though it is less vulnerable than newly induced LTP. Villarreal et al. (2002) also showed that very similar protective effects of an NMDA antagonist were observed when a spatial learning task was used (instead of inducing LTP) and memory performance was tested after a delay (instead of monitoring the maintenance of LTP).

The point is just that retroactive interference resulting from the formation of new memories may be a constantly applied, cumulative force that operates whenever a rat (or a human) is awake. Humans presumably make memories at a high rate, and it is hard to prevent that from happening (though it can be done using sleep or amnesia-inducing drugs). The rat hippocampus is presumably less taxed when in a familiar environment, but even that can be altered by enriching its environment. In a study by Abraham, Logan, Greenwood, and Dragunow (2002), LTP was induced in the hippocampus of rats, and the animals were then housed in their familiar home cage for two weeks. In this low-interference environment, LTP decayed, but it did so gradually (presumably because new memories were formed at a low rate—an explicitly arranged interfering task would have been needed to reverse it more quickly). In the following week, some of these animals were exposed to a more complex environment involving a larger cage, multiple objects, and other animals for 14 hours per day. Exposure to this environment for several days resulted in complete reversal of the previously induced LTP (presumably because the rate of new memory formation was substantially increased), whereas LTP in the control animals continued its very gradual decay.

All of these findings are consistent with the idea that the formation of new memories has a degrading effect on recently established memories (or recently established LTP). Over time, memories consolidate and become more resistant to such interference, but during that time they are confronted with—and degraded by—the interference associated with the encoding of other memories. Returning once again to the classic forgetting function presented by Ebbinghaus (1885), nonspecific retroactive interference associated with the formation of new memories may explain why forgetting occurs rapidly at first but occurs at an ever-slowing rate as time passes (Figure 5.1). As time passes, surviving memories become more resistant to the constantly applied, interfering force of new memory formation.

This way of thinking could also help to explain why forgetting functions have the shape they do even when plotted over a 50-year period. Bahrick (1984) reported long-term forgetting data for Spanish learned in high school. The data from various subtests in this study were aggregated (following Hintzman, 1990) and then fit with the same three-parameter power function that accurately described the Ebbinghaus savings data. The averaged data are somewhat variable, but the form

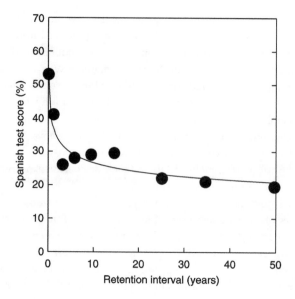

FIGURE 5.2 Retention of Spanish learned in high school, as reported by Bahrick (1984). The solid curve represents the least squares fit of the three-parameter Wickelgren power law (defined in the caption for Figure 5.1)

of forgetting over 50 years (Figure 5.2) looks much like the form of forgetting over 31 days (Figure 5.1). On both timescales, memories weaken rapidly at first and then weaken at an ever slower rate as time passes.

Bahrick (1984) proposed the concept of "permastore" to account for the shape of the 50-year retention function. According to this idea, memories start off in a somewhat labile state but then enter a different, more permanent state some years later. He implied that memories that had not yet transitioned into permastore were vulnerable to interference, whereas memories that had were essentially invulnerable. The consolidation account of forgetting that I have presented here is much the same, except that it does not envision a discontinuous transition into a qualitatively different state. Instead, memories continuously harden against the forces of interference as a result of synaptic and systems consolidation—perhaps reaching some maximum state of resistance after several years (after which they are still vulnerable to interference, just much less so than they were before). In addition, in the account I have described (and that Müller and Pilzecker described long ago), the interfering force against which memories harden over time is that associated with the formation of new memories—a process that degrades previously established memories, whether or not those previously established memories are related to the subsequently formed memories.

With all of the credit that Müller and Pilzecker (1900) justifiably receive for introducing the theory of consolidation (Lechner, Squire, & Byrne, 1999; McGaugh, 2000), it is sometimes forgotten that theirs was a theory of interference and forgetting, not a theory about how memories eventually become less dependent on one brain structure and more dependent on another. They were, after all, experimental psychologists, not neuroscientists. More than 100 years and thousands of studies later, their theory of forgetting is still standing.

Note

* This chapter originally appeared in the edited volume, *Forgetting*.

References

Abel, T., Nguyen, P.V., Barad, M., Deuel, T. A., Kandel, E. R., & Bourtchouladze, R. (1997). Genetic demonstration of a role for PKA in the late phase of LTP and in hippocampus-based long-term memory. *Cell, 88*, 615–626.

Abraham, W. C., Logan, B., Greenwood, J. M., & Dragunow, M. (2002). Induction and experience-dependent consolidation of stable long-term potentiation lasting months in the hippocampus. *Journal of Neuroscience, 22*, 9626–9634.

Bahrick, H. P. (1984). Semantic memory content in permastore: Fifty years of memory for Spanish learning in school. *Journal of Experimental Psychology: General, 113*, 1–29.

Bailey, C. H., & Chen, M. (1989). Time course of structural changes at identified sensory neuron synapses during long-term sensitization in *Aplysia. Journal of Neuroscience, 9*, 1774–1780.

Barrett, T. R., & Ekstrand, B. R. (1972). Effect of sleep on memory: III. Controlling for time-of-day effects. *Journal of Experimental Psychology, 96*, 321–327.

Bliss, T.V. P., & Collingridge, G. L. (1993). A synaptic model of memory: Long-term potentiation in the hippocampus. *Nature, 361*, 31–39.

Bramham, C. R., & Srebo, B. (1989). Synaptic plasticity in the hippocampus is modulated by behavioral state. *Brain Research, 493*, 74–86.

Bruce, K. R., & Pihl, R. O. (1997). Forget "drinking to forget": Enhanced consolidation of emotionally charged memory by alcohol. *Experimental and Clinical Psychopharmacology, 5*, 242–250.

Buzsaki, G. (1989). A two-stage model of memory trace formation: A role for "noisy" brain states. *Neuroscience, 31*, 551–570.

Coenen, A. M. L., & Van Luijtelaar, E. L. J. M. (1997). Effects of benzodiazepines, sleep and sleep deprivation on vigilance and memory. *Acta Neurologica Belgica, 97*, 123–129.

Davis, H. P., & Squire, L. R. (1984). Protein synthesis and memory: A review. *Psychological Bulletin, 96*, 518–559.

Del Cerro, S., Jung, M., & Lynch, L. (1992). Benzodiazepines block long-term potentiation in slices of hippocampus and piriform cortex. *Neuroscience, 49*, 1–6.

Dewar, M., Fernandez Garcia, Y., Cowan, N., & Della Sala, S. (2009). Delaying interference enhances memory consolidation in amnesic patients. *Neuropsychology, 23*(5), 627–634.

Dommett, E. J., Henderson, E. L., Westwell, M. S., & Greenfield, S. A. (2008). Methylphenidate amplifies long-term plasticity in the hippocampus via noradrenergic mechanisms. *Learning & Memory, 15*, 580–586.

Ebbinghaus, H. (1885). *Über das Gedchtnis. Untersuchungen zur experimentellen Psychologie.* Leipzig: Duncker & Humblot.

Ebbinghaus, H. (1913). *Memory. A contribution to experimental psychology.* New York: Teachers College, Columbia University. English edition of Ebbinghaus, 1885.

Ekstrand, B. R. (1967). The effect of sleep on memory. *Journal of Experimental Psychology*, *75*, 64–72.

Ekstrand, B. R. (1972). To sleep, perchance to dream (about why we forget). In C. P. Duncan, L. Sechrest, & A. W. Melton (Eds.), *Human memory: Festschrift for Benton J. Underwood* (pp. 59–82). New York: Appelton-Century-Crofts.

Evans, M. S., & Viola-McCabe, K. E. (1996). Midazolam inhibits long-term potentiation through modulation of GABA$_A$ receptors. *Neuropharmacology*, *35*, 347–357.

File, S. E., Fluck, E., & Joyce, E. M. (1999). Conditions under which lorazepam can facilitate retrieval. *Journal of Clinical Psychopharmacology*, *19*, 349–353.

Fillmore, M. T., Kelly, T. H., Rush, C. R., & Hays, L. (2001). Retrograde facilitation of memory by triazolam: Effects on automatic processes. *Psychopharmacology*, *158*, 314–321.

Fowler, M. J., Sullivan, M. J., & Ekstrand, B. R. (1973). Sleep and memory. *Science*, *179*, 302–304.

Frey, U., Krug, M., Reymann, K. G., & Matthies, H. (1988). Anisomycin, an inhibitor of protein synthesis, blocks late phases of LTP phenomena in the hippocampal CA1 region in vitro. *Brain Research*, *452*, 57–65.

Gais, S., Lucas, B., & Born, J. (2006). Sleep after learning aids memory recall. *Learning and Memory*, *13*, 259–262.

Ghoneim, M. M., Hinrichs, J. V., & Mewaldt, S. P. (1984). Dose-response analysis of the behavioral effects of diazepam: I. Learning and memory. *Psychopharmacology*, *82*, 291–295.

Givens, B., & McMahon, K. (1995). Ethanol suppresses the induction of long-term potentiation in vivo. *Brain Research*, *688*, 27–33.

Hinrichs, J. V., Ghoneim, M. M., & Mewaldt, S. P. (1984). Diazepam and memory: Retrograde facilitation produced by interference reduction. *Psychopharmacology*, *84*, 158–162.

Hintzman, D. (1990). *Permastore or grade inflation? Adjusting Bahrick's data for changes in academic standards*. (Tech. Rep. No. 90–15.) Eugene, OR: University of Oregon, Institute of Cognitive and Decision Sciences.

Hoffman, K. L., & McNaughton, B. L. (2002). Coordinated reactivation of distributed memory traces in primate neocortex. *Science*, *297*, 2070–2073.

Izquierdo, I., Schröder, N., Netto, C. A., & Medina, J. H. (1999). Novelty causes time-dependent retrograde amnesia for one-trial avoidance in rats through NMDA receptor- and CaMKII-dependent mechanisms in the hippocampus. *European Journal of Neuroscience*, *11*, 3323–3328.

Jenkins, J. G., & Dallenbach, K. M. (1924). Oblivescence during sleep and waking. *American Journal of Psychology*, *35*, 605–612.

Ji, D., & Wilson, M. A. (2007). Coordinated memory replay in the visual cortex and hippocampus during sleep. *Nature Neuroscience*, *10*, 100–107.

Jones Leonard, B., McNaughton, B. L., & Barnes, C. A. (1987). Suppression of hippocampal synaptic activity during slow-wave sleep. *Brain Research*, *425*, 174–177.

Jost, A. (1897). Die Assoziationsfestigkeit in ihrer Abhängigkeit von der Verteilung der Wiederholungen [The strength of associations in their dependence on the distribution of repetitions]. *Zeitschrift für Psychologie und Physiologie der Sinnesorgane*, *16*, 436–472.

Kamal, A., Spoelstra, K., Biessels, G., Urban, I. J. A., & Gispen, W. H. (1999). Effects of changes in glucose concentration on synaptic plasticity in hippocampal slices. *Brain Research*, *824*, 238–242.

Karlsson, M. P., & Frank, L. M. (2009). Awake replay of remote experiences in the hippocampus. *Nature Neuroscience*, *12*, 913–920.

Karni, A., Tanne, D., Rubenstein, B. S., Askenasy, J. J. M., & Sagi, D. (1994). Dependence on REM sleep of overnight improvement of a perceptual skill. *Science*, *265*, 679–682.

Keppel, G. (1968). Retroactive and proactive inhibition. In T. R. Dixon & D. L. Horton (Eds.), *Verbal behavior and general behavior theory* (pp. 172–213). Englewood Cliffs, NJ: Prentice-Hall.

Lamberty, G. J., Beckwith, B. E., & Petros, T. V. (1990). Posttrial treatment with ethanol enhances recall of prose narratives. *Physiology and Behavior, 48,* 653–658.

Lechner, H. A., Squire, L. R., & Byrne, J. H. (1999). 100 years of consolidation—Remembering Müller and Pilzecker. *Learning and Memory, 6,* 77–87.

Louie, K., & Wilson, M. A. (2001). Temporally structured replay of awake hippocampal ensemble activity during rapid eye movement sleep. *Neuron, 29,* 145–156.

McClelland, J. L., McNaughton, B. L., & O'Reilly, R. C. (1995). Why there are complementary learning systems in the hippocampus and neocortex: Insights from the successes and failures of connectionist models of learning and memory. *Psychological Review, 102,* 419–457.

McGaugh, J. L. (2000). Memory: A century of consolidation. *Science, 287,* 248–251.

Mann, R. E., Cho-Young, & Vogel-Sprott, M. (1984). Retrograde enhancement by alcohol of delayed free recall performance. *Pharmacology, Biochemistry and Behavior, 20,* 639–642.

Manning, C. A., Parsons, M. W., & Gold, P. E. (1992). Anterograde and retrograde enhancement of 24-h memory by glucose in elderly humans. *Behavioral and Neural Biology, 58,* 125–130.

Martin, S. J., Grimwood, P. D., & Morris, R. G. M. (2000). Synaptic plasticity and memory: An evaluation of the hypothesis. *Annual Review of Neuroscience, 23,* 649–711.

Morris, R. G. M. (1989). Synaptic plasticity and learning: Selective impairment of learning in rats and blockade of long-term potentiation in vivo by the N-methyl-D-aspartate receptor antagonist AP5. *Journal of Neuroscience, 9,* 3040–3057.

Morris, R. G. M., Anderson, E., Lynch, G. S., & Baudry, M. (1986). Selective impairment of learning and blockade of long-term potentiation by an N-methyl-D-aspartate receptor antagonist, AP5. *Nature 319,* 774–776.

Mueller, C. W., Lisman, S. A., & Spear, N. E. (1983). Alcohol enhancement of human memory: Tests of consolidation and interference hypotheses. *Psychopharmacology, 80,* 226–230.

Müller, G. E. & Pilzecker, A. (1900). Experimentelle Beiträge zur Lehre vom Gedächtnis. Ergänzungsband [Experimental contributions to the science of memory]. *Zeitschrift für Psychologie, 1,* 1–300.

Parker, E. S., Birnbaum, I. M., Weingartner, H., Hartley, J. T., Stillman, R. C., & Wyatt, R. J. (1980). Retrograde enhancement of human memory with alcohol. *Psychopharmacology, 69,* 219–222.

Parker, E. S., Morihisa, J. M., Wyatt, R. J., Schwartz, B. L., Weingartner, H., & Stillman, R. C. (1981). The alcohol facilitation effect on memory: A dose-response study. *Psychopharmacology, 74,* 88–92.

Peigneux, P., Laureys, S., Fuchs, S., Collette, F., Perrin, F., Reggers, J., et al. (2004). Are spatial memories strengthened in the human hippocampus during slow-wave sleep? *Neuron, 44,* 535–545.

Phihal, W., & Born, J. (1997). Effects of early and late nocturnal sleep on declarative and procedural memory. *Journal of Cognitive Neuroscience, 9,* 534–547.

Phihal, W., & Born, J. (1999). Effects of early and late nocturnal sleep on priming and spatial memory. *Psychophysiology, 36,* 571–582.

Pivik, T., & Foulkes, D. (1968). NREM mentation: Relation to personality, orientation time, and time of night. *Journal of Consulting and Clinical Psychology, 32,* 144–151.

Rasch, B., Buchel, C., Gais, S., & Born, J. (2007). Odor cues during slow-wave sleep prompt declarative memory consolidation. *Science, 315,* 1426–1429.

Ribot, T. (1881). *Les Maladies de la mémoire* [Diseases of memory]. New York: Appleton-Century-Crofts.

Ribot, T. (1882). *Diseases of memory: An essay in positive psychology.* London: Kegan Paul, Trench & Co.

Roberto, M., Nelson, T. E., Ur, C. L., & Gruol, D. L. (2002). Long-term potentiation in the rat hippocampus is reversibly depressed by chronic intermittent ethanol exposure. *Journal of Neurophysiology, 87,* 2385–2397.

Scoville, W. B., & Milner, B. (1957). Loss of recent memory after bilateral hippocampal lesions. *Journal of Neurology, Neurosurgery and Psychiatry, 20,* 11–21.

Simon, H. A. (1966). A note on Jost's Law and exponential forgetting. *Psychometrika, 31,* 505–506.

Sinclair, J. G., & Lo, G. F. (1986). Ethanol blocks tetanic and calcium-induced long-term potentiation in the hippocampal slice. *General Pharmacology, 17,* 231–233.

Skaggs, E. B. (1925). Further studies in retroactive inhibition. *Psychological Monographs* (Whole No. 161), *34,* 1–60.

Soetens, E., Casaer, S., D'Hooge, R., & Hueting, J. E. (1995). Effect of amphetamine on long-term retention of verbal material. *Psychopharmacology, 119,* 155–162.

Squire, L. R. (2009). The legacy of patient H.M. for neuroscience. *Neuron, 61,* 6–9.

Squire, L. R., & Alvarez, P. (1995). Retrograde amnesia and memory consolidation: A neuro-biological perspective. *Current Opinion in Neurobiology, 5,* 169–177.

Squire, L. R., Clark, R. E., & Knowlton, B. J. (2001). Retrograde amnesia. *Hippocampus, 11,* 50–55.

Sünram-Lea, S. I., Foster, J. K., Durlach, P., & Perez, C. (2002). The effect of retrograde and anterograde glucose administration on memory performance in healthy young adults. *Behavioural Brain Research, 134,* 505–516.

Talamini L. M., Nieuwenhuis, I. L., Takashima A., & Jensen O. (2008). Sleep directly following learning benefits consolidation of spatial associative memory. *Learning and Memory, 15,* 233–237.

Tulving, E., & Madigan, S. A. (1970). Memory and verbal learning. *Annual Review of Psychology, 21,* 437–484.

Tulving, E., & Pearlstone, Z. (1966). Availability versus accessibility of information in memory for words. *Journal of Verbal Learning and Verbal Behavior, 5,* 381–391.

Tulving, E., & Thomson, D. M. (1973). Encoding specificity and retrieval processes in episodic memory. *Psychological Review, 80,* 352–373.

Tyson, P., & Schirmuly, M. (1994). Memory enhancement after drinking ethanol: Consolidation, interference, or response bias? *Psychology and Behavior, 56,* 933–937.

Underwood, B. J. (1957). Interference and forgetting. *Psychological Review, 64,* 49–60.

Underwood, B. J. (1983). *Attributes of memory.* Glenview, IL: Scott, Foresman & Co.

Underwood, B. J., & Ekstrand, B. R. (1966). An analysis of some shortcomings in the interference theory of forgetting. *Psychological Review, 73,* 540–549.

Underwood, B. J., & Ekstrand, B. R. (1967). Studies of distributed practice: XXIV. Differentiation and proactive inhibition. *Journal of Experimental Psychology, 74,* 574–580.

Underwood, B. J., & Postman, L. (1960). Extraexperimental sources of interference in forgetting. *Psychological Review, 67,* 73–95.

Villarreal, D. M., Do, V., Haddad, E., & Derrick, B. E. (2002). NMDA receptor antagonists sustain LTP and spatial memory: Active processes mediate LTP decay. *Nature Neuroscience, 5,* 48–52.

Walker, M. P. (2005). A refined model of sleep and the time course of memory formation. *Behavioral and Brain Sciences, 28*, 51–104.

Watkins, C., & Watkins, M. J. (1975). Buildup of proactive inhibition as a cue-overload effect. *Journal of Experimental Psychology: Human Learning and Memory, 1*, 442–452.

Weingartner, H. J., Sirocco, K., Curran, V., & Wolkowitz, O. (1995). Memory facilitation following the administration of the benzodiazepine triazolam. *Experimental and Clinical Psychopharmacology, 3*, 298–303.

Whitlock J. R., Heynen A. J., Schuler M. G., & Bear M. F. (2006). Learning induces long-term potentiation in the hippocampus. *Science, 313*, 1058–1059.

Wickelgren, W. A. (1974). Single-trace fragility theory of memory dynamics. *Memory and Cognition, 2*, 775–780.

Wilson, M. A., & McNaughton, B. L. (1994). Reactivation of hippocampal ensemble memories during sleep. *Science, 265*, 676–679.

Wixted, J. T. (2004a). On common ground: Jost's (1897) law of forgetting and Ribot's (1881) law of retrograde amnesia. *Psychological Review, 111*, 864–879.

Wixted, J. T. (2004b). The psychology and neuroscience of forgetting. *Annual Review of Psychology, 55*, 235–269.

Wixted, J. T., & Carpenter, S. K. (2007). The Wickelgren power law and the Ebbinghaus savings function. *Psychological Science, 18*, 133–134.

Wixted, J.T., & Ebbesen, E. (1991). On the form of forgetting. *Psychological Science, 2*, 409–415.

Xu, L., Anwyl, R., & Rowan, M. J. (1998). Spatial exploration induces a persistent reversal of long-term potentiation in rat hippocampus. *Nature, 394*, 891–894.

Yaroush, R., Sullivan, M. J., & Ekstrand, B. R. (1971). The effect of sleep on memory: II. Differential effect of the first and second half of the night. *Journal of Experimental Psychology, 88*, 361–366.

Zola-Morgan, S., & Squire, L. R. (1990). The primate hippocampal formation: Evidence for a time-limited role in memory storage. *Science, 250*, 288–290.

6

AUTOBIOGRAPHICAL FORGETTING, SOCIAL FORGETTING, AND SITUATED FORGETTING*

Forgetting in context

Celia B. Harris, John Sutton, and Amanda J. Barnier

Introduction

We have a striking ability to alter our psychological access to past experiences. Consider the following case. Andrew "Nicky" Barr, OBE, MC, DFC (1915–2006), was one of Australia's most decorated World War II fighter pilots. He was the top ace of the Western Desert's 3 Squadron, the pre-eminent fighter squadron in the Middle East, flying P-40 Kittyhawks over Africa. From October 1941, when Nicky Barr's war began, he flew 22 missions and shot down eight enemy planes in his first 35 operational hours. He was shot down three times, once 25 miles behind enemy lines while trying to rescue a downed pilot. He escaped from prisoner of war camps four times, once jumping out of a train as it travelled from Italy into Austria. His wife Dot, who he married only weeks before the war, waited for him at home. She was told on at least three occasions that he was missing in action or dead.

For 50 years, Nicky Barr never spoke publicly, and rarely privately, of his wartime experiences. He was very much a forgotten and forgetting hero (for further details, see Dornan, 2002). In his first public interview in 2002 on the Australian documentary program "Australian Story", Nicky explained his 50-year silence by saying:

> I think my reluctance [to talk] comes from a very definite desire to forget all about the war as quickly as I could. I was concerned about how the regurgitating of all the things that I didn't like, things I wasn't very proud about, the things I had to do in order to survive—how that would really impact on us. … We found we couldn't quite cope … the memories got on top. I didn't need to go through the business of discussing all my adventures … some of the things should have stayed forgotten.

Forgetting the past has received a great deal of attention in recent years, both inside and outside psychology (e.g., Connerton, 2008; Erdelyi, 2006; Golding & MacLeod, 1998; McNally, 2005; Schacter, 1996). While the events Barr strived to forget are extraordinary (at least to a generation who has not lived through war), his desire to forget is not. Functioning in our day-to-day lives involves, or perhaps even requires, forgetting. We forget and remember events from our past in a goal-directed, strategic way (Bjork, Bjork, & Anderson, 1998; Conway, 2005). Bjork et al. (1998) defined goal-directed forgetting as "forgetting that serves some implicit or explicit personal need" (p. 103). Despite this definition, forgetting is often equated with failure (see also Cubelli's chapter, in *Forgetting*. This is probably because of the influence of the computer metaphor of human memory, which sees human information processing as a sequence of steps where information is encoded, stored, and then retrieved. By this view, recall is expected to be perfect or verbatim, just as a computer can output on command completely and accurately the contents saved in its memory system. But for human memory, this is neither plausible nor functional. Rather, it may be functional to forget certain information that is irrelevant, redundant, out-of-date, damaging, or distressing (see also the chapter by Markowistch & Brand, in *Forgetting*). In the decade since this chapter was first published, there has been increasing research attention on "motivated forgetting" (Anderson & Hanslmayr, 2014), or "active forgetting" (Anderson & Hulbert, 2021), and particularly on the neural processes involved. Indeed, some research has noted that intentional forgetting can require more neural effort than remembering (Cheng et al., 2012), emphasizing the role of control processes in determining what we remember and what we forget.

In this chapter, we focus on autobiographical memory, which relates to events and experiences in our personal past. We focus in particular on autobiographical forgetting. Autobiographical remembering and forgetting serve a range of functions, especially in maintaining our identity (Conway, 2005; Nelson, 2003) and guiding our behaviour into the future (Pillemer, 2003). In this chapter, we also extend our discussion of forgetting to social memory, which occurs in conversation or community with other people. We focus in particular on social forgetting—both what is not recalled during joint remembering and what is forgotten subsequent to joint memory activities. Social remembering and forgetting serve a range of functions, such as establishing and maintaining relationships, teaching or entertaining others (Alea & Bluck, 2003), and supporting group identity (Sahdra & Ross, 2007).

Although remembering and forgetting may be functional for individuals, groups or societies, across each of these levels different (and possibly competing) functions may be more or less important. For example, in recent years younger Australians have become increasingly involved in commemorating our wartime heroes, especially on ANZAC Day (April 25; which is the anniversary of Australian and New Zealand troops landing on the Turkish Peninsula at Gallipoli in World War I) and especially as the last of our World War I veterans pass away.

Commentators have noted a swell in the social or national desire to remember these events and individuals: attendance at ANZAC Day ceremonies has surged, descendants of servicemen are marching in greater numbers in ANZAC Day parades, and each year more and more young Australian make the journey to Turkey to pay their respects at the site of the Gallipoli landing (Wilson, 2008). This contrasts with the individual desire of many veterans, such as Nicky Barr, to forget their wartime experiences. Some war veterans, for instance, avoided ANZAC Day marches and ceremonies entirely (see "Marcel Caux, 105", 2004). In other words, an individual's goal to forget may be threatened by a broader goal to remember (or vice versa).

Forgetting may occur for a number of reasons (see Cubelli's and Levy, Kuhl & Wagner's chapters, in *Forgetting*). In this chapter, we focus on the inability to retrieve information that has been successfully stored in memory. That is, we assume that both encoding and storage were successful, and that forgetting occurs at the retrieval stage. When a particular memory has been encoded and stored successfully but cannot be retrieved, there are at least two possible reasons: reduced memory accessibility and/or reduced memory availability (Tulving & Pearlstone, 1966; see also Kihlstrom & Barnhardt, 1993). Memories that are both available and accessible can be consciously brought to awareness, and can be indexed by explicit memory tests (tests that involve the conscious, intentional recall of target material; Schacter, 1987). Memories that are available but not currently accessible remain outside awareness but can influence ongoing behaviour, and can be indexed by implicit memory tests (tests that do not require conscious recall but where prior learning can aid performance, e.g., priming; Schacter, 1987). Although memories may be inaccessible in a particular context or on a particular recall occasion, they may become accessible in another context, with repeated retrieval attempts or with an appropriate cue (Rubin, 2007). Memories that are neither available nor accessible do not influence either conscious or unconscious processing, such that the likelihood of recalling these memories is low and they may be effectively lost over time.

Adopting a functional view of autobiographical memory (Conway, 2005), in this chapter we consider research that has extended studies of remembering and forgetting to a broad range of "memory cases" (Barnier, Sutton, Harris, & Wilson, 2008). We describe experimental paradigms for studying goal-directed forgetting in the laboratory, and review research extending these paradigms toward more auto-biographical remembering and forgetting and toward more social remembering and forgetting. Finally, we link these experimental findings to interdisciplinary work from social science and philosophy on autobiographical forgetting and social forgetting.

Autobiographical memory: Forgetting the personal past

The self-memory system

Autobiographical memories are our recollections of specific episodes from the past. Tulving (2002) described autobiographical remembering as "mental time travel", in which we relive the best, the worst, and the everyday occurrences of our lives. In the absence of significant disruption, we remember many things from our past. However, autobiographical memory is selective. We tend to remember events that place us in a good light, support our current self-image, or promote ongoing activities. And we try to forget—with varying success—memories of experiences that undermine the current self, contradict our beliefs, plans, and goals, and increase anxiety or other negative emotions (Conway, 2005; Conway & Pleydell-Pearce, 2000).

Conway (2005; Conway & Pleydell-Pearce, 2000) proposed the Self-Memory System (SMS) to describe the structure of autobiographical memory and the relationship between autobiographical memory and self-identity. In the SMS, people's knowledge about their lives is organized hierarchically across three levels of increasing specificity: lifetime periods (e.g., when I was in high school), general events (e.g., going to Maths class), and event-specific knowledge (e.g., the day I had our final Maths exam). A specific autobiographical memory is generated by a stable pattern of activation across all three levels of knowledge. However, the construction of this pattern of activation is constrained by executive control processes that coordinate access to the knowledge base and modulate output from it (Conway, 2005; Conway & Pleydell-Pearce, 2000). These control processes are termed the "working self". The working self can facilitate or inhibit retrieval of certain memories depending on current goals. In the SMS, goals influence the encoding, storage, and retrieval of information to determine the content and accessibility of autobiographical memories (Conway, 2005; see also Conway, Justice, & D'Argembeau, 2019).

Conway (2005; Conway, Singer, & Tagini, 2004) identified two fundamental principles underlying autobiographical memory. The first is "coherence", which refers to the need to maintain an integrated and consistent sense of one's life experiences. The second is "correspondence", which refers to the need for episodic memory to correspond with reality. These principles are not mutually exclusive. Rather, a balance between them is required for a functioning autobiographical memory system. This distinction between coherence and correspondence is not new. Bartlett (1932) emphasized that the purpose of remembering, particularly in a social context, is to share our impressions with others, so people are likely to construct and embellish upon their memories rather than generate a strictly accurate representation of what happened. Conway (2005) argued that over time, in long-term memory, coherence takes precedence over correspondence.

One main idea from the SMS is that what is remembered from our lives, and what in turn is forgotten, is determined by our current working self (the image of ourselves we have at any given time). As noted above, autobiographical memories that are consistent with the goals and values of our working self are prioritized for remembering, whereas memories that conflict with our working self are likely to be forgotten (Barnier, Conway, Mayoh, Speyer, Avizmil, & Harris, 2007; Conway, 2005; Conway & Pleydell-Pearce, 2000). Within the SMS model then, autobiographical forgetting is a goal-directed, executive process, where certain memories are actively gated from consciousness. Those memories that are irrelevant, inconsistent with current identity goals, or upsetting are particularly likely to be forgotten.

Studying autobiographical forgetting

Research within different traditions and paradigms supports the view that certain kinds of memories are forgotten in apparently goal-directed ways. For instance, diary studies have suggested that whereas people are more likely to forget events about themselves that are negative rather than positive, they are more likely to forget events about others that are positive rather than negative (Thompson, Skowronski, Larsen, & Betz, 1996; Walker, Skowronski, & Thompson, 2003). Also, people tend to organize their life story in terms of well-remembered turning points (Thorne, 2000), and forget events that are inconsistent with their current goals and motivations (Habermas & Bluck, 2000). In the clinical domain, some people with posttraumatic stress disorder deliberately and persistently try to forget memories of their trauma (Brewin, 1998), people with functional amnesia forget whole chunks or even their entire autobiographical history following a traumatic experience (Kihlstrom & Schacter, 1995), and people with a repressive coping style (low reported anxiety but high defensiveness) are much more likely to forget negative childhood events than nonrepressors and will actively suppress negative life events whether instructed to or not (Barnier, Levin, & Maher, 2004; Myers & Brewin, 1994).

In the next sections, we review three major experimental paradigms of goal-directed forgetting: retrieval-induced forgetting (Anderson, Bjork, & Bjork, 1994), directed forgetting (Bjork, 1970; Bjork et al., 1998), and think/no think (Anderson & Green, 2001). Directed forgetting is claimed to operate at the level of accessibility, temporarily reducing access to the memory. Retrieval-induced forgetting and think/no-think are claimed to operate on availability, degrading the memory representation itself (for a review of these paradigms and their claims, see Anderson 2005). Each of these paradigms has been adopted and extended to explore the functional nature of memory, for example by using emotional words as stimuli or by examining specific clinical populations. Studies of clinical populations are important because it has been suggested that people with certain disorders develop memory biases that can maintain their illnesses; that is, their functional remembering and forgetting becomes dysfunctional (Starr & Moulds, 2006). Each of these paradigms has been extended also (to varying degrees) to study the forgetting of autobiographical memories. Studies involving autobiographical material are important because they index the extent to which these paradigms can tell us about everyday remembering and forgetting.

Retrieval-induced forgetting

The retrieval-induced forgetting (RIF) paradigm developed by Anderson, Bjork, and Bjork (1994; see also Anderson, 2005) models the kind of forgetting that occurs unconsciously in response to competition between memories, by practising some memories at the expense of others. Imagine the woman who thinks of her wedding day, and consistently remembers the things that went according to, rather than contrary to, her careful plans. After repeated rehearsals of the things that went right, she is less likely to remember the things that went wrong. Hence, retrieval-induced forgetting avoids cluttering memory with information that is unwanted, redundant, or out-of-date.

In the standard paradigm, participants learn a set of category-exemplar pairs, such as "fruit-apple", "fruit-banana", "instrument-flute", and "instrument-violin". Participants are then presented with the cue "fruit-a" a number of times, and practise retrieving "apple" repeatedly when presented with this cue. Finally, participants are presented with the categories (fruit, instrument) and asked to recall all the exemplars for each one (see Figure 6.1). Typically, participants are less likely to recall "banana" than they are to remember "flute" or "violin". This is the RIF effect: retrieval practice reduces recall of unpractised exemplars from the practised category, relative to exemplars from an unpractised category. It has been suggested that when presented with "fruit-a" all the fruit exemplars are activated to some extent, and so successful retrieval practice of "apple" requires the inhibition of the competing, irrelevant fruit exemplar "banana". This means that "banana" is subsequently more difficult to recall than non-competing irrelevant information (like flute, violin), which was not activated during retrieval practice (see Bjork et al., 1998; see also Levy et al.'s chapter, in *Forgetting*). It has been argued the RIF impairs both memory accessibility and availability. This is supported by evidence showing that recall of unpractised, related exemplars is still inhibited when tested with a novel, independent cue (Anderson, 2005; Anderson & Spellman, 1995; but see MacLeod, Dodd, Sheard, Wilson, & Bibi, 2003 for a non-inhibitory account).

RIF is considered an automatic, inevitable consequence of practising one piece of information at the expense of another. But researchers have examined whether RIF effects are influenced by motivation. Generally, this has taken the form of comparing RIF for emotional (positive or negative) material with RIF for unemotional material (the standard paradigm uses neutral word pairs). The logic is that people might be motivated to forget certain types of information (e.g., negative information), and so might show greater RIF for these words. Alternatively, people might have difficulty forgetting such information (e.g., in certain clinical populations),

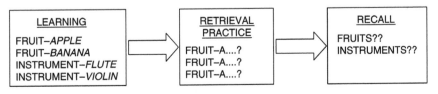

FIGURE 6.1 The retrieval-induced forgetting procedure (Anderson et al., 1994)

and so RIF may not occur for emotional material. In other words, are RIF effects selective consistent with the functional view of remembering and forgetting?

Moulds and Kandris (2006) investigated RIF of negative and neutral words in high and low dysphoric participants (dysphoria is a measure of negative mood, and is used as an analogue for depression in non-clinical samples). In general, high dysphoric participants tend to recall more negative than positive memories (Mineka & Nugent, 1995). However, Moulds and Kandris (2006) found that both high and low dysphoric participants showed RIF for neutral but not negative words; that is, in both groups negative words were not forgotten. Similarly, Kuhbandner, Bäuml, and Stiedl, (2009) examined RIF for negative pictures and found that the more intensely negative the picture was, the less likely participants were to show RIF for it; this was particularly so for participants in a negative mood. Relatedly, Amir, Coles, Brigidi, and Foa (2001) found that people with generalized social phobia showed RIF for non-social words and positive social words, but not for negative social words; in other words they had difficulty forgetting words that were particularly relevant to their phobia (category-exemplar pairs included, e.g., dating-rejection, dating-clumsy, conversation-babble, conversation-silence). Taken together, these results suggest that motivational factors do influence forgetting in the RIF paradigm: emotionally negative material may be less likely forgotten, and individual memory biases can moderate the effects of retrieval practice.

In updating our review, we note additional findings in the literature about the impact of emotional valence and memory biases on retrieval induced forgetting effects. Dehli and Brennan (2009) reported a RIF effect for neutral, but not positive or negative words. Kobayashi and Tanno (2013) reported RIF for neutral words but not negative words, noting that this was due to a reduced baseline in the negative condition. On the other hand, Barber and Mather (2012) reported similar RIF effects for emotional and neutral material, for both older and younger adults. Similarly, Kobayashi and Tanno (2015) found RIF effects for both negative and neutral word stimuli, when the retrieval practice involved semantic associates. Overall, with some exceptions, these findings continue to support the general conclusion that emotionality as well as individual characteristics and biases can influence RIF effects, such that RIF effects are not inevitable, but emotional material does not always abolish RIF effects. What then might this predict for RIF of autobiographical memories, which are not only emotional, but are meaningful, complex, and self-relevant?

Macrae and Roseveare (2002) suggested that the personal relevance of the information to be remembered vs. forgotten might influence RIF. In their study, participants learned a list of "gift" words by either imagining themselves purchasing the gift ("self" condition) or imagining another person purchasing the gift ("other" condition). Interestingly, whereas participants in the other condition showed a standard RIF effect, participants in the self condition did not; that is, participants did not forget the gifts they imagined themselves buying, even when these gifts competed for retrieval with practised items. Macrae and Roseveare (2002) argued that self-relevant material might be protected from RIF. Given that autobiograph-ical memories are by definition self-relevant (Conway, 2005), are they susceptible to RIF? Is RIF a good model of autobiographical forgetting?

To test this, Barnier, Hung, and Conway (2004) adapted the RIF paradigm to examine forgetting of positive, neutral, and negative autobiographical memories. In their procedure, participants elicited four memories for each of a number of cues such as "happy", "tidy", and "sickness". Subsequently, participants practised retrieving half their memories in response to half the cues, before being asked to remember all the memories for each cue. Barnier, Hung et al. (2004) found an overall RIF effect. Participants were less likely to recall unpractised memories that competed with practised memories than they were to recall baseline memories. That is, retrieval practice resulted in forgetting of competing, irrelevant autobio-graphical memories. However, in contrast to RIF research using words and other simple materials, Barnier, Hung et al. (2004) found that emotional valence of the memories did not influence the RIF effect. Rather, independent of retrieval prac-tice, participants were simply less likely to elicit and more likely to forget emotional than unemotional memories.

In a follow-up study, Wessel and Hauer (2006) replicated Barnier, Hung et al.'s (2004) finding of RIF for autobiographical memories. But unlike Barnier, Hung et al., however, they found RIF for negative but not positive memories. In con-trast, in a study of individuals experiencing normal and low mood, Harris et al. (2010) found that retrieval-induced forgetting occurred for negative but not posi-tive memories regardless of mood. Stone et al. (2013b) found RIF effects across both positive and negative autobiographical memories, but reported that practising related memories also reduced confidence in the accuracy of positive memories (mirroring the RIF effect), but actually increased confidence in negative memories (opposite to the RIF effect). Therefore the findings about emotion and forgetting of autobiographical memories remain mixed. It may be that manipulating memory valence—positive vs. negative. vs. neutral—does not fully capture memory biases (see Barnier et al., 2007; Harris et al., 2010), and that more subtle manipulations (such as whether memories are personally significant or not and whether memories are self-defining or not) may be required to determine when retrieval practice leads to forgetting of autobiographical memories.

Directed forgetting

The directed forgetting (DF) paradigm models the type of forgetting that occurs when we are explicitly instructed that certain information is unnecessary or unwanted (Bjork et al., 1998). This can occur when old information is updated with new, competing information. Imagine a jury is presented with one set of facts about a defendant, but then promptly told by a judge to forget this information and to focus on a new set of facts instead.

In the standard list-method directed forgetting (DF) paradigm, participants study two lists of words (List 1 and List 2). After studying List 1, half the participants

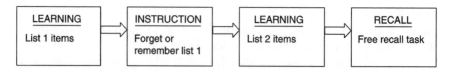

FIGURE 6.2 The list-method directed forgetting procedure (Bjork, 1970)

are told to forget List 1 items, and half are told to remember List 1 items. Both groups are told to remember List 2 items, which are subsequently presented (see Figure 6.2). Participants told to forget List 1 items recall fewer items from this list than participants told to remember List 1 items: this is the DF effect (Bjork et al., 1998). Notably, competition between to-be-forgotten (List 1) material and to-be-remembered (List 2) material is necessary for DF; there is no forgetting in the absence of List 2 learning (Bjork et al., 1998). DF impairs explicit memory while leaving implicit memory intact, as demonstrated by Basden, Basden, and Gargano (1993) using a word stem completion task. Also, DF can be abolished using a recognition test rather than a recall test (Basden et al, 1993; Bjork et al., 1998). Thus, it has been argued the DF impairs memory accessibility, but not availability, since these items can still be recalled given sufficient cues (as in a recognition task; but see Sahakyan & Delaney, 2005, for an alternative, non-inhibitory account of DF).

Like the RIF paradigm, researchers have examined whether DF effects are influenced by motivation. Again, this has generally taken the form of comparing DF for emotional (positive or negative) material with DF for unemotional material (for a review, see Koutstaal & Schacter, 1997). Are DF effects selective consistent with the functional view of remembering and forgetting? To test this Payne and Corrigan (2007), for example, examined DF of emotional and neutral pictures, and found a DF effect for neutral pictures but not for emotional pictures; that is, emotional stimuli were not forgotten. In contrast, Wessel and Merckelbach (2006) found DF effects for both emotional and unemotional words. More recently, Gamboa et al. (2017) reported significant DF effects for both neutral and negative stimuli, which was not influenced by giving participants mindfulness strategies to support their attentional control. As Payne and Corrigan (2007) argued, this might be because words are unlikely to elicit emotional responses in a normal population. Laying aside questions about the stimuli, Payne and Corrigan's (2007) findings, as well as some RIF findings, suggest that emotional material—particularly negative material—might be resistant to forgetting, although such findings are not universal. This conclusion is consistent with the functional, selective view of remembering and forgetting outlined above, although it remains controversial whether and why negative material would be particularly resistant to forgetting (Anderson & Levy, 2002; Brewin, 1998; Erdelyi, 2006; Kihlstrom, 2002, 2006; McNally, 2005).

Like RIF, much research on DF has focused on clinical populations. For example, Geraerts, Smeets, Jelicic, Merckelbach, and van Heerdan (2006b) compared DF of neutral words with DF of words associated with child sexual abuse in either participants who had reported continuous memories of abuse, participants who recovered memories of abuse, and control participants. Unexpectedly, all participants demonstrated less forgetting (no or reduced DF effects) for abuse-related words. This is similar to Payne and Corrigan's finding (2007), which suggested that emotional material may be immune to DF. In contrast, other researchers have reported that certain populations show more forgetting (greater DF effects) of negative material. For example, Moulds and Bryant (2002) examined patients with acute stress disorder. They found that these patients forgot more trauma-related words when given a forget instruction than controls (Moulds & Bryant, 2002). Myers, Brewin, and Power (1998) examined individuals with a repressive coping style (individuals characterized by low reported anxiety and high defensiveness). They found that repressive copers forgot more negative material when given a forget instruction than non-repressors (Myers et al., 1998). Similarly Myers and Derakshan (2004) found that repressive copers forgot more negative words when given a forget instruction than non-repressors, but only when they rated the words for self-descriptiveness; when they rated them for other descriptiveness there was no difference.

Taken together, these findings suggest that DF effects are selective: some research suggests that DF operates on all kinds of material, other research suggests that DF does not operate on emotional material, and still other research suggests that DF operates particularly for emotional material, and may depend on individuals' memory biases. Although, as suggested above for RIF, memory valence may not fully capture motivational effects on forgetting in the DF paradigm, these findings lead us to ask how DF (like RIF) might influence autobiographical memories.

Joslyn and Oakes (2005) conducted a diary study to examine this. They asked participants to record ten events from their lives each week over a two-week period. After one week, half the participants were told that the first week was for practice (Experiment 1), or that the first week memories were for a different experiment (Experiment 2). Finally, participants were asked to recall all the events they had recorded from both weeks. Joslyn and Oakes (2005) reported a significant DF effect; participants in the forget condition recalled fewer week one memories than participants in the remember condition. This effect occurred for positive and negative events, and for high intensity and low intensity events (Joslyn & Oakes, 2005). In a closer adaptation of the original DF procedure, Barnier et al. (2007) also examined directed forgetting of autobiographical memories. In our adaptation, participants elicited autobiographical memories in response to cue words such as "happy" and "sickness". Halfway through the words, participants were either told to forget or remember the first list, before eliciting memories for a second set of cues (List 2). Barnier et al. (2007) found a DF effect for positive, negative, and neutral autobiographical memories, although neutral memories were more likely forgotten overall than emotional memories. This contrasts with Barnier, Hung et al.'s (2004) findings for RIF, where emotional memories were *more* likely forgotten overall than neutral memories. Again, more targeted manipulations, such as whether memories are personally significant or not and whether memories are self-defining or not might help us to better understand these different patterns for emotional and unemotional memories (as well as emotional and unemotional simple material) and better capture the goal-directed nature of remembering and forgetting. Indeed, more recent research suggests that self-referential processing reduces or abolishes DF effects (Mao et al., 2017; Yang et al., 2013).

Think/no-think

The think/no-think paradigm models the kind of forgetting that occurs when we intentionally suppress or avoid remembering in response to strong reminders of a particular event (Anderson & Green, 2001; Levy & Anderson, 2002). Imagine a man who associates a particular song with an unhappy love affair. Each time he hears the song, he tries to avoid thinking of the failed relationship, and over time, he remembers less.

In this paradigm, participants learn a series of cue-target pairs (e.g. "ambition-ballet", "ordeal-roach", "fuss-poodle"). Subsequently, in the think/no-think phase, participants are presented with some of the cue words again. In this phase, for half the cues (e.g. "ambition") participants recall the associated target, and for half the cues (e.g. "ordeal") participants avoid letting the target come into their mind (see Figure 6.3). On a final cued recall test, Anderson and Green (2001) found that participants recalled fewer targets that they suppressed (e.g. "roach") than baseline targets (items that did not appear at all in the think/no-think phase, e.g. "poodle"). They concluded that this procedure might model Freudian repression, by showing that deliberate attempts to suppress may result in forgetting (Anderson & Levy, 2002; but see Kihlstrom, 2002; see also Erdelyi, 2006; Kihlstrom, 2006). TNT has been argued to impair both memory accessibility and availability. This is supported by evidence that participants show poorer recall for suppressed items even when recall is cued with a novel cue (e.g., "insect" for "roach"; Anderson & Green, 2001).

While some researchers have replicated the forgetting effect following suppression in this paradigm (for review, see Levy & Anderson, 2008), others have had difficulty. For example, across three attempted replications with increasingly precise adherence to Anderson and Green's (2001) original procedure, Bulevich, Roediger, Balota, and Butler (2006) failed to find a TNT effect. It is worth noting that, compared to RIF and DF, the magnitude of the TNT effect is quite small

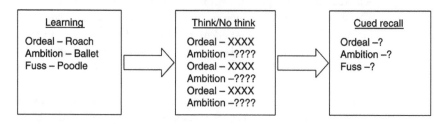

FIGURE 6.3 The think/no-think procedure (Anderson & Green, 2001)

(Anderson & Green, 2001; Levy & Anderson, 2008). Hertel and Calcaterra (2005) argued that the use of particular strategies during suppression may predict successful forgetting in TNT. They replicated the TNT effect only when participants used the strategy of thinking about an alternate word during suppression, either because they were instructed to do so or did so spontaneously (but see Levy & Anderson, 2008).

Like RIF and DF, some researchers have examined motivational influences on TNT; does TNT differentially impact recall of emotional material? Depue, Banich, and Curran (2006) compared TNT for negative and neutral stimuli, and found stronger forgetting effects for negative stimuli. They argued that cognitive control processes may be activated more strongly for emotional information. Although this finding is consistent with a functional view of forgetting, it contrasts with the mixed findings for emotional material in the RIF and DF paradigms. Also, like RIF and DF, other researchers have focused on whether specific populations might show stronger or weaker TNT effects. For example, Joormann, Hertel, LeMoult, and Gotlib (2009) examined TNT of positive and negative words in depressed and non-depressed participants. They found that, while non-depressed participants forgot positive and negative words they had suppressed, depressed participants did not show forgetting of negative words. However, when trained to think of an alternate word during suppression (as in Hertel & Calcaterra, 2005), depressed participants successfully forgot negative words. More recently, Noreen et al. (2020) reported that participants who were low in working memory and higher in depression symptoms showed weaker TNT effects, suggesting that individual differences might impact on effective suppression abilities. Finally, Noreen et al. (2014) gave participants hypothetical scenarios to read and to rate whether they would forgive a transgressor in each one. Following a suppression instruction, Noreen et al. (2014) found that people showed TNT effects for scenarios where they had forgiven the transgressor but not when they had not forgiven. These results suggest that both motivations and strategies may determine the success of suppression in the TNT paradigm.

As with RIF and DF, we have explored whether TNT influences autobiographical memories, using a similar adaptation. In a series of experiments that adapted the TNT procedure to autobiographical memories (similar to our adaptations of RIF and DF), we asked participants to generate autobiographical memories in response to cue words. Then, participants were presented with some of the words, half of which they responded to by recalling the associated memory, and half of which they avoided by suppressing the associated memory. To date, we have conducted five experiments. In the first, participants completed three suppression cycles during the TNT phase. In the second, participants completed 12 suppression cycles. In the third, we instructed participants to think about an alternative memory during suppression (as in Hertel & Calcaterra, 2005). In the fourth, we introduced competition between the memories: participants elicited six memories to each of six cues (as in the RIF paradigm, see Barnier, Hung et al., 2004), so that the respond memories directly competed for recall with the unwanted avoid memories via a shared cue. In our final experiment, we combined 12 suppression trials, a distraction condition, and a cue structure that created competition between the memories, plus a delay between memory elicitation and the TNT phase to reduce overall recall. We also asked participants about their life experiences, particularly about their exposure to trauma and attempts to suppress memories of this trauma in their daily lives (as suggested by Levy & Anderson, 2008). We have had difficulty finding a robust TNT effect. Overall, participants remember their autobiographical events despite repeated attempts to suppress (their memory performance is mostly at ceiling). However, introducing competition between the memories decreased memory overall and may have aided suppression (at least for a subset of participants) and in our most recent experiment, there is some indication that trauma exposure may predict suppression success (Levy & Anderson, 2008). More recently, Noreen and MacLeod (2013) did find TNT effects for positive and negative autobiographical memories, where participants recalled fewer details associated with memories they had intentionally suppressed, as well as slower recall latencies, suggesting that TNT effects can extend to autobiographical material.

Results with TNT are interesting in light of work in the related "thought suppression" paradigm (Wegner, Schneider, Carter, & White, 1987). In our lab, in a thought suppression study comparing repressive copers and nonrepressors, we found that nonrepressors were able to suppress positive memories during a suppression period, but experienced a rebound effect following suppression; they were unable to suppress negative memories at all (Barnier, Levin, & Maher, 2004). In other words, nonrepressors' initial suppression success, at least for positive memories, did not result in later forgetting, which contrasts with findings from the TNT paradigm. However, repressive copers were particularly successful in suppressing negative events, even when they weren't instructed to do so (Barnier, Levin, et al., 2004; see also Geraerts, Merckelbach, Jelicic, & Smeets, 2006a), and they showed no rebound effect (but see Geraerts et al., 2006a). This is similar to findings from the TNT paradigm. Thus, it remains unclear when and why suppression (whether in TNT or thought suppression) might result in successful forgetting of autobiographical memories.

More recently, Noreen and MacLeod (2013) did find TNT effects for positive and negative autobiographical memories, where participants recalled fewer details associated with memories they had intentionally suppressed, as well as slower recall latencies.

Conclusion

Based on this review, it is clear that the effects of RIF, DF, and TNT paradigms extend from the simple materials used to develop the original methodologies, to emotional words and sometimes to autobiographical memories. However, as the material increases in complexity (emotionality and personal meaningfulness) so do the effects. These paradigms can be argued to model different mechanisms of goal-directed forgetting and provide good laboratory analogues for everyday, real-world forgetting. As noted above, one assumption of a functional view of memory is that people might try to forget negatively valenced or upsetting memories. In general, results across these paradigms suggest that sometimes people remember more emotional than unemotional material, sometimes they remember as much, and sometimes they forget more emotional material than unemotional. This implies that in remembering and forgetting the past, people are not just influenced by the simple valence of a piece of information or of an event. Likely there are other dimensions predicting its self-relevance, and thus, whether it is prioritized for remembering or forgetting.

Social forgetting: Forgetting with others

While memory is motivated by individual goals such as maintaining a positive identity, it is also motivated by social goals such as promoting group cohesion, enhancing relationships, negotiating the meaning of shared experiences, and planning joint action or projects (Alea & Bluck, 2003; Barnier, et al., 2008). For instance, consider the following excerpts from interviews with two long-married couples who we asked (both individually and jointly) to describe their autobiographical memories and their remembering practices. One couple, married for 35 years, remembered together in a genuinely shared way, dynamically constructing the past, and often speaking directly to each other rather than to the interviewers. In his individual interview, the husband described the role of remembering in their relationship:

Interviewer: How often do you talk about the past together with [wife]?
Husband: A lot. We're big talkers. That has always been a big point of our lives, still is!

In contrast, another couple, who had recently experienced marital difficulties, did not seem to jointly remember in an efficient manner. The wife, in her individual interview, described how recent difficulties in their relationship had resulted in less day-to-day reminiscing with her husband:

Interviewer. Do you tend to reminisce together?
Wife. Not as much as we used to.
Interviewer. OK, so it's kind of changed you think.
Wife. Yeah I do. Yeah there were some circumstances that changed it, a couple of years ago, which were really not, not happy for me, and not happy for him.

Insights from these interviews support our view that studying social influences on remembering and forgetting is a natural extension of the functional approach to autobiographical memory.

We are likely to discuss a whole range of events with others: recent and distant, significant and mundane, shared and unshared. However, just as individual autobiographical memory is selective and goal-directed, social memory is also likely to be selective, depending on the norms and values of the group that might prioritize certain items for retrieval and others for forgetting. The social context might also shape what is remembered and what is forgotten more subtly, by dictating the appropriate style and contents of recall, the social dynamics of who speaks when and whose recollections are given the most weight, and the purpose of remembering (Weldon & Bellinger, 1997). According to Schudson (1995, p. 360), people remember "collectively, publicly and interactively", in the sense that remembering occurs for a particular audience and with input from that audience. Listeners' responses can guide what is recalled during conversation (Pasupathi, 2001), and recalling selectively in a social context can shape subsequent individual memory (Tversky & Marsh, 2000). Based on these ideas, autobiographical memory has been labelled "relational" (Campbell, 2003). It originates with an individual's experience of an event but is maintained, shaped, and elaborated through interaction with others (Hayne & MacDonald, 2003), as well as through individual identity goals.

In terms of forgetting, the selective nature of social remembering suggests that information that conflicts not just with individual goals, but also with social goals, is unlikely to be recalled during conversation. Fivush (2004) described "silencing", the self- or other-censorship that can occur when recalling the past with others. She argued that this silencing during social interaction can cause subsequent forgetting of material that was not mentioned during the conversation (Fivush, 2004). Thus, social influence may cause forgetting, particularly of memories that conflict with the group's goals. An alternative (but not conflicting) view is that social influence may reduce forgetting by providing social support for memory, and we elaborate further on this later in the chapter. We do not focus on social influences on misremembering, which have been extensively studied and are covered in detail elsewhere (see Loftus, 2005 for a review).

Studying social forgetting

Social aspects of remembering and forgetting have received a great deal of attention from psychologists, at least since Bartlett's (1932) *Remembering*. In the developmental domain, researchers have focused on how parents talk to children about the past and teach them the narrative structures of autobiographical remembering (Reese & Fivush, 2008). In the forensic domain, researchers have examined how eyewitnesses influence each others' memories, and whether interactions between witnesses can distort later testimony (Paterson & Kemp, 2006). In the organizational domain, researchers have focused on how groups coordinate performance to enhance workplace productivity (Brandon & Hollingshead, 2004). In contrast, cognitive psychology has traditionally been more individualistic in its approach to studying memory, and it is only relatively recently that cognitive, experimental paradigms have been developed to examine how remembering with others is different to remembering alone. Below, we review two major experimental paradigms that have been used to study social forgetting in the laboratory. The first is socially shared retrieval-induced forgetting, which is an extension of the RIF paradigm into a social context (Cuc, Koppel, & Hirst, 2007). The second is collaborative recall, which was developed to directly measure how what is remembered and forgotten in a group compares to what is remembered and forgotten by the same number of individuals recalling alone (Weldon & Bellinger, 1997). These paradigms demonstrate the ways in which individual and social processes combine to influence both remembering and forgetting.

Socially shared retrieval-induced forgetting (SS-RIF)

The RIF paradigm (described in the previous section) has been extended to examine forgetting in a social context. This paradigm models the kind of forgetting that is the result of selective remembering in conversation with others. Imagine a politician who repeatedly directs her audience's attention to her successful, popular policies, and avoids mentioning her unpopular policies and scandals. She might hope that this would cause her listeners to subsequently forget her misdeeds. Cuc et al. (2007) argued that the selective remembering that happens in a conversation (where only information consistent with conversational goals is mentioned; Tversky & Marsh, 2000) is a form of retrieval practice that should result in forgetting of unpractised, related information.

To test this, Cuc et al. (2007) replicated the standard RIF procedure of Anderson et al. (1994) but introduced a "listener" who observed the "speaker's" retrieval practice and monitored them for either accuracy or fluency. Speakers showed RIF as expected. Most importantly, listeners showed RIF as well but only when they monitored the speaker's accuracy, presumably because this encouraged listeners to perform the retrieval practice themselves as they observed the speaker. To examine whether SS-RIF might also operate in a natural discussion, where participants were not explicitly instructed to monitor for accuracy and where the role of speaker and listener shifted back and forth, in a second experiment Cuc et al. (2007) modified the SS-RIF procedure so that the retrieval practice phase consisted of a free-flowing conversation between two participants. They found that both speaker and listener showed RIF (Cuc et al., 2007). Thus, SS-RIF appears to be one plausible explanation for forgetting in social interactions, and in our lab we are currently extending this effect to autobiographical memories. This research suggests that the content of a conversation could be shaped either intentionally or unintentionally to induce forgetting of unwanted information. In this way, social interaction could lead to individual forgetting (Hirst & Manier, 2008).

More recently, SS-RIF has been extended to apply to autobiographical and emotional material as well as clinical populations. This includes people's memories for their experience of a highly emotional and impactful event (the 9/11 terrorist attack on the World Trade Center in New York; Coman et al., 2009). Stone et al. (2013b) found SS-RIF effects for positive, neutral, and negative autobiographical memories, regardless of memory valence, extending Barnier et al.'s (2004) paradigm to social interaction. Brown et al. (2012) found that people with PTSD showed SS-RIF for combat-relevant and neutral stimuli, but showed stronger forgetting for combat-relevant stimuli (unlike effects reported above for RIF, where clinically relevant stimuli tend to be immune to forgetting). In SS-RIF, there are additional motivational effects beyond the self-relevance of the information; namely, the relationship between the individuals in the social interaction. Coman and Hirst (2015) found that SS-RIF effects only occurred for a pair of in-group members (fellow Princeton students), but not for out-group members. Similarly, Barber and Mather (2012) found SS-RIF effects for same-gender but not mixed-gender pairs. Thus, social interactions can shape memory even for personal, emotional, autobiographical material, but depends on individual characteristics as well as relationship and similarity between group members.

Collaborative recall

Another major experimental paradigm used to measure the impact of recalling the past with others is collaborative recall (Basden, Basden, Bryner, & Thomas, 1997; Blumen & Rajaram, 2008; Finlay, Hitch, & Meudell, 2000; Weldon & Bellinger, 1997), which was designed to assess the "costs and benefits" of remembering in a group (Basden, Basden, & Henry, 2000; for review, see Harris, Paterson, & Kemp, 2008). Collaborative recall models the kind of remembering and forgetting that occurs around the dinner table when a family reminisces about the last holiday they took together. In this paradigm, the recall performance of collaborative groups (people recalling together) is compared to the recall performance of nominal groups (the pooled recall of the same number of individuals recalling alone; see Figure 6.4). We might assume that recalling with others should help our individual performance. But the opposite is true. Research on collaborative recall has consistently demonstrated that collaborative groups recall less than nominal groups; this effect is termed "collaborative inhibition" (Weldon & Bellinger, 1997; Basden et al., 2000).

The best supported explanation for collaborative inhibition is the retrieval strategy disruption hypothesis: recalling information in a group disrupts each individual's retrieval strategies, making them less efficient (Basden et al., 1997). That is, recalling with others results in each individual forgetting items that they would have been able to recall alone. Evidence for this account comes from research showing that collaborative inhibition is abolished when each group member is responsible for recalling a different part of a categorized list (Basden et al., 1997). Also, collaborative inhibition is abolished when recall is cued (Finlay et al. 2000), when group members are forced to organize their recall by category (and hence, presumably, use the same retrieval strategies, Basden et al., 1997), or when group members are unable to hear or see the items recalled by other group members (Wright & Klumpp, 2004). Essentially, collaborative inhibition is abolished when individuals in a group remember not as a group, but as individuals, that is, when the group cannot hinder, but also cannot help, recall.

Collaboration has ongoing influences on individual memory. Prior collaboration results in an inhibition of hypermnesia; participants who have collaborated are subsequently more likely to recall items mentioned in the collaboration, but less likely to recall new items from the original list (Basden et al., 2000). That is, collaboration shapes subsequent individual recall, both in terms of remembering (mentioned

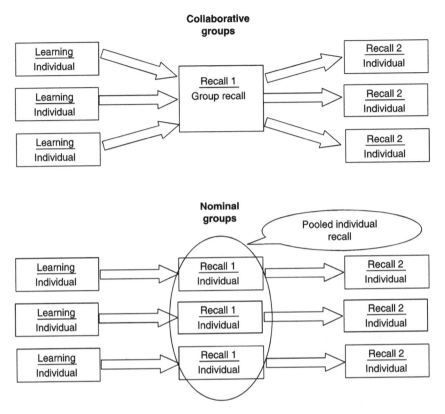

FIGURE 6.4 The collaborative recall procedure (Basden, et al., 2000)

items) and forgetting (unmentioned items). Interestingly, recent results from our lab suggest that collaboration can improve accuracy (if not amount recalled), both during collaboration and on subsequent individual tests, but only when collaborating groups are instructed to reach a consensus about each item recalled (Harris, Barnier, & Sutton, 2012).

Much like standard RIF, DF, and TNT, most of the research on collaborative recall has focused on relatively neutral material. If remembering with others does influence what we remember and forget, we might expect this influence to operate particularly for important or emotional memories, when recalling with our social groups (e.g., family, friends) or when recalling shared events. In terms of emotional events, Yaron-Antar and Nachson (2006) examined whether collaboration impaired recall of the details of the assassination of Israeli Prime Minister Rabin. It still did; collaborative groups still showed collaborative inhibition. In terms of recalling with our social groups, studies of whether collaborative inhibition is reduced or abolished when in groups of acquaintances have yielded mixed results: Andersson and Rönnberg (1995) reported less collaborative inhibition for groups of friends, while Gould, Osborn, Krein, and Mortenson (2002) reported no difference between married and unacquainted dyads. Other aspects of the group, apart from familiarity, may also be important in determining the outcomes of collaboration. Social and motivational factors—such as whether the interaction is face-to-face or electronic, and the perceived output level of the group—impact the amount remembered and forgotten by the individuals in a group (Ekeocha & Brennan, 2008; Reysen, 2003). Notably, in a recent study of collaboration between expert pilots, who are skilled at communicating in order to perform tasks together, Meade, Nokes, and Morrow (2009) found facilitation not inhibition. In terms of shared and unshared events, we recently conducted a study of collaborative recall among friends and strangers, who either encoded information together or individually. Our results suggest that, when information is encoded individually, collaboration results in inhibition for both groups of strangers and groups of friends. But when information is encoded as a group, collaboration results in no inhibition for groups of strangers or groups of friends (Harris, Barnier, & Sutton, 2009).

In an extension of the collaborative recall paradigm to memory for personal experiences, we examined how conversation about a shared, significant event might shape memory for and feelings about that event (Harris, Barnier, Sutton, & Keil, 2010). Following the sudden death of Australian celebrity, "Crocodile Hunter" Steve Irwin, we asked participants to come to the lab and either discuss their memories for hearing of Irwin's death in a group of three, or to spend time thinking about their memory alone. We indexed participants' memories for and feelings about the event on three occasions—before the discussion phase, one week later, and one month later. We found that, during discussion, references to personally being upset by Irwin's death were silenced. Consider the following excerpt from a group conversation between a female participants (K) and two male participants (M and E):

K: I know people that cried when they were watching the memorial service when Bindi was doing her speech.
M: Yeah, that was really sad! I don't know anybody who actually cried …
E: Did you cry?
K: Can't say that I did.
E: Do you know anybody that cares at all?
M: I don't think a lot of people …
K. I think people feel bad for him. A lot of people.
E. People die every day.

This excerpt illustrates the process of negotiation that occurred during conversations, such that personal emotion was silenced. This silencing influenced subsequent memory—participants who discussed their memory reduced their ratings of how upset they had been when they heard the news, relative to participants who thought about the event alone. In this case, discussion resulted in forgetting of emotion, rather than the factual details of the event. Indeed more recent research supports the view that collaboration selectively reduces remembered negative emotion (Maswood et al., 2019). While the collaborative recall paradigm suggests that remembering with others results in forgetting, our research suggests that this forgetting is targeted—that collaboration may result in forgetting of specific aspects of an event depending on the group norms that emerge during discussion (Harris et al., 2010). That is, social motivations, such as fitting into a group of peers or agreeing with others, can drive what is remembered and forgotten, even for emotional events that are well remembered (cf. Fivush, 2004) In the last ten years, studies of social remembering in various domains within psychology as well as across disciplines have flourished (see Meade, Harris, Van Bergen, Sutton, & Barnier, 2018).

Conclusion

Overall, research on SS-RIF and collaborative recall suggests that a range of individual and social factors can influence what is remembered and what is forgotten when people talk about the past together. This research highlights that laboratory paradigms of individual and social forgetting can be extended to examine more complex questions about ways in which our social interactions influence what we remember and what we forget.

Situated forgetting: Forgetting in context

As mainstream cognitive psychology has moved toward the functional (constructive, motivated, selective) view of remembering that we have described, it has increasingly stressed the central role of the "context" in determining what is remembered vs. forgotten. So far we have highlighted two aspects of the remembering context that might influence forgetting: individual motivations and goals, and social motivations and goals. In this section, we discuss a view of forgetting where context plays an even more pivotal role: situated forgetting. Over the last 20 years, philosophers of cognitive science have proposed that human cognitive processing is "hybrid": including not only the individual brain and body, but also the environment with its social and technological resources. This view has been labelled as "situated", "distributed", "extended", or "embedded" cognition, proposing that an individual's neural system does not act in causal isolation from its environmental and social context (see Barnier et al., 2008; Michaelian & Sutton, 2013).

Distributed cognition and situated forgetting

Within the situated cognition framework, the human brain is seen as embedded in and extended into its world (Clark & Chalmers, 1998; Wheeler, 2005), where it rarely performs cognitive operations in isolation. Rather, intelligent action is conceptualized as the outcome of the cooperation or "coupling" of neural, bodily and external systems in complex webs of "continuous reciprocal causation" (Clark 1997, pp. 163–6). Applying this framework to memory, philosophers argue that humans augment their relatively unstable individual memories, which are not typically stored as discrete, fully-formed units but as distributed representations, with more stable external "scaffolding" (Sutton, 2015a; Wilson, 2005). They form temporarily integrated larger cognitive systems that incorporate distinct, but complementary, internal and external components. As Andy Clark puts it, "our brains make the world smart so that we can be dumb in peace" (Clark, 1997, p. 180). Memory systems are seen as extending the natural, technological, and social environment. This approach builds on Bartlett's (1932) work on remembering as the context-dependent compiling of materials from changing "interest-carried traces"; Vygotsky's (1978) analysis of how children's memory is transformed as they incorporate the ability to use artificial signs and cultural operations; and Halbwachs's (1980) stress on "the necessity of an affective community" in structuring and maintaining memory. A rich interdisciplinary literature now seeks to update and implement these ideas (Bietti & Sutton, 2015; Brown & Reavey, 2015; Donald, 1991; Heersmink, 2018; Hirst & Manier, 2008; Nelson, 2003; Rowlands, 1999; Rubin, 1995; Sutton, 2015b; Wagoner, Brescó de Luna, & Zadeh, 2020; Welzer & Markowitsch, 2005; Wertsch, 2002).

Most discussions of situated or distributed cognition have focused on the way an individual's memory system might extend to incorporate various technologies. For instance, an abstract artist may work incessantly with a sketchpad because imagining an artwork *in the mind's eye* will not successfully allow the perception, creation, and transformation of the right aesthetic patterns (van Leeuwen, Verstijnen, & Hekkert, 1999). The sketchpad isn't just a convenient storage bin for pre-existing visual images: the ongoing externalizing and reperceiving is an intrinsic part of artistic cognition itself (Clark, 2001). Other frequently cited examples include the tools and objects used to process orders in a café, the notes and records used to write an academic paper, or the use of particular glasses by bartenders in remembering cocktail orders (Beach, 1988; Clark, 1997; Hutchins, 1995; Kirsh, 2006).

More recently, a growing body of research in cognitive psychology has examined the interaction between external resources and the remembering and forgetting that happens within the heads of individuals (Finley et al., 2018). Some of this research reiterates the assumptions that outsourcing memory to external resources and external storage—replacing internal storage—represents a negative outcome, a memory failure. For instance, recent findings suggest that taking photos during experiences reduce individuals' abilities to accurately recall details later (Henkel, 2014), labelled the "photo-taking impairment effect" (Soares & Storm, 2018). But in such studies, participants are not allowed to review or interact with these photos, and other research on automatic cameras suggests photos can provide valuable memory cues for people with memory impairments (Loveday & Conway, 2011). Sparrow et al. (2011) found that people who could save information for later had impaired memory for the contents of the information but enhanced memory for where to find it, suggesting that external tools can shape the value of different kinds of information for internal memory.

In this context, forgetting can be seen as complementary to remembering. The storage of information which is less self-relevant or which is computationally costly might be offloaded onto the world, so that individuals can safely forget some information that they would have to hold internally if the environment was less structured or stable (see also Risko & Gilbert, 2016). Nevertheless, it is fair to say that researchers' focus has generally been on how situated memory, memory extended beyond the brain, can reduce forgetting. There has been less discussion of ways in which the use of objects may promote forgetting of material that is redundant, unnecessary, or unwanted, consistent with the increasingly clearly articulated view of forgetting as active and motivated when applied to internal individual memory within cognitive science (e.g., Anderson & Hulbert, 2021). The functional approach to remembering and forgetting recognizes that what and how we forget is as important as what and how we remember. More work could be done to identify how people use technological resources to manage the balance between remembering and forgetting, and what kinds of new technologies could support the maintenance of this balance rather than a "store everything" approach.

An individual's memory is also situated more broadly in their physical and cultural environment. Broader cultural symbols—such as museums, memorials, and monuments—may serve to shape and support an individual's memory, which is seen in these interdisciplinary literatures as notoriously fallible. These external objects are considered relatively stable and secure supplements to our internal storage systems. By this view, because neural processes are active, constructive, and selective, we rely on information outsourced to more enduring and unchanging cultural symbols (Clark, 1998; Donald, 1998). Similar to the research on memory-supporting technologies, research has focused mostly on how cultural symbols promote remembering, with less discussion of the balance between remembering and forgetting.

There are some notable exceptions however, which promise an interesting integration of approaches to forgetting from the social sciences and from cognitive psychology (Connerton, 2008; Erdelyi, 2008; Singer & Conway, 2008; Wessel & Moulds, 2008). Objects that act as cultural symbols are not always intended to persist unchanged, and even those that are intended to last may not do so (Bowker 2005; Malafouris 2004; Sutton 2008b). By preserving or highlighting certain features of the past, or rendering others open to dispute or renegotiation, cultural symbols can act as agents of forgetting. This is most obvious in cases of "repressive erasure" (Connerton 2008, pp. 60–61) such as the politically motivated airbrushing of a person from a photograph (e.g., the case of Vladimír Clementis described by Milan Kundera; Kundera 1980). But objects can also play more subtle roles in encouraging forgetting. In certain African and Melanesian cultures, for example, some artifacts and structures "are made only to be abandoned immediately to decay", ephemeral monuments which may be the means by which "the members of the society get rid of what they no longer need or wish to remember" (Forty 1999, pp. 4–5). In the Melanesian society described by Küchler (1999), an elaborate memorial device called a "malangann" is carved after someone's death. But instead of being installed as a permanent physical reminder, it stands on the grave for one night only before being abandoned or destroyed. Likewise, while places, buildings, or other physical locations do often support remembering, acting as key features of the cognitive (and affective and social) environment in which we reinstate or reconstruct the past, geographical sites too are vulnerable to change, reinterpretation, or erasure (Casey, 1987, 1992). In many projects of "urban renewal", for example, the physical destruction of existing communities is accompanied by a loss of the memories and traditions of the neighbourhoods in question, leaving only partial clues in a land-scape of scars (Klein, 1997).

Socially situated forgetting and transactive memory

In our own work, we particularly focus on one form of situated or extended memory: how memory is shared among people in social groups. We investigate how small groups influence individual memory and how this reliance on the group may, in turn, lead to collective memory that is more than the sum of individual memories. Social influences on memory can be seen as so pervasive that some have argued that memory is inherently social and individual memory does not exist. For instance, Halbwachs (1980) suggested that, even when we are superficially alone, we carry our groups with us, so that nothing much like memory at all would be left if all the social contexts of autobiographical remembering were truly stripped away. This view may seem extreme, especially to cognitive psychologists, but it draws our attention to theoretical accounts that try to reconcile individual and social memory, and within which we might place our laboratory studies of forgetting (see also Barnier et al., 2008; Sutton, 2009; Tollefsen, 2006; Wilson, 2005).

For example, some theorists highlight the specific social and narrative envir-onments in which we first learn to think and talk about the past. These envir-onments, each with their own norms and dynamics, influence the subsequent selection principles and style of our own spontaneous remembering (Fivush 2019; Wang 2013). Other theorists argue that, as adults, "sharing memories is our default" (Campbell, 2008, p. 43; Sutton, 2009). Where there is a rich shared history of joint actions in a couple or a small group, this history of interactions and negotiations dictates what is most commonly and comfortably forgotten or passed over, and in what contexts. The common ground on which successful communication within a dyad or a group rests is itself partly constituted by shared memories, and in turn underlies the members' ongoing ways of about the past whether together or alone.

The theory of transactive memory, developed by Wegner and colleagues, emphasizes the potential benefits of sharing memories, and gives rise to a clear picture of the interpersonal dimensions of forgetting. A transactive memory system is a combination of the information held by the individuals in a group, and the communication processes that occur between them: transactive memory is a real property of the group, not merely the sum of its component members, because information is often transformed as it is encoded, modified, and retrieved across the distributed but coordinated system (Wegner, Giuliano, & Hertel, 1985; Wegner, 1986; Tollefsen, 2006). For example, as a couple struggle to recall information about something they did together years before, they may exchange suggestions (often partial or idiosyncratic) in an iterative process of interactive cueing which may, in the extreme, be the only way that either of them could have produced the item sought (Wegner, Giuliano, & Hertel, 1985, p. 257). Consider the following exchange from one of our own interviews with a couple who jointly discussed their honeymoon 40 years before.

Wife: And we went to two shows, can you remember what they were called?
Husband: We did. One was a musical, or were they both? I don't … no … one …
Wife: John Hanson was in it.
Husband: *Desert Song*.
Wife: *Desert Song*, that's it, I couldn't remember what it was called, but yes, I knew John Hanson was in it.
Husband: Yes.

This is a particularly striking example because neither member of the couple can remember the name of the show individually (they have both forgotten). Yet through a process of communicative cross-cueing the couple as a group can recall this information. Thus, the other person in such a long-standing and successful transactive system is a crucial component of the retrieval context. We have reported substantial benefits of shared remembering in couples in several more recent studies, consistent with the predictions of transactive memory theory and in contrast with typical findings of collaborative inhibition for laboratory groups (Barnier et al., 2018; Harris et al., 2011; Harris et al., 2017; Harris et al., 2019; Selwood, 2020).

Transactive memory theory focuses on the way in which socially shared remembering supports memory, and by extension, protects against forgetting. One application of transactive memory to problems of forgetting is in the arena of social-cognitive supports for memory in aging (Dixon, 1996). In transactive memory theory, the fact that I do not store certain detailed memories internally does not equate to memory failure, since the relevant information might still be accessible given the right reliable remembering environment, such as being in the company of my spouse (as in the example described above). "I forget" does not entail "we forget". As long as I retain sufficient "labelling" information about the location of the information, and as long as the external storage is in fact available, retrieval success can be achieved within the context of a broader transactive system. What would look like a failure of individual memory, particularly when people are tested in isolation from their usual contexts and supports, can in fact be a functional, computationally efficient distributed system (Wegner, 1986, p. 189).

Notably, transactive memory theory predicts that changes or disruptions to the remembering system should result in forgetting for the people who make up the group. This is the case in the breakdown of intimate relationships, for example, when an individual can no longer "count on access to a wide range of storage in their partner" and when their partner is no longer around to reinstate the settings of to-be-recalled experience (Wegner, 1986, p. 201). Further, one "loses access to the differentiated portion of transactive memory held by the other", so that in the extreme "because transactive retrieval is no longer possible, there will be entire realms of one's experience that merely slip away, unrecognized in their departure, and never to be retrieved again" (Wegner, Giuliano, & Hertel, 1985, p. 273). This theory predicts also that a decline in cognitive function in one partner, perhaps due to aging or disease, could result in reduced memory performance in both members of the couple, unless they update their transactive system based on new strategies to overcome the deficit.

Despite its origins in the study of intimate couples, transactive memory theory has arguably had its greatest influence in organizational psychology and small group research (Austin, 2003; Peltokorpi, 2008). In this context, change to the remembering system occurs when there is turnover in the personnel in teams or small groups, where a departing team member may remove knowledge from the whole transactive system. For example, Lewis and colleagues argued that groups tend to retain an earlier transactive memory system, developed by former members of the group, even when the distribution of expertise and knowledge has changed or needs to change; this ineffective transactive system would result in forgetting by the group. They suggest, however, that the negative effects of failing to update the transactive system can be overcome when group members are instructed to reflect on who knows what; that is, when they reflect on the nature and distribution of collective knowledge (Lewis, Belliveau, Herndon, & Keller, 2007).

It is interesting to note here that work on the socially situated and embedded nature of remembering, including the theory of transactive memory, emphasizes the benefits of shared remembering. Shared remembering is seen as a way of reducing forgetting by sharing the cognitive load between members of a stable social group, and thus improving joint memory performance consistent with their shared goals. However, in laboratory work, such as the work on collaborative recall reviewed above, shared remembering appears to be detrimental to the individual; individuals who remember in groups show collaborative inhibition (at least in terms of amount recalled; accuracy of recall may be boosted; Harris et al., 2008). How should we reconcile these laboratory findings and work on socially situated memory? Perhaps work in the laboratory does not yet fully capture the richly shared remembering that is the focus of other disciplines (see Barnier et al., 2008). For instance, transactive memory theory predicts that the benefits of remembering with others might only emerge over time in stable groups (see also Tollefsen, 2006), but our research in couples shows that, even in these groups, benefits of shared remembering depend on a complex interplay between individuals, their relationship, the memory task, and the broader context. Increasingly over the last ten years, we have seen that all experimental forgetting paradigms reviewed have moved from neutral words to more emotional and complex personal memories, with sometimes complex patterns of findings as the effects of personal meaning, motivations, emotion, and social processes interact.

Final thoughts

In this chapter, we have focused on ways that individuals and groups manage their memories. We have adopted a functional approach (Conway, 2005), which suggests that both remembering and forgetting are important and adaptive for individuals and groups. What is remembered vs. forgotten at any particular time is driven by a range of individual and social goals and motivations. For individuals and groups alike, the goals and motivations that influence access to memories of the past may compete and need to be balanced. Think back to the case of Nicky Barr, who reluctantly recalled long-past, distressing wartime experiences for a television interview, after years of trying to forget them. He described the personal cost of remembering these events. But was there a broader, cultural benefit of not letting him forget, of persuading him to let us commemorate his heroic actions? Equally, for many years, as individual Indigenous Australians remembered the trauma of being forcibly removed from their families as members of the Stolen Generation, there seemed to be a national climate of forgetting these events. This seemed to change when the Australian Government formally apologized for past wrongs in February 2008, signalling that we could now all "remember" (National Inquiry into the Separation of Aboriginal and Torres Strait Islander Children from their Families, 1997). Although ten years later, we can observe how private and public remembering and forgetting can be unstable, tenuous, and continuously negotiated. The functional, selective, constructive account of memory described above views neither remembering nor forgetting as necessarily intrinsically better; both serve important roles for individuals, groups, and societies but these functions can be in tension with each other.

In this chapter, we have walked through forgetting, from the individual, to individuals in groups, and finally to groups themselves. We have reviewed experimental paradigms and findings as well as broader theoretical views of social memory, situated cognition, and transactive memory, hopefully to give the sense that the forgetting that we as individuals experience lies on a continuum with the forgetting that happens between couples, families, members of community groups, and even nations. The challenge is to identify ways to investigate the processes that underlie these forms of forgetting and how they relate. We believe that laboratory paradigms from cognitive psychology can be extended to map a full range of remembering cases within a broader interdisciplinary framework (Barnier et al., 2008). We believe that a picture of remembering and forgetting as functional and selective can unify our understanding of both autobiographical and social memory. These forms of memory alike serve, drive, and reflect the goals and motivations of individuals and groups.

Note

* This chapter originally appeared in the edited volume, *Forgetting*. Author note: Since we first published this chapter in 2010, there have been a number of relevant additional investigations of the forgetting of emotional and autobiographical material, for individuals and in social contexts, as well as several substantive reviews. Although we have left the chapter largely intact for this republication, we have updated it where possible with some more recent references and findings to inform the main claims.

References

Alea, N., & Bluck, S. (2003). Why are you telling me that? A conceptual model of the social function of autobiographical memory. *Memory, 11,* 165–178.

Amir, N., Coles, M. E., Brigidi, B., & Foa, E. B. (2001). The effect of practice on recall of emotional information in individuals with generalized social phobia. *Journal of Abnormal Psychology, 110,* 76–82.

Anderson, M. C. (2005). The role of inhibitory control in forgetting unwanted memories: A consideration of three methods. In C. MacLeod & B. Uttl (Eds.), *Dynamic Cognitive Processes* (pp. 159–190). Tokyo: Springer-Verlag.

Anderson, M. C., & Green, C. (2001). Suppressing unwanted memories by executive control. *Nature, 410,* 366–369.

Anderson, M. C. & Hanslmayr, S. (2014). Neural mechanisms of motivated forgetting. *Trends in Cognitive Sciences, 18,* 279–292.

Anderson, M. C., and Hulbert, J. C. (2021). Active forgetting: Adaptation of memory by pre-frontal control. *Annual Review of Psychology.*

Anderson, M. C., & Levy, B. (2002). Repression can (and should) be studied empirically. *Trends in Cognitive Sciences, 6,* 502–503.

Andersson, J., & Rönnberg, J. (1995). Recall suffers from collaboration: joint recall effects of friendship and task complexity. *Applied Cognitive Psychology, 9,* 273–287.

Anderson, M. C., & Spellman, B. A. (1995). On the status of inhibitory mechanisms in cognition: memory retrieval as a model case. *Psychological Review, 102,* 68–100.

Anderson, M. C., Bjork, R. A., & Bjork, E. L. (1994). Remembering can cause forgetting: retrieval dynamics in long-term memory. *Journal of Experimental Psychology: Learning, Memory, and Cognition, 20,* 1063–1087.

Austin, J. R. (2003). Transactive memory in organizational groups: The effects of content, consensus, specialization, and accuracy on group performance. *Journal of Applied Psychology, 88,* 866–878.

Barber, S. J. & Mather, M. (2012). Forgetting in context: The effects of age, emotion, and social factors on retrieval-induced forgetting. *Memory and Cognition, 40,* 874–888.

Barnier, A. J., Harris, C. B., Morris, T., & Savage, G. (2018). Collaborative facilitation in older couples: Successful joint remembering across memory tasks. *Frontiers in Psychology, 9,* 1–21.

Barnier, A. J., Levin, K., & Maher, A. (2004). Suppressing thoughts of past events: are repressive copers good suppressors? *Cognition and Emotion, 18,* 513–531.

Barnier, A. J., Sutton, J., Harris, C. B., & Wilson, R. A. (2008). A conceptual and empirical framework for the social distribution of cognition: the case of memory. *Cognitive Systems Research, 9,* 33–51.

Barnier, A. J., Conway, M. A., Mayoh, L., Speyer, J., Avizmil, O, & Harris, C. B. (2007). Directed forgetting of recently recalled autobiographical memories. *Journal of Experimental Psychology: General, 136,* 301–322.

Barnier, A. J., Hung, L., & Conway, M.A. (2004). Retrieval-induced forgetting of autobiographical episodes. *Cognition and Emotion, 18,* 457–477.

Bartlett, F. C. (1932). *Remembering: A study in experimental and social psychology.* London: Cambridge University Press.

Basden, B. H., Basden, D. R., & Gargano, G. J. (1993). Directed forgetting in implicit and explicit memory tests: a comparison of methods. *Journal of Experimental Psychology: Learning, Memory, and Cognition, 19,* 603–616.

Basden, B. H., Basden, D. R., & Henry, S. (2000). Costs and benefits of collaborative remembering. *Applied Cognitive Psychology, 14,* 497–507.

Basden, B. H., Basden, D. R., Bryber, S., & Thomas, R. L., III. (1997). A comparison of group and individual remembering: does collaboration disrupt retrieval strategies? *Journal of Experimental Psychology: Learning, Memory and Cognition, 23,* 1176–1189.

Beach, K. (1988). The role of external mnemonic symbols in acquiring an occupation. In M. M. Gruneberg & R. N. Sykes (Eds.), *Practical aspects of memory* (pp. 342–346). New York: Wiley.

Bietti, L. & Sutton, J. (2015). Interacting to remember at multiple timescales: Coordination, collaboration, cooperation and culture in joint remembering. *Interaction Studies, 16,* 419–450.

Bjork, R. A. (1970). Positive forgetting: The noninterference of items intentionally forgotten. *Journal of Verbal Learning and Verbal Behavior, 9,* 255–268.

Bjork, R. A., Bjork, E. L., & Anderson, M. C. (1998). Varieties of goal-directed forgetting. In J. M. Golding & C. M. MacLeod (Eds.), *Intentional forgetting: Interdisciplinary approaches* (pp. 103–137). Mahwah, NJ: Lawrence Erlbaum.

Bloch, M. (1998). *How we think they think: Anthropological approaches to cognition, memory, and literacy.* Boulder, CO: Westview Press.

Blumen, H. M., & Rajaram, S. (2008). Re-exposure and retrieval disruption during group collaboration as well as repeated retrieval influence later individual recall. *Memory, 16,* 231–244.

Bowker. G. (2005). *Memory practices in the sciences.* Cambridge, MA: MIT Press.

Brandon, D. P., & Hollingshead, A. B. (2004). Transactive memory systems in organizations: matching tasks, expertise and people. *Organization Science, 15,* 633–644.

Brewin, C. R. (1998). Intrusive autobiographical memories in depression and post-traumatic stress disorder. *Applied Cognitive Psychology, 12,* 359–370.

Brown, A. D., Kramer, M. E., Romano, T. A., and Hirst, W. (2012). Forgetting trauma: Socially shared retrieval-induced forgetting and post-traumatic stress disorder. *Applied Cognitive Psychology, 26,* 24–34.

Brown, S. D., & Reavey, P. 2015. *Vital memories and affect: Living with a difficult past.* London: Routledge.

Browning, C.A., Harris, C.B., Bergen, P.V., Barnier, A.J., & Rendell, P.G. (2018). Collaboration and prospective memory: Comparing nominal and collaborative group performance in strangers and couples. *Memory, 26,* 1206–1219.

Bulevich, J. B., Roediger, H. L. III, Balota, D. A., & Butler, A. C. (2006). Failures to find suppression of episodic memories in the think/no-think paradigm. *Memory and Cognition, 34,* 1569–1577.

Campbell, S. (2003). *Relational remembering: Rethinking the memory wars.* Lanham, MD: Rowman & Littlefield.

Campbell, S. (2008). The second voice. *Memory Studies, 1,* 41–48.

Casey, E. S. (1987). *Remembering: A phenomenological study.* Bloomington, IN: Indiana University Press.

Casey, E. S. (1992). Forgetting remembered. *Man and World, 25,* 281–311.

Cheng, S. K, Liu, I. C., Lee, J. R., Hung, D. L., & Tzeng, O. J. L. (2012). Intentional forgetting might be more effortful than remembering: An ERP study of item-method directed forgetting. *Biological Psychology, 89,* 283–292.

Clark, A. (1997). *Being there: Putting brain, body, and world together again.* Cambridge, MA: MIT Press.

Clark, A. (1998). Author's response: Review symposium on *Being There. Metascience, 7,* 95–103.

Clark, A. (2001). Reasons, robots and the extended mind. *Mind and Language, 16*(2), 121–145.

Clark, A., & Chalmers, D. (1998). The extended mind. *Analysis, 58*(1), 7–19.

Coman, A., & Hirst, W. (2015). Social identity and socially shared retrieval-induced forgetting: The effects of group membership. *Journal of Experimental Psychology: General, 144,* 717–722.

Coman, A., Manier, D., & Hirst, W. (2009). Forgetting the unforgettable through conversation. *Psychological Science, 20,* 627–633.

Connerton, P. (1989). *How societies remember.* Cambridge: Cambridge University Press.

Connerton, P. (2008). Seven types of forgetting. *Memory Studies, 1,* 59–71.

Conway, M. A. (2005). Memory and the self. *Journal of Memory and Language, 53,* 594–628.

Conway, M. A., & Pleydell-Pearce, C. W. (2000). The construction of autobiographical memories in the self-memory system. *Psychological Review, 107,* 261–288.

Conway, M. A., Justice, L. V., & D'Argembeau, A. (2019). The self-memory system revisited. In J. Mace, *The organization and structure of autobiographical memory,* pp. 28–51. Oxford: Oxford University Press.

Conway, M. A., Singer, J. A., & Tagini, A. (2004). The self and autobiographical memory: Correspondence and coherence. *Social Cognition, 22,* 491–529.

Cuc, A., Koppel, J., & Hirst, W. (2007). Silence is not golden: A case for socially shared retrieval-induced forgetting. *Psychological Science, 18,* 727–733.

Dehli, L., and Brennen, T. (2009). Does retrieval-induced forgetting occur for emotional stimuli? *Cognition and Emotion, 23,* 1056–1068.

Depue, B. E., Banich, M. T., & Curran, T. (2006). Suppression of emotional and nonemotional content in memory: Effects of repetition on cognitive control. *Psychological Science, 17,* 441–447.

Dixon, R. A. 1996. Collaborative memory and aging. In D. J. Herrman, M. K. Johnson, C. L. McEvoy, C. Herzog, & P. Hertel (Eds.), *Basic and applied memory research: Theory in context* (pp. 359–383). Mahwah, NJ: Erlbaum.

Donald, M. (1991). *Origins of the modern mind: Three stages in the evolution of culture and cognition.* Cambridge, MA: Harvard University Press.

Donald, M. (1998). Material culture and cognition. In C. Renfrew & C. Scarre (Eds.), *Cognition and material culture: The archaeology of symbolic storage* (pp. 181–187). Cambridge: McDonald Institute for Archaeological Research.

Dornan, P. (2002). *Nicky Barr: An Australian air ace.* Sydney: Allen & Unwin.

Ekeocha, J. O., & Brennen, S. E. (2008). Collaborative recall in face-to-face and electronic groups. *Memory, 16,* 245–261.

Erdelyi, M. (2008). Forgetting and remembering in psychology: Commentary on Paul Connerton's "Seven Types of Forgetting" (2008). *Memory Studies, 1,* 273–278.

Erdelyi, M. H. (2006). The unified theory of repression. *Behavioral and Brain Sciences, 29,* 499–511.

Finlay, F., Hitch, G. J., & Meudell, P. (2000). Mutual inhibition in collaborative recall: Evidence for a retrieval-based account. *Journal of Experimental Psychology: Learning, Memory and Cognition, 26,* 1556–1567.

Finley, J. R., Naaz, F., & Goh, F. W. (2018). *Memory and technology: How we use information in the brain and in the world.* Cham: Springer.

Fitzgerald, J. M. (1992). Autobiographical memory and conceptualisations of the self. In M. A. Conway, D. C. Rubin, H. Spinnler, & W. A. Wagenaar (Eds.), *Theoretical perspectives on autobiographical memory* (pp. 99–114). Dordrecht: Kluwer Academic Publishers.

Fivush, R. (2004). Voice and silence: A feminist model of autobiographical memory. In J. Lucariello, J. A. Hudson, R. Fivush, & P. J. Bauer (Eds.), *The development of the mediated mind: Sociocultural context and cognitive development.* Mahwah, NJ: Erlbaum.

Fivush, R. (2019). *Family narratives and the development of an autobiographical self: Social and cultural perspectives on autobiographical memory*. London: Routledge.

Forty, A. (1999). Introduction: The art of forgetting. In A. Forty & S. Küchler (Eds.), *The art of forgetting* (pp. 1–18). Oxford: Berg.

Gamboa, O. L., Garcia-Campayo, J., Müller, T., & von Wegner, F. (2017). Suppress to forget: The effect of a mindfulness-based strategy during an emotional item-directed forgetting paradigm. *Frontiers in Psychology, 8,* 432.

Geraerts, E., Merckelbach, H., Jelicic, M., & Smeets, E. (2006a). Long term consequences of suppression of intrusive thoughts and repressive coping. *Behaviour Research and Therapy, 44,* 1451–1460.

Geraerts, E., Smeets, E., Jelicic, M., Merckelbach, H., & van Heerdan, J. (2006b). Retrieval inhibition of trauma-related words in women reporting repressed or recovered memories of childhood sexual abuse. *Behaviour Research and Therapy, 44,* 1129–1136.

Golding, J. M., & MacLeod, C. M. (Eds.), (1998). *Intentional forgetting: Interdisciplinary approaches*. Mahwah, NJ: Lawrence Erlbaum.

Gould, O. N., Osborn, C., Krein, H., & Mortenson, M. (2002). Collaborative recall in married and unacquainted dyads. *International Journal of Behavioral Development, 26,* 36–44.

Habermas, T., & Bluck, S. (2000). Getting a life: The emergence of the life story in adolescence. *Psychological Bulletin, 126,* 748–769.

Halbwachs, M. (1980). *The collective memory*. F. J. Ditter and V. Y. Ditter (Trans.), M. Douglas (Ed.). New York: Harper & Row.

Harris, C. B., Barnier, A. J., and Sutton, J. (2012). Consensus collaboration enhances group and individual recall accuracy. *Quarterly Journal of Experimental Psychology,* 65, 179–194.

Harris, C. B., Barnier, A. J., Sutton, J., and Keil, P. G. (2010). How did you feel when "The Crocodile Hunter" died? Voicing and silencing in conversation influences memory for an autobiographical event. *Memory, 18,* 185–197.

Harris, C. B., Paterson, H. M., & Kemp, R. I. (2008). Collaborative recall and collective memory: What happens when we remember together? *Memory, 16,* 213–230.

Harris, C. B., Sharman, S. J., Barnier, A. J., & Moulds, M. L. (2010). Mood and retrieval-induced forgetting of positive and negative autobiographical memories. *Applied Cognitive Psychology, 24,* 399–413.

Harris, C. B, Barnier, A. J., Sutton, J., Keil, P. G., & Dixon, R. A. (2017). "Going episodic": Collaborative inhibition and facilitation when long-married couples remember together. *Memory, 25,* 1148–1159.

Harris, C. B., Barnier, A. J., Sutton, J., and Savage, G. (2019). Features of successful and unsuccessful collaborative memory conversations in long-married couples. *Topics in Cognitive Science, 11,* 668–686.

Harris, C. B., Keil, P. G., Sutton, J., Barnier, A. J., and McIlwain, D. J. F. (2011). We remember, we forget: Collaborative remembering in older couples. *Discourse Processes, 48,* 267–303.

Hayne, H., & MacDonald, S. (2003). The socialization of autobiographical memory in children and adults: The role of culture and gender. In R. Fivush & C. A. Haden (Eds.), *Autobiographical memory and the construction of a narrative self: Developmental and cultural perspectives* (pp. 99–120). Mahwah, NJ: Lawrence Erlbaum Associates.

Heersmink, R. (2018). The narrative self, distributed memory, and evocative objects. *Philosophical Studies 175,* 1829–1849.

Henkel, L. A. (2014). Point-and-shoot memories: The influence of taking photos on memory for a museum tour. *Psychological Science, 25,* 396–402.

Hertel, P. T., & Calcaterra, G. (2005). Intentional forgetting benefits from thought substitution. *Psychonomic Bulletin and Review, 12,* 484–489.

Hirst, W., & Manier, D. (2008). Towards a psychology of collective memory. *Memory, 16,* 183–200.

Hutchins, E. (1995). *Cognition in the wild.* Cambridge, MA: MIT Press.

Johansson, N. O., Andersson, J., & Rönnberg, J. (2005). Compensating strategies in collaborative remembering in very old couples. *Scandinavian Journal of Psychology 46,* 349–359.

Joormann, J., Hertel, P.T., LeMoult, J., & Gotlib, I. H. (2009). Training forgetting of negative material in depression. *Journal of Abnormal Psychology, 118,* 34–43.

Joslyn, S. L., & Oakes, M. A. (2005). Directed forgetting of autobiographical events. *Memory and Cognition, 33,* 577–587.

Kihlstrom, J. F. (2002). No need for repression. *Trends in Cognitive Sciences, 6,* 502.

Kihlstrom, J. F. (2006). Repression: A unified theory of will-o-the-wisp. *Behavioral and Brain Sciences, 29,* 523.

Kihlstrom, J. F., & Barnhardt, T. M. (1993). The self regulation of memory: For better and for worse, with and without hypnosis. In D. M. Wegner and J. Pennebaker (Eds), *Handbook of mental control* (pp. 88–125). Englewood Cliffs, NJ: Prentice Hall.

Kihlstrom, J. F., & Schacter, D. L. (1995). Functional disorders of autobiographical memory. In A. D. Baddeley, B. A. Wilson, & F. N. Watts (Eds.), *Handbook of memory disorders* (pp. 337–364). Chichester: Wiley.

Kirsh, D. (2006). Distributed cognition: A methodological note. *Pragmatics and Cognition, 14,* 249–262.

Klein, N. M. (1997). *The history of forgetting: Los Angeles and the erasure of memory.* London: Verso.

Kobayashi, M., & Tanno, Y. (2013). Retrieval-induced forgetting of words with negative emotionality. *Memory, 21,* 315–323.

Kobayashi, M., & Tanno, Y. (2015). Remembering episodic memories is not necessary for forgetting of negative words: Semantic retrieval can cause forgetting of negative words. *Psychonomic Bulletin and Review, 22,* 766–771.

Koutstaal, W., & Schacter, D. L. (1997). Intentional forgetting and voluntary thought suppression: Two potential methods for coping with childhood trauma. In L. J. Dickstein, M. B. Riba, & J. M. Oldham (Eds.), *Review of Psychiatry* (vol. 16, pp. II-79–II-121). Washington, DC: American Psychiatric Press.

Krell, D. F. (1990). *Of memory, reminiscence, and writing: On the verge.* Bloomington, IN: Indiana University Press.

Küchler, S. (1999). The place of memory. In A. Forty & S. Küchler (Eds.), *The art of forgetting* (pp. 55–72). Oxford: Berg.

Kuhbandner, C., Bäuml, K.-H., & Stiedl, F. C. (2009). Retrieval-induced forgetting of negative stimuli: The role of emotional intensity. *Cognition and Emotion, 23,* 817–830.

Kundera, M. (1980). *The book of laughter and forgetting.* Harmondsworth: Penguin.

Levy, B. J., & Anderson, M. C. (2002). Inhibitory processes and the control of memory retrieval. *Trends in Cognitive Sciences, 6,* 299–305.

Levy, B. J., & Anderson, M. C. (2008). Individual differences in the suppression of unwanted memories: The executive deficit hypothesis. *Acta Psychologica, 127,* 623–635.

Lewis, K., Belliveau, M., Herndon, B., & Keller, J. (2007). Group cognition, membership change, and performance: Investigating the benefits and detriments of collective knowledge. *Organizational Behavior and Human Decision Processes, 103,* 159–178.

Loftus, E. F. (2005) Planting misinformation in the human mind: A 30-year investigation of the malleability of memory. *Learning and Memory, 12,* 361–366.

Loveday, C. & Conway, M. A. (2011). Using SenseCam with an amnesic patient: Accessing inaccessible everyday memories. *Memory, 19,* 697–704.

MacLeod, C. M., Dodd, M. D., Sheard, E. D., Wilson, D. E., & Bibi, U. (2003). In opposition to inhibition. In B. H. Ross (Ed.), *The psychology of learning and motivation* (pp. 163–214). San Diego, CA: Academic Press.

Macrae, C. N., & Roseveare, T. A. (2002). I was always on my mind: The self and temporary forgetting. *Psychonomic Bulletin and Review, 9,* 611–614.

Malafouris, L. (2004). The cognitive basis of material engagement: Where brain, body and culture conflate. In E. DeMarrais, C. Gosden, & C. Renfrew (Eds.), *Rethinking materiality: The engagement of mind with the material world* (pp. 53–62). Cambridge: McDonald Institute for Archaeological Research.

Mao, X., Wang, Y., Wu, Y., and Guo, C. (2017). Self-referential information alleviates retrieval inhibition of directed forgetting effects—an ERP evidence of source memory. *Frontiers in Behavioral Neuroscience, 11,* 187.

Marcel Caux, 105. (2004). *The Age,* April 25. Retrieved April 14, 2009, from http://www.theage.com.au/articles/2004/04/24/1082719676658.html.

Maswood, R., Rasmussen, A. S., & Rajaram, S. (2019). Collaborative remembering of emotional autobiographical memories: Implications for emotion regulation and collective memory. *Journal of Experimental Psychology: General, 148*(1), 65–79.

Meade, M. L., Harris, C. B., Van Bergen, P., Sutton, J., & Barnier, A. J. (2018). *Collaborative remembering: Theories, research, and applications.* Oxford: Oxford University Press.

McCulloch, K. C., Aarts, H., Fujita, K., & Bargh, J. A. (2008). Inhibition in goal systems: A retrieval-induced forgetting account. *Journal of Experimental Social Psychology, 44,* 857–865.

McNally, R. J. (2005). *Remembering trauma.* Cambridge, MA: Harvard University Press.

Meade, M. L., Nokes, T. J., & Morrow, D. G. (2009). Expertise promotes facilitation on a collaborative memory task. *Memory, 17,* 39–48.

Meudell, P. R., Hitch, G. J., & Boyle, M. M. (1995). Collaboration in recall: Do pairs of people cross-cue each other to produce new memories? *Quarterly Journal of Experimental Psychology, 48A,* 141–152.

Michaelian, K., & Sutton, J. (2013). Distributed cognition and memory research: History and current directions. *Review of Philosophy and Psychology, 4,* 1–24.

Middleton, D., & Brown, S. D. (2005). *The social psychology of experience: Studies in remembering and forgetting.* London: Sage.

Mineka, S., & Nugent, K. (1995). Mood-congruent biases in anxiety and depression. In D. L. Schacter (Ed.), *Memory distortion: How minds, brains and societies reconstruct the past.* Cambridge, MA: Harvard University Press.

Moulds, M. L., & Bryant, R. A. (2002). Directed forgetting in acute stress disorder. *Journal of Abnormal Psychology, 111,* 175–179.

Moulds, M. L., & Kandris, E. (2006). The effect of practice on recall of negative material in dysphoria. *Journal of Affective Disorders, 91,* 269–272.

Myers, L. B. & Brewin, C. R. (1994). Recall of early experience and the repressive coping style. *Journal of Abnormal Psychology, 103,* 288–292.

Myers, L. B., & Derakshan, N. (2004). To forget or not to forget: What do repressors forget and when do they forget? *Cognition and Emotion, 18,* 495–511.

Myers, L. B., Brewin, C. R., & Power, M. J. (1998). Repressive coping and the directed forgetting of emotional material. *Journal of Abnormal Psychology, 107,* 141–148.

National Inquiry into the Separation of Aboriginal and Torres Strait Islander Children from their Families (1997). *Bringing them home: Report of the national inquiry into the separation of Aboriginal and Torres Strait Islander children from their families.* Retrieved April 14, 2009, from http://www.hreoc.gov.au/pdf/social_justice/bringing_them_home_report.pdf.

Nelson, K. (2003). Self and social functions: Individual autobiographical memory and collective narrative. *Memory, 11,* 125–136.

Nelson, K., & Fivush, R. (2004). The emergence of autobiographical memory: A social cultural developmental theory. *Psychological Review, 111,* 486–511.

Noreen, S. & MacLeod, M. D. (2013). It's all in the detail: Intentional forgetting of autobiographical memories using the autobiographical think/no-think task. *Journal of Experimental Psychology: Learning Memory and Cognition, 39,* 375–393.

Noreen, S., Bierman, R. N. & MacLeod, M. D. (2014). Forgiving you is hard, but forgetting seems easy: Can forgiveness facilitate forgetting? *Psychological Science, 25,* 1295–1302.

Noreen, S., Cooke, R. & Ridout, N. (2020). Investigating the mediating effect of working memory on intentional forgetting in dysphoria. *Psychological Research, 84,* 2273–2286.

Olick, J. (1999). Collective memory: The two cultures. *Sociological Theory, 17,* 333–348.

Pasupathi, M. (2001). The social construction of the personal past and its implications for adult development. *Psychological Bulletin, 127,* 651–672.

Paterson, H., & Kemp, R. (2006). Comparing methods of encountering postevent information: The power of co-witness suggestion. *Applied Cognitive Psychology, 20,* 1083–1099.

Payne, B. K., & Corrigan, E. (2007). Emotional constraints on intentional forgetting. *Journal of Experimental Social Psychology, 43,* 780–786.

Peltokorpi, V. (2008). Transactive memory systems. *Review of General Psychology, 12,* 378–394.

Pillemer, D. B. (2003). Directive functions of autobiographical memory: The guiding power of the specific episode. *Memory, 11,* 193–202.

Reese, E. (2002). A model of the origins of autobiographical memory. In J. W. Fagen & H. Hayne (Eds.), *Progress in infancy research* (vol. 2, pp. 215–260). Hillsdale, NJ: Erlbaum.

Reese, E., & Fivush, R. (2008). The development of collective remembering. *Memory, 16,* 202–212.

Reysen, M. B. (2003). The effects of social pressure on group recall. *Memory and Cognition, 31,* 1163–1168.

Ricoeur, P. (2004). *Memory, history, forgetting.* Chicago, IL: Chicago University Press.

Risko, E. F., & Gilbert, S. J. (2016). Cognitive offloading. *Trends in Cognitive Sciences, 20,* 676–688.

Rowlands, M. (1999). *The body in mind: Understanding cognitive processes.* Cambridge: Cambridge University Press.

Rubin, D. C. (1995). *Memory in oral traditions: The cognitive psychology of epic, ballads, and counting-out rhymes.* Oxford: Oxford University Press.

Rubin, D. C. (2007). Forgetting: Its role in the science of memory. In H. L. Roediger III, Y. Dudai, & S. M. Fitzpatrick (Eds.), *Science of memory: Concepts* (pp. 325–328). Oxford: Oxford University Press.

Sahakyan, L., & Delaney, P. F. (2005). Directed forgetting in incidental learning and recognition testing: Support for a two factor account. *Journal of Experimental Psychology: Learning, Memory and Cognition, 31,* 789–801.

Sahdra, B., & Ross, M. (2007). Group identification and historical memory. *Personality and Social Psychology Bulletin, 33,* 384–395.

Sansom, B. (2006). The brief reach of history and the limitations of recall in traditional Aboriginal societies and cultures. *Oceania, 76,* 150–172.

Schacter, D. L. (1987). Implicit memory: History and current status. *Journal of Experimental Psychology: Learning, Memory, and Cognition, 13,* 501–518.

Schacter, D. L. (1996). *Searching for memory: The brain, the mind, and the past.* New York: Basic Books.

Schudson, M. (1995). Dynamics of distortion in collective memory. In D. L. Schacter (Ed.), *Memory distortions: How minds, brains and societies reconstruct the past* (pp. 346–364). Cambridge, MA: Harvard University Press.

Selwood, A., Harris, C. B., Barnier, A. J., and Sutton, J. (2020). Effects of collaboration on the qualities of autobiographical recall in strangers, friends, and siblings: Both remembering partner and communication processes matter. *Memory, 28*, 399–416.

Singer, J. A., & Conway, M. A. (2008). Should we forget forgetting? *Memory Studies, 1*, 279–285.

Sloboda, John A. (1985). *The musical mind: The cognitive psychology of music.* Oxford: Oxford University Press.

Soares, J. S., & Storm, B. C. (2018). Forget in a flash: A further investigation of the photo-taking-impairment effect. *Journal of Applied Research in Memory and Cognition, 7*, 154–160.

Sparrow, B., Liu, J., & Wegner, D. M. (2011). Google effects on memory: Cognitive consequences of having information at our fingertips. *Science, 333*, 776–778.

Starr, S., & Moulds, M. L. (2006). The role of negative interpretations of intrusive memories in depression. *Journal of Affective Disorders, 93*, 125–132.

Stone, C. B., Barnier, A. J., Sutton, J., & Hirst, W. (2013a). Forgetting our personal past: Socially shared retrieval-induced forgetting of autobiographical memories. *Journal of Experimental Psychology: General, 142*, 1084–1099.

Stone, C. B., Luminet, O., & Hirst, W. (2013b). Induced forgetting and reduced confidence in our personal past? The consequences of retrieving emotional autobiographical memories. *Acta Psychologica, 144*, 250–257.

Sutton, J. (2008a). Between individual and collective memory: Interaction, coordination, distribution. *Social Research, 75*, 23–48.

Sutton, J. (2008b). Material agency, skills, and history: Distributed cognition and the archaeology of memory. In C. Knappett & L. Malafouris (Eds.), *Material agency: Towards a non-anthropocentric approach* (pp. 37–55). New York: Springer.

Sutton, J. (2009). Remembering. In P. Robbins & M. Aydede (Eds.), *The Cambridge handbook of situated cognition* (pp. 217–235). Cambridge: Cambridge University Press.

Sutton, J. (2015a). Scaffolding memory: Themes, taxonomies, puzzles. In L. Bietti & C. B. Stone (Eds.), *Contextualizing human memory: An interdisciplinary approach to understanding how individuals and groups remember the past* (pp. 187–205). London: Routledge.

Sutton, J. (2015b). Remembering as public practice: Wittgenstein, memory, and distributed cognitive ecologies. In D. Moyal-Sharrock, A. Coliva, & V. Munz (Eds.), *Mind, language, and action: Proceedings of the 36th International Wittgenstein Symposium* (pp. 409–443). Berlin: Walter de Gruyter.

Thompson, C. P., Skowronski, J. J., Larsen, S. F., & Betz, A. (1996). *Autobiographical memory: Remembering what and remembering when.* Mahwah, NJ: Lawrence Erlbaum.

Thorne, A. (2000). Personal memory telling and personality development. *Personality and Social Psychology Review, 4*, 45–56.

Tollefsen, D. P. (2006). From extended mind to collective mind. *Cognitive Systems Research, 7*, 140–150.

Tulving, E., & Pearlstone, Z. (1966). Availability versus accessibility of information in memory for words. *Journal of Verbal Learning and Verbal Behavior, 5*, 381–391.

Tulving, E. (2002). Episodic memory: From mind to brain. *Annual Review of Psychology, 53*, 1–25.

Tulving, E., and Thomson, D. M. (1973). Encoding specificity and retrieval processes in episodic memory. *Psychological Review, 80*, 352–373.

Tversky, B., & Marsh, E. J. (2000). Biased retellings of events yield biased memories. *Cognitive Psychology, 40*, 1–38.

van Leeuwen, C., Verstijnen, I. M., & Hekkert, P. (1999). Common unconscious dynamics underly uncommon conscious effect: A case study in the iterative nature of perception and creation In J. S. Jordan (Ed.), *Modeling consciousness across the disciplines*. Baltimore, MD: University Press of America.

Vygotsky, L. (1978). *Mind in society: The development of higher psychological processes*. Cambridge, MA: Harvard University Press.

Wagoner, B., Brescó de Luna, I., & Zadeh, S. (Eds.), (2020). *Memory in the wild*. Charlotte, NC: Information Age Publishing.

Walker, W. R., Skowronski, J. J., & Thompson, C. P. (2003). Life is pleasant—and memory helps to keep it that way! *Review of General Psychology, 7*, 203–210.

Wang, Q. 2013. *The autobiographical self in time and culture*. Oxford: Oxford University Press.

Wegner, D. M. (1986). Transactive memory: a contemporary analysis of the group mind. In B. Mullen & G. R. Goethals (Eds.), *Theories of group behaviour* (pp. 185–208). New York: Springer-Verlag.

Wegner, D. M., Giuliano, T., & Hertel, P. T. (1985). Cognitive interdependence in close relationships. In W. Ickes (Ed.) *Compatible and incompatible relationships* (Springer Series of Social Psychology) (pp. 253–276). New York: Springer-Verlag.

Wegner, D. M., Schneider, D. J., Carter, S. R., III, & White, T. L. (1987). Paradoxical effects of thought suppression. *Journal of Personality and Social Psychology, 53*, 636–647.

Weldon, M. S., & Bellinger, K. D. (1997). Collective memory: Collaborative and individual processes in remembering. *Journal of Experimental Psychology: Learning, Memory and Cognition, 23*, 1160–1175.

Welzer, H., & Markowitsch, H. J. (2005). Towards a bio-psycho-social model of autobiographical memory. *Memory, 13*, 63–78.

Wertsch, J. V. (2002). *Voices of collective remembering*. Cambridge: Cambridge University Press.

Wessel, I., & Hauer, B. (2006). Retrieval-induced forgetting of autobiographical memory details. *Cognition and Emotion, 20*, 430–447.

Wessel, I., & Merckelbach, H. (2006). Forgetting "murder" is not harder than forgetting "circle": Listwise-directed forgetting of emotional words. *Cognition and Emotion, 20*, 129–137.

Wessel, I., & Moulds, M. 2008). How many types of forgetting? Comments on Connerton (2008). *Memory Studies, 1*, 287–294.

Wheeler, M. (2005). *Reconstructing the cognitive world: The next step*. Cambridge, MA: MIT Press.

Wilson, P. (2008). War pilgrims flock to the corner of a foreign field. *The Australian*, April 25. Retrieved April 14, 2009, from http://www.theaustralian.news.com.au/story/0,25197,23595543-22242,00.html.

Wilson, R. A. (2005). Collective memory, group minds, and the extended mind thesis. *Cognitive Processing, 6*, 227–236.

Wilson, R. A., & Clark, A. (2009). How to situate cognition: Letting nature take its course. In P. Robbins & M. Aydede (Eds.), *The Cambridge handbook of situated cognition* (pp. 55–77). Cambridge: Cambridge University Press.

Wright, D. B., & Klumpp, A. (2004). Collaborative inhibition is due to the product, not the process, of recalling in groups. *Psychonomic Bulletin and Review, 11*, 1080–1083.

Yang, W., Liu, P., Cui, Q., Wei, D., Li, W., Qiu, J., and Zhang, Q. (2013). Directed forgetting of negative self-referential information is difficult: An fMRI study. *PLoS ONE, 8(10)*, e75190.

Yaron-Antar, A., & Nachson, I. (2006). Collaborative remembering of emotional events: The case of Rabin's assassination. *Memory, 14*, 46–56.

7

TAKE THE FIELD!

Investigating prospective memory in naturalistic and real-life settings[*]

Jan Rummel and Lia Kvavilashvili

Early research on prospective memory (PM) employed several naturalistic tasks for studying PM (Kvavilashvili, 1992). However, with the development of the now standard laboratory paradigm by Einstein and McDaniel (1990), the field changed dramatically and, over the past decades, has been focused strongly on studying cognitive mechanisms of PM under controlled conditions. We argue that the time may now be ripe to return to the study of PM outside the laboratory, to reconnect and generalize laboratory findings to real life.

In the standard PM paradigm, participants engage in some ongoing task, which they perceive as their primary activity. In addition, they have to remember to respond to an infrequently occurring target event or target time (e.g., a certain word occurring in the ongoing task or a particular time-point) by carrying out a simple action. This paradigm, or its variants, have been used extensively for studying PM processes and applications (Loft, Dismukes, & Grundgeiger, Chapter 8 of this volume). Due to the importance of this paradigm to the field, some researchers have even informally referred to it as PM researchers' *drosophila*. Just like the drosophila model of human genetics, the laboratory PM paradigm has several advantages. It enables researchers to study PM efficiently and with limited resources, as laboratory PM tasks are usually completed in less than an hour while providing multiple observations of PM responses, which increases the reliability of PM measures (Kelemen, Weinberg, Alford, Mulvey, & Kaeochinda, 2006). Moreover, it allows for studying a wide range of factors meaningful to PM, as these can be easily manipulated (e.g., the nature of target events, ongoing-task complexity, etc.). Most importantly, the laboratory paradigm provides an excellent model for studying PM, as it reproduces the most critical features of real-life PM tasks (e.g., delayed intention-execution, self-initiated retrieval requirements, etc.). However, just as insights from drosophila models need to be reconnected to the human organism to evaluate their impact (Jackson, 2008), psychological insight about PM functioning gained in the laboratory should be reconnected to real-life environments to test the generalizability of these laboratory findings and the early naturalistic PM studies could be a starting point for how to achieve such a reconnection.

Currently, there is very little research addressing the important question of to which extent laboratory findings reconnect to real-life PM, but some positive findings do exist. For example, the typical pattern of time monitoring as well as superior performance in event-based compared to time-based tasks, which have often been reported in the laboratory, have also been observed outside of the laboratory (Kvavilashvili & Fisher, 2007; Niedźwieńska & Barzykowski, 2012; Sellen, Louie, Harris, & Wilkins, 1997). In contrast, Unsworth, Brewer, and Spillers (2012) found that participants' scores on two laboratory event-based tasks did not correlate with the number of PM failures recorded by the same participants in a one-week diary. Moreover, research on the age-PM paradox (Rendell & Thomson, 1999,) has shown that the negative effects of age on PM, typically obtained in laboratory PM tasks, can reverse in naturalistic PM tasks. These and similar findings emphasize the necessity of studying PM with both laboratory and naturalistic methods.

Taking this point into account, we consider the following issues to be of particular importance. First, it is necessary to keep in mind that laboratory situations are abstractions of real-life situations and that not all phenomena observed in the laboratory will map onto real-life phenomena one-to-one. For example, laboratory research has made a clear distinction between time-based and event-based PM, which might be less straightforward outside of the laboratory. Indeed, two naturalistic studies on self-assigned intentions yielded a clear dominance of time-based PM tasks and a remarkable absence of event-based tasks (Holbrook & Dismukes, 2009; Schnitzspahn, Altgassen, & Kvavilashvili, 2020). Considering that the vast majority of laboratory studies investigate event-based PM and the nature of target events (their focality, distinctiveness), this discrepancy merits closer attention. Second, naturalistic tasks, just like laboratory tasks, should provide reliable and valid measures of the variables of interest. Third, as real-life investigations do not allow for the same degree of control as experimental settings and often rely on less objective measures, researchers should be aware of potential biases associated with real-life investigations and learn how to minimize them. If these points are considered, the path from the laboratory to real life is not a one-way street. In other words, real-life studies will not only serve to reconnect laboratory findings to the real world, but they can also play an important role in suggesting novel hypotheses, which can then be tested in controlled experimental settings (Mortenson & Cialdini, 2010).

In this chapter, we will first review previous research that used more or less naturalistic tasks for studying PM and discuss the extent to which a reconnection from the laboratory to real life was achieved. We will then make the case that real-life studies on other types of future-oriented cognition (especially mind-wandering and involuntary future thinking) have identified certain processes that are relevant for PM and should thus be considered by PM researchers. We will briefly review some of the findings and methods from these research areas that seem most relevant for a naturalistic approach to PM. Finally, we will discuss pitfalls and promises of naturalistic PM studies.

Studying prospective memory in naturalistic and real-life settings

In the absence of a well-established laboratory paradigm, early studies of PM used a variety of naturalistic tasks in- and outside of the laboratory (see Kvavilashvili, 1992, for a methodological review). The majority of studies conducted outside of the laboratory involved asking participants to carry out simple actions on multiple occasions. For example, Meacham and colleagues introduced a simple task of posting a blank postcard (stamped and addressed to the researcher) on pre-specified dates, a method that allowed them to investigate the role of external reminders (Meacham & Leiman, 1982) and incentives (Meacham & Singer, 1977) in remembering time-based PM tasks over long periods. Another task involved asking participants to carry a small clock device for a week and push a button at predetermined times several times a day (Wilkins & Baddeley, 1978). Moscovitch and Minde (described in Moscovitch, 1982) introduced a task in which participants had to call the researcher at a predetermined time of the day and leave a message on the answering machine several times over a particular period of time (see also Maylor, 1990).

Whereas these studies were relatively easy to carry out and enabled researchers to obtain PM performance scores based on multiple observations, they lacked control over participants' daily activities and use of external memory aids (calendars or reminders). Moreover, although the tasks were executed in real-life environments (e.g., at home, post office, grocery store), the intentions themselves were not entirely natural (e.g., sending blank postcards is not something we do in everyday life) and participants knew that their PM was under scrutiny (cf. Kvavilashvili, 1992). However, some studies managed to investigate naturalistic PM without participants knowing about their performance being assessed. For example, Dobbs and Rule (1987) gave participants a questionnaire to complete at home and post back. Participants were told that it was important for the researchers to know when exactly they completed the questionnaire and, therefore, participants had to remember to indicate the completion time on the front page of the questionnaire. This PM task is more subtle than sending back postcards or making phone calls and it also minimizes the chances of using reminders (see also Bailey, Henry, Rendell, Phillips, & Kliegel, 2010; Kvavilashvili, Cockburn, & Kornbrot, 2013). Similarly, in a study by Somerville, Wellman, and Cultice (1983), caregivers (mostly mothers) asked toddlers to remind them of certain intentions at specific moments. Results showed that even 2 year olds remembered the intentions when they were of personal relevance to them (e.g., reminding the caregiver to buy sweets when being at the store). Here, the PM tasks were part of caregivers' meaningful everyday requests, with the added bonus of caregivers being able to monitor children's behavior during the delay interval.

Ellis (1988) pioneered yet another naturalistic method, which involved asking participants, over a period of several days, to list the activities they had themselves planned for the upcoming day, and to indicate, in the evening, which of these intended activities they had actually executed. Participants also kept a diary during the day to record any instances of spontaneous thoughts or recollections of their intentions specified in the morning (see also Marsh, Hicks, & Landau, 1998). In this approach, the intentions are naturalistic, but at the cost of giving up experimental control over the nature of the intentions, rendering them less comparable across participants. Additionally, the central outcome (intention-execution rate) relies upon retrospectively provided self-reports and can be thus prone to retrospective biases.

Despite the prevalence of naturalistic studies outside of the laboratory, several early researchers of PM opted for studying PM in the laboratory but used rather naturalistic tasks. In these studies, participants had to carry out an additional PM task while completing other experimental tasks during the laboratory session. A variety of simple PM tasks were used for this purpose. For example, participants in Loftus's (1971) experiment had to remember to tell the researcher the state in which they were born after completing a survey. In a study by Meacham and Dumitru (1976), children had to remember to post a drawing into a box on the way to their classroom. In other studies, participants had to remind the experimenter to carry out a particular activity, which was presented as a personal request rather than a study requirement (e.g., Kvavilashvili, 1987). Until today, many tests for functional PM impairments used in clinical settings rely on such naturalistic laboratory tasks (e.g., Wilson et al., 2005). Although some studies asked participants to carry out several requests during the experimental session, most of these studies involved assessing PM on single occasions, thereby increasing the demands on sample sizes.

Over the past 20 years, several new naturalistic methods have been developed. Most prominently, these involve virtual simulations of real-life PM tasks in the laboratory and in participants' everyday life. For example, Rendell and Craik (2000) developed a virtual week planning board game to investigate time- and event-based PM tasks (e.g., call the plumber), embedded in simulated daily activities, such as having breakfast, meeting a friend, or watching a TV program. Rendell and Craik (2000) also developed an actual week simulation, in which participants have to remember a set of experimenter-assigned time- and event-based intentions (i.e., they have to state at designated times that they "remembered" a PM assignment during a regular week in their everyday life). This *actual week task* has been shown to have good psychometric properties (Au, Vandermorris, Rendell, Craik, & Troyer, 2018). Other studies have used virtual simulations of PM in participants' work environment (see Loft et al., this volume) or specifically designed laboratory environments resembling everyday environments/tasks/situations, such as a laboratory kitchen (Altgassen et al., 2015) or a laboratory apartment (Schmitter-Edgecombe, McAlister, & Weakley, 2012). Thanks to progress in technology, some recent naturalistic PM tasks now even make use of virtual reality environments. For instance, Trawley, Stephens, Rendell, and Groeger (2017) asked participants to remember to run a certain errand when arriving at the gas station in a driving simulator.

Notably, the degree to which these "naturalistic" PM tasks overlap with real-life PM requirements varies considerably across studies. We therefore believe that PM tasks are not either naturalistic or not, but that there are different degrees of "naturalness" (Kvavilashvili & Ellis, 2004). We further argue that both the PM task's and the ongoing task's closeness to real life should be taken into account when judging the naturalness of a PM setting. Regarding the PM task, one could broadly differentiate between the requirement of merely enacting a simple and arbitrary action (writing one's initials on an envelope one will receive later; Huppert, Johnson, & Nickson, 2000), executing an experimenter-induced action resembling a real-life PM task (e.g., making a phone call in a couple of days; Maylor, 1990), or executing an action that originated in participants' natural future planning (Marsh et al., 1998). Regarding the ongoing-task context, the PM action may have to be executed while performing some laboratory task, which might correspond more or less strongly with real-life activities, while performing an experimenter-imposed daily task, either in an experimenter-provided setting or in a natural environment, or during a daily task one would naturally engage in anyway during the test period. Of course, different levels of naturalness may be desirable for answering different types of research questions. However, the "litmus test" for laboratory findings' generalizability are PM actions that are as naturalistic as possible and are to be executed in real-life environments.

PM studies using a fully naturalistic approach are still rare, but we believe that this is a particularly promising area for future research. On the one hand, psychology research does not aim to understand the cognitive processes necessary to solve a laboratory task, but rather the human cognitive abilities as reflected by a particular laboratory paradigm (Meiser, 2011). Therefore, generalizability of laboratory findings should speak to their (external) validity. On the other hand, naturalistic approaches may allow for the investigation of certain aspects of PM that are not easily accessible in the laboratory. Most obviously, real-life PM approaches allow the researcher to investigate how PM intentions are maintained over longer retention intervals (i.e., over several days rather than just several minutes), which appears to be a question of critical importance. In this regard, other areas that are interested in understanding future-oriented cognition, namely research on spontaneous future thoughts and future-oriented mind-wandering, can provide additional starting points for identifying and investigating these PM processes (Kvavilashvili & Rummel, 2020).

Research on future-oriented cognition and its relevance for prospective memory

Most studies on future-oriented cognition or prospection have been focused on voluntary constructions of plausible future events or scenarios in which future thoughts are generated in response to cues provided to the participants (for a recent review of this research, see Schacter, Benoit, & Szpunar, 2017). However, there is an increased realization among researchers that thinking about the future in everyday life may be fairly different from how it has been studied in the laboratory, both in terms of its occurrence and the contents of future thoughts. Therefore, emerging research on spontaneous future cognition concerns itself, on the one hand, with involuntary thoughts about the future that people frequently experience in their daily life (Berntsen, 2019; Cole & Kvavilashvili, 2019). Researchers in this area usually use various diary methods to investigate why some (future) thoughts occur involuntarily (e.g., whether they were triggered by a particular cue), how frequently they pop into our mind, and what their phenomenological characteristics are (Cole, Staugaard, & Berntsen, 2016). At this initial stage, such involuntary future thoughts are often contrasted or compared with involuntary thoughts about the past or involuntary autobiographical memories (Berntsen & Jacobsen, 2008; Cole et al., 2016).

Mind-wandering, on the other hand, describes the ubiquitous phenomenon of one's thoughts drifting away from the here-and-now (e.g., from a currently ongoing activity) towards inner thoughts or feelings (Smallwood & Schooler, 2015). Most mind-wandering episodes seem to occur involuntarily (Seli, Risko, Smilek, & Schacter, 2016), thus making spontaneous future thoughts and future-oriented mind-wandering related phenomena, as they are both concerned with spontaneous cognition. Mind-wandering is sometimes assessed with the self-caught method (i.e., by asking participants to indicate when they notice their thoughts trailing off). However, self-caught assessment requires participants to be aware of their wandering mind, which they are often not (Smallwood & Schooler, 2015). For this reason, mind-wandering is more frequently assessed with the probe-caught method, which randomly asks participants to report their momentary thoughts and experiences while performing a concurrent task (usually vigilance or go/no-go tasks). Although mind-wandering research strongly relies on self-report data, this momentary experience-sampling method has been proven to be valid and to minimize risks of retrospective biases (Schooler & Schreiber, 2004).

Several laboratory studies using this method have shown that mind-wandering episodes are often future-oriented, a finding that has been referred to as the prospective bias in mind-wandering (Stawarczyk, Majerus, Maj, Van der Linden, & D'Argembeau, 2011). Another interesting finding is that the majority (about 60%) of such future-oriented spontaneous thoughts, as obtained in a sample of young non-dysphoric participants, referred to upcoming PM tasks and plans (e.g., *need to start a diet after my revision period; must buy a new duvet cover set*) rather than future events without a PM component or wishful/hypothetical thinking (Plimpton, Patel, & Kvavilashvili, 2015).

Importantly, broadly similar results have been obtained in experience-sampling studies outside of the laboratory, where participants carried special devices or special smartphone applications that were set to probe participants' thoughts while they performed their daily activities. For example, using this method, Song and Wang (2012) demonstrated the prospective bias in mind-wandering in a sample of Chinese participants who were probed six times per day over a three-day period. Warden, Plimpton, and Kvavilashvili (2018) used 30 probes over a ten-hour period in one day (Study 2) and found that both young and old participants reported a significantly higher number of task-unrelated future thoughts about upcoming PM tasks than about future events without a PM component or hypothetical scenarios.

Taken together, these insights from research on spontaneous future thought have interesting implications for PM research. They suggest that the prospective bias in mind-wandering may at least partly be explained by participants' spontaneous thoughts about PM tasks that have to be carried out later in the day or in the near future. An important research question raised in the mind-wandering literature concerns the functional significance of such prospective thoughts and whether they actually help people to carry out their planned actions (Stawarczyk, 2018). Initial findings in relation to this question have emerged predominantly from research on PM. For example, a few studies that implemented the probe-caught method in laboratory PM paradigms found that periodically thinking about a pending intention while performing other tasks was beneficial for event-based and time-based intention-execution (Rummel, Smeekens, & Kane, 2017; Seli, Smilek, Ralph, & Schacter, 2018). Moreover, such intention-related thoughts occurred even after the PM task had been canceled or finished (Anderson & Einstein, 2017).

Investigating prospective-memory-related thoughts in real-life situations

Experience-sampling and diary methods will be particularly useful for investigating spontaneous PM-related thoughts over long retention intervals outside of the laboratory, more specifically for addressing the question of whether prospective bias in mind-wandering helps people to accomplish their daily plans and intentions. One early study on this topic was conducted by Kvavilashvili and Fisher (2007). Their participants formed the intention to call the experimenter (either at a certain time or when receiving a specific text message). During a one-week intention retention interval, they had to record every instance of them spontaneously thinking about this PM task and indicate whether these thoughts were triggered by stimuli in the environment, by their own thoughts, or whether there was no trigger. Results showed, among other things, that time-based PM-related thoughts more often seemed to occur with no apparent triggers than event-based PM-related thoughts. Most importantly, the number of such thoughts in young participants was positively correlated with remembering to make a phone call within ten minutes of the target time (Study 2 and 3), but this correlation was not significant for older adults (Study 2).

More recently, Mason and Reinholtz (2015) asked participants to send text messages or emails to the experimenter at certain times and meanwhile had them count their intention-related thoughts using a special smartphone application. They found more frequent PM-related thoughts to be associated with a higher likelihood of executing an intention. Szarras and Niedźwieńska (2011) used an even more naturalistic approach, asking participants to list ten intentions they wanted to execute within the next ten days and to collect PM-related thoughts that occurred to them in the meantime in a diary. They found that those intentions that were actually executed were more frequently mentioned in the diaries than those that were not executed.

Notably, in all these studies, PM-related thoughts were assessed via the self-caught method, meaning that only thoughts that participants were meta-cognitively aware of could be considered. In contrast, in two studies, Anderson and McDaniel (2019), who probed their participants six times over a five-day period, found that participants reported thinking about their intentions in 12–17% of the thought probes, and about the future in general (i.e., without a PM task in mind) in 13–18% of the thought probes. Importantly, about 60% of these PM-related thoughts were reported to have been deliberately (self-)generated rather than coming to mind spontaneously (cf. Warden et al., 2018). Another study that compared the frequency of intention-related thoughts in young and older adults, using an average of 220 prompts per participant over a three-week period, found that younger and older adults reported intention-related thought 10% and 21% of the time, respectively (Gardner & Ascoli, 2015). The reviewed studies show how experience-sampling methods and diary-like momentary thought assessment can be used to study real-life PM, particularly spontaneous PM-related thoughts. However, although these methods are very promising, there are also some limitations that should be taken into account.

Potential pitfalls associated with real-life prospective memory investigations

In comparison to hundreds of laboratory studies on PM, the amount of research on naturalistic PM is relatively modest (about 75 published articles at the point at which this chapter was written, according to searches on the Web-of-Science with the keywords "prospective memory" and "naturalistic" or "real-life"). The reader may wonder why there are fewer published studies on real-life PM, and we can only speculate about the reasons. To begin with, employing experience-sampling and momentary thought assessment methods in real life has only recently become a more standard method for psychology researchers (Trull & Ebner-Priemer, 2014). One important step in the development of these so-called ambulatory assessment techniques was certainly the growing use of smartphones, which meant that ambulatory assessments were no longer reliant upon participants carrying around special devices (Trull & Ebner-Priemer, 2014). A more mundane point may be that real-life investigations tend to be more costly. They regularly require higher monetary investments (e.g., to compensate participants for the often quite high time investment and the inconveniences associated with ambulatory assessment) as well as time investments (e.g., for the researcher to repeatedly interact with participants). However, on the bright side, recent findings from diary and experience-sampling studies by Laughland and Kvavilashvili (2018) and Warden et al. (2018) suggest that shorter periods of recording may be desirable as they produce more participant engagement and higher rates of recording compared to more standard one-week-long or longer recording periods.

Finally, naturalistic studies do not allow for strict experimental control (Kvavilashvili, 1992). Therefore, these methods seem less suitable to study cognitive processes via effective manipulation of different independent variables. Additionally, in the case of PM, these methods are particularly bias-prone, as participants could easily "cheat" in real-life PM studies by using external reminders or other memory aids to better remember their intentions. Even when participants do not cheat, researchers still have to rely on bias-prone self-reports. An easy solution to several of these problems may be to use more controlled (semi-)naturalistic approaches, like naturalistic laboratories or virtual environments. However, the problem with these approaches is that PM requirements still differ considerably from those in real-life environments, while experimental control is still reduced compared to laboratory settings. That is why we argue that fully naturalistic PM studies are nevertheless needed. Our recommendation would be to fight these pitfalls by using online rather than retrospective assessments, trying to minimize reactivity and various biases as well as to maximize participants' compliance, and considering not only collecting self-reports, but also objective data (e.g., on intention-execution) when possible. A detailed review of these methods would go beyond the scope of this chapter, but we recommend the *Handbook of Research Methods for Studying Daily Life* (Mehl & Conner, 2011) for this purpose. Some advice on studying spontaneous future thoughts using paper and smartphone diaries can be found in Laughland and Kvavilashvili (2018).

Conclusions and outlook

A brief review of research methods used to study PM since its inception in the 1970s appears to suggest that PM research may have come full circle. It started off by using naturalistic PM tasks in- and outside of the laboratory until the introduction of a standard laboratory paradigm in 1990, which greatly accelerated and transformed research on PM. However, with the increased popularity of ambulatory assessments of cognitive processes in everyday life over the past decade, PM researchers have started using these methods and naturalistic PM tasks to address a variety of research questions. Despite all the pitfalls of real-life PM investigations listed in the previous section, it seems that researchers are prepared to go the extra mile to investigate when and how the effects and mechanisms observed in the laboratory paradigm of PM transfer onto real-life PM. Most importantly, we hope that, in the near future, naturalistic methods can be used to investigate those PM processes that are particularly difficult to isolate in the laboratory. For example, the marked absence of event-based PM tasks when participants are asked to list their own real-life intentions (Schnitzspahn et al., 2020), the mechanisms behind the age-PM paradox (Rendell & Craik, 2000), and spontaneous self-reminding of intentions in everyday life (Anderson & McDaniel, 2019; Warden et al., 2018).

Note

* This chapter originally appeared in the edited volume, *Prospective Memory*. It has been updated for this compilation.

References

Altgassen, M., Rendell, P. G., Bernhard, A., Henry, J. D., Bailey, P. E., Phillips, L. H., & Kliegel, M. (2015). Future thinking improves prospective memory performance and plan enactment in older adults. *Quarterly Journal of Experimental Psychology, 68*, 192–204.

Anderson, F. T., & Einstein, G. O. (2017). The fate of completed intentions. *Memory, 25*, 467–480.

Anderson, F. T., & McDaniel, M. A. (2019). Hey buddy, why don't we take it outside: An experience sampling study of prospective memory. *Memory and Cognition, 47*, 47–62.

Au, A., Vandermorris, S., Rendell, P. G., Craik, F. I. M., & Troyer, A. K. (2018). Psychometric properties of the actual week test: A naturalistic prospective memory task. *Clinical Neuropsychologist, 32*, 1068–1083.

Bailey, P. E., Henry, J. D., Rendell, P. G., Phillips, L. H., & Kliegel, M. (2010). Dismantling the "age-prospective memory paradox": The classic laboratory paradigm simulated in a naturalistic setting. *Quarterly Journal of Experimental Psychology, 63*, 646–652.

Berntsen, D. (2019). Spontaneous future cognitions: An integrative review. *Psychological Research, 83*, 651–665.

Berntsen, D., & Jacobsen, A. S. (2008). Involuntary (spontaneous) mental time travel into the past and future. *Consciousness and Cognition, 17*, 1093–1104.

Cole, S. N., & Kvavilashvili, L. (2019). Spontaneous future cognition: Framework for an emerging topic. *Psychological Research, 83*, 631–650.

Cole, S. N., Staugaard, S. R., & Berntsen, D. (2016). Inducing involuntary and voluntary mental time travel using a laboratory paradigm. *Memory and Cognition, 44*, 376–389.

Dobbs, A. R., & Rule, B. G. (1987). Prospective memory and self-reports of memory abilities in older adults. *Canadian Journal of Psychology, 41*, 209–222.

Einstein, G. O., & McDaniel, M. A. (1990). Normal aging and prospective memory. *Journal of Experimental Psychology: Learning, Memory, and Cognition, 16*, 717–726.

Ellis, J. A. (1988). Memory for future intentions: Investigating pulses and steps. In M. M. Gruneberg, P. E. Morris, & R. N. Sykes (Eds.), *Practical aspects of memory: Current research and issues* (pp. 371–376). Chichester: John Wiley & Sons.

Gardner, R. S., & Ascoli, G. A. (2015). The natural frequency of human prospective memory increases with age. *Psychology and Aging, 30*, 209–219.

Holbrook, J. B. & Dismukes, R. K. (2009). Prospective memory in everyday tasks. In *Proceedings of the Human Factors and Ergonomics Society 53rd Annual Meeting* (pp. 590–594). Santa Monica, CA: Human Factors and Ergonomics Society.

Huppert, F. A., Johnson, T., & Nickson, J. (2000). High prevalence of prospective memory impairment in the elderly and in early stage dementia: Findings from a population-based study. *Applied Cognitive Psychology, 14*, 63–81.

Jackson, G. R. (2008). Guide to understanding drosophila models of neurodegenerative diseases. *PLOS Biology, 6*, 236–239.

Kelemen, W. L., Weinberg, W. B., Alford, H. S., Mulvey, E. K., & Kaeochinda, K. F. (2006). Improving the reliability of event-based laboratory tests of prospective memory. *Psychonomic Bulletin & Review, 13*, 1028–1032.

Kvavilashvili, L. (1987). Remembering intention as a distinct form of memory. *British Journal of Psychology, 78*, 507–518.

Kvavilashvili, L. (1992). Remembering intentions: A critical review of existing experimental paradigms. *Applied Cognitive Psychology, 6*, 507–524.

Kvavilashvili, L., Cockburn, J., & Kornbrot, D. E. (2013). Prospective memory and ageing paradox with event-based tasks: A study of young, young-old, and old-old participants. *Quarterly Journal of Experimental Psychology, 66*, 864–875.

Kvavilashvili, L., & Ellis, J. (2004). Ecological validity and twenty years of real-life/laboratory controversy in memory research: A critical (and historical) review. *History and Philosophy of Psychology, 6*, 59–80.

Kvavilashvili, L., & Fisher, L. (2007). Is time-based prospective remembering mediated by self-initiated rehearsals? Role of incidental cues, ongoing activity, age, and motivation. *Journal of Experimental Psychology: General, 136*, 112–132.

Kvavilashvili, L., & Rummel, J. (2020). On the nature of everyday prospection: A review and theoretical integration of research on mind-wandering, future thinking, and prospective memory, Review of General Psychology, 24, 210–237.

Laughland, A., & Kvavilashvili, L. (2018). Should participants be left to their own devices? Comparing paper and smartphone diaries in psychological research. *Journal of Applied Research in Memory and Cognition, 7*, 552–563.

Loftus, E. F. (1971). Memory for intentions: The effect of presence of a cue and interpolated activity. *Psychonomic Science, 23*, 315–316.

Marsh, R. L., Hicks, J. L., & Landau, J. D. (1998). An investigation of everyday prospective memory. *Memory and Cognition, 26*, 633–643.

Mason, M. F., & Reinholtz, N. (2015). Avenues down which a self-reminding mind can wander. *Motivation Science, 1*, 1–21.

Maylor, E. A. (1990). Age and prospective memory. *Quarterly Journal of Experimental Psychology 42*, 471–493.

Meacham, J. A., & Dumitru, J. (1976). Prospective remembering and external retrieval cues. *Catalog of Selected Documents in Psychology, 6*, 1284.

Meacham, J. A., & Leiman, B. (1982). Remembering to perform future actions. In U. Neisser (Ed.), *Memory observed: Remembering in natural contexts* (pp. 327–336). San Francisco, CA: Freeman.

Meacham, J. A., & Singer, J. (1977). Incentive effects in prospective remembering. *Journal of Psychology, 97*, 191–197.

Mehl, M. R., & Conner, T. S. (2011). *Handbook of research methods for studying daily life.* New York: Guilford Press.

Meiser, T. (2011). Much pain, little gain? Paradigm-specific models and methods in experimental psychology. *Perspectives on Psychological Science, 6*, 183–191.

Mortenson, C. R., & Cialdini, R. B. (2010). Full-cycle social psychology for theory and application. *Social and Personality Psychology Compass, 4,* 53–63.

Moscovitch, M. (1982). A neuropsychological approach to memory and perception in normal and pathological aging. In F. I. M. Craik & S. Trehub (Eds.), *Aging and cognitive processes* (pp. 55–78). New York: Plenum Press.

Niedźwieńska, A., & Barzykowski, K. (2012). The age prospective memory paradox within the same sample in time-based and event-based tasks. *Aging, Neuropsychology, and Cognition, 19,* 58–83.

Plimpton, B., Patel, P., & Kvavilashvili, L. (2015). Role of triggers and dysphoria in mind-wandering about past, present and future: A laboratory study. *Consciousness and Cognition, 33,* 261–276.

Rendell, P. G., & Craik, F. I. M. (2000). Virtual week and actual week: Age-related differences in prospective memory. *Applied Cognitive Psychology, 14,* 43–62.

Rendell, P. G., & Thomson, D. M. (1999). Aging and prospective memory: Differences between naturalistic and laboratory tasks. *Journals of Gerontology Series B-Psychological Sciences and Social Sciences, 54,* 256–269.

Rummel, J., Smeekens, B. A., & Kane, M. J. (2017). Dealing with prospective memory demands while performing an ongoing task: Shared processing, increased on-task focus, or both? *Journal of Experimental Psychology: Learning, Memory, and Cognition, 43,* 1047–1062.

Schacter, D. L., Benoit, R. G., & Szpunar, K. K. (2017). Episodic future thinking: Mechanisms and functions. *Current Opinion in Behavioral Sciences, 17,* 41–50.

Schmitter-Edgecombe, M., McAlister, C., & Weakley, A. (2012). Naturalistic assessment of everyday functioning in individuals with mild cognitive impairment: The day-out task. *Neuropsychology, 26,* 631–641.

Schnitzspahn, K. M., Altgassen, M., & Kvavilashvili, L. (2020). Redefining the pattern of age-prospective memory-paradox: New insights on age effects in lab-based, naturalistic and self-assigned tasks. *Psychological Research, 84,* 1370–1386.

Schooler, J. W., & Schreiber, C. A. (2004). Experience, meta-consciousness, and the paradox of introspection. *Journal of Consciousness Studies, 11,* 17–39.

Seli, P., Risko, E. F., Smilek, D., & Schacter, D. L. (2016). Mind-wandering with and without intention. *Trends in Cognitive Sciences, 20,* 605–617.

Seli, P., Smilek, D., Ralph, B. C. W., & Schacter, D. L. (2018). The awakening of the attention: Evidence for a link between the monitoring of mind wandering and prospective goals. *Journal of Experimental Psychology: General, 147,* 431–443.

Sellen, A. J., Louie, G., Harris, J. E., & Wilkins, A. J. (1997). What brings intentions to mind? An in situ study of prospective memory. *Memory, 5,* 483–507.

Smallwood, J., & Schooler, J. W. (2015). The science of mind wandering: Empirically navigating the stream of consciousness. *Annual Review of Psychology, 66,* 487–518.

Somerville, S. C., Wellman, H. M., & Cultice, J. C. (1983). Young children's deliberate reminding. *Journal of Genetic Psychology, 143,* 87–96.

Song, X., & Wang, X. (2012). Mind wandering in Chinese daily lives: An experience sampling study. *PLOS ONE, 7,* e44423.

Stawarczyk, D. (2018). Phenomenological properties of mind-wandering and daydreaming: A historical overview and functional correlates. In K. Christoff & K. C. R. Fox (Eds.), *The Oxford handbook of spontaneous thought.* New York: Oxford University Press.

Stawarczyk, D., Majerus, S., Maj, M., Van der Linden, M., & D'Argembeau, A. (2011). Mind-wandering: Phenomenology and function as assessed with a novel experience sampling method. *Acta Psychologica, 136,* 370–381.

Szarras, K., & Niedźwieńska, A. (2011). The role of rehearsals in self-generated prospective memory tasks. *International Journal of Psychology, 46,* 346–353.

Trawley, S. L., Stephens, A. N., Rendell, P. G., & Groeger, J. A. (2017). Prospective memory while driving: Comparison of time- and event-based intentions. *Ergonomics, 60*, 780–790.

Trull, T. J., & Ebner-Priemer, U. (2014). The role of ambulatory assessment in psychological science. *Current Directions in Psychological Science, 23*, 466–470.

Unsworth, N., Brewer, G. A., & Spillers, G. J. (2012). Variation in cognitive failures: An individual differences investigation of everyday attention and memory failures. *Journal of Memory and Language, 67*, 1–16.

Warden, E. A., Plimpton, B., & Kvavilashvili, L. (2018). Absence of age effects on spontaneous past and future thinking in daily life. *Psychological Research*, Advanced online publication. doi: 10.1007/s00426-018-1103-7

Wilkins, A. J., & Baddeley, A. D. (1978). Remembering to recall in everyday life: An approach to absentmindedness. In M. M. Gruneberg, P. E. Morris & R. N. Sykes (Eds.), *Practical aspects of memory* (pp. 27–34). London: Academic Press.

Wilson, B. A., Emslie, H., Foley, J., Shiel, A., Watson, P., Hawkins, K … Evans, J. (2005). *The Cambridge prospective memory test*. London: Harcourt-Assessment.

8

PROSPECTIVE MEMORY IN SAFETY-CRITICAL WORK CONTEXTS*

Shayne Loft, Key Dismukes, and Tobias Grundgeiger

Reliable prospective memory (PM) functioning of individuals is essential for safe and efficient outcomes of sociotechnical work systems such as air traffic control (ATC), commercial piloting, emergency healthcare, intensive care, submarine control rooms, and emergency response units. For example, air traffic controllers may need to remember to hold an aircraft when it reaches a specific way-point in their sector because of crossing traffic or bad weather. A pilot may need to report passing through a particular altitude when instructed by ATC. During shift handover in an intensive care unit, the departing nurse may need to remember to show the incoming nurse a patient's electrocardiogram.

Shorrock (2005) reported that 38% of memory errors made by air traffic controllers in the United Kingdom involved failures of PM (e.g., forgetting to perform deferred tasks such as instructing the aircraft to descend). Nowinski, Holbrook, and Dismukes (2003) found that 74 of 75 reports of memory errors airline pilots submitted to the Aviation Safety Reporting System involved PM rather than retrospective memory. In aircraft maintenance, the most common error technicians make is inadvertent omission of a critical procedural step when reassembling equipment after repair or inspection (Hobbs & Williamson, 2003). Rothschild et al. (2005) found that over 50% of errors made in intensive care units were due to failures to carry out intended plans of action such as the failure to discontinue a medication or skipping steps when administering medication.

Failure to perform deferred task actions in such safety-critical work settings can have dangerous consequences. Fortunately, in the vast majority of cases, system-safety barriers prevented single PM failure points from going on to cause accidents, but such barriers are no guarantee. For example, in 1991, a tower controller at Los Angeles International Airport cleared a SkyWest aircraft to hold on the runway while working to clear other aircraft to cross the far end of the runway.

Communication delays occurred, dusk-time visibility was poor, and the controller forgot to clear SkyWest to take off before clearing another aircraft to land while SkyWest was still on the runway, causing a collision that killed 34 people (National Transportation Safety Board, 1991). PM errors made by pilots, such as forgetting to set flaps to take-off position (at Madrid in 2008), forgetting to turn on the pitot heat to prevent icing (at LaGuardia airport in 1994), forgetting to set the hydraulic pumps to the high position (in Houston, 1996), have also led to major accidents. A further issue of concern, as reviewed in this chapter, is the growing evidence that PM task demands may decrease performance on other ongoing tasks.

Several studies have examined PM in workplaces using ethnographic observations, analyses of accident reports, diary reports, and related methods (e.g., Dismukes, Berman, & Loukopoulos, 2007; Grundgeiger, Sanderson, MacDougall, & Venkatesh 2009; Shorrock, 2005). These field study techniques are critical for identifying PM phenomena, understanding the constraints and affordances of complex work systems, and for determining strategies that individuals use. It is equally critical to conduct well-controlled use-inspired (Stokes, 1997) experiments, using simulations of PM demands found in the workplace, to further understand the cognitive processes underlying PM (Dismukes, 2012; Loft, 2014). Working back and forth between the field and the laboratory can enrich both approaches (Wickens, 1992). In addition, by applying theory and methods from the PM literature to simulations of work contexts such as aviation and healthcare, it is possible to establish the utility of PM theory and produce application-relevant information (Morrow, 2018).

Field studies examining PM in workplace settings, particularly those conducted by Dismukes and colleagues in commercial airline settings, have highlighted that PM tasks in the workplace can take a variety of forms (see Dismukes & Nowinski, 2007; Dismukes, 2010; also see Grundgeiger et al. 2009, and Fink, Pak, Bass, Johnston, & Battisto, 2010, for work in healthcare). Most basic laboratory PM studies have examined the ability of individuals to remember to perform a task in the future that is not habitually performed (*episodic PM task*). For example, participants may be asked to perform an ongoing task (e.g., deciding whether strings of letters are words) and to remember to make a separate PM response (e.g., press the "F1" key) when presented with a PM target event. This paradigm corresponds to everyday situations such as intending to give a message to a friend the next time one sees them. However, workplace situations often involve aspects missing from this paradigm, which have been studied far less. Among these aspects are remembering to perform disrupted habitual tasks, remembering to substitute atypical actions for habitual actions, remembering to perform PM tasks created by interruptions, and remembering to switch attention between concurrent tasks. Finally, despite the use of the term prospective *memory*, successful prospective remembering involves planning, attention, and task management, in addition to memory (Dobbs & Reeves, 1996). These components play an especially important role when investigating PM in workplace settings.

In the sections below, we review the literature regarding these aspects of PM, focusing in particular on aviation and healthcare. Although researchers have made considerable progress in understanding how individuals complete PM tasks in these workplaces, they have mainly focused on the cognitive processes of the individual mind. In this chapter we outline the need to also understand the interaction between the environment in which deferred tasks must be remembered and the individual; referred to as *distributed PM* (Grundgeiger et al., 2009; Grundgeiger, Sanderson & Dismukes, 2014). We then discuss how individual and system level vulnerabilities in PM can be identified and mitigated, and we conclude the chapter by identifying several themes for future research.

Disrupted habitual tasks

Much of the work of pilots, air traffic controllers, and healthcare professionals such as doctors and nurses, involves executing the sequential steps of highly practiced procedures. Normally, performance of each step in habitual procedures is reliable, but research suggests that individuals can inadvertently omit steps when their normal sequence is disrupted. For example, one crucial step in preparing a commercial aircraft for flight is to set the wing flaps to take-off position. Setting the flaps is a step embedded in one of several procedural sequences executed from memory, but also backed up with a checklist and cross-checked by both pilots. In spite of these procedural protections, several airline catastrophes have occurred when pilots attempted to take off with flaps not set correctly. Ordinarily, if pilots advance the throttle to take off without setting flaps, a take-off configuration warning system alerts them to abort the take-off, but in these accidents the warning system failed and the pilots continued the take-off roll (e.g., the MD-82 crash in Madrid in 2008).[1]

The Aviation Safety Reporting System (ASRS)[2] database includes a substantial number of reports from airline pilots who aborted a take-off after their warning system alerted them that their flaps were not properly set. The circumstances vary, but a frequent theme is that circumstances forced the pilots to defer setting flaps out of the normal sequence. For example, if the taxiway is covered with icy slush, company procedures may require the pilots to defer setting flaps until they reach the runway. But this altered procedure, which is needed only occasionally, removes cognitive aspects that usually help the pilots remember to set flaps. The immediately preceding actions associated in memory with setting flaps are now temporally remote, the runway environment is not associated with setting flaps but instead with actions to start the take-off, and time pressure is often an issue at this point. (See ASRS report #263589 for an example of this situation.)

Grundgeiger et al. (2013) investigated the ability of nurses to remember to perform deferred habitual tasks in simulated intensive care. Nurses were required to remember to check the content of an emergency drawer for completeness, a task that is conducted at the start of every shift and includes the same steps, while involved in a social conversation with the night-duty nurse (confederate).

Although the task of checking the emergency drawer for completeness is conducted frequently, the nurses have to remember to check for each item without external prompting. The missing visual cues and the additional distracting conversation resulted in incomplete checks in more than 80% of the cases. However, PM errors decreased by 20% when visual cues were provided. In addition to automatic triggering of sequential steps in highly practiced tasks and support by task context, visual cues for task step status seem to contribute to successful remembering of habitual PM tasks.

Remembering to substitute atypical actions for habitual actions

One common form of PM error is "habit capture" (Reason, 1990), in which individuals fail to remember to perform an atypical intended action, substituting the habitual action instead. Not only must the individual remember a new, episodic PM task, but the intended action must compete for retrieval with task responses more directly associated with the ongoing task. Of the PM errors airline pilots reported to the ASRS 19% involved habit capture (Nowinski et al., 2003).

Much of the empirical work on habit capture has been done in simulated ATC, but findings from ATC tasks are also potentially relevant to other work contexts in which individuals monitor perceptual displays with multiple task demands (e.g., naval radar tracking, air-battle management, unmanned vehicle control).

Stone, Dismukes, and Remington (2001) found that participants were less likely to remember to reroute an aircraft when the number of aircraft being handled increased or when they were required to complete an auditory shadowing task concurrently. Loft and Remington (2010) had participants perform ongoing ATC tasks, such as accepting aircraft entering the sector, handing-off aircraft leaving the sector, and detecting and resolving aircraft conflicts. For the PM task, participants needed to remember to press an alternative response key instead of the routine key when accepting target aircraft that had certain flight data (e.g., a certain altitude). Participants were less likely to remember to deviate from aircraft acceptance routines that had been more practiced, indicating that the PM response competes with the ongoing task response for response selection. However, PM errors were reduced when the flight information that needed to be assessed to accept an aircraft (e.g., altitude) was the same type of flight information that needed to be assessed to determine the PM status of an aircraft (focal targets) compared to when it was different (nonfocal targets). Loft, Smith, and Remington (2013) reported that PM errors were particularly prevalent under conditions in which the PM target presentation rate was reduced. This finding is relevant because controllers report that PM target events can sometimes be encountered after delays of many minutes or even hours (Dismukes, 2012; Shorrock, 2005).

Context is a powerful cue for experts. Controllers are trained on specific sectors and thus learn to recognize specific types of air traffic configurations (Loft, Sanderson, Neal, & Moiij, 2007). For example, if a controller intends to reroute incoming aircraft due to bad weather, the controller would know which area of the sector the weather is affecting, and this should allow attention to be focused to that region. In line with this, Loft, Finnerty, and Remington (2011) demonstrated that PM errors were reduced when individuals were informed about which display regions they could expect the PM target aircraft to appear in. These findings are consistent with basic laboratory research showing that PM improves when the retrieval context matches encoding context, apparently due to associative cueing (Cook, Marsh, & Hicks, 2005; Nowinski & Dismukes, 2005; see Smith & Skinner, in *Prospective Memory*).

A robust finding reported by Loft and colleagues has been that PM tasks can lead to costs to ongoing tasks in the form of slowed non-target aircraft acceptance and handoff, slowed conflict detection, and increased missed conflicts, compared to individuals without PM tasks (e.g., Loft, Finnerty, et al. 2011; Loft & Remington, 2010). These costs are consistent with theories of PM (see chapters by Shelton, Scullin, & Hacker, and by Strickland, Loft & Heathcote, in *Prospective Memory*) and human error (Norman, 1981; Reason, 1990) that assume that some form of cognitive control is required to inhibit habitual task responses and retrieve deferred task actions. Conditions in simulated ATC, in which participants are required to continuously monitor multi-item dynamic displays for events with variable onsets and durations, are quite different from the traditional basic laboratory paradigm, in which participants make rapid responses to static stimuli presented one at a time, and therefore costs may result from different underlying cognitive mechanisms in ATC compared to basic paradigms. Regarding the costs to aircraft conflict detection, it is possible that the cognitive load or the accumulative time commitment associated with checking the PM status of aircraft, or the fact that the PM-task goal needs to be held in mind, causes slower or less extensive scanning of the display or decreases the accuracy or efficiency of predicting future relative positions of the aircraft (Loft, Bolland, Humphreys, & Neal, 2009). Regardless of the underlying mechanisms, these studies demonstrate that the costs of maintaining a deferred intention while performing ongoing tasks have important implications for operational settings.

Interruptions create prospective memory tasks

A PM task can be formed when a primary task is interrupted, since the interruption makes it necessary to remember to resume the primary task after dealing with the interruption (Boehm-Davis & Remington, 2009). Individuals are more likely forget to resume interrupted tasks if they fail to encode an explicit intention to resume the interrupted task because the interruption occurs abruptly or needs immediate attention; if new pressing task demands draw attention immediately after the interruption has ended; or if suitable cues are not present to remind the individual of uncompleted tasks after the interruption has ended.[3] In line with this, Dodhia and Dismukes (2009) reported that participants in a computerized laboratory task context were more likely to resume an interrupted task when given a short pause or a reminder to complete unfinished tasks at the beginning of an interruption, or when provided a pause or an explicit cue when the interruption ended.

Healthcare professionals are often interrupted, which significantly increases the chance of PM error (Fong, Hettinger, & Ratwani, 2017; Westbrook, Woods, Rob, Dunsmuir, & Day, 2010). Grundgeiger, Sanderson, MacDougall, & Venkatesh (2010) investigated the PM demands associated with intensive care nurses resuming an interrupted task. The resumption lag was defined as the time from a nurse's last fixation on an object associated with the interrupting task to the nurse's first fixation on an object associated with the to-be-resumed primary task. Grundgeiger et al. (2010) found that longer interruptions and a context change due to the interrupting task increased primary task resumption time. Using a similar approach, Fong et al. (2017) were able to predict whether emergency physicians would forget to resume interrupted tasks. However, Grundgeiger et al. (2010) also reported that, in about 45% of the interrupted tasks, nurses used various behavioral strategies, such as retaining a task artifact associated with the PM task, while attending to the interruption, that changed the cognitive demands of the PM tasks. We will address these changes in cognitive demand later when discussing distributed PM. In an intensive care simulation, Grundgeiger et al. (2013) investigated whether visual cues could assist nurses in the resumption of interrupted tasks. The participating nurses were interrupted before checking the settings of the mechanical ventilator. In the visual cue condition, the settings tab on the display of the ventilator was open at the time of the interruption whilst, in the no visual cue condition, the tab was closed. The hypothesis was that nurses in the visual cue condition would resume the task more frequently compared to the no cue condition. However, nurses in the visual cue condition used a different strategy to manage the interruption and the associated PM demands. In the visual cue condition, nurses significantly more often blocked the interruption and asked the interrupting nurse to wait until the settings of the mechanical ventilator had been checked (see also Weng, Huber, Vilgan, Grundgeiger, & Sanderson, 2017).

In a recent field driving study, Gregory, Irwin, Faulks, and Chekaluk (2014) examined the speeding behavior of drivers who were interrupted shortly after they encountered a new lower speed limit. They found that 100 m after an interruption (caused by having to stop for a red traffic light), drivers exceeded the new 40 km/h speed limit by an average of 8 km/h. Drivers that were not interrupted, on the other hand, exceeded the speed limit by less than 2 km/h. Gregory et al. suggested that the speeding resulted from drivers forgetting to travel at the new lower speed limit following the traffic light interruption. Bowden, Visser, and Loft (2017) replicated and extended these findings using a driving simulator. Bowden et al. showed an increase in the probability of uncorrected speeding (speed limit exceeded by at least 5 km/h with no attempt to return below the limit) from 9% when uninterrupted to 26% when interrupted by a traffic light. Performing a cognitively demanding task during the interruption (i.e., an auditory n-back task), when compared to an unfilled interruption, further increased speeding. Providing drivers with 10 s longer to encode the new speed limit before interruption decreased speeding.

Wilson, Farrell, Visser, and Lof (2018; also see Wilson, Strickland, Farrell, Visser, & Loft, 2020) examined how interruptions—presented between encoding a deferred task action and the time to perform that action—influenced the probability and speed at which individuals remembered to perform deferred tasks in simulated ATC. Participants were required to accept/handoff aircraft, detect aircraft conflicts, and perform two deferred tasks: a deferred conflict detection task that required remembering to resolve a conflict, and a deferred handoff task that required substituting an alternative aircraft handoff action in place of a routine handoff action. Participants were either not interrupted during the time between encoding the PM task and the correct time for PM retrieval, or were interrupted by the ATC task being replaced by a blank display, an n-back task; or a secondary (independent) ATC task scenario. Relative to no interruption, interruptions slowed deferred conflict detection task resumption, and an ex-Gaussian model of task resumption times revealed that participants were slower to initiate responding to the deferred conflict in the interruption conditions compared to the no-interruption condition. In addition, individuals failed to detect deferred conflicts more often following an ATC task interruption compared to following no interruption. The ex-Gaussian model revealed that these resumption failures reflected true forgetting of the deferred task, rather than delayed retrieval of the deferred task.

Interleaving the monitoring of concurrent tasks

Experts at work often need to remember to periodically switch attention back and forth between concurrent tasks to check their status. The pattern of attention-switching required varies substantially with the particular tasks involved. Some situations are similar to laboratory studies of time-based PM. For example, in older airliners, pilots must occasionally pump fuel from one tank to another to correct imbalance, and this process may take several minutes, during which the pilots may perform other tasks and forget to turn off the pumps before going too far. Other situations require more regular back and forth switching of attention; for example, a pilot flying in manual control mode while climbing out from take-off must consistently switch attention back and forth from monitoring for traffic outside the cockpit to monitoring the altimeter to level off at an assigned altitude. With practice, pilots develop skill in interleaving specific combinations of monitoring tasks, but remain vulnerable to "cognitive tunneling", that is, focusing on one task that has become unexpectedly difficult and forgetting to switch attention on time.

Throughout a flight, pilots must monitor the status of multiple systems as well as the aircraft trajectory. The airline industry considers monitoring a crucial responsibility and skill for pilots; recently, an industry group issued a report on ways to improve training and procedures for monitoring (Active Pilot Monitoring Working Group, 2014).

This form of PM task is equally relevant to ATC, healthcare, and driving. In healthcare, during cardiopulmonary resuscitations, emergency physicians need to remember to switch between, for example, checking the patient's heart rhythm every two minutes, thinking about causes of the cardiac arrest, and managing several other tasks such as deciding on medication administration and interventions (Soar et al., 2015). Even highly qualified staff can be challenged by avoiding getting absorbed by one task and having to remember to switch attention (Abella et al., 2005).

When driving, we need to monitor and integrate information from outside the vehicle (steering, interpreting road signs, reacting to other cars and pedestrians) with information from inside the vehicle (checking instruments, checking GPS, adjusting temperature controls). One potential problem is that drivers can become absorbed in attending to information inside the vehicle and fail to monitor the visual environment frequently enough to respond to unexpected events, such as another car braking suddenly or a child crossing the road.

The less frequently an event occurs the more difficult humans find it to maintain vigilant monitoring for that event, even if the consequences of it occurring might be disastrous (Wickens, Hooey, Gore, Sebok & Koenicke, 2009). For example, in small aircraft a crucial harbinger of imminent engine failure is a rapid drop in oil pressure; however, this occurs so infrequently that pilots find it difficult to consistently monitor the oil pressure gauge. To improve monitoring skills, we need cognitive models of attention distribution among field tasks. The most relevant computational model of this sort is the Salience, Effort, Expectancy, Value (SEEV) model of visual attention (Wickens, 2015). Salience refers to the physical properties of events (the likelihood that events will capture attention), effort refers to both the effort involved in reallocating attention and to the current workload associated with the currently attended task, expectancy refers to the expectancy of gaining information from an event, and value refers to the value or cost of processing or failing to process information. This model could provide a foundation for practical ways to improve displays and monitoring training.

Encoding deferred intentions in operational settings

Some researchers might argue that some of the examples we have given do not truly involve PM because the individual did not form an explicit intention to perform the task. When interrupted, an individual may not explicitly think "I must remember to resume this interrupted task later." But, if asked, the individual would very probably say of course he or she intended to resume the interrupted task—the intention was implicit in the individual's goal structure. Similarly, a pilot correcting a fuel tank imbalance may not think explicitly "I must monitor the fuel gauges and turn off the fuel pump when the tanks are balanced", but the intention to do so is implicit in the pilot's goal structure. It does not matter whether we label such situations as PM, but it is important to understand why individuals forget to act in these situations and to develop ways to help them remember.

Individuals in operational and everyday settings often encode intentions incompletely, vaguely, or only implicitly. Nowinski et al. (2003) found that 19% of PM errors pilots reported involved poor encoding of intentions, such as not identifying all of the instruments that should be reset after being given a change in departure runways. A study of everyday deferred intentions found that individuals rarely formed a specific plan for how, where, and when they would perform self-generated deferred intentions, although doing so improved performance (Holbrook & Dismukes, 2009). Empirical studies have shown that forming specific implementation intentions improves PM dramatically in diverse everyday settings (Gollwitzer & Sheeran, 2006).

Distributed prospective memory

Sociotechnical settings have several features that are generally not replicated in basic PM research. First, situations can change quickly as a result of human control actions or external forces. Second, the environment is replete with specialized technological equipment and procedures (nonhuman agents). For example, airline pilots manage sophisticated control and navigation systems. Equipment in intensive care units includes patient monitors for monitoring vital signs such as heart rate and oxygen saturation, and electronic medical records for documentation. Third, individuals follow formal procedures such as checklists to organize work and protect them against errors. Fourth, completion of task goals in sociotechnical settings almost always involves coordination with other team members (human agents), rather than the functioning of one individual alone. For example, aircraft separation assurance is the responsibility of multiple human agents such as air traffic controllers, pilots, and supervisory controllers. Airline cockpits have two pilots who interact with air traffic controllers, dispatchers, flight attendants, and other personnel. Patient treatment and safety in hospitals is the joint responsibility of physicians, nurses, surgeons, physiotherapists, radiologists, and so on.

Due to these features of sociotechnical work settings, Grundgeiger et al. (2014) proposed that we need to take a *systems view* (Hutchins, 1995a, 1995b; Norman, 1993) to understand the interaction between the environment, in which deferred tasks must be remembered, and the cognition of the individual. Remembering to perform deferred task actions can be supported by both internal cognition and external cognition.

The internal cognitive processes that individuals rely on to remember to perform deferred intentions have been extensively studied. It is likely, however, that experts often rely less on internal cognition, and more on external representation, when faced with PM demands in sociotechnical work settings. For example, equipment or artifacts that are likely to be encountered in an environment may be directly associated with a PM task. Grundgeiger, Liu, Sanderson, Jenkins, and Leane (2008) reported that 60% of anesthesiologists remembered a pre-transfusion bedside check only after looking at the label attached to the blood bag (a natural and direct, and therefore a passive, external representation of the task).

Healthcare professionals sometimes create specific external representations as reminders. Grundgeiger et al. (2013) found that nurses place written notes or key equipment in frequently attended positions, such as on the keyboard of the computer terminal or on the medication bench, and line equipment up in the order of temporal use. Xiao, Milgram, and Doyle (1997) reported that anesthetists create "trigger cues" for remembering to administer a specific drug.

The benefit of external reminders of deferred task goals has also been experimentally studied in driving (Gregory et al., 2014) and in simulated ATC (Loft, Chapman, & Smith, 2016; Loft, Smith, Bhaskara, 2011; Loft et al., 2013; Vortac, Edwards, & Manning, 1995). In a naturalistic driving study, Gregory et al. found that speeding was reduced by placing a flashing LED sign immediately after the interruption to remind drivers to check their speed.

In simulated ATC, PM aids that presented the PM instruction (e.g., "Press 9 if speed > 48") on the display and flashed to alert participants when they needed to deviate from aircraft acceptance routines have been effective in reducing, but not eliminating, PM errors. The abrupt appearance of something new on a display is highly effective in capturing attention (Posner, 1980), and likely reduced the demands associated with "searching" for target aircraft or rehearsing the PM-task goal because participants can reliably depend on the PM aid to alert them when a target aircraft was present. It is important to note, however, that in operational settings human trust and appropriate behavioral reliance on PM reminders (which is, technically speaking, a form of task automation) is highly dependent on continued exposure to the reliability of that PM reminder (Lee & See, 2004).

PM tasks can also be externally represented in the environment by interactions with team members. Grundgeiger et al. (2010) reported that some PM tasks were done redundantly by other staff members; four to six bedside nurses are assisted by an additional "bay nurse" who conducts a redundant bedside area safety check, and the bay nurse indeed noticed previous PM failures (Grundgeiger et al. 2013). In an airline operation, the pilot not actively flying the aircraft is now designated the "monitoring pilot" to emphasize this pilot's role in monitoring the status of the aircraft and its systems and the actions of the flying pilot.

Using task analysis and operational experience, system designers try to anticipate PM demanding situations and to support operators by designing reminders into work systems. In healthcare, electronic patient records provide time-based reminders for patient care and medication tasks. Alarm limits of patient vital sign monitors reduce the burden of remembering to shift attention periodically to the monitor, reducing the internal cognitive demand for interleaving this PM task.

In the aviation industry, formalized operating procedures and checklists are used extensively to standardize procedures and protect against both retrospective memory lapses and PM lapses. Hutchins (1995a,b) argued that the cockpit, with its specifically designed displays and controls, operating manuals and checklists, which interacts with trained pilots, constitutes a memory system in itself.

Improving prospective memory in the workplace

Various countermeasures can help system designers and individuals reduce the probability of making PM errors in the workplace (see Dismukes, 2010, for detailed discussion). These countermeasures are based on existing PM research, but one should note that little empirical research has directly tested the effectiveness and practicality of countermeasures, with the exception of "implementation intentions" and external aids.

One critical intervention is to conduct task analyses of operating environments to determine situations in which PM and concurrent task demands are high, or where interruptions are likely to be frequent. If data are available, this process should include analysis of specific situations in which PM failures have occurred in the past and the factors contributing to those PM failures. This analysis can help organizations revise existing operating procedures and systems to reduce the frequency of PM demands and interruptions, and to educate individuals about vulnerability to PM failure. This education/training could discuss the importance of adhering to work procedures for checklist use, monitoring, and cross-checking; avoiding deferring crucial tasks unnecessarily; pausing to encode explicit intentions to resume interrupted tasks, creating reminder cues, and forming explicit implementation plans for deferred tasks.

Implementation planning[4] refers to elaborating an intention when initially formed by identifying where, when, and how one will execute the intention, and to visualize oneself executing that intention when the time comes (Gollwitzer & Sheeran, 2006). This sort of planning has been shown to improve performance as much as two to four-fold in tasks such as exercising, medication adherence, breast self-examination, and homework completion.

In situations in which PM vulnerability is unavoidable and the consequences of failing to perform a deferred task goal are high, displays and alerting systems can be designed to help individuals keep track of deferred task goals, for example, by providing external memory aids that are salient, distinctive, and highly related to the deferred task goal. However, designing effective external reminders is not necessarily easy. Operators often habituate to reminders over time, reducing their effectiveness. It is also not always practical or safe to introduce additional visual clutter to task displays (Moacdieh & Sarter, 2015). And lastly, an external reminder that is salient enough to guarantee attention may be overly distracting and subjectively annoying, and could potentially take an operator's attention away from other safety-critical tasks.

Interlocks that prevent operators from proceeding until previous steps are completed can also be effective PM aids, but like alerts and warnings, these must be carefully designed to work within the overall task environment.

A recent promising research area in acute healthcare is that of cognitive aids (Clebone, et al., 2017; Marshall, 2013). These aids are artifacts that help users performing a task reduce PM lapses and other errors and help increase speed and fluidity of performance (Reason, 1987). In healthcare, cognitive aids frequently come as checklists or medical decision algorithms and, from a PM perspective, are external reminders. However, recent electronic cognitive aids have been evaluated that, in addition to reminding operators of episodic PM tasks, can also support interleaving monitoring tasks. For example, during resuscitations, these electronic aids can provide information about the time elapsed since the last heart rhythm analyses or suggest possible causes of the cardiac arrest to consider during times of lower workload (Grundgeiger, Huber, Reinhardt, Steinisch, Happel, & Wurmb, 2019).

Conclusions and outlook

As reviewed in this chapter, PM tasks in complex work systems diverge in many ways from the manner in which PM has traditionally been studied in the basic PM literature. The research reviewed here has started exploration of the various constraints and affordances that complex work systems place on PM in safety-critical work contexts, but further work is needed, especially laboratory research to elucidate the mechanisms of effects identified in ethnographic studies.

For example, retention intervals are often far longer in the workplace than in the laboratory, and we need to understand how the intention to complete deferred actions can be maintained over longer delays. An under-researched but critical feature of complex sociotechnical work systems is that there can often be a fairly broad window of opportunity to perform a deferred task, and that opportunity may be defined by a conjunction of several events rather than a single event (e.g., if my supervisor starts to leave the hangar before I finish reassembling this engine, and if no one else is around, I will ask him which maintenance manual to use).

Empirical investigation will be also be important to elucidate cognitive processes underlying forms of PM tasks identified in work settings, such as when individuals need to periodically shift attention among multiple tasks to check their status (with or without the benefit of events in the environment prompting them to do so), or when sequential steps of highly practiced procedures are disrupted and individuals need to remember to resume them at the correct re-entry point. We also need to examine the role of incidental (vs. planned) cues in triggering retrieval of deferred task actions.

Various countermeasures have been suggested to support PM, but empirical research is required to determine the efficacy and practicality of these measures and to tune them for diverse operational settings.

Much of the research on health care and ATC reviewed in this chapter used simulations of task environments designed to have both high psychological fidelity and experimental control. Ecologically motivated work simulations combined with experimental control allow us to apply theories of memory and attention derived from basic research to complex domains that are not well captured by traditional laboratory research (Dismukes, 2012; Loft, 2014). PM research on piloting, to date, has been based primarily on accident reports, interviews, and *in situ* observations; a great deal more could be learned by applying this controlled simulation approach to studying PM in the cockpit.

Expertise is central in many respects to the performance of professionals in their domains. For example, the highly practiced skills of pilots, controllers, and surgeons rely heavily on automaticity, rather than the controlled processing of novices. Experts may also prioritize and interleave tasks in ways different than novices, and this divergence may not be captured in experimental designs or instructions to participants. With the exception of some of the health care simulations cited here, most basic research laboratory and simulation studies have not used expert participants, so the role of expertise in PM is as yet largely unexplored.

Finally, we hope that this chapter illustrates the benefits of combining ethnographic, simulation, and controlled laboratory studies of PM in an iterative manner. Each approach can inform the others. Applied studies can be shaped by theories arising from basic studies and can identify new and important phenomena to stimulate theory and experimentation.

Notes

* This chapter originally appeared in the edited volume, *Prospective Memory*. It has been updated for this compilation.

1 The investigation report, CIAIAC A032/2008, can be downloaded from http://www. aviation-accidents.net/report-download.php?id=18.

2 Information about ASRS can be found at https://asrs.arc.nasa.gov. Loukopoulos, Dismukes, & Barshi (2009) analyze many ASRS reports involving PM and attention management.

3 The effects of interruptions on task performance have been studied extensively, but most of the laboratory studies have used time to resume the interrupted task or subsequent errors as the dependent variables. For reviews see Trafton & Monk (2007) and Salvucci & Taatgen (2011).

4 Termed "implementation intentions" by the scientists who originally developed the technique.

References

Abella, B. S., Alvarado, J. P., Myklebust, H., Edelson, D. P., Barry, A., O'Hearn, N. ... Becker, L. B. (2005). Quality of cardiopulmonary resuscitation during in-hospital cardiac arrest. *Journal of the American Medical Association*, *293*, 305–310.

Active Pilot Monitoring Working Group (2014). *A practical guide to improving flight path monitoring*. Alexandria, VA: Flight Safety Foundation.

Boehm-Davis, D. A., & Remington R. W. (2009). Reducing the disruptive effects of interruption: A cognitive framework for analysing the costs and benefits of intervention strategies. *Accident Analysis and Prevention*, *41*, 1124–1129.

Bowden, V. K., Visser, T. A. W., & Loft, S. (2017). Forgetting induced speeding: Can prospective memory failure account for drivers exceeding the speed limit? *Journal of Experimental Psychology: Applied*, *23*, 180–190.

Clebone, A., Burian, B. K., Watkins, S. C., Gálvez, J. A., Lockman, J. L., & Heitmiller, E. S. (2017). The development and implementation of cognitive aids for critical events in pediatric anesthesia: The Society for Pediatric Anesthesia critical events checklist. *Anesthesia and Analgesia, 124*, 900–907.

Cook, G. K., Marsh, R. L., & Hicks, J. L. (2005). Associating a time-based prospective memory task with an expected context can improve or impair intention completion. *Applied Cognitive Psychology, 19*, 345–360.

Dismukes, R. K. (2010). Remembrance of things future: Prospective memory in laboratory, workplace and everyday settings. In D. H. Harris (Ed.), *Reviews of human factors and ergonomics* (vol. 6, pp. 79–122). Santa Monica, CA: Human Factors Society.

Dismukes, R. K. (2012). Prospective memory in workplace and everyday situations. *Current Directions in Psychological Science, 21*, 215–220.

Dismukes, R. K., Berman, B., & Loukopoulos, L. D. (2007). *The limits of expertise: Rethinking pilot error and the causes of airline accidents*. Burlington, VT: Ashgate.

Dismukes, R. K., & Nowinski, J. (2007). Prospective memory, concurrent task management, and pilot error. In A. Kramer, D. Wiegmann, & A. Kirlik (Eds.), *Attention: From theory to practice* (pp. 225–236). New York: Oxford University Press.

Dobbs, A. R., & Reeves, B. (1996). Prospective memory: More than memory. In M. Brandimonte, G. O. Einstein, & M. A. McDaniel (Eds.), *Prospective memory: Theory and applications* (pp. 199–225). Mahwah, NJ: Lawrence Erlbaum Associates.

Dodhia, R. M., & Dismukes, R. K. (2009). Interruptions create prospective memory tasks. *Applied Cognitive Psychology, 23*, 73–89.

Fink, N., Pak, R., Bass, B., Johnston, M., & Battisto, D. (2010). A survey of nurses self-reported prospective memory tasks: What must they remember and what do they forget. Paper presented at the 54th Annual Meeting of the Human Factors and Ergonomics Society, October 27–30, San Francisco, CA.

Fong, A., Hettinger, A. Z., & Ratwani, R. M. (2017). A predictive model of emergency physician task resumption following interruptions. Paper presented at the Proceedings of the 2017 CHI Conference on Human Factors in Computing Systems.

Gollwitzer, P. M. & Sheeran, P. (2006). Implementation intentions and goal achievement: A meta-analysis of effects and processes. *Advances in Experimental Social Psychology, 38*, 69–119.

Gregory, B., Irwin, J. D., Faulks, I. J., & Chekaluk, E. (2014). Speeding in school zones: Violation or lapse in prospective memory? *Journal of Experimental Psychology: Applied, 20*, 191–198.

Grundgeiger, T., Liu, D., Sanderson, P. M., Jenkins, S., & Leane, T. (2008). Effects of interruptions on prospective memory performance in anesthesiology. Paper presented at the 52nd Annual Meeting of the Human Factors and Ergonomics Society, New York.

Grundgeiger, T., Sanderson, P. M., Beltran Orihuela, C., Thompson, A., MacDougall, H. G., Nunnink, L., & Venkatesh, B. (2013). Prospective memory in intensive care nursing: A representative and controlled patient simulator study. *Ergonomics, 56*, 579–589.

Grundgeiger, T., Sanderson, P. M., & Dismukes, R. K. (2014). Prospective memory in complex sociotechnical systems. *Zeitschrift für Psychologie: Journal of Psychology, 222*, 100–109.

Grundgeiger, T., Sanderson, P. M., MacDougall, H. G. & Venkatesh, B. (2009). Distributed prospective memory: An approach to understanding how nurses remember tasks. Paper presented at the Proceedings of 53rd Annual Meeting of the Human Factors and Ergonomics Society, October, San Antonio, TX.

Grundgeiger, T., Sanderson, P. M., MacDougall, H. G., & Venkatesh, B. (2010). Interruption management in the intensive care unit: Predicting resumption times and assessing distributed support. *Journal of Experimental Psychology: Applied, 16*, 317–334.

Grundgeiger, T., Huber, S., Reinhardt, D., Steinisch, A., Happel, O., & Wurmb, T. (2019). Cognitive aids in acute care: Investigating how cognitive aids affect and support in-hospital emergency teams. Paper presented at the 2019 CHI Conference on Human Factors in Computing Systems, Glasgow, UK.

Hobbs, A. & Williamson, A. (2003). Associations between errors and contributing factors in aircraft maintenance. *Human Factors, 45*, 186–201.

Holbrook, J. B., & Dismukes, R. K. (2009). Prospective memory in everyday tasks. In *Proceedings of the Human Factors and Ergonomics Society 53rd Annual Meeting* (pp. 590–594). Santa Monica, CA: Human Factors and Ergonomics Society.

Hutchins, E. (1995a). *Cognition in the wild*. Cambridge, MA: MIT Press.

Hutchins, E. (1995b). How a cockpit remembers its speeds. *Cognitive Science, 19*, 265–288.

Lee, J. D., & See, K. A. (2004). Trust in automation: Designing for appropriate reliance. *Human Factors, 46*, 50–80.

Loft, S. (2014). Applying psychological science to examine prospective memory in simulated air traffic control. *Current Directions in Psychological Science, 23*, 326–331.

Loft, S., Bolland, S., Humphreys, M. S., & Neal, A. (2009). A theory and model of conflict detection in air traffic control: Incorporating environmental constraints. *Journal of Experimental Psychology: Applied, 15*, 106–124.

Loft, S., Chapman, M., & Smith, R. E. (2016). Reducing prospective memory error and costs in simulated air traffic control: External aids, extending practice, and removing perceived memory requirements. *Journal of Experimental Psychology: Applied, 22*, 272–284.

Loft, S., Finnerty, D., & Remington, R. W. (2011). Using spatial context to support prospective memory in simulated air traffic control. *Human Factors, 53*, 662–671.

Loft, S., & Remington, R. W. (2010). Prospective memory and task interference in a continuous monitoring dynamic display task. *Journal of Experimental Psychology: Applied, 16*, 145–157.

Loft, S., Sanderson, P., Neal, A., & Mooij, M. (2007). Modeling and predicting mental workload in en route air traffic control: Critical review and broader implications. *Human Factors, 49*, 376–399.

Loft, S. Smith, R. E., & Bhaskara, A. (2011). Prospective memory in an air traffic control simulation: External aids that signal when to act. *Journal of Experimental Psychology: Applied, 17*, 60–70.

Loft, S., Smith, R. E., & Remington, R. W. (2013). Minimizing the disruptive effects of prospective memory in simulated air traffic control. *Journal of Experimental Psychology: Applied, 19*, 254–265.

Loukopoulos, L. D., Dismukes, R. K., & Barshi, I. (2009). *The multitasking myth: Handling complexity in real-world operations*. Burlington, VT: Ashgate.

Marshall, S. (2013). The use of cognitive aids during emergencies in anesthesia: A review of the literature. *Anesthesia and Analgesia, 117*, 1162–1171.

Moacdieh, N., & Sarter, N. (2015). Display clutter: A review of definitions and measurement techniques. *Human Factors, 57*, 61–100.

Morrow, D. G. (2018). Publishing papers that matter. *Journal of Experimental Psychology: Applied, 24*, 1–2.

National Transportation Safety Board (1991). *Aircraft accident report (NTSB/AAR-91/08)*. Washington, DC: US Government Printing Office.

Norman, D. A. (1981) Categorization of action slips. *Psychological Review, 88*, 1–15.

Norman, D. A. (1993). *Things that make us smart: Defending human attributes in the age of the machine*. Reading, MA: Addison-Wesley.

Nowinski, J. L., & Dismukes, R. K. (2005). Effects of ongoing task context and target typicality on prospective memory performance: The importance of associative cueing. *Memory, 13*, 649–657.

Nowinski, J. L., Hobrook, J. B., & Dismukes, R. K. (2003). Human memory and cockpit operations: An ASRS study. *Proceedings of the 12th International Symposium on Aviation Psychology* (pp. 888–893). Dayton, OH: Wright State University.

Posner, M. I. (1980). Orienting of attention. *Quarterly Journal of Experimental Psychology, 32*, 3–25.

Reason, J. (1987). Cognitive aids in process environments: Prostheses or tools? *International Journal of Man-Machine Studies, 27*, 463–470.

Reason, J. (1990). *Human error.* Cambridge: Cambridge University Press.

Rothschild, J. M., Landrigan, C. P., Cronin, J. W., Kaushal, R., Lockley, S. W., Burdick, E. … Bates, D. W. (2005). The critical care safety study: The incidence and nature of adverse events and serious medical errors in intensive care. *Critical Care Medicine, 33*, 1694–1700.

Salvucci, D. D., & Taatgen, N. A. (2011). *The multitasking mind.* New York: Oxford University Press.

Shorrock, S. T. (2005). Errors of memory in air traffic control. *Safety Science, 43*, 571–588.

Soar, J., Nolan, J. P., Böttiger, B. W., Perkins, G. D., Lott, C., Carli, P.…Deakin, C. D. (2015). European Resuscitation Council guidelines for resuscitation 2015. *Resuscitation, 95*, 100–147.

Stokes, D. E. (1997). *Pasteur's quadrant: Basic science and technological innovation.* Washington, DC: Brookings Institution Press.

Stone, M., Dismukes, K., & Remington, R. (2001). Prospective memory in dynamic environments: Effects of load, delay, and phonological rehearsal. *Memory, 9*, 165–176.

Trafton, J. G., & Monk, C. A. (2007). Task interruptions. *Reviews of Human Factors and Ergonomics, 3*, 111–126.

Vortac, O. U., Edwards, M. B., & Manning, C. A. (1995). Functions of external cues in prospective memory. *Memory, 3*, 201–219.

Weng, M., Huber, S., Vilgan, E., Grundgeiger, T., & Sanderson, P. M. (2017). Interruptions, visual cues, and the microstructure of interaction: Four laboratory studies. *International Journal of Human-Computer Studies, 103*, 77–94.

Westbrook, J. I., Woods, A., Rob, M. I., Dunsmuir, W. T. M., & Day, R. O. (2010). Association of interruptions with an increased risk and severity of medication administration errors. *Archives of Internal Medicine, 170*, 683–690.

Wickens, C. D. (1992). *Engineering psychology and human performance.* New York: Harper Collins Publishers.

Wickens, C. D. (2015). Noticing events in the visual workplace: The SEEV and NSEEV models. In R. R. Hoffman, P. A. Hancock, M. W. Scerbo, R. Parasuraman, & J. L. Szalma (Eds.), *Cambridge handbook of applied perception research* (pp. 749–768). New York: Cambridge.

Wickens, C. D., Hooey, B. L., Gore, B. F., Sebok, A., & Koenicke, C. S. (2009). Identifying black swans in NextGen: Predicting human performance in off-nominal conditions. *Human Factors, 51*, 638–651.

Wilson, M. S., Farrell, S., Visser, T. A. W., & Loft, S. (2018). Remembering to execute deferred tasks in simulated air traffic control: The impact of interruptions. *Journal of Experimental Psychology: Applied, 24*, 360–379.

Wilson, M. S., Strickland, L., Farrell, S., Visser, T. A. W., & Loft, S. (2020). Prospective memory performance in simulated air traffic control: Robust to interruptions but impaired by retention interval. *Human Factors, 62*(8), 1249–1264.

Xiao, Y., Milgram, P., & Doyle, D. J. (1997). Planning behaviour and its functional role in interactions with complex systems. *IEEE Transactions on Systems, Man, and Cybernetics Part A: Systems and Humans, 27*, 313–324.

PART III

Memory limitations: False memories

9

FALSE MEMORIES MATTER

The repercussions that follow the development of false memory*

Cara Laney and Elizabeth F. Loftus

Many of our everyday memories have repercussions. This means that they can have consequences for our later thoughts, intentions, and even behaviors. Memories of a favorite childhood pet can give people warm feelings later in life. Memories of getting horrible food poisoning after eating leftover pizza from the fridge can make people avoid pizza (or at least cold pizza) for the rest of their lives. Memories of committing a wrong against a friend can lead to lifelong feelings of guilt. But what about false memories? Can they have repercussions too? If they did not, it might lead to a way to distinguish true from false memories.

Being able to differentiate between memories for events that truly happened and false memories would be highly beneficial, especially for the justice system. Finding a reliable distinguishing characteristic between true and false memories has been an important research goal for years (Heaps & Nash, 2001; Loftus & Bernstein, 2005; Bernstein & Loftus, 2009). Numerous potential characteristics have been tested, including confidence (Loftus & Pickrell, 1995; Laney & Takarangi, 2013), detail (e.g., Hyman & Pentland, 1996; Porter, Yuille, & Lehman, 1999), emotionality (Campbell & Porter, 2002; McNally, 2003; McNally et al., 2004; Laney & Loftus, 2008; see also Oulton & Takarangi, 2017), longevity (Geraerts et al., 2008; Laney, Bowman-Fowler, Nelson, Bernstein, & Loftus, 2008; see also later), and individual differences that might distinguish between people who are more versus less likely to form false memories (e.g., Porter, Birt, Yuille, & Lehman, 2000; Drivdahl & Zaragoza, 2001; Ost, Foster, Costall, & Bull, 2005; Zhu et al., 2010). Although many of these studies found some statistical differences between groups of true and false memories (or groups of people who did and did not form them in a particular case), none of these has been able to reliably determine whether a particular memory is true or false, especially to the degree of certainty necessary for the courts.

So would the presence or absence of consequences be a way to do so? If false memories are substantially less likely than true memories to have repercussions in people's lives, then measuring consequentiality could be a useful way to weed out false memories from true memories. In an important aside, it has long been known that false memories can wreak havoc in the lives of those who have them and their families, including interpersonal and legal upheavals (e.g., Gudjonsson, 1996, 2008). The kinds of repercussions that we are talking about in this instance are both smaller and more specific.

Early studies: Pickles, eggs, strawberry ice cream

In the initial published studies of false memory consequences, our research group gave subjects false memories for one of two food-related childhood events, getting sick after eating either dill pickles or hard-boiled eggs (Bernstein, Laney, Morris, & Loftus, 2005b). We chose getting sick after eating a particular food because this is a nicely concrete event that could reasonably happen at almost any time in childhood, and because there is an established literature demonstrating the psychological consequences that can occur when people genuinely get sick after eating a particular type of food (e.g., Gustavson, Garcia, Hankins, & Rusiniak, 1974; Broberg & Bernstein, 1987). We chose pickles and hard-boiled eggs because they were foods that we thought most kids would have had some experience with, but not everyday experience.

These initial studies, and indeed most of the studies described in this chapter, use the false feedback procedure for implanting false memories. This procedure involves three key phases, though with a host of variations (see also Laney & Loftus, 2010). In the first phase, subjects come into the lab and are given a cover story and a set of questionnaires to complete. The questionnaires all revolve around a common theme that supports the cover story but also provides key premanipulation measures for the specific study. In the second phase, which normally occurs approximately a week after the first phase (though in some studies happens as little as ten minutes later), subjects are given the false feedback manipulation. This takes the form of a supposedly computer-generated feedback profile that gives subjects information about events that happened in their childhoods. The content of this profile is determined not by subjects' answers to the phase 1 questionnaires (as they are told), but instead by random assignment. In particular, experimental (but not control) subjects are told that they had a specific experience as a child. In the studies described here, this is normally a specific experience with a particular food (e.g., you got sick eating a hard-boiled egg). Subjects are asked to read their profile and, in most studies, to answer some questions about it to ensure that they do actually read and understand it. In the third phase of the study, which normally immediately follows the second phase, subjects are given an additional set of questionnaires that assess whether the manipulation has produced changes in subjects' confidence that the suggested event occurred, as well as measuring the false memory consequences of interest in the particular study.

How do we decide that someone has developed a false belief or memory? In most false feedback, false memory studies, subjects are said to have developed false memories (termed "believers") if they meet three specific criteria: (1) their premanipulation confidence that the critical event happened is low (that is, they do not have arguably "true" memories), (2) that confidence increases after the manipulation, and (3) they report a specific "memory" or a less specific "belief" for the event at the end of the study (see Morris, Laney, Bernstein, & Loftus, 2006). Often, the key comparison for determining whether false memories have repercussions is between these "believers" and control subjects.

In the initial false memory consequence study (Bernstein et al., 2005b, Experiment 1), subjects first completed just one questionnaire (asking about their preferences for various foods) and then were told that their data would be analyzed by a special computer system. A few minutes later, subjects were given a feedback profile that the computer had supposedly generated. This profile contained three filler items for all subjects (that as young children they had disliked spinach and enjoyed fried foods and chocolate-covered almonds) and for experimental subjects also contained the suggestion that they had once gotten sick after eating either dill pickles or hard-boiled eggs (depending on condition). Subjects were then asked to briefly elaborate on their critical item (controls elaborated on a filler item) and then to complete a further set of questionnaires designed to assess whether their confidence that they had gotten sick on pickles or eggs had increased and whether these altered beliefs might have consequences (detailed later).

The methodology for Experiment 2 was similar, except that (a) subjects completed the confidence measure (called the Food History Inventory) and three filler questionnaires at premanipulation, (b) the delay between phase 1 and phase 2 was a week instead of a few minutes, (c) the food preferences questionnaire was used as a postmanipulation confidence measure instead, and (d) we used an additional postmanipulation questionnaire called the Memory or Belief form, on which they were instructed to judge their experiences of three different events (including their critical egg or pickle event) as specific memories, less specific beliefs that the event occurred, or neither of these.

In Experiment 1, subjects given the pickle feedback were more confident than egg feedback subjects or controls that they had indeed gotten sick eating pickles, though egg feedback subjects were no more confident than pickle feedback subjects that they had gotten sick after eating hard-boiled eggs. In Experiment 2, both types of feedback produced significant increases in confidence in their respective subjects from pre- to postmanipulation. In addition, the combination of confidence change and a "memory" or "belief" response on the Memory or Belief form became the criteria for labeling subjects as having false memories (being "believers") for their critical sickness event. Specifically, 25% of pickle feedback subjects and 31% of egg feedback subjects believed their feedback, reporting increased confidence that they had been sick after eating the food and reporting a specific memory or belief that they had been sick.

To determine whether subjects' new false memories were consequential, they were given a Party Behavior Questionnaire, on which they were asked how likely they were to consume a variety of foods (including dill pickle spears and salted hard-boiled eggs, as well as related items—pickle slices and egg salad finger sandwiches) in a backyard party situation. In Experiment 2 subjects were also asked to rate their preference for a list of foods, including both critical foods and several closely related foods. Experiment 1 did not produce significant differences in expressed desire to eat pickles or hard-boiled eggs at a party between people who were or were not exposed to false feedback about getting sick, but this may be because those who actually believed the feedback were lumped in with others who did not. That is, this study was not able to distinguish between those who believed versus did not believe the false feedback. This comparison was possible in Experiment 2, and we found that those who believed their feedback were indeed less interested in eating the food that they now believed they had gotten sick after eating. And these effects even carried over to other, closely related, foods like egg salad.

That is, false memories did seem to be consequential for those who developed them, in the same way that true memories can be consequential. So looking for evidence of consequentiality appears to be another dead-end in the search for categorical differences between true and false memories. Nonetheless, there is still much more to learn about the consequences of false memories and what they can tell us about memory processes more broadly. For details regarding the food items, manipulations, proportions of "believing" subjects, and basic results regarding two key kinds of false memory repercussions (preference consequences and action consequences) for each of the studies described in this chapter, see Table 9.1.

Once we had established that false memories, like true memories, could be consequential for those who possessed them, we looked at several other types of false memories and consequences. First we gave subjects false memories for getting sick on chocolate cake and potato chips, using essentially the same methodology as that of Bernstein et al. (2005b, Experiment 2) described earlier (Laney, Morris, Bernstein, & Loftus, 2004). Although we were able to plant false memories for getting sick on both of these foods, we did not see any consequences of these false memories. That is, although 24% of subjects falsely believed that they had once gotten sick after eating chocolate cake, these cake believers did not demonstrate any reduction in preference for cake or willingness to eat cake, relative to nonbelievers or nonexposed subjects. We also successfully convinced 49% of subjects they had once gotten sick after eating potato chips, but again, these believers were no less interested in eating potato chips than nonbelievers or nonexposed subjects. (Note that this doesn't undermine the previous claim that false memories cannot be distinguished from true memories on the basis of their consequentiality—in this study, true memories were also not distinguishable from other groups on the basis of their consequentiality.)

TABLE 9.1 Studies of false memory consequences

Study	Item(s)	Manipulation	% "believers"	Preference consequences	Consumption consequences
Bernstein et al. (2005b) Experiment 1	dill pickles; hard-boiled eggs	"you got sick"	n/a	n/a	none
Bernstein et al. (2005b) Experiment 2	dill pickles; hard-boiled eggs	"you got sick"	25% for pickles; 31% for eggs	less preference among believers	less reported willingness to eat food among believers
Laney et al. (2004)	chocolate cake; potato chips	"you got sick"	24% for cakes; 49% for chips	n/a	none
Bernstein et al. (2005a) Experiment 1	strawberry ice cream; chocolate chip cookies	"you got sick"	18% for ice cream; 9% for cookies	lower preference for strawberry ice cream (but not cookies) among believers	less reported willingness to eat strawberry ice cream (but not cookies) among believers
Bernstein et al. (2005a) Experiment 2	strawberry ice cream; chocolate chip cookies	"you got sick" plus elaboration or scenario choice	41% for ice cream; 22% for cookies	believers (combined) avoided (combination of preference and hypothetical action) more than nonbelievers and controls	
Scoboria et al. (2008)	peach yogurt	personalized "got sick" suggestion plus generic "heath alert" suggestion	not measured	lower reported desirability of peach yogurt (specifically) in experimental group	lower consumption of peach yogurt and two other flavors (but not crackers) in experimental group

(continued)

TABLE 9.1 Cont.

Study	Item(s)	Manipulation	% "believers"	Preference consequences	Consumption consequences
Laney, Morris et al. (2008) Experiment 1	asparagus	"you loved cooked asparagus"	48%	greater preference among believers	greater intention to eat and willingness to pay more among believers relative to controls
Laney, Morris et al. (2008) Experiment 2	Asparagus	"you loved asparagus the first time you ate it"	53%	greater preference among believers; more positive feelings toward picture of asparagus	n/a
Study Laney, Bowman-Fowler et al. (008)	*Item(s)* asparagus	*Manipulation* "loved"; "hated"; also 2-week delay phase	*% "believers"* for "loved": 34% immediately, 26% after 2 weeks; for "hated": 47% immediately, 40% after 2 weeks	*Preference consequences* greater preference among "love" believers and lower preference among "hate" believers immediately and after two weeks, relative to pre-manipulation levels	*Consumption consequences* greater intention to eat among "love" believers immediately and after 2 weeks; greater request to eat among "love" believers after 1 week
Geraerts et al. (2008)	egg salad	"got sick"; also 4-month delay phase	39% of manipulated subjects	lower preference for egg salad among believers	believers ate fewer egg salad sandwiches than controls, immediately and 4 months later
Berkowitz et al. (2008)	Pluto (Disney character)	"Bad Pluto" had "inappropriately" licked kids' ears; "Good Pluto" had licked ears to kids' delight	30% Bad Pluto; 39% Good Pluto	none	reduced willingness to pay for Pluto souvenir among Bad Pluto believers

Study	Food/Drink	Suggestion		Preference	Consumption
Scoboria et al. (2012)	peach yogurt	personalized "got sick" suggestion and/or generic "heath alert" suggestion; also 1-month delay phase	44% of personalized suggestions subjects indicated "memory" or "belief"	lower preference for peach yogurt in those given the personalized suggestion only	lower consumption of peach yogurt by those given the personalized suggestion only; at one week and one month delays
Clifasefi et al. (2013)	vodka; rum	"got sick"	20% of manipulated	lower preference for suggested alcohol type among believers	n/a
Mantonakis et al. (2013)	white wine	"loved" or "got sick"	46% of manipulated (not separated by manipulation)	n/a	greater actual consumption of wine in "loved condition" (only)

So why do false beliefs about some foods have consequences but false beliefs about other foods do not? After some thought, we hypothesized that most college students have lots of positive experiences with cake and chips. They like to eat cake and chips and know full well that they like to eat cake and chips. When faced with (new) knowledge that they had once become sick after eating one of these common and preferred foods, subjects in the study may have concluded that, even if they once got sick, it clearly hadn't affected their preference for these foods or willingness to eat them. After all, they had plenty of evidence from their own memories that they liked to eat these foods—much more than they likely had evidence about their feelings for rarer foods like dill pickles and hard-boiled eggs. This suggests that false memories may not be the next great diet fad (though see Bernstein, Pernat, & Loftus, 2011).

We next turned this bit of post-hoc reasoning into a hypothesis for a new study (Bernstein, Laney, Morris, & Loftus, 2005a). Specifically, we hypothesized that we would be able to give subjects false memories for getting sick after eating either a very common food, chocolate chip cookies, or a somewhat less common food, strawberry ice cream, but that we would only find false memory consequences for the less common food.

The procedures for the study were similar to those used by Bernstein et al. (2005b, Experiment 2). Subjects completed questionnaires and were told that their data would be analyzed by a special computer that would produce profiles before they returned a week later. All subjects' profiles told them that as young children they had liked bananas and hated spinach and that they had been happy when a classmate had brought sweets to school. Subjects in the experimental conditions were also told that they had once gotten sick after eating either strawberry ice cream or chocolate chip cookies. In fact we were really successful at giving people false memories only for getting sick from eating strawberry ice cream (18% of these subjects met our "believer" criteria). These people also demonstrated avoidance of strawberry ice cream, as hypothesized. No one avoided the more common food, chocolate chip cookies. Experiment 2 further demonstrated that the recency of eating the food did not, by itself, predict whether people would adopt false memories.

Can we make people want to eat more instead of less?

Once researchers had clearly demonstrated that planting false memories for getting sick on a particular food, could have negative consequences for how people felt about that food, we wondered whether we might be able to do the opposite. Could we plant a positive false memory about a (healthy) food and cause people to want to eat more of it (Laney, Morris, Bernstein, Wakefield, & Loftus, 2008)? We chose asparagus as our target food because we believed that it is not typically enjoyed by young children and, although not found on every dinner table, it is approximately equally common in the typical diets of Asian Americans and White Americans, the two largest groups in our student population at the time.

We used the same false feedback procedure as in the prior studies, but this time the false feedback item was "You loved to eat cooked asparagus" (in Experiment 1) and confidence on the item "Loved asparagus the first time you tried it" was measured. After the manipulation, 48% of relevant subjects met the criteria to be labeled "believers". These subjects expressed greater preference for asparagus and were more interested in eating asparagus in a hypothetical restaurant situation (similar to the early "Party Behavior" measure) than were controls. Interestingly, asparagus believers also reported willingness to pay more for asparagus in a store than did controls.

In Experiment 2 we started to look for underlying mechanisms that might explain the differences between believers and other subjects. This time, 53% of relevant subjects met the criteria to be labeled "believers", and again these individuals displayed significantly greater preference for asparagus than controls (the restaurant measure was not significant this time). In addition believers in this study rated a photograph of asparagus as somewhat more appetizing and significantly less disgusting than controls.

In the final asparagus study (to date), Laney, Bowman-Fowler et al. (2008) used the false feedback procedure to give subjects false memories for either loving or hating asparagus the first time they tried it and again assessed whether there were consequences of these false memories. But then, instead of debriefing people in the same (second) session, we asked people to come back to the lab for a third session two weeks later. Some 34% of "loved" subjects and 47% of "hated" subjects met our believer criteria in an immediate test; these numbers dropped to 26% and 40%, respectively, by the two-week follow-up. These believers' preferences for asparagus changed from pre- to postmanipulation in the expected directions (increasing for the "love" group and decreasing for the "hate" group) and essentially maintained these levels at the two-week follow-up. "Love" believers (but not "hate" believers) also demonstrated greater intention to eat asparagus in a hypothetical restaurant. One week after the manipulation (and one week before the last session of the study) subjects were informed (falsely) that we would be providing snacks during the final session of the study and asked to rank vegetables (including asparagus) according to how much they would like to eat them. Again, "love" believers (but not "hate" believers) were more interested in eating asparagus than were controls. Two additional studies have also looked for (and found) long-term consequences of false memories—see descriptions of Geraerts et al. (2008) and Scoboria, Mazzoni, Jarry, and Bernstein (2012) later.

This last asparagus study was also interesting because we explicitly compared true and false memories in terms of their consequentiality (Laney, Bowman-Fowler, et al., 2008; see also Laney & Loftus, 2010). True memory subjects in this study were those who started the study with and maintained high confidence that they had loved or hated asparagus the first time they had tried it. In summary, people with true memories for loving asparagus tended to behave like those with false memories for loving asparagus, but even more so (greater preference and greater willingness to eat, on average). People with true memories for hating asparagus the first time they tried it showed few consequences of this belief, just like people with false memories of hating asparagus.

Do false memories affect actual behavior?

The studies described so far use as a dependent measure intention to eat, reported by subjects via paper and pencil tasks, rather than actual eating behavior. Other researchers took the next step of actually putting food down in front of subjects and measuring how much they ate. Geraerts et al. (2008) tested whether false memories of getting sick after eating egg salad would affect subjects' subsequent consumption of egg salad sandwiches. They used the false feedback procedure and succeeded in giving 41% of experimental subjects false memories for getting sick on egg salad. In an immediate test after a bogus debriefing, manipulated subjects ate fewer egg sandwiches than did nonmanipulated subjects. Four months later, subjects were recontacted under the guise of a separate study and again offered egg salad and other sandwiches. This time believers ate fewer egg salad sandwiches than controls.

Scoboria, Mazzoni, and Jarry (2008) used a suggestion similar to those used in previous studies plus a "health alert" suggestion to convince subjects that they had once been exposed to and sickened by contaminated peach yogurt. A week later, in what subjects were led to believe was a separate study, subjects tasted actual peach yogurt, as well as strawberry yogurt, cherry yogurt, and three flavors of crackers. Although Scoboria et al. did not separate out their "believer" subjects, they found that manipulated subjects as a group liked peach yogurt less and ate less of all three types of yogurt (but not fewer crackers) than control subjects. Two critics (Pezdek & Freyd, 2009) argue that these results don't matter because yogurt "is not commonly consumed" (p. 179; we suggest that the shareholders of Yoplait, Danon, Chobani, and Oikos, among others, would disagree).

Scoboria et al. (2012) extended the findings of Scoboria et al. (2008) by separating out the two distinct manipulations (personal suggestion and generalized "heath alert" suggestion). Different subjects received each of these manipulations individually, or both, or neither. These authors found that the personalized suggestion worked best and that the generalized suggestion actually reduced the likelihood of forming false memories. This time Scoboria et al. also reported that 44% of their personalized suggestions subjects reported a "memory" or "belief" after the manipulation. Subjects given the personalized suggestion also reported lower preference for peach yogurt and consumed less peach yogurt (but not less strawberry yogurt, cherry yogurt, or crackers) when given the opportunity after one week or one month.

Bernstein, Scoboria, and Arnold (2015) conducted a mega-analysis (a type of meta-analysis where raw data from several studies are combined into a single data set) of eight food studies and found that the false suggestion directly affected some consequences (food preferences) but not others (intention to eat), that belief in the false suggestion predicted intention to eat, and that positive suggestions (loving on first consumption) were more powerful than negative suggestions (getting sick).

Does it only work on food?

Although our lab was never very successful at reducing hypothetical consumption of unhealthy foods (Bernstein et al., 2005a; Laney et al., 2004), other researchers have also attempted to alter negative consumption habits with false memories. Clifasefi, Bernstein, Mantonakis, and Loftus (2013) used the false feedback procedure to convince subjects that they had once been sick after drinking either vodka or rum (depending on condition) before the age of 16. Some 20% of subjects formed false memories, and subjects whose first drinking experience had occurred at a younger age were more likely to be believers. These believers' preference for the manipulated alcohol type (and indeed that of all those who were exposed to the "got sick" manipulation) decreased from pre- to postmanipulation. This suggests, but does not directly demonstrate, that alcohol consumption, like food consumption, may be affected by false memories.

Mantonakis, Wudarzewski, Bernstein, Clifasefi, and Loftus (2013) took things one step further by actually giving subjects alcohol to drink. These authors used a version of the false feedback procedure to convince some subjects that they had become sick after drinking (or had loved) white wine before the age of 20 (a more recent event than those used in prior studies). These researchers were able to convince 46% of subjects that they had had a specific experience with white wine (these authors did not say what proportion of these believers were in each of the two conditions). They also found that, when given the opportunity, "love" believers drank more wine than controls. Sick believers did not, however, drink less than controls.

Mantonakis et al. (2013) discuss the implications of their research for the field of advertising, suggesting that policy makers might want to attend to the research demonstrating that false beliefs can alter behavior. Rajagopal and Montgomery (2011) tested the relationship between advertising and false beliefs even more directly. These authors had subjects listen to radio advertisements that varied in their imagery. Subjects exposed to high imagery ads often believed that they had actually experienced a product that they had not. The researchers found that false beliefs (that subjects had actually tried the advertised product) led to similar outcomes (including favorable attitudes toward the product) to those produced by true beliefs.

In a rather different kind of false memory repercussion study, Berkowitz, Laney, Morris, Garry, and Loftus (2008) used the false feedback procedure to give subjects false memories for one of two experiences with the character Pluto at Disneyland (close to the UC Irvine campus where this research was conducted). Some subjects were told that, based on the outcome of their fear profile (similar to the food-related false feedback profiles described earlier), a news story might be relevant to them. The news story described an unpleasant and drug-fueled Pluto character who had inappropriately licked the ears of children who visited Disneyland during the childhoods of the subjects. Other subjects were given a happier profile and a story of a happy-go-lucky Pluto character who had licked the ears of children in a delightful way. Thirty percent of the "Bad Pluto" subjects and 39% of the "Good

Pluto" subjects formed false memories of being licked by Pluto. Although these manipulations did not affect subjects' feelings about the character of Pluto, the "Bad Pluto" subjects reported being less willing to pay for Pluto souvenirs at Disneyland.

Concluding remarks

Why does it matter whether false memories have repercussions? For starters, it means that this is yet another way (besides confidence, detail, emotionality, etc.) that false memories can be indistinguishable from true memories. In one sense, this is unsurprising. Because memory is reconstructive, even memories that are largely accurate may contain bits of fiction.

Smeets, Merckelbach, Horselenberg, and Jelicic (2005) argue that too many researchers who claim to be studying false memory are in fact studying something less concrete, like false beliefs, and suggest that in order to speak meaningfully about false memories we should only ever consider false memories that have real behavioral consequences. At the time these researchers made this argument, there were few studies of behaviorally consequential false memories available. More than ten years later, there is now a sizable body of work that supports the conclusion that false memories really do matter.

Note

* This chapter originally appeared in the edited volume, *False and Distorted Memories*. It has been updated for this compilation.

References

Berkowitz, S. R., Laney, C., Morris, E. K., Garry, M., & Loftus, E. F. (2008). Pluto behaving badly: False beliefs and their consequences. *American Journal of Psychology, 121*, 643–660.

Bernstein, D. M., Laney, C., Morris, E. K., & Loftus, E. F. (2005a). False beliefs about fattening foods can have healthy consequences. *Proceedings of the National Academy of Sciences, 102*, 13724–13731.

Bernstein, D. M., Laney, C., Morris, E. K., & Loftus, E. F. (2005b). False memories about food can lead to food avoidance. *Social Cognition, 23*, 10–33.

Bernstein, D. M., & Loftus, E. F. (2009). How to tell if a particular memory is true or false. *Perspectives on Psychological Science, 4*, 370–374.

Bernstein, D. M., Pernat, N. L. M., & Loftus, E. F. (2011). The false memory diet: False memories alter food preferences. In V. R. Preedy, R. R. Watson, & C. R. Martin (Eds.), *Handbook of behavior, food, and nutrition* (pp. 1645–1663). New York: Springer.

Bernstein, D. M., Scoboria, A., & Arnold, R. (2015). The consequences of suggesting false childhood food events. *Acta Psychologica, 156*, 1–7.

Broberg, D. J., & Bernstein, I. L. (1987). Candy as a scapegoat in the prevention of food aversions in children receiving chemotherapy. *Cancer, 60*, 2344–3647.

Campbell, M. A., & Porter, S. (2002). Pinpointing reality: How well can people judge true and mistaken emotional childhood memories? *Canadian Journal of Behavioural Science, 34*, 217–229.

Clifasefi, S. L., Bernstein, D. M., Mantonakis, A., & Loftus, E. F. (2013). "Queasy does it": False alcohol beliefs and memories may lead to diminished alcohol preferences. *Acta Psychologica, 143*, 14–19.

Drivdahl, S. B., & Zaragoza, M. S. (2001). The role of elaboration and individual differences in the creation of false memories for suggested events. *Applied Cognitive Psychology, 15*, 265–281.

Geraerts, E., Bernstein, D. M., Merckelbach, H., Linders, C., Raymaekers, L., & Loftus, E. F. (2008). Lasting false beliefs and their behavioral consequences. *Psychological Science, 19*, 746–753.

Gudjonsson, G. (1996). Accusations by adults of childhood sexual abuse: A survey of the members of the British False Memory Society (BFMS). *Applied Cognitive Psychology, 10*, 1–16.

Gudjonsson, G. (2008). Members of the British False Memory Society: The legal consequences of the accusations for the families. *Journal of Forensic Psychiatry, 8*, 348–356.

Gustavson, C. R., Garcia, J., Hankins, W. G., & Rusiniak, K. W. (1974). Coyote predation control by aversive conditioning. *Science, 184*, 581–583.

Heaps, C. M., & Nash, M. (2001). Comparing recollective experience in true and false autobiographical memories. *Journal of Experimental Psychology: Learning, Memory, and Cognition, 27*, 920–930.

Hyman, Jr., I. E., & Pentland, J. (1996). The role of imagery in the creation of false childhood memories. *Journal of Memory and Language, 35*, 101–117.

Laney, C., Bowman-Fowler, N., Nelson, K. J., Bernstein, D. M., & Loftus. E. F. (2008). The persistence of false beliefs. *Acta Psychologica, 129*, 190–197.

Laney, C., & Loftus, E. F. (2008). Emotional content of true and false memories. *Memory, 16*, 500–516.

Laney, C., & Loftus, E. F. (2010). Truth in emotional memories. In B. H. Bornstein & R. L. Wiener (Eds.), *Emotion and the law: Psychological perspectives* (pp. 157–183). New York: Springer.

Laney, C., Morris, E. K., Bernstein, D. M., & Loftus, E. F. (2004). Consequences of false memories for getting sick on potato chips and chocolate cake. Unpublished manuscript, University of California, Irvine.

Laney, C., Morris, E. K., Bernstein, D. M., Wakefield, B. M., & Loftus, E. F. (2008). Asparagus, a love story: Healthier eating could be just a false memory away. *Experimental Psychology, 55*, 291–300.

Laney, C., & Takarangi, M. K. T. (2013). False memories for aggressive acts. *Acta Psychologica, 143*, 227–234.

Loftus, E. F., & Bernstein, D. M. (2005). Rich false memories: The royal road to success. In A. F. Healy (Ed.), *Experimental cognitive psychology and its applications* (pp. 101–113). Washington, DC: American Psychological Association.

Loftus, E. F., & Pickrell, J. E. (1995). The formation of false memories. *Psychiatric Annals, 25*, 720–725.

Mantonakis, A., Wudarzewski, A., Bernstein, D. M., Clifasefi, S. L., & Loftus, E. F. (2013). False beliefs can shape current consumption. *Psychology, 4*, 302–308.

McNally, R. J. (2003). *Remembering trauma*. Cambridge, MA: Harvard University Press.

McNally, R. J., Lasko, N. B., Clancy, S. A., Maclin, M. L., Pitman, R. K., & Orr, S. P. (2004). Psychophysiological responding during script-driven imagery in people reporting abduction by space aliens. *Psychological Science, 15*, 493–497.

Morris, E. K., Laney, C., Bernstein, D. M., & Loftus, E. F. (2006). Susceptibility to memory distortion: How do we decide it has occurred? *American Journal of Psychology, 119*, 255–274.

Ost, J., Foster, S., Costall, A., & Bull, R. (2005). False reports of childhood events in appropriate interviews. *Memory, 13*, 700–710.

Oulton, J. M., & Takarangi, M. K. T. (2017). (Mis)remembering negative emotional experiences. In R. A. Nash & J. Ost (Eds.), *False and distorted memories* (pp. 9–22). Abingdon, Oxon: Routledge.

Pezdek, K., & Freyd, J. J. (2009). The fallacy of generalizing from egg salad in false-belief research. *Analyses of Social Issues and Public Policy, 9*, 177–183.

Porter, S., Birt, A. R., Yuille, J. C., & Lehman, D. R. (2000). Negotiating false memories: Interviewer and remplaceerer characteristics relate to memory distortion. *Psychological Science, 6*, 507–510.

Porter, S., Yuille, J. C., & Lehman, D. R. (1999). The nature of real, mistaken, and fabricated memories for emotional childhood events: Implication for the false memory debate. *Law and Human Behavior, 23*, 517–537.

Rajagopal, P., & Montgomery, N. V. (2011). I imagine, I experience, I like: The false experience effect. *Journal of Consumer Research, 38*, 578–594.

Scoboria, A., Mazzoni, G., & Jarry, J. L. (2008). Suggesting childhood food illness results in reduced eating behavior. *Acta Psychologica, 128*, 304–309.

Scoboria, A., Mazzoni, G., Jarry, J. L., & Bernstein, D. M. (2012). Personalized and not general suggestion produces false autobiographical memories and suggestion-consistent behavior. *Acta Psychologica, 139*, 225–232.

Smeets, T., Merckelbach, H., Horselenberg, R., & Jelicic, M. (2005). Trying to recollect past events: Confidence, beliefs, and memories. *Clinical Psychology Review, 25*, 917–934.

Zhu, B., Chen, C., Loftus, E. F., Lin, C., He, Q., Chen, C., Li, H., Xue, G., Lu, Z., & Dong, Q. (2010). Individual differences in false memory from misinformation: Cognitive factors. *Memory, 18*, 543–555.

10

PHOTOS AND MEMORY*

*Kimberley A. Wade, Sophie J. Nightingale,
and Melissa F. Colloff*

We live in a world where we witness news and international events as they happen. Information is sent and received rapidly, thanks to ever-advancing social networks and fiber-optic communication. But this process of passing information around is wide open to abuse, particularly when information is fabricated or irrelevant and uncritically passed on. Consider, for example, the photographs that circulated on the Internet in October 2012 as Hurricane Sandy swept across New York. Striking images of apocalyptic-looking clouds looming over Manhattan spread around Twitter and Facebook. Photos of a rogue shark swimming through the streets of New Jersey also popped up, but then again, this shark appears every time a major weather event occurs (see http://mashable.com/2012/10/29/fake-hurricane-sandy-photos/). These jaw-dropping images were compelling and dramatic, but the events they depicted were not real. It would be fine, of course, if we could dismiss such captivating, yet fake, images as light entertainment or jokes shared amongst friends. But psychological science suggests we don't. We place faith in photographs to accurately depict real-world events. We use images to inform our judgements, to make decisions, and to remind us who we are. And whilst we might carefully choose the friends, experts, and newspaper and media outlets we follow, we often pass over photographs uncritically, because photographs are entertaining, or provocative, or they—more dangerously—fit with our worldview. As British big-data artist Eric Drass points out: "The legitimacy of information is dependent on the trustworthiness of the source, but often this is unclear, and often overpowered by a compelling image."

Over the last 10 to 15 years, memory researchers have become increasingly interested in how photos—both doctored and real—affect human memory. Although doctoring images or circulating misleading photos might seem like harmless fun, we know that people often accept photographs as realistic depictions of events. As a result, photos can potentially change our memories of both childhood and recent experiences. They can also influence our decisions, our intentions, our behaviour, and even our willingness to confess to something we never did. Photos are powerful because we ascribe them more credibility than they often deserve. They can also make an event feel more familiar than it really is and promote vivid visual imagery, which can affect a number of common cognitive tasks. Here we describe the growing body of research into photographs and memory, and consider the crucial implications for criminal justice settings.

Photographs and childhood memories

Memory researchers have known for a long time that childhood memories are prone to error. One of the earliest attempts to plant a wholly false childhood memory in adults involved a procedure in which adult subjects were given short narrative descriptions of four childhood events and were asked to remember as much as they could about each experience. The subjects were led to believe that their families had provided the descriptions but, in reality, one event was a fake that the experimenters created. After two visits to the lab in which they worked at remembering the real and false childhood events, 25% of subjects came to believe, wholly or partially, that at the age of 5 or 6, they got lost in a shopping mall and were eventually helped by an elderly lady who reunited them with their parents (Loftus & Pickrell, 1995). This was the first systematic procedure for planting and examining false childhood memories, and the paradigm proved to be popular and robust. To date 16 published studies have used variants of the *familial-informant false-narrative procedure* (Lindsay, Hagen, Read, Wade, & Garry, 2004) to explore the power of suggestive techniques and repeated retrieval.

In the early 2000s, Wade and co-workers adapted the familial-informant false-narrative procedure to determine whether doctored photographs of childhood events, without any accompanying verbal description, might also lead people to develop false childhood memories (Wade, Garry, Read, & Lindsay, 2002). People often rely on photographs of significant, personal experiences to trigger stronger remembering and to remind themselves of who they are, which could make photographs a compelling source of misinformation (for early work into reviewing photos and false recollection, see Schacter, Koutstaal, Johnson, Gross, & Angell, 1997; Koutstaal, Schacter, Johnson, Angell, & Gross, 1998). In Wade et al.'s study, over one to two weeks, adult subjects worked at remembering events depicted in childhood photographs that their family members provided. The photos depicted moderately significant events, including childhood birthday parties, family holidays, and cultural celebrations. One was a fake and depicted the subject and a relative on a hot-air balloon ride—an event that subjects' family members confirmed never happened. To be categorized as having a *clear* false memory, subjects had to report memories of the balloon ride and provide consistent information beyond that depicted in the photo. For a *partial* false memory, subjects had to consistently elaborate on the false photo (e.g., report feelings, describe who was present, etc.) but did not have to indicate memories of taking the balloon ride per se. By the end of the study period, 20% of subjects remembered the balloon ride clearly and a further 30% remembered it partially— proof that doctored photographs, like narratives, could lead people to remember wholly false childhood experiences.

Subjects in the hot-air balloon study and in follow-up experiments typically developed false memories slowly over the duration of the study (Garry & Wade, 2005; Wade, Garry, Nash, & Harper, 2010). The subjects who ultimately reported illusory memories often began by offering visual snippets of the balloon event and then embellished these details over the study period until their reports became coherent, detailed, and clear. A clause-analysis of subjects' memory reports revealed an interesting fact: the information depicted in the fake photographs played a small role in determining the content of subjects' illusory memory reports. Fewer than 30% of the clauses in subjects' false memory reports were made up of information that subjects could have reasonably gleaned from the doctored photograph. Indeed, the vast majority of subjects' memory reports were made up of details they must have incorporated from other cognitive processes—presumably imagination and relevant, real memories.

In later research, Garry and Wade (2005) pitted verbal descriptions of a childhood balloon ride against doctored photos of the same event to determine which medium—images or descriptions—would foster more false memories. Counterintuitively, the descriptions proved to be more powerful. Of the subjects who reviewed the hot-air balloon description, 82% were categorized as reporting images or full-blown memories of the balloon ride, compared to 50% in the photo condition. One possible explanation for this pattern of results is that words afford people more freedom to imagine the suggested experience (e.g., the shape, size, and colour of the balloon) and to construct a memory that contains idiosyncratic and familiar information. We know from the source monitoring and perceptual fluency literatures that easily imagined events are more likely to be mistaken for genuine memories (Johnson, Hashtroudi, & Lindsay, 1993; Whittlesea, 1993, 2011; Lindsay, 2008; Newman's chapter in *False and Distorted Memories*). Consistent with this account, Hessen-Kayfitz and Scoboria (2012) showed that imbuing doctored photos with additional unfamiliar details lowers the rate of false recall. Their subjects were less likely to report false childhood memories of a hot-air balloon ride when they viewed doctored balloon images that contained an unfamiliar lighthouse digit-ally inserted into the background (see Figure 10.1). Thus doctored photos may be powerful, but research suggests they are no more so than descriptions of suggested events.

One question that frequently arises in the false memory domain is whether subjects are genuinely developing false memories or simply uncovering true mem-ories. This is an important point because the "lost in the mall" or even the "hot-air balloon" suggestion could conceivably be leading people to recall genuine events

	No self-relevant detail	Self-relevant detail
No unfamiliar detail		
Unfamiliar detail		

FIGURE 10.1 Hessen–Kayfitz and Scoboria's (2012) doctored photos

rather than to report false memories. This question has led researchers to examine false memories for implausible and even impossible events to determine whether suggestive manipulations really are creating false memories. In a clever series of experiments, Braun, Ellis, and Loftus (2002) used doctored images of company advertisements to induce impossible memories. Subjects evaluated advertisements for a Disney resort. Half viewed a generic ad that did not mention any cartoon characters, and half viewed a fake ad for Disney that featured Bugs Bunny—a Warner Brothers character. After a delay, subjects were asked about any childhood trips they took to Disney, and viewing the fake ad led 16% of subjects to falsely claim that they had personally met Bugs at Disney. Follow-up experiments by Grinley (2002) showed that multiple exposures to the fake ad boosted the likelihood of false memories (25% of subjects in one study, 36% in another).

Children can develop wildly implausible false memories too with the aid of doctored photos. In one study, 6 and 10 year olds were given doctored photographs of themselves, aged 2. One doctored photograph depicted them taking a hot-air balloon ride; the other depicted them having tea with Prince Charles (Strange, Sutherland, & Garry, 2006). The royal tea scenario is, of course, highly implausible, if only for the fact that the royal family live in England and the subjects were all New Zealanders. Yet, after reviewing the fake photos, the children were just as likely to have developed a memory for having tea with the prince as they were to develop a memory for the hot-air balloon ride. For example, one child remembered the following details about the fictitious balloon experience:

> This … is … this is me, Michael and Granddad and um we went in a balloon, in Christchurch somewhere. And it was a sixplay [display] of balloons. And

we had to pay like $5 or something for the ride. And we went in there for like half an hour or something and we went over Christchurch. And ... yeah. And we were down there for, on holiday ... And after ... I had done this I went and saw my Dad in the dairy [convenience store] and he gave, and my grandma gave me free lollies [candy] and all that.

(Strange et al., 2006, p. 944)

It is important to note that photographs do not have a particular power to make children believe in impossible events. Other studies have shown that suggestive descriptions of plausible events (almost choking on a candy) and implausible events (being abducted by a UFO) are equally likely to give rise to rich false memories in children (Otgaar, Candel, Merckelbach, & Wade, 2009).

Although doctored photos have become a useful tool for examining the mechanisms underlying false memory reports, on a more practical level, we know that people are unlikely to encounter doctored photos of themselves doing things they have never done in their day-to-day lives. This line of thinking led Lindsay et al. (2004) to wonder about the influence of *real* photographs on false memory creation. Using a variant of the familial-informant false-narrative procedure, Lindsay and colleagues attempted to plant a false memory of putting Slime—the bright green gooey toy—in a teacher's desk in grade 1 or 2 (age 5 or 6). Subjects were led to believe that the prank was committed with a classmate, and that the teacher was unhappy and made the subject and their accomplice sit facing a wall, legs and arms crossed, for 30 minutes. The procedure once again proved extremely powerful, with 23% of subjects stating that they remembered this event. But more importantly, this false memory rate almost tripled, to 65%, when subjects used their school class photo from grade 1 or 2 as an aide-mémoire. Several processes could account for why the class photo, which didn't depict the suggested Slime incident, worked so well. As Lindsay et al. argued, the photo may have boosted the credibility of the suggestion, enabled subjects to speculate about the event, or provided a visual springboard for imagination.

Photographs and recent memories

In familial-informant false-narrative (or photo) studies, subjects are asked to recall a suggested event that ostensibly happened during childhood, which may involve thinking back to 10, 20, or even 30 years ago. Of course, childhood memories are typically faded, sketchy, and difficult to recollect, so it is easy to see why people are prone to accepting suggestions and, with a little repeated imagination and social demand, reporting wholly false memories of distant events. Indeed, people are more prone to misremembering an event that ostensibly occurred at age 2 than at age 10 (Strange, Wade, & Hayne, 2008). So there are good reasons to believe that altering someone's memory for a recent event—something that occurred within the last few hours or the last few days—would be much more challenging. Or would it?

Sacchi, Agnoli, and Loftus (2007) explored the influence of doctored photos on memory for significant, recent public events. The researchers digitally doctored two photographs, one of a relatively old event—the 1989 Tiananmen Square protest in Beijing—and one that occurred only a year before the study was conducted—the 2003 Iraq war protest in Rome. For the Beijing event, an original photograph depicting a student standing in front of military tanks was doctored to include crowds of people standing on the sidelines. For the Rome event, aggressive-looking demonstrators and police officers wearing riot gear were digitally added to the original image of the peaceful demonstration march. Subjects viewed a photo of the Beijing event and a photo of the Rome event, each one either in its original or doctored format. In a recognition memory test, subjects who viewed the doctored Beijing image estimated that more people were involved in the protest than those who viewed the original photograph. Similarly, subjects who viewed the doctored Rome image were more likely to state that the protest involved physical confrontation, damage to property, and significant injuries. The doctored-photo subjects were also seven times more likely to state that people were killed during the demonstration. Directly instructing subjects to disregard the photographs didn't change these results, which illustrates the power of doctored photos to influence memory of even relatively recent events.

One limitation of the Sacchi et al. (2007) study is that subjects may not have been familiar with the Tiananmen Square or Iraq war protests. Indeed, 35% of Sacchi et al.'s younger sample and 5% of their older sample reported being "completely unfamiliar" with the Beijing event. Rather than reporting their memories of these events, some subjects may have simply guessed or fabricated their answers. Other research has avoided this problem by examining the persuasive effects of photographs when they are presented alongside a to-be-remembered event, and the results are strikingly similar. Garry, Strange, Bernstein, and Kinzett (2007) asked subjects to proofread a set of news articles and to indicate where an accompanying photograph should be placed. The critical article described a tropical hurricane that had destroyed properties when it hit a coastal town in Mexico. Some subjects received a photograph depicting the aftermath of the hurricane, and some received a photograph of the town before the hurricane had hit. Later on, subjects were given a surprise recognition test to determine whether their memories of the article had been influenced by the content of the photograph. About a third of subjects who viewed the "aftermath" photograph claimed to remember that the hurricane had caused death and serious injuries. Only 9% of those who had seen the "before" photograph claimed to have read statements about death in the original article. Garry et al. concluded that spending two minutes with a photograph depicting property damage was enough to facilitate speculation or mental images about the outcomes of a hurricane. These speculations or images were subsequently incorporated into memory, and subjects came to believe that they had read about, rather than imagined, some serious personal injuries.

Another compelling example of people developing false memories based on inferences they have drawn from photographs comes from work conducted by

Linda Henkel (2012). Subjects read short stories that induced them to infer certain scenarios. "Sabrina dropped the delicate vase", for example, induces the inference that the vase broke. Each story was accompanied by a photograph depicting the likely inference (e.g., a broken vase), a photograph depicting a different aspect of the story (e.g., a vase before it was dropped), or no photograph at all. As expected, subjects were more likely to claim that they had read the inference—that the vase was broken—in the story when the story was accompanied by a broken-glass photograph, compared to when it was accompanied by a vase photograph or no photograph. In fact, subjects falsely recognized inferences almost 75% of the time after seeing inference-consistent photographs (Experiment 1). These false inferences, induced by the presence of a photograph, were made with high confidence and were enduring. The errors occurred even when memory was strong (i.e., when subjects were tested after five minutes) and when memory was not prompted (i.e., when subjects were tested using free recall). When recounting memories of recent events, we seem to find it difficult to determine which information we have gleaned from photographs and which information we have read about or experienced.

Further research has shown that photographs don't have to infer a particular outcome to create havoc in memory. Even seemingly innocuous photographs set alongside news headlines can have a marked impact. Strange, Garry, Bernstein, and Lindsay's (2011) subjects were presented with genuine headlines from recent significant international events, along with a number of headlines that were created by the researchers. Some headlines were accompanied by a photograph that was loosely related to the event. The headline "Bin Laden Offers Truce to Europe, Not US", for example, was accompanied by a headshot photo of Osama Bin Laden. The remaining headlines were presented without photographs. The mere presence of a tangentially related photo encouraged people to confidently and immediately state that they remembered both the true and the fictitious events. Critically, 38% of the false events with photographs were "remembered", whereas only 16% of the false events without photographs were "remembered".

Similar results were reported by Newman, Garry, Bernstein, Kantner, and Lindsay (2012) who presented familiar and unfamiliar celebrity names with either a photograph of that person or no photograph. Subjects had to quickly respond either "true" or "false" to the claim "This famous person is alive" or "This famous person is dead". For unfamiliar celebrities, the presence of the photograph increased the likelihood that subjects would report the statement was true. In a second experiment, general knowledge claims (e.g. "Macadamia nuts are in the same evolutionary family as peaches") that were accompanied by a nonprobative photograph (e.g. macadamia nuts) were also judged as more likely to be true than similar claims without photos. The photo-induced *truth bias* is robust and persistent. When subjects were invited back to the lab 48 hours after making "true" or "false" judgements about general knowledge claims, the statements that had previously been presented with photos were *still* more likely to be deemed true (Fenn, Newman, Pezdek, & Garry, 2013).

Thus, even nonprobative photographs can have enduring and misleading effects on people's judgements.

Newman and co-workers have investigated the mechanisms underlying the photo-induced truth bias (Newman et al., 2012). One possibility is that photos increase "truthiness"—the subjective and intuitive feeling that something is true—because they provide a semantically rich context that facilitates the generation of related thoughts and images. These thoughts and images are then misconstrued as evidence to suggest that something is true. Another possibility is that the photos themselves drive the effect because they are deemed to be inherently credible. As photos are interpreted as evidence of reality (Kelly & Nace, 1994; Wright, 2013), they may have simply given the statements an aura of plausibility. To test these competing accounts, Newman and colleagues used a variant of the celebrity names study described earlier to compare the effect of presenting celebrity names with either nonprobative photos or verbal descriptions of those photos. Subjects tended to respond "true", regardless of whether the celebrity name was accompanied by a photo or a verbal description of the photo. Therefore, the truth bias effect is not restricted to photographs, per se, but rather any technique that facilitates elaboration by generating related ideas and images can lead people to conclude that claims are true. As the authors report, photos (and words) inflate "truthiness" (Newman et al., 2012; Fenn et al., 2013).

Although photographs can influence what we remember, research suggests that we aren't all equally prone to the same memory distortions. Recent research by Frenda, Knowles, Saletan, and Loftus (2013), for instance, shows how our political beliefs can influence the likelihood of false memories for different political scenarios. In an online study incorporating over 5,000 individuals, Frenda et al. presented subjects with descriptions of three true and one (out of a possible five) fabricated political events. An authentic photo accompanied each of the true events, and images were doctored to accompany the fabricated events (see Figure 10.2). Nearly all of the subjects (98%) stated that they remembered at least two of the true events occurring, and half of the subjects reported that they remembered the false event, with 27% of these people even stating that they had seen it happen on the news. Interestingly, Frenda et al. showed how subjects' political orientation influenced which suggestion they fell prey to. Liberals, for instance, were more likely than Conservatives to falsely remember that George W. Bush holidayed with a baseball celebrity during the Hurricane Katrina catastrophe. Similarly, Conservatives were more likely than Liberals to falsely remember that Barack Obama shook hands with the president of Iran. Frenda and colleagues concluded that false events are more easily implanted in memory when they are congruent with one's pre-existing attitudes. Of course, it could have been political ideology or other factors that are confounded with political ideology that led to these differences. However, the study used a large general population sample, and the findings converge with those from smaller-scale college sample studies (e.g. Garry et al., 2007; Sacchi et al., 2007). All these studies suggest that photographs transform not only our memories, but also our judgements of recent experiences.

FIGURE 10.2 Frenda et al.'s (2013) doctored photos

Implications for criminal justice

It should be clear by now that photographs—both real and doctored—can affect what we recall about events across the lifespan and, in some cases, lead people to develop elaborate false memories. This raises important questions about whether photographs might also have consequences for how we behave and, if so, what the implications are for legal settings. For example, could photographs encourage people to testify about or confess to things that never happened?

Henkel (2011) explored whether photos can make people falsely claim that they have performed an action. Subjects performed and imagined performing various actions (e.g., breaking a pencil). One week later, they viewed photographs depicting some of these performed or imagined actions in their completed state (e.g., a broken pencil) and some photos depicting the completed state of "new" actions that were neither performed nor imagined. In a final session another week later, subjects were given a surprise memory test in which they had to determine which actions they had originally performed and which they had imagined. When subjects had viewed a photo of the completed action, they were more likely to falsely claim that they had performed, rather than merely imagined, that action. Moreover, viewing photos of a new action in session 2 induced some subjects to report performing or imagining those actions in session 1. Of course, it's possible that increased familiarity with the actions through repeated exposure to them caused the effect. However, using a similar procedure, Henkel found that viewing a photograph of an action once had approximately the same effect on memory errors as reading a textual description of the action four times. Thus, it appears that the photographs are the driving force of the errors and that photographs can cause people to state with high confidence that they remember doing things they did not actually do.

The fact that photographs can elicit false memories of mundane actions does not speak closely to situations in which people might testify about events that never occurred. There are no ramifications for misremembering a broken pencil. However, law enforcement officers sometimes use photographs when interviewing suspects in criminal investigations (Inbau, Reid, Buckley, & Jayne, 2005; Kassin et al., 2007). Concerns about these techniques led Nash and colleagues to develop an experimental procedure for exposing mock witnesses to doctored evidence and then attempting to obtain false testimony.

In Nash and co-workers' false-video procedure, subjects are filmed while completing a computerized gambling task in which they take fake money from a "bank" when they answer questions correctly, and return fake money to the bank when they answer questions incorrectly. Later, subjects are told that the person sitting next to them during the gambling task (a research confederate) had cheated and took money from the bank when they should have returned it. In reality, the confederate didn't cheat, but subjects are told that the "other participant" was clearly trying to earn more money in order to win a cash prize. Subjects are then randomly assigned to one of the experimental conditions. In Wade, Green, and Nash (2010), some subjects watched a digitally manipulated video of the confederate cheating. Some were told that incriminating video evidence existed. The remaining subjects were told nothing about video evidence. Finally, subjects were asked if they could corroborate the (false) accusation that the other subject cheated by signing a statement confirming that they had actually witnessed the other subject cheating. Overall, 20% of subjects signed the witness statement, knowing that their corroboration would result in disciplinary action against the accused student. Most importantly, though, subjects who saw the false video evidence were more likely to sign the statement than those who were told the video existed and were significantly more likely to sign the statement than those who were told nothing about the video evidence. A third of the subjects who signed the witness statement (from the see-video and told-video conditions) also provided additional incriminating details, such as: "I saw the 'X' sign crossed out on her screen and she reached out for a note from the bank."

In a modified version of the false-video procedure, Nash and Wade (2009) illustrated how doctored video footage could induce people to falsely confess to cheating on the task. When accused of cheating, all of the subjects complied and signed a confession form stating that they had cheated. Yet those who viewed a doctored video of themselves apparently cheating were more likely to confess on the first request and were more likely to confabulate details than those who were just told that incriminating video evidence existed. Perhaps most importantly, those who viewed the doctored video were more likely to internalize (come to believe) that they had actually cheated. Given that the same pattern of results emerged when subjects were accused of cheating on three separate occasions, it is unlikely that they simply signed the confession because they thought it was plausible they had unknowingly cheated.

In another study designed with criminal justice applications in mind, Wright, Wade, and Watson (2013) showed that timing and repetition both serve to increase the power of false video evidence. Subjects who were shown false video evidence of themselves cheating on a computerized driving test after a brief nine-minute delay were more likely to believe that they had cheated than those who were shown false video evidence immediately after they had been told that they had been caught. Presenting the false evidence more than once also resulted in subjects being more likely to believe that they had cheated. Repetition over time was particularly persuasive: when the false evidence was repeated with a delay, subjects were 20% more likely to confabulate details about how they cheated than when evidence was repeated without a delay. Again, these findings raise concerns about police techniques such as presenting suspects with false evidence, persistent questioning, and repeatedly stating that the suspect is guilty (Inbau et al., 2005; National Policing Improvement Agency, 2009). In sum, these studies suggest that doctored image evidence, particularly when presented repeatedly over a delay, might affect the reliability of people's memory reports in forensic settings.

Images are powerful

What is it about images that can make us misremember significant, personal experiences? Why do images lead us to think, for example, that fictitious statements are true? How can images lead us to confess to a misdemeanour we never committed? Scientists are starting to understand the complex social and cognitive mechanisms underlying the creation of false memories, and the growing body of research on photos and memories is highlighting the role that images play.

The prevalent theoretical approach to understanding false memories is the source monitoring framework (SMF; Johnson et al., 1993). Given that memories are not stored with a label to help us later identify their source, we must determine the source of our mental experiences in some other way. The SMF proposes that we make such source judgements using various cues—qualitative characteristics—within our memories, such as perceptual detail (e.g., sound) and contextual detail (e.g., time), to differentiate between memories of events we perceive and events we internally generate (i.e., imagine or think about). Usually we judge the source of our memories automatically and effortlessly based on these qualitative cues because memories of real events are, on average, richer in the qualitative characteristics than memories of internally generated events. Based on this framework, the chances of making a source misattribution increase when internally generated events take on more of the qualitative characteristics typically associated with actual memories. When this happens, confusion about the correct source of the mental experience can lead to false memories. As we know from research already discussed in this chapter, images are extremely powerful in making people more prone to source monitoring errors, but why?

Based on the SMF, Nash, Wade, and Brewer (2009) advanced three possible cognitive mechanisms that might account for the role images play in memory distortions: *familiarity*, *imagery*, and *credibility*. First, we know that memories of perceived (real) events usually come to mind fluently and quickly, which results in a feeling of familiarity. If imagined or suggested events come to mind with such fluency, they can also be prone to being misattributed to memory rather than to their actual source (Jacoby, Kelley, & Dywan, 1989; Newman, 2017). When thinking about this in the context of photographs, it might be that the visual depiction of an event causes images to come to mind fluently, generating feelings similar to those experienced when remembering a real event. This can create an illusion of familiarity and result in a source misattribution. Second, images may make it easier for people to imagine the suggested event because they act as a scaffold for other related imagery from real memories. The imagery generated from the photograph and the imagery of real memories become intertwined, embellishing the former with qualitative characteristics that are typically only associated with memories of real events (Johnson, Foley, Suengas, & Raye, 1988). In short, false memories occur when the distinction between imagery generated from the photograph and imagery from real memories becomes blurred. Finally, images are often perceived to be evidence of reality (Kelly & Nace, 1994; Wright, 2013), and therefore may provide a credible indication that the suggested event has occurred. This can result in people lowering their criteria for accepting an imagined event as a real memory (Mazzoni & Kirsch, 2002). As a consequence, the lowered criteria can explain why even an imagined event low in perceptual and contextual detail might be incorrectly accepted as a real memory.

Which mechanism—familiarity, imagery, or credibility—best accounts for the power of photographs to influence memory? Nash, Wade, & Lindsay (2009) tested these three mechanisms directly using a simple procedure. Subjects were videoed as they observed and copied a research assistant (RA) performing various actions such as clapping his hands or performing a salute. Subjects were then shown video clips of the actions and video clips of two "new" critical actions. In the video, subjects either saw the RA performing the actions with the subject ostensibly in the room (Self+RA), the RA performing the actions without the subject in the room (RA-Only), or a stranger performing the actions in an unfamiliar room (Stranger-Only). In all three conditions subjects gave higher memory ratings to the critical actions than to the control actions (that the subject neither observed nor performed). This suggests that simply seeing the critical actions being performed in the video clip increases their familiarity and results in false memories of performing these actions. Further, the Self+RA condition was most powerful in creating memories of performing the critical actions. With the subject ostensibly in the room, this condition provides the most persuasive false evidence and thereby gives some weight to the credibility mechanism.

Frenda et al.'s (2013) research, described earlier, on the power of doctored photos to distort people's memories for political events, also supports a credibility account. When subjects viewed doctored images of events that had not actually happened, their personal attitudes affected how credible they felt the suggested event was. If the event depicted in the image was congruent with their political beliefs, subjects perceived the event to be more believable and presumably lowered their threshold for accepting any internally generated "memory" of the event as real. If the event depicted in the image was incongruent with their political beliefs, subjects perceived the event to be less believable and raised their threshold for accepting any internally generated "memory" of the event as real.

Curiously, the perception that images are credible sources of information is a paradox given that images are (and always have been) manipulated. There are two main reasons we should worry about this pervading misconception. First, as we alluded to at the start of this chapter, image-editing technology and image-sharing facilities are developing at a phenomenal pace. As a result, we are increasingly exposed to sophisticated doctored images. Second, research using computer-generated images (Farid, 2009; Farid & Bravo, 2010; Nightingale, Wade, & Watson, 2019) and images of real-world scenes (Nightingale, Wade, & Watson, 2017) demonstrates just how remarkably poor people are at detecting digital manipulations. What is more, we know that even warnings and previous experience of personally altering photographs don't appear to protect people from being fooled (Kelly & Nace, 1994). We might assume the misplaced credibility attributed to photos is set to persist; thus, future research should further examine this process and its contribution to belief, memory, and judgement distortion.

However, we know that the credibility mechanism cannot explain the effect of photos in every situation. Recall that Newman et al. (2012) presented famous names with a photo of the famous person or a text description of the person, and subjects were equally likely to respond "true" to the statement "This famous person is alive", regardless of the format of the additional information. Therefore, in this instance, photos didn't afford any more credibility in the information than did text. In fact, these findings fit with an imagery mechanism—both photos and text descriptions might facilitate people's ability to bring to mind related images and ideas leading to an inflated feeling of "truthiness". Thus, it isn't necessarily the case that one single mechanism—familiarity, imagery, or credibility—prevails. In fact, some empirical evidence suggests a combination of processes could be at play (Nash, Wade, & Lindsay, 2009).

Concluding remarks

It is clear that photographs can readily distort our memories for both distant and recent experiences. Photos can also influence our decisions, our judgements, and even our behaviour. On a theoretical level, we still have a lot to learn about how and why photos can affect our memories so much. Although photos carry with them an unwarranted degree of credibility and authenticity, clearly other cognitive processes are at play that make them persuasive. On a more practical level, we know that taking, sharing, and altering photographs is only becoming easier, more affordable, and more popular amongst people all over the world. And although the effects of photos on memory, cognition, and behaviour are often minor, in certain circumstances—for example, in criminal justice settings—we believe these effects could have major ramifications. Of course, your own chances of experiencing such severe negative consequences are fairly slim, but the next time you see a news article or posting on a social network site that is accompanied by a photograph, we invite you to remember the shark swimming through New Jersey and to view that photo with a critical eye.

Note

* This chapter originally appeared in the edited volume, *False and Distorted Memories*. It has been updated for this compilation.

References

Braun, K. A., Ellis, R., & Loftus, E. F. (2002). Make my memory: How advertising can change our memories of the past. *Psychology and Marketing, 19*, 1–23.

Farid, H. (2009). Image forgery detection. *Signal Processing Magazine, IEEE, 26*, 16–25.

Farid, H., & Bravo, M. J. (2010). Image forensic analyses that elude the human visual system. *Proceedings of SPIE, 7541*, 1–10.

Fenn, E., Newman, E. J., Pezdek, K., & Garry, M. (2013). The effect of nonprobative photographs on truthiness persists over time. *Acta Psychologica, 144*, 207–211.

Frenda, S. J., Knowles, E. D., Saletan, W., & Loftus, E. F. (2013). False memories of fabricated political events. *Journal of Experimental Social Psychology, 49*, 280–286.

Garry, M., Strange, D., Bernstein, D. M., & Kinzett, T. (2007). Photographs can distort memory for the news. *Applied Cognitive Psychology, 21*, 995–1004.

Garry, M., & Wade, K. A. (2005). Actually, a picture is worth less than 45 words: Narratives produce more false memories than photographs. *Psychonomic Bulletin and Review, 12*, 359–366.

Grinley, M. J. (2002). Effects of advertising on semantic and episodic memory. Unpublished Master's thesis, University of Washington.

Henkel, L. A. (2011). Photograph-induced memory errors: When photographs make people claim they have done things they have not. *Applied Cognitive Psychology, 25*, 78–86.

Henkel, L. A. (2012). Seeing photos makes us read between the lines: The influence of photos on memory for inferences. *Quarterly Journal of Experimental Psychology, 65*, 773–795.

Hessen-Kayfitz, J. K., & Scoboria, A. (2012). False memory is in the details: Photographic details differentially predict memory formation. *Applied Cognitive Psychology, 26*, 333–341.

Inbau, F. E., Reid, J. E., Buckley, J. P., & Jayne, B. C. (2005). *Essentials of the Reid technique: Criminal interrogation and confessions*. Sudbury, MA: Jones & Bartlett Publishers.

Jacoby, L. L., Kelley, C. M., & Dywan, J. (1989). Memory attributions. In H. L. Roediger, III & F. I. M. Craik (Eds.), *Varieties of memory and consciousness: Essays in honour of Endel Tulving* (pp. 391–422). Hillsdale, NJ: Erlbaum.

Johnson, M. K., Foley, M. A., Suengas, A. G., & Raye, C. L. (1988). Phenomenal characteristics of memories for perceived and imagined autobiographical events. *Journal of Experimental Psychology: General, 117*, 371–376.

Johnson, M. K., Hashtroudi, S., & Lindsay, D. S. (1993). Source monitoring. *Psychological Bulletin, 114*, 3–28.

Kassin, S. M., Leo, R. A., Meissner, C. A., Richman, K. D., Colwell, L. H., Leach, A., & La Fon, D. (2007). Police interviewing and interrogation: A self-report survey of police practices and beliefs. *Law and Human Behavior, 31*, 381–400.

Kelly, J. E., & Nace, D. (1994). Digital imaging and believing photos. *Visual Communication Quarterly, 1*, 4–18.

Koutstaal, W., Schacter, D. L., Johnson, M. K., Angell, K. E., & Gross, M. S. (1998). Post-event review in older and younger adults: Improving memory accessibility of complex everyday events. *Psychology and Aging, 13*, 277–296.

Lindsay, D. S. (2008). Source monitoring. In H. L. Roediger (Ed.), *Cognitive psychology of memory* (vol. 2, pp. 325–348). Oxford: Elsevier.

Lindsay, D. S., Hagen, L., Read, J. D., Wade, K. A., & Garry, M. (2004). True photographs and false memories. *Psychological Science, 15*, 149–154.

Loftus, E. F., & Pickrell, J. E. (1995). The formation of false memories. *Psychiatric Annals, 25*, 720–725.

Mazzoni, G., & Kirsch, I. (2002). False autobiographical memories and beliefs: A preliminary metacognitive model. In T. Perfect & B. Schwartz (Eds.), *Applied metacognition* (pp. 121–145). Cambridge: Cambridge University Press.

Nash, R. A., & Wade, K. A. (2009). Innocent but proven guilty: Eliciting internalized false confessions using doctored video evidence. *Applied Cognitive Psychology, 23*, 624–637.

Nash, R. A., Wade, K. A., & Brewer, R. J. (2009). Why do doctored images distort memory? *Consciousness and Cognition, 18*, 773–780.

Nash, R. A., Wade, K. A., & Lindsay, D. S. (2009). Digitally manipulating memory: Effects of doctored videos and imagination in distorting beliefs and memories. *Memory and Cognition, 37*, 414–424.

National Policing Improvement Agency. (2009). *National investigative interviewing strategy*. Retrieved from www.npia.police.uk/en/docs/National_Investigative_Interviewing_Strategy_09.pdf.

Newman, E. J. (2017). Cognitive fluency and false memories. In R. A. Nash & J. Ost (Eds.), *False and distorted memories* (pp. 112–124). London and New York: Routledge.

Newman, E. J., Garry, M., Bernstein, D. M., Kantner, J., & Lindsay, D. S. (2012). Nonprobative photographs (or words) inflate truthiness. *Psychonomic Bulletin & Review, 19*, 969–974.

Nightingale, S. J., Wade, K. A., Farid, H., & Watson, D. G. (2019). Can people detect errors in shadows and reflections? *Attention, Perception, and Psychophysics, 81*, 2917–2943.

Nightingale, S. J., Wade, K. A., & Watson, D. G. (2017). Can people identify original and manipulated photos of real-world scenes? *Cognitive Research: Principles and Implications, 2*, 30.

Otgaar, H., Candel, I., Merckelbach, H., & Wade, K. A. (2009). Abducted by a UFO: Prevalence information affects young children's false memories for an implausible event. *Applied Cognitive Psychology, 23*, 115–125.

Sacchi, D. L. M., Agnoli, F., & Loftus, E. F. (2007). Changing history: Doctored photographs affect memory for past public events. *Applied Cognitive Psychology, 21*, 1005–1022.

Schacter, D. L., Koutstaal, W., Johnson, M. K., Gross, M. S., & Angell, K. E. (1997). False recollection induced by photographs: A comparison of older and younger adults. *Psychology and Aging, 12*, 203–215.

Strange, D., Garry, M., Bernstein, D. M., & Lindsay, D. S. (2011). Photographs cause false memories for the news. *Acta Psychologica, 136*, 90–94.

Strange, D., Sutherland, R., & Garry, M. (2006). Event plausibility does not determine children's false memories. *Memory, 14*, 937–951.

Strange, D., Wade, K. A., & Hayne, H. (2008). Creating false memories for events that occurred before versus after the offset of childhood amnesia. *Memory, 16*, 475–484.

Wade, K. A., Garry, M., Nash, R. A., & Harper, D. (2010). Anchoring effects in the development of false childhood memories. *Psychonomic Bulletin and Review, 17*, 66–72.

Wade, K. A., Garry, M., Read, J. D., & Lindsay, D. S. (2002). A picture is worth a thousand lies: Using false photographs to create false childhood memories. *Psychonomic Bulletin and Review, 9*, 597–603.

Wade, K. A., Green, S. L., & Nash, R. A. (2010). Can fabricated evidence induce false eyewitness testimony? *Applied Cognitive Psychology, 24*, 899–908.

Whittlesea, B. W. A. (1993). Illusions of familiarity. *Journal of Experimental Psychology: Learning, Memory, and Cognition, 19*, 1235–1253.

Whittlesea, B. W. A. (2011). Remembering under the influence of unconscious expectations. In P. A. Higham & J. P. Leboe (Eds.), *Constructions of remembering and metacognition: Essays in honor of Bruce Whittlesea* (pp. 225–236). Houndmills: Palgrave Macmillan.

Wright, D. S. (2013). The mediating and moderating factors of fabricated evidence on false confessions, beliefs and memory. Unpublished doctoral dissertation, University of Warwick, UK.

Wright, D. S., Wade, K. A., & Watson, D. G. (2013). Delay and déjà vu: Timing and repetition increase the power of false evidence. *Psychonomic Bulletin and Review, 20*, 812–818.

11

FORCED FABRICATION AND FALSE EYEWITNESS MEMORIES*

Maria S. Zaragoza, Patrick Rich, Eric Rindal, and Rachel DeFranco

For decades, the suggestibility of eyewitness memory has been an extremely active research area, and there is now an extensive literature documenting that exposure to false or misleading postevent information can lead to confidently held false memories of having witnessed events that were never actually experienced (see Loftus, 2005; Zaragoza, Belli, & Payment, 2007, for reviews). Our research program on forced fabrication stems from the observation that in real-world forensic investigations, suggestive interviews are not restricted to situations where an interviewer surreptitiously implants, or exposes a witness to, a piece of false information. Rather, in many cases, interviewers attempt to elicit from the witnesses testimony that can assist them in their investigation or in prosecuting a crime. In such cases, interviewers may pressure witnesses to speculate or even fabricate information about events the interviewer believes transpired, even when the witness does not remember or never witnessed the events he or she is asked to describe (see, e.g., Lassiter & Meissner, 2010, for a recent volume on the related topic of interrogation practices used to elicit confessions). In such highly coercive interview contexts, witnesses may succumb to this pressure in an attempt to satisfy the interviewer and knowingly provide a fabricated account. Although this may occur unwittingly— as in the case of spontaneous inference—our research has been concerned with cases where participants are pressed to fabricate information they would not have provided had they not been forced to do so. In all of these studies, the central research question has been whether participant-witnesses might eventually develop false memories of having witnessed the events they had earlier fabricated knowingly and under duress. As we will show, there is now a substantial body of evidence that they do.[1]

An experimental paradigm for investigating the consequences of forced fabrication

To investigate whether participants might develop false memories of their forced fabrications, we have employed a modified version of the misinformation paradigm originally developed by E. Loftus (e.g., Loftus, Miller, & Burns, 1978). As in the typical eyewitness suggestibility study, in the forced fabrication paradigm, all participants view an eyewitness event, are subsequently exposed to a suggestive manipulation, and are later tested on their memory for the witnessed event, with the goal of assessing whether the suggestive manipulation has contaminated the originally witnessed memory. Where the forced fabrication paradigm differs from the traditional paradigm is in the nature of the suggestive manipulation. In the traditional paradigm, the experimenter provides some piece of false or misleading information, typically by presupposing its existence in an interview questionnaire or narrative description of the event the participant is asked to read. In the forced fabrication paradigm, by contrast, rather than being told some falsehood, participant-witnesses engage in face-to-face interviews with the experimenter where, in addition to answering questions about true events they did witness, they are asked "false event" questions about blatantly nonexistent objects or events and are pressed to provide answers to these unanswerable questions. Importantly, the participant-witness is not permitted to evade the interviewer's request to provide an answer to the false-event questions. Rather, participants are informed ahead of time that they must respond to all questions, even if they have to guess. Although participants resist answering these false-event questions, the interviewer "forces" them to comply by repeatedly insisting that they just "give their best guess" until participants eventually acquiesce by providing a relevant response.

To illustrate the coercive nature of these interviews and participants' resistance to answering these false-event questions, we provide here a transcribed portion of an interview with a participant from one of our initial studies (Zaragoza, Payment, Ackil, Drivdahl, & Beck, 2001). In the example, the participant had witnessed a video clip from a movie involving two brothers at a summer camp (see also Ackil & Zaragoza, 1998). In one of the scenes that the participant actually witnessed, a camp counselor named Delaney stands on a chair to make an announcement in the dining hall, when he loses his balance and falls to the floor. The scene was used as the basis for a false-event question that asked participants where Delaney was bleeding, when there was no evidence that Delaney had injured himself (or bled) at all. The exchange between the interviewer and the participant is as follows:

INTERVIEWER: After he fell, where was Delaney bleeding?
PARTICIPANT: He wasn't. He was? I didn't see any blood.
INTERVIEWER: What's your best guess?
PARTICIPANT: Where was he bleeding?
INTERVIEWER: Yeah.

PARTICIPANT: But he wasn't bleeding. Oh … I don't have a best guess. I didn't think he was bleeding. His knee?

This transcript illustrates several characteristic features of forced fabrication interviews. First, in order to comply with the experimenter's demands, participants have to make up, or fabricate, a response to the false-event questions (in this case, the participant had to invent that it was Delaney's knee that was bleeding, because no bleeding was depicted in the video clip). Second, participants' resistance to answering such false-event questions clearly indicates their awareness that they do not know the answer. In the previous example, the participant repeatedly states that she didn't see any blood, and in fact, directly states that Delaney wasn't bleeding at all. Moreover, as is typically the case, the resistance is so strong that it takes several conversational turns before the interviewer is able to elicit any information relevant to the question. Clearly, this participant would never have stated that Delaney's knee was bleeding had she not been forced to do so, even though it is plausible that the character bled given the fall the participant witnessed. Although participants overtly express resistance to responding to false-event questions about half the time (by verbally stating that they didn't know the answer, didn't see the queried info, etc.), in the vast majority of cases where participants don't overtly resist, they evidenced more passive forms of resistance, such as evading the question or refraining from answering the question until prompted (sometimes repeatedly) by the interviewer to provide their best guess.

In the typical forced fabrication experiment, false memory for the fabricated events is assessed by giving participants a delayed (typically five to seven days) yes/no recognition test of their memory for the witnessed event, where they are presented with the items they had earlier fabricated, and asked if they remember witnessing them in the original event. Other studies have used tests of free recall, and assessed whether participants incorporate their fabrications into their freely provided accounts of the witnessed event.

Methodological considerations

The goal of the research described in this chapter is to assess whether forcing witnesses to fabricate fictitious items and events leads them to develop false memories of having witnessed these knowingly fabricated events. To answer this question, we have designed all of our studies with the following methodological considerations in mind. In this chapter, we restrict our review to studies conducted with adult participants who meet these methodological requirements.

Ensuring testimony is forced rather than freely provided

The goal of forced fabrication studies is to mimic forensic situations where witnesses are pressed to fabricate testimony they would not have provided had they not been pressured to do so (for related paradigms where participants sometimes voluntarily respond to false-event questions, see Pezdek, Sperry, & Owens, 2007; Pezdek, Lam, & Sperry, 2009; Gombos, Pezdek, & Haymond, 2011). To that end, participants are asked questions about objects and events that they clearly never witnessed and that are not readily guessed. Although the resistance participants display when pressed to provide fabricated responses provides compelling evidence that they are being "forced", we have also sought more direct evidence. To this end, in two of our forced fabrication studies (Ackil & Zaragoza, 1998; Zaragoza et al., 2001), we included a second group of participants (the "free" group) who were instructed that they should respond "don't know" if they did not know the answer to a question posed by the interviewer, and should refrain from guessing. In both studies, none of the participants in the free group spontaneously provided answers to any of the false-event questions, thus verifying that participants do not answer these questions unless forced to do so.

Assessing the extent to which false memories are caused by the forced fabrication interview

Because our central concern is determining whether forced fabrication leads to memory distortions, an important methodological issue is isolating memory errors that result from the suggestive interview from memory errors that might result from other causes (e.g., spontaneous inference). To do so requires assessing the extent to which control participants, who were never asked to fabricate these events, might claim to remember witnessing the fabricated events on the final memory test (i.e., to establish the base rate of assenting to the fabricated events). If forced fabrication leads to false memory, participants' claims of having witnessed the fabricated events should reliably exceed the base rate of these false claims, and this is the measure of false memory we employed in all of the studies reviewed here. Across studies, we have consistently found that the base rate of false assents to the fabricated events is low (on yes/no recognition tests typically 10% or less; on measures of free recall, it was consistently at floor), thus providing further evidence that participants witnessing these events do not infer the fabricated events spontaneously. Rather, these false memory errors are a direct consequence of the forced fabrication interview.

Differentiating between false reports and false beliefs/memories

In studies of forced fabrication, as in all eyewitness suggestibility studies, the experimenter is in a position of authority, and participants may feel some pressure to go along with the suggestions provided by the experimenter. Moreover, participants in forced fabrication studies might feel pressure to respond consistently across interviews because they may find it unflattering to admit that their responses during the initial interview were mere fabrications. Because the goal of our studies is to assess false memory, we have designed our studies such that these social demands are eliminated or at least minimized. In particular, in all studies of forced fabrication reviewed here, the experimenter who tested participants' memory on the delayed tests was different from the one who carried out the forced fabrication interview, thus minimizing any perceived pressure to respond consistently across test sessions. More importantly, virtually all studies have used a warning that explicitly informs participants before taking the memory test that the person who had interviewed them initially had asked them some questions about events that never actually happened, thus disabusing participants of the belief that all of the information provided by the interviewer was accurate. Finally, participants were instructed that their task was to differentiate between those events they specifically remembered witnessing in the video and information they may have encountered during the interviews.

A more difficult question to answer conclusively is whether suggestive interviews involving forced fabrications lead to false recollections of having witnessed the fabricated events, or whether participants simply come to develop strong beliefs that they witnessed the fabricated events (without being able to consciously recollect having witnessed the fabricated event). One potential method for distinguishing between false recollections and false beliefs is to employ measures of phenomenological experience (see Frost, LaCroix, & Sanborn, 2003, for evidence that participants do sometimes recollect having witnessed their forced fabrications). However, because most of the studies reviewed here did not include measures of phenomenological experience, it is unclear whether these false memory effects reflect false recollections or a confident belief in having witnessed the fabricated events. Hence, in this chapter, we use the term "false memory" to mean instances where participants claim to remember witnessing their fabrications; our use of the term "false memory" is not meant to imply anything specific about the nature of the phenomenological experience that accompanies these claims.

Empirical evidence that forced fabrication leads to false memories

Intuitively, it would seem that the experience of being coerced into providing descriptions of fictitious items or events would be salient and memorable to participants, and that they would remember that their fabricated responses were mere speculations that they had been forced to provide. To the contrary, there is now considerable evidence that after retention intervals of just one week, participants are prone to developing false memories of having witnessed their forced fabrications even when warned before taking the test (Ackil & Zaragoza, 1998, 2011; Zaragoza et al., 2001; Frost et al., 2003; Hanba & Zaragoza, 2007; Memon, Zaragoza, Clifford, & Kidd, 2010). In what follows, we review the factors that have been shown to mitigate false memory development in the forced fabrication paradigm, and the factors that have been shown to promote these false memories.

Factors that mitigate false memory development

Overt resistance and warnings

As we have shown, one of the unique features of suggestive interviews involving forced fabrication is that participants are pressed to provide responses to unanswerable questions (and hence must fabricate a response). Not surprisingly, participants resist doing so. In several studies we have sought to assess whether there is a relationship between participants' resistance to providing a fabricated response and later false memory for that fabricated response. We have found that in some cases, and for some types of resistance, there is. Specifically, several studies have shown that overt, verbal resistance (e.g., "I didn't see that", or "His knee wasn't bleeding") is associated with lower false memory development, but more passive forms of resistance (long latency or refusals to respond) are not (Zaragoza et al., 2001; Ackil & Zaragoza, 2011). Relative to passive resistance, we have found that in those fabrications that were generated following overt resistance, false memory development is substantially reduced (Ackil & Zaragoza, 2011) and in some cases not evident at all (Zaragoza et al., 2001).

It should be noted, however, that this apparent protective benefit of overt resistance occurs under restricted circumstances only. Ackil and Zaragoza (2011) manipulated whether or not participants received a warning before the final test and manipulated whether the final test was recognition or free recall. Relative to fabrications provided without verbal resistance, false memory for verbally resisted fabrications was significantly lower, but this reduction in false memory was observed only if two conditions were met jointly: participants received a pretest warning, and the final test was a recognition test. If only one of these conditions was met, overt resistance did not confer any benefit. That is, neither participants who were unwarned and given a recognition test nor those who were warned but tested with free recall evidenced any reduction in false memory when fabrications were generated following verbal resistance (Ackil & Zaragoza, 2011). Finally, as we will show later in this chapter, the association between overt resistance and reduced false memory disappears when participants receive confirmatory interviewer feedback following their fabricated responses, as well as when they are tested after very long retention intervals (Chrobak & Zaragoza, 2008).

Collectively, the data reviewed here are consistent with the conclusion that resistance is most likely to offer protection against false memory development under conditions that encourage participants to remember their uncertainty in their fabricated response. We interpret these findings as evidence that publicly expressing resistance (as opposed to keeping such thoughts internal) enhances memory for the resistance and for having fabricated the response. We further propose that pretest warnings prompt participants to retrieve their uncertainty in their fabricated response in cases where they do not spontaneously do so. Finally, we propose that because tests of narrative free recall are more cognitively demanding than yes/no recognition, participants are less likely to spontaneously retrieve memories of resistance when providing free recall.

Improving memory for the witnessed event with the cognitive interview

Participants may resist providing a fabricated response for a number of reasons. Some participants may resist because they are highly confident that the events they are being asked to describe never transpired. Other participants may accept the interviewer's false presupposition as truth (e.g., Delaney fell because someone pulled a prank) because they assume that they either failed to notice or have forgotten the false information. For these latter participants, resistance may reflect discomfort with guessing, reluctance to publicly state a guess that may be wrong, or difficulty generating an appropriate guess (i.e., because there is a large pool of possible answers). Although in both cases participants are aware that the response they are providing is mere conjecture, it seems reasonable to predict that participants who are highly confident that they are being asked about events that never happened might be more resistant to the effects of forced fabrication. Hence, one strategy that might mitigate the contaminating effects of forced fabrication interviews is to enhance participants' memory for the witnessed event. A study by Memon et al. (2010) did just that.

The cognitive interview (hereafter, CI; Fisher & Geiselman, 1992) is an investigative tool that produces detailed reports from an eyewitness without reducing accuracy. Memon et al. (2010) hypothesized that administering a CI after a witnessed event (but before participants underwent a forced fabrication interview) would solidify participants' memory for the witnessed event and counteract the memory-distorting effects of the forced fabrication interview. The findings supported this hypothesis: relative to free recall, the CI significantly reduced false assents to fabricated items, but only if it was administered before the forced fabrication interview; the CI administered after the forced fabrication interview had no effect on false memory for forced fabrications.

Factors that promote false memory development: The role of confirmatory feedback

In an effort to elicit cooperation from witnesses and set them at ease, it is natural for interviewers to reinforce reluctant or unsure witnesses when they comply with the interviewer's request for information. However, research has shown that when interviewers reinforce unsure or erroneous testimony, it has the potential of inflating witnesses' confidence in their mistaken testimony and distorting their memories (see Steblay, Wells, & Douglass, 2014, for a recent review of research on confirmatory interviewer feedback and erroneous lineup identifications).

Of particular relevance here is the finding in several studies that confirmatory interviewer feedback provided in the context of forced fabrication interviews is a potent catalyst to false memory creation (Zaragoza et al., 2001; Frost et al. 2003; Hanba & Zaragoza, 2007). For example, in Zaragoza et al. (2001), participants witnessed a video event and underwent a forced fabrication interview where they were pressed to respond to both true-event and false-event questions. As in the typical forced fabrication study, participants resisted providing fabricated responses, but eventually acquiesced. The novel manipulation was that immediately following their fabricated responses the experimenter provided feedback that was either confirmatory (e.g., "That's right, __ is the correct answer!"), or neutral/noninformative (e.g., "__, OK", delivered with flat affect). Participants were tested on their memories of the witnessed event with a yes/no recognition test accompanied by a warning that was administered one week later. Relative to neutral feedback, confirmatory interviewer feedback led to significant increases in the incidence of false memories, increased confidence in those false memories, and increased the likelihood that participants would incorporate their forced fabrications into their freely provided accounts one month later (Zaragoza et al., 2001). Importantly, even those participants who could not remember the confirmatory feedback showed increased false memory, thus showing that participants were not simply going along with the feedback. In addition, Zaragoza et al. found that although overt verbal resistance was associated with reduced false memory when participants received neutral feedback following their fabrications, there was no advantage associated with overt verbal resistance when their fabrications had earlier been reinforced with confirmatory feedback. We interpret these findings as evidence that confirmatory feedback leads participants to suppress or discount their uncertainty in their fabricated responses.

Additional evidence that confirmatory feedback increases participants' confidence in their fabricated responses comes from a study that examined how confirmatory interviewer feedback provided during an initial interview affects participants' behavior in subsequent interviews involving the same questions (Hanba & Zaragoza, 2007). The finding of interest was that when confirmatory feedback was provided during the initial interview, participants later provided fabricated responses with a speed and confidence that resembled their responses to the true-event questions. Collectively, the results showed that, when earlier reinforced by confirmatory feedback, the apparent confidence with which participants later reported their fabricated response and the perceived credibility of their fabricated testimony were inflated considerably.

Can the effects of confirmatory feedback be reversed? Recent unpublished studies from our laboratory have attempted to address this question by asking participants to disregard the feedback. The consistent finding, however, is that the effects of confirmatory feedback persist even when attempts are made to discredit the validity of the feedback. Regardless of whether participants are given a mild warning that the feedback may not have been accurate or a very strong warning that the feedback was completely random, confirmatory feedback increases false memory and the speed with which participants endorse their false memories for the fabricated events.

Extensions of the forced fabrication paradigm: Does forcing witnesses to fabricate entire fictitious events lead to false memories?

The purpose of many forensic interviews is to elicit from the witness a complete account of the actions and events that caused an adverse outcome, such as a crime or an accident. Accordingly, witnesses will often be pressed to describe events that are broad in scope and extended in time. The forced fabrication studies discussed earlier assessed false memory in situations where participants were forced to fabricate isolated items that were somewhat incidental to the storyline. However, we have also assessed whether these false memory effects generalize to situations where participants are required to fabricate entire fictitious events that are extended in time, and involve people engaging in actions that they never witnessed. As reviewed later, even when pushed to fabricate entire fictitious events that are broad in scope, people will sometimes develop robust false memories for these fictitious accounts (Chrobak & Zaragoza, 2008, 2013; Chrobak, Rindal, & Zaragoza, 2015).

To illustrate how we have implemented forced fabrication of entire events (hereafter referred to as *event fabrications*), we provide next a portion of an interview with a participant from one of our studies (Chrobak & Zaragoza, 2008). In the example, the participant had witnessed the same scene discussed earlier, where Delaney stands up to make an announcement, loses his balance, and falls on the floor. However, rather than asking participants where he was bleeding (as in the earlier item fabrication studies), participants were asked to describe a fictitious practical joke that the experimenter claimed had caused him to fall. In the video clip participants witnessed, there was no evidence of a practical joke—the clip simply depicts him losing his balance and falling to the floor. Nevertheless, participants were pressed to describe a fictitious practical joke that caused the fall, including a description of what the joke was, who did it, and how. The exchange between the experimenter (E) and the participant (P) appears here:

E: The next scene takes place in the dining hall. Delaney is asked to stand up and give an announcement. A practical joke is pulled on him that causes him to fall and end up on the floor. What was it?

P: Uhh, I'm not sure what the practical joke was, ehh … I know that he fell, I thought he did it on purpose though.

E: Just give your best guess about the practical joke.

P: Umm uh no one was paying attention to him, and then I guess he slipped. I don't know. Yeah I really don't, like I thought like he did it on purpose to get everyone's attention. I didn't know there was a practical joke going on.

E: Just give your best guess.

P: Umm, let's see, I really don't remember, like I don't.

E: Well, what did he slip on?

P: A piece of food?

E: Ok what was the practical joke that they pulled?

P: Umm, like what do you mean like?

E: How did it get there?

P: I guess someone put it there.

E: Who might have put it there?

P: Probably, umm, not his little brother but what's that other guy that's causing trouble in the beginning?

E: Ratface?

P: Yeah probably Ratface.

E: And what food did he put there?

P: Uhh maybe a banana? I don't know.

E: And how might he have put it there?

P: Uh, sneaking up there.

E: How did he sneak up there?

P: (laughs) I don't remember. Umm …

E: Just give your best guess.

P: Umm he just was, doing it when no one was looking.

E: Ok so your answer was: Delaney slipped on some food, it was a banana that Ratface put there, and he might have sneaked it up there when no one was looking. Is there anything else you remember about the practical joke played on Delaney?

P: No, uhh yeah there was that lady that yelled at him and said that his foolishness isn't going to help them get donations from those ladies that were visiting.

A comparison of this transcript with the earlier example shows that, as expected, participants are much more resistant to fabricating entire fictitious events than they are to fabricating an isolated item. As we will see, this high level of resistance reduces false memory development over the short term, but does not prevent rather substantial levels of false memory over the longer term.

We have now shown in several event fabrication studies that, when participants are tested at a relatively short retention interval of one week and are provided a warning before taking the test, they evidence no false memory for their fabricated accounts (Chrobak & Zaragoza, 2008; Chrobak et al., 2015). However, when the same participants returned six to eight weeks later, almost half of the participants *who correctly rejected their forced fabrications on a one-week recognition* test freely incorporated their forced fabrications into their testimony (Chrobak & Zaragoza, 2008; see also Chrobak & Zaragoza, 2013 for similar findings when a six- to eight-week free recall test is used without an intervening recognition test). To be clear, what has been assessed in these studies is whether participants freely recall the specific events they fabricated when forced to do so (e.g., Ratface put a banana peel on the floor). In those cases where participants merely reported the suggestion provided by the experimenter (that someone pulled a prank), the report, although false, was not counted as false memory for their fabrications.

Factors that influence the incidence and magnitude of false memory for event fabrications

Relative to situations where participants are asked to fabricate isolated items, participants who are pressed to fabricate entire fictitious events are likely to have greater awareness and conviction that they did not witness or do not remember the events they are being asked to fabricate, thus enhancing their memory that these accounts are mere fabrications. However, even when participants fabricate entire fictitious events, they eventually forget that these accounts are fabricated, as evidenced by the fact that robust false memories for these fabricated accounts emerge when these same participants are retested six to eight weeks later. If the foregoing account is correct, then what predicts false memory for event fabrications is not necessarily the retention interval, but whether or not participants retrieve their uncertainty in their fabricated accounts. As we discuss next, the evidence is consistent with this prediction.

Multifaceted questions and limited processing resources

Lawyers will frequently use complex question forms, such as multifaceted questions (single questions that contain both a true and a false proposition) when cross-examining witnesses, and research has shown that the use of such questions reduces testimonial accuracy. We assume that the cognitive load induced by having to concurrently evaluate the validity of multiple propositions impairs people's ability to answer correctly. A recent study by Chrobak et al. (2015) showed that, when testing participants about their memory for the witnessed event, the use of multifaceted questions led to increased false memory for event fabrications, even when tested at short retention intervals of one week. In the same study, they were able to replicate Chrobak and Zaragoza's (2008) finding of no false memory when, at the time of the test, participants were presented with their fabrications in isolation. In sum, the previous findings show that, when cognitive resources were taxed, participants evidenced reliable false memory for entire fictitious events, even at short retention intervals.

The role of confirmatory interviewer feedback

As we have seen, one consequence of confirmatory interviewer feedback is that it leads participants to discount their uncertainty in their fabricated responses, such that it increases false memory for fabricated events and leads participants to endorse witnessing fabricated items with the same speed and confidence that they endorse actually witnessed items. In a recent unpublished study (Rich & Zaragoza, 2016) we assessed whether confirmatory interviewer feedback would also catalyze false memory development in situations where participants are forced to fabricate entire fictitious events. A clear finding was that confirmatory interviewer feedback accelerated the development of false memory for event fabrications, even when participants were warned prior to taking the test. Although prior event fabrication studies have consistently shown that participants are resistant to false memory at short retention intervals, we found that, when participants received confirmatory interviewer feedback following their event fabrications, they evidenced reliable false memory effects at retention intervals of one week, even when participants were warned that they had been misled and even when the analysis was restricted to participants who did not remember the feedback.

The fabricated event's explanatory role

One factor that contributed to the high level of false recall in the experiments involving event fabrications is the explanatory role these fabrications served (see Chrobak & Zaragoza, 2013). In all of the experiments where we have forced participants to fabricate entire fictitious events, participants' fabrications served an explanatory function, in that the fabricated accounts helped to provide a more complete explanation for an outcome they had witnessed. For example, as described earlier, some participants were pressed to fabricate a fictitious prank that caused Delaney to fall to the floor in the dining hall. Relative to the events participants had witnessed (Delaney losing his balance and falling), the events participants were forced to fabricate (a prank that precipitated the fall) provided a richer, more plausible, and more complete explanation of the events that caused the witnessed outcomes. Several pieces of evidence support the hypothesis that a fabrication's explanatory role is one factor that contributes to false memory development. For example, Chrobak and Zaragoza (2013) showed that participants were less likely to develop false memories for their event fabrications when the explanatory strength of the fabricated account had been reduced by the presence of a potential alternative explanation for the same outcome (see Chrobak & Zaragoza, 2013, for additional evidence that supports this explanatory role hypothesis). Given that the purpose of forensic interviews is to seek an explanation for an adverse outcome (e.g., a crime or an accident), much of the information that witnesses are asked to provide serves an explanatory function. To the extent that this testimony is forced, its explanatory role is one factor that contributes to false memory development.

An uncertainty monitoring account of false memories that result from forced fabrication

One potential explanation for the false memories that result from forced fabrication is that people are prone to forgetting the source of their fabrications (for reviews of research and theory on source monitoring see Johnson, Hashtroudi, & Lindsay, 1993; Lindsay, 2008). The evidence suggests, however, that the memory deficit that underlies the forced fabrication effect is much more selective than a general "source amnesia" hypothesis would suggest. In studies where we have directly assessed participants' memory for the source of their fabricated events, we find that an overwhelming majority of participants accurately remember having provided the fabricated information during the postevent interview. For example, Ackil and Zaragoza (2011) gave participants a source recognition test and found that participants tested after a two-week retention interval correctly attributed their fabricated items to the postevent interview 81% of the time. Even more impressive was the finding by Chrobak and Zaragoza (2013) that after a six- to eight-week retention interval, 89% of participants were able to reproduce their fabricated account when asked to recall what answer they had given earlier in response to the false-event question. Also interesting was the finding that confirmatory interviewer feedback (which increases false memory) also has the seemingly paradoxical effect of improving participants' memory for the fact that the fabricated event was from the postevent interview (Zaragoza et al., 2001).

How is it possible that the very same participants who incorrectly claim to remember witnessing their forcibly fabricated events in the video nevertheless also accurately remember providing these items/events as responses during the postevent interview? It is important to remember that the witnessed event and postevent interview are not mutually exclusive sources of information. To the contrary, because the interview is about the witnessed event, most of the information the participant encounters during the postevent interview is an accurate description of the events he or she witnessed. Hence, even if participants know that they were interviewed about things that never happened, the mere knowledge that an item was provided as a response during the interview is not diagnostic with regard to its validity.

What appears to underlie participants' claims that they remember their fabricated event from both the video and the interview is that, although they remember providing the fabricated response, they selectively forget (or fail to retrieve) that the response they provided was fabricated under duress. This failure to remember having fabricated the response renders it susceptible to misattribution for a number of reasons. First, as in all eyewitness suggestibility situations, there is a great deal of overlap between the witnessed event and subsequent interviews about the event, thus rendering the two sources highly confusable. In addition, pressing participants to describe fictitious events forces participants to create concrete, perceptually detailed memory representations that have characteristics typical of witnessed events (e.g., Johnson et al., 1993). Moreover, given the well-documented mnemonic advantage enjoyed by self-generated information (Slamecka & Graf, 1978), the content of participants' self-generated fabrications is likely well remembered and highly familiar at the time of the test, thus rendering it confusable for a real event. Finally, the fabrications that participants generated are likely constrained by their own idiosyncratic knowledge, making them particularly plausible.

In summary, many factors render a self-generated fabrication about the witnessed event confusable with a witnessed memory. The one factor that should prevent false memory is the knowledge that the item/event was fabricated under duress. As we have seen, memory for having fabricated these events is particularly vulnerable to forgetting/retrieval failure. Moreover, our review of the available evidence shows that situations that promote retrieval of participants' uncertainty in their fabricated responses (overt verbal resistance, warnings, short retention intervals, strong memory for the witnessed event) are associated with reduced false memory development, and, conversely, situations that discourage retrieval of this uncertainty (protracted retention intervals, complex question formats, and confirmatory interviewer feedback) all serve to promote false memory development. Unfortunately, however, as we have shown, the factors that promote false memory, such as long retention intervals and confirmatory feedback, can override the protective factors.

Concluding remarks

In forensic interview situations, the stakes associated with solving a crime can be very high. As a consequence, forensic investigators may push witnesses beyond their actual memories, encouraging and even coercing them to provide testimony about events they cannot remember or perhaps never witnessed. The research reviewed here shows that, over time, people are prone to developing false memories for events that were at one time mere speculation or even coerced fabrications, especially when these fabrications have been reinforced by confirmatory interview feedback or serve an explanatory function. We propose that people's vulnerability to these false memory errors is related to the particular difficulty they have monitoring uncertainty. Although people remember many aspects of their experiences extraordinarily well, they are especially prone to forgetting the reasons why they were at one time unsure of the validity of their fabricated responses.

Notes

* This chapter originally appeared in the edited volume, *False and Distorted Memories*.
1 We use the words "coercive," "forced," and "pressure" here, and indeed many of our subjects do strongly resist confabulating information. Nevertheless, as researchers we have an ethical duty to ensure that the kinds of interrogative pressure we aim to emulate do not cause our participants distress. We take considerable measures to avoid any such distress, and all of our study procedures have been approved by the relevant research ethics committees.

References

Ackil, J. K., & Zaragoza, M. S. (1998). Memorial consequences of forced confabulation: Age differences in susceptibility to false memories. *Developmental Psychology, 34*, 1358–1372.

Ackil, J. K., & Zaragoza, M. S. (2011). Forced fabrication versus interviewer suggestions: Differences in false memory depend on how memory is assessed. *Applied Cognitive Psychology, 25*, 933–942.

Chrobak, Q. M., Rindal, E. J., & Zaragoza, M. S. (2015). The impact of multifaceted questions on eyewitness accuracy following forced fabrication interviews. *Journal of General Psychology, 142*, 150–166.

Chrobak, Q. M., & Zaragoza, M. S. (2008). Inventing stories: Forcing witnesses to fabricate entire fictitious events leads to freely reported false memories. *Psychonomic Bulletin and Review, 15*, 1190–1195.

Chrobak, Q. M., & Zaragoza, M. S. (2013). When forced fabrications become truth: Causal explanations and false memory development. *Journal of Experimental Psychology: General, 142*, 827–844.

Fisher, R. P., & Geiselman, R. E. (Eds.) (1992). *Memory enhancing techniques for investigative interviewing: The cognitive interview.* Springfield, IL: Charles C. Thomas.

Frost, P., Lacroix, D., & Sanborn, N. (2003). Increasing false recognition rates with confirmatory feedback: A phenomenological analysis. *American Journal of Psychology, 116*, 515–525.

Gombos, V., Pezdek, K., & Haymond, K. (2011). Forced confabulation affects memory sensitivity as well as response bias. *Memory and Cognition, 40,* 127–134.

Hanba, J. M., & Zaragoza, M. S. (2007). Interviewer feedback in repeated interviews involving forced confabulation. *Applied Cognitive Psychology, 21,* 433–455.

Johnson, M. K., Hashtroudi, S., & Lindsay, D. S. (1993). Source monitoring. *Psychological Bulletin, 114,* 3–28.

Lassiter, G. D., & Meissner, C. A. (Eds.), (2010). *Police interrogations and false confessions: Current research, practice, and policy recommendations.* Washington, DC: American Psychological Association.

Lindsay, D. S. (2008). Source monitoring. In J. Byrne (Series Ed.) & H. L. Roediger III (Volume Ed.), *Learning and memory: A comprehensive reference,* vol. 2. *Cognitive psychology of memory* (pp. 325–348). Oxford: Elsevier.

Loftus, E. F. (2005). Planting misinformation in the human mind: A 30-year investigation of the malleability of memory. *Learning and Memory, 12,* 361–366.

Loftus, E. F., Miller, D. G., & Burns, H. J. (1978). Semantic integration of verbal information into a visual memory. *Journal of Experimental Psychology: Human Learning and Memory, 4,* 19–31.

Memon, A., Zaragoza, M., Clifford, B. R., & Kidd, L. (2010). Inoculation or antidote? The effects of cognitive interview timing on false memories for forcibly fabricated events. *Law and Human Behavior, 34,* 105–117.

Pezdek, K., Lam, S. T., & Sperry, K. (2009). Forced confabulation more strongly influences event memory if suggestions are other-generated than self-generated. *Legal and Criminological Psychology, 14,* 241–252.

Pezdek, K., Sperry, K., & Owens, S. M. (2007). Interviewing witnesses: The effect of forced confabulation on event memory. *Law and Human Behavior, 31,* 463–478.

Rich, P., & Zaragoza, M. S. (2016). Interviewing witnesses: Effects of confirmatory feedback on freely provided reports of event fabrications. Manuscript in preparation.

Slamecka, N. J., & Graf, P. (1978). The generation effect: Delineation of a phenomenon. *Journal of Experimental Psychology: Human Learning and Memory, 4,* 592–604.

Steblay, N. K., Wells, G. L., & Douglass, A. B. (2014). The eyewitness post identification feedback effect 15 years later: Theoretical and policy implications. *Psychology, Public Policy, and Law, 20,* 1–18.

Zaragoza, M. S., Belli, R. F., & Payment, K. E. (2007). Misinformation effects and the suggestibility of eyewitness memory. In M. Garry & H. Hayne (Eds.), *Do justice and let the sky fall: Elizabeth Loftus and her contributions to science, law, and academic freedom* (pp. 35–63). Mahwah, NJ: Erlbaum.

Zaragoza, M. S., Payment, K. E., Ackil, J. K., Drivdahl, S. B., & Beck, M. (2001). Interviewing witnesses: Forced confabulation and confirmatory feedback increase false memories. *Psychological Science, 12,* 473–477.

12

WHEN CHILDREN ARE THE WORST AND BEST EYEWITNESSES

Factors behind the development of false memory[*]

Henry Otgaar, Mark L. Howe, Nathalie Brackmann, and Jianqin Wang

One pertinent question in many legal proceedings concerns whether children's memory is sufficiently reliable to depend on as evidence in legal cases. This is a vital issue because the centrepiece of many criminal trials rests on the reliability of eyewitness statements. When grappling with the reliability of children's accounts, one is confronted with a persistently held undifferentiated assumption among legal professionals. That is, children's memory reports are frequently deemed to be highly vulnerable to errors (i.e., false memory) and should at face value be inferior to adults' memory reports (Brainerd, 2013). In the current synopsis, we discuss recent experimental evidence that challenges this assumption, showing that proneness to false memories is highly malleable and changes in age-dependent predictable ways.

In the first part of this chapter, we discuss several false memory methods and theories that have frequently been employed to study and explain false memories and their development. Then, we direct our attention to relevant precursors of children's false memories. After this, we focus on the developmental aspects of the formation of different types of false memories. Our conclusion will revolve around the legal implications of this new line of investigation into children's proneness to false memory.

Evoking false memories

Several methods have been constructed to elicit false memories in children. One branch of methods has predominantly focused on the production of false memories in children using suggestive pressure (Poole, Dickinson, & Brubacher, 2014). These studies were largely inspired by legal cases in which the authenticity of children's claims of sexual abuse was questioned (Bottoms & Goodman, 1996). One influential example that occurred in 1983 in the Netherlands was the Oude

Pekela case in which many children reported having been abused by satanic clowns (Jonker & Jonker-Bakker, 1991). It became evident that their reports were probably tainted due to suggestive questioning and (partly) based on mere fantasy (see also Kleijwegt, 2011).

Misinformation paradigm

Many studies that use suggestion to instigate false memories follow a procedure called the *misinformation paradigm* (Loftus, 2005; Otgaar, Candel, Smeets, & Merckelbach, 2010) in which participants are exposed to erroneous information (i.e., misinformation). Research that has implemented this paradigm with child participants has tended to focus on children's susceptibility to suggestive questioning when the suggestion is repeated or when a person of authority delivers the suggestion. For example, in one study, 5-year-old children received a vaccination from a paediatrician (Bruck, Ceci, Francoeur, & Barr, 1995). Children were repeatedly interviewed about this visit one year later. One group of children who were interviewed in a nonsuggestive, neutral manner provided accurate reports of the visit. However, the group of children who were interviewed suggestively using misinformation often falsely remembered certain details (e.g., that a female researcher, not the male paediatrician, inoculated them).

The influence of suggestion on children's memory can also be subtler. In a study conducted by Poole and Lindsay (1995), 3 to 4 year olds and 5 to 7 year olds interacted individually with Mr Science, a person who demonstrated certain "science facts" to children. Three months later, parents suggested to some of the children details that did not occur during the Mr Science event. The authors found that many children erroneously remembered details that were not part of the original event.

Implantation paradigm

An extension of the misinformation paradigm is the *false memory implantation paradigm* in which entire fictitious events are injected into memory (Frenda, Nichols, & Loftus, 2011; Otgaar & Candel, 2011). Loftus and Pickrell (1995) were the first to demonstrate the contaminating impact of personalized suggestions on memory. In their study, adult participants were suggestively told that they were lost in a shopping mall when they were 5. Participants were asked about this false event during two suggestive interviews. A quarter of participants ($n = 6$) developed implanted false memories for the suggested event and even provided additional event-related details.

False memory implantation studies have also been undertaken using child participants. For example, Ceci, Huffman, Smith, and Loftus (1994) presented preschool children (3 to 6 year olds) with fictitious events suggesting that their hands got stuck in a mousetrap or that they went on a hot-air balloon ride. Children had to try to recollect the events on numerous occasions. About a third of the children eventually were confident that the fabricated stories truly happened to them. Similar results were obtained when it was suggested that children had fallen off a tricycle and had received stitches in their leg (Ceci, Loftus, Leichtman, & Bruck, 1994). These results show that children are highly vulnerable to the creation of implanted false memories and that they can falsely assent to both negative (e.g., mousetrap) and positive (e.g., hot-air balloon ride) events (Ceci et al., 1994).

Deese-Roediger-McDermott paradigm

The *Deese-Roediger-McDermott (DRM) paradigm* (Deese, 1959; Roediger & McDermott, 1995) has proven to be a robust tool to induce false memories without exposing participants to suggestive pressure. In this method, participants are presented with word lists containing concepts that are semantically related to each other (e.g., *tiger, circus, jungle, cub*). These words are all associatively related to a nonpresented word called the critical lure (i.e., *lion*). People frequently falsely recall and recognize the critical lure with rates comparable to the recall and recognition of presented words (Roediger, Watson, McDermott, & Gallo, 2001). The DRM paradigm has been conducted with both child and adult participants. One of the principal reasons this paradigm has been used with children is that it has been predicted this method should produce developmental increases, not decreases, in false memory rates (e.g., Brainerd, Reyna, & Forrest, 2002; Brainerd, Reyna, & Ceci, 2008; Howe, Wimmer, Gagnon, & Plumpton, 2009). Indeed, many studies have now confirmed that false memories evoked by the DRM paradigm follow an age-related increase; an effect also dubbed a *developmental reversal* (Brainerd, 2013).

False memory theories

Fuzzy trace theory

One influential theory that has explicated the development of false memories is *Fuzzy Trace Theory* (FTT; Brainerd et al., 2008). FTT stipulates that memories are stored in two distinct memory traces called *gist* and *verbatim*. Gist traces are involved in the processing of the underlying meaning (associative and semantic structure) of events, whereas verbatim traces store item-specific, detailed characteristics of an event. FTT assumes that false memories rely on the retrieval of gist traces when verbatim traces are unavailable to be retrieved. For example, an eyewitness to an armed robbery will—according to FTT—store two memory traces. A gist trace could be one of the culprits carrying a certain weapon, whereas the verbatim trace would specify which weapon (e.g., gun). Because verbatim traces fade faster over time, people often rely more on gist traces. As a result, the eyewitness might falsely recollect that the culprit was carrying a knife rather than a gun.

Associative activation theory

Another important false memory theory builds on the concept of spreading activation to explain the formation of false memories. In *Associative Activation Theory* (AAT; Howe et al., 2009; Otgaar, Howe, Peters, Smeets, & Moritz, 2014) it is assumed that false memories are caused by associative activation spreading throughout an individual's knowledge base. As they age, people gain more experience and knowledge and, as a consequence, associative activation through a knowledge base will spread more quickly and automatically. A knowledge base contains nodes representing parts of information and experiences. When these nodes are activated, they will—depending on the strength of the link—activate other nodes as well. According to AAT, false memories are the result of nodes (especially nodes representing themes, that is, general subsets of concepts) being incorrectly activated. In the example of the armed robbery, the memory of the violent event involving weapons could have activated weapon-related theme nodes, whose links to other weapons (e.g., a knife) that were not present could have led the witness to falsely remember that the culprit had been carrying a knife.

Source monitoring

Another influential framework used to explain the formation of false memories is the *source monitoring framework* (SMF; Johnson, Hashtroudi, & Lindsay, 1993). Source monitoring refers to the mechanisms involved in making inferences about the origins of our memories. According to SMF, memories from different origins have different characteristics. For example, memories for experienced events contain more visual, spatial, auditory, temporal, and affective information compared to memories based on imagination. False memories arise when so-called source monitoring errors occur and people attribute incorrect sources to their memories (e.g., somebody reports having been involved in a robbery, when, in fact, she or he had only imagined it; Shaw & Porter, 2015). The ability to monitor the sources of memories improves with age and, hence, the SMF can accurately predict developmental decreases in false memories that are evoked using suggestive pressure (Lindsay, Johnson, & Kwon, 1991). However, the SMF fails to predict developmental increases in false memories, such as the developmental reversal in which adults are more susceptible to false memory formation than children.

Precursors of children's false memory

False memory implantation studies have shown that it is relatively easy to induce implanted false memories in children. However, during the advent of these studies, one lingering unanswered issue concerned the precise precursors that determine the production of implanted false memories. Specifically, one unsolved issue was whether implanted false memories could also take place for *implausible* and *negative* events of which children had *limited knowledge*. Interest in this issue was heightened by well-known legal proceedings, such as the Oude Pekela case in which children reported having experienced bizarre and negative actions—experiences that one might assume children do not have much knowledge about (i.e., satanic abuse by clowns).

False memory models have emphasized that, in order to fuel false memory formation of fictitious events, people should first believe that the event is something plausible that could have happened to them (e.g., Pezdek, Blandon-Gitlin, Lam, Hart, & Schooler, 2006). According to this interpretation, events should first be judged to be true before details related to the event (schema-congruent information) can be retrieved. This view postulates that plausible events are frequently experiences that consist of considerable script knowledge. So when information is retrieved that is highly related to the general knowledge of such an event (i.e., script knowledge), participants are more likely to believe and come to remember that a false event had actually happened to them. Furthermore, how the emotional aspects of experiences might interact with plausibility and script knowledge was not obvious. Clearly, negative events are more likely to be recollected because of their distinctiveness and increased arousal, yet whether such events are also more likely to be distorted was at that time unclear (Porter, ten Brinke, Riley, & Baker, 2014).

Plausibility

One of the first studies that examined the effect of plausibility on the formation of implanted false memories (in adults) was conducted by Pezdek, Finger, and Hodge (1997). In two experiments, they manipulated the degree of plausibility and assessed its influence on whether participants succumbed to suggestive pressure. Specifically, in Experiment 1, Jewish and Catholic students received three true and two false descriptions of (non)experienced events. The false events described religious rituals: one specific for the Jewish community (Shabbot) and one directed at the Catholic community (Communion). The researchers found that both Jewish and Catholic students were most likely to falsely recollect the ritual that was deemed plausible for them (Shabbot or Communion, respectively). In the second experiment, adult participants heard two false stories, with one story depicting a plausible event (i.e., lost in a shopping mall) and the other an implausible occasion (i.e., receiving an enema). Like the first experiment, the plausible event gave rise to significantly more false memories relative to the implausible event. Using a similar procedure as in Experiment 2, Pezdek and Hodge (1999) extended their approach and tested 5- to 7-year-old and 9- to 12-year-old children as well. The pattern of findings was nearly identical. The authors once more showed that plausible events were more easily planted into children's memory than implausible events.

Although these findings concerning plausibility and false memory propensity seemed to provide a coherent picture, Pezdek and colleagues assumed that plausible events are events for which people have considerable script knowledge. That is, they suggested that "in most real cases, [plausibility and schematic knowledge] are highly correlated" (p. 888; Pezdek & Hodge, 1999). Work by Scoboria, Mazzoni,

Kirsch, and Relyea (2004), however, revealed that plausibility and script know-ledge were unrelated to each other. In their study, participants were asked about several events (e.g., losing a toy) and rated the plausibility, belief, and memory of those events. Some of the participants also had to provide schematic knowledge of the events. The main finding was that having a memory of an event implies that one also believes in the occurrence of the event, and this in turn implies that the event is considered to be plausible. More importantly, no relationship was found between plausibility and script knowledge.

Another important consideration is that research has shown that perceived plausibility is not fixed, but highly malleable. For example, Mazzoni, Loftus, and Kirsch (2001) examined in three experiments whether people's judgments of the likelihood that an implausible event (i.e., witnessing demonic possession) occurred could be altered. Specifically, in one of their experiments (Experiment 1), participants were asked to indicate how likely it was that certain events could have occurred to them. Three months later, some of these participants received stories suggesting that witnessing a demonic possession was quite common in the general population, thereby manipulating the base rate information. One week after the second session, these participants were falsely told that they showed signs of having witnessed such a possession before the age of 3. Finally, one week after this meeting, participants were asked to indicate again how likely it was that they had witnessed demonic possession. Strikingly, participants increased their confidence in how likely it was such an event could have occurred to them compared to a control group who was not presented with base rate information. Thus, the experiment revealed that perceived plausibility is not fixed, but can be changed depending on manipulations such as focusing on the base rate of events occurring in the general population.

Following this line of reasoning, we examined whether such base rate manipulations could actually affect the creation of children's false memories for an implausible event. We first conducted a pilot study to examine how certain events (e.g., UFO abduction) were rated on plausibility and valence and what people knew about them (i.e., script knowledge). Based on the results of this pilot study, we selected two events that differed in perceived plausibility but were equal in terms of valence and script knowledge.

In the subsequent implantation experiment, younger (7- to 8-year-old) and older (11- to 12-year-old) children were falsely told that they were abducted by a UFO or almost choked on a candy when they were 4 (Otgaar, Candel, Merckelbach, & Wade, 2009). Importantly, half of the children received false newspaper articles ostensibly suggesting that UFO abduction or almost choking on a candy happened quite frequently where they lived when they were 4. During two interviews, we measured the likelihood that children would form false memories. Interestingly, we found that at the second interview, children were more likely to falsely recollect that they were abducted by a flying saucer when they received the newspaper article relative to children who did not receive this manipulation. We also demonstrated that children were equally likely to produce false memories for the plausible or implausible event. The bottom-line message of these studies is that, although plausible events are extremely likely to be misremembered, even implausible events can be falsely implanted in memory. Furthermore, these experiments reveal that under certain circumstances, plausibility does not catalyze false memory propensity and that both children and adults are equally likely to produce plausible and implausible false memories (see also Strange, Sutherland, & Garry, 2006).

Valence

We also examined children's false memory propensity for a negative (i.e., copying someone's homework) or neutral event (i.e., moving to another classroom) (Otgaar, Candel, & Merckelbach, 2008). Interestingly, based on previous work, two contrasting hypotheses exist. One line of evidence suggested that emotionally negative material was more likely to be contaminated by false memories than neutral or positive material (Porter, Spence, & Birt, 2003). The idea underlying this was that emotionally negative material contained more networks of interrelated nodes and information than other types of material (Talmi & Moscovitch, 2004). The consequence of such dense and well-integrated networks is that information spreads extremely fast. This heightens the probability that related but not-experienced information is activated (Howe et al., 2009; Otgaar, et al., 2014). Such incorrect associations might lead to false memories. Another stream of empirical work indicated, however, that people are less likely to err when it comes to negatively laden information (e.g., Goodman, Quas, & Ogle, 2010). According to these studies, children make fewer errors when being confronted with negative suggestions that might make them feel embarrassed or that revolve around a taboo (e.g., abuse).

In our false memory implantation study, 7-year-old children received false narratives that they copied their neighbour's homework or had to move to another classroom. We made sure that the events were comparable in terms of plausibility and script knowledge. At both interviews, our results showed that children were more likely to falsely recollect the negative than the neutral event. Since then, studies using suggestion-based false memory paradigms or other paradigms have found comparable results in children as well in adults (e.g., Howe, Candel, Otgaar, Malone, & Wimmer, 2010; Porter et al., 2014). When emotionally negative information is presented containing dense networks of nodes, false memories seem more likely to be engendered for negative than neutral material. The legal implications of such findings are serious. Legal cases are typically about negative occasions, and this work shows that, when suggestion is provided about negative experiences, children and adults are more likely to create false memories.

Script knowledge

Because former studies on plausibility were likely confounded by events differing in script knowledge (Pezdek & Hodge, 1999), the question remained about the impact of script knowledge on the formation of children's false memories. Earlier studies have primarily concentrated on the impact of script knowledge on true memory and false beliefs. For example, Ornstein et al. (1998) examined whether script knowledge affected children's memory for a paediatric examination. After an interval of 12 weeks, details of the physical examination were extremely well remembered, implying that knowledge of this event led to coherent and structured memory representations.

Experimentation in adults has found that, although script knowledge affects the formation of false beliefs, it is not a prerequisite for false beliefs to occur (Hart & Schooler, 2006; Scoboria, Mazzoni, Kirsch, & Jimenez, 2006). However, because plausibility and script knowledge might have been confounded in previous false memory implantation studies and because the degree of familiarity of an event limits the effect of script knowledge on false beliefs (Pezdek et al., 2006), we assessed the contribution of script knowledge on children's implanted false memories while holding plausibility constant (Otgaar, Candel, Scoboria, & Merckelbach, 2010).

Based on our pilot study, we selected two events that differed in the amount of script knowledge but were equated on plausibility and valence. Younger (7-year-old) and older (11-year-old) children were presented with false narratives describing either a high-knowledge event (i.e., finger being caught in a mousetrap) or low-knowledge event (i.e., receiving an enema) that supposedly happened when they were 4. During two interviews, they were suggestively questioned about what they could recollect about the events. We demonstrated that, at both interviews, more false memories were observed for the event that contained high rather than low script knowledge. Presumably, both younger and older children's extended knowledge base about the mousetrap event resulted in a higher acceptance rate for the suggestion because of its increased relatedness with their knowledge about the event. Our results also revealed that younger children were more likely to accept the suggestion than older children, a finding that accords well with developmental false memory research (Ceci & Bruck, 1993).

However, although our results indicated that script knowledge might simultaneously facilitate true *and* false memory production, these results merely elucidated the role of *existing* knowledge on false memory formation. In many cases, children receive *extra* knowledge about nonexperienced events apparently because interviewers assume that events were experienced (Garven, Wood, & Malpass, 2000). For example, interviewers might provide suggestive information about details concerning sexual abuse, details that might not be evident for children. To address this issue empirically, we provided 7 to 9 year olds with additional script knowledge about a false event and examined its impact on false memory propensity. Specifically, children were falsely told that they had visited a burns centre when they were 4 (Otgaar, Smeets, & Peters, 2012). Two-thirds of the children received a video that showed what happens during such an event. This manipulation served to stimulate script knowledge about the event. Half of these children had to view this material daily. Interestingly, at the second interview, children who received additional knowledge about the event were more susceptible to incorporating the suggestion that they had visited a burns centre as having occurred to them than the control group.

To conclude, our results imply that one's knowledge base about an event might boost false memories. This line of work comes close to recent research showing that false memory development between children and adults can change depending on one's knowledge base.

Knowledge base and false memory development

Numerous studies reveal that false memories follow a clear developmental pattern. Specifically, these studies showed that children are more likely to produce false memories than adults (e.g., Ceci & Bruck, 1993). Importantly, this pattern is predominantly evident for false memories caused by suggestive pressure. These *suggestion-based false memories* are the result of a mixture of endogenous and exogenous mechanisms (Mazzoni, 2002; Brainerd et al., 2008). Endogenous mechanisms refer to internal mechanisms related to memory such as spreading activation and gist extraction. Exogenous mechanisms are related to external influences on memory such as compliance. The combination of these influences leads to the often-detected pattern in the false memory field that false memory propensity decreases with age.

This false memory view has been the cornerstone of much developmental false memory work. Even more, this view has penetrated practically relevant fields such as the legal arena. Legal professionals have adopted the assumption that false memory decreases with age and that this necessarily implies that children are more vulnerable eyewitnesses than adults (Knutsson & Allwood, 2014). In a sense, memory researchers and legal professionals have embraced this assumption as established science. Recent experimentation has, however, brought a shift in this view by showing that, under certain circumstances, another type of false memories, called *spontaneous false memories*, increases with age (e.g., Brainerd et al., 2008; Howe, 2011; Brackmann, Otgaar, Sauerland, & Merckelbach, 2015).

This effect—also termed *developmental reversal*—was predicted by relying on theoretical principles derived from FTT and AAT. One of the basic factors underlying this developmental reversal is the age-related differences in the knowledge base and the consequence of these differences on false memory generation. Specifically, FTT stipulates that the ability to extract the gist from experienced events serves as the major component of the developmental reversal effect (Brainerd et al., 2008). When children become older, the ability to extract the gist or underlying meaning of events improves. Also, because over time verbatim traces fade faster, people rely more frequently on gist traces. The net effect of this is that, when focusing on the meaning of events, false memory can dramatically increase with age.

The idea of extracting the underlying meaning of an event is closely linked to AAT's claims regarding automatic associative activation in one's knowledge base (Howe et al., 2009; Howe, 2011; Otgaar et al., 2014). According to AAT, children have acquired less experience and knowledge about the world than adults and, hence, are less likely to produce false memories because their knowledge base (i.e., schematic knowledge) is more poorly organized and less well integrated and interconnected than adults'. Furthermore, AAT proposes that associative activation running through a knowledge base becomes more automatic and spreads faster across development in childhood and adolescence. This ultimately means that throughout development, increases in speed and automaticity of spreading activation also enhance the chances that nodes of nonpresented information are incorrectly activated. Such erroneous links can form the basis for constructing false memories.

The notion that developmental differences in gist extraction and associative activation in one's knowledge base might affect false memory rates has resulted in counterintuitive findings in the false memory field. That is, the developmental reversal effect has predominantly appeared when using connected-meaning procedures such as the DRM paradigm (Brainerd et al., 2002; Howe et al., 2010). Since the first studies on this effect, several lines of research have emerged to assess this effect in greater depth.

One line of work has concentrated on whether rates of spontaneous false memories might be affected by the emotionality of stimuli and whether this might interact with development. In one study, Howe et al. (2010) examined children's and adults' false memory development for negative and neutral DRM lists after an immediate or delayed (one-week) test. Although false recall was higher for neutral than negative lists, false recognition was highest for the negatively charged material. More intriguingly, whereas false recognition of neutral lists remained virtually unchanged after a one-week delay, false memories for negative lists increased significantly over time. Another notable result was that developmental reversal effects appeared for both types of lists, thereby showing that valence does not interact with the development of false memories.

Another branch of research has assessed the malleability of developmental reversal effects when taking into account developmental changes in the knowledge base. The lion's share of work on spontaneous false memories has employed connected-meaning procedures such as the DRM paradigm. Recent work has, however, concentrated on implementing other connected-meaning procedures to foster the creation of spontaneous false memories. We, for example, presented younger (6- to 8-year-old) and older (10- to 12-year-old) children and adults with two procedures to stimulate the production of spontaneous false memories (Otgaar, Howe, Peters, Sauerland, & Raymaekers, 2013). That is, we presented them with DRM lists and with several videos in which certain critical elements were not presented. After this, all participants received a recognition task. For example, one video was about a street fight. During the recognition task, an example of a nonpresented but related item was about a policeman on a motorcycle. For the DRM paradigm, the standard developmental reversal emerged, whereas for the video false memory paradigm, spontaneous false memories were more evident in children than in adults.

Although our results concerning the video false memory paradigm seem to contrast with experimentation on the developmental reversal effect, it closely matches work using story contexts to induce spontaneous false memories. For example, in a study by Dewhurst, Pursglove, and Lewis (2007), children aged 5, 8, and 11 years were either presented with standard DRM lists or stories in which DRM stimuli were embedded. The principal reason for using stories was to make the underlying theme linking the stimuli clearer. Like the findings from our video false memory work, Dewhurst and colleagues found that 5 year olds falsely remembered more items than did older children when being presented with the story (see Howe & Wilkinson, 2011, for similar results). The idea behind this effect is that younger children profited more from this contextual embedding in terms of increased associative activation in their knowledge base; this in turn led to increased false recollections. For older children, such theme manipulations were redundant because their knowledge base was already sufficiently integrated in relation to the DRM stimuli.

To examine the effects of theme availability on the production of spontaneous false memory development in more depth, we recently conducted three experiments in which we presented children and adults with stimuli containing obvious themes (Otgaar et al., 2014). We confronted children and adults with visual scenes (e.g., beach, funeral) in which certain critical items were left out (i.e., beach ball, priest). After the presentation of these stimuli, a recognition task was provided. We found in three experiments that when using such related stimuli, the developmental reversal effect in spontaneous false memories itself reversed, demonstrating that children evinced higher false memory levels than adults. In general, such research shows that the development of spontaneous false memories is highly flexible and that in many circumstances, developmental reversal effects are revealed, whereas in situations that focus on principles such as theme extraction, developmental reversal effects can even entirely flip (see also Holliday, Brainerd, & Reyna, 2011).

The issue of the malleability of developmental reversal effects brings us back to the starting point of research in the area of false memory. That is, interest in the development of false memories arose out of forensic questions concerning the reliability of eyewitnesses' statements (Ceci & Friedman, 2000; Goodman, 2006). In these cases, the question emerged as to whether suggestive tactics might taint the memory performance of witnesses. As has been said before, research in this domain painted a consistent picture—children were more likely to succumb to suggestive pressure than were adults.

The research into developmental reversal effects begs the question as to whether the development of suggestion-induced false memories is just as malleable as that of spontaneous false memories. Interestingly, one of the main forensically relevant methods to elicit suggestion-induced false memories is the aforementioned misinformation paradigm (Loftus, 2005). This paradigm can be easily adjusted to resemble conditions in which a developmental reversal is likely to be found. Specifically, during the encoding phase, children and adults should be presented with connected-meaning stimuli. Following this, misinformation should be provided about related but not-presented items. The prediction is that adults are more likely to incorrectly link misinformation with encoded stimuli relative to children leading to a developmental reversal effect in suggestion-induced false memories.

We have recently investigated whether using such an approach would indeed lead to adults being the most vulnerable to suggestion (Otgaar, Howe, Smeets, & Garner, 2013; Otgaar, Howe, Brackmann, & Smeets, 2016). In these adapted misinformation experiments, participants saw videos (e.g., of a robbery) containing associatively related details (e.g., bullets), but several critical related details were removed (e.g., gun). In the second stage, participants received misinformation in which the critical (but not presented) related details were presented. Following this, participants were given a recognition task. Intriguingly, in all experiments, our expectations were supported. When participants were involved in this adapted misinformation experiment, susceptibility to suggestion-induced false memories increased, not decreased, with age. Overall, like spontaneous false memories, developmental trends in suggestion-induced false memories are not fixed, but rather are highly flexible depending on the development of associative activation in one's knowledge base.

Concluding remarks

In the current synopsis, we have outlined evidence that several precursors underlie the formation of suggestion-induced or implanted false memories. We have shown that implanted false memories can occur for a variety of plausible and implausible events. We have also demonstrated that negative events are more readily implanted in memory than positive or neutral events. Furthermore, one of these precursors—knowledge base (e.g., script knowledge)—has also played a vital role in new developmental work in the field of spontaneous false memories.

More precisely, the default assumption among many memory scholars and legal professionals is that false memories are more likely to develop in children and become less pronounced when getting older. This assumption has been partially based on developmental false memory work showing that resistance to suggestion-induced false memories increases with age (e.g., Ackil & Zaragoza, 1998; Sutherland & Hayne, 2001). This assumption has driven some legal professionals to argue that expert evidence about the memory functioning of younger witnesses is not necessary in the courtroom (Brainerd, 2013; Howe & Knott, 2015).

New investigations into the field of spontaneous false memories have turned this traditional view on false memory development on its head. Deriving theoretical principles from FTT and AAT that emphasize the role of gist extraction and knowledge base on false memory development, empirical demonstrations have revealed that under certain conditions, both spontaneous and suggestion-induced false memories do increase with age. The ultimate consequence of this novel work is that our view concerning false memory development should be revisited, and that memory experts who are conversant with current findings should testify in the courtroom when decisions solely rely on eyewitness reports (Brackmann, Otgaar, Sauerland, & Jelicic, 2016).

A logical next step is to delineate the precise factors that lead to increases and decreases in false memory development. Although factors such as gist extraction and associative activation have played an especially important role in predicting and understanding false memory development, other related factors might be vital as well. One promising factor that potentially influences false memory development is metacognition. Research shows that young children lack the ability to provide accurate judgments about their own memory functioning. Such lack of metacognition makes children especially vulnerable to the acceptance of false autobiographical events, but perhaps less vulnerable to the creation of spontaneous false memories (Ghetti & Alexander, 2004). One interesting research avenue is to examine whether training in metacognition might make children less prone to suggestion, yet more prone to spontaneous false memory production.

To conclude, recent empirical investigations have revealed that much of the work on false memory development needs rethinking, as the development of false memories is not as fixed as was previously assumed. Such new directions might ultimately lead to a reconsideration of how children's and adults' accounts in court are weighted. The relevance of these directions becomes obvious when considering that the majority of legal decisions are based on the weight of eyewitness statements.

Note

* This chapter originally appeared in the edited volume, *False and Distorted Memories*. The writing of this chapter was supported by a grant from the Netherlands Organization for Scientific Research (NWO 415–12–003) to H.O.

References

Ackil, J. K., & Zaragoza, M. S. (1998). Memorial consequences of forced confabulation: Age differences in susceptibility to false memories. *Developmental Psychology, 34*, 1358–1372.

Bottoms, B. L., & Goodman, G. S. (1996). *International perspectives on child abuse and children's testimony: Psychological research and law.* Thousand Oaks, CA: Sage.

Brackmann, N., Otgaar, H., Sauerland, M., & Jelicic, M. (2016). When children are the least vulnerable to false memories: A true case or a case of autosuggestion? *Journal of Forensic Sciences, 61*, S271–S275.

Brackmann, N., Otgaar, H., Sauerland, M., & Merckelbach, H. (2015). Children are poor witnesses: Or are they? *In Mind, 24*, 1–6.

Brainerd, C. J. (2013). Developmental reversals in false memory: A new look at the reliability of children's evidence. *Current Directions in Psychological Science, 22*, 335–341.

Brainerd, C. J., Reyna, V. F., & Ceci, S. J. (2008). Developmental reversals in false memory: A review of data and theory. *Psychological Bulletin, 134*, 343–382.

Brainerd, C. J., Reyna, V. F., & Forrest, T. J. (2002). Are young children susceptible to the false-memory illusion? *Child Development, 73*, 1363–1377.

Bruck, M., Ceci, S. J., Francoeur, E., & Barr, R. (1995). "I hardly cried when I got my shot!" Influencing children's reports about a visit to their pediatrician. *Child Development, 66*, 193–208.

Ceci, S. J., & Bruck, M. (1993). Suggestibility of the child witness: A historical review and synthesis. *Psychological Bulletin, 113*, 403–439.

Ceci, S. J., & Friedman, R. D. (2000). Suggestibility of children: Scientific research and legal implications. *Cornell Law Review, 86*, 33–108.

Ceci, S. J., Huffman, M. L. C., Smith, E., & Loftus, E. F. (1994). Repeatedly thinking about a non-event: Source misattributions among preschoolers. *Consciousness and Cognition, 3,* 388–407.

Ceci, S. J., Loftus, E. F., Leichtman, M. D., & Bruck, M. (1994). The possible role of source misattributions in the creation of false beliefs among preschoolers. *International Journal of Clinical and Experimental Hypnosis, 42,* 304–320.

Deese, J. (1959). On the prediction of occurrence of particular verbal intrusions in immediate recall. *Journal of Experimental Psychology, 58,* 17–22.

Dewhurst, S. A., Pursglove, R. C., & Lewis, C. (2007). Story contexts increase susceptibility to the DRM illusion in 5-year-olds. *Developmental Science, 10,* 374–378.

Frenda, S. J., Nichols, R. M., & Loftus, E. F. (2011). Current issues and advances in misinformation research. *Current Directions in Psychological Science, 20,* 20–23.

Garven, S., Wood, J. M., & Malpass, R. S. (2000). Allegations of wrongdoing: The effects of reinforcement on children's mundane and fantastic claims. *Journal of Applied Psychology, 85,* 38–49.

Ghetti, S., & Alexander, K. W. (2004). "If it happened, I would remember it": Strategic use of event memorability in the rejection of false autobiographical events. *Child Development, 75,* 542–561.

Goodman, G. S. (2006). Children's eyewitness memory: A modern history and contemporary commentary. *Journal of Social Issues, 62,* 811–832.

Goodman, G. S., Quas, J. A., & Ogle, C. M. (2010). Child maltreatment and memory. *Annual Review of Psychology, 61,* 325–351.

Hart, R. E., & Schooler, J. W. (2006). Increasing belief in the experience of an invasive procedure that never happened: The role of plausibility and schematicity. *Applied Cognitive Psychology, 20,* 661–669.

Holliday, R. E., Brainerd, C. J., & Reyna, V. F. (2011). Developmental reversals in false memory: Now you see them, now you don't! *Developmental Psychology, 47,* 442–449.

Howe, M. L. (2011). *The nature of early memory: An adaptive theory of the genesis and development of memory.* New York: Oxford University Press.

Howe, M. L., Candel, I., Otgaar, H., Malone, C., & Wimmer, M. C. (2010). Valence and the development of immediate and long-term false memory illusions. *Memory, 18,* 58–75.

Howe, M. L., & Knott, L. M. (2015). The fallibility of memory in judicial processes: Lessons from the past and their modern consequences. *Memory, 23,* 633–656.

Howe, M. L., & Wilkinson, S. (2011). Using story contexts to bias children's true and false memories. *Journal of Experimental Child Psychology, 108,* 77–95.

Howe, M. L., Wimmer, M. C., Gagnon, N., & Plumpton, S. (2009). An associative-activation theory of children's and adults' memory illusions. *Journal of Memory and Language, 60,* 229–251.

Johnson, M. K., Hashtroudi, S., & Lindsay, D. S. (1993). Source monitoring. *Psychological Bulletin, 114,* 3–28.

Jonker, F., & Jonker-Bakker, P. (1991). Experiences with ritualist child sexual abuse: A case study from the Netherlands. *Child Abuse and Neglect, 15,* 191–196.

Kleijwegt, M. (2011). *Terug naar Oude Pekela [Back to Oude Pekela].* Amsterdam: Balans.

Knutsson, J., & Allwood, C. M. (2014). Opinions of legal professionals: Comparing child and adult witnesses' memory report capabilities. *European Journal of Psychology Applied to Legal Context, 6,* 79–89.

Lindsay, D. S., Johnson, M. K., & Kwon, P. (1991). Developmental changes in memory source monitoring. *Journal of Experimental Child Psychology, 52,* 297–318.

Loftus, E. F. (2005). Planting misinformation in the human mind: A 30-year investigation of the malleability of memory. *Learning and Memory, 12*, 361–366.

Loftus, E. F., & Pickrell, J. E. (1995). The formation of false memories. *Psychiatric Annals, 25*, 720–725.

Mazzoni, G. (2002). Naturally occurring and suggestion-dependent memory distortions: The convergence of disparate research traditions. *European Psychologist, 7*, 17–30.

Mazzoni, G. A. L., Loftus, E. F., & Kirsch, I. (2001). Changing beliefs about implausible autobiographical events: A little plausibility goes a long way. *Journal of Experimental Psychology: Applied, 7*, 51–59.

Ornstein, P. A., Merritt, K. A., Baker-Ward, L., Furtado, E., Gordon, B. N., & Principe, G. (1998). Children's knowledge, expectation, and long-term retention. *Applied Cognitive Psychology, 12*, 387–405.

Otgaar, H., & Candel, I. (2011). Children's false memories: Different false memory paradigms reveal different results. *Psychology, Crime and Law, 17*, 513–528.

Otgaar, H., Candel, I., & Merckelbach, H. (2008). Children's false memories: Easier to elicit for a negative than for a neutral event. *Acta Psychologica, 128*, 350–354.

Otgaar, H., Candel, I., Merckelbach, H., & Wade, K. A. (2009). Abducted by a UFO: Prevalence information affects young children's false memories for an implausible event. *Applied Cognitive Psychology, 23*, 115–125.

Otgaar, H., Candel, I., Scoboria, A., & Merckelbach, H. (2010). Script knowledge enhances the development of children's false memories. *Acta Psychologica, 133*, 57–63.

Otgaar, H., Candel, I., Smeets, T., & Merckelbach, H. (2010). "You didn't take Lucy's skirt off": The effect of misleading information on omissions and commissions in children's memory reports. *Legal and Criminological Psychology, 15*, 229–241.

Otgaar, H., Howe, M. L., Brackmann, N., & Smeets, T. (2016). The malleability of developmental trends in neutral and negative memory illusions. *Journal of Experimental Psychology: General, 145*, 31–55.

Otgaar, H., Howe, M. L., Peters, M., Sauerland, M., & Raymaekers, L. (2013). Developmental trends in different types of spontaneous false memories: Implications for the legal field. *Behavioral Sciences and the Law, 31*, 666–682.

Otgaar, H., Howe, M. L., Peters, M., Smeets, T., & Moritz, S. (2014). The production of spontaneous false memories across childhood. *Journal of Experimental Child Psychology, 121*, 28–41.

Otgaar, H., Howe, M. L., Smeets, T., & Garner, S. R. (2013). Developmental trends in adaptive memory. *Memory, 22*, 103–117.

Otgaar, H., Smeets, T., & Peters, M. (2012). Children's implanted false memories and additional script knowledge. *Applied Cognitive Psychology, 26*, 709–715.

Pezdek, K., Blandon-Gitlin, I., Lam, S., Hart, R. E., & Schooler, J. W. (2006). Is knowing believing? The role of event plausibility and background knowledge in planting false beliefs about the personal past. *Memory and Cognition, 34*, 1628–1635.

Pezdek, K., Finger, K., & Hodge, D. (1997). Planting false childhood memories: The role of event plausibility. *Psychological Science, 8*, 437–441.

Pezdek, K., & Hodge, D. (1999). Planting false childhood memories in children: The role of event plausibility. *Child Development, 70*, 887–895.

Poole, D. A., Dickinson, J. J., & Brubacher, S. P. (2014). Sources of unreliable testimony from children. *Roger Williams University Law Review, 19*, 382–1006.

Poole, D. A., & Lindsay, D. S. (1995). Interviewing preschoolers: Effects of nonsuggestive techniques, parental coaching, and leading questions on reports of nonexperienced events. *Journal of Experimental Child Psychology, 60*, 129–154.

Porter, S., Spencer, L., & Birt, A. R. (2003). Blinded by emotion? Effect of the emotionality of a scene on susceptibility to false memories. *Canadian Journal of Behavioural Science / Revue Canadienne des Sciences du Comportement, 35*, 165–175.

Porter, S., ten Brinke, L., Riley, S. N., & Baker, A. (2014). Prime time news: The influence of primed positive and negative emotion on susceptibility to false memories. *Cognition and Emotion, 28*, 1422–1434.

Roediger, H. L., & McDermott, K. B. (1995). Creating false memories: Remembering words not presented in lists. *Journal of Experimental Psychology: Learning, Memory, and Cognition, 21*, 803–814.

Roediger, H. L., Watson, J. M., McDermott, K. B., & Gallo, D. A. (2001). Factors that determine false recall: A multiple regression analysis. *Psychonomic Bulletin and Review, 8*, 385–407.

Scoboria, A., Mazzoni, G., Kirsch, I., & Jimenez, S. (2006). The effects of prevalence and script information on plausibility, belief, and memory of autobiographical events. *Applied Cognitive Psychology, 20*, 1049–1064.

Scoboria, A., Mazzoni, G., Kirsch, I., & Relyea, M. (2004). Plausibility and belief in autobiographical memory. *Applied Cognitive Psychology, 18*, 791–807.

Shaw, J., & Porter, S. (2015). Constructing rich false memories of committing crime. *Psychological Science, 26*, 291–301.

Strange, D., Sutherland, R., & Garry, M. (2006). Event plausibility does not determine children's false memories. *Memory, 14*, 937–951.

Sutherland, R., & Hayne, H. (2001). Age-related changes in the misinformation effect. *Journal of Experimental Child Psychology, 79*, 388–404.

Talmi, D., & Moscovitch, M. (2004). Can semantic relatedness explain the enhancement of memory for emotional words? *Memory and Cognition, 32*, 742–751.

13

FACTORS AFFECTING THE RELIABILITY OF CHILDREN'S FORENSIC REPORTS

An updated review*

Kamala London, Sarah Kulkofsky, and Christina O. Perez

Child maltreatment is a major societal problem. In the United States, over four million cases of child maltreatment are investigated each year (Pipe, Lamb, Orbach, & Cederborg, 2007a). Propelled by a rash of high-profile infamous childcare and satanic ritualistic abuse cases from the 1980s and 1990s, a corpus of research has emerged to outline the interview contexts that help and hinder children's reports of past events. In this chapter, we update our review of the contemporary research findings on factors affecting the reliability of children's forensic reports with relevant research released in the decade since the publication of our original chapter. In the first half of the chapter, we review the literature on autobiographical memory and suggestibility. In the second half of the chapter, we review contemporary research findings regarding whether and how sexually abused children tend to tell others about the abuse.

Autobiographical memory

Understanding children's ability to provide complete and accurate reports of past events in forensic contexts requires an understanding of children's developing memory systems. Crucially important in this regard is research on the development of *autobiographical memory*. Autobiographical memory refers to memory about personally experienced events. Some authors specify that autobiographical memories are only those memories that are long-lasting and centrally involve the self (e.g., Nelson, 1993b; Nelson & Fivush, 2004). Memories of personally experienced events that may be more likely to be forgotten or do not centrally involve the self are sometimes referred to as *event memories* or *episodic memories*. Autobiographical memories and more general event memories appear to rely on the same underlying neurological systems (Nelson & Fivush, 2004) and thus appear only to differ in the meaning or significance of the event. Thus, research on both autobiographical memory and event memory is relevant here.

The research on the development of autobiographical memory has shown that, by around 2 years of age, as children begin to develop stable self-concepts and the language of narrative, they begin to show the ability to talk about past events (Nelson & Fivush, 2004). At this young age, however, children's reports often require a great deal of adult prompting. Children's responses to open-ended prompts such as "Tell me what happened" tend to include very little detail (Fivush, 1993). Throughout early childhood children's ability to provide detailed and elaborate accounts of past events continues to improve so that, by about age 6, children are able to provide more complete and elaborate accounts of past events (Fivush, Haden, & Adam, 1995; Hamond & Fivush, 1991).

Many studies of children's autobiographical memory focus on naturally occurring events, and thus memory accuracy cannot be assessed since the researchers themselves do not know what happened. However, maternal reports tend to confirm the accuracy of children's statements (e.g., Fivush, Gray, & Fromhoff, 1987). Other work using staged events for which statements can be verified has also shown high rates of accuracy (e.g., Leichtman, Pillemer, Wang, Koreishi, & Han, 2000). As such, young children's spontaneous recall of personally experienced past events is often characterized as accurate albeit incomplete.

However, the enthusiasm for the accuracy of children's spontaneous statements should be tempered to some degree. It is certainly not the case that all spontaneous statements made by young children are accurate. In particular, if the child is interviewed about confusing events or events that run counter to their knowledge, then the accuracy of the child's report may be compromised. For example, Ornstein and colleagues (Ornstein, Merrit, Baker-Ward, Furtado, Gordon, & Principe, 1998) had children experience a mock medical examination in which some common features (such as listening to the child's heart) were omitted and atypical features (such as wiping the child's belly button with alcohol) were added. When children were interviewed about the event after a 12-week delay, 42% of 4 year olds and 74% of 6 year olds spontaneously reported that at least one of the common features was part of the examination although it was not. Similarly, Goodman and colleagues (Goodman, Quas, Batterman-Faunce, Riddelsburger, & Kuhn 1994) interviewed children about a painful genital catheterization procedure. Among the children who were 3 to 4 years old, 23% of free recall statements were incorrect. Finally, Kulkofsky, Wang, and Ceci (2008) had preschool-aged children engage in a pizza-baking activity that included a number of unusual, non-schematic elements (e.g., the pizza was baked in a refrigerator). At one week 24% of children's free recall statements were classified as incorrect. Thus, although children in the above studies were largely accurate, children's spontaneous statements are not completely error-free. Given that in forensic settings young children are often interviewed about events that may be ambiguous and may not fit their current knowledge base, these findings may be particularly concerning.

In addition to often being incomplete, young children's recall of personal memories are also dominated by scripts. Scripts are generalized accounts of what usually happens in a given situation (Nelson, 1993a). For example, an adult's script for going to a restaurant may include waiting to be seated, reviewing the menu, ordering the meal, eating, and paying the bill. Very young children show better performance in reporting scripted information compared to information about specific events (Hudson & Nelson, 1986). Further, young children have more difficulty distinguishing between specific episodes of repeated events (Farrar & Goodman, 1992). When forensic interviewers are interested in a single novel event, children's reliance on scripts may not prove problematic; however, in the context of child maltreatment cases, children often are interviewed about repeated events. Thus, children's reliance on scripts in these contexts may create difficulties in obtaining complete and accurate accounts of specific episodes.

Finally, although children are able to report memories of childhood experiences, and may report memories of younger ages than adults are able to recall (Fivush & Schwarzmueller, 1999), there does appear to be a limit to how early in childhood children can remember. Specifically, children show difficulty with remembering events that occurred prior to the onset of language. For example, Peterson and Rideout (1998) interviewed young children about a visit to an emergency room that occurred when children were between 13 and 34 months old. Eighteen months later, only children who were 25 months and older at the time of the injury were able to verbally recall any details of the event, even though at the time of the interview these children had the requisite verbal ability to do so. Similarly, Bauer, Wenner, and Kroupina (2002) interviewed 3 year olds about a previous experience in the lab when they were between 13 and 20 months of age. Only children who had been 20 months of age spontaneously provided verbalizations that indicated memory for the event, although children at all age groups showed non-verbal evidence of memory. In a related study, Simcock and Hayne (2002) exposed children who were 27, 33, and 39 months old to a novel event and then tested their memories six months and one year later. At both the initial exposure and at the memory interviews parents reported children's vocabulary, including their vocabulary that was pertinent to the novel event. At both the six-month and one-year tests, no child used words to describe the event that had not been part of the child's vocabulary at the time of the original event. Taken together, these results suggest that later verbal recall of an event is, in part, dependent on children's language ability at the time of encoding.

Children's language abilities also play a significant role in the accurate recall of autobiographical memories. In the decade since the publication of our chapter, language abilities have emerged as an important cognitive factor in the accurate retrieval of autobiographical memories. Klemfuss (2015) argued task demands differ between various methods of questioning children (e.g., open-ended prompts vs. direct/misleading questions) and thus draw upon separate domains of language abilities. In theory, spontaneously recalling memories calls on children's *expressive* language abilities, while understanding and responding appropriately to direct questions targets children's *receptive* language abilities. Among a sample of 64 preschoolers, Klemfuss (2015) found increases in children's expressive language skills predicted more correct responses during free recall, whereas increases in their receptive language skills predicted more correct responses to misleading questions. In a review of the eyewitness literature spanning approximately 30 years, Perez, London, and Otgaar (under review) found support for Klemfuss's (2015) theory regarding the differential contributions of language abilities to children's eyewitness memory. Across 35 studies, children's accurate free recall was most consistently related to measures of expressive language, while accurate responses to direct (non-leading) questions were most associated with measures of receptive language. These findings are important given research indicates that maltreatment hinders children's language development and thereby limits their ability to recount their experiences (Beers & De Bellis, 2002; Benedan, Powell, Zajac, Lum, & Snow, 2018; Cicchetti, Rogosch, Howe, & Toth, 2010; Howe, Cicchetti, & Toth, 2006; Otgaar, Howe, Merckelbach, & Muris, 2018; Porter, Lawson, & Bigler, 2005).

When children participate in the forensic arena, they frequently are asked to provide details about events that occurred months or even years ago. This raises concerns about how well children can remember events after a significant delay. The results of a number of studies of children's memories of unique naturalistic events (e.g., hurricanes, medical procedures, trips to Disneyland) indicate that, although there is forgetting, preschool and school-aged children do accurately recall details about personally experienced events with delays of months and even years (e.g., Bahrick, Parker, Fivush, & Levitt, 1998; Hammond & Fivush, 1991). For example, Peterson and colleagues (e.g., Peterson, 1996; Peterson & Bell, 1996; Peterson & Whalen, 2001) examined children's long-term memory for emergency room visits. Children (ages 2 to 13 years) were interviewed as soon after the visit as possible and then, depending on the study, they were interviewed six months to five years later. Preschoolers reported fewer details than older children did, but even 3 year olds (but not 2 year olds) recalled some central information about highly salient events.

The research on autobiographical memory development suggests that in general young children's spontaneous reports of personally experienced past events are largely accurate although they can be quite sparse. However, accuracy is impaired when children are asked to recall confusing or ambiguous events and children's reliance on scripts may lead to further memory errors. Furthermore, recent research suggests children's language abilities are important predictors for retrieval of autobiographical memories. Findings regarding the differential contributions of language in children's accurate recall highlight the importance of keeping children's language abilities in mind during interviews as well as in competency assessments (Klemfuss & Ceci, 2012). Finally, there is a limit to how far back children can remember, and thus, the veracity of memories recalled before the onset of language should be considered suspect.

Suggestibility

Since the 1980s a great deal of developmental research has focused on the issue of suggestibility. Ceci and Bruck (1993) defined suggestibility as "the degree to which children's encoding, storage, retrieval, and reporting of events can be influenced by a range of social and psychological factors" (p. 404). This broad definition of suggestibility allows for information that is presented both before and after an event to taint children's recall, and further allows for the possibility that children's reports may be inaccurate even without any underlying memory impairment. That is, children may accept an interviewer's suggestion while knowing that the suggestion is not correct.

While the literature implies that children's spontaneous reports are largely accurate, reports that emerge as a result of suggestive interviewing techniques tend to be error-prone. In the classic sense, suggestive techniques involve asking leading questions. Studies of actual investigative interviews indicate that forensic interviewers frequently ask children leading questions (Ceci, Kulkofsky, Klemfuss, Sweeney, & Bruck, 2007a). Moreover, extensive training programs designed to teach best practices for interviewing young witnesses do not appear to be effective in reducing the number of leading questions interviewers ask (Sternberg, Lamb, Davies, & Westcott, 2001a). Leading questions are even used when interviewers are using a scripted interview protocol, although using an interview protocol does appear to reduce the number of suggestive utterances and increase the amount of information that is obtained from non-suggestive means (e.g., Orbach, Hershkowitz, Lamb, Sternberg, Esplin, & Horowitz, 2000; for a recent review, see Berg, Munthe-Kaas, Baiju, Muller, & Brurberg, 2019). Leading questions are likely used, particularly with young children, because, as noted above, their spontaneous reports are often skeletal in nature and provide very little detail about the specific event. However, in general children are less accurate when answering direct questions compared to open-ended questions (Ornstein et al., 1998; Peterson, Dowden, & Tobin, 1999). Further, young children are less likely to respond to leading questions with "I don't know" compared with simply picking an answer choice, even to nonsensical questions (Hughes & Grieve, 1980). Leading questions are particularly problematic because the interviewer presupposes certain events occurred (e.g., "He took your clothes off, didn't he?"). However, without knowing exactly what happened, which is almost always the case in forensic interviews, an interviewer's leading question may actually be misleading.

The suggestiveness of an interview goes beyond simply indexing the number of leading questions. Rather, one must consider how the concept of interviewer bias plays out in the interview. Interviewer bias characterizes those interviewers who hold a priori beliefs about what has occurred and mold the interview to maximize disclosures that are consistent with those beliefs. Interviewer bias may be communicated through other suggestive techniques including providing positive and negative reinforcement (e.g., praising the child for providing disclosures or withholding benefits such as trips to the restroom for not disclosing), using peer or parental pressure (e.g., telling the child that his or her classmates or parents have already disclosed), creating a negative or accusatory emotional tone (e.g., urging the child to help keep the defendant in jail), inducing stereotypes about the accused (e.g., referring to the accused as a "bad person"), and repeating questions or interviews until the child provides the desired answer.

Research indicates that combining suggestive techniques tends to result in heightened levels of suggestibility. For example, Leichtman and Ceci (1995) showed that when children had been exposed to stereotypes about a classroom visitor they were more likely to incorporate an interviewer's misleading suggestion than children who were not exposed to stereotypes. In another set of studies, Garven and colleagues (Garven, Wood, Malpass, & Shaw, 1998; Garven, Wood, & Malpass, 2000) examined how the techniques that were used by investigators in the now infamous McMartin Preschool Case (*State of Calif. v. Buckey*, 1990) can taint children's testimony beyond that of misleading questions alone. In one study (Garven et al., 2000), the researchers asked kindergarten children to recall details from when a visitor named Paco came to their classroom and read a story, gave out treats, and wore a funny hat. Half of the children were given interviews that included misleading questions about plausible events (e.g., "Did Paco break a toy?") and bizarre events (e.g., "Did Paco take you to a farm in a helicopter?"). In this group children assented to 13% of the plausible questions and 5% of the fantastic questions. A second group of children were also questioned but these children were given negative feedback to their "no" responses and positive feedback to their "yes" responses. This latter group of children falsely assented to the plausible items 35% of the time and the bizarre items 52% of the time. Furthermore, these group differences remained when children were interviewed neutrally two weeks later. London, Bruck, and Melnyk (2009) found suggestive questions negatively affected children's recognition reports during an unbiased interviewing following a delay of 15 months. Thus, it appears that interviewer bias in earlier interviews can taint later interviews even if these later interviews are conducted in an unbiased manner.

However, we would be remiss if we implied that a combination of highly suggestive techniques is necessary in order to taint children's reports. Children can incorporate misleading information into their accounts even after a single suggestive interview (Ceci et al., 2007a; London et al., 2009). Further, other milder forms of suggestions have been shown to influence the accuracy of children's reports. In a set of studies, Principe and colleagues have shown how rumors spread among peers may produce false reports (Principe & Ceci, 2002; Principe, Guiliano, & Root, 2008; Principe, Haines, Adkins, & Guiliano, 2010; Principe, Kanaya, Ceci, & Singh, 2006; Principe & Schindewolf, 2012). In one study (Principe et al., 2008), 3- to 6-year-old children watched a magic show that included two failed tricks. Some of the children saw clues to provide them with hints about why these two tricks failed. When interviewed later about the events, both the children who were exposed to the clues and their classmates reported inaccurate details consistent with the clues, whereas control children who were not exposed to clues, either directly or through their classmates, rarely reported such details. Not only did children report false details, but many maintained they had seen the false events themselves. These results suggest that children need only to be exposed to conversations with peers with false beliefs developed through the children's own causal inferences in order to distort the accuracy of their reports.

Another interesting aspect of Principe et al.'s (2008) study was that older children were more likely to report false details as a result of their own inferences than were younger children. In most typical suggestibility studies there are reliable age differences, with younger children being more suggestible than older children and adults (Ceci & Bruck, 1993). In fact, age appears to be the single best predictor of suggestibility (Geddie, Fradin, & Beer, 2000; Poole, Dickinson, Brubacher, Liberty, & Kaake, 2014). However, this is not to say that only young children are suggestible. There is a great deal of evidence that older children and adults can fall prey to suggestive techniques (Ceci et al., 2007a; Finnillä, Mahlberga, Santtilaa, & Niemi, 2003; London et al., 2009). Further, as the Principe et al. (2008) study shows, there are situations when older children may actually be more suggestible than younger children. In particular, in some cases older children's more advanced cognitive capabilities actually lead to increased incorporation of false information.

In the case of the Principe et al. (2008) study, older children were likely providing more false details as a result of their own inferences because older children are more capable of developing causal inferences compared to younger children. Children's underlying knowledge representations (e.g., schemas, associative structures) may also play a role in influencing reverse age trends in suggestibility (Ceci, Bookbinder, Bruck, Perez, & London, in preparation). For example, in one study by Ceci and colleagues (Ceci, Papierno, & Kulkofsky, 2007b), 4 year olds and 9 year olds were read a story that included a series of objects. Later children were given misinformation about the objects in the story. They were subsequently asked to recall the objects that were part of the original story. The direction of the age differences in suggestibility was predicted by children's semantic representations of the similarity between the actual and suggested objects. For example, compared with younger children, older children were more likely to erroneously report that there had been an orange tree in the story when there had actually been a lemon tree. This is because older children found oranges and lemons to be more similar than younger children did. Similarly, in DRM studies, where lists of semantically related words are presented, false reports of target semantically related but non-presented words rise with age (e.g., Brainerd, Holliday, & Reyna, 2004). London et al. (2009) found similar levels of suggestibility among 4 to 9 year olds. They suggest the mode delivering suggestions may also affect age findings in suggestibility studies. In their study, they used a forced confabulation paradigm where children were given false information rather than simply being asked whether the false details occurred (also see Zaragoza, Payment, Kichler, Stines, & Drivdahl, 2001).

One argument that is often made against much of the research on suggestibility is that children are only suggestible about inconsequential, peripheral details of events. However, the effects of suggestive questioning are not limited to irrelevant and peripheral details of unemotional events. Children's erroneous reports as a result of suggestive techniques include central details of negative and painful events, such as doctor's office and emergency room visits (Bruck, Ceci, Francoeur, & Barr, 1995; Bruck, Ceci, & Francoeur, 2000; Burgwyn-Bales, Baker-Ward, Gordon, & Ornstein, 2001) and other forms of bodily touching (Poole & Lindsay, 1995; White, Leichtman, & Ceci, 1997).

Finally, it is important to note that children's false reports that emerge through suggestive techniques may be indistinguishable from true statements. Both Ceci, Loftus, Leichtman, and Bruck (1994) and Leichtman and Ceci (1995) had legal and psychological experts watch videos of children's true and false reports that emerged as a result of suggestive questioning techniques. Experts were asked to attempt to classify the true and false events. In both cases, the professionals were no better than chance at distinguishing true from false memories. Furthermore, Bruck and colleagues (Bruck, Ceci, & Hembrooke, 2002) systematically compared children's true and false narratives. In this study, children were repeatedly and suggestively interviewed about two true and two false events. Children's subsequent narratives were then coded for a number of characteristics including number of spontaneous utterances, contradictory statements, narrative cohesion, and aggressive or improbable details. Bruck et al. (2002) found that false narratives contained more spontaneous details, more temporal markers, more elaborations, and more aggressive details than true narratives. In a similar study, Powell and colleagues (Powell, Jones, & Campbell, 2003) found that, like Bruck et al. (2002), false narratives were similar to true narratives in number of details, structure, and quality. Furthermore, Principe and Ceci (2002) found that false narratives were actually more elaborate than children's true narratives, and further Kulkofsky and colleagues (2008) found that increases in narrative quality were associated with decreases in accuracy.

Even when experts attempt to apply more systematic methods to distinguish true from false reports elicited through suggestive questions, their decisions are not reliable. For instance, criterion-based content analysis (CBCA) has been touted as one way to distinguish true from false reports in forensic contexts (e.g., Vrij, 2005). In CBCA, experts code the witness's statement for the presence of specific contents that are expected to occur more frequently in true reports. Although there is some limited evidence that CBCA can distinguish truthful statements from intentional lies, it cannot reliably distinguish true statements from false statements that were developed as a result of suggestive questioning techniques (Kulkofsky, 2008).

The research on children's suggestibility paints a somewhat grim picture of young children's reliability as witnesses in forensic contexts. Children are vulnerable to leading questions and other suggestive techniques, including some very mild forms of suggestion. Although young children appear to be the most suggestible, older children are also susceptible to suggestive techniques. Further, children may be suggestible about central details of events and events that involve pain or bodily touch. Finally, children's reports that emerge through suggestive questioning often appear quite credible.

We should note, though, in this section we have focused primarily on aspects of interviewing contexts that tend to impair the accuracy of children's reports.

As noted in the previous section, children can often provide highly accurate accounts of past events. Also, concerns about memory accuracy do not only pertain to children, adults' autobiographical memory also undergoes memory reconstruction. When interviews are neutral in tone and include few or no suggestive questions children can provide accurate and useful information about past events, including traumatic events (Fivush, 1993; Goodman, Batterman-Faunce, & Kenney, 1992; Peterson, 1996; Peterson & Bell, 1996). Best-practice guidelines have been developed to encourage forensic interviewers to avoid the pitfalls of suggestive interviewing techniques while still encouraging children to provide as much information as possible (Sternberg, Lamb, Orbach, & Esplin, 2001b; Orbach et al., 2000; Poole & Lamb, 1998). To the degree to which actual forensic and therapeutic interviews follow these practices, we can have greater confidence in the veracity of children's statements.

Disclosure patterns among sexually abused children

In most cases where child sexual abuse (CSA) is suspected, children's statements are the central evidence by which to evaluate abuse allegations (London, Bruck, Ceci, & Shuman, 2005). As reviewed above, a corpus of studies indicates that open-ended questions, where children provide reports in their own words, produce the most trustworthy reports. However, sometimes there are reasons to suspect abuse has occurred in cases where children have not disclosed abuse. For example, perhaps someone gets convicted for sexually abusing one of his step-children, and investigators are concerned that other children in the family might also have been abused. During an initial forensic interview, the other children in the family do not make abuse allegations. In these cases, the investigator must decide whether and how to continue interviewing the child and at what point they should end the investigation.

Some professionals have expressed the view that children may be highly reticent to disclose sexual abuse and that sexually abused children may only disclose abuse in a lengthy process, if at all. In 1983 Roland Summit published a theoretical view based on his clinical experiences with his adult psychiatric patients, termed child sexual abuse accommodation syndrome (CSAAS). He postulated that children who have experienced intra-familial sexual abuse may be reluctant to disclose abuse because of motivational reasons such as being ashamed, scared, or embarrassed. As a result, he argued, abused children may delay abuse disclosure, deny abuse when asked, make partial disclosures, and retract abuse disclosures. He later extended the theory to include children who have experienced extra-familial sexual abuse (Summit, 1992).

Summit's theory (1983, 1992) has exerted a tremendous influence on forensic interview practices with children. The paper was rated as one of the most influential in the field of child maltreatment and continues to be taught internationally in many contemporary training seminars for child abuse professionals (e.g., see www. secasa.com.au; www.ndaa.org). For example, CSAAS is on the topic list for the

April 2008 training course held by the Advanced Trial Advocacy for Child Abuse Prosecutors in conjunction with the National District Attorneys Association.

In 1992 Summit published a paper entitled "Abuse of the Child Sexual Abuse Accommodation Syndrome" where he cautioned practitioners that CSAAS was a clinical opinion not a scientific or diagnostic instrument and that his model was being misused by practitioners who used it as such. Unfortunately, some investigators have grasped onto the idea that sexually abused children deny abuse, and that denial in and of itself is diagnostic or indicative of abuse. In some of these cases, children were interviewed with misleading and even coercive methods (see Schreiber et al., 2006, for details on the infamous Kelly Michaels and McMartin investigations). In instances such as the rash of suspected ritualistic satanic abuse cases in Salt Lake City (Sorensen & Snow, 1991),[1] themes emerged whereby the investigators reported refusing to believe children despite their repeated denials of abuse (see London et al., 2005, for details that call into question the validity of Sorensen & Snow's 1991 findings). Such cases are not historical artifacts but continue today, both in terms of newly adjudicated cases as well as cases still undergoing appeal. Many clinicians and forensic interviewers continue to interpret abuse denials or inconsistencies in children's statements as consistent with the stages postulated in the CSAAS. For example, in recent testimony from a director of an advocacy center who has interviewed over 800 children:

> Well, it's my understanding from reviewing those five areas that she did keep it a secret for a number of years. That, you know, she was helpless; she didn't fight back, things like that. That she just kind of accommodated to the situation. You know, her disclosure was, you know, different at times, and she did not retract, but, you know, she did minimize when she did her first interview about what had happened to her. So, you know, from my—just view of the information and the research, you know, it seems that she has gone through those stages.
>
> (*State of North Dakota v. Art Tibor*, 2007)

Considering CSAAS frequently is taught to forensic interviewers as evidence supporting the notion of extreme reticence among children undergoing forensic interviews, the tenets postulated by CSAAS have undergone little scientific scrutiny to date. This is perhaps because, when originally submitted for publication, Summit's theory was seen as being quite obvious and as consistent with forensic interview practices and general intuition about abuse disclosure (Summit, 1992).

In several papers, London and colleagues (London et al., 2005; London, Bruck, Ceci, & Shuman, 2007; London, Bruck, Wright, & Ceci, 2008) reviewed the literature on disclosure patterns among sexually abused children. The goal of these reviews was to examine the contemporary empirical findings regarding the nature and timing of children's sexual abuse disclosures.[2] London et al. reviewed two main sources of data: adults' retrospective accounts of CSA and whether they disclosed the abuse to anyone, and case records from children undergoing contemporaneous forensic evaluation. Below, we first present a summary of research findings from adults' retrospective reports. Then we discuss conclusions that can be drawn from the research on children undergoing forensic evaluations.

Adults' retrospective accounts of CSA and childhood disclosure: Evidence on delayed disclosure

Data from the retrospective accounts yield two central findings: Many adults report that they never told anyone during childhood about the CSA they experienced, and even fewer reported that the abuse came to the attention of authorities. Across 13 retrospective abuse disclosure studies reviewed, 21–87% of participants reported they disclosed the sexual abuse during childhood (see London et al., 2008, table 1, for studies and citations). A childhood disclosure rate of 87% (reported by Mullen, Martin, Anderson, Romans, & Herbison, 1993) was much higher than the other studies and might be accounted for through methodological factors in their study (London et al., 2005). Of the 13 studies reviewed, 11 found that 34–54% of their adult sample who experienced CSA reported that they had ever told anyone about the abuse during childhood.

Fewer studies reported data on adults' retrospective reports of whether the abuse disclosure involved authorities such as police or social workers. Across seven studies to provide data on disclosure to authorities, 5–18% of adults who reportedly experienced CSA indicated the abuse was brought to the attention of authorities, with four of the seven studies reporting rates between 10 and 13% (London et al., 2008). Though the retrospective accounts are subject to problems inherent in any retrospective account, London et al. (2008) concluded extant data support Summit's notion of secrecy among sexually abused children. According to retrospective reports, only about one third to one half of children ever tell anyone and even fewer cases come to the attention of authorities.

Many of the retrospective studies reported very long delays between the abusive episodes and children's disclosure, sometimes of several years. Though there are limited data at present, adults' retrospective reports suggest that some children disclose relatively close in time to the abuse (e.g., within the first six months), while others wait many years or never tell anyone during childhood (London et al., 2008).

The adult retrospective literature yields few individual difference variables (e.g., severity of abuse, presence of threats, intra-familial vs. extra-familial perpetrators, race and gender of child) that predicted whether and when children disclosed the abuse. We suspect such variables do exist (and some have been identified in the literature examining contemporaneous abuse investigations, see London et al., 2005). Likely there are multiple reasons why such findings have not emerged in the retrospective literature. First, only some of the retrospective studies reported relevant data. Second, samples sometimes were not adequately diverse to allow individual difference analyses. Third, individual difference variables may not be detected if adults have difficulties precisely pin-pointing the time at which the disclosure was made. Finally, multivariate methods may be necessary to reveal abuse, child, and perpetrator characteristics that predict CSA disclosure (e.g., see Goodman-Brown, Edelstein, Goodman, Jones, & Gordon, 2003).

While the retrospective accounts indicate a minority of children disclose abuse to authorities, the retrospective accounts do not yield information about the disclosure patterns among the minority of children to undergo forensic interviews. Among adults who retrospectively reported disclosing CSA during childhood, most reported telling a non-offending parent or a friend. Considering that only 10–15% of CSA cases appear to reach authorities, cases that come before forensic interviewers may have different features and characteristics from cases where children disclosed only to friends or family. In the next section, we discuss research findings on children under going contemporaneous abuse assessments.

Studies of children undergoing forensic evaluation for suspected abuse: Evidence on abuse denials and recantations

Studies of children undergoing assessment for suspected CSA provide the second source of data on disclosure patterns of abused children. These studies generally examined archival records of children undergoing assessment by police, social workers, physicians, or abuse assessment teams. Such samples allow an exploration of the extent to which children make denials and recantations during forensic assessment.

Unlike the retrospective studies reviewed above, London and colleagues (2005, 2007, 2008) reported a wide range of disclosure rates during forensic or medical interviews across 21 different studies. The reported disclosure rates ranged from a low of about 25% (Gonzalez, Waterman, Kelly, McCord, & Oliveri, 1993; Sorensen & Snow, 1991)[3] to a high of 96% (Bradley & Wood, 1996). Methodological features, particularly sample choices and interview methods, appear to play a primary role in accounting for these discrepant rates. Because of its importance, in this section, we focus on this issue. Findings on disclosure rates and specific child/perpetrator and abuse context characteristics have been reviewed and discussed elsewhere (most notably see edited volume on abuse disclosure by Pipe, Lamb, Orbach, & Cederborg, 2007b; also see London et al., 2005).

In order to calculate true rates of disclosures and denials during forensic interviews, information is needed that accurately classifies children as abused or non-abused regardless of whether the child makes an allegation during the interview. At the same time, the chosen sample should be representative of all children who come before forensic interviewers. For example, sampling methods that eliminate children from their sample who readily disclose to forensic interviewers would not provide accurate estimates of the overall rates of disclosure among all children who come before interviewers. At the same time, because abuse substantiation is highly reliant on children's disclosures, samples that only include highly probable or prosecuted cases suffer the limitation of excluding possible true cases where the child denies abuse during interview (see Lyon, 2007). Of course, there could also be cases where the child comes to make an abuse allegation despite not having experienced abuse.

Because of these real-world constraints, disclosure rates in founded and unfounded cases to come before forensic interviewers are unknown and likely vary temporally and across communities (according to varying factors like abuse education, mandatory reporting laws, and community thresholds of what signs constitute abuse suspicion). As reviewed in this chapter, the reliability of children's forensic reports is directly contingent upon the questioning methods employed. Hence, the sensitivity and specificity of abuse diagnoses vary according to interview methods. The difficult task for estimating CSA denial and recantation rates is choosing a sample that is both representative of children to come before forensic interviewers but also one that provides some meaningful measure of abuse certainty.

London et al. (2005, 2007, 2008) argued that disclosure rates during forensic interviews vary systematically according to the certainty with which children in the study samples were abused. They divided the child literature into four major groupings that correspond with ascending disclosure rates: Group 1—cases of dubious validity, Group 2—select subsamples, Group 3—all children to come before forensic interviewers, and Group 4—cases that come before forensic interviewers that are rated as founded or highly probable.

Group 1 studies reported the lowest disclosure rates. These rates came from studies with very dubious or overturned cases and documented poor interview techniques (Gonzalez et al., 1993; Sorensen & Snow, 1991). In these studies, the abuse denials may have been true denials rather than evidence of reluctant disclosure, for which the two articles frequently are cited. Many of the children from Gonzalez et al.'s sample were from the infamous McMartin case (see Schreiber et al., 2006, for a systematic evaluation of the methods employed in those interviews). Sorensen and Snow's (1991) children were from a rash of neighborhood ritualistic satanic abuse cases, most of which either were not prosecuted or later were thrown out of court. Based on the documented highly suggestive techniques used in these studies, we argue these studies do not provide any information about disclosure patterns among abused children.

Group 2 is composed of studies which reported disclosure rates among select subsamples of children who come before authorities. These studies provide the second tier of disclosure rates with between 43% and 61% of children disclosing abuse when interviewed (for the study citations see London et al., 2008, table 2). There are two types of cases in this grouping: (1) children undergoing extended evaluation for non-disclosure with high suspicion of abuse, and (2) children who come to the attention of authorities because of strong evidence of abuse (videotaped abuse evidence or sexually transmitted disease [STD] diagnoses who have not made prior disclosures). While these studies yield important information on abuse disclosure among their specific subsamples, caution is warranted in generalizing the results beyond the context under which these interviews occur. The rates are not based on studies of all children who come before forensic interviewers but rather a select subsample.

Also in this second major grouping of studies, some studies have reported disclosure rates in children who present with an STD (e.g., Lawson & Chaffin, 1992). Lyon (2007) reviewed 21 studies that presented data on children presenting to medical settings with gonorrhea. These studies were published between 1965 and 1993 with all but two being from 1982 and earlier. Across these 21 studies, Lyon (2007) reported a mean disclosure rate of 43%. There are a number of problems with generalizing results from these medical studies to all cases who come before forensic interviewers (Lawson & Chaffin, 1992). Some of the studies that are in this grouping purposely excluded a very large number of girls who were examined and readily disclosed and instead focused on a small number of girls with no prior disclosure. For example, in one study, from over 800 girls to undergo STD evaluation, disclosure rates were reported on 28 girls who were diagnosed with gonorrhea but who did not make a disclosure at the initial medical evaluation (as aptly noted by Lawson & Chaffin, 1992). Also, disclosure was a peripheral issue in these pediatric gonorrhea publications reviewed by Lyon (2007), and in some of these reports it was unclear (a) if the medical professional even attempted to ascertain directly from the child the nature of the abuse—especially considering the questioning took place before the burgeoning research on interviewing children, (b) if the child was pubertal and engaged in sexual activity with a same-aged peer, (c) the rate of false positives on the gonorrhea tests especially those conducted in the 1960s and 1970s, and (d) whether some of the children contacted gonorrhea via fomite transmission. Among cases to come before forensic interviewers, less than 1% of girls are estimated to fall into the category of testing positive for gonorrhea and not having previously disclosed abuse (London et al., 2008). While Lyon's (2007) review provides compelling evidence that some children in fact do deny abuse in the face of incontrovertible evidence of abuse, we argue these rates are not representative of all children who come before forensic interviewers. That is, it would be faulty reasoning for forensic interviewers to expect that fewer than half of children presenting before them who truly were abused would readily disclose abuse, as will become evident in the third grouping of studies.

Group 3 studies reported data among all children to come before forensic interviewers regardless of abuse substantiation. In several provocative studies by Lamb, Pipe, and colleagues, among all children with CSA suspicions to come before highly trained forensic interviewers using the NICHD protocol (in the United States and Israel), 71–83% made disclosures (Hershkowitz, Horowitz, & Lamb, 2005; Pipe, Lamb, Orbach, Stewart, Sternberg, & Esplin, 2007c). These findings reveal that disclosure rates in the 40–60% range do not approach the lowest level of disclosure rates found among all children to come before highly trained forensic interviewers. Importantly, with the 71–83% disclosure rates, no efforts were made to weed out unfounded suspicions.

We argue that the rates reported in studies in Group 3 reflect the lower boundary of disclosure rates that should be expected among large general groups of children interviewed by highly trained forensic interviewers (London et al., 2007). One important caveat to this finding is that most children who come before forensic interviewers had made disclosures prior to the interviews (and continue to do so during formal interviews), which was the impetus to the investigation. This factor probably contributes to the much higher disclosure rates found in studies where children come before forensic interviewers versus medical professionals in Group 2.

Group 4 represents studies which reported disclosure rates among highly probable cases that came before investigators. In these studies, efforts were taken by abuse assessment teams to rate the certainty of abuse in light of all the case materials available (e.g., children's disclosure, medical evidence, perpetrator confession, eyewitness reports, etc.). The highest rates of disclosure, 85–96%, are found among studies that report disclosure rates among cases classified as highly probable. We argue these rates provide the best estimate of disclosure rates among general samples of abused children who come before forensic interviewers as some effort must be made to classify founded and unfounded cases in order to give meaningful abuse disclosure estimates.

Lyon (2007) points out that these studies provide elevated disclosure rates since abuse substantiation often is dependent upon a disclosure. Hence, in true abuse cases where no disclosure is made, the case might get classified as an improbable abuse case. Using substantiated cases to estimate disclosure rates becomes circular, then, if substantiation is largely driven by abuse disclosure, and then disclosure rates are estimated based on substantiated cases. At the same time, some effort must be made to distinguish true and false cases or else the rates simply reflect disclosure among all children interviewed (as in the studies in Group 3). Clearly, each sampling method has limitations.

Finally, we turn to the issue of abuse recantations. Once children have disclosed abuse, how likely are they to recant the allegations? There is much less data on recantation rates than on disclosure rates. Like abuse disclosure rates, recantation rates depend on sampling methods and abuse substantiation. Two of the highest recantation rates (27% and 22%, respectively) were reported in the Gonzalez et al. (1993) and Sorensen and Snow (1991) papers. As discussed above and elsewhere (e.g., London et al., 2005, 2007, 2008; Schreiber et al., 2006), due to serious concerns about the forensic interview methods employed and uncertainty of abuse substantiation in the cases, we argue these rates are not representative of cases that come before forensic interviewers who have been highly trained with contemporary interview protocols. Recantation rates of 5–9% are reported in general samples of highly probable abuse cases. A higher rate was reported by Malloy, Lyon, and Quas (2007), who found a rate of 23% among children with substantiated CSA cases facing dependency hearings. Dependency hearings often involve removing the child from the home for reasons stemming from the CSA. There may be different motivations for recanting in these circumstances than in other situations. While these cases are important, it is also important to differentiate the types of samples used and not generalize from samples that are not representative of the wider population of interest.

Could factors independent of forensic contexts drive children to recant allegations of maltreatment? Malloy and colleagues (Malloy & Mugno, 2016; Malloy, Mugno,

Rivard, Lyon, & Quas, 2016) propose various sociomotivational factors, including familial reactions to disclosures, may predict recantations. In the first experimental study on children's recantation, Malloy and Mugno (2016) explored the impact of caregiver reactions on children's recantations of adult wrongdoing. Children (ages 6–9 years, $n = 73$) participated in an interactive health and safety demonstration individually with an unfamiliar adult experimenter. During the event, the experimenter appeared to break a puppet and asked children to keep the transgression a secret. Children were interviewed twice about the event using a series of open-ended prompts and direct questions. Interviewers were trained to elicit a disclosure of the transgression during the first interview. Between interviews, children's mothers met with them individually and delivered a set of scripted lines regarding children's initial disclosures (mothers were randomly assigned to be supportive or unsupportive). Supportive mothers praised children for disclosing and instructed them to continue telling the truth if asked about the event again. Unsupportive mothers urged children to change their initial statement in order to prevent the experimenter from getting in trouble. Overall, 23.3% of children recanted their previous disclosure. Although almost half (46%) of children who received the unsupportive caregiver manipulation recanted their initial disclosure about the puppet breaking, no child in the supportive condition recanted. Notably, of the children who recanted, only three mentioned the conversation with their mother to the second interviewer. In a second study, Malloy et al. (2016) examined a sample of substantiated CSA cases ($n = 58$ cases, ages 3–16 years) involving recantations. Their findings revealed children are less likely to recant when access to potential familial influences is limited (i.e., removal from the home and separation from siblings post-disclosure) and family members (other than the nonoffending caregiver) express belief. Alternatively, children were at increased risk of recantation when family members (other than the nonoffending caregiver) expressed disbelief and when visits with the alleged perpetrator were recommended at the first hearing. These findings suggest children who experience negative reactions following disclosure are at increased risk of recanting previous statements, but children who receive support are unlikely to spontaneously recant truthful allegations.

Overall, extant data on recantation of CSA disclosures suggest (a) recantations occur in a minority of cases and do not typify abuse disclosure patterns, and (b) recantation may be more common in certain situations (e.g., one with pressure or motivation to make recantation such as having a non-supportive non–abusing caregiver; e.g., Elliott & Briere, 1994; Malloy & Mugno, 2016, Malloy et al., 2016). When evaluating the minority of cases where abuse recantation occurs, like evaluating disclosure evidence, all of the evidence in the case, including potential motivators for recantation, should be considered.

Conclusions

Legal researchers and practitioners have made great strides over the past 40 years in devising forensic interviewing protocols that are sensitive to children's developing social and cognitive abilities. In this chapter, we have reviewed the contemporary literature on three main areas related to forensic reports from children: autobiographical memory development, suggestibility, and disclosure of child sexual abuse.

Prior to 1980, children rarely were allowed to give courtroom testimony. Beginning in the late 1980s, a rash of childcare center and satanic ritualistic abuse cases were prosecuted. The pendulum swung in the opposite direction, where laypeople and protective services workers sometimes seemed to blindly accept testimony elicited from highly suggestive interviews from children as young as ages 2 or 3. The scientific evidence shows that neither of these extreme views is supported. Instead, research indicates that children can give accurate reports of past events, even traumatic events following delays. At the same time, factors external (e.g., misleading questions) and internal (e.g., reliance on scripts) to children can taint their memory and produce erroneous reports.

In the first half of this chapter, we reviewed the literature on autobiographical memory and suggestibility. Evidence indicates even preschoolers can provide some information about central salient details of personally experienced events. Many studies have found children's free recall reports to be more accurate than recognition responses, though free recall in young children often is very sparse. The natural tendency of an adult interviewer, then, may be to resort to a series of forced-choice or yes/no questions. However, when there are high stakes attached to obtaining correct information, as in the case of forensic interviews, the use of option-posing questions runs a higher risk of eliciting erroneous information. When given forced choice options, young children tend to choose a response rather than indicating they do not know or do not understand a question.

One concern in evaluating forensic interviews with children is the extent to which the interviewers believed they knew what happened before eliciting children's narratives. When interviewers believe they know what happened in a given event, they tend to employ various suggestive interview techniques that are powerful in shaping children's responses to be in accord with their beliefs. Researchers have shown that a variety of suggestive techniques, beyond simply giving leading questions, can detrimentally affect children's reports. Researchers have found suggestive questioning can taint children's reports not just about peripheral details regarding inconsequential events but also about central details regarding events such as doctor's visits or bodily touching.

Children often do not simply parrot back the misinformation to which they have been exposed. Instead they may provide many elaborations that interfere with fact-finders' ability to distinguish true events from suggestively induced false reports. Hence, the first interviews with children are crucial. Numerous forensic interview protocols have emerged over the past 15 years to provide guidelines for maximizing accurate reports from children. Videotaping forensic interviews with children can help fact-finders evaluate the extent to which information was elicited from children in ways that produce accurate versus inaccurate reports.

Given the large body of work documenting the detrimental effects of repeated suggestive questioning, the following vignette illustrates one pattern of child sexual abuse disclosure that is particularly concerning. An adult develops a suspicion about abuse. Initially the child says nothing. After exposure to repeated questioning by parents and forensic interviewers who doggedly pursue the child for a certain report, the child eventually comes to make some statements that are consistent with the adults' a priori beliefs. Interviewers sometimes contend that such methods are justified because of children's extreme reluctance to disclose abuse. We argue that, for two reasons, such a conclusion is unwise.

First, in the event the adults' suspicions are inaccurate, the suggestive questioning may elicit erroneous information from children. Even if there is strong suspicion of abuse, suggestive misleading questioning strategies have been shown to elicit inaccurate information. Second, among high probability cases to come before forensic interviewers, most children make abuse disclosures during the initial open-ended phases of the interview process. Studies that provide data on general samples of CSA cases considered highly probable that come before forensic interviewers report disclosure rates of about 85%. Among the 15–30% of children who do not make a disclosure, some unknown and likely variable percentage of these children are reluctant disclosers and some are making true denials. Evidence from highly probable cases (e.g., see Cederborg, Lamb, & Laurell, 2007; Dickinson, Del Russo, & D'Urso, 2008; Lawson & Chaffin, 1992; Lyon, 2007; Malloy et al., 2007) indicates some sexually abused children do deny abuse during forensic or medical interviews, and a minority of truly abused children do falsely retract abuse.

While there is some disagreement about the overall rates of denial and recantation due to difficulties inherent in the scientific investigation of this issue, several researchers have opined that, while some children may deny or recant abuse, the term "syndrome" does not well characterize CSA disclosures (London et al., 2007; Lyon, 2007; Pipe et al., 2007a; Summit, 1992). We argue that the notion that sexually abused children typically progress through a series of syndrome-like stages from secrecy to partial disclosures and retractions, or that denials and retractions justify highly suggestive and coercive interview strategies, is not scientifically supported.

There are data supporting the notion that many sexually abused children fail to ever come forward to anyone about the abuse. Studies of adults' retrospective reports of their CSA disclosure patterns indicate that only one-third to one-half of sexually abused children ever tell anyone about the abuse during childhood; stated another way, 50–70% of adults report they never told anyone during childhood that they experienced CSA. There appears to be consensus among researchers at this point that Summit's notion of secrecy among sexually abused children has empirical support (e.g., Dickinson et al., 2008; London et al., 2008; Lyon, 2007).

Although the trend is that high probability abuse cases disclose early in well-conducted interviews, there are certain populations where denial (and recantation) during formal interviews may be more common. Some researchers have begun to elucidate variables that predict non-disclosure and recantation among founded abuse cases (e.g., see Cederborg et al., 2007; Horowitz, 2007; Lawson & Chaffin, 1992; Malloy et al., 2007; Orbach, Shiloach, & Lamb, 2007; Pipe et al., 2007c).

Identifying social and cognitive factors that interfere with disclosure is an important first step toward exploring interview methods that will motivate reluctant disclosers to come forward[4] without running a high risk of eliciting false reports from non-abused children.

A major advance in better understanding disclosure patterns among sexually abused children are the studies by Michael Lamb and colleagues who employ the empirically driven NICHD interview protocol (see edited volume by Pipe et al., 2007b, for several examples). Since the accuracy of children's reports (and classification as abused or non-abused) is driven by interview quality, estimates of CSA disclosure rates are most accurate under optimal interview conditions. Lamb and colleagues have recently published data showing the majority of children who make an abuse disclosure during forensic interviews do so at the beginning stages of the interview, during open-ended questions. The answer, then, to overcoming reluctance in disclosure among abused children undergoing forensic interviews does not lie in exposing them to repeated suggestive interviews or suggestive influences from non-professionals such as parents. While these techniques might act to overcome reluctance among abused children, they also run the risk of eliciting false allegations in non-abused children. Instead, techniques must be devised that encourage abused children to disclose without elevating false allegations among non-abused children. Fortunately, there is much exciting data emerging on abuse disclosure that can be used to refine and revise best-practice standards.

Notes

* This chapter originally appeared in the edited volume, *Current Issues in Applied Memory Research*. It has been updated for this compilation. Author Note: Our co-author passed away shortly after the publication of the original chapter, in January 2011, due to complications from the flu. She is sorely missed.
1 On February 19, 2008, Barbara Snow's license to practice as a clinical social worker was placed on a four-year probation due to unprofessional conduct (Falk, 2008).
2 Because forensic interview practices have undergone much transformation in recent years, we have limited our reviews to findings published in 1990 or later.
3 Of Sorensen and Snow's therapy clients 25% disclosed during initial interviews; eventually, after sometimes months of questionable interview techniques, 96% came to make abuse disclosures. Most of these cases either were overturned or did not go to trial. Similarly, Gonzalez et al.'s (1993) sample included children from the infamous McMartin case.
4 Given that the vast majority of CSA cases never reach authorities even when children do disclose to a friend or family member, top-down sexual abuse prevention efforts and community efforts aimed toward adults to whom children might disclose could have far-reaching implications for child protection.

References

Bahrick, L. E., Parker, J. F., Fivush, R., & Levitt, M. (1998). The effects of stress on young children's memory for a natural disaster. *Journal of Experimental Psychology: Applied, 4,* 308–331.

Bauer, P. J., Wenner, J. A., & Kroupina, M. G. (2002). Making the past present: Later verbal accessibility of early memories. *Journal of Cognition and Development, 3*, 21–47.

Beers, S. R., & De Bellis, M. D. (2002). Neuropsychological function in children with maltreatment-related posttraumatic stress disorder. *American Journal of Psychiatry, 159*, 483–486.

Benedan, L., Powell, M. B., Zajac, R., Lum, J. A. G., & Snow, P. (2018). Suggestibility in neglected children: The influence of intelligence, language, and social skills. *Child Abuse and Neglect, 79*, 51–60.

Berg, R., Munthe-Kaas, H. M., Baiju, N., Muller, A. E., & Brurberg, K. G. (2019). *The accuracy of using open-ended questions in structured conversations with children: a systematic review.* Norwegian Institute of Public Health.

Bradley, A. R., & Wood, J. M. (1996). How do children tell? The disclosure process in child sexual abuse. *Child Abuse and Neglect, 20*, 881–891.

Brainerd, C. J., Holliday, R. E., & Reyna, V. F. (2004). Behavioral measurement of remembering phenomenologies: So simple a child can do it. *Child Development, 75*, 505–522.

Bruck, M., Ceci, S. J., & Francoeur, E., (2000). Children's use of anatomically detailed dolls to report genital touching in a medical examination: Developmental and gender comparisons. *Journal of Experimental Psychology: Applied, 6*, 74–83.

Bruck, M., Ceci, S. J., Francoeur, E., & Barr, R. J. (1995). "I hardly cried when I got my shot!": Influencing children's reports about a visit to their pediatrician. *Child Development, 66*, 193–208.

Bruck, M., Ceci, S. J., & Hembrooke, H. (2002). The nature of children's true and false memories. *Developmental Review, 22*, 520–554.

Burgwyn-Bales, E., Baker-Ward, L., Gordon, B. N., & Ornstein, P. A. (2001). Children's memory for emergency medical treatment after one year: The impact of individual difference variables on recall and suggestibility. *Applied Cognitive Psychology, 15*, S25–S48.

Ceci, S. J., Bookbinder, S., Bruck, M., Perez, C. O., & London, K. (in preparation). Normative developmental vs. reverse developmental trends: A theoretical framework. Manuscript in preparation.

Ceci, S. J., & Bruck, M. (1993). Suggestibility of the child witness: A historical review and synthesis. *Psychological Bulletin, 113*, 403–439.

Ceci, S. J., Kulkofsky, S., Klemfuss, J. Z., Sweeney, C. D., & Bruck, M. (2007a). Unwarranted assumptions about children's testimonial accuracy. *Annual Review of Clinical Psychology, 3*, 311–328.

Ceci, S. J., Loftus, E. F., Leichtman, M. D., & Bruck, M. (1994). The possible role of source misattributions in the creation of false beliefs among preschoolers. *International Journal of Clinical and Experimental Hypnosis, 62*, 304–320.

Ceci, S. J., Papierno, P., & Kulkofsky, S. (2007b). Representational constraints on children's suggestibility. *Psychological Science, 18*, 503–509.

Cederborg, A. C., Lamb, M. E., & Laurell, O. (2007). Delay of disclosure, minimization, and denial when the evidence is unambiguous: A multi-victim case. In M. E. Pipe, M. E. Lamb, Y. Orbach, & A. C. Cederborg (Eds.), *Child sexual abuse: Disclosure, delay, and denial* (pp. 159–173). Mahwah, NJ: Lawrence Erlbaum Associates, Inc.

Cicchetti, D., Rogosch, F. A., Howe, M. L., & Toth, S. L. (2010). The effects of maltreatment and neuroendocrine regulation on memory performance. *Child Development, 81*, 1504–1519.

Dickinson, J., Del Russo, J., & D'Urso, A. (2008, March). Children's disclosure of sex abuse: A new approach to answering elusive questions. Paper presented at the annual meeting of the American Psychology—Law Society, Jacksonville, FL.

Elliott, D. M., & Briere, J. (1994). Forensic sexual abuse evaluations of older children: Disclosures and symptomatology. *Behavioral Sciences and the Law, 12,* 261–277.

Falk, A. (February 21, 2008). Controversial therapist put on probation. *Deseret Morning News.* Salt Lake City, UT.

Farrar, M. J., & Goodman, G. S. (1992). Developmental changes in event memory. *Child Development, 63,* 173–187.

Finnillä, K., Mahlberga, N., Santtilaa, P., Sandnabba, K., & Niemi, P. (2003). Validity of a test of children's suggestibility for predicting responses to two interview situations differing in their degree of suggestiveness. *Journal of Experimental Child Psychology, 85,* 32–49.

Fivush, R. (1993). Developmental perspectives on autobiographical recall. In G. S. Goodman & B. Bottoms (Eds.), *Child victims and child witnesses: Understanding and improving testimony* (pp. 1–24). New York: Guilford.

Fivush, R., Gray, J. T., & Fromhoff, F. A. (1987). Two year olds talk about the past. *Cognitive Development, 2,* 393–410.

Fivush, R., Haden, C., & Adam, S. (1995). Structure and coherence of preschoolers' personal narratives over time: Implications for childhood amnesia. *Journal of Experimental Child Psychology, 60,* 32–56.

Fivush, R., & Schwarzmueller, A. (1999). Children remember childhood: Implications for childhood amnesia. *Applied Cognitive Psychology, 12,* 455–473.

Garven, S., Wood, J. M., & Malpass, R. S. (2000). Allegations of wrongdoing: The effects of reinforcement on children's mundane and fantastic claims. *Journal of Applied Psychology, 85,* 38–49.

Garven, S., Wood, J. M., Malpass, R., & Shaw, J. S. (1998). More than suggestion: Consequences of the interviewing techniques from the McMartin preschool case. *Journal of Applied Psychology, 83,* 347–359.

Geddie, L., Fradin, S., & Beer, J. (2000). Child characteristics which impact accuracy of recall in preschoolers: Is age the best predictor? *Child Abuse and Neglect, 24,* 223–235.

Gonzalez, L. S., Waterman, J., Kelly, R., McCord, J., & Oliveri, K. (1993). Children's patterns of disclosures and recantations of sexual and ritualistic abuse allegations in psychotherapy. *Child Abuse and Neglect, 17,* 281–289.

Goodman, G. S., Batterman-Faunce, J. M., & Kenney, R. (1992). Optimizing children's testimony: Research and social policy issues concerning allegations of child sexual abuse. In D. Cicchetti & S. Toth (Eds.), *Child abuse, child development, and social policy* (pp. 65–87). Norwood, NJ: Ablex.

Goodman, G. S., Quas, J. A., Batterman-Faunce, J. M., Riddelsberger, M. M., & Kuhn, J. (1994). Predictors of accurate and inaccurate memories of traumatic events experienced in childhood. *Consciousness and Cognition, 3,* 269–294.

Goodman-Brown, T. B., Edelstein, R. S., Goodman, G. S., Jones, D. P. H., & Gordon, D. S. (2003). Why children tell: A model of children's disclosure of sexual abuse. *Child Abuse and Neglect, 27,* 525–540.

Hamond, N. R., & Fivush, R. (1991). Memories of Mickey Mouse: Young children recount their trip to Disney World. *Cognitive Development, 6,* 433–448.

Hershkowitz, I., Horowitz, D., & Lamb, M. E. (2005). Trends in children's disclosure of abuse in Israel: A national study. *Child Abuse and Neglect, 29,* 1203–1214.

Horowitz, D. (2007). The silence of abused children in Israel: Policy implications. In M. E. Pipe, M. E. Lamb, Y. Orbach, & A. C. Cederborg (Eds.), *Child sexual abuse: Disclosure, delay, and denial* (pp. 281–290). Mahwah, NJ: Lawrence Erlbaum Associates, Inc.

Howe, M. L., Cicchetti, D., & Toth, S. L. (2006). Children's basic memory processes, stress, and maltreatment. *Development and Psychopathology, 18,* 759–769.

Hudson, J., & Nelson, K. (1986). Repeated encounters of a similar kind: Effects of familiarity on children's autobiographic memory. *Cognitive Development, 1*, 253–271.

Hughes, M., & Grieve, R. (1980). On asking children bizarre questions. *First Language, 1*, 149–160.

Klemfuss, J. Z. (2015). Differential contributions of language skills to children's episodic recall. *Journal of Cognition and Development, 16*, 608–620.

Klemfuss, J. Z., & Ceci, S. J. (2012). Legal and psychological perspectives on children's competence to testify in court. *Developmental Review, 32*, 262–286.

Kulkofsky, S. (2008). Credible but inaccurate: Can Criterion-Based Content Analysis (CBCA) distinguish true and false memories? In M. J. Smith (Ed.), *Child sexual abuse: Issues and challenges* (p. 21–42). New York; Nova Science Publishers.

Kulkofsky, S., Wang, Q., & Ceci, S. J. (2008). Do better stories make better memories? Narrative quality and memory accuracy in preschool children. *Applied Cognitive Psychology, 22*, 21–38.

Lawson, L., & Chaffin, M. (1992). False negatives in sexual abuse disclosure interviews: Incidence and influence of caretaker's belief in abuse in cases of accidental abuse discovery by diagnosis of STD. *Journal of Interpersonal Violence, 7*, 532–542.

Leichtman, M. D. & Ceci, S. J. (1995). The effects of stereotypes and suggestions on preschoolers' reports. *Developmental Psychology, 31*, 568–578.

Leichtman, M. D., Pillemer, D. B., Wang, Q., Korieshi, A., & Han, J. J. (2000). When Baby Maisy came to school: Mother's interview styles and children's event memories. *Cognitive Development, 15*, 99–114.

London, K., Bruck, M., Ceci, S. J., & Shuman, D. (2005). Children's disclosure of sexual abuse: What does the research tell us about the ways that children tell? *Psychology, Public Policy, and the Law, 11*, 194–226.

London, K., Bruck, M., & Ceci, S. J., & Shuman, D. (2007). Disclosure of child sexual abuse: A review of the contemporary empirical literature. In M. E. Pipe, M. E. Lamb, Y. Orbach, & A. C. Cederborg (Eds.), *Child sexual abuse: Disclosure, delay, and denial* (pp. 11–39). Mahwah, NJ: Lawrence Erlbaum Associates, Inc.

London, K., Bruck, M., & Melnyk, L. (2009). Post-event information affects children's autobiographical memory after one year. *Law and Human Behavior, 33*(4), 344–355.

London, K., Bruck, M., Wright, D. B., & Ceci, S. J. (2008). How children report sexual abuse to others: Findings and methodological issues. *Memory, 16*, 29–47.

Lyon, T. D. (2007). False denials: Overcoming methodological biases in abuse disclosure research. In M. E. Pipe, M. E. Lamb, Y. Orbach, & A. C. Cederborg (Eds.), *Child sexual abuse: Disclosure, delay, and denial* (pp. 41–62). Mahwah, NJ: Lawrence Erlbaum Associates, Inc.

Malloy, L. C., & Mugno, A. P. (2016). Children's recantation of adult wrongdoing: An experimental investigation. *Journal of Experimental Child Psychology, 145*, 11–21.

Malloy, L. C., Lyon, T. D., & Quas, J. A. (2007). Filial dependency and recantation of child sexual abuse allegations. *Journal of the American Academy of Child and Adolescent Psychiatry, 46*, 162–170.

Malloy, L. C., Mugno, A. P., Rivard, J. R., Lyon, T. D., & Quas, J. A. (2016). Familial influences on recantation in substantiated child sexual abuse cases. *Child Maltreatment, 21*(3), 256–261.

Mullen, P. E., Martin, J. L., Anderson, J. C., Romans, S. E., & Herbison, G. P. (1993). Child sexual abuse and mental health in adult life. *British Journal of Psychiatry, 163*, 721–732.

Nelson, K. (1993a). Events, narratives, memory: What develops? In C. A. Nelson (Ed.), *Memory affect in development* (pp. 1–24). Hillsdale, NJ: Lawrence Erlbaum Associates, Inc.

Nelson, K. (1993b). The psychological and social origins of autobiographical memory. *Psychological Science, 4*, 7–14.

Nelson, K., & Fivush, R. (2004). The emergence of autobiographical memory: A social cultural developmental theory. *Psychological Review, 111*, 486–511.

Orbach, Y., Hershkowitz, I., Lamb, M. E., Sternberg, K. J., Esplin, P. W., & Horowitz, D. (2000). Assessing the value of structured protocols for forensic interviews of alleged child abuse victims. *Child Abuse and Neglect, 24*, 733–752.

Orbach, Y., Shiloach, H., & Lamb, M. E. (2007). Reluctant disclosers of child sexual abuse. In M. E. Pipe, M. E. Lamb, Y. Orbach, & A. C. Cederborg (Eds.), *Child sexual abuse: Disclosure, delay, and denial* (pp. 115–134). Mahwah, NJ: Lawrence Erlbaum Associates.

Ornstein, P. A., Merrit, K. A., Baker-Ward, L., Furtado, E., Gordon, B. N., & Principe, G. F. (1998). Children's knowledge, expectation, and long-term retention. *Applied Cognitive Psychology, 12*, 387–405.

Otgaar, H., Howe, M. L., Merckelbach, H., & Muris, P. (2018). Who is the better eyewitness? Sometimes adults, but at other times children. *Current Directions in Psychological Science, 27*, 378–385.

Perez, C. O., London, K., & Otgaar, H. (under review). A review of the differential contributions of language abilities to children's eyewitness memory and suggestibility. Manuscript submitted for publication.

Peterson, C. (1996). The preschool child witness: Errors in accounts of traumatic injury. *Canadian Journal of Behavioral Science, 28*, 36–42.

Peterson, C., & Bell, M. (1996). Children's memory for traumatic injury. *Child Development, 67*, 3045–3070.

Peterson, C., Dowden, C., & Tobin, J. (1999). Interviewing preschoolers: Comparisons of yes/no and wh- questions. *Law and Human Behavior, 23*, 539–555.

Peterson, C., & Rideout, R. (1998). Memory for medical emergencies experienced by 1- and 2-year-olds. *Developmental Psychology, 34*, 1059–1072.

Peterson, C., & Whalen, N. (2001). Five years later: Children's memory for medical emergencies. *Applied Cognitive Psychology, 15*, 7–24.

Pipe, M. E., Lamb, M. E., Orbach, Y., & Cederborg, A. C. (2007a). Seeking resolution in the disclosure wars: An overview. In M. E. Pipe, M. E. Lamb, Y. Orbach, & A. C. Cederborg (Eds.), *Child sexual abuse: Disclosure, delay, and denial* (pp. 1–10). Mahwah, NJ: Lawrence Erlbaum Associates, Inc.

Pipe, M. E., Lamb, M. E., Orbach, Y., & Cederborg, A. C. (Eds.), (2007b), *Child sexual abuse: Disclosure, delay, and denial*. Mahwah, NJ: Lawrence Erlbaum Associates, Inc.

Pipe, M. E., Lamb, M. E., Orbach, Y., Stewart, H. L., Sternberg, K. L., & Esplin, P. W. (2007c). Factors associated with nondisclosure of suspected abuse during forensic interviews. In M. E. Pipe, M. E. Lamb, Y. Orbach, & A. C. Cederborg (Eds.), *Child sexual abuse: Disclosure, delay, and denial* (pp. 77–96). Mahwah, NJ: Lawrence Erlbaum Associates, Inc.

Poole, D. A., Dickinson, J. J., Brubacher, S. P., Liberty, A. E., & Kaake, A. M. (2014). Deficient cognitive control fuels children's exuberant false allegations. *Journal of Experimental Child Psychology, 118*, 101–109.

Poole, D. A., & Lamb, M. E. (1998). *Investigative interviews of children: A guide for helping professionals*. Washington, DC: American Psychological Association.

Poole, D. A., & Lindsay, D. S. (1995). Interviewing preschoolers: Effects of non-suggestive techniques, parental coaching, and leading questions on reports of non-experienced events. *Journal of Experimental Child Psychology, 60*, 129–154.

Porter, C., Lawson, J. S., & Bigler, E. D. (2005). Neurobehavioral sequelae of child sexual abuse. *Child Neuropsychology, 11*, 203–220.

Powell, M. B., Jones, C. H., & Campbell, C. (2003). A comparison of preschoolers' recall of experienced versus non-experienced events across multiple interviewers. *Applied Cognitive Psychology, 17*, 935–952.

Principe, G. F., & Ceci, S. J. (2002). "I saw it with my own ears": The influence of peer conversations and suggestive questions on preschoolers' event memory. *Journal of Experimental Child Psychology, 83*, 1–25.

Principe, G. F., Giuliano, S., & Root, C. (2008). Rumor mongering and remembering: How rumors originating in children's inferences can affect memory. *Journal of Experimental Child Psychology, 99*, 135–155.

Principe, G. F., Haines, B., Adkins, A., & Guiliano, S. (2010). False rumors and true belief: Memory processes underlying children's errant reports of rumored events. *Journal of Experimental Child Psychology, 107*(4), 407–422.

Principe, G. F., Kanaya, T., Ceci, S. J., & Singh, M. (2006). Believing is seeing: How rumors can engender false memories in preschoolers. *Psychological Science, 17*, 243–248.

Principe, G. F., & Schindewolf, E. (2012). Natural conversations as a source of false memories in children: Implications for the testimony of young witnesses. *Developmental Review, 32*(3), 205–223.

Schreiber, N., Bellah, L. D., Martinez, Y., McLaurin, K. A., Strok, R., Garven, S., & Wood, J. M. (2006). Suggestive interviewing in the McMartin Preschool and Kelly Michaels daycare abuse cases: A case study. *Social Influence, 1*, 16–47.

Simcock, G., & Hayne, H. (2002). Breaking the barrier? Children fail to translate their pre-verbal memories into language. *Psychological Science, 13*, 225–231.

Sorensen, T., & Snow, B. (1991). How children tell: The process of disclosure of child sexual abuse. *Child Welfare, 70*, 3–15.

State of Calif. v. Buckey. 1990. Sup. Ct., Los Angeles County, #A750900.

State of North Dakota v. Art Tibor. 2007. N.D. 146.

Sternberg, K. J., Lamb, M. E., Davies, G. M., & Westcott, H. L. (2001a). The memorandum of good practice: Theory versus application. *Child Abuse and Neglect, 25*, 669–681.

Sternberg, K. J., Lamb, M. E., Orbach, Y., & Esplin, P. W. (2001b). Use of a structured investigative protocol enhances young children's responses to free-recall prompts in the course of forensic interviews. *Journal of Applied Psychology, 86*, 997–1005.

Summit, R. C. (1983). The Child Sexual Abuse Accommodation Syndrome. *Child Abuse and Neglect, 7*, 177–193.

Summit, R. (1992). Abuse of the Child Sexual Abuse Accommodation Syndrome. *Journal of Child Sexual Abuse, 1*, 153–163.

Vrij, A. (2005). Criteria-based content analysis: A qualitative review of the first 37 studies. *Psychology, Public Policy, and Law, 11*, 3–41.

White, T. L., Leichtman, M. D., & Ceci, S. J. (1997). The good, the bad, and the ugly: Accuracy, inaccuracy, and elaboration in preschoolers' reports about a past event. *Applied Cognitive Psychology, 11*, S37–S54.

Zaragoza, M. S., Payment, K., Kichler, J., Stines, L., & Drivdahl, S. (2001). Forced confabulation and false memory in child witnesses. Paper presented at the 2001 biennial meeting of the Society for Research in Child Development, Minneapolis, MN.

PART IV

Memory augmentations: How can memory capacities be improved?

14

INDIVIDUAL DIFFERENCES IN WORKING MEMORY AND AGING*

Timothy A. Salthouse

This chapter reviews research conducted in my laboratory over the past 25 years in which aspects of working memory (WM) have been examined in adults of different ages. My thinking has been strongly influenced by Welford's discussions of the role of WM in age differences in cognitive functioning in his 1958 book *Ageing and Human Skill*. Although I don't believe he used the term working memory, his description in the following passage of a fundamental age-related limitation clearly resembles contemporary ideas about the relation between aging and working memory:

> It is conceived that data are somehow held in a form of short-term storage while other data are being gathered. Obviously, unless data can be so held, the amount of information that can be simultaneously applied to any problem is very small indeed. It would appear that in old people the amount that can be stored tends to diminish, and that what is stored is more liable than it is in younger people to interference and disruption from other activity going on at the same time. Such a decline in short-term retention would be capable of accounting for a very wide range of observed age changes in learning and problem solving …
>
> (p. 285)

As implied by the quotation above, WM has been of interest primarily because of its relation to other aspects of cognition; in fact, WM can be defined as memory in the service of cognition. Because a wide range of cognitive tasks have been reported to have negative age relations, WM has been postulated to be a critical limiting factor, or a processing resource, that could be contributing to adult age differences in many different cognitive tasks. This view was articulated by Salthouse and Skovronek (1992) in their statement that:

[I]ncreased age seems to be associated with progressively greater difficulties when information must be simultaneously stored and either transformed or abstracted. This decreased ability to keep the intermediate products of earlier processing available, while also transforming or abstracting information, necessarily impairs the identification of abstract relations among sets of elements ... Because the solution of many cognitive tasks requires abstraction of higher order relations, people with smaller working-memory capacities, such as older adults, are likely to be less successful than those with larger capacities, such as young adults.

(pp. 119–120)

Indirect evidence for a role of WM in age differences in cognition is available in numerous studies in which larger age differences favoring young adults have been found when conditions in the tasks could be assumed to make greater demands on working memory. Examples of this phenomenon in my research are findings that the age differences in performance were larger with: more complex (i.e. alternating or second-order relations compared to simple sequential relations) series completion problems (Salthouse & Prill, 1987), larger angular discrepancy between cubes in a cube comparison task (Salthouse & Skovronek, 1992), more operations in spatial integration tasks (Salthouse, 1987, 1988; Salthouse & Mitchell, 1989), geometric analogy tasks (Salthouse, 1988), paper folding tasks (Salthouse, 1988, 1992a; Salthouse et al. 1989b), integrative reasoning tasks (Salthouse, 1992a; Salthouse et al. 1989b) and cube assembly tasks (Salthouse, 1992a).

A more detailed investigation of the phenomenon of larger age differences at greater levels of task complexity with integrative reasoning and paper folding tasks was conducted by Salthouse et al. (1989b). The specific goal in that project was to investigate whether this "complexity effect" at least in part reflected a failure to preserve earlier information during the performance of the task. The procedure consisted of comparing decision accuracy when all relevant information was available in a single display with accuracy when the relevant information was distributed across multiple displays, and therefore information integration was presumably required. The critical finding was that the slopes of the functions relating decision accuracy to number of premises or number of folds were very similar when only a single premise or fold was relevant to the decision as when the relevant information was distributed across multiple displays, and that this was equally true at all ages. Because no integration is required when the relevant information is presented in a single display, poorer performance with additional premises or folds can be presumed to reflect inability to preserve earlier information during the presentation and processing of later information. These results are therefore consistent with the interpretation that most of the age differences in these tasks are attributable to a failure to retain information from early premises or folds during the presentation of subsequent premises or folds, and that they are unlikely to be due to a limitation associated with integrating information.

A related finding was reported by Salthouse, Mitchell, and Palmon (1989a) with a spatial integration task. In this case, no age differences were evident in the accuracy of merely recognizing information, but young adults were more accurate than older adults when the trials involved several displays but all of the relevant information was contained in a single display. As in the other study, these results imply that the age-related difficulty was in maintaining information during the performance of the task. In both situations the inability to preserve relevant information during the processing of other information is consistent with a failure of working memory.

Assessment of WM

Different conceptualizations of WM have guided how it has been measured, and many of the measurement methods have been incorporated in studies comparing adults of different ages. As elaborated below, the assessments can be categorized as either within-context methods, including measurement of redundant information requests and accuracy of recognizing probes of earlier information, or out-of-context methods, including measures evaluating updating of continuously changing information or measures involving simultaneous storage and processing.

Within-context measures

In an article published in 1990, within-context assessments of working memory were described as follows:

> Within-context assessments of working memory consist of information about memory functioning derived during the performance of ongoing cognitive tasks. That is, these evaluations are not obtained from tasks deliberately designed to assess specific attributes of memory capacity, but instead are inferred from observations collected while research participants are performing other cognitive tasks.
>
> (Salthouse, 1990, p. 104)

Redundant information requests

Several examples of within-context assessments of working memory in tasks involving sequential presentation of relevant information were described by Welford (1958). For example, in different experiments subjects were asked to locate a target cell in a matrix, to determine the correspondence between elements in an electrical circuit, or to determine the relative positions of horses in a horse race. In each case, older adults were reported to make more uninformative or redundant information inquiries than young adults.

Salthouse and Skovronek (1992) investigated within-context assessments of working memory with a cube comparison task in which the subject was to decide if two displays portraying 3-D cubes could represent the same object. In some conditions the subjects were required to make explicit requests (via commands on a computer) to view the contents of specific cube faces, and the number of times the same cube face was re-examined was recorded. These repeated cube face examinations were assumed to occur because the subject was unable to maintain relevant information while it was being processed, and hence a larger number of repeated information requests might be symptomatic of a smaller, or less effective, working memory. As expected, older adults made more redundant (i.e. repeated) requests for information in the cube comparison task than young adults, and they also made more redundant information requests in a successive version of the Raven's Progressive Matrices task. That is, in contrast to the traditional format in which all information is simultaneously available, in the successive version the participant selected specific cells in the matrix to be examined sequentially. Repetition of a previously examined cell was designated a redundant information request. A particularly interesting result in this study was that the number of redundant requests in the Raven's Matrices task and in the cube comparisons task were significantly correlated in both young adults ($r = .41$) and older adults ($r = .34$), which suggests that the tendency to make redundant information requests is a meaningful individual difference dimension not restricted to a specific cognitive task.

The sequential version of the Raven's task was also administered in a later study (Salthouse, 1993), and once again older adults were found to make more redundant cell examinations than young adults. Two complex span WM tasks were also administered to the subjects in this study and, surprisingly, the number of redundant information requests was only weakly related to the WM measures (i.e. $r = -.12$ for young adults and $r = -.09$ for older adults). These results raise the possibility that a greater number of information requests may reflect lack of confidence or excess cautiousness as much as, or more than, a failure to preserve prior information. However, this inference should be considered tentative because no information about the reliability of the measures was available, and therefore it is possible that the weak correlations might simply have been a consequence of low reliability.

Probes

If WM reflects the ability to preserve information during ongoing processing, individuals with high levels of WM might be expected to have better recognition of earlier presented information in the task than individuals with lower levels of WM. Salthouse and Mitchell (1989) applied this logic in a spatial integration task in which sequentially presented line segments were to be synthesized into a composite figure and compared with a target pattern. In addition to complete comparison figures, probes of the line segments from a prior frame were occasionally presented to test for recognition of the earlier information. Somewhat surprisingly, no significant age differences were found in the accuracy of recognizing probes. Salthouse and Skovronek (1992) also did not find significant age differences in probe recognition of prior cube faces in a sequential version of the cube comparison task.

However, young adults were more accurate in probe recognition than older adults in other studies. For example, Salthouse (1992b) found that older adults were less accurate than young adults when recognizing probes of prior premises during the performance of an integrative reasoning task. And in two separate studies involving a sequential version of the Raven's matrix reasoning task, Salthouse (1993) found older adults to be less accurate than young adults in recognizing contents of prior cells. Furthermore, the correlations of probe recognition accuracy with age in the two studies were −.50 and −.70, and the correlations with Raven's accuracy were .67 and .60, and thus the results are consistent with the possibility that age differences in preserving relevant information contributed to the age differences in task performance.

The preceding review reveals that results comparing adults of different ages on within-context assessments of WM have been somewhat inconsistent. Among the possible reasons for the inconsistencies are potentially low reliability of the measures, or uncontrolled variations in task strategy. Despite the inconsistencies, more research investigating within-context WM measures is nevertheless desirable because these types of measures are likely to be informative about the mechanisms involved in the relations between WM and cognitive functioning, and the impact of age on these mechanisms.

Out of context WM assessment

Tasks deliberately designed to evaluate properties of WM rather than other aspects of cognitive functioning can be considered as out-of-context WM assessments. Two major categories of out-of-context assessments have been employed: measures of the accuracy of updating the status of continuously changing information; and measures of the accuracy of remembering information while processing the same or other information in various complex span tasks.

Updating

Updating tasks require the subject to maintain the status of several continuously changing variables. Welford (1958) described early versions of what is now known as the *n*-back task, and one of the first published studies using this task was an age-comparative study by Kirchner (1958). A version of the *n*-back was used in a study by Salthouse, Atkinson and Berish (2003) and, as in Kirchner's study, significant age differences were found, favoring younger adults.

Tasks requiring updating of numbers with arithmetic operations, and of spatial positions with arrows indicating location transformations, have been examined in several studies in my laboratory (e.g. Salthouse, Babcock, & Shaw, 1991; Salthouse,

1992c; Salthouse, 1995). In every case, older adults were found to be less accurate than young adults. Significant negative age correlations were also reported in a spatial updating task used in Salthouse, Atkinson and Berish (2003) and Salthouse, Pink, and Tucker-Drob (2008), and in a color counters numeric updating task in Salthouse, Pink, and Tucker-Drob (2008).

Yntema and Trask (1963) may have been the first to use a keeping track task involving sequential presentation of exemplars from categories with occasional probes of the most recent exemplar from a target category. A version of this task was used in a study by Salthouse, Atkinson, and Berish (2003) and, as with most WM tasks, significant age differences were found, favoring younger adults.

Talland (e.g. 1968) described tasks in which the participant was to recall the non-repeated item in a list last, or an adaptation of the running memory task introduced by Pollack, Johnson, and Knaff (1959) in which the requirement was to recall the last n items in a list of unpredictable length. Talland reported age differences in both types of tasks, and the running memory finding was replicated by Siedlecki, Salthouse, and Berish (2005) in a task in which the participant was instructed to recall the last three words in the list. Running memory tasks in which the participant was to recall the last four letters or dot positions were also administered in Salthouse, Pink, and Tucker-Drob (2008), and in both tasks there were significant negative correlations between age and performance accuracy.

Simultaneous storage and processing

Case, Kurland, and Goldberg (1982), and Daneman and Carpenter (1980) developed complex span WM tasks with both storage and processing requirements, in that the subject was to remember some information while processing the same or other information. Several versions of complex span tasks have been developed in my laboratory, including computation span (Salthouse & Prill, 1987; Salthouse & Mitchell, 1989; Salthouse et al., 1989), reading span and listening span (Salthouse & Babcock, 1991), and line span (Babcock & Salthouse, 1990; Salthouse & Skovronek, 1992). One or more of these tasks have been included in numerous studies, and age differences favoring young adults have consistently been found. Other variants of complex span tasks developed by Engle and colleagues (e.g. Conway et al., 2005) were used in Salthouse, Pink, and Tucker-Drob (2008) and, again, moderately large age differences were found.

Although research from my laboratory represents only a small proportion of the research concerned with age differences in WM, it is clear from the results reviewed above that increased age is often associated with lower levels of performance in tasks postulated to measure WM. Many of the studies in my laboratory involved moderately large samples of adults across a wide age range, and therefore the age trends with these data may provide good estimates of the relations between age and WM. Figure 14.1 portrays the age relations with six WM tasks in samples of 724 adults (for the operation span and symmetry span tasks), 1,460 adults (for the computation span and reading span tasks), and 1,563 adults (for the running memory tasks).

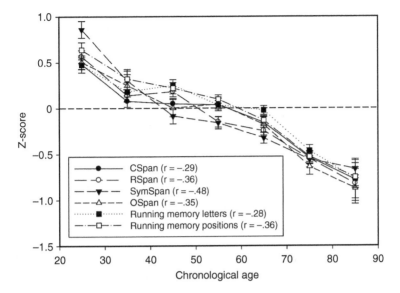

FIGURE 14.1 Means and standard errors of z-scores representing performance in six working memory tasks as a function of age

Source: Data from various Salthouse studies.

It can be seen that for every measure the age trends were nearly linear between 25 and 85 years of age.

WM relations

The information in the preceding sections indicates that most measures postulated to assess WM have been found to have significant age relations, and thus it is reasonable to conclude that there are age differences in WM as the construct is assessed by these tasks. However, because a large number of cognitive variables have been found to have significant age differences, it is possible that the measures may not represent anything special. Information relevant to this point is illustrated in Figure 14.2, which portrays age trends in measures of reasoning, memory, and speed in the same format as Figure 14.1. Note that the age trends with these measures were all quite linear and, if anything, were more strongly negative than those for the WM measures in Figure 14.1. A key question with respect to aging and WM, therefore, is not whether WM measures are related to age, because that certainly seems to be the case, but rather the nature of the relations of WM measures with measures of other types of cognition.

Internal relations

Internal relations can be conceptualized as relations among hypothesized components within the same task, or among measures from similar tasks. As

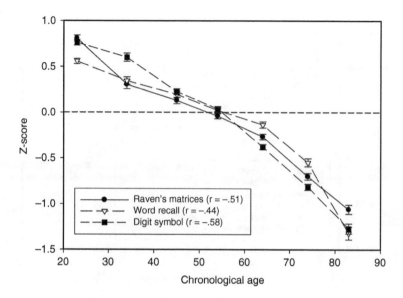

FIGURE 14.2 Means and standard errors of z-scores representing performance in tests of reasoning (Raven's Matrices), memory (Word Recall), and speed (Digit Symbol) as a function of decade

Source: Data from various Salthouse studies.

an example, Salthouse and Babcock (1991) proposed that processing efficiency, storage capacity, and coordination effectiveness are the primary components of complex span tasks, and they obtained measures of each hypothesized component from adults across a wide age range. Path analysis models suggested that a large proportion of the age differences in WM were mediated through components postulated to reflect processing efficiency and coordination effectiveness. Reanalyses of these data were conducted by Salthouse (1994) to identify the proportional contributions of the different components to individual differences in WM. The results revealed that the combination of the three components accounted for 60% of the variance in complex span measures of WM, with 50% accounted for by the processing efficiency component alone. Furthermore, the largest contribution to the age-related variance in complex span WM measures was variability in processing efficiency.

Motivated in part by this discovery of strong relations between processing efficiency and WM, a number of studies were conducted to investigate the reduction in cross-sectional age-related variance in WM after controlling the variance in various measures of speed (e.g. Salthouse, 1991, 1992b, 1993; Salthouse & Babcock, 1991; Salthouse & Meinz, 1995). In every case the results revealed a moderate to large attenuation of the age-related variance in WM, and the following interpretation of these results was proposed:

One possible interpretation of the relation between speed and working memory is that working memory has a dynamic quality, perhaps somewhat analogous to someone trying to juggle several objects simultaneously. That is, just as the number of items that can be successfully juggled depends on the rate at which they can be caught and tossed, so might the limits on the number of distinct ideas that can be kept active (or mentally juggled) in working memory be set by the rate at which information can be processed. From this perspective, therefore, working memory might be interpreted as the set of items currently active in consciousness, and age differences in working memory might be hypothesized to originate because increased age is associated with a reduction either in the ability to activate new information or in the ability to maintain the activation of old information.

(Salthouse, 1992b, p. 422)

A key aspect of this conceptualization of WM is that aspects of processing efficiency or effectiveness are at least as important as aspects of information storage, particularly with respect to age differences in WM.

Although complex span tasks are distinguished from simple span tasks by a requirement for simultaneous processing in addition to storage of information, most studies in which complex span tasks have been used have only considered storage measures in their analyses, and have either ignored the processing component, or have treated it as an exclusionary criterion by discarding data from participants with low levels of processing accuracy. However, it may only be meaningful to neglect one component if there is little variation across people in the measures of that component, or if the measures of that component have a weak relation to the relevant construct. Research from my laboratory and from other laboratories suggests that neither of these conditions is likely to be true (e.g. Babcock & Salthouse, 1990; Duff & Logie, 2001; Salthouse & Babcock, 1991; Waters & Caplan, 1996). For example, Salthouse, Pink, and Tucker-Drob (2008) found substantial individual difference variance, and significant age differences, on measures of both storage and processing in complex span tasks. Moreover, an unpublished study (Salthouse & Tucker-Drob, 2008) found significant relations between the storage and processing measures. Three models of possible organizations among the storage and processing measures from different complex span tasks (i.e. operation span, symmetry span, and reading span) considered in that study are portrayed in Figure 14.3. The model in the top panel represents the possibility that all of the measures reflect a single modality-independent WM construct. The model in the bottom left panel postulates that the measures are best organized in terms of the modality-specific WM tasks from which they were derived, and the model in the bottom right panel postulates the existence of separate constructs corresponding to storage and processing components. The models were examined with data from the two studies in Salthouse, Pink, and Tucker-Drob (2008).

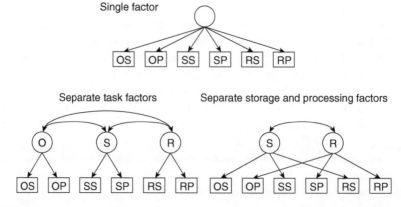

Single factor

Separate task factors   Separate storage and processing factors

FIGURE 14.3 Three alternative models of the organization of storage and processing measures in complex span WM tasks
Key: OS = operation span storage, OP = operation span processing, SS = symmetry span storage, SP = symmetry span processing, RS = reading span storage, RP = reading span processing

The best-fitting model in both studies had separate, but moderately correlated (r = .73 and .47 in the two studies), storage and processing constructs. Similar results were reported by Unsworth et al. (2009) in a study involving 138 young adults. That is, in the Unsworth et al. study a model based on separate task constructs did not fit the data very well, but a model with separate processing and storage constructs had a good fit, with an estimated correlation of .61 between the processing accuracy and storage constructs. These results have at least two important implications. First, they suggest that it can be misleading to ignore the processing measures in analyses of complex span performance because people differ in their levels of processing accuracy, and individual differences in processing accuracy are related to individual differences in the storage measures. And second, at least with these types of complex span WM tasks, it appears that the individual differences are more consistent with a general, modality-independent WM factor rather than with several separate modality-specific factors.

Another issue relevant to internal WM relations concerns the magnitude of correlations of WM measures with each other because moderate correlations would be expected if the various measures represent a single coherent construct. Initial information relevant to this question based on small samples of 20 young and 20 old adults who each performed several WM tasks was reported in Salthouse (1988). The WM tasks consisted of: repeating a digit sequence in reverse order (backwards digit span), repeating digits after subtracting two from each digit (subtract 2 span), identifying the missing digit when the sequence was repeated in random order (missing digit span), and remembering digits while simultaneously performing arithmetic operations (computation span). Large age differences favoring young adults were found in all except the missing digit span task. Most importantly in the current context was the finding that the measures were moderately correlated with one another, and to a similar extent in the two age groups. Similar results with a somewhat different combination of WM tasks were reported by Waters and Caplan (2003).

Subsequent studies in my lab have revealed correlations between measures from computation span and listening or reading span tasks ranging from .40 to .79 (e.g. Salthouse, 1991, 1992c, 1993; Salthouse & Babcock, 1991; Salthouse, Babcock, & Shaw, 1991; Salthouse & Kersten, 1993; Salthouse & Meinz, 1995), and similar values have been reported in studies by other researchers (e.g. de Frias, Dixon, & Strauss, 2009; McCabe et al., 2010). Correlations between measures from other complex span tasks ranging from .52 between operation span and symmetry span to .71 between operation span and reading span were reported by Salthouse and Pink (2008).

One issue relevant to age differences in WM measures is whether the structure is similar at different ages. Studies by Park et al. (2002) and Hale et al. (2011) found similar patterns of interrelations of WM measures at different ages. Johnson, Logie, and Brockmole (2010) also found a strong common WM factor at all ages, although there was also evidence of age differences in the residual variances in some measures. No formal comparisons were conducted on the data from Study 2 in Salthouse, Pink, and Tucker-Drob (2008), but inspection of the standardized coefficients among the WM measures in Table 14.1 reveals that the pattern was similar in three different age groups, with very strong relations of the WM construct with a Gf construct in each group, suggesting qualitatively similar WM constructs at each age.

It is clear from the results summarized in Table 14.1 that there are moderate correlations among different measures postulated to assess WM. Although these results are consistent with the assumption that the measures represent a common construct or dimension of individual differences, that information is only relevant to the convergent validity of a construct, and information about discriminant validity is also needed to establish that the construct is distinct. That is, in addition to determining that the measures presumed to represent the same construct are moderately correlated with one another, it is also important to determine if they have weaker correlations with measures assumed to represent different constructs because otherwise the constructs may not be truly distinct, and they could reflect the same underlying dimension of individual differences.

External relations

External relations refer to relations of WM measures with other cognitive abilities, either in the role of a mediator of the cross-sectional age-cognition relations, or in other types of correlational analyses. Early studies in which WM was examined as a mediator of the age differences in other cognitive tasks were reviewed by Salthouse (1990). Many of the studies published at that time had a number of limitations, such as the use of a single variable as a mediator, which includes task-specific influences

TABLE 14.1 Standardized coefficients for Gf and WM relations with a hierarchical WM model in three age groups

			Age group		
			18–39	*40–59*	*60–98*
Study 1, N = 708					
WM	→	Storage	.70	.93	.73
	→	Processing	1.02	.92	.79
Storage	→	OSpan storage	.56	.54	.66
	→	SymSpan storage	.80	.64	.75
Processing	→	OSpan processing	.43	.44	.62
	→	SymSpan processing	.51	.57	.57
WM	← →	Gf	.90	.94	1.03
Fit statistics					
	CFI		.95	.95	.97
	RMSEA		.08	.08	.06

Source: Data from Salthouse, Pink and Tucker-Drob (2008)

and measurement error in addition to the construct of interest, and consideration of only one mediator at a time, which means that the mediator absorbs all of the variance that it shares with other potential mediators in addition to any unique variance it might have. Furthermore, the sample sizes in most of the early studies were often rather small, which resulted in low power and imprecise estimates of the relations. Finally, few of the studies considered alternative models of the relations among the measures to evaluate the plausibility of different patterns of influence (cf. Salthouse, 2011a). Despite these limitations, a sizable reduction in the cross-sectional relation of age to the measure of cognitive performance when the variation in the WM measure was controlled was found in every study conducted in my lab (e.g. Salthouse et al., 1989; Salthouse, 1991; Salthouse, 1992b; Salthouse & Kersten 1993).

The focus in more recent studies in my laboratory has been on identifying the cognitive abilities involved in WM tasks, and investigating whether the WM–ability relations were similar at different ages. The analytical approach has been termed contextual analysis because the target variables, in this case measures assumed to assess WM, are analyzed in the context of other cognitive abilities.

A schematic illustration of the contextual analysis approach is portrayed in Figure 14.4. The bottom portion of the figure illustrates that the target variables in this type of analysis can be single variables, first-order latent constructs, or second-order latent constructs. Although not included in the figure, each of four abilities was represented by three to six measures from separate cognitive tests, and thus the assessment of the constructs was not only relatively broad, but had minimal measurement error. The portion of the model in which the cognitive abilities and age are simultaneous predictors of the target variable is

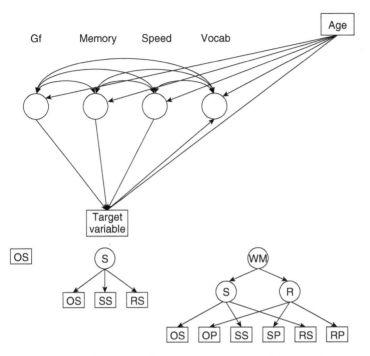

FIGURE 14.4 Schematic illustration of contextual analysis model (see main text for details)

essentially equivalent to multiple regression, and therefore the coefficients for these paths indicate the unique influences of each predictor when influences of other predictors are controlled. Advantages of contextual analyses over other types of analyses are better representation of the cognitive abilities by relying on latent constructs instead of single variables, and information about the unique influences of each predictor because the predictors are considered simultaneously rather than separately.

Results of contextual analyses on a variety of different WM measures, including *n*-back, backwards digit span, complex span, and updating, were reported in Salthouse (2005), Salthouse, Atkinson, and Berish (2003) and Salthouse, Pink, and Tucker-Drob (2008). As in many reports by other researchers (e.g. Ackerman, Beier, & Boyle, 2005; Colom et al., 2005), the analyses revealed strong relations of individual WM measures with a reasoning or fluid ability (Gf) construct.

Contextual analysis results with the Salthouse, Pink, and Tucker-Drob (2008) data are reported in Table 14.2. The results with individual variables were reported in the original article, but those with latent constructs representing storage and processing, and with a hierarchical WM construct, have not been published before. Two results of the contextual analyses summarized in Table 14.2 are particularly noteworthy. First, none of the unique age relations was significant when considering influences on the reference cognitive abilities. These findings suggest

TABLE 14.2 Contextual analysis results with the model in Figure 14.4 applied to data from Table 14.1

	Age			Cognitive Ability		
	Total	Unique	Gf	Mem	Speed	Voc
Study 1, N = 708						
Single variables						
Operation span storage	−.33★	.03	.40★	.07	.20★	.03
Operation span processing	−.23★	−.08	.37★	.11	−.04	.19★
Symmetry span storage	−.50★	−.10	.71★	−.05	.01	−.13★
Symmetry span processing	−.21★	.01	.69★	−.08	−.15	.06
Latent constructs						
Storage	−.49★	−.09	.77★	−.03	.10	−.12
Processing	−.26★	−.07	.98★	−.02	−.26★	.16
Hierarchical WM	−.59★	−.09	.97★	−.02	−.02	−.04
Study 2, N = 213						
Single variables						
Operation span storage	−.32★	−.01	.57★	.14	−.07	−.06
Operation span processing	−.18★	.20	.74★	.02	−.06	−.14
Symmetry span storage	−.60★	−.11	.65★	−.04	.14	−.27★
Symmetry span processing	−.18★	−.03	.57★	.13	−.25	.05
Reading span storage	−.22★	−.12	.40★	.05	−.03	.21
Reading span processing	−.05	−.22	−.05	.25	−.10	.45★
Keeping track	−.15★	.08	.55★	.15	−.20	−.09
Running memory letters	−.17★	.24	.78★	−.03	.02	−.12
Running memory positions	−.35★	.15	.81★	.04	.03	−.19
Latent constructs						
Storage	−.50★	−.09	.69★	.03	.01	−.12
Processing	−.28★	.16	.82★	.22	−.17	.01
Hierarchical WM	−.56★	−.01	1.10★	.15	−.17	−.10
Updating	−.41★	.27	1.09★	.06	.03	−.16

Source: Data from Salthouse, Pink and Tucker-Drob (2008)

Note

★ $p<.01$. The signs have been reversed for the processing measures based on errors such that higher scores with all variables represent better performance.

that all of the age-related influences on the WM variables or constructs were shared with age-related influences on other cognitive abilities. In other words, these results imply that, if people were equated on the levels of these cognitive abilities, little or no cross-sectional age differences would be expected on the WM measures.

The second noteworthy finding in Table 14.2 is that the Gf relations were stronger with processing constructs than with storage constructs, and when both types of measures were included in a hierarchical model of WM. An implication of these results is that the relations of complex span measures to Gf may be underestimated when only storage measures are used to assess WM.

It is clear from the results just discussed, and from similar results in many studies from other laboratories, that the WM and Gf constructs are strongly related to one another. An important question therefore concerns the nature of that relation. In particular, is WM the critical constituent of Gf, and possibly of age differences in many different cognitive tasks, or is WM merely another aspect of a broader Gf construct? Because it is not easy to distinguish these possibilities on the basis of behavioral observations at a single point in time, positions on this issue have primarily been based on theoretical arguments rather than empirical data.

Although not definitive, one type of empirical information relevant to this issue can be derived from comparisons of the unique prediction of WM and Gf on other cognitive measures. The logic of this asymmetric prediction procedure is schematically represented in Figure 14.5. Panel A indicates that the WM and Gf constructs have been found to be correlated with each other, and Panel B indicates that each construct has been found to be correlated with other cognitive variables, represented as the target variable in the figure. The most interesting information concerns the three proportions of variance in a target variable that can be identified when two constructs are used as simultaneous predictors, as illustrated in Panel C.

The rationale underlying the procedure is as follows. If the WM and Gf constructs represent essentially the same dimension of individual differences, then most of the

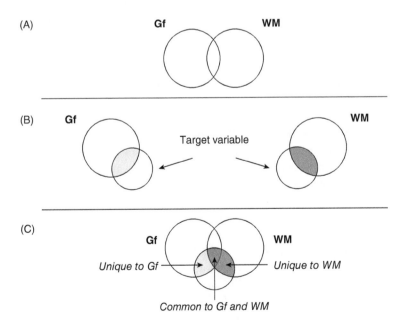

FIGURE 14.5 Schematic illustration of the logic underlying the asymmetric prediction procedure to identify unique influences of Gf and WM

variance in the target variable should be shared across the two predictors, with little that is unique to either predictor. Another possible outcome is that the constructs might each have some unique prediction, perhaps with proportions in the same ratio as the simple correlations of the constructs with the target variable because level of reliability might impose similar constraints on the total and unique influences. What might be the most interesting outcome would be if one construct dominates the prediction of the target variable, with much greater unique influences than those associated with the other construct.

That is, an asymmetric pattern such as this would be informative in indicating which construct had the greater overlap with, and possibly was more central to, the target variable.

The asymmetric prediction method was recently applied by Salthouse (2011b), with scores on the connections variant of the trail-making test serving as the target variable. The major finding was an asymmetric pattern, with no unique prediction of WM on the connections variables when variance in the Gf construct was controlled, but significant unique prediction of Gf when the variance in the WM construct was controlled.

In order to explore the generalizability of this asymmetric pattern, different combinations of variables from Study 2 in Salthouse, Pink, and Tucker-Drob (2008) were examined. Four variables were hypothesized to reflect Gf, but they involved different types of stimulus material and processing operations than the variables used to define the Gf construct. Five updating measures were examined, two involving verbal information (keeping track and running memory letters), and three involving visual-spatial information (color counters, matrix monitoring, and running memory positions).

Because simultaneous prediction results could vary according to the particular manner in which the Gf and WM constructs were operationalized, the analyses were repeated with different operationalizations of the constructs. One analysis was conducted with the most comprehensive assessment of the constructs, consisting of six Gf measures (i.e. Raven's, Shipley, letter sets, spatial relations, paper folding, and form boards), and six WM measures (i.e. both storage and processing measures from three complex span tasks). The second analysis was conducted with a narrower Gf construct based on only Raven's, Shipley, and letter sets tests, and a narrower WM construct based on only storage measures from the three complex span tasks.

Results of these asymmetric prediction analyses are presented in Table 14.3. Inspection of the entries in the table reveals that the results were very similar with the broad and narrow assessments of the Gf and WM constructs, which suggests that the results of simultaneous prediction analyses are not specific to a particular method of operationalizing the relevant constructs. The most important finding was that for most of the target variables the only significant unique influences were with the Gf construct. This might have been expected for the new Gf variables, but it was surprising to find that this was also true for many of the variables selected

TABLE 14.3 Simultaneous prediction of new Gf variables from Gf and WM constructs based on the model in panel C of Figure 14.5

Target Variable Model	Total	Gf	Unique	Total	WM	Unique
Analysis synthesis Broad Gf and WM	.68★		.73★	.48★		−.06
Narrow Gf and WM	.69★		.75★	.42★		−.09
Mystery codes						
Broad Gf and WM	.79★		.74★	.63★		.07
Narrow Gf and WM	.77★		.67★	.60★		.13
Logical steps						
Broad Gf and WM	.78★		.83★	.57★		−.06
Narrow Gf and WM	.81★		.89★	.50★		−.12
Concept formation						
Broad Gf and WM	.48★		.46★	.37★		.03
Narrow Gf and WM	.47★		.42★	.35★		.07
Keeping track						
Broad Gf and WM	.49★		.54★	.34★		−.06
Narrow Gf and WM	.46★		.43★	.32★		.03
Color counters						
Broad Gf and WM	.62★		.34★	.61★		.36★
Narrow Gf and WM	.64★		.44★	.58★		.28★
Matrix monitoring						
Broad Gf and WM	.60★		.77★	.34★		−.22
Narrow Gf and WM	.59★		.71★	.30★		−.18
Running memory letters Broad Gf and WM	.54★		.27	.54★		.35★
Narrow Gf and WM	.57★		.39★	.52★		.25
Running memory positions Broad Gf and WM	.67★		.70★	.50★		−.03
Narrow Gf and WM	.67★		.67★	.46★		−.00

Note

★ $p<.01$. Values in the "total" columns are simple correlations and values in the "unique" columns are β coefficients obtained in a regression equation with both Gf and WM as simultaneous predictors. Variables used in the Broad Gf and Wm assessments included those in the narrow assessments plus spatial relations, form boards, and paper folding in Gf, and processing measures from operation span, symmetry span, and reading span. Variables used in the narrow Gf and WM assessments were Raven's, Shipley abstraction, and letter sets for Gf and storage measures from operation span, symmetry span, and reading span.

to represent the updating aspect of WM (with the exception of the color counters and running memory letters tasks). Because the pattern of results was very similar across narrow and broad operationalizations of each construct, it is not the case that Gf is simply a more amorphous, or less coherent, construct than WM. Instead these results suggest that Gf may represent a superordinate or broader dimension of individual differences than WM, and that it encompasses the WM construct as well as a variety of other types of controlled processing.

Conclusion

Strong relations of age have been found with many measures hypothesized to reflect WM, and the WM measures have frequently been found to have moderate to strong correlations with a variety of cognitive measures. This combination of results is consistent with the proposal that decline in WM functioning contributes to age-related cognitive differences. However, the conclusion must still be considered tentative because of questions about the construct validity of WM, and particularly if and how the WM construct is distinct from other constructs such as fluid ability (Gf). Rather than merely assuming that WM is the core of cognition, or the driving force underlying age-related differences in cognitive functioning, the nature of the relations of WM to other constructs needs to be systematically investigated in adults of different ages.

Because results are most convincing when they are obtained with strong methods, several suggestions can be offered to improve future research on relations of aging and WM from an individual differences perspective. First, it is desirable to rely on multivariate assessment of all relevant constructs, and to conduct analyses on latent constructs rather than single observed variables to minimize measurement error (and maximize reliability) and obtain a broader representation of the constructs. It is widely acknowledged that no single measure is a pure reflection of a theoretical construct or process, but it may be possible to converge on a good approximation of the construct by aggregating across multiple measures. This is a different approach to the "process purity" problem than reliance on methods designed to isolate the critical process, but results obtained with a broader construct based on variance shared across different cognitive measures may be more generalizable than those based on a single measure.

Second, moderately large samples, involving hundreds of participants, should be employed because many of the individual difference analyses are based on correlations, and the confidence interval around a correlation coefficient depends on sample size. Third, the research questions should be investigated with theoretically relevant models and analyses, and not exclusively with simple correlations. And finally, future research should examine possible moderators of WM relations. Much of the currently available research suggests that WM has similar meaning and relations with other aspects of cognitive functioning at all ages, but much more information about the potential moderating effects of age on WM-cognition relations is needed before the role of WM in age-related differences in cognition can be considered to be understood.

Note

* This chapter originally appeared in the edited volume, *Working Memory and Ageing*.

References

Ackerman, P. L., Beier, M. E. & Boyle, M. O. (2005). Working memory and intelligence: The same or different constructs? *Psychological Bulletin, 131*, 30–60.

Babcock, R. L. & Salthouse, T. A. (1990). Effects of increased processing demands on age differences in working memory. *Psychology and Aging, 5*, 421–428.

Case, R., Kurland, D. M. & Goldberg, J. (1982). Operational efficiency and the growth of short-term memory span. *Journal of Experimental Child Psychology, 33*, 386–404.

Colom, R., Abad, F. J., Rebollo, I. & Shih, P. C. (2005). Memory span and general intelligence: A latent-variable approach. *Intelligence, 33*, 623–642.

Conway, A. R. A., Kane, M. J., Bunting, M. F., Hambrick, D. Z., Wilhelm, O. & Engle, R. W. (2005). Working memory span tasks: A methodological review and user's guide. *Psychonomic Bulletin and Review, 12*, 769–786.

Daneman, M. & Carpenter, P. A. (1980). Individual differences in working memory and reading. *Journal of Verbal Learning and Verbal Behavior, 19*, 450–466.

de Frias, C. M., Dixon, R. A. & Strauss, E. (2009). Characterizing executive functioning in older special populations: From cognitively elite to cognitively impaired. *Neuropsychology, 23*, 778–791.

Duff, S. C. & Logie, R. H. (2001). Processing and storage in working memory span. *Quarterly Journal of Experimental Psychology, 54A*, 31–48.

Hale, S., Rose, N. S., Myerson, J., Strube, M. J., Sommers, M., Tye-Murray, N. & Spehar, B. (2011). The structure of working memory abilities across the adult life span. *Psychology and Aging, 26*, 92–110.

Johnson, W., Logie, R. H., Brockmole, J. R. (2010). Working memory tasks differ in factor structure across age cohorts: Implications for differentiation. *Intelligence, 38*, 513–528.

Kirchner, W. K. (1958). Age differences in short-term retention of rapidly changing information. *Journal of Experimental Psychology, 55*, 352–358.

McCabe, D. P., Roediger, H. L., McDaniel, M. A., Balota, D. A. & Hambrick, D. Z. (2010). The relationship between working memory capacity and executive functioning: Evidence for a common executive attention construct. *Neuropsychology, 24*, 222–243.

Park, D. C., Lautenschlager, G., Hedden, T., Davidson, N. S., Smith, A. D. & Smith, P. K. (2002). Models of visuospatial and verbal memory across the adult life span. *Psychology and Aging, 17*, 299–320.

Pollack, I., Johnson, L. B. & Knaff, P. R. (1959). Running memory span. *Journal of Experimental Psychology, 57*, 137–146.

Salthouse, T. A. (1987). Adult age differences in integrative spatial ability. *Psychology and Aging, 2*, 254–260.

Salthouse, T. A. (1988). The role of processing resources in cognitive aging. In M. L. Howe & C. J. Brainerd (Eds.), *Cognitive Development in Adulthood*. New York: Springer-Verlag.

Salthouse, T. A. (1990). Working memory as a processing resource in cognitive aging. *Developmental Review, 10*, 101–124.

Salthouse, T. A. (1991). Mediation of adult age differences in cognition by reductions in working memory and speed of processing. *Psychological Science, 2*, 179–183.

Salthouse, T. A. (1992a). Why do adult age differences increase with task complexity? *Developmental Psychology, 28*, 905–918.

Salthouse, T. A. (1992b). Working memory mediation of adult age differences in integrative reasoning. *Memory and Cognition, 20*, 413–423.

Salthouse, T. A. (1992c). Influence of processing speed on adult age differences in working memory. *Acta Psychologica, 79*, 155–170.

Salthouse, T. A. (1993). Influence of working memory on adult age differences in matrix reasoning. *British Journal of Psychology, 84*, 171–199.

Salthouse, T. A. (1994). The aging of working memory. *Neuropsychology, 8*, 535–543.

Salthouse, T. A. (1995). Influence of processing speed on adult age differences in learning. *Swiss Journal of Psychology, 54*, 102–112.

Salthouse, T. A. (2005). Relations between cognitive abilities and measures of executive functioning. *Neuropsychology, 19*, 532–545.

Salthouse, T. A. (2011a). Neuroanatomical substrates of age-related cognitive decline. *Psychological Bulletin, 137,* 753–784.

Salthouse, T. A. (2011b). What cognitive abilities are involved in trail-making performance? *Intelligence, 39,* 222–232.

Salthouse, T. A. & Babcock, R. L. (1991). Decomposing adult age differences in working memory. *Developmental Psychology, 27,* 763–776.

Salthouse, T. A. & Kersten, A. W. (1993). Decomposing adult age differences in symbol arithmetic. *Memory and Cognition, 21,* 699–710.

Salthouse, T. A. & Meinz, E. J. (1995). Aging, inhibition, working memory, and speed. *Journal of Gerontology: Psychological Sciences, 50B,* P297–P306.

Salthouse, T. A. & Mitchell, D. R. D. (1989). Structural and operational capacities in integrative spatial ability. *Psychology and Aging, 4,* 18–25.

Salthouse, T. A. & Pink, J. E. (2008). Why is working memory related to fluid intelligence? *Psychonomic Bulletin and Review, 15,* 364–371.

Salthouse, T. A. & Prill, K. A. (1987). Inferences about age impairments in inferential reasoning. *Psychology and Aging, 2,* 43–51.

Salthouse, T. A. & Skovronek, E. (1992). Within-context assessment of age differences in working memory. *Journal of Gerontology: Psychological Sciences, 47,* 110–120.

Salthouse, T. A. & Tucker-Drob, E. (2008). Aging, cognitive abilities, and working memory. Unpublished manuscript.

Salthouse, T. A., Atkinson, T. M. & Berish, D. E. (2003). Executive functioning as a potential mediator of age-related cognitive decline in normal adults. *Journal of Experimental Psychology: General, 132,* 566–594.

Salthouse, T. A., Babcock, R. L. & Shaw, R. J. (1991). Effects of adult age on structural and operational capacities in working memory. *Psychology and Aging, 6,* 118–127.

Salthouse, T. A., Mitchell, D. R. D. & Palmon, R. (1989a). Memory and age differences in spatial manipulation ability. *Psychology and Aging, 4,* 480–486.

Salthouse, T. A., Mitchell, D. R. D., Skovronek, E. & Babcock, R. L. (1989b). Effects of adult age and working memory on reasoning and spatial abilities. *Journal of Experimental Psychology: Learning, Memory, and Cognition, 15,* 507–516

Salthouse, T. A., Pink, J. E. & Tucker-Drob, E. M. (2008). Contextual analysis of fluid intelligence. *Intelligence, 36,* 464–486.

Siedlecki, K. L., Salthouse, T. A. & Berish, D. E. (2005). Is there anything special about the aging of source memory? *Psychology and Aging, 20,* 19–32.

Talland, G. A. (1968). Age and the span of immediate recall. In G. A. Talland (Ed.), *Human Aging and Behavior* (pp. 93–129). New York: Academic Press.

Unsworth, N., Redick, T. S., Heitz, R. P., Broadway, J. M. & Engle, R. W. (2009). Complex working memory span tasks and higher-order cognition: A latent-variable analysis of the relationship between processing and storage. *Memory, 17,* 635–654.

Waters, G. S. & Caplan, D. (1996). The measurement of verbal working memory capacity and its relation to reading comprehension. *Quarterly Journal of Experimental Psychology, 49A,* 51–79.

Waters, G. S. & Caplan, D. (2003). The reliability and stability of verbal working memory measures. *Behavior Research Methods, Instruments, and Computers, 35,* 550–564.

Welford, A. T. (1958). *Ageing and human skill.* New York: Oxford University Press.

Yntema, D. B. & Trask, F. P. (1963). Recall as a search process. *Journal of Verbal Learning and Verbal Behavior, 2,* 65–74.

15

WORKING MEMORY TRAINING IN LATE ADULTHOOD

A behavioral and brain perspective*

Anna Stigsdotter Neely and Lars Nyberg

A wealth of evidence has shown that aging is associated with decline in various cognitive abilities. For decades, cognitive aging research has focused on explaining age-related cognitive decline with less emphasis on how to support the aging mind and brain. Recently, this has changed noticeably where issues related to how cognitive functions can be successfully maintained and improved throughout the adult life span have entertained increased interest (see Hertzog et al., 2009, for a comprehensive review). This is certainly welcomed from both a theoretical and a practical standpoint. In the face of an aging population the motivation has grown to find methods to support cognitive health, vital for coping with the challenges of everyday life. This chapter will provide an overview of the efforts that have been undertaken to ameliorate decline in cognitive functions in healthy older adults through practice and training with a particular focus on working memory and its processes. Working memory has long been viewed as a memory system not amendable in any significant way by training or practice. However, recent studies are questioning this trait-like view of working memory by showing that training can improve working memory performance in ways that may suggest more general alterations in working memory capacity (Klingberg, 2010). This field is rapidly developing and the results to date are promising but also mixed. We will begin this review by discussing the multitude of training paradigms that have been used to address working memory and related processes as well as the theoretical motivations behind them. This is followed by findings from neuroimaging studies concerning the neural underpinnings of working memory plasticity and age-related differences thereof. The success of working memory training lies in its ability to give rise to generalized gains that are maintained over time: the question is whether it does.

Early cognitive training studies

It has not been until quite recently that more focused attempts to train working memory have become the very topic of cognitive training for both young and old adults. In a well-cited review article by Verhaeghen, Marcoen, and Goossens (1992) it was shown that the majority of cognitive training studies undertaken up to that point focused predominately on episodic memory and fluid intelligence.

The motivation in many of these studies was to teach strategies such as the method of loci to support encoding and retrieval of words or reasoning skills to help solve problems (Stigsdotter Neely & Bäckman, 1993; Verhaeghen, 2000). This line of work has generally demonstrated that older adults show substantial and long-lasting improvements in the tasks trained, but more limited gain in tasks not trained (Lustig et al., 2009; Rebok, Carlson & Langbaum, 2007). Also, when training gains have been compared to those of young adults, older adults show less gain after training, suggesting that age differences are magnified not reduced after training. Overall, these studies have shown that learning after strategy training in old age is possible but rather task-specific in nature.

The lack of more generalized gain after strategy-based training programs has sparked an interest in issues related to the scope and nature of transfer effects (Lövdén et al., 2010). Is it so that cognitive training mainly fosters acquisition of skills beneficial to the specific tasks used in training with limited applicability outside that context (Owen et al., 2010), as results from strategy-training studies may imply? Or can training also affect more general cognitive mechanisms and capacities targeted in training? If so, the training may stand a greater chance to affect a wider range of tasks. To find ways to alter more fundamental ability levels through training has been the driving force behind the recent interest in working memory training and more process-oriented training approaches to cognition in old age.

As the volume *Working Memory and Ageing* attests, working memory can be conceptualized in several ways but is commonly referred to as a limited multicomponent memory system that actively holds and manipulates information over brief periods of time (Baddeley & Hitch, 1974; Miyake & Shah, 1999). The centrality of working memory to human cognition and behavior has been illustrated extensively (Unsworth, Heitz, & Engle, 2005). Working memory capacity as measured by complex span tasks has been found to correlate with higher order cognition such as episodic memory, reading comprehension, multi-tasking, reasoning, and measures of fluid intelligence to name but a few (Unsworth & Engle, 2007). Moreover, working memory performance is sensitive to many conditions affecting the brain, such as Alzheimer's and Parkinson's disease, but is also negatively affected by normal aging (Gabrieli et al., 1996; Kempler et al., 1998; McCabe et al., 2010). As a matter of fact, one prominent theory of cognitive aging suggested that decline in working memory capacity underlies much of the observed negative relationship between age and cognitive performance (Hasher, Lustig, & Zacks, 2007). Hence, a person's working memory capacity is essential for successfully being able to carry out a wide variety of cognitive tasks important for everyday life. Given the importance of working memory for cognition and the aging mind it is surprising that working memory plasticity (here defined as positive change in performance as a function of training) has not until recently enjoyed more scientific interest.

We will present the behavioral studies that have been conducted with older adults to address whether prolonged practice and training of working memory leads to improved, maintained, and widespread effects on trained and untrained tasks.

Working memory intervention studies: Behavioral results

As will be evident from this review, working memory performance has been trained in many different ways. There are most likely many reasons for this, one being that researchers in this field have used different conceptualizations of working memory as well as holding different views on what specific processes need to be addressed in old age. As mentioned above, perhaps one of the most influential models of the working memory system was proposed by Baddeley and Hitch in 1974. The model comprises three components for brief storage and maintenance of verbal, visuo-spatial and integrated episodic information (the phonological loop, the visuo-spatial sketchpad, and the episodic buffer) as well as a domain-general component (the central executive) responsible for coordinating use of the storage systems and for controlling attention. This model has inspired many of the working memory training studies that will be reviewed here and will help classify the reviewed training protocols according to their main focus: is the purpose of the training to expand the capacity to store and maintain information, or is the focus to improve the central executive abilities for controlled attention and the coordination of information in the storage systems, or are the protocols addressing both aspects of working memory function?

The main focus for this review is to evaluate whether working memory training gives rise to improvements in the ability level and not only in the particular task used in training. In other words, the training should foster skilled performance outside the immediate context of the training. In order to be able to draw such a conclusion the benefits of the training should be assessed on three dimensions. First, the magnitude of task-specific gains should be addressed, that is, did the training lead to improvements in the trained tasks? Second, the generalizability or transfer of positive gains to tasks not trained needs to be investigated. The battery of transfer tests should optimally tap both near- and far-transfer tests, where near-transfer tests commonly refer to tasks measuring the ability of interest (here working memory and its processes) and far-transfer tests tap other ability domains related to working memory such as fluid intelligence or everyday life skills. And finally, the durability or maintenance of positive task-specific as well as transfer effects over time should be assessed to evaluate whether there have been more fundamental effects on the cognitive system. Furthermore, to protect against several sources of potential confounds such as test-retest and Hawthorne effects, a pretest-training-posttest design with random assignment of participants to a treatment group and to one or more control groups is recommended in order to minimize alternative explanations. Hence working memory intervention studies designed accordingly provide a controlled way to assess the nature of cognitive training effects.

Training executive cognitive control processes: Dual-tasking

As pronounced age differences have commonly been observed in various processes related to the central executive, several training paradigms have specifically addressed one or more of these cognitive control abilities such as dual-tasking, updating, inhibition, and shifting. As has been made clear since the original Baddeley and Hitch (1974) proposal, the central executive is not a unitary system and can be subdivided into several component processes. Miyake and colleagues (2000) provided evidence for a division of the central executive into three separate but moderately correlated processes, namely updating, shifting and inhibition. This model has influenced some of the training studies below.

In the mid-1990s Kramer and colleagues started off a series of studies that examined the effects of dual-task training in young and old adults (Kramer, Larish, & Strayer, 1995; Kramer et al., 1999). A number of research questions have been addressed in this research and here we will only focus on the issues related to training gains, maintenance, and transfer in old and young adults.

The dual-task training protocol used in this research has varied slightly between studies but generally consists of two tasks performed concurrently such as a tracing task combined with an alphabet-arithmetic task or letter discrimination combined with tone discrimination (Bherer et al., 2005, 2006, 2008; Kramer, Larish, & Strayer, 1995). Several of their studies have assessed the impact of variable-priority strategy training in which the participants were to vary their response priorities between the two tasks by prioritizing one task over the other as compared to a fixed-priority strategy where both tasks were to be equally emphasized. The variable-priority strategy is thought to foster different ways to perform a complex task, which may be beneficial for learning and transfer of skill (see also Schmidt & Bjork, 1992). Also, adaptive individual feedback on performance is an integral part of their protocol. The number of training sessions provided has usually been around five one-hour sessions. The results from these studies have convincingly shown that both young and old adults can improve substantially in the trained dual-task, measured as lower task-set costs and dual-task costs after training. The results are, however, mixed concerning the benefits of the variable-priority strategy over the fixed-priority instruction, with some showing clear benefits (Kramer, Larish & Strayer, 1995) and others not (Bherer et al., 2005). A possibility that has been suggested to resolve the discrepant findings may be that different dual tasks have been used in these studies where the variable-priority strategy seems more beneficial when applied to more complex dual tasks. Long-term effects have been addressed in two studies showing maintenance for one and two months respectively following training, indicating that the effects show some stability and do not wear off immediately (Bherer et al., 2005; Kramer et al., 1999). The transfer of positive gains to tasks not trained has usually been addressed by including two near-transfer dual tasks, where results have consistently shown positive effects. Far transfer effects have been addressed to a lesser extent—although, in two recent studies on older adults the effects of dual-task training on simulated driving performance as well as on motoric performance were examined. In both studies positive effects of dual-task training were demonstrated, suggesting that far transfer is possible in task domains requiring the coordination of multiple sub-skills (Li et al., 2010; Cassavaugh & Kramer, 2009). But no far transfer to mental speed was seen in a study by MacKay-Brandt (2011) using a dual-task training protocol similar those in the above studies. More studies are clearly needed to examine a broader range of transfer effects after dual-task training. Finally, age-related differences in dual-task training gains have been addressed in several studies most of which have shown parallel gains or an advantage for the older adults (Kramer, Larish, & Strayer, 1995; Bherer et al., 2006). This pattern of similar or a reduction of age differences as a function of training is at odds with much of strategy-training research, which more often yields a magnification of age differences following training (Verhaeghen & Marcoen, 1996).

In sum, dual-task training shows promise as a viable method to train one critical aspect of working memory, namely dual-tasking, by showing substantial immediate and near transfer effects in both young and old adults. However, the evidence is more limited concerning long-lasting and far-transfer effects. Maintenance has only been observed after a couple of months and transfer has only been addressed with a limited transfer battery. For example, no measures of working memory capacity have been included in these studies, making it hard to draw firm conclusions about whether working memory capacity in a more general sense has been improved. Hence strong conclusions about whether these effects indicate a more general improvement of working memory or dual-task ability, rather than just strengthen a stimulus-response relationship specific to the trained task, cannot be convincingly made and need further scientific attention.

Training in updating, shifting, and inhibition

Another line of research that in recent years has enjoyed increased interest is training that targets updating of information in working memory. Updating refers to the ability to monitor incoming information for relevance to the task in hand and when necessary updating old no longer relevant information with newer more relevant information. Previous research has implicated the importance of updating for learning (Collette & Van der Linden, 2002) and intelligence (Friedman et al., 2006).

A study by Jaeggi and colleagues (2008) with young adults has attracted a high degree of attention as it was one of the first studies reporting far transfer to a measure of intelligence after updating working memory training (see also Olesen, Westerberg, & Klingberg, 2004). In this study updating was trained in four groups receiving 8, 12, 17, or 19 sessions respectively using a dual n-back task. This task required participants to attend to a changing stream of information (here positions and numbers) and to decide if the items currently shown were the same as n-items ago. The results showed, in a dose-response manner, greater gains with more practice in the trained dual n-back task and in an untrained non-verbal reasoning task but not in a complex working memory task (Jaeggi et al., 2008). As far as we know these results have not been replicated nor has the stability of these effects across time been established. The study has also been criticized due to its unconventional way of administering the far transfer test (see Moody, 2009). The fact that no effects were seen in complex working memory task performance makes it hard to argue that the training has improved working memory capacity more broadly. Therefore the mechanism by which dual-updating training may enhance intelligence remains somewhat unclear. Nevertheless, the findings are encouraging and deserve further attention.

In two studies we have used a slightly different approach in training updating of working memory in both young and old adults (Dahlin et al., 2008a; Dahlin et al., 2008b). Our program provided training in four running span tasks where the task was to constantly update a stream of single items in order to be able to remember the four last presented items in correct order. Also a keep-track task was used where the participant had to associate a stream of words to categories and to be able to remember the most recently presented word associated with the categories. Fifteen sessions of adaptive practice over a five-week period were given. A large transfer battery was given, covering tasks tapping mental speed, short-term memory, working memory, inhibition, episodic memory, and intelligence. In contrast to the Jaeggi study, our findings (Dahlin et al., 2008a) were more limited for the young adults showing near-transfer to an untrained updating task (n-back) and far-transfer to an episodic memory task, where only the near-transfer effect was maintained 18 months later (Dahlin et al., 2008a). We have interpreted the finding of a maintained transfer effect to n-back to suggest that transfer is facilitated only when the trained task and the untrained transfer task overlap in terms of shared processes (e.g. updating) and may reflect an ability-specific effect for updating, which will be further discussed below in relation to brain data. Moreover, the older adults only showed improvement in the trained task that was maintained 18 months later. Hence no transfer effects were seen in the old. With regard to age-related differences in gain after training both young and old improved to a similar degree in the trained task. Despite equal gains, the performance level for the older adults was significantly below that of the young adults at post-test. This may suggest that not only the magnitude of gain but also the level of performance obtained after training may be one important aspect behind transfer.

Also a study by Li and colleagues (2008) has examined the effects of updating training with older and younger adults. Here 45 daily practice sessions of 15 minutes were given and a limited transfer battery of two untrained updating tasks as well as two complex working memory span tasks were administered. Also a follow-up assessment was made after three months. The program focused on a spatial n-back task with two levels of difficulty that was not adaptive to performance. In line with our study above, only near-transfer effects were seen to the two untrained updating tasks for both age groups. These effects were maintained three months later. Hence, no evidence for far-transfer effects were obtained for young or for old. Also, the older adults showed a pattern of equal and slightly greater gains as a function of training. This pattern, however, may be explained by a functional ceiling effect for the young adults.

In an ongoing study, we have addressed the question of whether a training program that taps the central executive more broadly by addressing three critical executive control processes—updating, inhibition, and shifting—would give rise to more broad transfer effects in both young and old adults (Sandberg et al., 2013).

Our assumption is that a training program focused on several critical cognitive control functions, and assumed to engage a common core of domain-general executive processes, may give rise to more generalized transfer effects. The experimental set-up was the same as in the Dahlin et al. (2008a) studies in which 15 sessions of training over a five-week period were given. The same transfer battery was also employed. Six different tasks were used in training that increased in difficulty. Two tasks were used to train updating, inhibition, and shifting respectively. The results showed pronounced gains in the trained tasks, where both the young and old gained equally across training. Also, near transfer was seen for both the young and old adults to non-trained updating and inhibition tasks. However, only the young adults showed transfer to two complex working memory tasks, suggesting greater transfer effects in the young. No far-transfer effects were seen to episodic memory or to intelligence. Maintenance effects have so far only been examined for the older adults and suggest stability of task-specific and near-transfer effects 18 months after completion of training. Our data suggest that when the training is focused on a wider range of process, here three instead of one executive process as in the Dahlin at al. study (2008a), more generalized improvements occur at least for the young adults. At the same time transfer was limited to the working memory domain and did not affect measures of intelligence, reflecting a highly selective effect.

A notable exception to the finding of limited transfer in old adults after executive process training has recently been shown in a study by Karbach and Kray (2009). In this study task-shifting was trained which taps the ability to flexibly switch between two simple tasks such as deciding whether a picture is a fruit or a vegetable (task A) or if it is small or large (task B). Four different training groups were compared to address potential benefits of self-instructions (e.g., verbalize the upcoming task vs not) and of variable training (one vs several tasks) in groups of children, and young and old adults (Karbach & Kray, 2009; see also Karbach, Mang, & Kray, 2010). The training was not adaptive in terms of difficulty and an active control group was used. A broad transfer battery was administered tapping shifting, inhibition, verbal and spatial working memory, and fluid intelligence. The findings yielded near-transfer to an untrained shifting-task, but more striking was the transfer to all far-transfer tasks and across all age groups and training conditions. This suggests that far-transfer was broad and similar for young and old and not related to type of training. One reason for the broad transfer effects offered by the authors was that the trained shifting task engaged a multitude of critical processes, such as goal maintenance, interference control, and task-set selection, as well as the ability to switch between tasks. This explanation is not easy to accept when contrasted with the above study by Sandberg et al., where shifting was trained in a similar fashion over 15 sessions and did not result in broad transfer effects. A replication of these findings is desirable to further cast light on what factors might drive the far-transfer effects.

In sum, the dominant finding from the studies presented above on executive process training in older adults was strong and long-lasting task-specific and near-transfer effects to the trained ability. Only one study (Karbach & Kray, 2009) showed broad far-transfer effects in older as well as younger adults after executive process training. Based on these data the evidence is not in favor of broad improvements after training in updating, shifting, or inhibition in older adults. As for dual-task training, gains across training were similar for both young and old adults in the above studies (Dahlin et al., 2008a; Li et al., 2008; Sandberg et al., 2013).

Training in maintenance and cognitive control: The complex working memory span task

Another task that has been used in the working memory training literature is the complex working memory span task introduced by Daneman and Carpenter (1980). In the original version the subjects had to read sentences while remembering the final words of all the sentences for later serial recall. Since then many versions of the complex working memory task have been developed but core features are that these tasks jointly tap storage and processing in working memory. Moreover this task has served as the foundation of many studies linking working memory capacity to complex cognition (e.g. Unsworth, Heitz, & Engle, 2005), making it an interesting task as a target for training.

In a study by Borella and colleagues (2010) they offered three sessions of training to a group of older adults in a categorization working memory span task. Here, the participants were presented with lists of words and had to tap their hand if the presented word belonged to the category of animals (processing) while trying to remember the last word presented in each list (storage). The training increased in difficulty and was adaptive to the performance of the subject. No feedback was provided. A contact control group was used, filling in questionnaires related to autobiographical memory and well-being. The test-battery included near- and far-transfer tests tapping mental speed, short-term memory, working memory, inhibition, and fluid intelligence. Follow-up assessment was carried out eight months after completion of training. The results were impressive, showing transfer effects to all tasks administered to assess short-term memory, working memory, inhibition, mental speed, and fluid intelligence. These effects were still present for fluid intelligence and mental speed eight months later. One factor raised by the authors as critical for obtaining the positive effects was, besides focusing on critical WM processes, that the training was variable and flexible (Borella et al., 2010).

A slightly different version of the complex span task was used in a recent study by Richmond and colleagues (2011). Here they provided 20 sessions of training in one verbal and one visuo-spatial complex span task to a group of older adults. The training was adaptive to the participant's performance level and feedback was provided. Also an active control group, engaged in solving trivia quizzes, was used. The results indicated performance gains in both trained complex span tasks and near transfer to a similar complex working memory span task (reading span). Far transfer was only seen in an episodic memory task where fewer repetitions of recalled items were made after training (Richmond et al., 2011). Moreover the results of the older trained group were also compared to younger adults who had been part of an earlier study receiving a very similar training protocol (see Chein & Morrison, 2010). In line with the above results, older adults performed at a lower level but the magnitude of gain as function of training was similar for young and old adults.

Finally, a study by Buschkuehl and colleagues (2008) used a training protocol with three tasks to train working memory—one simple span task and two complex span tasks. They also included two simple reaction time tasks mainly to make the training more variable and attractive. The participants were 80 years old and took part in 23 sessions. As for the above studies they used an active control group receiving light physical training. The results only showed a near-transfer effect to an untrained simple span task similar to the task used in training but no far-transfer effects to episodic memory. A one-year follow-up assessment did not reveal any maintenance effects. Hence the results indicate slim transfer effects with limited durability in older samples.

First of all, these studies enjoy several positive design characteristics by including active control groups, adaptive training protocols, and the use of more extensive transfer batteries to evaluate training effects. However, given that all three studies offered training in rather similar complex working memory span tasks in healthy older adults, the finding of impressive far-transfer effects after three practice sessions reported in the Borella et al. (2010) study is intriguing in relation to the more humble near-transfer effects seen after 20 sessions or more of training in the studies by Richmond et al. (2011) and Buschkuehl et al. (2008) respectively. As mentioned above, Borella et al. (2010) offered two tentative explanations for their positive far-transfer effects, namely that the training was challenging and variable and that the short time frame of the training phase had a facilitating effect on performance. However, the training protocols used in both the Richmond et al. (2011) and Buschkuehl et al. (2008) studies were also challenging and variable, in that several training tasks were used and the training was adaptive to the performance of the subjects. Hence training variability does not seem like a strong candidate for driving the effects. Also it is hard to reconcile that a few practice sessions should have a more facilitating effect on performance over several sessions (see Jaeggi et al., 2008). Clearly more research is needed on the factors important to foster far-transfer effects as well as the replication and extension of successful training protocols.

Conclusions: The behavioral training studies of working memory

The main question for this review was whether working memory training for healthy older adults produces generalized gains that are maintained over time. As evidenced by the review of the literature, the support for a broad generalized improvement is limited. The majority of studies show near-transfer to the same ability trained, reflecting a restricted view on transfer. This is very much in line with a study by Owen and colleagues (2010) where over 11,000 participants took part in an online training program focusing on several cognitive functions. The study showed that on average 25 sessions of online cognitive training distributed over a six-week period did not result in any transfer effects as compared to an active control group. Needless to say, this is an impressive demonstration of the lack of generalized improvements. Why this may be the case will be the topic of the next section.

However, two studies have been successful in obtaining broad generalization following working memory training in older adults (Borella et al., 2010; Karbach & Kray, 2009). What may account for these positive effects? Here, it is interesting to note that in both studies the training was short and limited to one task. Is it so that a brief and focused approach to training leads to greater gains? This seems highly unlikely since it runs contrary to many findings within the field, suggesting that both task-specific and transfer gains are more evident after longer training periods (see Jaeggi et al., 2008) and that more variable and complex training experiences tend to optimize transfer (see Schmidt & Bjork, 1992). The driving force behind these positive far-transfer effects remains unclear.

The relatively recent interest in working memory training in aging has resulted in a body of literature that is very diverse. Type of training, the number of sessions, the duration of sessions, and spacing of practice sessions provided are just a few of the many characteristics of training programs which have varied between studies— making it a challenge when reviewing the entire body of work to understand how these factors may contribute to positive training effects (see also Morrison & Chein, 2011; Shipstead, Redick, & Engle, 2010). Hopefully, however, the field has started to mature to a point where critical training characteristics can be more systematic- ally examined in order to find out how to best support the aging mind. Finally, it is interesting to note that most studies did not find age differences in the magnitude of training-related improvements in the trained tasks. This finding is at odds with much earlier research showing that training more often amplifies preexisting age differences in performance (Verhaeghen & Marcoen, 1996). One reason for similar age trajectories as a function of working memory training may be due to fewer demands on self-initiated processing, as most training tasks employed require very little strategy acquisition and application (Craik & Byrd, 1982).

Working memory plasticity: Brain imaging studies

To the best of our knowledge, the first functional brain imaging study of the neural correlates of cognitive training in adulthood and aging targeted the method of

LOCI mental imagery mnemonic (Nyberg et al., 2003). In keeping with previous behavioral studies (Baltes & Kliegl, 1992), age differences in memory performance were found to be magnified after as compared to before the intervention. Analyses of functional brain activity patterns, based on positron emission tomography (PET) recordings, revealed that one basis for the age-related difference implicated putative task-specific processes such as creating visual images and binding of cue-target information. These processes were related to occipito-temporal cortex and medial-temporal lobe regions, and significant age differences were observed in these regions (Nyberg et al., 2003; see also Jones et al., 2006). A second basis for the observed age differences and their magnification following training was found to be age-related processing deficits (e.g. executive), which affected the older adults' ability to effectively make use of the LOCI mnemonic (Nyberg et al., 2003; see also Jones et al., 2006). The apparent age-related processing deficit was linked to diminished frontal brain activity.

Thus, age-related differences in fronto-parietal brain activity, and associated executive processes, seem to underlie constraints in benefitting from mnemonic support. In a subsequent project, we therefore targeted training of executive processes (cf. section above, Dahlin et al., 2008a). The basic idea was that, if we could strengthen executive processes and related fronto-parietal circuits, then older adults might show similar training-related gains to those of younger adults. A second motivation behind targeting general executive processes was to test the hypothesis that training of executive functions might lead to stronger and potentially broader transfer effects than more domain-specific interventions such as the method of LOCI. Numerous brain-imaging studies converge to show that a common characteristic of many cognitive tasks is that they engage fronto-parietal networks (for reviews, see Cabeza & Nyberg, 2000; Naghavi & Nyberg, 2005). At least in part, this commonality may reflect shared executive processes (Collette et al, 2006; Marklund et al., 2007). Hence, by strengthening executive processes and associated fronto-parietal networks by a certain type of cognitive training program, transfer to non-trained tasks that also rely on fronto-parietal regions might be expected (cf. Klingberg et al., 2005). However, as was reviewed above, cognitive transfer effects are typically weak or non-existent (e.g. Owen et al., 2010; Lee et al., 2012), which apparently conflicts with the notion that training a specific executive task and associated fronto-parietal recruitment will benefit other executive (fronto-parietal) tasks. An alternative possibility, then, is that training affects much more specific processes and brain systems, which accounts for the general finding of limited transfer.

Figure 15.1A schematically outlines our experimental protocol for testing whether executive functions training might broadly enhance the performance of older adults and lead to transfer via fronto-parietal networks. We targeted *updating* of information in working memory, a process related to fronto-parietal cortical regions as well as the striatum (Collette et al., 2006; Marklund et al., 2007; O'Reilly, 2006). Before and after five weeks of updating training (Dahlin et al., 2008b), functional magnetic resonance imaging (fMRI) was used to assess training-related changes in functional brain activity. Three different tasks were scanned: a letter-memory updating task which served as the criterion task and two transfer tasks: an n-back working memory task and a Stroop inhibition task. All three tasks were expected to engage executive control processes and fronto-parietal circuits (Collette et al., 2006; Miyake et al., 2000), and our fMRI findings supported this prediction (Figure 15.1B). The letter-memory task and the n-back task were expected to involve updating and engage the striatum (Miyake et al., 2000; O'Reilly, 2006), whereas the Stroop inhibition task was not, and the fMRI results confirmed this prediction (Figure 15.1B). Thus, to the degree that transfer was based on a shared fronto-parietal network, we would expect to find transfer from letter memory to both n-back and Stroop, whereas if transfer instead was based on the striatal updating network we would expect transfer to n-back only. The findings showed a highly selective behavioral transfer effect to n-back along with a training-related modulation of the fMRI signal in the striatum. These results confirm the hypothesis that a prerequisite for transfer is that the transfer task taxes the same basic process as supported by the intervention and related brain areas (Jonides, 2004; Thorndike & Woodworth, 1901)—in the present case updating and basal ganglia circuits.

An additional goal of the experiment was to examine whether executive processing training would lead to similar training-related gains for older as for younger adults. The results were positive by showing parallel gains for both age groups, i.e. there was no magnification of age differences. However, the older adults' level of performance on the letter-memory criterion task after five weeks of training was similar to the level reached by younger adults after two weeks. Moreover, the older adults did not show a significant transfer effect to the n-back task. The age-related constraints on learning and transfer after updating training were related to age-related changes in the striatum, thereby providing further support for a critical role of this brain region for updating.

Theoretical and computational models of the role of striatum in updating of information in working memory indicate that dopaminergic neurotransmission is a key factor (Drustewitz, 2006; O'Reilly, 2006). A recent PET study provided empirical support for this prediction (Bäckman et al., 2011). PET was used to assess dopamine D2 binding potential before and after five weeks of updating training, and an extensive neuropsychological battery was administered before and after the training period (cf. the fMRI protocol above). The behavioral results replicated the findings from the fMRI study by showing highly selective transfer to an n-back task only. The PET recordings were done during a baseline task as well as during a period when information was updated in working memory. Updating processing was found to affect bilateral striatal dopamine binding. Critically, a training-related influence on dopaminergic activity was observed in the left striatum, closely overlapping the region where a training-related effect was seen in the fMRI study. These findings extend related observations for the dopamine D1 system (McNab et al., 2009), and show that the dopamine system is modifiable by directed training. Physical activity (exercise) has been demonstrated to have beneficial effects on learning and cognition (Hillman et al., 2009), and the exercise-induced cognitive

A

FMRI session I
- letter memory
- n-back
- Stroop

Five weeks of
updating training

FMRI session II
- letter memory
- n-back
- Stroop

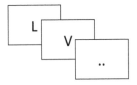

B

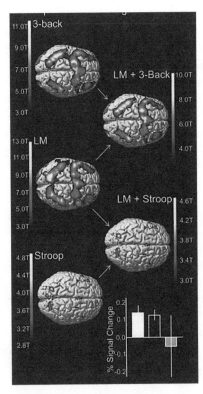

FIGURE 15.1 (A) An outline of the experimental protocol. (B) To the left, brain maps showing activation of common fronto-parietal circuits for all three tasks. The bar graph shows overlapping activation at pretest for both updating tasks (letter memory and 3-back) but not for the Stroop task

Source: Reproduced with permission from Dahlin et al. (2008b)

facilitation may in part be mediated by stimulation of dopaminergic neurotransmission by physical activity (Winter et al., 2007).

Taken together, the brain-imaging findings converge with behavioral findings of weak transfer effects, and indicate that a critical underlying factor is that the criterion and transfer tasks must engage overlapping *specific* processes and brain regions (cf. Boot et al., 2010), such as updating and the striatum as focused on here. Quite likely, other forms of training will critically depend on other processes and related brain circuits, but together with the rich set of behavioral studies showing limited transfer effects the imaging data reviewed here predict that attempts at developing training programs that lead to broad transfer effects are likely to fail.

Important questions for future research

A central message of the present chapter is that transfer-of-learning effects are highly selective and limited in magnitude. At the same time, it is important to stress that reliable and reproducible transfer can be demonstrated, as in the original study by Dahlin et al. (2008a) and in the independent replication by Bäckman et al. (2011). Thus, for the future, an important task will be to determine what training conditions lead to best transfer effects (Jaeggi et al., 2011).

Relatedly, the transfer to everyday activities requires further examination. Based on the experimental findings, broad transfer seems unlikely (cf. Ball et al., 2002), indicating that analyses of key component processes underlying the targeted everyday behavior is vital for setting up an optimal training program.

The durability of training effects is a key issue that warrants further examination (Dahlin et al., 2008a; also Dahlin et al., 2009). As for physical activities, there are reasons to believe that cognitive training needs to be maintained. At the same time, some long-lasting effects have been reported (Dahlin et al., 2008a). The determining factor may be the length of the initial training program, as longer programs are more likely to establish new cognitive skills of substantial durability. In conclusion, the present review indicates that cognitive training in general and working-memory training in particular cannot be expected to have very broad and general effects. At the same time, by now it seems firmly established that training of working memory is possible, and that some such effects do transfer. Therefore, although caution is warranted in view of commercial claims of training being a "low-hanging fruit" (cf. Owen et al., 2010), we are optimistic about future intervention studies.

Note

* This chapter originally appeared in the edited volume, *Working Memory and Ageing*.

References

Bäckman, L., Nyberg, L., Soveri, A., Johansson, J., Andersson, M., Dahlin, E., Stigsdotter Neely, A., Virta, J., Laine, M. & Rinne J. (2011). Effects of working-memory training on striatal dopamine release. *Science, 333*, 718.

Baddeley, A. D. & Hitch, G. (1974). Working memory. In G. H. Bower (Ed.), *The psychology of learning and motivation* (vol. 8, pp. 47–89). New York: Academic Press.

Ball, K., Berch, D. B., Helmers, K. F., Jobe, J. B., Leveck, M. D., Marsiske, M. ... Willis, S. L. (2002). Effects of cognitive training interventions with older adults: A randomized controlled trial. *Journal of the American Medical Association, 288*, 2271–2281.

Baltes, P. B. & Kliegl, R. (1992). Testing-the-limits research suggests irreversible aging loss in memory based on mental imagination. *Developmental Psychology, 28*, 121–125.

Bherer, L., Kramer, A. F., Peterson, M. S., Colcombe, S., Erickson, K. & Becic, E. (2005). Training effects on dual-task performance: Are there age-related differences in plasticity of attentional control? *Psychology and Aging, 20*, 695–709.

Bherer, L., Kramer, A. F., Peterson, M. S., Colcombe, S., Erickson, K. & Becic, E. (2006). Testing the limits of cognitive plasticity in older adults: Application to attention control. *Acta Psychologica, 123*, 261–278.

Bherer, L., Kramer, A. F., Peterson, M. S., Colcombe, S., Erickson, K. & Becic, E. (2008). Transfer effects in task-set cost and dual-task set cost after dual-task training in older and younger adults: Further evidence for cognitive plasticity in attentional control in late adulthood. *Experimental Aging Research, 34*, 188–219.

Boot, W. R., Basak, C., Basak, C., Erickson, K. I., Neider, M., Simons, D. J. ... Kramer, A. F. (2010). Transfer of skill engendered by complex task training under conditions of variable priority. *Acta Psychologica, 135*, 349–357.

Borella, E., Carretti, B., Riboldi, F. & De Beni, R. (2010). Working memory training in older adults: Evidence of transfer and maintenance effects. *Psychology and Aging, 25*, 767–778.

Buschkuehl, M., Jaeggi, S., Hutchinson, S., Perrig-Chiello, P., Sapp, C., Muller, M. ... Perrig, W. (2008). Impact of working memory training on memory performance in old-old adults. *Psychology and Aging, 23*, 743–753.

Cabeza, R. & Nyberg, L. (2000). Imaging cognition II: An empirical review of 275 PET and fMRI studies. *Journal of Cognitive Neuroscience, 12*, 1–47.

Cassavaugh, N. D. & Kramer, A. F. (2009). Transfer of computer-based training to simulated driving in older adults. *Applied Ergonomics, 40*, 943–952.

Chein, J. M. & Morrison, A. B. (2010). Expanding the mind's workspace: Training and transfer effects with a complex working memory span task. *Psychonomic Bulletin and Review, 17*, 193–199.

Collette, F. & Van der Linden, M. (2002). Brain imaging of the central executive component of working memory. *Neuroscience and Biobehavioral Reviews, 26*, 105–125.

Collette, F., Hogge, M., Salmon, E. & Van der Linden, M. (2006). Exploration of the neural substrates of executive functioning by functional neuroimaging. *Neuroscience, 139*, 209–221.

Craik, F. I. M. & Byrd, M. (1982). Aging and cognitive deficits: The role of attentional resources. In F. I. M. Craik & S. E. Trehub (Eds.), *Aging and cognitive processes* (pp. 191–211). New York: Plenum Press.

Dahlin, E., Bäckman, L., Stigsdotter Neely, A. & Nyberg, L. (2009). Training of the executive component of working memory: Subcortical areas mediate transfer effects. *Restorative Neurology and Neuroscience, 27*, 405–419.

Dahlin, E., Nyberg, L., Bäckman, L. & Stigsdotter Neely, A. (2008a). Plasticity of executive functioning in young and older adults: Immediate training gains, transfer and long-term maintenance. *Psychology and Aging, 23*, 720–730.

Dahlin, E., Stigsdotter Neely, A., Larsson, A., Bäckman, L. & Nyberg, L. (2008b). Transfer of learning after updating training mediated by the striatum. *Science, 320*, 1510–1512.

Daneman, M. & Carpenter, P. A. (1980). Individual difference in working memory and reading. *Journal of Verbal Learning and Verbal Behavior, 19*, 450–466.

Drustewitz, D. (2006). A few important points about dopamine's role in neural network dynamics. *Pharmacopsychiatry, 39*, 72–75.

Friedman, N. P., Miyake, A., Corley, R. P., Young, S. E., DeFries, J. C. & Hewitt, J. K. (2006). Not all executive functions are related to intelligence. *Psychological Science, 17*, 172–179.

Gabrieli, J. D. E., Singh, J., Stebbins, G. T. & Goetz, C. G. (1996). Reduced working memory span in Parkinson's disease: Evidence of the role of a frontostriatal system in working and strategic memory. *Neuropsychology, 10*, 322–332.

Hasher, L., Lustig, C. & Zacks, R. T. (2007). Inhibitory mechanisms and the control of attention. In A. R. A. Conway, C. Jarrold, M. J. Kane, A. Miyake & L. N. Towse (Eds.), *Variations in working memory*. New York: Oxford University Press.

Hertzog, C., Kramer, A. F., Wilson, R. S. & Lindenberger, U. (2009). Enrichment effects on adult cognitive development: Can the functional capacity of older adults be preserved and enhanced? *Psychological Science, 9*, 1–65.

Hillman, C. H., Pontifex, M. B., Raine, L. B., Castelli, D. M., Hall, E. E. & Kramer, A. F. (2009). The effect of acute treadmill walking on cognitive control and academic achievement in preadolescent children. *Neuroscience, 159*, 1044–1054.

Jaeggi, S. M., Buschkuehl, M., Jonides, J. & Perrig, W. J. (2008). Improving fluid intelligence with training on working memory. *Proceedings of the National Academy of Sciences, 105*, 6829–6833.

Jaeggi, S. M., Buschkuehl, M., Jonides, J. & Shah, P. (2011). Short- and long-term benefits of cognitive training. *Proceedings of the National Academy of Sciences, 108*, 10081–10086.

Jones, S., Nyberg, L., Sandblom, J., Stigsdotter Neely, A., Ingvars, M., Peterssons, K. M. & Bäckman, L. (2006). Cognitive and neural plasticity in aging: General and task-specific limitations. *Neuroscience and Biobehavioral Reviews, 30*, 864–871.

Jonides, J. (2004). How does practice makes perfect? *Nature Neuroscience, 7*, 10–11.

Karbach, J. & Kray, J. (2009). How useful is executive control training? Age differences in near and far transfer of task-switching training. *Developmental Science, 12*, 978–990.

Karbach, J., Mang, S. & Kray, J. (2010). Transfer of task-switching training in older age: The role of verbal processes. *Psychology and Aging, 25*, 677–683.

Kempler, D., Almor, A., Tyler, L. K., Andersen, E. S. & MacDonald, M. C. (1998). Sentence comprehension deficits in Alzheimer's disease: A comparison of off-line and on-line processing. *Brain and Language, 64*, 297–316.

Klingberg, T. (2010). Training and plasticity of working memory. *Trends of Cognitive Sciences, 14*, 317–324.

Klingberg, T., Fernell, E., Olesen, P. J., Johnson, M., Gustafsson, P., Dahlström, K., Gillberg, C. G., Forssberg, H. & Westerberg, H. (2005). Computerized training of working memory in children with ADHD—a randomized, controlled trial. *Journal of the American Academy of Child and Adolescence Psychiatry, 44*, 177–186.

Kramer, A. F., Larish, J. F. & Strayer, D. L. (1995). Training for attentional control in dual task settings: A comparison of young and old adults. *Journal of Experimental Psychology: Applied, 1*, 50–76.

Kramer, A. F., Larish, J. F., Weber, T. A. & Bardell, L. (1999). Training for executive control: Task coordination strategies and aging. In D. Gopher & A. Koriat (Eds.), *Attention and performance XVII: Cognitive regulation of performance: Interaction of theory and application* (pp. 617–652). Cambridge, MA: MIT Press.

Lee, H., Boot, W. R., Basak, C., Voss., M. W., Prakash, R. S., Neider, M. … Kramer, A. F. (2012). Performance gains from direct training do not transfer to untrained tasks. *Acta Psychologica, 139*, 146–158.

Li, K. Z. H., Roudaia, E., Lussier, M., Bherer, L., Leroux, A. & McKinley, P. A. (2010). Benefits of cognitive dual-task training on balance performance in healthy older adults. *Journal of Gerontology: Medical Sciences, 12*, 1344–1352.

Li, S.-C., Schmiedek, F., Huxhold, O., Röcke, C., Smith, J. & Lindenberger, U. (2008). Working memory plasticity in old age: Transfer and maintenance. *Psychology and Aging, 23,* 731–742.

Lustig, C., Shah, P., Seidler, R. & Reuter-Lorenz, P.A. (2009). Aging, training, and the brain: A review and future directions. *Neuropsychological Review, 19,* 504–522.

Lövdén, M., Bäckman, L., Lindenberger, U., Schaefer, S. & Schmiedek, F. (2010). A theoretical framework for the study of adult cognitive plasticity. *Psychological Bulletin, 136,* 659–676.

McCabe, D. P., Roediger III, H. L., McDaniel, M.A., Balota, D.A. & Hambrick, D. Z. (2010). The relationship between working memory capacity and executive functioning: Evidence for a common executive attention construct. *Neuropsychology, 24,* 222–243.

MacKay-Brandt, A. (2011). Training attentional control in older adults. *Aging Neuropsychology and Cognition, 18,* 432–451.

McNab, F., Varrone, A., Farde, L., Jucaite, A., Bystritsky, P., Forssberg, H. & Klingberg, T. (2009). Changes in cortical dopamine D1 receptor binding associated with cognitive training. *Science, 323,* 800–802.

Marklund, P., Fransson, P., Cabeza, R., Larsson, A., Ingvar, M. & Nyberg, L. (2007). Unity and diversity of tonic and phasic executive control components in episodic and working memory. *NeuroImage, 36,* 1361–1373.

Miyake, A. & Shah, P. (1999). *Models of working memory: Mechanisms of active maintenance and executive control.* Melbourne: Cambridge University Press.

Miyake, A., Friedman, N. P., Emerson, M. J., Witzki, A. H., Howerter, A. & Wager, T. D. (2000). The unity and diversity of executive functions and their contributions to complex "Frontal Lobe" tasks: A latent variable analysis. *Cognitive Psychology, 41,* 49–100.

Moody, D. E. (2009). Can intelligence be increased by training on a task of working memory? *Intelligence, 37,* 327–328.

Morrison, A. B. & Chein, J. M. (2011). Does working memory training work? The promise and challenges of enhancing cognition by training working memory. *Psychonomic Bulletin and Review, 18,* 46–60.

Naghavi, H. R. & Nyberg, L. (2005). Common fronto-parietal activity in attention, memory, and consciousness: Shared demands on integration? *Consciousness and Cognition, 14,* 390–425.

Nyberg, L., Sandblom, J., Jones, S., Stigsdotter Neely, A., Petersson, K. M., Ingvars, M. & Bäckman, L. (2003). Neural correlates of training-related memory improvement in adulthood and aging. *Proceedings of the National Academy of Sciences, 100,* 13728–13733.

Olesen, P. J., Westerberg, H., Klingberg, T. (2004). Increased prefrontal and parietal activity after training of working memory. *Nature Neuroscience, 7,* 75–79.

O'Reilly, R. C. (2006). Biologically based computational models of high-level cognition. *Science, 314,* 91–94.

Owen, A. M., Hampshire, A., Grahn, J. A., Stenton, R., Dajani, S., Burns, A. S., Howard, R. J. & Ballard, C. G. (2010). Putting brain training to the test. *Nature, 465,* 775–778.

Rebok, G. W., Carlson, M. C. & Langbaum, J. B. S. (2007). Training and maintaining memory abilities in healthy older adults: Traditional and novel approaches. *Journal of Gerontology: Series B, 62b,* 53–61.

Richmond, L. L., Morrison, A. B., Chein, J. M. & Olson, I. R. (2011). Working memory training and transfer in older adults. *Psychology and Aging, 26,* 813–822.

Sandberg, P., Rönnlund, M., Nyberg, L. & Stigsdotter Neely, A. (2013). Executive process training in young and old adults. *Aging, Neuropsychology, and Cognition* [Epub ahead of print]. DOI: 10.1080/13825585.2013.839777

Schmidt, R. A. & Bjork, R. A. (1992). New conceptualizations of practice: Common principals in three paradigms suggest new concepts for training. *Psychological Science, 3,* 207–217.

Shipstead, Z., Redick, T. S. & Engle, R. W. (2010). Does working memory training generalize? *Psychologica Belgica, 50,* 245–276.

Stigsdotter Neely, A. & Bäckman, L. (1993). Long-term maintenance of gains from memory training in older adults: Two 3½ year follow-up studies. *Journal of Gerontology: Psychological Sciences, 48,* 233–237.

Thorndike, E. L. & Woodworth, R. S. (1901). The influence of improvement in one mental function upon the efficiency of other functions. *Psychological Review, 8,* 247–261.

Unsworth, N. & Engle, R. W. (2007). The nature of individual differences in working memory capacity: Active maintenance in primary memory and controlled search from secondary memory. *Psychological Review, 114,* 104–132.

Unsworth, N., Heitz, R. P., Engle, R. W. (2005). Working memory capacity in hot and cold cognition. In R. W. Engle, G. Sedek, U. Hecker & D. N. McIntosh (Eds.), *Cognitive limitations in aging and psychopathology: Attention, working memory, and executive functions* (pp. 19–43). New York: Oxford University Press.

Verhaeghen, P. (2000). The interplay of growth and decline: Theoretical and empirical aspects of plasticity of intellectual and memory performance in normal aging. In R. D. Hill, L. Bäckman & A. Stigsdotter Neely (Eds.), *Cognitive rehabilitation in old age* (pp. 3–22). New York: Oxford University Press.

Verhaeghen, P. & Marcoen, A. (1996). On the mechanisms of plasticity in young and older adults after instruction in the method of loci: Evidence for an amplification model. *Psychology and Aging, 11,* 164–178.

Verhaeghen, P., Marcoen, A. & Goossens, L. (1992). Improving memory performance in the aged through mnemonic training: A meta-analytic study. *Psychology and Aging, 7,* 242–251.

Winter, B., Breitenstein, C., Mooren, F. C., Voelker, K., Fobker, M., Lechtermann, A. … Knecht, S. (2007). High impact running improves learning. *Neurobiology of Learning and Memory, 87,* 597–609.

16

MORE THAN JUST A MEMORY

The nature and validity of working memory in educational settings[*]

Darren S. Levin, S. Kenneth Thurman, and Marissa H. Kiepert

Since its origins in the 1960s cognitive revolution, "short-term" or "primary" memory has developed into the more sophisticated concept of working memory, in which information is not only retained for a brief period of time, but is also manipulated and closely involved in higher order processing activities such as comprehension, problem solving, and reasoning. While the dominant model of working memory has been Baddeley and Hitch's multiple-component model (1974; Baddeley, 2000, 2007), there are several other theoretical views including Cowan's embedded-processes model (1988, 1999, 2005) and Ericsson and Kintsch's long-term working memory theory (1995). Assessments of working memory in children and adults are typically grounded or validated in light of a particular theoretical viewpoint. Research with children has focused on the relationship of working memory to academic achievement. This chapter reviews how working memory has been defined, assessed, and measured in experimental and applied (i.e., educational) settings with children. In light of this review, it raises serious questions regarding the ecological validity of much current research into the measurement of working memory in the classroom.

Models of working memory

How working memory is defined, assessed, and measured in laboratory or applied settings is guided by and closely related to a particular theoretical framework of working memory; moreover, how researchers define, assess, and measure working memory has implications for its applicability in real-world situations. Thus, it is necessary to briefly present several theoretical views of working memory prior to discussing how this construct is used in educational settings.

Baddeley and Hitch's multicomponent model

The dominant theory of working memory is the multicomponent Baddeley and Hitch model which was promulgated in 1974, and later revised by Baddeley (2000, 2007). This model defines working memory as "a limited capacity temporary storage system that underpins complex human thought" (Baddeley, 2007, p. 7). In contrast to Atkinson and Shiffrin's (1968) "modal model" which depicted short-term memory as a temporary but unitary store of information, Baddeley and Hitch (1974) proposed a multicomponent system to account for several of the inconsistencies found between the modal model and existing data. Baddeley (2007) suggests that the modal model could not account for (1) evidence that short-term and long-term memory could not be neatly distinguished based on codes (i.e., semantic, phonetic, and visual), (2) findings from studies indicating that short-term memory could be severely disrupted, yet the transfer of information to long-term memory remained largely unaffected, and (3) data showing that concurrent tasks could selectively interfere with the uptake of information into long-term memory.

Baddeley and Hitch's (1974) original model of working memory consisted of three components, each of which is responsible for different tasks. The "central executive" is the attentional control, decision-making system and is supported by two temporary storage subsystems (or "slave systems") that are domain specific. The first slave system, the "phonological loop", has received the most empirical investigation and support. The function of the phonological loop is to store and manipulate speech-based information through a subvocal rehearsal process known as articulatory control. The second slave system, the visuospatial sketchpad, stores and manipulates visual and spatial information. In 2000, Baddeley extended this model to include a third temporary storage subsystem known as the episodic buffer. This fourth component was proposed to account for data indicating that visual and phonological information are combined in some way (e.g., Logie, Della Sala, Val Wynn, & Baddeley, 2000; Saito, Logie, Morita, & Law, 2008), and helps explain data that could not be supported solely by these two existing slave systems. Thus, the episodic buffer was added as a subsystem that formed an interface between the other components and long-term memory (Baddeley, 2007).

Early research on the model focused heavily on the phonological loop. Initial laboratory evidence supporting the existence of a phonological loop includes:

- the *irrelevant speech* effect: the effect occurring when subject performance on remembering printed verbal items is disrupted by irrelevant spoken material presented at the same time (Colle & Welsh, 1976),
- the *word length* effect: a phenomenon in which memory span coincides with the spoken length of the word such that memory span for long words is smaller than for short (Baddeley, Thomson, & Buchanan, 1975),

- the *phonological similarity* effect: the effect that occurs when similar sounding words impair immediate serial recall (Conrad & Hull, 1964), and
- *articulatory suppression*, which occurs when the prevention of the subvocal rehearsal processes severely disrupts performance on a memory list and also abolishes the word length effect (Baddeley, Lewis, & Vallar, 1984).

The concept of a phonological loop has not gone unchallenged, however. To date, the theoretical underpinnings of the phonological loop continue to be researched and have produced interesting developments in our understanding of language acquisition and processing (see Baddeley, 2007 for review).

The visuospatial sketchpad, researched to a lesser degree than the phonological loop, is also empirically supported. Evidence for the visuospatial sketchpad comes from studies on visual imagery (e.g., Baddeley, Grant, Wight, & Thompson, 1975) and more recently from neuropsychology research using brain-imaging techniques (e.g., Jonides et al., 1993; Smith & Jonides, 1997; Della Sala & Logie, 2002). Recent reviews of the advancements of the visuospatial sketchpad are given by Logie (1995, 2003), and Fletcher and Henson (2001).

Despite being at the core of the model, attempts to analyze the central executive came later than developments on these two subcomponents. However, great strides have been made in understanding the functions of the central executive since Baddeley's first attempt in 1986, which comprised only a single book chapter. Review of recent developments in research on the central executive can be found in Baddeley (2007).

Other models of working memory have emerged in response to criticisms of Baddeley and Hitch's multicomponent theory. Two of the most influential are Cowan's embedded-processes model and Ericsson and Kintsch's long-term working memory theory.

Cowan's embedded-processes model

Cowan's embedded-processes model of working memory (1988, 1999, 2005) has been developing since 1988, although the term "embedded processes" did not appear until 1999. One of the most notable differences between Cowan's model of working memory and Baddeley's model is in the *level* of analysis: Cowan uses more generic terms to explain working memory rather than explicit terms favored by Baddeley. For example, rather than supporting specific slave systems, Cowan's model uses vaguer terminology such as "activated memory", which according to him is a more all-embracing term. Activated memory is not limited to phonological or visual-spatial information, but can include representations of tactile sensory information, which is lacking from Baddeley's model, even with the inclusion of an episodic buffer (Cowan, 2005).

Two key elements play a role in Cowan's model (1988, 1999, 2005). The first is activated memory, or sensory and categorical features from long-term memory that are currently in an activated state. The second element is the focus of attention, which is a portion of the activated memory that is in conscious awareness and of limited capacity. It functions to form new episodic links between items that are activated at the same time and which are subsequently integrated into long-term memory. Like Baddeley, Cowan (2005) suggests that the central executive controls, at least in part, the focus of attention through orienting responses that can either attract attention when information is new or interesting, or counteract the central executive when information is not novel. Recently Cowan (2005) has asserted that working memory is "a set of processes that hold a limited amount of information in a readily accessible state for use in an active task" (p. 39). However, there are clear conceptual similarities between the rival theories and Cowan has stated that: "Practically, there may be only subtle (though potentially important) differences between a distinct-buffers view and a more integrated approach" (2005, p. 43).

Ericsson and Kintsch's long-term working memory theory

Another rival to the multicomponent view is Ericsson and Kintsch's (1995) theory of long-term working memory (LT-WM). Unlike the models just discussed, LT-WM is meant to describe a specific *instance* of working memory capacity. Specifically, LT-WM theory accounts for the extensive working memory capacity often displayed by experts and skilled performers as well as the large working memory demands made by text comprehension. Like Cowan's model, LT-WM theory developed in response to Baddeley's model, or rather, the inadequacies of Baddeley's model. In particular, Ericsson and Kintsch (1995) made the case that Baddeley's model (1986) left unexplained the working memory processes of highly skilled activities (such as piano playing, typing, and reading). It is noteworthy, however, that the LT-WM theory of Ericsson and Kintsch was formulated in 1995, before Baddeley added the episodic buffer as the fourth component of his model in 2000—a component he deemed necessary to help account for "the temporary storage of material in quantities that seemed clearly to exceed the capacity of either the verbal or visual-spatial peripheral subsystems. This shows up particularly clearly in the retention of prose passages" (Baddeley, 2003, p. 202).

In their theory, Ericsson and Kintsch (1995) refer to the temporary storage of information (the traditional view of working memory) as short-term working memory (or ST-WM), which differs from LT-WM in "the durability of the storage it provides and the need for sufficient retrieval cues in attention for access to information in long-term memory" (Ericsson & Kintsch, 1995, p. 211). In highly skilled activities retrieval cues in ST-WM make accessible relevant information in long-term memory. Thus, Ericsson and Kintsch stress the importance of efficient and reliable storage of information, as well as its organization.

Assessment of working memory

The theories of working memory described above provide the foundations and theoretical underpinnings for the design of empirical (i.e., experimental) working memory tasks. Empirical working memory tasks attempt to delineate *how* humans use the basic functions of working memory to solve problems and adapt to their environments. In addition, such empirical findings provide data that support, refute, or otherwise shape the original theories. Such is the typical evolution of knowledge (Kuhn, 1962); each step shapes the previous step allowing for theory modification and evolution.

With regard to working memory, experimental findings have allowed for further construct development and the differentiation of working memory from short-term memory and verbal working memory from visual-spatial working memory. As empirical support is established for theoretical and empirical working memory task validity, working memory tasks are further developed for educational practice, most notably to predict or establish linkages between working memory and academic achievement such as general reasoning ability (e.g., Kyllonen & Christal, 1990), reading comprehension (e.g., Coltheart, 1987), arithmetic problem solving (e.g., Logie, Gilhooly, & Wynn, 1994), vocabulary acquisition (e.g., Gathercole & Baddeley, 1993), and learning disabilities (e.g., Reid, Hresko, & Swanson, 1996) (all as cited in Roid, 2003, p. 43). The previous section provided a history of the theoretical underpinnings of empirical working memory tasks. In this section, we explore the empirical tasks themselves, as well as the educationally relevant assessments that have evolved from them and are currently used in educational settings. In doing so, we wish to emphasize the breadth and depths of empirical working memory tasks, and thus their potential contributions to educational applications. However, we also underscore the chasm that actually exists between empirical and educational assessment practices, and therefore, the specific educational conclusions that can be drawn regarding the interpretation of educational working memory tasks.

In empirical assessment of working memory, respondents are typically required to combine memory for a sequence of items while simultaneously processing other information. This activity is increased over successive trials until criteria errors are committed (Gathercole & Alloway, 2008). Conventionally, many of the empirical assessments of working memory have been referred to as "span tasks", including reading span, digit span, listening span, computation span, counting span, and other types of visual-spatial spans.

Laboratory assessment of verbal working memory

Reading span tasks

Modern empirical assessment of working memory can be traced to Daneman and Carpenter's (1980) landmark study, which used a reading span test that assessed college students' use of both processing and storage capacity. Sets of sentences of approximately the same length were printed on cards, which were then read aloud by the students at a normal reading pace. Students were unable to view their previously read sentences. Presentation of a blank card signaled to the students to recite the last word of each sentence that was shown on the cards. Longer sets of sentences were presented in ensuing sets, until students failed all trials within a given set. Reading span was calculated based on the largest list size of perfectly recalled final words.

Tirre and Peña (1992) expanded on Daneman and Carpenter's test by presenting sentences on a computer screen. In their task, respondents, who were US Air Force personnel, were required to answer "True" or "False" to each sentence before proceeding; this ensured meaningful processing and provided a measure of knowledge which was also correlated with working memory. Unlike the previous studies, respondents in de Jong's (1998) study were children who were required to read sentences ranging from four to seven words. All these studies directly related working memory to reading skills, but Friedman and Miyake (2004) concluded that reading span tasks may be mediated by variables other than working memory capacity, such as time of processing.

Digit, letter, and word span tasks

Digit span tasks typically require the respondent to listen to verbally presented digits, and then recall them either in the same order in which they are presented (digits forward) or in backwards order (digits backward). Ramsay and Reynolds (1995) reviewed 27 articles on the separate scaling of the Digits Forward and Digits Backward subtests of the Test of Memory and Learning. Using factor analysis, Ramsay and Reynolds concluded that, despite similarities, the two tasks reflect different abilities. Similarly, Reynolds (1997) confirmed that the two tasks differ in that digits backward span requires the use of transformation (i.e., working memory), whereas the digits forward span does not. Despite Reynolds' warning that "separate scaled scores for forward and for backward memory span tasks should be provided routinely on any standardized assessment" (1997, p. 39), raw scores on the two tasks continue to be summed on some commercially available assessments of working memory to produce a single standard score.

There is a multitude of other span tasks that are derived from the digits forward/backward tasks, such as letter spans, number–letter combinations, and various word spans. All of these require participants to respond selectively according to certain criteria: for instance, the letters in alphabetical order or words according to prescribed categories (e.g., body parts followed by non-body parts).

Listening span tasks

Listening span tests are analogous to reading span tests in that they typically require a respondent to listen to a series of sentences and then recall the last word spoken in each sentence. Listening span tests have the advantage of not taxing reading skills which may be suspect in some children with educational disabilities. There are many varieties of listening span test, including the cloze procedure and knowledge verification procedures described below.

Siegel and Ryan (1989) explored working memory differences in children with a reading, math, or attention disability using a cloze procedure (Savage, Lavers, &

Pillay, 2007). Children were verbally presented with a set of sentences in which the last word in each sentence was missing. After each sentence the children were required to say the missing word and subsequently verbally recall all the missing words in the set. Example sentences from Seigel and Ryan include: "In summer it is very ___"; "People go to see monkeys in a ___"; "With dinner we sometimes eat bread and ___." In this case, the child was then required to repeat the words that he or she had chosen (i.e., hot, zoo, butter).

Under the knowledge verification procedure, a respondent is required to answer a question about sentences (e.g., by responding "true" or "false"; "yes" or "no") before being asked to recall the last word of the sentence. For example, Gathercole and Pickering (2000a) asked students to listen to a pair of sentences and judge the veracity of each spoken sentence (e.g., Oranges live in water) before recall. Whereas the cloze procedure has been used to establish a linkage between working memory and a reading disability (e.g., Siegel & Ryan, 1989), studies that have used a knowledge verification procedure have generally not supported such a link (e.g., Gathercole & Pickering, 2000b; Stothard & Hulme, 1992).

Computation span test

Based on the Operation Word task used by Turner and Engle (1989), de Jong (1998) employed the computation span test to distinguish differences in memory processing and storage. Analogous to the reading span tests employed in the same study (de Jong, 1998), each computation span test item required the child to first read and solve aloud a simple mathematical computation (e.g., 3 + 1) immediately before listening to a single digit spoken by the test administrator. Each computation consisted of either the addition or subtraction of 1 from a number less than 10, and the correct answer was always less than 10. After the digit was presented, the child was required to immediately begin the next computation, so as to minimize the possibility of rehearsal. As the number of computations increased from two to seven, so the list of numbers that had to be stored also increased.

Counting span task

In the same study, de Jong (1998) used a counting span test based on Case, Kurland, and Goldberg's (1982) design. The counting span test requires respondents to retain and reproduce a series of digits while counting. In de Jong's design, a card was presented to each child, on which an irregular pattern of green and yellow dots was printed. Each child was required to count aloud the number of green dots on each card; these numbers were to be stored and subsequently recalled in the correct order.

Assessment of visual-spatial working memory

Pentland, Anderson, Dye, and Wood (2003, pp. 144–145) define nonverbal memory as a "process that relates to the encoding and retrieval of spatial representations" and suggest that "nonverbal memory is more precisely defined in terms of a synthesis of visual and spatial (visuo-spatial) information". They suggest that, whereas the visual processing system processes object properties such as shape and color, the spatial processing unit assesses properties such as location and size (Pentland et al., 2003).

Historically, assessing visual-spatial working memory has been more challenging than assessing verbal working memory, due to the relative difficulty of designing tasks that are pure measures of visual-spatial constructs (Pickering, 2001). For example, verbal mediation is often used by respondents when performing many tasks of visual-spatial working memory (Pulos & Denzine, 2005). Two measures that are relatively free of verbal mediation, however, are the Corsi Block Test (Milner, 1971) and the Visual Patterns Test, devised by Wilson, Scott, and Power (1987), developed by Logie and Pearson (1997), and normed by Della Sala, Gray, Baddeley, Allamano, and Wilson (1999).

The Corsi Block Test (CBT) was designed in the early 1970s to be used in neuropsychology practice, and is an extension of the Cube Imitation Test, developed by Knox (1913) to diagnose "mental retardation" in early twentieth-century immigrants to the United States (Vecchi & Richardson, 2001). The CBT typically consists of wooden pegs arranged in a nonsymmetrical pattern, which are attached to a wooden board. The examiner taps specific blocks in a predetermined sequence (usually at the rate of one block per second), and upon cue, the respondent repeats the sequence. By increasing the number of blocks tapped, the examiner controls for the difficulty of the task (Pickering, 2001). Although the Corsi Block Test has been used extensively to assess individuals suspected of neuropsychological deficits, standardization of the assessment has been lacking (Kessels, van Zandvoort, Postma, Kappelle, & de Haan, 2000). In fact, Berch, Krikorian, and Huha (1998) identified significant variations in their review of 38 empirical studies utilizing the CBT. Such variations were associated with physical characteristics such as the color of the board, number of blocks positioned on the board, block size, block placement, and display area. Also noted in their review were significant administrative differences, for example, pointing procedure, block-tapping rate, starting point, trials per level, discontinue criterion, and block-tapping sequences. By using a computerized version of the CBT, Vandierendonck, Kemps, Fastame, and Szmalec (2004) investigated the CBT's potential load on working memory and concluded that the "findings are clear and fit in well with the working memory framework of Baddeley and Hitch (1974)".

Whereas the CBT is purported to measure visual and spatial working memory, the Visual Patterns Test (VPT) is designed to be a "purer" assessment of visual working memory (Della Sala et al., 1999). The VPT consists of crossword puzzle-like grids (without the numbers) that increase in the number of cells from four (i.e., a 2 × 2 matrix) to 30 (i.e., a 5 × 6 matrix). In each grid, the individual cells are either black or white. Each grid is displayed on a card, which is presented to the respondent for three seconds. When it is removed from view, the respondent is asked to reproduce the grid by marking the cells in an empty grid of the same size as that presented. Scoring is based on the number of correctly filled cells in the most complex pattern accurately recalled.

Star Counting Test

Based on Baddeley and Hitch's (1974) working memory model and Norman and Shallice's (1986) theory of central executive functioning, the Star Counting Test was "directly aimed at measuring the ability to activate, modulate, and inhibit processes of working memory" (de Jong, 1998, p. 84). For example, de Jong and Das-Smaal (1995) used nine rows of three to five stars in each item. A number was inserted at the beginning of the item, and plus and minus signs were inserted between some stars. The child was instructed to begin counting starting with the number presented at the beginning of the item, and count the stars from left to right, and top to bottom. However, the plus sign indicated to count the subsequent stars in forward sequence, whereas the minus sign clued the respondent to continue counting the subsequent stars in a backward order. Empty spaces took the place of some stars to prevent the child from counting by fives. Although the SCT does load on working memory skills, the authors concluded that SCT is "probably not a completely pure measure of working memory capacity" due to its demand of attention, counting speed, and sustained effort (de Jong, & Das-Smaal, 1995, p. 89).

Direction Span Test

Lecerf and Roulin (2006) designed the Direction Span Test (DST) to distinguish visual-spatial short-term memory from visual-spatial working memory. A 5 × 5 computerized matrix was presented on a computer monitor to each respondent. Directional arrows appeared randomly, one at a time, in different cells, which were to be encoded by the respondent. On tasks of short-term memory (Location Span Test), respondents were instructed to memorize the cells that contained the arrows. On tasks of working memory (DST), respondents were instructed to memorize the cells that were *pointed at* by the directional arrow. These two tasks were both subjected to different manipulations (e.g., encoding time, interval time, and order of presentation). Use of the DST established further support for the differentiation of short-term visual-spatial memory from visual-spatial working memory, and that encoding time, but not interval time, can enhance performance on visual-spatial working memory tasks.

Other spatial tasks

Shah and Miyake (1996) and Handley, Capon, Copp, and Harper (2002) also concluded that spatial and verbal working memory represent distinct systems, utilizing different pools of resources. Both studies incorporated a reading span test derived from Daneman and Carpenter (1980) and a spatial span task. The spatial span for both studies required participants to view normal and mirror-imaged capitalized English letters. However, the letters were rotated to various degrees, and the respondent was required to quickly and effectively judge which letter was normal, and which was a mirror image. Furthermore, the respondent was subsequently asked to recall the orientations of the images in the correct order in which they appeared.

Educational applications of working memory

Of the many instruments that are available to measure working memory, the Wechsler Intelligence Scale for Children—Fourth Edition (WISC-IV), the Woodcock–Johnson III Tests of Cognitive Abilities (WJ III COG), and the Stanford–Binet Intelligence Scales, Fifth Edition (SB5) are the most widely used today (Leffard et al., 2006). The following is a brief review of subtests that measure working memory, and, although not exhaustive, represents widely used subtests that have been distinguished by literature review and expert consensus (i.e., Flanagan, Ortiz, & Alfonso, 2007; Leffard et al., 2006) to measure working memory.

Wechsler assessments

The Wechsler Intelligence Scale for Children—Fourth Edition (WISC-IV) and the Wechsler Adult Intelligence Scale—Third Edition (WAIS-III) both include subtests that purport to measure working memory. Whereas the WISC-IV is normed for children aged 6.0–16.11, the WAIS-III is normed for individuals aged 16.0–89.0. The WISC-IV technical manual defines working memory as "the ability to actively maintain information in conscious awareness, perform some operation or manipulation with it, and produce a result" (Wechsler, 2003, p. 8). The WISC-IV test developers indicate that the Baddeley model of working memory serves as the basis for the working memory assessments (Leffard et al., 2006), and furthermore that working memory on these assessments can be assessed with three separate subtests: Digit Span, Letter–Number Sequencing, and Arithmetic. The Digit Span subtest is composed of Digits Forward and Digits Backward. The numbers cued increase for both tasks, and the tasks are terminated when the respondent fails a specific number of trials according to established criteria. Of significant mention is that the Digits Forward "involves rote learning and memory, attention, encoding, and auditory processing" whereas Digits Backward involves "working memory, transformation of information, mental manipulation, and visual-spatial imaging" (Wechsler, 2003, p. 16). Because Digits Backward (but not Digits Forward) emphasizes working memory and transformation of information, the Digit Span subtest does not appear to separate working memory from short-term memory. Thus, although the clinician can statistically separate respondents' performance on these tasks, interpreting the entire subtest as a construct of working memory is inadvisable. A similar issue regarding construct validity exists for the Arithmetic subtest, albeit for different reasons. On this subtest, the respondent is verbally presented with arithmetic problems to solve within a specified time limit without the use of paper or pencil. This subtest involves mental manipulation, concentration, attention, short- and long-term memory, numerical reasoning ability, and mental alertness (Wechsler, 2003, p. 17). Furthermore, Groth-Marnat, Kaufman, and Sattler also suggest that Arithmetic "may involve sequencing, fluid reasoning, and logical reasoning" (as cited in Wechsler, 2003, p. 17). It is worth noting that "working memory" is absent in both of these descriptions. Because of the many different cognitive domains that may be used on these tasks, Leffard et al. (2006) warn that the Arithmetic subtest is a "less pure" measure of working memory, and should therefore not be used as a measure of working memory.

The Letter–Number Sequencing task best exemplifies a valid working memory task from the Wechsler series. This subtest requires the respondent to listen to a series of letters and numbers, and then recall the numbers in ascending order and the letters in alphabetical order until he or she fails a specific number of trials according to criteria. Because of the transformations skills required of the respondent, higher-order processing demands are thus required (Leffard et al., 2006), especially when compared to those skills required for the Digit Span task.

The Woodcock–Johnson III Tests of Cognitive Abilities (WJ III COG)

The Woodcock–Johnson III Tests of Cognitive Abilities (WJ III COG) were designed and developed to measure broad and narrow abilities according to the Cattell–Horn–Carroll theory (see Carroll, 1993; Mather & Woodcock, 2001) of cognitive abilities. Mather and Woodcock (2001) define working memory as the narrow "ability to hold information in mind for a short time while performing some operation on it" (as cited in Leffard et al., 2006, p. 237). Two subtests of the WJ III COG, the Auditory Working Memory and Numbers Reversed, are aggregated to reflect the working memory Clinical Cluster. The Auditory Working Memory subtest requires the respondent to listen to a series of nouns and numbers, and to then repeat the nouns in the same order followed by the numbers in the same order. The Numbers Reversed subtest is analogous to the Digits Backward task of the Wechsler scales. Both working memory subtests on the WJ III COG are normed for persons aged 4 to 90 years.

Stanford–Binet Intelligence Scales, Fifth Edition (SB5)

In the Stanford–Binet Intelligence Scales, Fifth Edition (SB5), Roid (2003, p. 137) defines working memory as "a class of memory processes in which diverse information in short-term memory is inspected, sorted, or trans formed." The Last Word subtest was adapted from Daneman and Carpenter's (1980) seminal work. On levels 1–3, the respondent is required to repeat brief phrases and sentences. However, levels 1–3 appear to assess short-term memory only, as opposed to levels 4–6, which appear to more accurately reflect working memory. On levels 4–6, the respondent is required to provide brief responses to sentences (i.e., "yes" or "no") before recalling the last word in each sentence. The questions and their subsequent answers thus serve as the "transformation" requirement of working memory.

In order to provide a nonverbal alternative to traditional working memory tasks, the Block Span task was adapted from the original Corsi Block Test, developed by Knox (1913). On this task, the examiner taps a series of blocks with a separate block in a specified order. Then, the respondent taps the same blocks in the same order. On later tasks, the examiner taps specified blocks that are located in either red or yellow rows, and the respondent must tap the same blocks in order, but in one row (e.g., yellow) before the other row (e.g., red). Similar to the Last Word task, early levels of the Block Span task (i.e., 1–2) appear to assess short-term memory only, whereas levels 3–6 require the additional demands of working memory. As such, great care must be used when interpreting the SB5 subtests that purport to measure both verbal and nonverbal working memory, as respondents' scores may actually be more reflective of short-term memory. These two subtests are normed for individuals aged 2 to 85 years.

Differential Ability Scales, Second Edition (DAS-II)

Revised in 2007, the Differential Ability Scales, Second Edition (DAS-II) contains a working memory cluster for the Early Years Battery (Upper Level) and the School-Age Battery. For both batteries, the working memory cluster score is composed of two subtests: Recall of Sequential Order, and Recall of Digits Backward. In the Recall of Sequential Order subtest, the respondent is presented with an oral list of body parts, and is required to verbally sequence the list in order from the highest part on the body to the lowest. Older children are also presented with non-body parts, and must sequence the body parts (again from highest to lowest) followed by the non-body parts. The Recall of Digits Backward subtest is analogous to the Digits Backward task of the Wechsler scales. The two working memory subtests on the DAS-II are normed for children aged 5.0–17.11. Although the DAS-II was not developed to directly reflect current Cattell–Horn–Carroll (CHC) theory, "the factor structure of the DAS-II fits the seven-factor CHC model well" (Elliott, 2007, p. 13), and the working memory subtests were included in the current edition to reflect the general importance of research in the area of working memory.

Wide Range Assessment of Memory and Learning, Second Edition (WRAML2)

In addition to the six Core Subtests, the Wide Range Assessment of Memory and Learning Second Edition (WRAML2) includes two optional subtests that specifically address working memory: Verbal Working Memory and Symbolic Working Memory. Both subtests are normed for individuals aged 5–90. The Verbal Working Memory subtest requires respondents to complete two distinct, but related tasks. Respondents are verbally presented with a list of words that include animals and non-animals. The respondent is first asked to repeat the list, recalling all the animals followed by the non-animals. Then, after hearing another list, the respondent is asked to recall the animals in order of their typical sizes (smallest to largest), followed by the non-animals in any order. Respondents over 14 years of age are asked to verbally list the non-animals in relative size as well.

On the Symbolic Working Memory subtest, respondents are verbally presented with a series of random numbers, and are required to point out the numbers in ascending order on a stimulus card. Respondents are also verbally presented with random numbers–letters, and then asked to point out the numbers followed by the letters in correct order on another stimulus card. These two subtests are normed for individuals aged 9–85 years and older.

Working Memory Test Battery for Children (WMTB-C)

The Working Memory Test Battery for Children (WMTB-C) assesses working memory in children aged 5 to 15 (Pickering & Gathercole, 2001). Three of the nine subtests on the WMTB-C directly measure working memory: Listening Recall, Counting Recall, and Backward Digit Recall tasks. These subtests reflect the empirical and educational tasks described throughout this chapter. The other six subtests address the visual-spatial sketchpad and the phonological loop.

By examining the relationships between working memory tasks used in empirical research and tasks used in actual educational practice (delineated in Table 16.1) a number of conclusions can be drawn. First, of the 15 most widely used subtests in educational practice, 11 are based either directly or indirectly on digit span tasks, leaving results derived from the majority of the empirical studies unaccounted for in educational assessment. Second, the Digit Span subtest (WISC-IV, WAIS-III), arguably the most widely used subtest purporting to measure working memory, contains many items (i.e., Digits Forward) that reflect memory span, not working memory. This was included on the WISC-IV (2003) despite Reynolds' (1997) caveats published six years previously. Third, the Arithmetic subtest (WISC-IV, WAIS-III) likely loads on other cognitive factors to such an extent that Leffard et al. (1996) caution that it does not accurately measure working memory. Fourth, both working memory subtests on the SB5 may or may not reflect working memory, depending on which particular items are presented to the respondent. Fifth, of the 15 subtests described, only the Block Span (SB5) addresses visual-spatial working memory (and as just mentioned, only depending on specific items presented). Sixth, many of the educational subtests were derived from empirical studies that used adult subjects, raising concerns regarding the developmental applicability of such tasks.

By using these subtests during the educational assessment of working memory, our conclusions regarding children's cognitive skill sets are compromised. Furthermore, and perhaps more importantly, such educational assessments may not accurately assess the day-to-day demands of working memory, especially related to children's learning within educational milieus.

TABLE 16.1 Relationship between empirical support, laboratory, and educational assessment of working memory

Task	Relevant empirical assessment	Educational application
Reading span tasks	Daneman & Carpenter (1980, 1983) Daneman & Green (1986) Masson & Miller (1983) Tirre and Peña (1992) de Jong (1998) Friedman & Miyake (2004)	SB5: Last Word[a] WMTB-C: Listening Recall
Listening span tasks	Siegel & Ryan (1989) Gathercole & Pickering (2000a, 2000b) Stothard & Hulme (1992)	
Computation span tasks	Turner & Engle (1989) de Jong (1998)	
Counting span tasks	de Jong (1998) Case, Kurland, & Goldberg (1982)	WMTB-C: Counting Recall
Corsi Block Test/ Cube Imitation Test	Vandierendonk, Kemps, Fastame, & Szmalec (2004)	SB5: Block Span[a]
Visual Patterns Test		
Direction Span Test	Lecerf & Roulin (2006)	
Other spatial tasks	Shah & Miyake (1996) Handley, Capon, Copp, & Harper (2002)	
Digit span tasks and derivatives	Ramsay & Reynolds (1995) Reynolds (1997)	Wechsler: Digit Span[b] Wechsler: Letter Number Sequencing Wechsler: Arithmetic[c] WJ: Auditory WM WJ: Numbers Reversed DAS-II: Recall of Sequential Order DAS-II: Recall of Digits Backward WRAML2: Verbal Working Memory WRAML2: Symbolic Working Memory CMS: Sequences WMTB-C: Backward Digit Recall

[a]Working memory tapped on later items only.
[b]Working memory tapped on Digits Backward only.
[c]Additional constructs tapped other than working memory.

Ecological validity

In the first section of this chapter we examined the various models of working memory before focusing on the various measures employed and their potential problems, and then considering their application both in laboratory studies and in the domain of assessment. Before we consider the application of working memory to elementary classrooms, it is first necessary to address the issue of ecological validity.

The notion of ecological validity grows from the early work of Brunswik (1943, 1956). Brunswik's (1956) concern was with the over-generalization of perceptual cues in the laboratory to the real-world performance. Brunswik's view of ecological validity focused on how well a cue predicted a perceptual state in the environment. Brunswik's basic assertion was that generalizability depends not only on the representativeness of the sample but also on the representativeness of the cues presented in perceptual experiments. Over time the use of the term "ecological validity" has experienced some shift from Brunswik's original conceptualization to which certain authors have objected (e.g., Araujo, Davids, & Passos, 2007; Hammond, 1999). Be this as it may, these newer concepts of ecological validity are more to the point of the current discussion.

For example, Bronfenbrenner (1979) suggested that developmental researchers had to have greater concern with the study of human development in real-life situations. He espoused the view that research had to take place in both representative as well as natural settings. Similarly, Neisser (1976) has suggested that "cognitive psychologists must make a greater effort to understand cognition as it occurs in the ordinary environment and in the context of purposeful activity" (p. 7). More recently other authors (e.g., Savage et al., 2007 and Thurman & Kiepert, 2008) have made similar assertions regarding the study of working memory. Thurman and Kiepert stress that "with respect to applied cognitive research [including studies of working memory], the issue of ecological validity is particularly paramount because the success of an intervention oftentimes relies on our understanding of a child's functioning in everyday life" (p. 269). Similarly, Savage et al. (2007) assert that "empirically, the most popular current measures of WM [working memory] … can be criticized on a range of theoretical grounds including … the lack of ecological validity" (p. 197). Pickering (2006) has recently pointed out that, in spite of the concerns expressed regarding ecological validity, working memory function is still assessed primarily using things like nonsense words, numbers, or other equally meaningless information. The previous section of this chapter further validates Pickering's point.

Another view of ecological validity likens the construct to predictive validity. For example, Sbordone (1996) has suggested that ecological validity is characterized as a "functional and predictive relationship" between a person's test performance and their behavior in real-world settings (p. 16). To make such predictions it is necessary to understand the constructs being studied, in this case working memory, in the natural environment. In fact, Isquith, Gioia, and Espy (2004) have asserted that, when considering the assessment of executive function in young children, "the child's everyday environments, both at home and at school or day care, are important venues for observing routine manifestations of executive functions" (p. 406). Such observations typically culminate in the process of collecting and quantifying behavioral data that accurately reflect the construct under study. For example, the Behavior Rating Inventory of Executive Functioning (BRIEF) (Gioia, Isquith, Guy, & Kenworthy, 2000) may be an effective tool for measuring children's executive functions as they are manifested in children's natural environments. Used in this way, observational data help ensure the ecological validity of the constructs under study, as well as the generalizability and applicability of the construct to the targeted populations within their natural environments. Moreover, this approach is likely to enhance the power of these types of assessments for predicting real-world function (Thurman & McGrath, 2008).

Verisimilitude and veridicality

Ecological validity is relevant for applied cognitive research in general, and for understanding how children use working memory in academic settings. The concept of verisimilitude reflects an aspect of ecological validity, and refers to how closely the demands required by an experiment or assessment tool resemble the demands required of the individual in day-to-day functioning (Frazen & Wilhelm, 1996). This is an especially salient issue when drawing conclusions based on traditional educational assessments of working memory. As others (e.g., Gathercole & Alloway, 2008) discuss and as we have pointed out in the previous section, multifarious span tasks have been commonly used to assess working memory in research and educational settings. For example, many of the commercially available educational assessments of working memory are replete with tasks requiring backward digit recall and derivatives of it. However, one would be hard pressed to demonstrate when, if ever, students are actually required to perform such a task within classroom settings. As such, it appears that the vast majority of the ways that working memory has been conceptualized, measured, and assessed lack verisimilitude. Although we acknowledge that working memory is used to a substantial degree during the active processes of learning, we also suggest that there seems to be a schism between working memory's theoretical, empirical, and educational underpinnings and the way in which it is actually used, especially within the educational milieu. There is little doubt regarding the predictive power of working memory on academic achievement. A plethora of studies (see Gathercole & Alloway, 2008) convincingly demonstrates this relationship. However, with regard to verisimilitude, we suggest that it may be more ecologically valid to examine the behavioral manifestations of working memory, rather than the underlying construct, so that realistic, practical, and ecologically valid interventions can be designed and implemented, with (potentially) long-lasting, positive behavioral and academic consequences.

Table 16.2 provides some classroom examples requiring the use of working memory skills. Examination of Table 16.2 should provide the reader with insight

TABLE 16.2 Examples of the use of working memory skills in the classroom[a]

Subtraction problems requiring borrowing, especially when done mentally Following a
   multi-step command in the proper order
Writing a complex sentence
Identifying rhyming words after listening to a four-line passage Comprehending a read
   passage
Word decoding and supplying its meaning Writing a spelling word after its oral
   presentation Translating a passage from English to French

---

[a]The authors would like to thank Dr. Catherine Fiorello for some of these examples.

into how the tasks used to measure working memory in the laboratory and during
educational assessments (see Table 16.1) contrast with the use of working memory
skills in the classroom. These examples we hope are helpful to researchers and
practitioners in meeting the challenge of understanding and assessing working
memory in an ecologically valid manner.

Consideration needs to be given not only to whether assessments contain items
that are similar to those in the classroom environment (Frazen & Wilhelm, 1996),
but also to whether actual *performance (i.e., obtained scores)* on the assessments predicts
performance of actual classroom tasks that require working memory. Furthermore,
it is important to determine whether or not working memory skills are used
and applied in a similar manner to the way they manifest in classroom learning
tasks. Thus, although the approaches espoused by Isquith et al. (2004) specifically
address the issue of verisimilitude, an assessment's construct validity, generalizability, and practicality must be further explored. Assessment approaches must also
be interpreted within the context of the settings, people, and situational circumstance in which the behaviors are exhibited. It is possible, for example, that a child
might appear to have a working memory deficit in the classroom when, in fact,
his/her behavior might be a function of other more situational variables. By not
controlling or addressing these variables, hypotheses that what has been observed
is due to specific neurocognitive variables may be mitigated. By addressing these
issues during educational assessment, however, more ecologically valid conclusions
regarding working memory can be formulated. Because working memory abilities
increase with development, assessment tools used to measure working memory
must respect the changing demands of a child's environment as he or she matures
(Anderson, 2002; Silver, 2000). As Anderson (2002) suggests, assessments of cognitive abilities (including executive functioning) must be "suitable for children and
valid for specific developmental stages" (p. 75). Being cognizant of age appropri-
ateness of assessment tasks is critical for assuring ecological validity. As previously
discussed, many studies of working memory have used adults rather than children
in their experimental procedures, thus attenuating any conclusions that may be
generalized to children's skill sets. Moreover, the demands required by an assessment
tool must be reflective of specific, relevant, and everyday environmental demands
that are salient from the child's perspective, and not necessarily from the perspective

of the researcher. When interpreting ecologically valid working memory assessment results, any and all inconsistencies must be addressed. For example, observations that a student often "forgets" teachers' questions while taking notes yet easily "recalls" sequences of chemistry laboratory skills while conducting experiments will need to be rectified. By approaching working memory assessment in this way, proper construct measurement is ensured, rather than merely describing and documenting observed behaviors at specific moments of time or place.

Not only must assessments depict real-world events, but they must also *predict* behavioral functioning in authentic situations. This issue, termed veridicality, reflects the significance of correlational power: the greater the correlation between working memory assessment and performance of real-world tasks, the greater is our ability to predict, and therefore plan appropriate interventions. For example, behaviors exhibited in isolated testing situations by individuals with central nervous system lesions may not be particularly strong predictors of a person's ability to carry out activities of daily living in their natural environments (Chaytor & Schmitter-Edgecombe, 2003).

Conclusions

Understanding working memory is essential in designing effective classroom instruction. Thus, when empirically and educationally assessing working memory, it is essential to consider the verisimilitude and veridicality of an assessment instrument. By approaching working memory assessment in this way, we establish as much congruence as possible between the cognitive demands of the assessment environment and those found in the natural environment (Frazen & Wilhelm, 1996). In accordance with previous studies with children (Gioia & Isquith, 2004; Isquith et al., 2004), Chaytor, Schmitter-Edgecombe, and Burr (2006) also stress the importance of assessing cognitive demands in the environment with the purpose of obtaining ecologically valid assessment of executive functions. It is hoped that, in doing so, researchers and educators can maximize authentic data-driven decisions, and therefore plan more appropriate, effective, and efficient interventions for the children they serve. Recently, Thurman and McGrath (2008) have provided insight into the techniques for assessing children in the natural environment. They suggest that environmentally based assessment practices are essential for assuring ecological validity.

Although a plethora of findings indicates that working memory deficits are associated with poor academic performance, there is less agreement on the actual components of these deficits that might be responsible for this suppression of performance (Gathercole, Lamont, & Alloway, 2006). Consequently, greater understanding of working memory is needed within the classroom context and would result in an increased degree of ecological validity especially in light of data that suggest that teachers may not have a good understanding of working memory (Fiorello, Thurman, Zavertnick, Sher, & Coleman, 2009).

Note

* This chapter originally appeared in the edited volume, *Current Issues in Applied Memory Research*.

References

Anderson, P. (2002). Assessment and development of executive function during childhood. *Child Neuropsychology, 8*, 71–82.

Araujo, D., Davids, K., & Passos, P. (2007). Ecological validity, representative design and correspondence between experimental task constraints and behavior setting: Comment on Rogers, Kadar, and Costall (2005). *Ecological Psychology, 19*, 69–78.

Atkinson, R. C., & Shiffrin, R. M. (1968). Human memory: A proposed system and its control processes. In K. W. Spence & J. T. Spence (Eds.), *The psychology of learning and motivation: Advances in research and theory* (vol. 2, pp. 89–195). New York: Academic Press.

Baddeley, A. D. (1986). *Working memory*. London: Oxford University Press.

Baddeley, A. (1996). Exploring the central executive. *Quarterly Journal of Experimental Psychology, 49A*, 5–28.

Baddeley, A. (2000). The episodic buffer: A new component of working memory? *Trends in Cognitive Sciences, 4*, 417–423.

Baddeley, A. (2003). Working memory and language: An overview. *Journal of Communication Disorders, 36*, 189–208.

Baddeley, A. D. (2007). *Working memory in thought and action*. New York: Oxford University Press.

Baddeley, A. D., & Hitch, G. J. (1974). Working memory. In G. Bower (Ed.), *The psychology of learning and motivation* (vol. 8, pp. 47–90). New York: Academic Press.

Baddeley, A. D., Grant, S., Wight, E., & Thompson, N. (1975). Imagery and visual working memory. In P. M. A. Rabbitt & S. Dornic (Eds.), *Attention and performance V* (pp. 205–217). Hillsdale, NJ: Lawrence Erlbaum Associates.

Baddeley, A. D., Lewis, V. J., & Vallar, G. (1984). Exploring the articulatory loop. *Quarterly Journal of Experimental Psychology, 36*, 233–252.

Baddeley, A. D., Thomson, N., & Buchanan, M. (1975). Word length and the structure of short-term memory. *Journal of Verbal Learning and Verbal Behavior, 14*, 575–589.

Berch, D. B., Krikorian, R., & Huha, E. M. (1998). The Corsi block-tapping task: Methodological and theoretical considerations. *Brain and Cognition, 38*, 317–338.

Bronfenbrenner, U. (1979). *The ecology of human development: Experiments by nature and design*. Cambridge, MA: Harvard University Press.

Brunswik, E. (1943). Organismic achievement and environmental probability. *Psychological Review, 50*, 255–272.

Brunswik, E. (1956). *Perception and the representative design of psychological experiments*. Berkeley, CA: University of California Press.

Carroll, J. B. (1993). *Human cognitive abilities: A survey of factor-analytic studies*. New York: Cambridge University Press.

Case, R., Kurland, D. M., & Goldberg, J. (1982). Operational efficiency and the growth of short-term memory span. *Journal of Experimental Child Psychology, 33*, 386–404.

Chaytor, N., & Schmitter-Edgecombe, M. (2003). The ecological validity of neuropsychological tests: A review of the literature on everyday cognitive skills. *Neuropsychology Review, 13*, 181–197.

Chaytor, N., Schmitter-Edgecombe, M., & Burr, R. (2006). Improving the ecological validity of executive function assessment. *Archives of Clinical Neuropsychology*, *21*, 217–227.

Colle, H. A., & Welsh, A. (1976). Acoustic masking in primary memory. *Journal of Verbal Learning and Verbal Behavior*, *15*, 17–31.

Conrad, R., & Hull, A. J. (1964). Information, acoustic confusion and memory span. *British Journal of Psychology*, *55*, 429–432.

Cowan, N. (1988). Evolving conceptions of memory storage, selective attention, and their mutual constraints within the human information processing system. *Psychological Bulletin*, *104*, 163–191.

Cowan, N. (1999). An embedded-processes model of working memory. In A. Miyake & P. Shah (Eds.), *Models of working memory: Mechanisms of active maintenance and executive control* (pp. 62–101). Cambridge: Cambridge University Press.

Cowan, N. (2005). *Working memory capacity*. New York: Psychology Press.

Daneman, M., & Carpenter, P. A. (1980). Individual differences in working memory and reading. *Journal of Verbal Learning and Verbal Behavior*, *19*, 450–466.

Daneman, M., & Carpenter, P. A. (1983). Individual differences in integrating information between and within sentences. *Journal of Experimental Psychology: Learning, Memory, and Cognition*, *9*, 561–584.

Daneman, M., & Green, I. (1986). Individual differences in comprehending and producing words in context. *Journal of Memory and Language*, *25*, 1–18.

de Jong, P. F. (1998). Working memory deficits of reading disabled children. *Journal of Experimental Child Psychology*, *70*, 75–96.

de Jong, P. F., & Das-Smaal, E. A. (1995). Attention and intelligence: The validity of the star counting test. *Journal of Educational Psychology*, *87*, 80–92.

Della Sala, S., Gray, C., Baddeley, A., Allamano, N., & Wilson, L. (1999). Pattern span: A tool for unwelding visuo-spatial memory. *Neuropsychologia*, *37*, 1189–1199.

Della Sala, S., & Logie, R. H. (2002). Neuropsychological impairments of visual and spatial working memory. In A. D. Baddeley, M. D. Kipelman, & B. A. Wilson (Eds.), *Handbook of memory disorders* (2nd ed., pp. 271–292). Chichester: Wiley.

Elliott, C. D. (2007). *Examiner's manual. Differential ability scales* (2nd ed.). San Antonio, TX: Harcourt Assessment.

Ericsson, K. A., & Kintsch, W. (1995). Long-term working memory. *Psychological Review*, *102*, 211–245.

Fiorello, C. A., Thurman S. K., Zevertnik, J., Sher, R., & Coleman, S. (2009). A comparison of teachers' and school psychologists' views of the importance of CHC abilities in the classroom. *Psychology in the Schools*, *46*, 489–500.

Flanagan, D. P., Ortiz, S. O., & Alfonso, V. C. (2007). *Essentials of cross-battery assessment* (2nd ed.). Hoboken, NJ: Wiley.

Fletcher, P., & Henson, R. (2001). Frontal lobes and human memory: Insights from functional neuroimaging. *Brain*, *124*, 849–881.

Frazen, M. D., & Wilhelm, K. L. (1996). Conceptual foundations of ecological validity in neurological assessment. In R. J. Sbordone & C. J. Long (Eds.), *Ecological validity of neuropsychological testing* (pp. 91–112). Delray Beach, FL: GR Press/St. Lucie Press.

Friedman, N. P., & Miyake, A. (2004). The reading span test and its predictive power for reading comprehension ability. *Journal of Memory and Language*, *51*, 136.

Gathercole, S. E., & Alloway, T. (2008). Working memory and classroom learning. In S. K. Thurman & C. A. Fiorello (Eds.), *Applied cognitive research in k-3 classrooms* (pp. 17–40). New York: Routledge.

Gathercole, S. E., & Pickering, S. J. (2000a). Assessment of working memory in six- and seven-year-old children. *Journal of Educational Psychology*, *92*, 377–390.

Gathercole, S. E., & Pickering, S. J. (2000b). Working memory deficits in children with low achievements in the national curriculum at 7 years of age. *British Journal of Educational Psychology*, *70*, 177–194.

Gathercole, S. E., Lamont, E., & Alloway, T. P. (2006). Working memory in the classroom. In S. J. Pickering (Ed.), *Working memory and education* (pp. 220–241). New York: Academic Press.

Gioia, G. A., & Isquith, P. K. (2004). Ecological assessment of executive function in traumatic brain injury. *Developmental Neuropsychology*, *25*, 135–158.

Gioia, G. A., Isquith, P. K., Guy, S. C., & Kenworthy, L. (2000). *The behavior rating inventory of executive function*. Lutz, FL: Psychological Assessment Resources.

Hammond, K. (1999). *Ecological validity: Then and now*. Retrieved February 2008, from www.brunswik.org/notes/essay2.html.

Handley, S. J., Capon, A., Copp, C., & Harper, C. (2002). Conditional reasoning and the tower of Hanoi: The role of spatial and verbal working memory. *British Journal of Psychology*, *93*, 501–518.

Isquith, P. K., Gioia, G. A., & Espy. K. A. (2004). Executive function in preschool children: Examination through everyday behavior. *Developmental Neuropsychology*, *26*, 403–422.

Jonides, J., Smith, E. E., Koeppe, R. A., Awh, E., Minoshima, S., & Mintun, M. (1993). Spatial working memory in humans as revealed by PET. *Nature*, *363*, 623–625.

Kessels, R. P. C., van Zandvoort, M. J. E., Postma, A., Kappelle, L. J., & de Haan, E. H. F. (2000). The Corsi block-tapping task: Standardization and normative data. *Applied Neuropsychology*, *7*, 252–258.

Knox, H. A. (1913). The differentiation between moronism and ignorance. *New York Medical Journal*, *98*, 564–566.

Kuhn, T. S. (1962) *The structure of scientific revolutions*. Chicago, IL: University of Chicago Press.

Kyllonen, P. C., & Christal, R. E. (1990) Reasoning ability is (little more than) working-memory capacity?! *Intelligence*, 14(4), 389–433.

Lecerf, T., & Roulin, J. (2006). Distinction between visuo-spatial short-term-memory and working memory span tasks. *Swiss Journal of Psychology/Schweizerische Zeitschrift für Psychologie/Revue Suisse de Psychologie*, *65*, 37–54.

Leffard, S. A., Miller, J. A., Bernstein, J., DeMann, J. J., Mangis, H. A., & McCoy, E. L. B. (2006). Substantive validity of working memory measures in major cognitive functioning test batteries for children. *Applied Neuropsychology*, *13*, 230–241.

Logie, R. H. (1995). *Visuo-spatial working memory*. Hove: Lawrence Erlbaum Associates.

Logie, R. H. (2003). Spatial and visual working memory: A mental workspace. In D. Irwin and B. Ross (Eds.), *Cognitive vision: The psychology of learning and motivation* (vol. 42, pp. 37–78). San Diego, CA: Academic Press.

Logie, R. H., Della Sala, S., Wynn, V., & Baddeley, A. D. (2000). Visual similarity effects in immediate verbal serial recall. *Quarterly Journal of Experimental Psychology A: Human Experimental Psychology*, *5*, 626–646.

Logie, R. H., & Pearson, D. G. (1997). The inner eye and the inner scribe of visuo-spatial working memory: Evidence from developmental fractionation. *European Journal of Cognitive Psychology*, *9*, 241–257.

Masson, M. E., & Miller, J. A. (1983). Working memory and individual differences in comprehension and memory of text. *Journal of Educational Psychology*, *75*, 314–318.

Mather, N., & Woodcock, R. W. (2001). *Examiner's manual. Woodcock-Johnson III Tests of Cognitive Abilities*. Itasca, IL: Riverside.

Milner, B. (1971). Interhemispheric differences in the localisation of psychological processes in man. *British Medical Bulletin, 27,* 272–277.

Neisser, U. (1976). *Cognition and reality: Principles and implications of cognitive psychology.* San Francisco, CA: W. H. Freeman & Co.

Norman, D. A., & Shallice, T. (1986). Attention to action: Willed and automatic control of behavior. In G. E. Schwartz, R. J. Davidson, & D. Shapiro (Eds.), *Consciousness and self-regulation: Advances in research and theory* (vol. 4, pp. 1–18). New York: Plenum Press.

Pentland, L. M., Anderson, V. A., Dye, S., & Wood, S. J. (2003). The nine box maze test: A measure of spatial memory development in children. *Brain and Cognition, 52,* 144–154.

Pickering, S. J. (2001). The development of visuo-spatial working memory. *Memory, 9,* 423–432.

Pickering, S. J. (2006). Assessment of working memory in children. In S. J. Pickering (Ed.), *Working memory and education* (pp. 242–273). New York: Academic Press.

Pickering, S., & Gathercole, S. (2001). *Working memory test battery for children.* San Antonio, TX: The Psychology Corporation.

Pulos, S., & Denzine, G. (2005). Individual differences in planning behavior and working memory: A study of the Tower of London. *Individual Differences Research, 3,* 99–104.

Ramsay, M. C., & Reynolds, C. R. (1995). Separate digits tests: A brief history, a literature review, and a re-examination of the factor structure of the test of memory and learning (TOMAL). *Neuropsychology Review, 5,* 151–171.

Reynolds, C. R. (1997). Forward and backward memory span should not be combined for clinical analysis. *Archives of Clinical Neuropsychology, 12,* 29–40.

Roid, G. H. (2003). *Examiner's manual. Stanford-Binet Intelligence Scales, Fifth Edition.* Itasca, IL: Riverside.

Saito, S., Logie, R. H., Morita, A., & Law, A. (2008). Visual and phonological similarity effects in verbal immediate serial recall: A test with Kanji materials. *Journal of Memory and Language, 59,* 1–17.

Savage, R., Lavers, N., & Pillay, V. (2007). Working memory and reading difficulties: What we know and what we don't know about the relationship. *Educational Psychology Review, 19,* 185.

Sbordone, R. J. (1996). Ecological validity: Some critical issues for neuropsychologists. In R. J. Sbordone & C. J. Long (Eds.), *Ecological validity of neuropsychological testing* (pp. 15–41). Delray Beach, FL: GR Press/St. Lucie Press.

Shah, P., & Miyake, A. (1996). The separability of working memory resources for spatial thinking and language processing: An individual differences approach. *Journal of Experimental Psychology: General, 125,* 4–27.

Siegel, L. S., & Ryan, E. B. (1989). The development of working memory in normally achieving and subtypes of learning disabled children. *Child Development, 60,* 973–980.

Silver, C. H. (2000). Ecological validity of neurological assessment of childhood traumatic brain injury. *Journal of Head Trauma Rehabilitation, 15,* 973–988.

Smith, E. E., & Jonides, J. (1997). Working memory: A view from neuroimaging. *Cognitive Psychology, 33,* 5–42.

Stothard, S. E., & Hulme, C. (1992). Reading comprehension difficulties in children: The role of language comprehension and working memory skills. *Reading and Writing: An Interdisciplinary Journal, 4,* 245.

Thurman, S. K., & Kiepert, M. H. (2008). Issues and concerns in conducting applied cognitive research. In S. K. Thurman & C. A. Fiorello (Eds.), *Applied cognitive research in k-3 classrooms* (pp. 265–288). New York: Routledge.

Thurman, S. K., & McGrath, M. C. (2008). Environmentally based assessment practices: Viable alternatives to standardized assessment for assessing emergent literacy skills in young children. *Reading and Writing Quarterly: Overcoming Learning Difficulties, 24,* 7–24.

Tirre, W. C., & Peña, C. M. (1992). Investigation of functional working memory in the reading span test. *Journal of Educational Psychology, 84,* 462–472.

Turner, M. L., & Engle, R. W. (1989). Is working memory capacity task dependent? *Journal of Memory and Language, 28,* 127–154.

Vandierendonck, A., Kemps, E., Fastame, M. C., & Szmalec, A. (2004). Working memory components of the Corsi blocks task. *British Journal of Psychology, 95,* 57–79.

Vecchi, T., & Richardson, J. T. E. (2001). Measures of visuospatial short-term memory: The Knox cube imitation test and the Corsi blocks test compared. *Brain and Cognition, 46,* 291–294.

Wechsler, D. (2003). *Examiner's manual: Wechsler Intelligence Scale for Children—Fourth Edition.* San Antonio, TX: Harcourt Assessment.

Wilson, J. T. L., Scott, J. H., & Power, K. G. (1987). Developmental differences in the span of visual memory for pattern. *British Journal of Developmental Psychology, 5,* 249–255.

17

BENEFITS OF TESTING MEMORY

Best practices and boundary conditions*

*Henry L. Roediger, III, Pooja K. Agarwal,
Sean H. K. Kang, and Elizabeth J. Marsh*

The idea of a memory test or of a test of academic achievement is often circumscribed. Tests within the classroom are recognized as important for the assignment of grades, and tests given for academic assessment or achievement have increasingly come to determine the course of children's lives: score well on such tests and you advance, are placed in more challenging classes, and attend better schools. Against this widely acknowledged backdrop of the importance of testing in educational life (not just in the US, but all over the world), it would be difficult to justify the claim that testing is not used enough in educational practice. In fact, such a claim may seem to be ludicrous on the face of it. However, this is just the claim we will make in this chapter: Education in schools would greatly benefit from additional testing, and the need for increased testing probably increases with advancement in the educational system. In addition, students should use self-testing as a study strategy in preparing for their classes.

Now, having begun with an inflammatory claim—we need more testing in education—let us explain what we mean and back up our claims. First, we are not recommending increased use of standardized tests in education, which is usually what people think of when they hear the words "testing in education". Rather, we have in mind the types of assessments (tests, essays, exercises) given in the classroom or assigned for homework. The reason we advocate testing is that it requires students to retrieve information effortfully from memory, and such effortful retrieval turns out to be a wonderfully powerful mnemonic device in many circumstances.

Tests have both indirect and direct effects on learning (Roediger & Karpicke, 2006b). The indirect effect is that, if tests are given more frequently, students study more. Consider a college class in which there is only a mid-term and a final exam compared to a similar class in which weekly quizzes are given every Friday, in addition to the midterm and the final. A large research program is not required to determine that students study more in the class with weekly quizzes than in the class without them. Yet tests also have a direct effect on learning; many studies have shown that students' retrieval of information on tests greatly improves their later retention of the tested material, either compared to a no-intervention control or even compared to a control condition in which students study the material for an equivalent amount of time to that given to students taking the test. That is, taking a test on material often yields greater gains than restudying material, as we document below. These findings have important educational implications, ones that teachers and professors have not exploited.

In this chapter, we first report selectively on findings from our lab on the critical importance of testing (or retrieval) for future remembering. Retrieval is a powerful mnemonic enhancer. However, testing does not lead to improvements under all possible conditions, so the remainder of our chapter will discuss qualifications and boundary conditions of test-enhanced learning, as we call our program (McDaniel, Roediger, & McDermott, 2007b). We consider issues of test format in one section, such as whether multiple-choice or short answer tests produce greater enhancements in performance. Another critical issue, considered in the next section, is the role of feedback: When is it helpful, or is it always helpful? We then discuss how to schedule tests and whether tests should occur frequently with short spacings between them—should we strike memory again when the iron is hot, as it were? Or should tests be spaced out in time, and, if so, how? In the next section, we ask if true/false and multiple-choice tests can ever have negative influences on learning. These tests provide students with erroneous information, either in the form of false statements (in true/false tests) or plausible alternatives that are nearly, but not quite, correct (in multiple-choice tests). Might students pick up misinformation from these kinds of tests, just as they do in other situations (e.g., Loftus, Miller, & Burns, 1978)? We then turn to the issue of metacognition, and examine students' beliefs and practices about testing and how they think it compares to other study strategies. Finally, we discuss how the findings on testing reviewed in this chapter might be applied in the classroom, as recent studies show that test-enhanced learning works in actual classrooms from middle school to college. We end with a few reflections on the role of testing in enhancing educational attainment.

Test-enhanced learning

Psychologists have studied the effects of testing on later memory, off and on, for 100 years (Abbott, 1909). In this section we report two experiments from our own lab to illustrate the power of testing to readers who may not be familiar with this literature and to blunt one main criticism of some testing research (see Roediger & Karpicke [2006b] for a thorough review).

Consider first a study by Wheeler and Roediger (1992). As part of a larger experiment, students in one condition studied 60 pictures while listening to a story. The subjects were told that they should remember the pictures, because they would be tested on the names of the pictures (which were given in the story). The test was free recall, meaning that students were given a blank sheet of paper and asked to recall as many of the items as possible. After hearing the story, one group of students was permitted to leave the lab and asked to return one week later for the test. A second group was given a single test that lasted about seven minutes. A third group was given three successive tests. That is, a minute after their first test, they were given a new blank sheet of paper and asked to recall as many of the 60 pictures as they could for a second time. After they were finished, the procedure was repeated a third time. The group that was given a single recall test produced 32 items on the test; the group that took three tests recalled 32, 35, and 36, respectively. The improvement in recall across repeated tests (even though each later test is further delayed from original study) is called hypermnesia. However, the real interest for present purposes is how students performed on a final test a week later. All subjects had studied the same list of pictures while listening to a story, so the only difference was whether they had taken no, one, or three tests just after the study phase of the experiment.

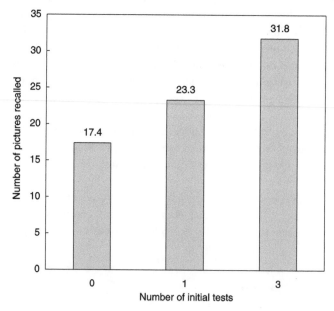

FIGURE 17.1 Number of pictures recalled on a one-week delayed test, adapted from Table 17.1 in Wheeler and Roediger (1992). The number of tests given just after learning greatly affected performance a week later; three prior tests raised recall over 80% relative to the no-test condition, and the act of taking three tests virtually eliminated the forgetting process

The results from the one-week delayed test are shown in Figure 17.1. Subjects who did not take a test during the first session recalled 17 items, those who had taken one test recalled 23 items, whereas those who had taken three tests recalled 32 items. The number of tests given just after learning greatly affected performance a week later; three prior tests raised recall over 80% relative to the no-test condition (i.e., $(32 - 17)/17 \times 100$). Looked at another way, immediately after study about 32 items could be recalled. If subjects took three tests just after recall, they could still recall 32 items a week later. The act of taking three tests essentially stopped the forgetting process in its tracks, so testing may be a mechanism to permit memories to consolidate or reconsolidate (Dudai, 2006).

Critics, however, could pounce on a potential flaw in the Wheeler and Roediger (1992) experiment just reported. Perhaps, they would carp, repeated testing simply exposes students to information again. That is, all "testing" does is allow for repeated study opportunities, and so the testing effect is no more surprising than the fact that when people study information two (or more) times they remember it better than if they study it once (e.g., Thompson, Wenger, & Bartling, 1978). This objection is plausible, but has been countered in many experiments that compared subjects who were tested to ones who spent the same amount of time restudying the material. The consistent finding is that taking an initial test produces greater recall on a final test than does restudying material (see Roediger & Karpicke, 2006b). Here we report only one experiment that makes the point.

Roediger and Karpicke (2006a, Experiment 1) had students read brief prose passages about a variety of topics, many having to do with science ("The Sun" or "Sea Otters") and other topics. After reading the passage, students either took a 7-minute test on the passage or read it again. Thus, in one condition, students studied the passage twice, whereas in the other they studied it once and took a test. The test consisted of students being given the title of the passage and asked to recall as much of it as possible. The data were scored in terms of the number of idea units recalled. The students taking the test recalled about 70% of the idea units during the test; on the other hand, students who restudied the passage were of course exposed to all the ideas in the passage. Thus, students who reread the passage actually received a greater exposure to the material than did students who took the test. The final test on the passages was either five minutes, two days, or seven days later, and was manipulated between subjects.

The results are shown in Figure 17.2 and several notable patterns can be seen. First, on the test given after a short (five-minute) delay, students who had repeatedly studied the material recalled it better than those who had studied it once and taken a test. Cramming (repeatedly reading) does work, at least at very short retention intervals. However, on the two delayed tests, the pattern reversed; studying and taking an initial test led to better performance on the delayed test than did studying the material twice. Testing enhanced long-term retention. Many other experiments, some of which are discussed below, have reported this same pattern (see Roediger & Karpicke, 2006b, for a review).

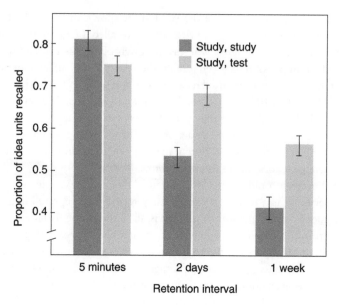

FIGURE 17.2 Results from Roediger and Karpicke (2006a, Experiment 1). On the five-minute delayed test, students who had repeatedly studied the material recalled it better than those who had studied it once and taken a test. Cramming (repeatedly reading) does work, at least at very short retention intervals. However, on the two delayed tests, the pattern reversed; studying and taking an initial test led to better performance on the delayed test than did studying the material twice

The results reviewed above, along with many others dating back over a century, establish the reality of the testing effect. However, not all experiments reveal testing effects. In the sections below, we consider variables that modulate the magnitude of the testing effect, beginning with the format of tests.

The format of tests

The power of testing to increase learning and retention has been demonstrated in numerous studies using a diverse range of materials; but both study and test materials come in a multitude of formats. Although the use of true/false and multiple-choice exams is now commonplace in high school and college classrooms, there was a time (in the 1920s and 1930s) when these kinds of exams were a novelty and referred to as "new-type", in contrast to the more traditional essay exams (Ruch, 1929). Given the variety of test formats, one question that arises is whether all formats are equally efficacious in improving retention. If we want to provide evidence-based recommendations for educators to utilize testing as a learning tool, it is important to ascertain if particular types of tests are more effective than others.

In a study designed to examine precisely this issue, Kang, McDermott, and Roediger (2007) manipulated the formats of both the initial and final tests—multiple-choice (MC) or short answer (SA)—using a fully-crossed, within-subjects design. Students read four short journal articles, and immediately afterwards they were given an MC quiz, an SA quiz, a list of statements to read, or a filler task. Feedback was given on quiz answers, and the quizzes and the list of statements all targeted the same critical facts. For instance, after reading an article on literacy acquisition, students in the SA condition generated an answer to "What is a phoneme?" (among other questions), students in the MC condition selected one of four possible alternatives to answer the same question, and students in the read-statements condition read "A phoneme is the basic sound unit of a language." This last condition allowed the effects of testing to be compared to the consequences of focused re-exposure to the target information (i.e., similar to receiving the test answers, without having to take the test). This control condition was a very conservative one, given that students in real life generally do not receive the answers to upcoming exams. A more typical baseline condition (i.e., having a filler task after reading the article) was also compared to the testing and focused rereading conditions. Three days later, subjects took a final test consisting of MC and SA questions.

Figure 17.3 shows that final performance was best in the initial SA condition. The initial MC condition led to the next best performance, followed by the read-statements condition and finally the filler-task condition. This pattern of results

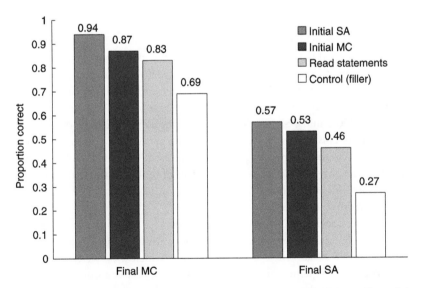

FIGURE 17.3 Results from Kang, McDermott, and Roediger (2007). Regardless of the format of the final test, the initial test format that required more effortful retrieval (i.e., the SA condition) yielded the best final performance, which was significantly better than being given the test answers without having to take a test. Although taking an initial MC test did benefit final performance relative to the filler-task control condition, the boost was not significantly above the read-statements condition

held for both final MC and final SA questions. Final test scores were significantly worse in the filler-task condition than the other three conditions, indicating that both testing (with feedback) and focused re-exposure aid retention of the target information. Importantly, only the initial SA condition produced significantly better final performance than the read-statements condition; the initial MC and read-statements conditions did not differ significantly. Retrieval is a potent memory modifier (Bjork, 1975). These results implicate the processes involved in actively producing information from memory as the causal mechanism underlying the testing effect. Regardless of the format of the final test, the initial test format that required more effortful retrieval (i.e., short answer) yielded the best final perform-ance, and this condition was significantly better than having read the test answers in isolation.

Similar results from other studies provide converging evidence that effortful retrieval is crucial for the testing effect (Carpenter & DeLosh, 2006; Glover, 1989). Butler and Roediger (2007), for example, used art history video lectures to simulate classroom learning. After the lectures, students completed short answer or multiple-choice tests, or they read statements as in Kang et al. (2007). On a final SA test given 30 days later, Butler and Roediger found the same pattern of results: (1) retention of target facts was best when students were given an initial SA quiz, and (2) taking an initial MC test produced final performance equivalent to reading the test answers (without taking a test). As discussed in a later section of this chapter, these findings have been replicated in an actual college course (McDaniel, Anderson, Derbish, & Morrisette, 2007b).

Although most evidence suggests that tests that require effortful retrieval yield the most memorial benefits, it should be noted that this depends upon successful retrieval on the initial test (or the delivery of feedback). Kang et al. (2007) had another experiment identical to the one described earlier except that no feedback was provided on the initial tests. Without corrective feedback, final test perform-ance changed: the initial SA condition yielded poorer performance than the initial MC condition. This difference makes sense when performance on the initial tests is considered: accuracy was much lower on the initial SA test ($M = .54$) than on the initial MC test ($M = .86$). The beneficial effect of testing can be attenuated when initial test performance is low (Wenger, Thompson, & Bartling, 1980) and no cor-rective feedback is provided.

This same conclusion about the role of level of initial performance can be drawn from Spitzer's (1939) early mega-study involving 3605 sixth-graders in Iowa. Students read an article on bamboo, after which they were tested. Spitzer manipulated the frequency of testing (students took between one and three tests) and the delay until the initial test (which ranged from immediately after reading the article to 63 days later). Most important for present purposes is that the benefit of prior testing became smaller the longer one waited after studying for the initial test; i.e., performance on the initial test declined with increasing retention interval, reducing the boost to performance on subsequent tests. In a similar vein, it has been shown that items that elicit errors on a cued recall test have almost no chance of being recalled correctly at a later time unless feedback is given (Pashler, Cepeda, Wixted, & Rohrer, 2005). In other words, learning from the test is handicapped when accuracy is low on the initial test (whereas this problem does not occur with rereading, where there is re-exposure to 100% of the target information). For the testing effect to manifest itself fully, feedback must be provided if initial test performance is low. Recent research showing that retrieval failure on a test (i.e., attempting to recall an answer but failing to) can enhance future encoding of the target information (Kornell, Hays, & Bjork, 2009; Richland, Kornell & Kao, 2009) emphasizes further the utility of providing feedback when initial test performance is poor.

A recent study (Agarwal, Karpicke, Kang, Roediger, & McDermott, 2008) delved more deeply into the issue of whether the kind of test influences the testing effect. In a closed-book test, students take the test without having concurrent access to their study materials, and this is the traditional way in which tests have been administered. In recent years, open-book tests—where students are permitted to consult their notes and textbooks during the test—have grown in popularity, with the belief that such tests promote higher-level thinking skills (e.g., Feller, 1994). The final test only involved short answer questions. We examined the issue of whether administering the initial test open- or closed-book made a difference to later retention of target facts. For the sake of brevity, only the second experiment will be described here (the results replicate the first experiment, which was similar in design). Students studied expository passages in various learning conditions: three study-only conditions (read the passage once, twice, or three times) and four test conditions (a closed-book test, a closed-book test with feedback, or an open-book test after reading the passage once, or a test completed simultaneously while reading the passage).

A final closed-book test was given a week later, and the key results are summarized in Table 17.1. Just taking a closed-book test (without feedback) resulted in final performance that was roughly equivalent to reading the passage three times (.55 vs. .54), and significantly better than reading the passage twice (.55 vs. 50), once again demonstrating the power of testing. The two learning conditions that tied for the best performance, however, were the closed-book test with feedback and the open-book test conditions ($Ms = .66$), both of which produced significantly more correct responses on the final test than all the other conditions. In our view, these two learning conditions contained two critical components—testing (retrieval) and feedback—that the other learning conditions lacked (or had only one or the other), and this combination contributed to best performance on the delayed test.

Although the current data suggest the equivalence of closed-book tests with feedback and open-book tests in enhancing later retention, further investigation into this issue is warranted, because on theoretical grounds one might expect a closed-book test to involve more retrieval effort than an open-book test. Perhaps a difference between these two conditions will emerge with a longer delay for the final test, an outcome that has occurred in other experiments (e.g., Roediger & Karpicke, 2006a). Such a finding would probably further depend on how students

TABLE 17.1 Mean proportion recalled in Agarwal et al.'s (2008) Experiment 2 on test formats. Proportion correct was greater for test conditions than study conditions; however, subjects predicted learning would be greater for study conditions relative to test conditions. Learning conditions that contained both testing and feedback, namely the closed-book test with feedback and the open-book test conditions, contributed to best performance on the delayed test

Condition	Proportion correct	
	Initial test	One-week delayed test
Study 1×		.40
Study 2×		.50
Study 3×		.54
Closed-book test	.67	.55
Closed-book test with feedback	.65	.66
Open-book test	.81	.66
Simultaneous answering	.83	.59
Non-studied control		.16

approach the open-book tests (e.g., whether they attempt retrieval of an answer before consulting the study material for feedback, or whether they immediately search the study material in order to identify the target information). Future research in our lab will tackle this topic.

In summary, one reason why testing benefits memory is that it promotes active retrieval of information. Not all formats of tests are equal. Test formats that require more effortful retrieval (e.g., short answer) tend to produce a greater boost to learning and retention, compared to test formats that engage less effortful retrieval (e.g., multiple-choice). However, tests that are more effortful or challenging also increase the likelihood of retrieval failure, which has been shown to reduce the beneficial effect of testing. Therefore, to ameliorate low performance on the initial test, corrective feedback should be provided. The practical implications of these findings for improving learning in the classroom are straightforward: instead of giving students summary notes to read, teachers should implement more frequent testing (of important facts and concepts)—using test formats that entail effortful retrieval—and provide feedback to correct errors. We turn now to a greater consideration of the issue of how and when feedback should be given after tests.

Testing and feedback

Broadly defined, feedback is information provided following a response or recollection, which informs the learner about the status of current performance, often leading to improvement in future performance (Roediger, Zaromb, & Butler, 2008). A great deal of laboratory and applied research has examined the conditions under which feedback is, and is not, effective in improving learning and perform-ance. We have already mentioned the critical importance of feedback when initial performance is low, as well as the benefit of feedback regardless of test format. In a later section, we discuss the benefits of feedback in reducing the negative effects of multiple-choice tests. For now, we focus on the effect of feedback type (e.g., cor-rective or right/wrong) and delay (e.g., immediate vs. delayed) on a learner's future responses and confidence regarding their own performance.

To begin, feedback can encompass a range of information: representation of the original material, information regarding whether the learner is simply correct or incorrect, or specific information regarding the correct response, just to name a few. In a study by Pashler et al. (2005), subjects studied Luganda–English word pairs (e.g., *leero—today*) and received no feedback, right/wrong feedback, or correct answer feedback following each response on an initial test. After one week, per-formance following the correct answer feedback condition was significantly greater than performance in either of the other conditions. In addition, right/wrong feed-back did not benefit retention over and above the absence of feedback, a finding replicated in other studies (e.g., see Bangert-Drowns, Kulik, Kulik, & Morgan, 1991, for a review). Furthermore, Moreno (2004) demonstrated that explanatory feedback (e.g., providing students with the correct answer and an explanation) increased final retention and transfer relative to corrective feedback (e.g., only providing students with the correct answer). In general, in order to improve performance, feedback must include corrective information, and the learner may further benefit when an explanation follows the corrective feedback.

Although Pashler et al. (2005) found the benefits of corrective feedback to be limited to revising errors, Butler, Karpicke, and Roediger (2007) found that feed-back benefits initially correct answers as well as incorrect responses. This recent finding is consistent with earlier research, which demonstrated that subjects who receive feedback are more likely to fix initial errors and remember initially correct responses on a final criterial test (Kulhavy, Yekovich, & Dyer, 1976, 1979). More specifically, subjects spend more time processing feedback following errors made with high confidence and correct answers made with low confidence. Butterfield and Metcalfe (2006) held feedback time constant, and still found subjects were more likely to later correct errors made with high confidence than those made with low confidence. They named this the hypercorrection effect, and argued that subjects attend more to feedback that is at odds with their expectations (see also Fazio & Marsh, 2009). Similarly, Butler, Karpicke, and Roediger (2008) suggested that feed-back reinforces the association between a cue and its target response, increasing the likelihood that an initially low-confidence correct response will be produced on a final criterial test.

Regarding the best time to deliver feedback, there exists a great deal of debate and confusion, as immediate and delayed feedback are operationalized differently across studies. For instance, the term "immediate feedback" has been used to imply feedback given just after each test item or feedback provided immediately after a test. On the other hand, "delayed feedback" can take place anywhere from eight seconds after an item to two days after the test (Kulik & Kulik, 1988), although in many educational settings the feedback may actually occur a week or more later.

Butler et al. (2007) investigated the effects of type and timing of feedback on long-term retention. Subjects read prose passages and completed an initial multiple-choice test. For some responses, they received standard feedback (i.e., the correct answer); for others they received feedback by answering until correct (labeled AUC: i.e., each response was labeled as correct or incorrect, and if incorrect they chose additional options until they answered the question correctly). Half of the subjects received the feedback immediately after each question, while the rest received the feedback after a one-day delay. One week later, subjects completed a final cued recall test, and these data are shown in Figure 17.4. On the final test, delayed feedback led to substantially better performance than immediate feedback, while the standard feedback condition and the answer-until-correct feedback condition resulted in similar performance. Butler et al. discussed why some studies find immediate feedback to be more beneficial than delayed feedback (e.g., see Kulik & Kulik, 1988, for a review). Namely, this inconsistency might occur if learners do not fully process delayed feedback, which would be particularly likely in applied studies where less experimental control is present. That is, even if students receive delayed feedback they may not look at it or look only at feedback on questions that they missed. When feedback processing is controlled, as in the Butler et al. study, a benefit for delayed feedback on long-term retention emerges.

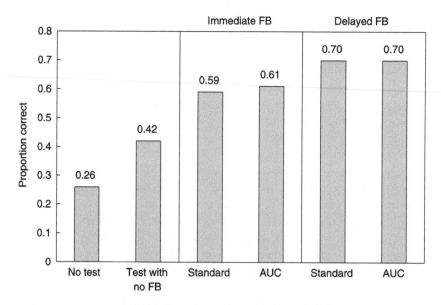

FIGURE 17.4 Results from Butler, Karpicke, and Roediger (2007). On the final test, delayed feedback (FB) led to substantially better performance than immediate feedback, while the standard feedback condition and the answer–until–correct (AUC) feedback condition resulted in similar performance. When feedback processing is controlled, a benefit for delayed feedback on long-term retention emerges

In sum, the provision of feedback leads to substantial increases in long-term learning. Delayed feedback virtually always boosts final performance if the feedback includes both the correct answer as well as an explanation of that answer. Feedback also serves a variety of purposes: correcting errors, improving retention of correct responses, and enhancing metacognition. Feedback should be incorporated into all educational testing.

Schedules for testing

The great bulk of the literature on testing effects shows the benefit of a single initial test relative to either no test or to a reading control condition. The fact that the testing effect occurs robustly in such situations indicates the power of testing, but one can ask whether students would learn better if they received multiple tests on the same material. For example, the Wheeler and Roediger (1992) data shown in Figure 17.1 indicate that three tests shortly after study led to better recall a week later relative to one test. Is this effect general?

Anecdotally, one might expect that it is. For example, when children in the early primary grades are taught their multiplication tables, they often use or construct flashcards. All problems up to 9×9 (or even higher) are created so that one side of the card might say $6 \times 8 = ??$ and the other side has 48. Students are instructed to test themselves repeatedly on the cards, flipping over to the other side when they need feedback. Students are usually instructed to do this until answering the item becomes quick and effortless, but it takes repeated practice to reach this state.

Flashcards are used in many other situations to learn large bodies of factual information, and educational companies make flashcards for a huge number of purposes, including learning foreign language vocabulary, the parts of the skeletal system, birds and their names, and so on. Research on how to effectively use flashcards is relatively new, however. One instruction often given in mastering a set of flashcards is to learn to give the correct answer, then practice it once, and then to drop that card from the pile to concentrate on others that have not yet been learned. The assumption is that learning to a criterion of one correct recitation means that the item is learned and that further practice on it will be for naught.

Karpicke and Roediger (2008) published a study that questions this common wisdom. In their study, students learned foreign language vocabulary in the form of Swahili–English word pairs. (Swahili was used because students were unfamiliar with the language, and yet the word forms were easily pronounceable for English speakers, such as *mashua–boat*). Students learned 40 pairs under one of four conditions. In one condition, students studied and were tested on the 40 pairs in the usual multitrial learning situation favored by psychologists (study–test, study–test, study–test, study–test, labeled the ST condition). In a second condition, students received a similar first study–test cycle, but if they correctly recalled pairs on the test, these pairs were dropped from the next study trial. Thus, across the four trials, the study list got smaller and smaller as students recalled more items. However, in this condition, labeled $S_N T$, students were tested on all 40 pairs during each test period. Thus, relative to the ST condition, the $S_N T$ condition involved fewer study opportunities but the same number of tests. In a third condition, labeled ST_N, students studied and were tested the same way as in the other conditions on the first trial, but after the first trial they repeatedly studied the pairs three more times, but once they had recalled a pair, it was dropped from the test. In this condition, the study sequence stayed the same on four occasions, but the number of items tested became smaller and smaller. Finally, in a fourth condition denoted $S_N T_N$, after the first study–test trial, items that were recalled were dropped both from the study and test phase of the experiment for the additional trials. In this case, then, the study list and the test sequence became shorter over trials. This last condition is most like standard advice for using flashcards—students studied and were tested on the pairs until they were recalled, and then they were dropped so that attention could be devoted to unlearned pairs.

Initial learning on the 40 pairs in the four conditions is shown in Figure 17.5, where it can be seen that all four conditions produced equivalent learning. The data in Figure 17.5 show cumulative performance, such that students were given credit the first time they recalled a pair and not again (for those conditions in which multiple recalls of a pair were required, ST and $S_N T$). At the end of the learning phase, students were told that they would come back a week later to be tested again

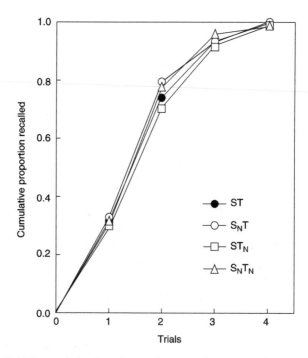

FIGURE 17.5 Initial cumulative learning performance from Karpicke and Roediger (2008). All four conditions produced equivalent learning

and were asked to predict how many pairs they would recall. Students in all four groups estimated that they would recall about 20 pairs, or 50% of the pairs, a week later. After all, the learning curves were equal, so why would we expect students' judgments to differ?

Figure 17.6 shows the proportion of items recalled 1 week later, in each of the four conditions. Students in two conditions did very well (ST and S_NT, around 80%) and in the other two conditions students did much more poorly (ST_N and S_NT_N, around 35%). What do the former two conditions have in common that the latter two conditions lack? The answer is retrieval practice.

In both the ST and S_NT conditions, students were tested on all 40 pairs for all four trials. Note that in the ST condition students studied all 40 items four times, whereas in the S_NT condition, the items were dropped from study. However, this reduced amount of study did not matter a bit for retention a week later. Students in the ST_N and S_NT_N conditions had only enough testing for each item to be recalled once and, without repeated retrieval, final recall was relatively poor. Once again, the condition with many more study opportunities (ST_N) did not lead to any

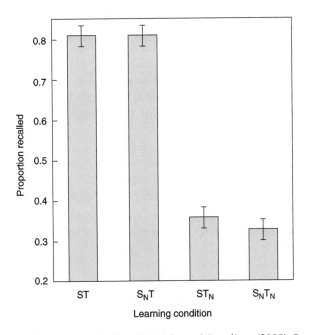

FIGURE 17.6 Final learning results from Karpicke and Roediger (2008). Students in the ST and S_NT conditions performed very well, and students in the ST_N and S_NT_N conditions did much more poorly. In both the ST and S_NT conditions, students were tested on all 40 pairs for all four trials. Students in the ST_N and S_NT_N conditions had only enough testing for each item to be recalled once and, without repeated retrieval, recall was relatively poor. The condition with many more study opportunities (ST_N) did not lead to any appreciably better recall a week later than the condition that had minimal study opportunities (S_NT_N)

appreciably better recall a week later than the condition that had minimal study opportunities ($S_N T_N$).

The bottom line from the Karpicke and Roediger (2008) experiment is that, after students have retrieved a pair correctly once, repeated retrieval is the key to improved long-term retention. Repeated studying after this point does not much matter.

Recall that the students in the four conditions predicted that they would do equally well, and recall about 50% after a week. As can be seen in Figure 17.6, the students who were repeatedly tested actually outperformed their predictions, so they underestimated the power of testing. On the other hand, the students who did not have repeated testing overestimated how well they would do. In a later section, we return to the issue of what students know about the effects of testing and whether they use testing as a study strategy when left to their own devices.

Repeated testing seems to be great for consolidating information into long-term memory, but is there an optimal schedule for repeated testing? Landauer and Bjork (1978) argued that a condition they called expanding retrieval was optimal, or at least was better than two other schedules called massed practice and equal interval practice. To explain, let us stick with our foreign-language vocabulary learning example above, *mashua–boat*, and consider patterns in which three retrievals of the target might be carried out. In the immediate test condition, after the item has been presented, *mashua* would be presented three times in a row for boat to be recalled each time. This condition might provide good practice because, of course, performance on each test would be nearly perfect. (In fact, in most experiments, this massed testing condition leads to 98% or higher correct recall with paired-associates.)

The massed retrieval condition will be denoted a 0-0-0 to indicate that the three retrievals occurred back to back, with no other study or test items between retrievals of the target.

A second condition is the equal interval schedule, in which tests are given after a delay from study and at equal intervals after that. So, in a 5-5-5 schedule, a pair like *mashua–boat* would be presented, then five other pairs or tests would occur, and then *mashua –??* would be given as a cue. This same process would occur two more times. Although distributed retrieval could be beneficial relative to massed retrieval, just as distributed study practice is beneficial relative to massed practice, one looming problem occurs in the case of retrieval—if the first test is delayed, recall on the first test may be low and, as discussed above, low performance on a test can reduce or eliminate the power of the testing effect. To overcome this problem, Landauer and Bjork (1978) introduced the idea of expanding retrieval practice, to insure a nearly errorless early retrieval with a quick first test while at the same time gaining advantages of distributed testing or practice. So, to continue with our example, in an expanding schedule of 1-4-10, students would be tested with *mashua –??* after only one intervening item, then again after four intervening items, and then after ten intervening items. The idea behind the expanding schedule is familiar to psychologists because it resembles the idea of shaping behavior by successive approximations (Skinner, 1953); just as schedules of reinforcement (Ferster & Skinner, 1957) exist to shape behavioral responses, so schedules of retrieval may shape the ability to remember. If a student wants to be able to retrieve a vocabulary word long after study, the expanding retrieval schedule may help to shape its retrieval.

Landauer and Bjork (1978) conducted two experiments pitting massed, equal interval, and expanding interval schedules of retrieval against one another. For the latter conditions, they used 5-5-5 spacing and 1-4-10 spacing. Note that this comparison equates the average interval of spacing at 5. The materials in one experiment were fictitious first and last names, such that students were required to produce a last name when given the first name. Landauer and Bjork measured performance on the three initial tests and then on a final test given at the end of the experimental session. The results for the expanding and equal interval retrieval sequences are shown in Table 17.2 for the three initial tests and then the final, criterial, test. Expanding retrieval schedules were better than equal interval schedules, as Landauer and Bjork predicted, on both the initial three tests and then the final criterial test. The 7% advantage of expanding interval retrieval to equally spaced retrieval on the final test was small but statistically significant, and this is the comparison that the authors emphasized in the paper. They replicated the effect in a separate experiment with face–name pairs. However, note a curious fact about the data in Table 17.2: Over the four tests shown, performance drops steadily in the expanding interval condition (from .61 to .47) whereas in the equal interval condition performance is essentially flat (.42 to .40). This pattern suggests that on a more delayed final test, the curves might cross over and equal interval retrieval might prove superior to expanding retrieval.

Strangely, for some years researchers did not investigate Landauer and Bjork's (1978) intriguing findings, perhaps because they made such good sense. Most of the studies on retrieval schedules compared expanding and massed retrieval, but did not include the critical equal interval condition needed to compare expanding retrieval to another distributed schedule (e.g., Rea & Modigliani, 1985). All studies making the massed versus expanding retrieval comparison showed expanding retrieval to be more effective, and Balota, Duchek, and Logan (2007)

TABLE 17.2 Mean proportion recalled in Landauer and Bjork's (1978) experiment on schedules of testing; data are estimated from Figures 17.1 and 1.2. Expanding retrieval schedules were better than equal interval schedules on both the initial three tests and the final criterial test

	Initial tests			Final test
	1	2	3	
Expanding	.61	.55	.50	.47
Equal	.42	.42	.43	.40

have provided an excellent review of this literature. They show conclusively that massed testing is a poor strategy relative to distributed testing, despite the fact that massed testing produces very high performance on the initial tests (much higher than equal interval testing). Although this might seem commonplace to cognitive psychologists steeped in the literature of massed versus spaced presentation (the spacing effect), from a different perspective the outcome is surprising. Skinner (1958) promoted the notion of errorless retrieval as being the key to learning, and he implemented this approach in his teaching machines and programmed learning. However, current research shows that distributed retrieval is much more effective in promoting later performance than is massed retrieval, even though massed retrieval produces errorless performance.

On the other hand, when comparisons are made between expanding and equal interval schedules, the data are much less conclusive. The other main point established in the Balota et al. (2007) review is that no consistent evidence exists for the advantage of expanding retrieval schedules over equal interval testing sequences. A few studies after Landauer and Bjork's (1978) seminal study obtained the effect, but the great majority did not. For example, Cull (2000) reported four experiments in which students learned difficult word pairs. Across experiments, he manipulated variables such as intertest interval, feedback or no feedback after the tests, and testing versus restudying the material. The general conclusion drawn from the four experiments was that distributed retrieval produced much better retention on a final test than did massed retrieval, but that it did not matter whether the schedule had uniform or expanded spacing of tests.

Recent research by Karpicke and Roediger (2007) and Logan and Balota (2008) actually shows a more interesting pattern. On tests that occur a day or more after original learning, equal interval schedules of initial testing actually produce greater long-term retention than do expanding schedules (just the opposite of Landauer and Bjork's findings). Recall the data in Table 17.2 and how the expanding retrieval testing condition showed a steady decline with repeated tests whereas the equal interval schedule showed essentially no decline. Because the final test in these studies occurred during the same session as initial learning, the retention interval for the final test was fairly short, leaving open the possibility that on a long-delayed test the functions would actually cross. This is just what both Karpicke and Roediger and Logan and Balota found.

Karpicke and Roediger (2007) had students learn word pairs taken from practice tests for the Graduate Record Exam (e.g., *sobriquet–nickname*, *benison–blessing*) and tests consisted of giving the first member of the pair and asking for the second. Their initial testing conditions were massed (0-0-0), expanding (1-5-9) and equal interval (5-5-5). In addition, they included two conditions in which students received only a single test after either one intervening pair or five. The design and initial test results are shown on the left side of Table 17.3. Initial test performance was best in the massed condition, next in the expanding condition, and worst in the equally spaced condition, the usual pattern, and students in the single test condition recalled less after a delay of five intervening items than after one. There are no surprises in

TABLE 17.3 Mean proportion recalled in Karpicke and Roediger's (2007) experiment on schedules of testing. Expanding retrieval in the initial phase produced better recall than the equal interval schedule on the 10-minute delayed test, and both of these schedules were better than the massed retrieval schedule. However, after a 2-day delay, recall was best in the equal interval condition relative to the expanding condition, although both conditions still produced better performance than in the massed condition

	Initial tests			Final tests	
	1	2	3	10 min	48 h
Massed (0-0-0)	.98	.98	.98	.47	.20
Expanding (1-5-9)	.78	.76	.77	.71	.33
Equal (5-5-5)	.73	.73	.73	.62	.45
Single-immediate (1)	.81			.65	.22
Single-delayed (5)	.73			.57	.30

the initial recall data. Half the students took a final test ten minutes after the initial learning phase, whereas the rest received the final test two days later. These results are shown in the right side of Table 17.3. First consider data at the ten-minute delay. The top three rows show a very nice replication of the pattern reported by Landauer and Bjork (1978): Expanding retrieval in the initial phase produced better recall on the final test than the equal interval schedule, and both of these schedules were better than the massed retrieval schedule. Also, the single-immediate test produced better delayed recall than the single-delayed test. However, the startling result in this experiment appeared for those subjects who took the test after a two-day delay. Recall was now best in the equal interval condition ($M = .45$) relative to the expanding condition ($M = .33$), although both conditions still produced better performance than in the massed condition ($M = .20$). Interestingly, performance also reversed across the delay for the two single test conditions: recall was better in the single-immediate condition after ten minutes, but was reliably better in the single-delayed condition after two days.

Karpicke and Roediger (2007) argued that, congenial as the idea is, expanding retrieval is not conducive to good long-term retention. Instead, what seems to be important for long-term retention is the difficulty of the first retrieval attempt. When subjects try to retrieve an item after five intervening items, they exert more effort during retrieval than after one intervening item, which in turn is more difficult than after no intervening items (the massed condition). Notice that the same pattern occurs for items that were tested only once, after either one or five intervening items. Karpicke and Roediger (2007) replicated these results in a second experiment in which feedback was given after the initial tests. A third experiment confirmed that delaying the first test is the critical ingredient in enhancing long-term retention and that the method of distributing retrieval (expanding or equal interval) does not matter. Logan and Balota (2008) reported similar data and reached the same general conclusion.

The conclusion that retrieval difficulty is the key element promoting better long-term retention for equal interval (relative to expanding or massed) schedules fits well with data reviewed in previous parts of the chapter, such as recall tests producing a greater testing effect than recognition tests. However, as Balota et al. (2007) have noted, the literature on expanding retrieval sequences has used a relatively small array of conditions (three tests, paired associate learning of one sort or another, relatively immediate tests). One can imagine that an expanding retrieval schedule could be better than equal intervals if there were more presentations and these occurred over longer periods of time. However, this conjecture awaits future testing.

Dangers of multiple-choice and true/false tests

We have established that students learn from tests, and that this learning seems to be especially durable. However, the fact that we learn from tests can also pose a danger in some situations. Although professors would never knowingly present wrong information during lectures or in assigned readings, they do it routinely when they give certain types of tests, namely, true/false and multiple-choice tests. If students learn from tests, might they learn wrong information if it is presented on the tests? On true/false tests it is common for half the statements to be right and half to be wrong, and normally false items are plausible in order to require rather fine discriminations. Similarly, for multiple-choice tests, students receive a question stem and then four possible completions, one of which is correct and three others that are erroneous (but again, statements that might be close to correct). Because erroneous information is presented on the tests, students might learn that incorrect information, especially if no feedback is given (as is often the case in college courses). If the test is especially difficult (meaning a large number of wrong answers are selected), the students may actually leave a test more confused about the material than when they walked in. However, even if conditions are such that students rarely commit errors, it might be that simply reading and carefully considering false statements on true/false tests and distractors on multiple-choice tests can lead later to erroneous knowledge. Several studies have shown that having people simply read statements (whether true or false) increases later judgments that the statements are true (Bacon, 1979; Begg, Armour, & Kerr, 1985; Hasher, Goldstein, & Toppino, 1977). This effect underlies the tactics of propagandists using "the big lie" technique by repeating a statement over and over until the populace believes it, and is also a favored tactic in most US presidential elections. If you repeat an untruth about an opponent repeatedly, the statement comes to be believed.

Remmers and Remmers (1926) first discussed the idea that incorrect information on tests might mislead students, when the "new" techniques of true/false and multiple-choice testing were introduced into education (Ruch, 1929). They called this outcome the negative suggestibility effect, although not much research was done on it for many years. Much later Toppino and his colleagues showed that statements presented as distractors on true/false and multiple-choice tests did indeed accrue truth value from their mere presentation, because these statements were judged as more true when mixed with novel statements in appropriately designed experiments (Toppino & Brochin, 1989; Toppino & Luipersbeck, 1993). In a similar vein, Brown (1988) and Jacoby and Hollingshead (1990) showed that exposing students to misspelled words increased misspelling of those words on a later oral test.

Roediger and Marsh (2005) asked whether giving a multiple-choice test (without feedback) would lead to a kind of misinformation effect (Loftus et al., 1978). That is, if students take a multiple-choice test on a subset of facts, and then take a short answer test on all facts, will prior testing increase intrusions of multiple-choice lures on the final test? Roediger and Marsh conducted a series of experiments to address this question, manipulating the difficulty of the material (and hence level of performance on the multiple-choice test) and the number of distractors given on the multiple-choice test. Three experiments were submitted using these tactics, but the editor asked us to drop our first two experiments (which established the phenomenon) and report only a third, control, experiment that showed that the negative suggestibility effect occurred under tightly controlled but not necessarily realistic conditions. We complied and published the third experiment, but the two most interesting experiments (in our opinion) were not reported. We present them here to show that negative effects of testing do accrue from taking multiple-choice tests and to have the experiments published, albeit in terse form.

Our first experiment was exploratory, just to make sure we could get the effects we sought. We predicted that we would see a positive testing effect to the extent students were able to answer the multiple-choice questions. Of interest was whether selecting distractors on the multiple-choice test would lead to their intrusion on a later test. We selected 80 easy and 80 hard general knowledge questions from the Nelson and Narens (1980) norms. Subjects in the norming study correctly answered an average of 72% of easy questions ("What sport uses the terms 'gutter' and 'alley'?" [bowling]) and 13% of the difficult items ("Which union general defeated the Confederate Army at the Civil War battle of Gettysburg?" [Meade]). Because the norms are for short answer questions, we generated three plausible distractors for each item. Four sets of 40 items (20 easy and 20 hard) were created and rotated through four multiple-choice test conditions: 40 items were not tested, 40 were tested with one distractor, 40 with two distractors, and 40 with three distractors. Thus the multiple-choice test consisted of 120 questions, and no feedback was given as to the correctness of the answers. Following this test, the 40 subjects in the experiment spent five minutes doing a visuospatial filler task before they took a final short answer (cued recall) test. They were given the 160 general knowledge questions (120 items previously tested with multiple-choice and the 40 nontested items).

Performance on the multiple-choice test is shown in the top panel of Table 17.4, in the section devoted to Experiment 1 data. Not surprisingly, performance was better on easy than difficult items and declined with the number of alternatives. However, we did succeed in manipulating the level of multiple-choice performance,

TABLE 17.4 Proportion correct on a multiple-choice test as a function of question difficulty and number of alternatives (including correct) for each question in Experiments 1 and 2 of Roediger and Marsh (reported in this chapter). Performance was better on easy than difficult items and declined with the number of alternatives. Similarly, performance on unread passages was lower than for read passages, and performance generally declined with the number of distractors (albeit more for unread than read passages)

| | Number of alternatives | | |
	Two	Three	Four
Experiment 1			
Easy questions	.91	.85	.85
Hard questions	.66	.55	.48
Experiment 2			
Passages read	.86	.86	.84
Passages not read	.68	.62	.51

and this allowed us to see if any negative effects of testing were limited to conditions in which subjects made more errors on the multiple-choice test (i.e., difficult items and relatively many distractors).

The interesting data are contained in Tables 17.5 and 17.6 (again, the top panels devoted to Experiment 1). Table 17.5 shows the proportion of short answer questions answered correctly ("bowling" in response to "What sport uses the terms 'gutter' and 'alleys'?"). A strong positive testing effect appeared: Relative to the nontested questions, subjects correctly answered more previously tested questions, for both easy and hard items. When previously tested with more multiple-choice distractors, the size of the positive effect dropped a bit for the hard items. However, the positive testing effect was robust in all conditions. Subjects had been required to guess on the short answer test (and they provided confidence ratings), but when we removed the "not sure" responses from the data, the same pattern held (for both high confidence and medium confidence answers). These data with "not sure responses removed" are shown in parentheses in Table 17.5.

Table 17.6 shows errors committed on the short answer test, and we found that prior multiple-choice testing also led to a negative effect (in addition to the positive testing effect just documented). The prior multiple-choice test led to more multiple-choice lure answers on the final test and this effect grew larger when more distractors had been presented on the multiple-choice test. Again, removing the "not sure" responses reduced the size of the negative suggestibility effect, but left the basic pattern intact. Those data are again in parentheses.

The data show clearly that taking a multiple-choice test can simultaneously enhance performance on a later cued recall test (a positive testing effect) and harm performance (a negative suggestibility effect). The former effect comes from questions answered correctly on the multiple-choice test, whereas the latter effect arises from errors committed on the multiple-choice test. In fact, 78% of the

TABLE 17.5 Proportion correct on the cued recall test as a function of question difficulty and number of alternatives (including the correct answer) on the prior multiple-choice test. Non-guess responses are in parentheses (proportion correct not including those that received a "not sure" rating). A positive testing effect is evident for both easy and hard questions, and read and unread passages, although the effect declined with the number of distractors on the prior multiple-choice test for the unread items. In both experiments, a positive testing effect was observed under all conditions, and the effect was maintained even when "not sure" responses were removed

| | Number of previous alternatives | | | |
	Zero (not-tested)	Two	Three	Four
Experiment 1 Easy questions	.69	.86	.84	.84
	(.65)	(.83)	(.81)	(.80)
Hard questions	.18	.44	.41	.38
	(.16)	(.40)	(.36)	(.33)
Experiment 2 Read passages	.56	.79	.79	.75
	(.52)	(.73)	(.72)	(.70)
Non-read passages	.23	.56	.53	.44
	(.14)	(.43)	(.40)	(.31)

TABLE 17.6 Proportion target incorrect answers on the cued recall test as a function of question difficulty and number of alternatives (including the correct answer) on the prior multiple-choice test. Non-guess responses are in parentheses (proportion correct not including those that received a "not sure" rating). The prior multiple-choice test led to more errors on the final test and this effect grew larger when more distractors had been presented on the multiple-choice test. Removing the "not sure" responses reduced the size of the negative suggestibility effect, but left the basic pattern intact

| | Number of previous alternatives | | | |
	Zero (not-tested)	Two	Three	Four
Experiment 1 Easy questions	.08	.09	.11	.11
	(.05)	(.06)	(.09)	(.08)
Hard questions	.17	.26	.34	.36
	(.10)	(.20)	(.21)	(.24)
Experiment 2 Read passages	.05	.09	.10	.11
	(.01)	(.06)	(.05)	(.07)
Non-read passages	.11	.24	.25	.37
	(.03)	(.13)	(.12)	(.15)

multiple-choice lure answers on the final test had been selected erroneously on the prior multiple-choice test. This result is noteworthy because it suggests that any negative effects of multiple-choice testing require selection of an incorrect answer, and that simply reading the lures (and then selecting the correct answer) is not problematic.

In Experiment 2 we examined whether students would show the same effects when learning from prose materials. We used 20 nonfiction passages on a wide variety of topics (the sun, Mt. Rainier, Louis Armstrong). For each passage we constructed four questions, each of which could be tested in both multiple-choice and short answer formats. Students read half the passages and not the other half, and then took a multiple-choice test where the number of multiple-choice lures was manipulated from zero (the item was not tested) through three alternatives. Thus, the design conformed to a 2 (studied, non-studied passages) × 4 (number of distractors on the test, 0–3) design. Five minutes after completing the multiple-choice test, the students took the final short answer test that contained 80 critical items (60 from the previous multiple-choice test and 20 previously nontested items). As in the first experiment, they were required to answer all questions and to rate their confidence in each answer.

The multiple-choice data are displayed in the bottom part of Table 17.4. Again, the results are straightforward: Not surprisingly, performance on unread passages was lower than for read passages, and performance generally declined with the number of distractors (albeit more for unread than read passages). Once again, the manipulations succeeded in varying multiple-choice performance across a fairly wide range.

The consequences of multiple-choice testing can be seen in the bottom of Table 17.5, which shows the proportion of final short answer questions answered correctly. A positive testing effect occurred for both read and unread passages, although for unread passages the effect declined with the number of distractors on the prior multiple-choice test. Still, as in the first experiment, a positive testing effect was observed in all conditions, even when "not sure" responses were removed (the data in parentheses).

As can be seen in Table 17.6, the negative suggestibility effect also appeared in full force in Experiment 2, although it was greater for the nonread passages, with their corresponding higher rate of errors on the multiple-choice test than for the read passages. For the read passages, the error rate nearly doubled after the multiple-choice test, from 5% to 9%. When the "not sure" responses were removed, the difference grew from 1% (not tested) to 6% (tested). This is not large, but is statistically significant. Also, note that students in this experiment were tested under conditions that usually do not hold in actual educational settings—they had carefully read the relevant passages only moments before the multiple-choice test and only 20 or so minutes before taking the final criterial test. The data from the nonread passages with their higher error rates may in some ways be more educationally informative, as unfortunately students are often unprepared for exams. The negative suggestibility effect was much larger in the nonread condition whether or not the "not sure" responses were included.

The generalization that may be taken from these two experiments is that, when multiple-choice performance is relatively high, a large positive testing effect and a relatively small negative suggestibility effect will be found. Correspondingly, under conditions of relatively poor multiple-choice performance, the positive testing effect will be diminished and the negative effect will be increased. These conclusions hold over more recent experiments, and also agree with the third experiment conducted, the one that did appear in the Roediger and Marsh (2005) paper. In this study, we replicated Experiment 2 but changed the instruction on the final short answer test from forced recall with confidence ratings to recall with a strong warning against guessing. That is, subjects were told to give an answer on the final test only if they were reasonably sure they were right. Under these stricter conditions, we still obtained the negative suggestibility effect (and, of course, the positive testing effect). These strict conditions are unlike those used in educational settings, though, where students are typically free to respond without fear of penalty for wrong answers.

The subjects in the three experiments just described were all from Washington University, a highly selective university, and therefore these expert test takers are unrepresentative of test takers in general. To take a step towards a more typical sample, we (Marsh, Agarwal, & Roediger, 2009) recently tested high school juniors at a suburban high school in Illinois, on practice SAT II questions on chemistry, biology, and history. SAT II tests (now renamed SAT subject tests) are often taken by high school juniors and used for college admissions and class placement decisions. We examined the effects of answering SAT II questions on a later short answer test, in both the high school students and a Duke University sample tested with similar procedures. Duke University students are expert test takers, who took tests similar to the SAT II for admission. Not surprisingly, the undergraduates did much better on the initial multiple-choice questions than did the high school students; undergraduates answered 55% correctly whereas high schoolers only answered 34% correctly. High schoolers also endorsed far more multiple-choice lures than did the university students; SAT II questions always offer a "don't know" option as the test penalizes wrong answers. So even if high school students didn't know the answers, they still could have responded "don't know" rather than endorsing a distractor—but they endorsed distractors for 56% of the multiple-choice questions! The results on the final short answer test were consistent with what we predicted— the negative testing effect was much larger in the group (high school students) who endorsed more multiple-choice lures. Testing led to a smaller positive testing effect in high school students, and a larger negative testing effect, emphasizing the need for future research to include populations other than undergraduates.

None of the experiments described thus far in this section provided any corrective feedback to students. Importantly, Butler and Roediger (2008) showed that feedback given shortly after a multiple-choice test enhanced the positive testing effect and neutralized the negative suggestibility effect. However, it is critical that feedback be provided under conditions in which it is carefully processed to have this positive impact (see too Butler et al., 2007). Giving feedback is thus one obvious method of preventing the negative suggestibility effect. However, in our experience feedback is rarely given in university and college settings and when provided it occurs under suboptimal conditions. In large introductory courses using multiple-choice and short answer tests, professors often want to protect items in their test banks (so they do not have to create new tests and can refine their old tests with the data students provide). Even when professors do give feedback on tests, it is often given relatively long after taking the test (due to time for grading) and/or the feedback is provided under conditions in which students may not attend to it (e.g., just giving back the marked tests or requiring students to stop by the professor's office to see the corrected tests).

Most professors we know give credit (and partial credit) as deserved, but do not deduct points for bad answers—the worst possible score on an item is a zero, not some negative number. However, giving a penalty for wrong answers sounds more interesting when one thinks about the importance of endorsing multiple-choice lures for the negative suggestibility effect. We examined this more directly in another experiment using SAT II practice questions and Duke undergraduates (Marsh et al., 2009). One group of undergraduates was warned they would receive a penalty for wrong answers and that they should choose a "don't know" option if they were not reasonably sure of their answer. Another group was required to answer all of the multiple-choice questions. Both groups showed large positive testing effects, and smaller negative testing effects. Critically, the penalty instruction significantly reduced the negative testing effect, although it was still significant.

Research on negative suggestibility is just beginning, and only a few variables have been systematically investigated. Three classes of variables are likely to be interesting: ones that affect how likely subjects are to select multiple-choice lures (e.g., reading related material, a penalty for wrong answers on the MC test), ones that affect the likelihood that selected multiple-choice lures are integrated with related world knowledge (e.g., corrective feedback), and ones that affect monitoring at test (e.g., the warning against guessing on the final test used in Roediger & Marsh, 2005). The negative testing effect could change in size for any of these reasons. For example, consider one recent investigation involving the effects of adding a "none of the above" option to the MC test (Odegard & Koen, 2007). When "none of the above" was the correct answer on the MC test, the negative testing effect increased. It turned out that subjects were less willing to endorse "none of the above" than a specific alternative, meaning that MC performance was worst for items containing a "none of the above" option (and MC lure endorsements increased), with consequences for later performance.

In summary, most experiments show that the positive testing effect is larger than any negative testing effect; even if subjects learn some false facts from the test, the net effect of testing is positive (see Marsh, Roediger, Bjork, & Bjork, 2007, for a review). The exception may be when students are totally unprepared for the test and endorse many multiple-choice lures—this is a scenario that needs further research. The best advice we can give is to make sure the students receive corrective feedback, and to consider penalizing students for wrong answers.

Metacognition and self-regulated learning

While we have focused on testing as a pedagogical tool to enhance learning in the classroom, we are mindful that the bulk of learning in real life takes place outside the classroom. More often than not learning is self-regulated—the learner has to decide what information to study, how long to study, the kind of strategies or processing to use when studying, and so on. All these decisions depend on the learner's goals (e.g., the desired level of mastery), beliefs (e.g., that a particular type of study strategy is more effective), external constraints (e.g., time pressure), and online monitoring during the learning experience (i.e., subjective assessments of how well the material has been learned; Benjamin, 2007). In other words, a student's beliefs about learning and memory and his or her subjective evaluations during the learning experience are vital to effective learning (Dunlosky, Hertzog, Kennedy, & Thiede, 2005). In this section we shall discuss the metacognitive factors concomitant with testing, how testing can improve monitoring accuracy, as well as the use of self-testing as a study strategy by students.

Research on metacognition provides a framework for examining how students strategically monitor and regulate their learning. *Monitoring* refers to a person's subjective assessment of their cognitive processes, and *control* refers to the processes that regulate behavior as a consequence of monitoring (Nelson & Narens, 1990). One indirect way in which testing can enhance future learning is by allowing students to better monitor their learning (i.e., discriminate information that has been learned well from that which has not been learned). Enhanced monitoring in turn influences subsequent study behavior, such as having students channel their efforts towards less well-learned materials. A survey of college students' study habits revealed that students are generally aware of this function of testing (Kornell & Bjork, 2007). In response to the question "If you quiz yourself while you study, why do you do so?" 68% of respondents chose "To figure out how well I have learned the information I'm studying," while only 18% selected "I learn more that way than through rereading," suggesting that relatively few students view testing as a learning event (see too Karpicke, Butler, & Roediger, 2009).

To gain insight into subjects' monitoring abilities, researchers ask them to make judgments of learning (JOLs). Normally done during study, students predict their ability to remember the to-be-learned information at a later point in time (usually on a scale of 0–100%), and then these predictions are compared to their actual performance. Usually people are moderately accurate when making these predictions in laboratory paradigms (e.g., Arbuckle & Cuddy, 1969), but JOLs are inferential in nature and can be based on a variety of beliefs and cues (Koriat, 1997). The accuracy of one's metacognitive monitoring depends on the extent to which the beliefs and cues that one uses are diagnostic of future memory performance—and some of students' beliefs about learning are wrong. For example, subjects believe that items that are easily processed will be easy to retrieve later (e.g., Begg, Duft, Lalonde, Melnick, & Sanvito, 1989), whereas we have already discussed that more effortful retrieval is more likely to promote retention. Similarly, students tend to give higher JOLs after repeated study than after receiving initial tests on the to-be-remembered material, but actual final memory performance exhibits the opposite pattern (i.e., the testing effect; Agarwal et al., 2008; Kang, 2009a; Roediger & Karpicke, 2006a).

Repeated studying of the material probably engenders greater processing fluency, which leads to an overestimation of one's future memory performance.

Students' incorrect beliefs about memory mean that they often engage in sub-optimal learning strategies. For example, JOLs are often negatively correlated with study times during learning, meaning that students spend more time studying items that they feel are difficult and that they still need to master (Son & Metcalfe, 2000; although see Metcalfe & Kornell [2003] for conditions that produce an exception to this generalization). Not only is testing a better strategy, but sometimes substantial increases in study time are not accompanied by equivalent increases in performance, an outcome termed the "labor-in-vain" effect (Nelson & Leonesio, 1988).

Consider a study by Karpicke (2009) that examined subjects' strategies for learning Swahili–English word pairs. Critically, the experiment had repeated study–test cycles (multi-trial learning) and once subjects were able to correctly recall the English word (when cued with the Swahili word) they were given the choice of whether to restudy, test, or drop an item for the upcoming trial, with the goal of maximizing performance on a final test one week later. Subjects chose to drop the majority of items (60%), while about 25% and 15% of the items were selected for repeated testing and restudy, respectively. Subjects also made JOLs before making each choice, and items selected for restudy were subjectively the most difficult (i.e., lowest JOLs), dropped items were perceived to be the easiest, and items selected for testing were in between. As expected, final performance increased as a function of the proportion of items chosen to be tested, whereas there was no relationship between the proportion of items chosen for restudy and final recall. Finally, there was a negative correlation between the proportion of items dropped and final recall, indicating that subjects dropped items before they had firmly registered the pair.

These results suggest that learners often make suboptimal choices during learning, opting for strategies that do not maximize subsequent retention. Also, the tendency to drop items once they were recalled the first time reflects overconfidence and under-appreciation of the value of practicing retrieval. Follow-up research in our lab (Kang, 2009b) is investigating whether experiencing the testing effect (i.e., performing well on a final test for items previously tested, relative to items that were previously dropped or restudied) can induce learners to select preferentially self-testing study strategies that enhance future recall. We suspect this may be possible, given that testing can help improve metacognitive monitoring and sensitize learners to retrieval conditions, as described in the next two experiments.

Comparisons between immediate and delayed JOLs suggest an important role for testing in improving monitoring accuracy. Delayed JOLs refer to ones solicited at some delay after the items have been studied, whereas immediate JOLs are solicited immediately after each item has been studied. Delayed JOLs are typically more accurate than immediate JOLs (e.g., Nelson & Dunlosky, 1991). This delayed JOL effect is obtained only under certain conditions, specifically when the JOLs are "cue-only" JOLs. This term refers to the situation in which studied items are A–B pairs and subjects are provided only with A when asked to make their prediction for later recall of the target B; the effect does not occur when JOLs are sought with intact cue-target pairs presented (Dunlosky & Nelson, 1992). One explanation for this finding is that subjects attempt retrieval of the target for cue-only delayed JOLs, and success or failure at retrieval then guides subjects' predictions (i.e., a high JOL is given if the target is successfully retrieved; if not then a low JOL is given). This enhanced ability to distinguish well-learned from less well-learned items, coupled with the testing effect on items retrieved successfully during the delayed JOL, has been proposed to account for the increased accuracy of delayed JOLs (Spellman & Bjork, 1992; Kelemen & Weaver, 1997).

Testing can also augment monitoring accuracy by sensitizing learners to the actual conditions that prevail at retrieval. Consider one study where JOLs were not always accurate: Koriat and Bjork (2005) had subjects learn paired associates, including forward-associated pairs (e.g., *cheddar–cheese*), backwards-associated pairs (e.g., *cheese–cheddar*), and unrelated pairs. During learning, subjects were asked to judge how likely it was that they would remember the second word in the pair. Subjects over-predicted their ability to remember the target in the backwards-associated pairs, and the authors dubbed this an "illusion of competence". When subjects see *"cheese–cheddar"* they think they will easily remember *cheddar* when they later see *cheese* because the two words are related. However, when *cheese* occurs on the later test, it does not cue *cheddar* because the association between them is asymmetric and occurs in the opposite direction (*cheddar* reminds people of *cheese*, but *cheese* is much less likely to remind people of *cheddar*). Castel, McCabe, and Roediger (2007) reported the same overconfidence in students believing they would remember identical pairs of words (*cheese–cheese*). Critically, Koriat and Bjork (2006) found that study–test experience could alleviate this metacognitive illusion. On the first study–test cycle, subjects showed the same overconfidence for the backward-associated pairs, but JOLs and recall performance became better calibrated with further study–test opportunities. This finding suggests that prior test experience can enhance learners' sensitivity to retrieval conditions on a subsequent test, and can be a way to improve metacognitive monitoring.

The studies discussed in this section converge on the general conclusion that the majority of college students are unaware of the mnemonic benefit of testing: When students monitor their learning they feel more confident after repeated reading than after repeated testing, and when allowed to choose their study strategies self-testing is not the dominant choice. Students' self-reported study strategies mirror these laboratory findings (Karpicke et al., 2009). When preparing for tests, rereading notes or textbooks was by far the most preferred strategy (endorsed by almost 55% of students completing the survey), whereas strategies that involve retrieval practice (e.g., doing practice problems, using flashcards, self-testing) were preferred by fewer than 20% of students. It is clear that, when left to their own devices, many students engage in suboptimal study behavior. Even though college students might be expected to be expert learners (given their many years of schooling and experience preparing for exams), they often labor in vain (e.g., rereading the text) instead of employing strategies that contribute to robust learning and retention. Self-testing may be unappealing to many students because of the greater effort required compared to rereading, but this difficulty during learning turns out to be beneficial for long-term performance (Bjork, 1994). Therefore, the challenge for future research is to uncover conditions that encourage learners to set aside their naïve intuitions when studying and opt for retrieval-based strategies that yield lasting results.

Applications of testing in classrooms

Recently, several journal articles have highlighted the importance of using tests and quizzes to improve learning in real educational situations. The notion of using testing to enhance student learning is not novel, however, as Gates employed this practice with elementary school students in 1917 (see too Jones [1923] and Spitzer [1939]). One cannot, however, assume that laboratory findings necessarily generalize to classroom situations, given that some laboratory parameters (e.g., relatively short retention intervals, tight experimental control) do not correspond well to naturalistic contexts. This distinction has garnered interest recently and we will outline a few studies that have evaluated the efficacy of test-enhanced learning within a classroom context.

Leeming (2002) adopted an "exam-a-day" procedure in two sections of Introductory Psychology and two sections of his summer Learning and Memory course, for a total of 22 to 24 exams over the duration of the courses. In comparable classes taught in prior semesters, students had received only four exams. Final retention was measured after six weeks. Leeming found significant increases in performance between the exam-a-day procedure and the four-exam procedure in both the Introductory Psychology sections (80% vs. 74%) and Learning and Memory sections (89% vs. 81%). In addition, the percentage of students who failed the course decreased following the exam-a-day procedure. Leeming's students also participated in a survey, and students in the exam-a-day sections reported increased interest and studying for class.

McDaniel et al. (2007a) described a study in an online Brain and Behavior course that used two kinds of initial test questions, short answer and multiple-choice, as well as a read-only condition. Weekly initial quizzes were administered via the Web; questions were followed by immediate feedback and in the read-only condition, the facts were represented. Two-unit examinations in multiple-choice format were given after three weeks of quizzes, and a final cumulative multiple-choice assessment at the end of the semester covered material from both units. Although facts targeted on the initial quizzes were repeated on the unit/final exams, the question stems were phrased differently so that the learning of concepts was assessed rather than memory for a prior test response. On the two-unit exams, retention for quizzed material was significantly greater than that for non-quizzed material, regardless of the initial quiz format. On the final exam, however, only short answer (but not multiple-choice) initial quizzes produced a significant benefit above non-quizzed and read-only material. The results from this study provide further evidence of the strength of the testing effect in classroom settings, as well as replicating prior findings showing that short answer tests produce a greater testing effect than do multiple-choice tests (e.g., Butler & Roediger, 2007; Kang et al., 2007).

McDaniel and Sun (2009) replicated these findings in a more traditional college classroom setting, in which students took two short-answer quizzes per week. The quizzes were emailed to the students, who had to complete them by noon the next day. After emailing their quiz back to the professor, students received an email with the quiz questions and correct answers. Retention was measured on unit exams, composed of quizzed and non-quizzed material, and administered at the end of every week. Performance for quizzed material was significantly greater than performance on non-quizzed material.

Finally, Roediger, McDaniel, McDermott, and Agarwal (2010) conducted various test-enhanced learning experiments at a middle school in Illinois. The experiments were fully integrated into the classroom schedules and used material drawn directly from the school and classroom curriculum. In the first study, 6th grade social studies, 7th grade English, and 8th grade science students completed initial multiple-choice quizzes over half of the classroom material. The other half of the material served as the control material. The teacher in the class left the classroom during administration of quizzes, so she did not know the content of the quizzes and could not bias her instruction toward (or against) the tested material. The initial quizzes included a pre-test before the teacher reviewed the material in class, a post-test immediately following the teacher's lecture, and a review test a few days after the teacher's lecture. Upon completion of a three- to six-week unit, retention was measured on chapter exams composed of both quizzed and non-quizzed material. At all three grade levels, and in all three content areas, significant testing effects were revealed such that retention for quizzed material was greater than for non-quizzed material, even up to nine months later (at the end of the school year). The results from 8th grade science, for example, can be seen in Figure 17.7.

This experiment was replicated with 6th grade social studies students who, instead of completing in-class multiple-choice quizzes, participated in games online using an interactive website at their leisure. This design was implemented in order to minimize the amount of class time required for a test-enhanced learning program. Despite being left to their own devices, students still performed better on quizzed material available online than non-quizzed material on their final chapter exams. Furthermore, in a subsequent experiment with 6th grade social studies students, a read-only condition was included, and performance for quizzed material was still significantly greater than read-only and non-quizzed material, even when the number of exposures were equated between the quizzed and read-only condition.

In sum, recent research is beginning to demonstrate the robust effects of testing in applied settings, including middle school and college classrooms. Future research extending to more content areas (e.g., math), age groups (e.g., elementary school students), methods of quizzing (e.g., computer-based and online), and types of material (e.g., application and transfer questions), we expect, will only provide further support for test-enhanced learning programs.

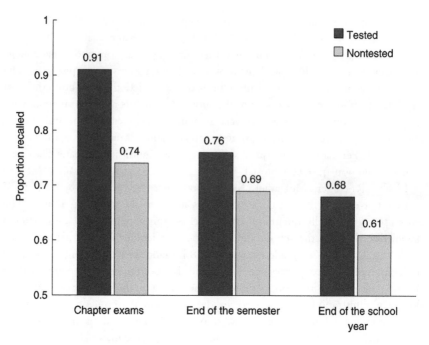

FIGURE 17.7 Science results from McDaniel et al. (2011). Significant testing effects in a middle school setting were revealed such that retention for quizzed material was greater than for non-quizzed material, even up to 9 months later (at the end of the school year)

Conclusion

In this chapter, we have reviewed evidence supporting test-enhanced learning in the classroom and as a study strategy (i.e., self-testing) for improving student performance. Frequent classroom testing has both indirect and direct benefits. The indirect benefits are that students study for more time and with greater regularity when tests are frequent, because the specter of a looming test encourages studying. The direct benefit is that testing on material serves as a potent enhancer of retention for this material on future tests, either relative to no activity or even relative to restudying material. Providing correct answer feedback on tests and insuring that students carefully process this feedback greatly enhances this testing effect. Feedback is especially important when initial test performance is low. Multiple tests produce a larger testing effect than does a single test. In addition, tests requiring production of answers (short answer or essay tests) produce a greater testing effect than do recognition tests (multiple-choice or true/false). The latter tests also have the disadvantage of exposing students to erroneous information, but giving feedback eliminates this problem. Test-enhanced learning is not limited to laboratory materials; it improves performance with educational materials (foreign language vocabulary, science passages) and in actual classroom settings (ranging from middle school classes in social studies, English, and science, to university classes in introductory psychology and biological bases of behavior). We believe that the application of frequent testing in classrooms can greatly improve academic performance across the curriculum.

Note

* This chapter originally appeared in the edited volume, *Current Issues in Applied Memory Research*. It has been updated for this compilation.

References

Abbott, E. E. (1909). On the analysis of the factors of recall in the learning process. *Psychological Monographs, 11*, 159–177.

Agarwal, P. K., Karpicke, J. D., Kang, S. H. K., Roediger, H. L., & McDermott, K. B. (2008). Examining the testing effect with open- and closed-book tests. *Applied Cognitive Psychology, 22*, 861–876.

Arbuckle, T. Y., & Cuddy, L. L. (1969). Discrimination of item strength at time of presentation. *Journal of Experimental Psychology, 81*, 126–131.

Bacon, F. T. (1979). Credibility of repeated statements: Memory for trivia. *Journal of Experimental Psychology: Human Learning and Memory, 5*, 241–252.

Balota, D. A., Duchek, J. M., & Logan, J. M. (2007). Is expanded retrieval practice a superior form of spaced retrieval? A critical review of the extant literature. In J. S. Nairne (Ed.), *The foundations of remembering: Essays in honor of Henry L. Roediger, III* (pp. 83–105). New York: Psychology Press.

Bangert-Drowns, R. L., Kulik, C. C., Kulik, J. A., & Morgan, M. (1991). The instructional feedback in test-like events. *Review of Educational Research, 61*, 213–238.

Begg, I., Armour, V., & Kerr, T. (1985). On believing what we remember. *Canadian Journal of Behavioral Science, 17*, 199–214.

Begg, I., Duft, S., Lalonde, P., Melnick, R., & Sanvito, J. (1989). Memory predictions are based on ease of processing. *Journal of Memory and Language, 28*, 610–632.

Benjamin, A. S. (2007). Memory is more than just remembering: Strategic control of encoding, accessing memory, and making decisions. In A. S. Benjamin & B. H. Ross (Eds.), *The psychology of learning and motivation: Skill and strategy in memory use* (vol. 48, pp. 175–223). London: Academic Press.

Bjork, R. A. (1975). Retrieval as a memory modifier: An interpretation of negative recency and related phenomena. In R. L. Solso (Ed.), *Information processing and cognition: The Loyola Symposium* (pp. 123–144). New York: Wiley.

Bjork, R. A. (1994). Memory and metamemory considerations in the training of human beings. In J. Metcalfe and A. Shimamura (Eds.), *Metacognition: Knowing about knowing* (pp. 185–205). Cambridge, MA: MIT Press.

Brown, A. S. (1988). Encountering misspellings and spelling performance: Why wrong isn't right. *Journal of Educational Psychology, 4*, 488–494.

Butler, A. C., Karpicke, J. D., & Roediger, H. L. (2007). The effect of type and timing of feedback on learning from multiple-choice tests. *Journal of Experimental Psychology: Applied, 13*, 273–281.

Butler, A. C., Karpicke, J. D., & Roediger, H. L. (2008). Correcting a metacognitive error: Feedback increases retention of low-confidence correct responses. *Journal of Experimental Psychology: Learning, Memory, and Cognition, 34*, 918–928.

Butler, A. C., & Roediger, H. L. (2007). Testing improves long-term retention in a simulated classroom setting. *European Journal of Cognitive Psychology, 19*, 514–527.

Butler, A. C., & Roediger, H. L. (2008). Feedback enhances the positive effects and reduces the negative effects of multiple-choice testing. *Memory and Cognition, 36*, 604–616.

Butterfield, B., & Metcalfe, J. (2006). The correction of errors committed with high confidence. *Metacognition and Learning, 1*, 69–84.

Carpenter, S. K., & DeLosh, E. L. (2006). Impoverished cue support enhances subsequent retention: Support for the elaborative retrieval explanation of the testing effect. *Memory and Cognition, 34*, 268–276.

Castel, A. D., McCabe, D. P., & Roediger, H. L. (2007). Illusions of competence and overestimation of associative memory for identical items: Evidence from judgments of learning. *Psychonomic Bulletin and Review, 14*, 107–111.

Cull, W. L. (2000). Untangling the benefits of multiple study opportunities and repeated testing for cued recall. *Applied Cognitive Psychology, 14*, 215–235.

Dudai, Y. (2006). Reconsolidation: The advantage of being refocused. *Current Opinion in Neurobiology, 16*, 174–178.

Dunlosky, J., Hertzog, C., Kennedy, M. R. T., & Thiede, K. W. (2005). The self-monitoring approach for effective learning. *Cognitive Technology, 10*, 4–11.

Dunlosky, J., & Nelson, T. O. (1992). Importance of the kind of cue for judgments of learning (JOL) and the delayed-JOL effect. *Memory and Cognition, 20*, 374–380.

Fazio, L. K., & Marsh, E. J. (2009). Surprising feedback improves later memory. *Psychonomic Bulletin and Review, 16*, 88–92.

Feller, M. (1994). Open-book testing and education for the future. *Studies in Educational Evaluation, 20*, 235–238.

Ferster, C. B., & Skinner, B. F. (1957). *Schedules of reinforcement.* New York: Appleton-Century-Crofts.

Gates, A. I. (1917). Recitation as a factor in memorizing. *Archives of Psychology, 6*(40).

Glover, J. A. (1989). The "testing" phenomenon: Not gone but nearly forgotten. *Journal of Educational Psychology, 81*, 392–399.

Hasher, L., Goldstein, D., & Toppino, T. (1977). Frequency and the conference of referential validity. *Journal of Verbal Learning and Verbal Behavior, 16*, 107–112.

Jacoby, L. L., & Hollingshead, A. (1990). Reading student essays may be hazardous to your spelling: Effects of reading incorrectly and correctly spelled words. *Canadian Journal of Psychology, 44*, 345–358.

Jones, H. E. (1923). The effects of examination on the performance of learning. *Archives of Psychology, 10*, 1–70.

Kang, S. H. K. (2009a). Enhancing visuo-spatial learning: The benefit of retrieval practice. Manuscript under revision.

Kang, S. H. K. (2009b). The influence of text expectancy, test format and test experience on study strategy selection and long-term retention. Unpublished doctoral dissertation, Washington University, St Louis, MO.

Kang, S. H. K., McDermott, K. B., & Roediger, H. L. (2007). Test format and corrective feedback modify the effect of testing on long-term retention. *European Journal of Cognitive Psychology, 19*, 528–558.

Karpicke, J. D. (2009). Metacognitive control and strategy selection: Deciding to practice retrieval during learning. *Journal of Experimental Psychology: General, 138*(4), 469–486.

Karpicke, J. D., Butler, A. C., & Roediger, H. L. (2009). Metacognitive strategies in student learning: Do students practise retrieval when they study on their own? *Memory, 17*, 471–479.

Karpicke, J. D., & Roediger, H. L. (2007). Expanding retrieval practice promotes short-term retention, but equally spaced retrieval enhances long-term retention. *Journal of Experimental Psychology: Learning, Memory, and Cognition, 33*, 704–719.

Karpicke, J. D., & Roediger, H. L. (2008). The critical importance of retrieval for learning. *Science, 319*, 966–968.

Kelemen, W. L., & Weaver, C. A. (1997). Enhanced memory at delays: Why do judgments of learning improve over time? *Journal of Experimental Psychology: Learning, Memory, and Cognition, 23*, 1394–1409.

Koriat, A. (1997). Monitoring one's own knowledge during study: A cue-utilization approach to judgments of learning. *Journal of Experimental Psychology: General, 126*, 349–370.

Koriat, A., & Bjork, R. A. (2005). Illusions of competence in monitoring one's knowledge during study. *Journal of Experimental Psychology: Learning, Memory, and Cognition, 31*, 187–194.

Koriat, A., & Bjork, R. A. (2006). Illusions of competence during study can be remedied by manipulations that enhance learners' sensitivity to retrieval conditions at test. *Memory and Cognition, 34*, 959–972.

Kornell, N., & Bjork, R. A. (2007). The promise and perils of self-regulated study. *Psychonomic Bulletin and Review, 14*, 219–224.

Kornell, N., Hays, M. J., & Bjork, R. A. (2009). Unsuccessful retrieval attempts enhance subsequent learning. *Journal of Experimental Psychology: Learning, Memory, and Cognition, 35*, 989–998.

Kulhavy, R. W., Yekovich, F. R., & Dyer, J. W. (1976). Feedback and response confidence. *Journal of Educational Psychology, 68*, 522–528.

Kulhavy, R. W., Yekovich, F. R., & Dyer, J. W. (1979). Feedback and content review in programmed instruction. *Contemporary Educational Psychology, 4*, 91–98.

Kulik, J. A., & Kulik, C. C. (1988). Timing of feedback and verbal learning. *Review of Educational Research, 58*, 79–97.

Landauer, T. K., & Bjork, R. A. (1978). Optimal rehearsal patterns and name learning. In M. M. Gruneberg, P. E. Harris, & R. N. Sykes (Eds.), *Practical aspects of memory* (pp. 625–632). New York: Academic Press.

Leeming, F. C. (2002). The exam-a-day procedure improves performance in Psychology classes. *Teaching of Psychology, 29*, 210–212.

Loftus, E. F., Miller, D. G., & Burns, H. J. (1978). Semantic integration of verbal information into a visual memory. *Journal of Experimental Psychology: Human Learning and Memory, 4*, 19–31.

Logan, J. M., & Balota, D. A. (2008). Expanded vs. equal interval spaced retrieval practice: Exploring different schedules of spacing and retention interval in younger and older adults. *Aging, Neuropsychology, and Cognition, 15*, 257–280.

McDaniel, M. A., & Sun, J. (2009). The testing effect: Experimental evidence in a college course. Manuscript under revision.

McDaniel, M. A., Anderson, J. L., Derbish, M. H., & Morrisette, N. (2007a). Testing the testing effect in the classroom. *European Journal of Cognitive Psychology, 19*, 494–513.

McDaniel, M. A., Roediger, H. L., III, & McDermott, K. B. (2007b). Generalizing test-enhanced learning from the laboratory to the classroom. *Psychonomic Bulletin and Review, 14*, 200–206.

McDaniel, M. A., Agarwal, P. K., Huelser, B. J., McDermott, K. B., & Roediger III, H. L. (2011). Test-enhanced learning in a middle school science classroom: The effects of quiz frequency and placement. *Journal of Educational Psychology, 103*(2), 399–414.

Marsh, E. J., Agarwal, P. K., & Roediger, H. L., III (2009). Memorial consequences of answering SAT II questions. *Journal of Experimental Psychology: Applied, 15,* 1–11.

Marsh, E. J., Roediger, H. L., III, Bjork, R. A., & Bjork, E. L. (2007). The memorial consequences of multiple-choice testing. *Psychonomic Bulletin and Review, 14,* 194–199.

Metcalfe, J., & Kornell, N. (2003). The dynamics of learning and allocation of study time to a region of proximal learning. *Journal of Experimental Psychology: General, 132,* 530–542.

Moreno, R. (2004). Decreasing cognitive load for novice students: Effects of explanatory versus corrective feedback in discovery-based multimedia. *Instructional Science, 32,* 99–113.

Nelson, T. O., & Dunlosky, J. (1991). When people's judgments of learning (JOLs) are extremely accurate at predicting subsequent recall: The "delayed-JOL effect". *Psychological Science, 2,* 267–270.

Nelson, T. O., & Leonesio, R. J. (1988). Allocation of self-paced study time and the "labor-in-vain effect". *Journal of Experimental Psychology: Learning, Memory, and Cognition, 14,* 676–686.

Nelson, T. O., & Narens, L. (1980). Norms of 300 general-information questions: Accuracy of recall, latency of recall, and feeling-of-knowing ratings. *Journal of Verbal Learning and Verbal Behavior, 19,* 338–368.

Nelson, T. O., & Narens, L. (1990). Metamemory: A theoretical framework and new findings. In G. H. Bower (Ed.), *The psychology of learning and motivation* (vol. 26, pp. 125–173). New York: Academic Press.

Odegard, T. N., & Koen, J. D. (2007). "None of the above" as a correct and incorrect alternative on a multiple-choice test: Implications for the testing effect. *Memory, 15,* 873–885.

Pashler, H., Cepeda, N. J., Wixted, J. T., & Rohrer, D. (2005). When does feedback facilitate learning of words? *Journal of Experimental Psychology: Learning, Memory, and Cognition, 31,* 3–8.

Rea, C. P., & Modigliani, V. (1985). The effect of expanded versus massed practice on the retention of multiplication facts and spelling lists. *Human Learning: Journal of Practical Research and Applications, 4,* 11–18.

Remmers, H. H., & Remmers, E. M. (1926). The negative suggestion effect on true-false examination questions. *Journal of Educational Psychology, 17,* 52–56.

Richland, L. E., Kornell, N. & Kao, L. S. (2009). The pretesting effect: Do unsuccessful retrieval attempts enhance learning? *Journal of Experimental Psychology: Applied, 15,* 243–257.

Roediger, H. L., & Karpicke, J. D. (2006a). Test enhanced learning: Taking memory tests improves long-term retention. *Psychological Science, 17,* 249–255.

Roediger, H. L., & Karpicke, J. D. (2006b). The power of testing memory: Basic research and implications for educational practice. *Perspectives on Psychological Science, 1,* 181–210.

Roediger, H. L., & Marsh, E. J. (2005). The positive and negative consequences of multiple-choice testing. *Journal of Experimental Psychology: Learning, Memory, and Cognition, 31,* 1155–1159.

Roediger, H. L., McDaniel, M. A., McDermott, K. B., & Agarwal, P. K. (2010). Test-enhanced learning in the classroom: Long-term improvements from quizzing. *Journal of Experimental Psychology: Applied, 17*(4), 382–395.

Roediger, H. L., Zaromb, F. M., & Butler, A. C. (2008). The role of repeated retrieval in shaping collective memory. In P. Boyer and J. V. Wertsch (Eds.), *Memory in Mind and Culture* (pp. 29–58). Cambridge: Cambridge University Press.

Ruch, G. M. (1929). *The objective or new-type examination: An introduction to educational measurement.* Chicago, IL: Scott, Foresman, and Co.

Skinner, B. F. (1953). *Science and human behavior.* New York: Macmillan.

Skinner, B. F. (1958). Teaching machines. *Science, 128*, 969–977.

Son, L. K., & Metcalfe, J. (2000). Metacognitive and control strategies in study-time allocation. *Journal of Experimental Psychology: Learning, Memory, and Cognition, 26*, 204–221.

Spellman, B. A., & Bjork, R. A. (1992). When predictions create reality: Judgments of learning may alter what they are intended to assess. *Psychological Science, 3*, 315–316.

Spitzer, H. F. (1939). Studies in retention. *Journal of Educational Psychology, 30*, 641–656.

Thompson, C. P., Wenger, S. K., & Bartling, C. A. (1978). How recall facilitates subsequent recall: A reappraisal. *Journal of Experimental Psychology: Human Learning and Memory, 4*, 210–221.

Toppino, T. C., & Brochin, H. A. (1989). Learning from tests: The case of true–false examinations. *Journal of Educational Research, 83*, 119–124.

Toppino, T. C., & Luipersbeck, S. M. (1993). Generality of the negative suggestion effect in objective tests. *Journal of Educational Research, 86*, 357–362.

Wenger, S. K., Thompson, C. P., & Bartling, C. A. (1980). Recall facilitates subsequent recognition. *Journal of Experimental Psychology: Human Learning and Memory, 6*, 135–144.

Wheeler, M. A., & Roediger, H. L. (1992). Disparate effects of repeated testing: Reconciling Ballard's (1913) and Bartlett's (1932) results. *Psychological Science, 3*, 240–245.

INDEX

Note: Page numbers in *italics* indicate figures and in **bold** indicate tables on the corresponding pages.

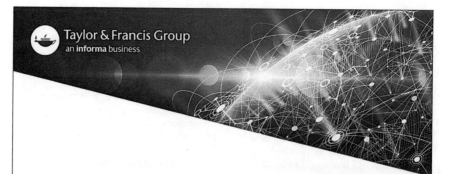